THE THEORY AND PRACTICE OF CHANGE MANAGEMENT

The theory and practice of change management

Third edition

John Hayes

First published 2010 by
PALGRAVE MACMILLAN

Palgrave Macmillan in the UK is an imprint of Macmillan Publishers Limited, registered in England, company number 785998, of Houndmills, Basingstoke, Hampshire RG21 6XS.

Palgrave Macmillan in the US is a division of St Martin's Press LLC, 175 Fifth Avenue, New York, NY 10010.

Palgrave Macmillan is the global academic imprint of the above companies and has companies and representatives throughout the world.

Palgrave® and Macmillan® are registered trademarks in the United States, the United Kingdom, Europe and other countries

ISBN 978–0–230–21069–1

This book is printed on paper suitable for recycling and made from fully managed and sustained forest sources. Logging, pulping and manufacturing processes are expected to conform to the environmental regulations of the country of origin.

A catalogue record for this book is available from the British Library.

A catalog record for this book is available from the Library of Congress.

10 9 8 7 6 5 4 3 2 1
19 18 17 16 15 14 13 12 11 10

Printed in China

To Martha, Ruby, Izaac, Isabel and Miranda

Contents

List of figures and tables

Figures

Tables

List of case studies

List of research reports, examples and change tools

Research reports

Examples

Change tools

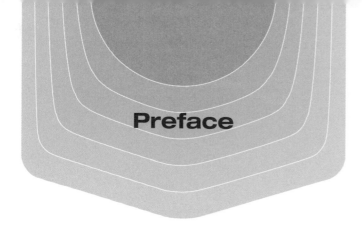

Preface

On many academic programmes, change management is positioned as the integrating course because it requires students to reflect on and synthesize the various perspectives on organizational functioning offered by other modules studied, such as finance, operations management, marketing, organizational behaviour and strategic management.

Studying change management is important because factors such as the availability of credit, technological advances, increasing competitive pressures, changes in the boundaries of organizations, the development of new organizational forms, regulatory reforms and globalization are creating opportunities and threats that organizations need to address if they are to survive and prosper. Managers, at all levels, have to be competent at identifying the need for change. They also have to be able to act in ways that will secure change. Getting it 'wrong' can be costly. It is imperative, therefore, that managers get it 'right', but getting it right is not easy. There is no single 'recipe' that can be applied to all organizations at all times. This book addresses a broad range of issues that will affect the likelihood that change efforts will be successful.

Studying change management will provide you with an opportunity to reflect on what you have learned from other courses and from your work experience about:

▶ sense making – drawing on different perspectives of organizational functioning
▶ ways of knowing – sources of data and evaluating evidence
▶ shaping behaviours – ways of influencing and coordinating behaviour
▶ designing interventions – ways of 'doing' that purposely disrupt the status quo in order to move the organization towards a more effective state.

The Theory and Practice of Change Management is designed to help you to:

▶ develop your investigative and diagnostic skills so that you will be more effective in assessing what is going on in organizations
▶ extend your ability to manage issues arising from internally planned and externally imposed organizational changes
▶ improve your awareness of how people can facilitate or resist change and extend your ability to manage human resources in the context of change.

Features of the book

The book has the following distinctive features, and includes the use of logos:

▶ *Underlying model:* In Chapter 2, 'change' is conceptualized as a process. A conceptual model is presented to help you think about the theory and practice of change management, and to provide a framework that will help you act effectively to bring about change.

▶ *Clear signposting:* The process model of change, presented at the end of this Preface and again in the Introduction, the Part I opener and at the end of Chapter 2, is elaborated to show how each part of the book and each chapter in each part relates to this model. The model is referred to in the introduction to each part and a smaller version of the model is included at the beginning of each chapter, with the relevant part of the model highlighted to show how that chapter relates to the process model.

▶ *Exercises* 🖊 : These draw on your personal experience of change. Some are presented at the beginning of a chapter and invite you to articulate and critically examine your own implicit theories of change and change management before studying the literature on the topic. Others are presented later and invite you to apply concepts and theories to your own experience of change.

▶ *Change tools* 🔧 : Change management is most effective when the use of tools and techniques is guided by theory. Throughout the book, a number of carefully selected change tools are presented alongside theory to provide change managers with some ideas about the kinds of practical tools and techniques that might be useful in specific circumstances.

▶ *Research reports* 🔍 : Much of the knowledge about the management of change that is available to managers is practice based. There is, however, a growing body of research evidence that can complement, and in some cases challenge, this craft-based expertise. Throughout the book, embedded in the text, there are frequent references to research studies, but from time to time, selected studies are presented in research reports. These give a flavour of some of this research-based knowledge and how research is contributing to our knowledge about change management. They also indicate some of the different approaches that researchers have adopted to the study of change.

▶ *Examples* 👉 : These illustrate a point. They describe an instance or refer to a pattern of behaviour that demonstrates the relevance, or aids the understanding, of a concept or theory.

▶ *Case studies* 🗋 : These invite you to apply theory to a variety of problematic situations unrelated to your own experience of change. The case studies are all based on actual events, although in some instances, the name of the organization has been changed.

Research reports

This is not a text on research methods but the research reports do provide material that can be used to stimulate debate about how we can develop a theory of change management. Some of the research reports focus on studies that seek to test a theory and explain causal relationships between variables. They adopt a deductive approach. An example is Research report 1.1 on Romanelli and Tushman's study of organizational transformation as punctuated equilibrium. Starting with a theory, they deduced a set of hypotheses, expressed them in operational terms and conducted an empirical inquiry to test them. Other research reports point to a number of issues students of change need to be aware of when designing studies. For example, Research report 10.1 on Greenberg's study of communicating bad news provides a good illustration of expressing a hypothesis in a way that facilitates measurement, wherein the effect of bad news is measured using pilfering rates and labour turnover. Research report 11.1 on Coch and French's study of resistance to change provides an example of using controls to facilitate hypothesis testing.

Inductive studies adopt a different approach. They involve moving from data to theory. Researchers involve themselves in a situation to understand what is going on. They collect data, often using interviews and observation, and use this understanding to formulate theory. Trist and Bamforth's study (Research report 16.1) involved them following and maintaining relatively continuous contact with 20 coalface workers over a period of two years in order to gain a deep understanding of why the introduction of the longwall method of coal getting failed to yield improvements in performance. This study led to the formulation of a theory of sociotechnical systems.

Some studies combine deductive and inductive approaches. Denis et al's research on the dynamics of collective leadership (Research report 9.1) involved five case studies over a five-year period. Based on their initial case studies, they developed some theoretical ideas about the collective nature of leadership. In their later studies, they went on to examine how these ideas could be generalized and enriched to aid the understanding of leadership in more complex and pluralistic settings.

Case studies

This book was originally written for MBA students and practising managers and others who have considerable experience of working in organizations. In the second edition, the many exercises designed to help experienced managers apply theory to their own practice of management were supplemented with a range of examples and case studies that could aid understanding for those without much direct experience of managing change. In this third edition, the range of case studies has been extended.

The case studies are used in different ways. Sometimes they are presented at the end of a chapter to test your understanding of theory. For example, at the end of Chapter 1, you are invited to use a typology of change presented in the chapter to identify the kind of change confronting the BBC, UK Coal, Leicester Royal Infirmary, McDonald's and GNER (Case studies 1.1.1–1.1.5). In some chapters, the case studies are presented at the beginning or early in the chapter to encourage you to think about how you might manage a situation before you are introduced to theory that will help you to diagnose the problem and formulate a course of action. Examples include Case study 3.1 on the Active Sports Equipment Company and Case study 14.1 on Asda. Sometimes a case study is broken down into a series of related mini-cases to help you to discover ways in which theory can improve your practice of change management. An example in Chapter 8 involves the merger of two hospitals. First, Case study 8.1 invites you to identify all those who might be affected by and/or could affect the outcome of the change. Later on, Case study 8.2 involves mapping stakeholders in accordance with how much power and influence they have and their attitude towards the change. Lastly, Case study 8.3 involves developing strategies for managing relationships with each group of stakeholders.

Sometimes cases relate to a part of the book rather than specific chapters. At the end of Chapter 17, four case studies invite you to imagine that you are a consultant who has been asked to design an intervention that will address the issues raised in Part VI, Implementing change. Case study 17.1 is set in southwest India and involves improving the effectiveness of primary healthcare centres. Case study 17.2 involves designing an intervention to increase the motivation and flexibility of the workforce of a Danish dairy company operating in the UK. Case study 17.3 involves designing an intervention to improve the treatment offered by the trauma orthopaedic care department of a large UK hospital. Case study 17.4 involves reducing absenteeism in the elderly care sector of Silkeborg Council in Denmark.

Chapter 30 introduces a concluding case study designed to provide you with an opportunity to review what you have read and to think about how the many theories, models, techniques and tools can be applied to the management of a single case. You can do this on your own or with others.

The case studies relate to public and private sector organizations, operating in a variety of areas such as healthcare, local government, broadcasting, energy, chemicals, dairy, fast foods, leisure, manufacturing and security. The case studies also relate to situations in the UK, Denmark, Germany, India and elsewhere, and to multinational companies that operate in several countries. Although not presented as a case study, enterprise-level training in Australia is discussed in some detail in Chapter 21.

Changes to the content of the third edition

The content of the book is organized into eight parts and 30 chapters. This structure reflects some of the theoretical and practical issues that have been important in my experience consulting with a wide variety of clients on a range of change-related issues.

New chapters

The third edition includes six new chapters, three in Part VI, Implementing change:

▶ Chapter 24 – Lean
▶ Chapter 25 – Restructuring for strategic gain
▶ Chapter 26 – Merging groups

and three in Part VIII, Sustaining change:

▶ Chapter 28 – Making change stick
▶ Chapter 29 – Spreading change
▶ Chapter 30 – Pulling it all together: the concluding case.

Reorganization

The first part of the second edition entitled Core concepts has been reduced from five to two chapters and retitled The nature of change. Two of the remaining original chapters in Part I have been moved. Open systems models and alignment is now the first chapter in Part III. Collective learning is now the first chapter in Part VI. Material from the chapter on organizational effectiveness has been incorporated into Chapter 3, Recognizing the need for change, at the beginning of Part III.

The final part of the second edition has been replaced by a new final part on sustaining change. The chapter Modes of intervening, the penultimate chapter in the second edition, has been moved to Part IV, and has been expanded to included material from the final chapter in the second edition. This revised structure supports the underlying model presented in Chapter 2.

The following are changes to other chapters:

▶ Chapter 6 has been extended to include a discussion of life cycle models of organizational growth and development.
▶ Chapter 9 has been extended to include a discussion of leadership styles, situational leadership and 'new genre' models including charismatic leadership.

▸ Chapter 15 has been extended to include a discussion of the danger of adopting a fragmented approach to leading change.
▸ Chapter 17 includes the addition of trans-organization to the levels included in the three-dimensional model for selecting interventions.

In addition there have been minor additions to most other chapters.

Pathways

One of the strengths of this book is its wide scope. Not everybody, however, will want to read all 30 chapters. Some may want a quick overview of the 'essentials' of change management and others may want to focus on a particular issue.

The 'essentials'

If you want to use the book to quickly grasp the essentials of change management, you might find it helpful to begin by reading Chapter 2. This chapter presents a process model and briefly describes the key steps in the process of change management. Each step is covered in much greater detail in Parts II–VIII, but you might find it helpful to begin by focusing attention on a few chapters that provide more information about diagnosis, managing people through change and planning for implementation. An essentials pathway might therefore include:

▸ The process model of change management: Chapter 2
▸ Diagnosis: Chapters 5 and 6
▸ Managing people issues: Chapters 8–10
▸ Shaping implementation strategies: Chapter 14
▸ Ways of intervening: Chapters 16 and 17.

Implementing change

If you want to quickly review the theory and practice that relates to implementation, you might find the following pathway helpful:

▸ The process of change management: Chapter 2
▸ Stakeholder management: Chapter 8
▸ Planning and preparing for change: Chapters 14–17
▸ Implementation: Some or all of the nine chapters in Part VI – Chapters 18–20 address interventions that focus on human process problems, Chapters 21 and 22 focus on interventions that address human resource issues, Chapters 23 and 24 focus on technostructural interventions and Chapters 25 and 26 on interventions that address strategic issues.
▸ Reviewing and keeping the change on track: Chapter 27.

Other ways to access content relevant to your needs

While most readers will find it helpful to begin by reading Chapters 1 and 2, you might want to start by dipping into chapters that relate to an immediate concern. Consulting the Introduction and overview, which follows this Preface, might help you to identify relevant chapters. For example, if your concern is sustaining change, Chapters 28 and 29 might provide a relevant start. If your immediate concern relates to mergers or acquisitions, you might want to begin by looking at Chapters 25 and 26. If you want some ideas about who should lead the change process, you might find it helpful to look at Chapters 4, 9 and 15.

A tutor's guide is available for those who adopt this book at www.palgrave.com/business/hayes3. It includes a set of PowerPoint slides and a full debrief of many of the case studies, including Case study 14.1 and Case studies 17.1–17.4.

JOHN HAYES

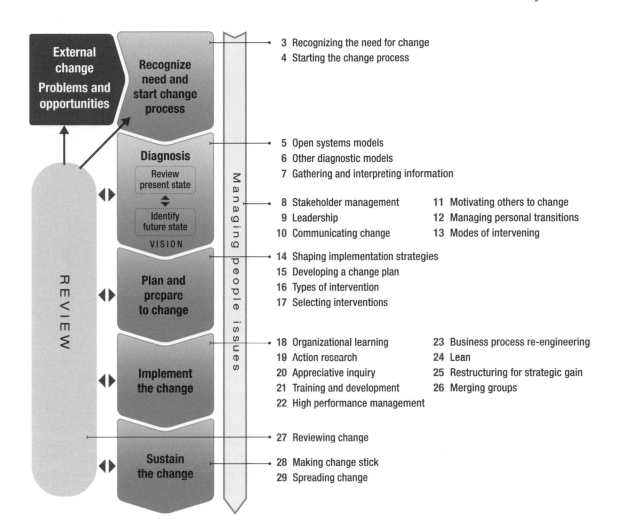

The relationship between Chapters 3–29 and the generic process model of change

Acknowledgements

The author and publishers wish to thank the following for permission to reproduce copyright material:

Harvard Business Review for Figure 6.2 'Greiner's five phases of growth', Greiner, L.E. (1972) Evolution and revolution as organisations grow, *Harvard Business Review*, **50**(4): 41.

Sage Publications for Figure 6.6 'Weisbord's six-box model', Weisbord, M.R. (1976) Organization diagnosis: six places to look for trouble with or without a theory, *Group and Organization Management*, **1**(4): 432; Figures 6.7 and 6.8 'The Burke-Litwin causal model of organizational performance and change' and 'The transformational factors', Burke, W.W. and Litwin, G.H. (1992) A causal model of organizational performance and change, *Journal of Management*, **18**(3): 528.

The Academy of Management for Figure 10.1 'Effectiveness of communication strategies', Clampitt, P.G., DeKoch, R.J. and Cashman, T. (2000) A strategy for communicating about uncertainty, *Academy of Management Executive*, **14**(4): 48; Figure 10.2 'Dynamics giving rise to organisational silence', adapted from Morrison, E.W. and Milliken, F. J. (2000) Organizational silence: a barrier to change and development in a pluralistic world, *Academy of Management Review*, **25**(4): 709; Figure 24.2 'The Toyota Production System house', Liker, J.K. and Morgan, J.M. (2006) The Toyota way in services: the case of lean product development, *Academy of Management Perspectives*, **20**(2): 7; Figures 26.1 and 26.2 'Acquired firm's preferred mode of acculturation' and 'Acquiring firm's preferred mode of acculturation', Nahavandi, A. and Malekzadeh, A.R. (1988) Acculturation in mergers and acquisitions, *Academy of Management Review*, **13**(1): 83–4; Table 29.1 'Implementation climate and innovation/values fit', Klein, K.L. and Sorra, J.S. (1996) The challenge of innovation implementation, *Academy of Management Review*, **21**(4): 1066.

Elsevier Publishers for Table 12.1 'The social readjustment rating scale', adapted from Holmes, T. and Rahe, R. (1967) The social readjustment rating scale, *Journal of Psychosomatic Research*, 11: 215.

Cengage Publishers for Figure 16.2 'Cummings and Worley's typology of interventions based on focal issues', adapted from Cummings, T.G. and Worley, C.G. (2001) *Organizational Development and Change*, 7th edn.

Emerald Group Publishing for Table 25.1 'Post-merger integration tasks', Shrivastava, P. (1986) 'Postmerger integration', *Journal of Business Strategy*, 7(1): 67; Figures

28.1 and 28.2 'Classes of sustainability at cell level' and 'Factory-level improvement model', Bateman, N. and David, A. (2002) Process improvement programmes: a model for assessing sustainability, *International Journal of Operations and Production Management*, **22**(5/6): 520.

Wiley for Figure 1.3 'Types of organizational change', adapted from Nadler, D. and Shaw, R. (1995) Change leadership, in Nadler, D., Shaw, R. and Walton, A.E. (eds) *Discontinuous Change*, Jossey-Bass; Figure 3.1 'The trap of success', Nadler, D. and Shaw, R. (1995) Change leadership, in Nadler, D., Shaw, R. and Walton, A.E. (eds) *Discontinuous Change*, Jossey-Bass; Exercise 5.1 'Raising awareness of your implicit model of organizational functioning', described in Tichy, N.M. and Hornstein, H.A. (1980) Collaborative model building, in Lawler, E.E., Nadler, D.A. and Cammann, C. (eds) *Organizational Assessment*, Wiley; Figure 5.3 'Kotter's integrative model of organizational dynamics', Nadler, D. and Tushman, M. (1980) Congruence model for organizational assessment, in Lawler, E.E., Nadler, D.A. and Cammann, C. (eds) *Organizational Assessment*, Wiley; Table 5.5 'Examples of element states that do and do not facilitate system adaptation', adapted from Nadler, D. and Tushman, M. (1980) Congruence model for organizational assessment, in Lawler, E.E., Nadler, D.A. and Cammann, C. (eds) *Organizational Assessment*, Wiley; Figure 5.4 'Congruence model', Nadler, D and Tushman, M. (1980) Congruence model for organizational assessment, in Lawler, E.E., Nadler, D.A. and Cammann, C. (eds) *Organizational Assessment*, Wiley; Figure 6.3 'Flamholtz's pyramid of organizational development', Flamholtz, E. (1995) Managing organizational transition: implications for corporate and human resource management, *European Management Journal*, **13**(1): 44; Figure 6.4 'The absorptive capacity/ tipping point framework for growth firm states', Phelps, R., Adams, R. and Bessant, J. (2007) Life cycles of growing organizations: a review with implications for knowledge and learning, *International Journal of Management Reviews*, **9**(1): 13; Figure 16.1 'Developments in types of intervention over the past century', Weisbord, M. (1987) *Productive Workplaces: Organising and Managing for Dignity, Meaning and Community*, Jossey-Bass.

Simon & Schuster for Figure 6.5 'The 7S model', Pascale, R. and Athos, A. (1981) *The Art of Japanese Management*.

Every effort has been made to trace rights holders, but if any have been inadvertently overlooked the publishers would be pleased to make the necessary arrangements at the first opportunity.

Abbreviations

AAA	after action review
A&E	accident and emergency
BPR	business process re-engineering
CE	chief executive
CEO	chief executive officer
ERP	enterprise resource planning
HR	human resources
HRM	human resource management
IT	information technology
JIT	just in time
NHS	National Health Service
OD	organization development
PDSA	plan, do, study, act
PEST	political, economic, social, technological
SARS	severe acute respiratory syndrome
SWOT	strengths, weaknesses, opportunities, threats
TQM	total quality management

Introduction
and overview

The Theory and Practice of Change Management is designed to help you:

▶ develop your investigative and diagnostic skills so that you will be more effective in assessing what is going on in organizations

▶ extend your ability to manage issues arising from internally planned and externally imposed organizational changes

▶ improve your awareness of how people can facilitate or resist change and extend your ability to manage the human resource in the context of change.

The book is divided into eight parts. The first examines the nature of change and in Chapter 2 presents a model of change as a process. The following seven parts of the book address each stage of this process in turn. Part II focuses on recognizing the need for change and starting the change process. Part III looks at diagnosis and how change managers identify what it is that needs to be changed. Part IV explores the many people issues that have to be attended to. Part V is concerned with planning and preparing to implement a change. Part VI focuses on implementation. Part VII looks at how change managers can monitor and review how well the change is progressing and how feedback can draw attention to unanticipated consequences and the need for corrective action. Part VIII is about sustaining change, hanging on to gains and spreading good practice.

Part I The nature of change

The first part of this book reviews some important theoretical perspectives on the nature of change and a range of the issues and choices that need to be considered when developing an approach to managing change.

Chapter 1 Patterns of change

The first chapter examines the nature of change, reviews theories relating to patterns of change, considers some of the factors that facilitate or limit change and explores some of the implications of different types of change for change management practice.

Until recently almost all received models of change were incremental and cumulative. The gradualist paradigm posits that organizations can adapt and transform themselves, as required, through a process of continuous adjustment. This is in stark contrast to the punctuated equilibrium paradigm, which posits that systems (organizations) evolve through the alternation of periods of equilibrium, in which persistent 'deep structures' only permit limited incremental change, and periods of revolution, in which these deep structures are fundamentally altered. It is argued that, with a few exceptions, most organizations experience change as a pattern of punctuated equilibrium.

After reading this chapter, you will be invited to assess your understanding of some of the issues discussed by identifying the nature of change involved in Case studies 1.1–1.5. You will also be invited to reflect on the nature of the changes confronting the organization you work for, or another organization you know well.

Chapter 2   The process of change

This chapter opens with an activity designed to explore the issues and choices involved in developing an approach to managing organizational change. It then moves on to consider change from a process perspective and presents a generic model that provides the structure for Chapters 3–29 of this book.

The way in which chapters relate to the generic model is illustrated below.

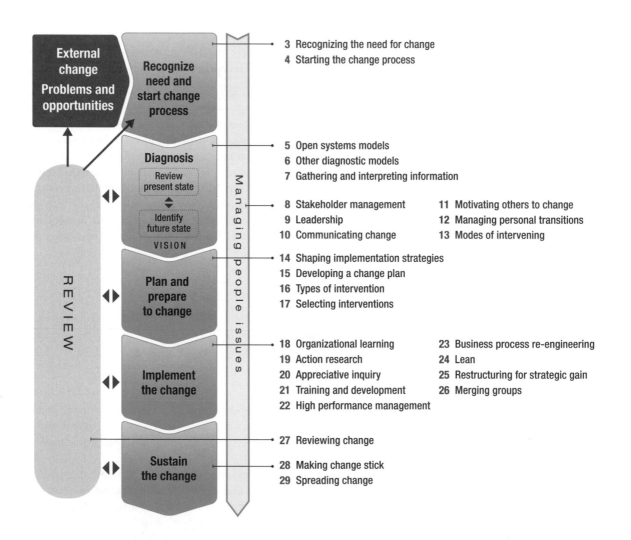

The relationship between Chapters 3–29 and the generic process model of change

Part II Recognizing the need for change and starting the change process

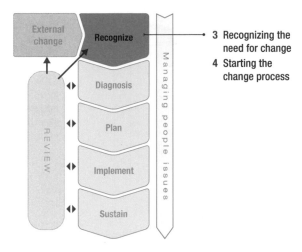

Chapter 3   Recognizing the need for change

The focus of this chapter is recognizing the need for change. Particular attention is given to how internal factors can affect this. These include strong organizational ideologies that inhibit learning, the composition of the top team, the way the agenda for change is formulated and the extent to which organizational members are encouraged or allowed to contribute to the change agenda.

Chapter 4   Starting the change process

This chapter examines some of the issues associated with starting the change process. Most important is translating the need for change into a desire for change. Organizational members may be reluctant to pursue change because they lack confidence in their own and others' ability to make a difference. This chapter (and book) adopts a 'voluntaristic' perspective and argues that organizational members are not powerless pawns, unable to affect change, but are independent actors able to intervene in ways that can make an important difference. To do this they need concepts and theories that will help them to understand the process of changing and ways of intervening, but they also need to believe in their own ability to affect outcomes.

Attention is given to who should lead the change and how they can build effective change relationships.

Part III   Diagnosis

Organizational diagnosis is concerned with identifying what it is that needs to be changed. Organizational behaviour, at all its different levels, is a complex phenomenon and it is impossible for managers to pay attention to every aspect of organizational functioning. Diagnostic models help change managers to cope with this complexity.

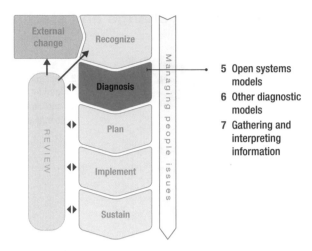

Chapter 5   Open systems models and alignment

This chapter opens with an examination of the role of models in organizational diagnosis and introduces an exercise designed to help raise your awareness of the implicit models you use when thinking about organizations and assessing the need for change.

Often our implicit models provide a good basis for understanding what is going on and predicting what kinds of actions or interventions will produce desired change. Sometimes, however, they are subjective and biased; they overemphasize some aspects of organizational functioning and completely neglect others. The aim of the model-building exercise is to help you to develop a greater awareness of your own model of organizational functioning, assess whether it is consistent with or relevant to the problems or opportunities you may need to address, and consider ways in which you can improve the efficacy of your approach to diagnosing and identifying what needs to be changed.

The second part of Chapter 5 considers the attributes of holistic models of organizational functioning, summarizes the main features of open systems models and discusses the utility of the concept of alignment.

Chapter 6   Other diagnostic models

This chapter presents a range of other models that can be used to aid diagnosis.

It is argued that 'good' diagnostic models are those that are relevant to the issues under consideration, help to identify critical cause-and-effect relationships and focus attention on elements that change managers can affect.

Chapter 7   Gathering and interpreting information for diagnosis

This chapter examines the process of gathering and interpreting information for the purpose of diagnosis. Attention is focused on five main steps:

1 selection of an appropriate conceptual model for diagnosis
2 clarification of information requirements
3 information gathering
4 analysis
5 interpretation.

Attention is also drawn to the political issues associated with data collection that can frustrate attempts to gain an accurate impression of organizational functioning.

At the end of this chapter, you are invited to think about a recent occasion when you, or somebody working close to you attempted to introduce and manage a change, and reflect on the extent to which this change initiative was based on an accurate diagnosis of the need for change, as well as consider the extent to which the accuracy of the diagnosis was related to the appropriateness of the diagnostic model used, the nature of the information collected and the way in which it was interpreted.

Part IV Managing the people issues

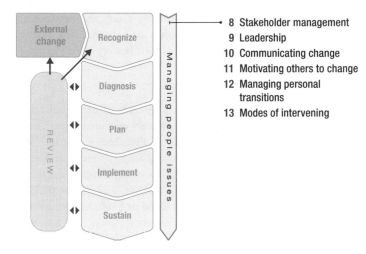

8 Stakeholder management
9 Leadership
10 Communicating change
11 Motivating others to change
12 Managing personal transitions
13 Modes of intervening

People issues need to be attended to throughout the whole change process. Just because 'managing people issues' is presented as Part IV does not mean that they are unimportant prior to implementation. A common mistake is to treat the early stages of starting the change and diagnosis and goal setting as purely technical activities. Too often, too little attention is given to political and motivational issues early on. It is not unusual for 'expert' change agents to decide when and where change is required and to define change objectives without taking into account the concerns of stakeholders or recognizing the ways in which they can contribute to or sabotage the change process. The six chapters in Part IV examine some of the people issues that change managers need to address.

Chapter 8 Power, politics and stakeholder management

This chapter explores the politics of organizational change and the need to enlist the support of key stakeholders. An instrumental theory of stakeholder management is elaborated with reference to resource dependence theory, prospect theory and life cycle models. It provides a conceptual framework for identifying which stakeholders are likely to be most important at various stages of a change project and for selecting appropriate ways of managing relationships with them. After completing an exercise designed to help you to explore some of the issues involved in stakeholder management, you will be invited to think about a recent change in your organization or elsewhere and, with the advantage of hindsight:

▸ identify the stakeholders involved in the change

▶ classify them according to their power to influence and their attitude towards the change
▶ assess the extent to which the change manager was aware of these stakeholders and took proper account of them when managing the change.

Chapter 9 The role of leadership in change management

This chapter examines the role of leadership in change management. Special attention is given to the leader's role in terms of creating a vision, aligning relationships around the vision and inspiring others to achieve the vision. Leadership is also considered as a collective process and some of the issues associated with maintaining coherence in the leadership group and between the leadership group and internal and external stakeholders are reviewed. The chapter closes with a review of Kotter's eight-point checklist of what leaders can do to promote change.

Chapter 10 Communicating change

This chapter considers the role of communication in the management of change. Often the focus is exclusively on the 'what, when, who and how' of communicating from the perspective of the change manager communicating to others. In this chapter, attention is also given to issues associated with change managers perceiving, interpreting and using information communicated to them by others.

After studying this chapter, you will be invited to consider how the quality of communication has helped or hindered change in your organization, or some other situation with which you are familiar.

Chapter 11 Motivating others to change

This chapter considers how the general level of commitment in an organization can affect the level of support for change and identifies some of the most common sources of resistance to change. The utility of expectancy theory for assessing and managing resistance to change is explored.

The second half of the chapter involves an exercise designed to help you to use expectancy and equity theory to motivate others to change.

Chapter 12 Managing personal transitions

This chapter addresses the way organizational members experience change. It examines the response to change, irrespective of whether the change is viewed as an opportunity or a threat, as a progression through a number of stages of psychological reaction. It also considers how an understanding of the way individuals react to change can help managers to plan and implement organizational change in ways that will maximize benefit and minimize cost for the organization and those affected by the change.

In this chapter, you will be invited to reflect on how you reacted to a change that was lasting in its effects, took place over a relatively short period of time and affected a number of key assumptions you made about how you related to the world around you. The information generated by this exercise will be used to validate a generic stage model of transition.

Chapter 13   Modes of intervening

This chapter argues that the most effective way of facilitating change is to intervene in a way that helps others to help themselves. Usually this involves adopting a collaborative approach but sometimes there may be special circumstances that call for a more prescriptive approach. Five different modes of intervening are discussed. One of these, advising, is prescriptive and the other four – supporting, theorizing, challenging and information gathering – are collaborative.

Part V   Planning and preparing for implementation

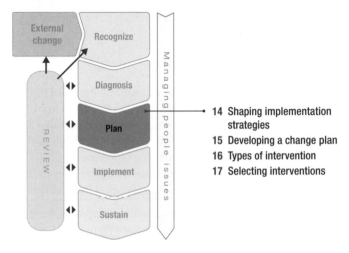

The four chapters in Part V examine some of the issues that change managers need to attend to, after they have diagnosed what needs to be changed, in order to decide how to achieve the required change.

Chapter 14   Shaping the implementation strategy

This chapter looks at the broad picture and considers the strengths and weaknesses of three approaches to managing change, explores some of the situational variables that need to be considered when shaping an implementation strategy and considers how and why a change strategy may need to change over time. The chapter concludes with a brief review of some alternative start points for change.

After reading this chapter, you will be invited to critically assess the strategy used to manage a recent change within your organization or some other situation with which you are familiar.

Chapter 15   Developing a change plan

It is not unusual for change to disrupt normal work and undermine existing management systems. This chapter considers some of the steps that need to be considered when developing a change plan. These are:

▶ appoint a transition manager
▶ identify what needs to be done
▶ produce an implementation plan, with clear targets and goals, which can indicate progress and signal a need for any remedial action
▶ use multiple and consistent leverage points for change

▶ schedule activities
▶ ensure that adequate resources are allocated to the change and that an appropriate balance is maintained between keeping the organization running and implementing the changes necessary to move towards the desired future state
▶ implement reward systems that encourage experimentation and change
▶ develop feedback mechanisms that provide the information required to ensure that the change programme moves forward in a coordinated manner, especially where the plan calls for change in a number of related areas.

After reading this chapter, you will be invited to reflect on an occasion when you were involved in the management of a change, at work or elsewhere, and consider what you or others might have done differently to develop an effective implementation plan.

Chapter 16   Types of intervention

Interventions are intentional acts designed to disrupt the status quo and move the organization towards a more effective state. Change efforts can be less successful than they might be because those responsible for managing the change are unaware of the full range of interventions available to them. This chapter reviews interventions using two contrasting typologies.

The first focuses attention on who does the intervening and what it is they do to bring about change. Four classes of intervention are discussed:

▶ experts applying scientific principles to solve specific problems
▶ groups working collaboratively to solve their own problems
▶ experts working to solve system-wide problems
▶ everybody working to improve the capability of the whole system for future performance.

The second classifies interventions in terms of the issues they address. Again, four main types of intervention are identified, which focus on:

▶ human process issues
▶ technology/structural issues
▶ human resource issues
▶ strategic issues.

Chapter 17   Selecting interventions

This chapter reviews some of the factors that need to be considered when selecting which kind of intervention to use. They include the nature of the diagnosed problem, the level of change target – individual, group, organization and so on – and the required depth of intervention. These factors are combined to provide a three-dimensional model to aid choice.

Attention is also given to the factors that can affect the sequencing of interventions. These include the intent or purpose of the change, organizational politics and how they can affect the support for different interventions, the need for an early success to maintain motivation, the stakes involved, and causal links that affect the dynamics of change.

Part VI Implementing change

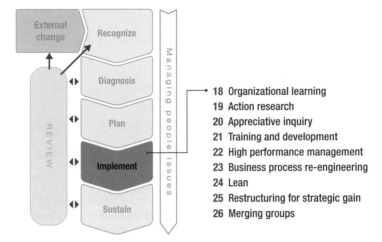

18 Organizational learning
19 Action research
20 Appreciative inquiry
21 Training and development
22 High performance management
23 Business process re-engineering
24 Lean
25 Restructuring for strategic gain
26 Merging groups

Implementation is the step in the change process that involves taking action to bring about change. Part VI reviews the theory that underpins nine types of intervention and considers how each can be used to secure change. The first three interventions (chapters) address human process problems, the next two focus on human resource issues, the following two on technostructural problems and the final two on strategic issues.

Chapter 18 Collective learning in organizations

This chapter reviews how collective learning can contribute to organizational effectiveness and presents examples of interventions that promote learning in different situations.

Different kinds of collective learning are discussed. Single loop learning is concerned with continuous improvement through doing things better. Double loop learning involves challenging current thinking and exploring the possibility of doing things differently or doing different things. Attention is also given to the role of knowledge transfer within and between organizations.

Chapter 19 Action research

Action research is the basic model underpinning most organizational change interventions. It involves the application of scientific methods (fact finding and experimentation) to organizational problems and underpins the generic process model of change presented in Chapter 2.

Action research is based on the premise that people learn best and are more willing to apply what they have learned when they manage the problem-solving process for themselves. The learning process involves:

▶ observing what is going on
▶ developing hypotheses that specify cause-and-effect relationships and point to actions that could help organizational members to manage their problem more effectively
▶ taking action
▶ collecting data to evaluate the effect of the action and test the hypothesis.

Chapter 20   Appreciative inquiry

Appreciative inquiry is a process that involves exploring the best of what is and amplifying this best practice. It seeks to accentuate the positive rather than eliminate the negative; it focuses attention on what is good and working rather than on what is wrong and not working.

Whereas action research promotes learning through attending to dysfunctional aspects of organizational functioning (problems), appreciative inquiry is concerned with embracing possibilities. This involves:

▶ Discovering the best of whatever is the focus of the inquiry, for example team working, leadership
▶ Understanding what creates the best of …
▶ Amplifying the people or processes that create the best of … .

This chapter examines appreciative inquiry from three perspectives: a philosophy of knowledge, an intervention theory, and a methodology for intervening in organizations to improve performance and the quality of life.

Chapter 21   Training and development

This chapter considers how training can contribute to the change process. Attention is directed towards the main elements of an effective approach to training. These are:

1 A training needs analysis, which involves three steps:
   • a system-level review to determine which parts of the organization will be affected by the change
   • a more focused task analysis to determine how the pattern of task demands and required competencies will change
   • a person analysis to identify the extent to which existing organizational members possess the required competencies.
2 The design and delivery of training.
3 The evaluation of the training.

The final section reviews the development of training practice in Australia over a 10-year period and highlights a number of trends in training provision.

Chapter 22   High performance management

This chapter considers how people management practices can affect performance by:

1 improving employees' knowledge and skills
2 motivating them to engage in discretionary behaviours that draw on their knowledge and skill
3 modifying organizational structures in ways that enable employees to improve the way they perform their jobs.

Rather than focusing on separate people management practices, high performance management involves developing and implementing a 'bundle' or system of practices that are internally consistent, aligned with other business processes, and aligned with the organization's business strategy.

Alignment is the defining feature of high performance management interventions.

Chapter 23 Business process re-engineering

This chapter examines the nature of business process re-engineering (BPR). While it is often regarded as a fundamental rethinking and radical redesign of business processes to achieve dramatic change, the benefits of less ambitious approaches that adopt BPR principles to improve existing processes are also considered.

The seven stages of BPR are discussed. These are:

1 process mapping
2 identifying processes for re-engineering
3 understanding the selected process
4 defining key performance objectives
5 designing new processes
6 testing
7 implementation.

Chapter 24 Lean

This chapter traces the development of lean thinking and presents Womark and Jones's five lean principles:

▶ specifying value for each product or product family
▶ identifying value streams for each product to expose waste
▶ making value flow without interruption
▶ letting customers pull value from the producer
▶ pursuing perfection by searching out and eliminating further waste.

A number of lean tools and techniques are reviewed along with issues to be considered when implementing lean. The chapter ends with an exploration of how lean has been applied in manufacturing and non-manufacturing settings.

Chapter 25 Restructuring for strategic gain: mergers and acquisitions

Acquisition success depends on both strategic and organization fit. This chapter adopts a process perspective and considers some of the conditions and critical junctures that can affect the quality of strategic fit and the integration process. Some of the issues that those leading the acquisition need to recognize and address are identified.

Many of the problems that undermine the acquisition process can be avoided, or at least minimized, if careful attention is given to:

▶ specifying acquisition objectives
▶ developing an acquisition overview that provides the bridge between the acquisition objectives and what needs to happen if they are to be achieved
▶ elaborating this overview to develop an implementation plan
▶ taking care to avoid managing the actual implementation in a heavy-handed way.

Chapter 26 Merging groups: combining people for effective performance

This chapter draws on social identity and acculturation theories to provide a conceptual framework for thinking about how managers can intervene to promote people synergy and achieve merger success. Attention is focused on three types of intervention:

▶ culture profiling – to pre-screen potential merger partners and, later in the merger process, guide the integration process

▶ change communication – to provide organizational members with clear and unambiguous information about what is going to change as a result of the merger

▶ socioemotional support – to care for those affected by the change, minimize alienation and promote post-merger organizational identity.

Part VII   Reviewing change

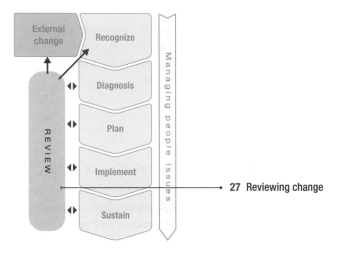

Chapter 27   Reviewing change

This chapter focuses special attention on how the process of reviewing progress can provide change managers with feedback they can use to assess whether interventions are being implemented as intended, whether the chosen interventions are having the desired effect and whether the change plan continues to be valid.

Part VIII   Sustaining change

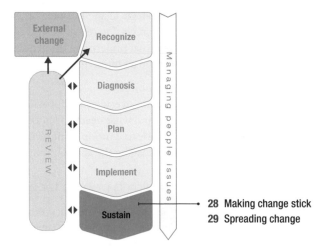

Lewin (1951) argued that all too often change is short-lived. After a 'shot in the arm', life returns to the way it was before. In his view, it is not enough to think of change in terms of simply reaching a new state. The first two chapters look at what managers

can do to sustain change. The final chapter presents a case study that provides an opportunity to reflect on and pull together all the concepts and ideas discussed in the book.

Chapter 28   Making change stick

This chapter looks at 'stickability' and what managers can do to consolidate a change and hold on to gains. Attention is focused on two key issues:

1 The way the change process is managed from the beginning. It is argued that tough top-down (push) strategies are more likely to foster compliance than commitment and ownership. Compliance often evaporates when the pressure to maintain the change is eased.
2 How change managers can act to sustain change after the initial change goals have been achieved.

Chapter 29   Spreading change

This chapter looks at 'spreadability', the extent to which new methods and processes that have delivered gains in one location are applied, or adapted and then applied elsewhere across the organization. Attention is given to what managers can do to promote the spread of change.

Chapter 30   Pulling it all together: a concluding case study

This book covers a lot of ground. Chapter 30 introduces a concluding case study designed to provide you with an opportunity to review what you have read and think about how the many theories, models, techniques and tools can be applied to the management of a single case. You can do this on your own or with others.

THE NATURE OF CHANGE

The first part of this book reviews some important theoretical perspectives on the nature of change and a range of the issues and choices that need to be considered when developing an approach to managing change.

The way in which chapters relate to the generic model is illustrated below.

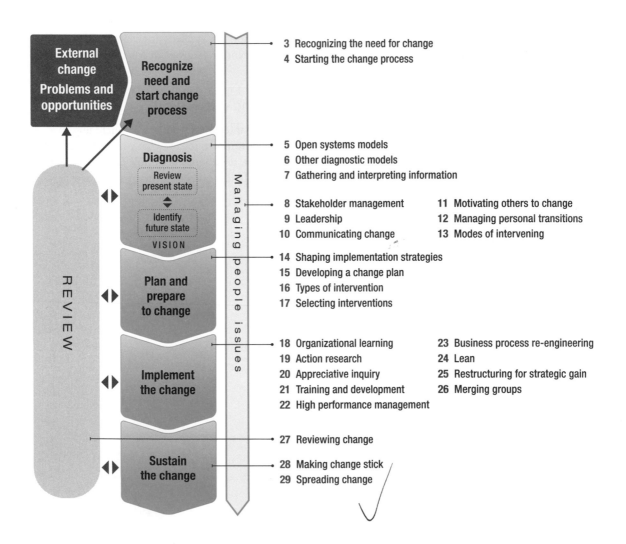

External change Problems and opportunities

Recognize need and start change process
- 3 Recognizing the need for change
- 4 Starting the change process

Diagnosis
Review present state
Identify future state
VISION
- 5 Open systems models
- 6 Other diagnostic models
- 7 Gathering and interpreting information

- 8 Stakeholder management
- 9 Leadership
- 10 Communicating change
- 11 Motivating others to change
- 12 Managing personal transitions
- 13 Modes of intervening

Plan and prepare to change
- 14 Shaping implementation strategies
- 15 Developing a change plan
- 16 Types of intervention
- 17 Selecting interventions

Implement the change
- 18 Organizational learning
- 19 Action research
- 20 Appreciative inquiry
- 21 Training and development
- 22 High performance management
- 23 Business process re-engineering
- 24 Lean
- 25 Restructuring for strategic gain
- 26 Merging groups

Sustain the change
- 27 Reviewing change
- 28 Making change stick
- 29 Spreading change

REVIEW

Managing people issues

The relationship between Chapters 3–29 and the generic process model of change

Chapter 1   Patterns of change

The first chapter examines the nature of change, reviews theories relating to patterns of change, considers some of the factors that facilitate or limit change and explores some of the implications of different types of change for change management practice.

Until recent times almost all received models of change were incremental and cumulative. The gradualist paradigm posits that organizations can adapt and transform themselves, as required, through a process of continuous adjustment. This is in stark contrast to the punctuated equilibrium paradigm, which posits that systems (organizations) evolve through the alternation of periods of equilibrium, in which persistent deep structures only permit limited incremental change, and periods of revolution, in which these deep structures are fundamentally altered. It is argued that, with a few exceptions, most organizations experience change as a pattern of punctuated equilibrium.

After reading this chapter, you will be invited to assess your understanding of some of the issues discussed by identifying the nature of change involved in Case studies 1.1.1–1.1.5. You will also be invited to reflect on the nature of the changes confronting the organization you work for, or another organization that you know well.

Chapter 2   The process of change

This chapter opens with an activity designed to explore the issues and choices involved in developing an approach to managing organizational change. It then moves on to consider change from a process perspective and presents a generic model that provides the structure for Chapters 3–29 of this book.

Patterns of change

The *Shorter Oxford Dictionary* offers several definitions of change, ranging from the 'substitution or succession of one thing in place of another' to the 'alteration in the state or quality of anything'. Changes can be large or small, evolutionary or revolutionary, sought after or resisted. This chapter examines the nature of change, reviews theories relating to patterns of change, considers some of the factors that facilitate or limit change and explores some of the implications of different types of change for change management practice. Attention is also given to the effects of change on individuals.

The chapter ends with two exercises. The first invites you to analyse the nature of the change involved in four case studies. The second invites you to reflect on the nature of the changes confronting the organization you work for, or another organization that you know well, and classify these changes using the conceptual frameworks presented in this chapter.

Until recently almost all received models of change were incremental and cumulative. This theoretical consensus had implications for change management practice. The aim of planned change efforts tended to be continuous improvement (what the Japanese refer to as 'kaizen') and most attention was focused on changing subsystems or parts of the organization in turn, rather than attempting to change the whole organization at once. Over the past 30 years, however, many traditional assumptions about the incremental nature of change have been revised.

The rate of change is not constant

Starting in the late 1970s, Tushman and his colleagues at Columbia University studied hundreds of companies in several industries over time (see Tushman and Romanelli, 1985; Tushman et al., 1986). They found evidence to support what many already knew. The rate of change, as an industry evolves, is not constant. It follows a sigmoidal (s-shaped) curve, with a slow beginning (lag phase) associated with experimentation and slow market penetration, a middle period of rapid growth (log phase) as the product gains acceptance and as dominant designs emerge, and finally a tapering off as more advanced or completely different products attract consumers' attention (Figure 1.1). The pattern then starts all over again.

Similar variations in the rate of change were identified much earlier by Ryan and Gross (1943), when they studied how 259 farmers in Iowa responded to the introduction of a new superior hybrid seed corn. The new seed was available in 1928 but it was 1932 before the first farmers began planting. In 1934, 16 farmers adopted the new seed, followed by slightly higher numbers in the following two years. But it was nine years after the seeds were first available before there was widespread acceptance. The breakthrough came in 1937. The first users were innovators who 'infected' the early adopters, a group who carefully monitored the success of the initial trials before deciding what to do. This group was followed by a mass of movers, the early and the late majority. The last group to adopt the seeds were the laggards and it was 1942 before all but two of the 259 farmers were planting the new seeds.

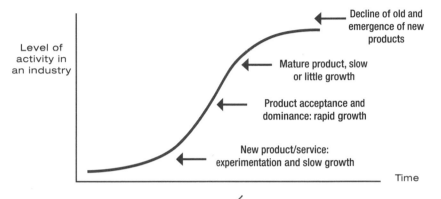

Figure 1.1 *Pattern of industry evolution*

Gladwell (2000), in his book *The Tipping Point*, cites some more dramatic examples – including the sudden and dramatic decline in crime in New York in 1990 and the takeoff of fax machines in the USA, when, only three years after they were first introduced, over a million machines were sold – to support his assertion that many social changes do not occur gradually. They spread like viral epidemics and change, when it happens, is sudden. The 'tipping point' is the name he gives to the dramatic moment in an epidemic when everything changes at once.

The proposition that some changes happen quickly, over relatively short periods of time, whereas others gradually evolve suggests that the tempo of change might provide a useful basis for thinking about the nature of change and the implications of different types of change for change management practice.

The punctuated equilibrium paradigm

Gould (1978) challenges the notion of incremental, cumulative change. He is a natural historian with an interest in Darwin's theory of evolution. Traditionalists assert that evolution involves a slow stream of small changes (mutations) that are continuously being shaped over time by environmental selection. While Gould accepts the principle of natural selection, he rejects the proposition that change is gradual and continuous. Gould (1978: 15) asserts that the evidence points to 'a world punctuated with periods of mass extinction and rapid origination among long stretches of relative tranquillity'. Some of his essays focus on the two greatest 'punctuations'. After four billion years of almost no change, there was the Cambrian explosion of life (about 600 million years ago) and, after another longish period of very slow change, the Permian extinction that wiped out half the families of marine invertebrates (225 million years ago).

Gersick (1991) has studied models of change in six domains – individual change, group development, organization development, history of science, biological evolution and physical science – and found support for the punctuated equilibrium paradigm in every domain. According to Gersick (1991: 12), the paradigm has the following components: 'relatively long periods of stability (equilibrium), punctuated by compact periods of qualitative, metamorphic change (revolution)'. She goes on to assert that in all the models she studied across the six domains:

> the relationship of these two modes is explained through the construct of a highly durable underlying order or deep structure. This deep structure is what persists and limits change during equilibrium periods and is what disassembles, reconfigures, and enforces wholesale transformation during revolutionary periods. (Gersick, 1991: 12)

The essence of the punctuated equilibrium paradigm is that systems (organizations) evolve through the alternation of periods of equilibrium, in which persistent 'deep structures' only permit limited incremental change, and periods of revolution, in which these deep structures are fundamentally altered. This is in stark contrast to the traditional gradualist paradigm, which suggests that:

▶ an organization (or an organizational subsystem) can accommodate any change at any time so long as it is a relatively small change
▶ a stream of incremental changes can, over a period of time, fundamentally transform the organization's deep structure.

Deep structure

Gersick (1991: 16) refers to deep structure as the fundamental choices an organization makes that determine the basic activity patterns that maintain its existence. She argues that deep structures are highly stable because the trail of choices made by a system (organization) rule out many options and rule in those that are mutually contingent – 'early steps in the decision tree are the most fateful'. She also argues that the activity patterns of a system's deep structure reinforce the system as a whole through mutual feedback loops.

Tushman and Romanelli (1985) identify five key domains of organizational activity that might be viewed as representing an organization's deep structure. These are organizational culture, strategy, structure, power distribution and control systems. Romanelli and Tushman (1994) go on to assert that it takes a revolution to alter a system of interrelated organizational parts when it is maintained by mutual dependencies among the parts, and when competitive, regulatory and technological systems outside the organization reinforce the legitimacy of the managerial choices that produced the parts.

Greenwood and Hinings (1996) offer a slightly different perspective based on neo-institutional theory, but the core argument is the same; there is a force for inertia that limits the possibility for incremental change, and that this resistance to change will be strongest when the network of mutual dependencies is tightly coupled. Greenwood and Hinings' (1996: 1023) argument is that a major source of resistance to change stems from the 'normative embeddedness of an organization within its institutional context'. Organizations must accommodate institutional expectations in order to survive. They illustrate this point with reference to the way institutional context has influenced the structure and governance of accounting firms. They were (and most still are) organized as professional partnerships, not because that form of governance facilitated efficient and effective task performance, but because it was defined as the appropriate way of organizing the conduct of accounting work.

The parameters offered by such an archetypal template provide the context for convergent change. Greenwood and Hinings (1996: 1025) suggest, for example, that an accounting firm operating as a professional partnership could, as it grows, introduce some form of representative democracy in place of the traditional broadly based democratic governance. This kind of incremental change could be achieved because it is perceived to be consistent with prevailing core ideas and values. However, a move towards a more a bureaucratic form of authority and governance might encounter strong resistance because it is perceived to be inconsistent with the prevailing template. Such a radical change would involve the organization moving from one template-in-use to another.

These templates work in the same way as Gersick's deep structures. However, the degree of embeddedness and the strength of these templates may vary between sectors, and this will affect the power of the template to limit the possibility for incremental cumulative change in any particular organization. In the case of the accounting profession, the partnership organizational form, with its commitment to independence, autonomy and responsible conduct, is supported by a strong network of reciprocal exchanges between professional associations, universities, state agencies and accounting firms. The outcome is a situation where individual accounting firms are tightly coupled to the prevailing archetypal template. Greenwood and Hinings (1996) argue that radical change in tightly coupled fields will be unusual, but if it does occur, it will be revolutionary. However, in loosely coupled fields, radical change will be more common and will tend to be evolutionary and could unfold over a relatively long period of time.

Equilibrium periods

Gersick (1991: 16) introduces the analogy of the playing field and the rules of the game to describe an organization's deep structure, and the game in play to describe activity during an equilibrium period. How a game of football is played may change over the course of a match, but there is a consistency that is determined by the nature of the playing field and the rules of the game. The coach and the players can intervene and make changes that will affect team performance, but they cannot intervene to change the nature of the playing field or the rules of the game (the deep structure). In terms of organizational change, during periods of equilibrium, change agents can intervene and make incremental adjustments in response to internal or external perturbations, but these interventions will not fundamentally affect the organization's deep structure.

An important question is: 'Why do organizations find it hard to change?' According to the punctuated equilibrium paradigm, organizations are resistant to change in equilibrium periods because of forces of inertia that work to maintain the status quo. Gersick argues that so long as the deep structure is intact, it generates a strong inertia to prevent the system from generating alternatives outside its own boundaries. Furthermore, these forces for inertia can pull any deviations that do occur back into line.

Gersick (1991) identifies three sources of inertia: cognitive frameworks, motivation and obligations. Organizational members often develop shared cognitive frameworks and mental models that influence the way they interpret reality and learn. Shared mental models can restrict attention to thinking 'within the frame'. With regard to change, attention may be restricted to searching for ways of doing things better. In periods of equilibrium, assumptions about the organization's theory of business (Drucker, 1994) often go unchallenged and organizational members fail to give sufficient attention to the possibility of doing things differently or even doing different things. (See Hodgkinson and Healey, 2008, for details of studies that have considered the role of mental representations in both organizational inertia and strategic adaptation.)

Motivational barriers to change are often related to the fear of loss, especially with regard to the sunk costs incurred during periods of equilibrium. Gersick (1991: 18) refers to the fear of losing control over one's situation if the equilibrium ends and argues that this contributes heavily to the human motivation to avoid significant system change. Thaler and Sunstein (2009) draw on the work of Samuelson and Zeckhauser to argue that for lots of reasons people prefer to stick with their current situation.

Obligations can also limit change. Tushman and Romanelli (1985: 177) note that even if a system can overcome its own cognitive and motivational barriers against realizing a need for change, the networks of interdependent resource relationships and value commitments generated by its structure will often prevent it being able to achieve the required change. This view, at least in part, adds support to Greenwood and Hining's (1996) proposition that the normative embeddedness of an organization can limit change.

Episodes of discontinuous change occur when inertia, that is, the inability of organizations to change as rapidly as their environment, triggers some form of revolutionary transformation.

Revolutionary periods

Gersick (1991) asserts that the definitive element of the punctuated equilibrium paradigm is that organizations do not shift from one 'kind of game' to another through incremental steps. This, according to Romanelli and Tushman (1994), is because resistance to change prevents small changes in organizational units from taking hold and substantially influencing activities in related subunits. Consequently, small changes do not accumulate incrementally to transform the organization.

Weick and Quinn (1999) note that punctuated equilibrium theorists posit that episodes of revolutionary change occur during periods of divergence when there is a growing misalignment between an organization's deep structure and perceived environmental demands. They report that the metaphor of the firm implied by conceptions of episodic change is an organization that comprises a set of interdependencies that converge and tighten (become more closely aligned) as short run adaptations are pursued in order to achieve higher levels of efficiency. This focus on internal alignment deflects attention away from the need to maintain external alignment and, consequently, the organization is slow to adapt to environmental change. Inertia maintains the state that Lewin (1947) described as stable, quasi-stationary equilibrium until misalignment reaches the point where major changes are precipitated. The only way forward is for the organization to transform itself. Gersick (1991: 19) argues that the transformation of deep structures can only occur through a process of wholesale upheaval:

> According to this logic, the deep structures must first be dismantled, leaving the system temporarily disorganized, in order for any fundamental change to be accomplished. Next, a subset of the system's old pieces, along with some new pieces, can be put back together into a new configuration, which operates according to a new set of rules.

This process of revolutionary change and organizational transformation provides the basis for a new state of equilibrium. However, because of forces of resistance that inhibit continuous adaptation, this new equilibrium gives rise to another period of relative stability that is followed by a further period of revolutionary change. This process continues to unfold as a process of punctuated equilibrium.

Those who subscribe to the punctuated equilibrium paradigm argue that revolutionary episodes may affect a single organization or a whole sector. Marks & Spencer is an organization that was faced with the need to reinvent itself when, even after a long period of incremental change, it found itself misaligned with its environment and performing less well than other leading retailers. An example of a whole sector that was faced with the need to change its deep structure is the electricity supply sector in the UK. When the Conservative government decided to privatize the industry, this created a new playing field and a new set of rules for all the utility companies in the sector.

Support for the punctuated equilibrium paradigm

Numerous case histories offer support for the punctuated equilibrium paradigm. Pettigrew (1987) reports a study of change in ICI over the period 1969–86. He found that radical periods of change were interspersed with periods of incremental adjustment and that change in core beliefs preceded changes in structure and business strategy. Tushman et al. (1986) examined the development of AT&T, General Radio, Citibank and Prime Computers and observed periods during which organizational systems, structures and strategies converged to be more aligned with the basic mission of these organizations. They also observed that these equilibrium periods were punctuated by brief periods of intense and pervasive change that led to the formulation of new missions and then the initiation of new equilibrium periods. The first direct test of the paradigm was Romanelli and Tushman's (1994) empirical study of microcomputer producers, the key elements of which are summarized in Research report 1.1.

Research report 1.1 ⟩ **Study of microcomputer producers**

Romanelli, E. and Tushman, M.L. (1994) Organizational transformation as punctuated equilibrium: an empirical test, *Academy of Management Journal*, **37**(5): 1141–66

According to the punctuated equilibrium model, radical and discontinuous change of all or most organizational activities is necessary to break the grip of strong inertia. This provides the basis of Romanelli and Tushman's first hypothesis:

> Organizational transformations will most frequently occur in short, discontinuous bursts of change involving most or all key domains of organizational activity.

Resistance to change is critical to punctuated equilibrium theory in that it establishes the key condition that supports revolutionary transformation. Resistance prevents small changes in organizational subunits from taking hold or substantially influencing activities in related subunits. This gives rise to their second hypothesis:

> Small changes in individual domains of organizational activity will not accumulate incrementally to yield a fundamental transformation.

Their final set of three hypotheses addressed how organizational transformation is stimulated. Since the punctuated equilibrium model posits strong inertia as the common state of organizational affairs, they hypothesized that this inertia will be broken by a severe crisis in performance, major changes in the organization's environment, and succession of its chief executive officer (CEO).

Method

Romanelli and Tushman studied the life histories of 25 minicomputer producers founded in the USA between 1967 and 1969. The firms were selected to maximize organizational similarities on dimensions of organizational age and the environmental characteristics that the organizations faced during founding and later in their lives.

Data were collected for all years of the organizations' lives from a variety of sources, including information required by the Securities and Exchange Commission, annual reports, prospectuses, and industry and business press reports. They found that detailed information about strategies, structures and power distributions was available for all organizations throughout their lives. However, they also found that organizations reported information about cultures and control systems infrequently and inconsistently. Consequently, Romanelli and Tushman dropped the culture and control system domains of activity from further analysis and focused their attention on structure, strategy and power distributions.

Fundamental organizational transformations, which could be either revolutionary or non-revolutionary, were identified as occurring whenever substantial changes were observed in the strategy, structure and power distribution domains of organizational activity. Revolutionary transformations were defined as occurring whenever changes in all three strategy, structure, and power distributions occurred within any two-year time period. NB: Two years was selected because some of the data were presented for corporate fiscal years and some for calendar years; however, they found that the majority of the revolutionary transformations actually occurred within a single year. Non-revolutionary transformations were identified in two ways. First, whenever there were substantial changes over a period longer than two years and, second, when small changes accumulated to a 30% change and when all three domains exhibited this level of change.

Results

The key findings of the study were that:

1 A large majority of organizational transformations were accomplished via rapid and discontinuous change.
2 Small changes in strategies, structure and power distribution did not accumulate to produce fundamental transformations. This finding provides additional evidence that fundamental organizational transformations tend to occur in short, discontinuous bursts.
3 Triggers for transformations were major environmental changes and CEO succession.

The gradualist paradigm

The gradualist paradigm posits that fundamental change (organizational transformation) can occur through a process of continuous adjustment, and does not require some major discontinuous jolt to the system in order to trigger a short episode of revolutionary change. Change is evolving and cumulative.

Brown and Eisenhardt (1997) argue that many firms compete by changing continuously. They cite companies such as Intel, Wal-Mart, 3M, Hewlett-Packard and Gillette and suggest that for them the ability to change rapidly and continuously is not just a core competence but is at the heart of their cultures. They refer to Burgelman (1991) and Chakravarthy (1997), who suggest that continuous change is often played out through product innovation as companies change and sometimes transform through a process of continually altering their products. Hewlett-Packard is identified as a classic case. The company changed from an instruments company to a computer firm through rapid, continuous product innovation, rather than through a sudden punctuated change.

Continuous change, when it occurs, involves the continuous updating of work processes and social practices. Weick and Quinn (1999) argue that this leads to new patterns of organizing in the absence of a priori intentions on the part of some change agent. It is emergent in the sense that there is no deliberate orchestration of change. It is continuous and is the outcome of the everyday process of management. They cite Orlikowski (1996), who suggests that continuous change involves individuals and groups accommodating and experimenting with everyday contingencies, breakdowns, exceptions, opportunities and unintended consequences, and repeating, sharing and amplifying them to produce perceptible and striking changes.

Weick and Quinn (1999) observe that the distinctive quality of continuous change is the idea that small continuous adjustments, created simultaneously across units, can cumulate and create substantial change. They identify three related processes associated with continuous change: improvisation, translation and learning:

▶ *Improvising* facilitates the modification of work practices through mutual adjustments in which the time gap between planning and implementing narrows towards the point where composition (planning) converges with execution (implementation).
▶ *Translation* refers to the continuous adoption and editing of ideas as they travel through the organization.
▶ *Learning* involves the continuous revision of shared mental models, which facilitates a change in the organization's response repertoire.

Weick and Quinn (1999: 372) suggest that

> organisations produce continuous change by means of repeated acts of improvisation involving simultaneous composition and execution, repeated acts of translation that convert ideas into useful artefacts that fit purposes at hand, or repeated acts of learning that enlarge, strengthen, or shrink the repertoire of responses.

Brown and Eisenhardt (1997) studied product innovation in six firms in the computer industry at a time of rapid product development associated with the Pentium processor, multimedia, internet and the convergence of telephony with consumer electronics. Three of their case studies related to firms with a record of successful product innovation and business performance and three related to firms with a relatively poor record of developing multi-product portfolios. They identified three characteristics of the firms that were able to manage change as a continuous process of adjustment: semi-structures that facilitated improvisation, links in time that facilitated learning, and sequenced steps for managing transitions.

While the punctuated equilibrium paradigm stresses the interdependence of organizational subunits and a web of interdependent relationships with buyers, suppliers and others that legally and normatively constrain organizations to established activities and relationships (Romanelli and Tushman, 1994), the gradualist paradigm emphasizes the relative independence of organizational subunits. This loose coupling facilitates change within subunits. Over time, as unit managers repeatedly alter their goals and relationships to accommodate changes in local environments, the organization as a whole can be transformed. As noted above, Greenwood and Hinings (1996) support the view that tightly coupled relationships are resistant to change and when change does occur, it tends to be revolutionary, but recognize that in loosely coupled fields, radical change can be evolutionary. Weick and Quinn (1999), however, suggest that when interdependencies are loose, continuous adjustments tend to be confined within subunits and remain as pockets of innovation. Continuous adjustment, therefore, may not always lead to fundamental change.

Burke (2002) speculates that more that 95% of organizational changes are, in some way, evolutionary, but he questions Orlikowski's assumption that this can lead to sufficient modification to achieve fundamental change. He asserts that it is difficult to overcome inertia and equilibrium without a discontinuous 'jolt' to the system:

Organisation change does occur with continuous attention and effort, but it is unlikely that fundamental change in the deep structure of the organization would happen. (Burke, 2002: 69)

The nature of change confronting most organizations

Dunphy (1996) argues that planned change is triggered by the failure of people to create a continuously adaptive organization, the kind of organization that is referred to in Chapter 18 as an effective learning organization. Weick and Quinn (1999) suggest that this holds true whether the focus is episodic or continuous change, and they propose that the ideal organization in both cases would resemble the successful self-organizing and highly adaptive firms that Brown and Eisenhardt found in the computer industry. However, while some organizations might achieve this ideal and become so effective at double loop collective learning (see Chapter 18) that they are never misaligned with their environment, most do not. The majority of organizations, if they survive long enough, experience episodes of discontinuous revolutionary as well as continuous incremental change.

There are three main categories of organizations that may not experience periods of discontinuous change. These are:

1 The kind of self-organizing and continuously changing learning organizations identified by Brown and Eisenhardt.
2 Companies operating in niche markets or slow-moving sectors where they have not yet encountered the kind of environmental change that requires them to transform their deep structures.
3 Organizations that are able to continue functioning without transforming themselves because they have sufficient 'fat' to absorb the inefficiencies associated with misalignment.

With these exceptions, most organizations experience change as a pattern of punctuated equilibrium. This pattern involves relatively long periods of equilibrium, during which an organization may only engage in incremental change, punctuated with short episodes of discontinuity during which an organization's survival may depend on its ability to transform itself.

Incremental change

According to the punctuated equilibrium paradigm, incremental change is associated with those periods when the industry is in equilibrium and the focus for change is 'doing things better' through a process of continuous tinkering, adaptation and modification. Nadler and Tushman (1995) make the point that incremental changes are not necessarily small changes. They can be large in terms of the resources needed and the impact on people. A key feature of this type of change is that it builds on what has already been accomplished and has the flavour of continuous improvement. According to the gradualist paradigm, incremental change can be cumulative and, over time, can lead to an organization transforming its deep structures and reinventing itself. However, according to the punctuated equilibrium paradigm, incremental change is incapable of fundamentally transforming the deep structures of an organization.

Transformational change

According to the punctuated equilibrium paradigm, transformational change occurs during periods of disequilibrium. Weick and Quinn (1999) and Gersick (1991) refer to this kind of change as 'revolutionary', but most writers, for example Tichy and Devanna (1986), Kotter (1999) and Burke and Litwin (1992), use the term 'transformational change'. It involves a break with the past, a step function change rather than an extrapolation of past patterns of change and development. It is based on new relationships and dynamics within the industry that may undermine core competencies, and question the very purpose of the enterprise. This kind of change involves doing things differently rather than doing things better. It might even mean doing different things. The reprographics industry provides a good example of a sector that was faced with a major discontinuity. Companies found that their core competence in optical reproduction was undermined when digital scanning technology was developed and made available to their customers.

The studies undertaken by Tushman and colleagues (summarized in Nadler and Tushman, 1995) suggest that most companies not only go through periods of continuous incremental and discontinuous transformational change, but that:

▶ this pattern of change repeats itself with some degree of regularity
▶ patterns vary across sectors, for example periods of discontinuity may follow a 30-year cycle in cement, but a 5-year cycle in minicomputers
▶ in almost all industries the rate of change is increasing and the time between periods of discontinuity is decreasing (Figure 1.2).

This last point is important because it predicts that all managers will be confronted with an ever greater need to manage both incremental and transformational change.

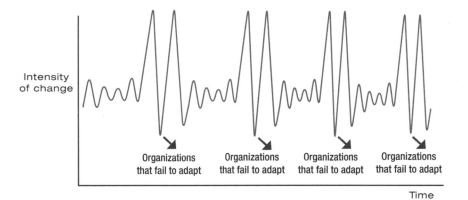

Figure 1.2 *Punctuated equilibrium: a recurring pattern of continuous and transformational change*

Not all organizations are able to successfully negotiate episodes of discontinuity and those that fail to adapt may drop out or be acquired by others. Forester and Kaplan (2001) provide chilling evidence of the consequences of failing to adapt. They refer to changes in the *Forbes* top 100 companies between 1917 and 1987. Out of the original 100 companies, only 18 were still in the list in 1987 and 61 no longer existed.

The possibility of anticipating change

Sometimes it is relatively easy to anticipate the need for change. For example, companies operating in the European Union can, if they pay appropriate attention, anticipate the impact of new regulations that are currently being discussed in

Brussels. Companies competing in markets where margins are being squeezed can anticipate the need to secure greater efficiencies or generate new income streams. There are, however, occasions when organizations are confronted with changes that are difficult to anticipate, for example the effects of the 9/11 terrorist attacks or the SARS epidemic.

Some organizations are much better at anticipating the need for change than others. They are proactive. They search out potential threats and opportunities. They prepare for destabilizing events that might occur or anticipate changes they could initiate to gain competitive advantage. Other organizations are much more reactive and only act when there is a clear and pressing need to respond.

Whether the need is for incremental or transformational change, the earlier the need is recognized, the greater the number of options managers will have when deciding how to manage it. Whenever managers are forced to react to an urgent and pressing need to change, they are relatively constrained in what they can do. For example:

▶ *There is less time for planning:* Careful planning takes time, something that is more likely to be available to those who are proactive and anticipate the need for change.
▶ *There is unlikely to be sufficient time to involve many people:* Involving people and encouraging participation in the change process can aid diagnosis, reduce resistance and increase commitment, but this also takes time.
▶ *There will be little time to experiment:* Early movers not only have time to experiment, they may also have the time to try again if the first experiment fails. When there is a pressing need for change, it is more difficult to search for creative solutions.
▶ *Late movers may have little opportunity to influence shifts in markets and technologies:* Early movers may have the opportunity to gain a competitive advantage by not only developing but also protecting, for example through patents, new products or technologies.

A typology of organizational change

Combining two of the dimensions of change discussed so far, the extent to which change involves incremental adjustment or transformational change and the extent to which the organization's response to change is proactive or reactive, provides a useful typology of organizational change (see Figure 1.3).

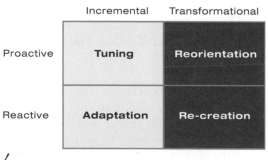

Figure 1.3 *Types of organizational change*
Source: Adapted from Nadler et al., 1995: 24

Nadler et al. (1995) identify four types of change:

1 *Tuning* is change that occurs when there is no immediate requirement to change. It involves seeking better ways of achieving and/or defending the strategic vision,

for example improving policies, methods, procedures; introducing new technologies; redesigning processes to reduce cost, time to market and so on; or developing people with required competencies. Most organizations engage in a form of fine-tuning much of the time. This approach to change tends to be initiated internally in order to make minor adjustments to maintain alignment between the internal elements of the organization and between the organization's strategy and the external environment.

2 *Adaptation* is an incremental and adaptive response to a pressing external demand for change. It might involve responding to a successful new marketing strategy adopted by a competitor or to a change in the availability of a key resource. Essentially, it broadly involves doing more of the same but doing it better in order to remain competitive. An example of adaptive change might be what happens when one company, for example Nestlé, is forced to respond to a competitive move by another, for example Mars may have either increased the size or reduced the price of some of its confectionary products. This kind of change is not about doing things in fundamentally different ways or about doing fundamentally different things.

While tuning and adaptation can involve minor or major changes, they are types of change that occur within the same frame, they are bounded by the existing paradigm. Reorientation and re-creation, on the other hand, are types of change that, to use Gersick's analogy, target the playing field and the rules of the game rather than the way a particular game is played. They involve transforming the organization and bending or breaking the frame to do things differently or to do different things.

3 *Reorientation* involves a redefinition of the enterprise. It is initiated in anticipation of future opportunities or problems. The aim is to ensure that the organization will be aligned and effective in the future. It may be necessary to modify the frame but, because the need for change has been anticipated, this could involve a gradual process of continuous frame bending. Nestlé offered a good example of reorientation in the mid-1980s. At a time when it was doing well, it embarked on a major change programme to ensure that it would remain aligned to its environment over the medium term. It initiated a top-down review to decide which businesses it should be in. Should it, for example, be in the pet foods business, continue to manufacture baked beans at a time when margins on that product were diminishing, or, as a major consumer of tin cans, supply its own or buy them in on a just in time basis? It also embarked on a major project to re-engineer the supply chain across the business and a bottom-up analysis of the added value contributed by each main activity. British Gas provides another example. After it had been privatized as a monopoly supplier of gas, the company was referred to the Monopolies and Mergers Commission. It was obvious to the top team that when the commission delivered its report, the company would be forced to change and might even be broken up. In order to prepare for this, a team of 10 senior managers was created to explore and test possible scenarios and help the organization to develop the capability to respond to the inevitable, but at that time unspecified, changes it would have to face.

In those cases where the need for change is not obvious to all and may not be seen as pressing by many, senior management (as in the British Gas example) may need to work hard in order to create a sense of urgency and gain widespread acceptance of the need to prepare for change.

4 *Re-creation* is a reactive change that involves transforming the organization through the fast and simultaneous change of all its basic elements. Nadler and Tushman (1995) state that it inevitably involves organizational frame breaking

and the destruction of some elements of the system. It can be disorienting. An often cited example of this kind of change is that introduced by Lee Iacocca when he became the new CEO at Chrysler. He embarked on a process of revolutionary change that involved replacing most of the top team, withdrawing the company from the large car market and divesting many foreign operations.

The most common type of change is incremental (either fine-tuning or adaptation) but it is not unusual for a single organization to be involved in more than one type of change at the same time. Confronted with ever diminishing opportunities to grow the mining business, UK Coal reappraised its assets and considered how it might revise its theory of business. The way forward was to explore the possibility of redefining the company as a land and property management and mining company. This reorientation involved many changes including bringing in new people with competencies in the area of land and property management. However, while this transformational change was being implemented at the highest level, the company was also pursuing incremental continuous improvement programmes to increase the efficiency of individual deep mines.

Implications of these different types of change for change management practice

Different types of change can affect the focus for change efforts, the sequence of steps in the change process and the locus for change, as discussed below.

The focus for change efforts

With incremental change, the aim is to improve alignment between existing organizational components in order to do things better and improve the efficiency of the organization (see Figure 1.4). With transformational change, the aim is to seek a new configuration of organizational components in order to realign the organization with its changing environment. As noted above, this often leads to doing things differently or doing different things.

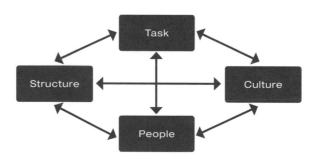

Figure 1.4　*Internal alignment*

The sequence of activities required to achieve a desired outcome

Inertia is often one of the major barriers to change. As an organization moves through a period of equilibrium, interdependencies tighten, ideologies that prescribe the best way of operating become more widely accepted and the fear of losing benefits associated with the status quo strengthens the resistance to change. The first step in the change process, therefore, involves equilibrium breaking, a step that Lewin (1947) referred to as 'unfreezing' (Figure 1.5). This unfreezing creates the conditions that facilitate transitioning, moving the organization to a new state.

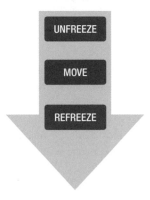

Figure 1.5 *Lewin's three-step change process*

The need to unfreeze is not limited to transformational change. Even when the change is a relatively small incremental change, there may still be resistance from 'local' organizational members and other stakeholders. Thus with most types of change, unfreezing is an essential first step in the change process. However, in a minority of cases, where constantly adapting organizations (of the type identified by Brown and Eisenhardt, 1997) are operating in high-velocity environments, the issue might not be overcoming inertia and unfreezing the organization but redirecting the continuous process of change that is already underway. Weick and Quinn (1999: 379) suggest that the appropriate change sequence required to redirect this kind of continuous change starts with 'freezing' in order to take stock and highlight what is happening, then moving on to 'rebalancing', a process that involves reinterpreting history and rese-quencing patterns so that they unfold with fewer blockages, followed by 'unfreezing' to resume improvisation, translation and learning 'in ways that are more mindful of sequences, more resilient to anomalies, and more flexible in their execution'.

The locus for change

Nadler and Tushman (1995) argue that an important factor that determines how change will be managed is the intensity, that is, level of trauma and dislocation, of the change. With reference to the typology of change presented above, transforma-tional change is more intense than incremental change. Gersick (1991) observes that since organizations are no longer directed by their old deep structures, and do not yet have future directions, organizational members (including senior managers) experience uncertainty, often accompanied by powerful emotions. Reactive change is also more intense than proactive change. Nadler and Tushman (1995) contend that during reactive change, everybody is aware that failure may threaten survival. Furthermore, organizational members may find that their efforts are constrained by time pressures, and often by a shortage of resources. They go on to argue that tuning is the least intense, followed by adaptation. There is a jump in intensity associated with reorientation but the highest level of intensity is associated with re-creation (see Figure 1.6).

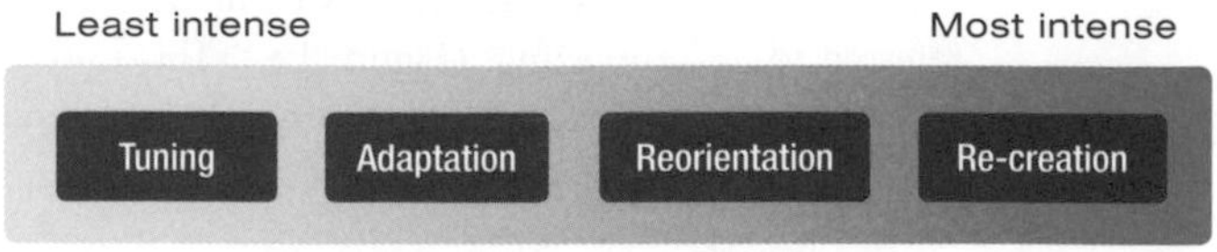

Least intense   Most intense

| Tuning | Adaptation | Reorientation | Re-creation |

Figure 1.6 *Intensity of change*

The main thrust of their argument is that when the intensity of change is low, it can usually be managed through project management and other forms of implementation associated with normal management processes and systems of accountability. As the intensity of change increases, so does the burden of change management until it reaches a point where it cannot easily be managed through normal management processes. When the intensity of change reaches this level, senior management often create special structures and roles to aid the process and they may even appoint an internal or external change agent to facilitate the change. Nadler and Tushman (1995: 32) refer to this approach to change management as 'transition management':

> It involves mechanisms specially created for the purpose of managing a specific change ... the senior team plays a supporting role, and the organization continues to be run as it was before. If the change is intense enough, it may appear on the senior team's agenda as one of a number of important items to be reviewed and managed over time.

However, as the intensity of changes increases still further, change management is no longer just one of the items on the senior team's agenda, it is the senior team's agenda and the CEO assumes responsibility for directing the change rather than delegating it to others.

New patterns of change

Gersick's (1991) multi-level and multi-domain exploration of punctuated equilibrium suggests that this pattern of change is not new. What is new is how people are experiencing it. When the pace of change was slower, a good number of people could spend their entire working life in organizations that were never significantly misaligned with their environment. Consequently, their experience of organizational change might have been confined to incremental fine-tuning and adaptation. However, with the increasing pace of change, many more organizations have experienced periods of strategic drift (Johnson et al., 2008) and misalignment with their environment to the point where the only way forward requires some form of radical transformation.

Nadler and Tushman (1995) report research findings indicating that the periods between episodes of revolutionary change are becoming shorter and shorter. Therefore, while the underlying pattern of change may not be changing, an acceleration in the pace of change is affecting the way many organizations and organizational members are experiencing change.

The impact of change on organizational members

It is 40 years since Toffler, an eminent futurologist, published his book *Future Shock* in which he discussed three aspects of change and speculated about how they would affect people. Addressing the title of his book, Toffler (1970) argues that, in many respects, 'future shock' is similar to culture shock, but with one important difference – there is no going back. If people find it difficult to adapt to a new culture, there is often the alternative of returning to the familiar culture they left behind. For example, if emigrants fail to settle in a new country (national culture), it might be possible for them to return home. However, when confronted with future shock, this option is unlikely to be as available.

Future shock is the product of three related trends:

1 *Transience:* Impermanence and transience are increasingly becoming important features of modern life because of a major expansion in the scale and scope of change and the accelerating pace of change. The accelerating pace of change affects people's relationships with things, places, people, organizations and ideas. As acceleration occurs, these relationships become foreshortened, telescoped in time. People respond to this increase in the pace of change in different ways. Those who internalize the principle of acceleration make an unconscious compensation for the compression of time – they modify their durational expectancies. But some find this more difficult than others.

2 *Novelty:* Toffler argues that having to live at an accelerating pace is one thing when life situations are more or less familiar, but having to do so when faced by unfamiliar, strange or unprecedented situations is distinctly another. And this is the reality for increasing numbers of people. Today, the balance between the familiar and the unfamiliar is changing. In Toffler's words, the 'novelty ratio is rising'.

3 *Diversity:* According to Toffler, the Orwellian view that people will become mindless consumer creatures, surrounded by standardized goods, educated in standardized schools, fed a diet of standardized mass culture and forced to adopt standardized styles of life could not be further from the truth. The reality is that most of us are faced with a paralysing surfeit of choice that, especially at work, complicates decision making.

Toffler (1970: 285) summarizes the consequence of these trends:

> When diversity converges with transience and novelty we rocket society toward an historical crisis of adaptation. We create an environment so ephemeral, unfamiliar and complex as to threaten millions with adaptive breakdown. This breakdown is future shock.

The changes that confront individuals and groups as a consequence of organizational adjustments are often incremental. People may be required to develop additional competencies or modify their ways of working. Such changes might be regarded as incremental in that they build on what is already there. However, sometimes a change can destroy, rather than modify, the relationship that exists between individuals and the organization. The change might undermine the assumptions that people make about themselves and how they relate with the world around them. Just as an organization might have to redefine its theory of business, individual organizational members might find that, as a result of an organizational change, they have to redefine their theory of being. This may not always be easy and, as Toffler points out, leads to the possibility of adaptive breakdown. Many reports document the increasing levels of stress experienced by workers. Much attention has also been focused on those who believe the psychological contract between themselves and their organization has been violated.

All these developments affect performance, commitment and the physical and psychological wellbeing of individual employees, and they also create problems for managers, supervisors and co-workers. They have to manage people who are upset by change at a time when the same changes are increasing their own workloads.

With increasing frequency, especially in times of discontinuous transformational change, organizational members have to cope with multiple and concurrent changes. At such times, having to cope with other people's emotional response to change is an added burden that is sometimes difficult to manage. This issue will be given more consideration in Chapter 12.

Conclusion

The management of change poses many challenges for managers. Burnes (2005: 85) observes that:

> Managing and changing organizations appears to be getting more rather than less difficult, and more rather than less important. Given the rapidly changing environment in which organizations operate, there is little doubt that the ability to manage change successfully needs to be a core competence for organisations.

Many, and some argue the majority of, change projects fail to achieve their intended outcomes. This book addresses this problem and explores how theory can help to improve the practice of change management.

This chapter ends with a series of case studies of organizations adapting to changing circumstances. You are invited to reflect on the content of this chapter and consider how it applies to these cases.

Case study 1.1

Types of change

Read the following five case studies and use the typology of change presented below to identify the type of change described in each case.

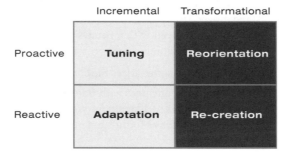

Types of organizational change
Source: Adapted from Nadler et al., 1995: 24

---

1 **The BBC**

2 **UK Coal**

3 **Leicester Royal Infirmary**

4 **McDonald's**

5 **GNER**

Case study 1.1.1) **The BBC**

After a long period of stability, during which the BBC had developed a reputation for honest reporting and programmes of outstanding quality, it had become complacent. Staff believed that the BBC was financially secure and that it was the best programme maker and broadcaster in the world. But then the world began to change and the BBC was slow to respond.

The situation when John Birt came to the BBC

John Birt came to the BBC, as deputy director general, in 1987 and was appointed director general in December 1992. In his autobiography, *The Harder Path* (2000), he reports that he was surprised to learn that there was little hard information about the BBC's basic business. He described the culture within the BBC as a kind of imperialism, where every regional commander in every part of the corporation acquired a full fleet of facilities, irrespective of need. The result was a vast excess of facilities: 'We could have covered Wimbledon, the World Cup and a world war, and still have had unused resources to spare.' He also found that staff utilization was low and that in some areas there was between 25 and 50% more staff than necessary. Part of the problem was that facilities, overheads and support services were funded by the centre and not charged to particular programmes. One result of this was that nobody had the slightest idea how much it cost to make a programme.

Until the mid-1980s, the BBC was able to survive in spite of its inefficiencies because, for a period of 60 years, its income from the licence fee had grown, on average, 4% per annum. But, because of a new political climate, this changed in 1985.

Political pressures for change

In 1979, Margaret Thatcher and a Conservative government came to power with an agenda for change that included plans to privatize much of the public sector. Thatcher viewed the BBC as a bloated bureaucracy that was overmanned, inefficient and, therefore, ripe for reform.

In 1985, the government froze the license fee (paid to the BBC by everybody in the UK who owns a radio or television) in order to force the BBC to become more efficient. Although the licence fee remained constant or was reduced in value over the next decade, costs continued to rise. Thatcher's intention of delivering a 'rude shock' to the BBC did not have the intended immediate impact, because Birt's predecessor had begun his term of office with a huge cash surplus that he spent on funding the growing gap between licence fee income and costs. When this surplus was used up, the BBC started borrowing until, in 1992, it faced a deficit of £100m. Birt recognized that this situation could not continue and that major changes were required.

Technological developments and new market pressures

The problem was further complicated by a wave of technological developments that threatened to undermine the BBC's traditional ways of working. The biggest challenge came from the development of digital technologies that opened up the possibility of many more channels, better technical quality, video on demand and interactivity. There was also increased competition from new players, for example Murdoch's launch of BSkyB.

Birt's strategy for change

Birt felt that he had no option other than to introduce radical reforms as quickly as possible in order to ensure the BBC's survival.

Case study 1.1.2

UK Coal

The state-owned coal industry in the UK was privatized in 1994/5. At that time, UK Coal operated about 20 deep mines and the same number of surface (opencast) mines. By 2004, turnover was down by half and the number of mines had reduced by more than 50%.

The main reason for the closure of many of UK Coal's deep mines was the exhaustion of economically viable reserves. New mines were not developed to replace those that had been closed because the continuing downward trend in world coal prices had undermined the business case for new investment.

The exhaustion of economically viable reserves was not the only problem. Other problems included environmental opposition to the burning of coal with high sulphur content. Imported coal was more attractive to major customers (the power generators) on this count as well as on price. Another factor was the considerable capital investment required to develop a new deep mine.

The change strategy

The reduction in the number of deep and surface mines encouraged UK Coal to begin looking for ways of improving the company's operating efficiency. One way of achieving this was to reduce the overhead cost of its central corporate headquarters by making each mine more autonomous and delegating to each unit a wider range of activities than used to be the case. Alongside this restructuring, UK Coal introduced a continuous improvement programme across all the remaining deep mines in order to make them more efficient and ensure their long-term survival.

Confronted with ever diminishing opportunities to grow the mining business, UK Coal also began to reappraise its assets and consider how it might revise its theory of business. It decided to explore the possibility of redefining the company as a land and property management and mining company. This reorientation involved many changes, including bringing new senior managers into the organization with competencies in the area of land and property management.

However, while this change was being implemented at the highest level, the company continued to pursue continuous improvement programmes to increase the efficiency of individual deep mines.

Case study 1.1.3

Leicester Royal Infirmary

The hospital is one of the largest teaching hospitals in England, with 1,100 beds and 4,200 staff. By the late 1980s, it had developed a reputation for being well run and it was near the top of the NHS efficiency league tables. However, even though the hospital was at the forefront of change, for example it was one of the first hospitals to introduce general managers in the mid-1980s, it was an early adopter of clinical directorates in 1986, and it gained NHS trust status in 1993, there were growing pressures for further change.

The new pressures for change

The city of Leicester had three acute hospitals located close to each other and integrated by a common medical school. When the opportunity of gaining more independence presented itself, the original proposal was that all three hospitals would become a single NHS trust. The Department of Health rejected this proposal and in the end three separate trusts were established. This created the possibility for competition between the three hospitals. For example, the district health authority (the body that purchased services from providers – hospitals – on behalf of the community) adopted a policy of service rationalization, which raised the prospect of the Leicester Royal losing contracts to one of the other hospitals.

The NHS internal market, introduced in 1991, led to another competitive pressure from the primary care sector, as community-based doctors (those who were GP fundholders with delegated budgets to purchase certain elective services) began 'shopping around' the three hospitals to obtain the most cost-effective and best quality provision. Purchasers also began to put considerable pressure on the hospitals to reduce patient waiting times.

In addition, the introduction of national targets to improve efficiency placed new demands on all hospitals to make year on year savings.

The change strategy

The Leicester Royal was much better placed than most hospitals to face these challenges and the leadership team proactively sought additional funding from the government to embark on a major change programme (see McNulty and Ferlie, 2002).

Because of the Leicester Royal Infirmary's earlier success in eliminating inefficiencies, there were few easy targets for further cost cutting. McNulty and Ferlie (2002) quote one member of the trust board as saying: 'I believe that there is no way we could improve the effectiveness and efficiency of this hospital simply by trying to do better that which we already do.'

Leicester Royal Infirmary, like hospitals generally, was organized according to functional principles. However, early experiments that involved introducing process-based principles of organizing led to some dramatic improvements in parts of the organization. In neurology, for example, the introduction of a single visit clinic reduced the time from visit to diagnosis from twelve weeks to one day, and in hearing services, the time to fit a hearing aid was reduced from fourteen months to six weeks.

These early successes encouraged the hospital to embark on an ambitious organization-wide programme of business process re-engineering. It was introduced in 1994 as a top-down programme to redesign two of the hospital's core processes, patient visits and diagnostic tests. The aim was to transform the organization from one that was characterized by fragmented functional thinking that directed attention and activity towards narrow departmental priorities to one where everybody worked together across functional boundaries to achieve wider organizational goals.

Case study 1.1.4 **McDonald's**

McDonald's is the world's largest fast-food restaurant chain. In 2004, it operated 1,250 outlets in the UK, of which 35% were franchised. McDonald's experienced rapid growth in the UK market from the early 1970s until the late 1990s. However, from the late 1990s, it began to experience a slowdown in growth, leading, in 2000, to a fall in both total sales and market share.

Over the past 45 years, its core business had been selling burgers, fries and soft drinks. Over this period, McDonald's only introduced occasional and relatively minor changes to its menu. Some commentators have suggested that because of its track record of sustained success, McDonald's was slow to recognize and respond to changes in its external environment.

Several factors appear to have contributed to the change in the company's fortunes:

- Greater competition from new entrants into the market, including new chains of coffee shops and sandwich bars.
- A desire on the part of consumers for a wider choice of food.
- A greater awareness of the importance of leading a healthy lifestyle and eating healthy foods.
- New evidence on the causes of obesity.
- Media interest that had publicized possible links between certain kinds of fast food and obesity.

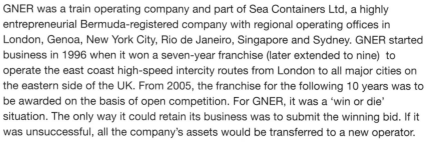

An additional threat that had received media attention, which could affect the company in the future, was the possibility that the UK government might introduce restrictions on advertising to children. There were rumours that it might consider imposing new taxes on those foods that were deemed to be 'unhealthy'.

McDonald's response to the new situation

In 2004, the company broadened its food offering and focused more attention on healthy eating with the launch of 'Salads Plus'. This was the biggest change to the McDonald's menu since it started business in the UK in 1974. The 'Good Food Fast' menu strategy involved the simultaneous introduction of eight new items to the McDonald's menu: Caesar salad, bacon ranch salad, mixed salad, quorn sandwiches, chicken filled sandwiches, yogurt and berry pot, fresh apples and muffins.

This major change to the company's product line involved a series of related changes:

- The introduction of new cooking equipment in all 1,250 outlets.
- Training 70,000 staff to cook and serve the new products.
- Training restaurant managers how to order and store new raw ingredients, and how to manage the introduction of the new menu in a way that enhanced profitability.
- Preparing managers at all levels, who had a wealth of experience of how to manage in a steady-state environment, to lead the introduction of these changes.

Case study 1.1.5

GNER

GNER was a train operating company and part of Sea Containers Ltd, a highly entrepreneurial Bermuda-registered company with regional operating offices in London, Genoa, New York City, Rio de Janeiro, Singapore and Sydney. GNER started business in 1996 when it won a seven-year franchise (later extended to nine) to operate the east coast high-speed intercity routes from London to all major cities on the eastern side of the UK. From 2005, the franchise for the following 10 years was to be awarded on the basis of open competition. For GNER, it was a 'win or die' situation. The only way it could retain its business was to submit the winning bid. If it was unsuccessful, all the company's assets would be transferred to a new operator.

The company's response was to establish a new development team, headed by a director of development, charged with preparing the company's bid for the east coast franchise. The bid was successful and GNER won the franchise up until 2015. The company decided to build on this experience and grow its business through bidding for other railway franchises as and when opportunities presented themselves. Its first venture was to join forces with the MTR Corporation, which runs the highly successful mass transit railway in Hong Kong, to bid for the integrated Kent franchise that includes the commuter rail services between southeast England and London and the new high-speed line from London to the Channel Tunnel. This first bid for new business was unsuccessful as was a second for the South Western franchise.

The change strategy

GNER's change strategy was to develop the existing east coast railway and generate additional revenue through the provision of enhanced services. Plans included rebuilding all the electric fleet carriages, introducing an innovative on-board wireless internet service on all trains and increasing the number of daily intercity services to London from 53 to 80. Alongside this development of the intercity east coast business, the company planned to grow by acquiring more franchises in the UK. It was anticipated that these would include different types of railway (intercity, regional and commuter), each with different risk patterns, and a portfolio of franchises with different expiry dates that would help to provide the company with greater stability.

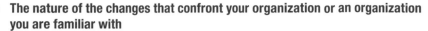

Exercise 1.1 **The nature of the changes that confront your organization or an organization you are familiar with**

You might find it useful to reflect on the nature of the changes that have confronted the total organization or the part of the organization you know best over the last year.

- Overall, would you describe the main type of change as incremental or discontinuous?

  In terms of the organization's typical response to change, think back and consider how the organization responded to change over the past few years. How does this compare with the organization's current way of responding to change?

- Is the organization's typical response to change reactive or proactive?

  Make a note of your answers in the space provided below.

Notes on the nature of change confronting your organization

Summary

This chapter has examined the nature of change, reviewed theories relating to patterns of change, considered some of the factors that facilitate or limit change and explored some of the implications of different types of change for change management practice.

Until recently almost all received models of change were incremental and cumulative. The gradualist paradigm posits that organizations can adapt and transform themselves, as required, through a process of continuous adjustment. This is in stark contrast to the punctuated equilibrium paradigm, which posits that systems (organizations) evolve through the alternation of periods of equilibrium, in which persistent deep structures only permit limited incremental change, and periods of revolution, in which these deep structures are fundamentally altered. It is argued that, with a few exceptions, most organizations experience change as a pattern of punctuated equilibrium.

▶ *The punctuated equilibrium paradigm:* Evidence supporting the theory of punctuated equilibrium is provided by Romanelli and Tushman. They examined the life histories of 25 minicomputer producers and found a pattern of discontinuous, episodic change. Changes in strategy, structure and power distribution tended to be clustered in time, as would be predicted by the punctuated equilibrium model, rather than spread over relatively long periods as would be predicted by a model of incremental changes that accumulate to transform the organization over time.

▷ *The gradualist paradigm:* This posits that fundamental change (organizational transformation) can occur through a process of continuous adjustment, and does not require some major discontinuous jolt to the system in order to trigger a short episode of revolutionary change. According to the gradualist paradigm, change is evolving and cumulative.

▷ *The nature of change confronting most organizations:* While the ideal pattern of change might be incremental and cumulative, the reality for many organizations appears to be a pattern of episodic change, which involves alternating between periods of equilibrium, where the focus for change is 'doing things better' through a process of continuous tinkering, adaptation and modification, and periods of discontinuous change, which involve a break with the past and doing things differently or doing different things.

▷ *Recognizing the need for change:* Some organizations are much better at anticipating the need for change than others. The earlier the need for change is recognized, the greater the number of options managers will have when deciding how to manage it. Whenever managers are forced to react to an urgent and pressing need for change, they are relatively constrained in what they can do. Nadler and colleagues have identified four types of change – tuning, adaptation, reorientation and recreation.

▷ *Implications of these different types of change for change management practice:* Different types of change can affect the focus for change efforts, the sequence of steps in the change process and the locus for change.

References

Birt, J. (2000) *The Harder Path*, London: Time Warner.

Brown, S.L. and Eisenhardt, K.M. (1997) The art of continuous change: linking complexity theory and time-paced evolution in relentlessly shifting organizations, *Administrative Science Quarterly*, 42: 1–34.

Burgelman, R.A. (1991) Intraorganizational ecology of strategy making and organizational adaptation: theory and field research, *Organizational Science*, 22: 239–62.

Burke, W.W. (2002) *Organizational Change: Theory and Practice*, Thousand Oaks, CA: Sage.

Burke, W.W. and Litwin, G.H. (1992) A causal model of organizational performance and change, *Journal of Management*, **18**(3): 523–45.

Burnes, B. (2005) Complexity theories and organizational change, *International Journal of Management Reviews*, **7**(2): 73–90.

Chakravarthy, B. (1997) A new strategy framework for coping with turbulence, *Sloan Management Review*, **38**(2): 69–82.

Drucker, P.F. (1994) The theory of the business, *Harvard Business Review*, **72**(5): 95–104.

Dunphy, D. (1996) Organisational change in corporate settings, *Human Relations*, **49**(5): 541–52.

Forester, R.N. and Kaplan, S. (2001) *Creative Destruction: Why Companies that are Built to Last Under-perform in the Market – and How to Successfully Transform Them*, New York: Currency.

Gersick, C.J. (1991) Revolutionary change theories: a multilevel exploration of the punctuated equilibrium paradigm, *Academy of Management Review*, 16: 10–36.

Gladwell, M. (2000) *The Tipping Point: How Little Things Can Make a Big Difference*, London: Little, Brown.

Gould, S.J. (1978) *Ever Since Darwin: Reflections in Natural History*, London: Burnett Books.

Greenwood, R. and Hinings, C.R. (1996) Understanding radical organizational change: bringing together the old and the new institutionalism, *Academy of Management Review*, 21: 1022–54.

Hodgkinson, G.P. and Healey, M.P. (2008) Cognition in organizations, *Annual Review of Psychology*, **59**(1): 387–417.

Johnson, G., Scholes, K. and Whittington, R. (2008) *Exploring Corporate Strategy*, London: Prentice Hall.

Kotter, J.P. (1999) *On What Leaders Really Do*, Boston, MA: Harvard Business School Press.

Lewin, K. (1947) New frontiers in group dynamics, in D. Cartwright (ed.) (1952) *Field Theory in Social Science*. London: Social Science Paperbacks.

McNulty, T. and Ferlie, E. (2002) *Reengineering Health Care: The Complexities of Organisational Transformation*, Oxford: Oxford University Press.

Nadler, D.A. and Tushman, M.L. (1995) Types of organizational change: from incremental improvement to discontinuous transformation, in D.A. Nadler, R.B.

Shaw and A.E. Walton (eds) *Discontinuous Change: Leading Organizational Transformation,* San Francisco, CA: Jossey-Bass.

Nadler, D., Shaw, R.B. and Walton, A.E. (1995) *Discontinuous Change: Leading Organizational Transformation,* San Francisco, CA: Jossey-Bass.

Orlikowski, W.J. (1996) Improvising organisational transformation over time: a situated change perspective, *Information Systems Research,* **7**(1): 63–92.

Pettigrew, A.M. (1987) Context and action in the transformation of the firm, *Journal of Management Studies,* **24**(6): 649–69.

Romanelli, E. and Tushman, M.L. (1994) Organizational transformation as punctuated equilibrium: an empirical test, *Academy of Management Journal,* **37**(5): 1141–66.

Ryan, B. and Gross, N. (1943) The diffusion of hybrid seed corn in two Iowa communities, *Rural Sociology,* 8: 15–24.

Samuelson, W. and Zeckhauser, R.J. (1988) Status quo bias in decision making, *Journal of Risk and Uncertainty,* 1: 7–59.

Thaler, R.H. and Sunstein, C.R. (2009) *Nudge: Improving Decisions about Health, Wealth, and Happiness,* London: Penguin.

Tichy, N.M. and Devanna, M.A. (1986) *The Transformational Leader,* Chichester: Wiley.

Toffler, A. (1970) *Future Shock,* New York: Random House.

Tushman, M.L. and Romanelli, E. (1985) Organizational evolution: a metamorphosis model of convergence and reorientation, in B. Staw and L. Cummings (eds) *Research in Organization Behavior,* vol. 7, Greenwich, CT: JAI Press.

Tushman, M.L., Newman, W. and Romanelli, E. (1986) Convergence and upheaval: managing the unsteady pace of organization evolution, *California Management Review,* **29**(1): 29–44.

Weick, K.E. and Quinn, R.E. (1999) Organizational change and development, *Annual Review of Psychology,* 50: 361–86.

This chapter opens with an activity designed to explore the issues and choices involved in developing an approach to managing organizational change. It then moves on to consider the main features of some frequently cited models for conceptualizing the change process and presents a generic model that will provide the structure for Chapters 3–29 of this book.

Exercise 2.1

Managing a branch closure programme: an exercise in planning and managing the process of change

The aim of this activity is to explore the issues and choices involved in developing an overall strategy for large-scale change.

The scenario

A long-established bank is facing strong competition from new entrants into the retail banking market. The new entrants specialize in the provision of telephone and internet banking services and have a lower cost base because they do not carry the overheads associated with a large branch network.

A director of the branch network in the traditional bank has proposed a strategy for responding to this competition. It involves closing down 20% of the branch network in order to reduce overheads and increase net revenue per customer. At this stage, the details of the strategy have not been finalized. For example, the branches targeted for closure could be city centre branches occupying expensive properties or small rural branches occupying low-cost premises but with relatively few customers of high net worth to the bank.

Imagine that you are a consultant who has been engaged by the director who initiated the proposal. Your role is to help her to explore the feasibility of the proposal to increase profitability by contracting the branch network

Step 1

You have brainstormed, with the director and her immediate colleagues, a list of possible actions that could provide the basis for a strategy for managing this change. These are listed in Table 2.1.

You are invited to review the list of actions presented in Table 2.1 and use your experience to:

- Delete any items that, on reflection, you feel are unimportant or irrelevant.
- Add, in the space provided in Table 2.1, any other actions that you feel should be included. You are allowed to add up to four additional actions.
- Think about how the actions might be sequenced from start to finish. For each action, identify whether you think it should occur early or late in the change management process. You can record this view in the space provided on the right-hand side of Table 2.1.

Table 2.1 *Possible actions*

		Early	Later
1	Identify key stakeholders who might be affected by the change		
2	Provide counselling service and retraining for those who will be displaced		
3	Inform staff how they, personally, will be affected by the closure plan		
4	Persuade those who are in a position to champion the favoured closure plan to support it		
5	Identify a project leader and set up a branch closure team		
6	Announce the scope and scale of the closure plan to all staff		
7	Brief key managers about the closure plan		
8	Identify which branches are to be closed		
9	Review success, or otherwise, of the closure programme and disseminate throughout the organization any lessons learned about change management		
10	Identify the information that will be required in order to decide the number and location of branches to be closed in order to achieve targeted benefits		
11	Announce closure plan to existing customers		
12	Train members of the branch closure team in change management skills		
13	Identify and quantify benefits sought from closures		
14	Develop personnel package for displaced staff		
15	Assess effects of the closures on other aspects of the bank's functioning		
16	Plan any training that may be required for staff who are to be reassigned to other work		
17	Hold team meetings to brief staff about how the closure plans will affect staff and indicate when they will be informed about how they (personally) will be affected by the change		
18	Identify what steps could be taken to retain high value customers affected by the closures		
19	Provide training for managers and supervisors to assist them to help others and themselves to cope with the change		
20	Issue newsletter outlining progress towards full implementation		
21	Decide who should be involved in analysing the information relating to whether a closure plan will deliver sufficient benefits to justify the costs		
22	Seek views of customers who might be affected by the closures about what issues should be given attention		
23	Seek views of branch staff about the issues that will have to be given attention if the closure plan is to be successfully accomplished		
24	If it is decided to implement the closure plan, decide who should be involved in identifying which branches are to be closed		
25	Initiate programme to make properties suitable for disposal, for example remove vaults		
26	Celebrate successes and build on them in order to motivate people to continue working to improve the bank's competitive position		
27	Decide on date for first closures		
28	Identify any personal gains or losses that might be perceived by those employees who will be affected by the closures		
29	Specify timetable for implementing the closure plan		
30	Consider what might be done to motivate employees to accept the change		
31	Issue a press release about the closure plan		
32	Monitor progress against timetable and anticipated benefits		
33	Explore the best way of disposing of redundant properties		
34	Identify social banking issues raised by the closures, for example what will happen to customers without transport when their local branch closes		
35	Plan what will happen to displaced staff – redeployment, early retirement, redundancy		
36			
37			
38			
39			

Step 2

Consider your list of action statements and assemble them into a plan:

- Identify the sequence of actions from start to finish, recognizing that some actions may occur in parallel or be repeated.
- Identify relationships between actions in your plan and consider how different actions might be categorized as separate steps or distinctive parts of your plan.
- Summarize your plan in the space provided below as a flow diagram, including descriptive labels for the main aspects or stages of your plan.

You might find it helpful to print out all the actions listed in Table 2.1 onto separate Post-it notes so that it will be easier to move them about and experiment with different ways of sequencing them and grouping them into categories that reflect the mains steps in your approach to managing the change process.

Your model, showing the main steps in the process of managing change

---

The next part of this chapter will consider some process issues associated with the management of change and will conclude by presenting a generic model that can be used as a guide when thinking about the best way to manage a particular change.

You might find it useful to compare this generic model with the model you developed in Exercise 2.1 to manage the branch closures.

As you read the rest of this book, you might also find it helpful to reflect on how the content of each chapter might influence your approach to managing this kind of change.

The nature of change as a process

Open systems theory provides a framework for thinking about organizations and parts of organizations as a system of interrelated components that are embedded in, and strongly influenced by, a larger system. The key to any system's prosperity and long-term survival is the quality of the fit (state of alignment) between the internal components of the focal system, for example in an organization or a department within an organization, and between the focal system and the wider system of which it is a part. Internal and external alignment promotes organizational effectiveness because, when aligned, the various elements of the system reinforce rather than disrupt each other, thereby minimizing the loss of system energy and resources (see Schneider et al., 2003).

Miles and Snow (1984) suggest that rather than viewing alignment as a state, because perfect alignment is rarely achieved, it might be better to think of it as a process – a dynamic search that seeks to align the organization with its environment and the various internal elements of the organization with each other. However, this quest for internal and external alignment is not an easy process to manage. As noted in Chapter 1, while organizations that recognize or anticipate shifts in their external environment may be better placed to initiate internal changes that could improve external alignment, recognition may not be enough to ensure that these changes will be secured. Forces for inertia within the organization can make it difficult to achieve and maintain a sufficient level of internal and external alignment. (See Chapter 5 for a more detailed discussion of alignment as a determinant of organizational effectiveness.)

The intentional management of change

These forces for inertia within organizations can inhibit the natural process of adaptation and lead to a state of misalignment that triggers a need for planned change (see Dunphy, 1996). Ford and Ford (1995: 2) argue that the intentional management of change occurs when a change agent 'deliberately and consciously sets out to establish conditions and circumstances that are different from what they are now'.

Lewin (1951) provided some useful insights into the nature of change that are relevant for those who seek intentionally to change the status quo. He argued that the state of no change does not refer to a situation in which everything is stationary. It involves a condition of 'stable quasi-stationary equilibrium' comparable to that of a river that flows with a given velocity in a given direction. A change in the behaviour of an individual, group or organization can be likened to a change in the river's velocity or direction. In a work situation, for example, certain hostile and friendly actions may occur between two groups in interdepartmental meetings. If the level of hostile behaviour is defined as a problem, a desired change may involve a reduction in hostile and an increase in friendly behaviours, in other words a move from one state of stable quasi-stationary equilibrium to another.

Lewin argued that any level of behaviour is maintained in a condition of quasi-stationary equilibrium by a force field comprising a balance of forces pushing for and resisting change. This level of behaviour can be changed by either adding forces for change in the desired direction or by diminishing the opposing or resisting forces (see Figure 2.1).

Figure 2.1 *A force field*

Both these approaches can result in change but, according to Lewin, the secondary effects associated with each approach will be different. Where change is brought about by increasing the forces pushing for change, this will result in an increase in tension. If this rises beyond a certain level, it may be accompanied by high aggressiveness (especially towards the source of the increased pressure for change), high emotionality and low levels of constructive behaviour. On the other hand, where change is brought about by diminishing the forces that oppose or resist change, the secondary effect will be a state of relatively low tension.

This argument led Lewin to advocate an approach to managing change that emphasized the importance of reducing the restraining forces in preference to a high pressured approach that only focused on increasing the forces pushing for change. He argued that approaches involving the removal of restraining forces within the individual, group or organization are likely to result in a more permanent change than approaches involving the application of outside pressure for change.

Achieving a lasting change

Lewin highlighted the concept of permanency. He suggested that successful change requires a three-step procedure that involves the stages of unfreezing, moving and refreezing, known as his three-step model of change.

Burnes (2004a, 2004b) has observed a tendency in recent years to play down the significance of Lewin's work for contemporary organizations. For example, Dawson (2003) and Kantor et al. (1992) argue that the notion of refreezing is not relevant for organizations operating in turbulent environments. They argue that organizations need to be fluid and adaptable and that the last thing they need is to be frozen into some given way of functioning. Lewin's point, however, is that all too often change is short-lived. After a 'shot in the arm', life returns to the way it was before. In his view, it is not enough to think of change in terms of simply reaching a new state, for example revised management practices that include a new pattern of behaviour towards subordinates. He asserted that permanency, for as long as it is relevant, needs to be an important part of the goal. This state may be brief and involve little more than taking stock before moving on to yet more change. It is, however, important to think in terms of consolidation in order to minimize the danger of slipping back to the way things were before.

Managing change, therefore, involves helping an individual, group or organization, unfreeze or unlock from the existing level of behaviour, move to a new level, and refreeze behaviour at this new level:

1 *Unfreezing* involves destabilizing the balance of driving and restraining forces. Kotter (1996) argues that the current state of equilibrium can be destabilized by alerting organizational members to the need for change. Creating a vision of a more desirable future state and providing information that creates a sense of urgency can weaken restraining and strengthen driving forces. Such action can motivate individuals and groups to let go of current ways of behaving and encourage them to search out more effective alternatives. Schein (1996) also points to how disconfirming people's assessment of the benefits of the current state can motivate learning and change.

2 *Movement* is where the balance of driving and restraining forces is modified to shift the equilibrium to a new level. Although these forces can assume many forms, they tend to manifest in terms of behaviours that affect performance (Ford and Greer, 2006). Consequently, movement tends to be achieved by adjusting attitudes and beliefs, and modifying the processes, systems and structures that shape behaviour.

3 *Refreezing* involves reinforcing new behaviours in order to maintain new levels of performance and avoid regression. Feedback that signals the effectiveness and consistency of new behaviours and incentives that reward new levels of performance can help to embed new practices.

Hendry (1996) testifies to Lewin's lasting contribution to change management. He notes:

Scratch any account of creating and managing change and the idea that change is a three stage process which necessarily begins with a process of unfreezing will not be far below the surface. (Hendry, 1996: 624)

However, as Burnes (2004a) has observed, the strength of Lewin's contribution to the theory and practice of organizational change is when this three-step model is viewed as part of an integrated theory that includes field theory, group dynamics (see Chapter 16) and action research (see Chapter 19). Research report 2.1 presents the results of an empirical test of Lewin's theory and the three-step model of change.

Research report 2.1

Testing Lewin's three-step model of change

Ford, M.W. and Greer, B.M. (2006) Profiling change: an empirical study of change process patterns, *Journal of Applied Behavioral Science*, 42: 420–46

This study uses profile analysis to investigate the validity of Lewin's three-phase model of change. The model implies that activities relating to unfreezing should be observable before activities relating to movement and refreezing. Unfreezing to destabilize the status quo needs to occur first, otherwise the organization will be poorly prepared for change. Movement requires that at least some old ways of doing things be discarded in favour of new behaviours. It is only after these new behaviours have been established that refreezing will facilitate the stabilization of the organization at a new equilibrium. Ford and Greer argue that if such a progression or sequence exists, then intensity levels of factors linked to each of the three stages of Lewin's (1947) model should change as implementation proceeds. Their first hypothesis is that:

> As implementation progresses, change process profiles will display higher levels of 'movement' and 'refreezing' factors.

Their second hypothesis relates to the levels of unfreezing-moving-refreezing activity associated with the degree of implementation success. Lewin's theory does not suggest that any of the three phases will dominate, for example refreezing, even though it occurs late in the change process, is just as important as unfreezing, so it follows that implementation success will be associated with more intense use of all change process factors. Their second hypothesis is:

> Change process profiles associated with higher degrees of implementation success will display higher levels of unfreezing, movement, and refreezing factors than change process profiles associated with lower degrees of success.

Method

After studying conceptualizations of change, Ford and Greer developed a set of change process factors that could be linked to Lewin's three phases:

1 *Goal setting* was identified as a measure of *unfreezing*, on the grounds that it is an activity that challenges extant expectations and motivates an analysis and assessment of the organization's relationship with its environment. A three-item scale was developed to measure this factor and similar scales were developed to measure the other factors listed below.

2 *Skill development* was identified as a measure of *movement*, on the grounds that moving an organization towards a new and improved state requires behavioural adjustment, and new behaviours require the development and delivery of new skills and competencies.

3 *Feedback and management control* were identified as measures of *refreezing*, on the grounds that refreezing requires confirmatory feedback and rewards to reinforce desired behaviours. Consistent with this need for feedback is the development of management control systems that monitor behaviour and keep the change on track.

A measure of implementation success was also developed and data were gathered from a cross-sectional sample of more than 100 managers involved in change implementation.

To test the first hypothesis, the data were split into four groups representing different levels of change implementation (percentage completion). Findings indicated that early in the implementation process, the use of feedback and management control, that is, the refreezing variables, was significantly below that of the other change process variables. As implementation progressed, the use of refreezing variables increased relative to the other change process variables. Movement activities also increased as implementation progressed, but to a lesser degree.

To test the second hypothesis, the data were split into three groups representing different levels of implementation success. Results indicated a highly significant overall difference across the outcome groups, with higher levels of use of all process variables (goal setting, skill development, feedback and management control) being associated with implementation success. A particularly interesting finding (pointing to the importance of sustaining change, discussed in Chapter 28) was that when the success of change implementation was low, the use of refreezing activities, such as feedback and management control, was significantly lower than in the change profiles associated with implementation success.

Ford and Greer's findings support the general progression from unfreezing to refreezing as theorized by Lewin. They also found, as implied by Lewin's framework, that organizations that achieve higher levels of implementation employ unfreezing, movement and refreezing activities at a higher level of intensity.

Models of stages in the process of managing change

This section briefly reviews three other process models of change that can be viewed as elaborations of Lewin's basic model:

1 Lippitt et al. (1958) expanded Lewin's three-stage model. After reviewing descriptions of change in persons, groups, organizations and communities, they felt that the moving phase divided naturally into three substages. These were:
 • the clarification or diagnosis of the client's problem
 • the examination of alternative routes and goals, and the establishment of goals and intentions for action
 • the transformation of intentions into actual change efforts.

They also argued that change managers can only be effective when they develop and maintain an appropriate relationship with those involved in or affected by the change. This led them to introduce two further stages into the helping process, one concerned with the formation and the other with the termination of relationships.

2 Egan (1996) developed a model that is based on Lewin's three stages, but it focuses most attention on the unfreezing and moving phases, with detailed consideration being given to the assessment of the current scenario (diagnosis), the creation of a preferred scenario (visioning) and the design of plans that move the system from the current to the preferred scenario (planning for change). The essential elements of each of these three stages are:
 • *The current scenario:* assessing problems and opportunities, developing new perspectives, and choosing high impact problems or opportunities for attention.
 • *The preferred scenario:* developing a range of possible futures, evaluating alternative possibilities to establish a viable agenda for change, and gaining commitment to the new agenda.
 • *Strategies and plans for moving to the preferred scenario:* brainstorming strategies for getting there, choosing the best strategy or best-fit package of strategies, and turning these strategies into a viable plan.

3 Beckhard and Harris (1987) present a three-stage model that focuses on defining the present and the future, managing the transition, and maintaining and updating the change. Special consideration is given to some of the issues associated with the moving or transitional stage, including the need for management mechanisms, the development of activity plans and the gaining of commitment from key stakeholders.

These models highlight the importance of:

▶ *Diagnosis* – change managers need to give attention to where the organization is now and to what a more desirable and attainable state would look like.
▶ *Strategies and plans* – to move the organization towards the desired state.
▶ *Implementation* – translating intentions (strategies and plans) into actual change efforts. Implementation also involves managing the interpersonal and political issues associated with change.

Key steps in the change process

Change is often managed less effectively than it might be because those responsible for managing it fail to attend to some of the critical aspects of the change process. The model presented below provides a conceptual framework for thinking about the management of change. It incorporates many of the features of the process models reviewed above. While the context here is organizational change, the same model can be applied to change at the level of the individual and the group.

At first glance this model suggests that change is a neat, rational and linear process. This is rarely the way it unfolds and is experienced in practice. Example 2.1 illustrates this point.

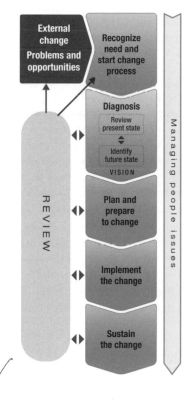

Figure 2.2 *Steps in the change process*
Source: Adapted from Hayes and Hyde, 1998

Example 2.1

> ### Car importer case
>
> Over several years, an importer of value for money, low-priced cars had built up a network of independent dealers to retail the vehicles to customers with relatively low disposable incomes. It was a successful business.
>
> Early in 2008, the manufacturer alerted the importer to a forthcoming change. In order to counter anticipated competition from even cheaper imported cars from India and China, it had decided to reposition its brand. It wanted to widen its market to include customers who normally bought more expensive vehicles, such as Ford or Opel. The manufacturer had already announced the launch of a new model that was technically superior to other cars in its range, but the early 2008 announcement made it clear that it intended to follow this up by rebranding and repositioning the entire range.
>
> The importer quickly recognized that this would require a lot of changes to its own business. Many of the retailers who were part of its dealer network had started out selling second-hand cars. Their showrooms tended to be located in premises adjacent to their original petrol retailing or repair shop businesses. They had long-standing relationships with many of their customers who had first come to them to buy second-hand cars and then moved on to purchase models from their range of inexpensive imported cars. An initial diagnosis indicated that the importer would have to encourage many of these dealers to refurbish and modernize their premises, and in some cases, relocate in order to attract the type of customer who would be interested in more expensive and better quality cars. Some dealers also had a relatively unsophisticated approach to selling, indicating a need for training and development. The importer quickly began to formulate a change strategy, but initial approaches to a sample of dealers to test out plans for change met with strong resistance.
>
> This triggered a rethink. The problem was reframed and another diagnostic exercise was undertaken to explore the possibility of replacing some of the existing dealers with dealers who were already selling more upmarket vehicles and who might be interested in either transferring their allegiance or taking on an additional brand and selling the imported cars alongside their existing range. When this strategy was tested, another set of problems was identified, prompting yet another rethink.
>
> This third way forward involved working with some (maybe a majority) of the existing dealers to help them to make the changes required to sell the rebranded cars and, alongside this approach, exploring the possibility of developing a new relationship with an Indian manufacturer of cheap cars. The plan was to establish a related business to import and distribute its vehicles using the rump of its existing dealer network.
>
> Before plans to pursue this strategy were well advanced, the credit crunch hit car sales and the Indian manufacturer announced a delay in its plans to launch its low-cost vehicles in European markets, calling for a further rethink of the situation.

Often new pressures for change emerge before the current change initiative has been completed, for example the credit crunch in the car importer case, and sometimes a desired end state is not obvious at the beginning of the process, a point that will be elaborated later. The arrows between the various stages of the change and the 'review process' in Figure 2.2 represent feedback loops and possible iterations. Typically, change is a messy and constantly evolving rather than a neat and linear process.

Recognition and start of the change process

The start of the process is the recognition that external events or internal circumstances require a change to take place. Recognition involves complex processes of perception, interpretation and decision making that, if not managed carefully, can lead to inappropriate outcomes, for example the organization might fail to change when it needs to or it may change when change is not required.

Following recognition, the next step involves translating the need for change into a desire for change, deciding who will manage the change and, especially where an external change agent is introduced to help with this process, establishing a workable and effective change relationship.

These early steps may be more or less explicit and formal, but, at some point, they typically involve a review, feasibility study or project. Critical questions that need to be considered at this stage are:

▶ Who to involve
▶ What to make public (if anything)
▶ Who should have management responsibility?

It is also important to begin thinking about how to unfreeze others, who, so far, may not be aware of the need for change, and gain their acceptance that change is needed.

Diagnosis: reviewing the present state and identifying the preferred future state

Although reviewing the present and identifying the future state may seem at first sight to be separate and distinct activities, they are often integrated in practice. These two steps frequently go through several iterations, progressing from broad concepts towards a vision of a more desirable state that is sufficiently concrete and detailed to be implemented.

There is also some debate about whether the process should in fact start with looking at the present or the future. The argument for starting with the present is to ensure that the change is not a 'utopian leap' to an unrealistic future that cannot be reached from the current situation. On the other hand, focusing too heavily on the present may limit horizons and lead to the goals of change being too cautious and constrained by current experience. Where radical or transformational change is needed, it may be better to consider the direction of change than to concentrate on the starting point. For these reasons, Figure 2.2 shows these two elements interacting in the same box.

Reviewing the present state

The present state of the organization can often only be understood in terms of the context of its past history and its external environment. The precise objectives for reviewing the present state will depend on the type of change that is being managed. Common reasons are to:

▶ help to identify the required change by diagnosing the cause of a problem, identifying current deficiencies or clarifying opportunities
▶ establish a baseline so that it is clear what is changing
▶ help to define the future direction.

Data gained from this kind of review can also be used to help to assess how organizational members and other stakeholders will react, and to prepare people for change.

Identifying the future state

What is required when identifying the future state depends on the kind of change that is being undertaken and the change managers' role in the overall process. If the change managers are responsible for initiating the change, their task is likely to involve developing a view or 'vision' of what they, and others involved in the diagnostic process, think the organization ought to look like in the future. If, on the other hand, their role is to implement a vision that is being imposed from elsewhere, their task might be more limited to thinking through and visioning the likely impact of the change for their part of the organization, and doing whatever is needed to implement this.

Quality of the vision

The vision of a more desirable future state provides a focus for attention and action. It can mobilize energy and effort. Locke and Latham (1984) argue that people are motivated to achieve goals to which they are committed and they try harder and are less willing to give up when goals are both clear and realistic.

Despite the obvious importance of the vision, those leading the change sometimes lock on to the first vision they generate, and in so doing, lock out the possibility of considering alternatives. The first vision may not be the best, either in terms of the desirability of the envisioned end state or its power to motivate those who need to be engaged with the change.

The way the diagnostic stage is managed can affect the way the need for change is (or is not) translated into a desire for change. Organizational members are more likely to be motivated to let go of the status quo and seek a more desirable state if:

▶ the diagnostic process disconfirms their view that all is well with the existing state of affairs
▶ this challenge produces a sufficient level of anxiety to motivate organizational members to search for new possibilities
▶ the vision of what might be offers sufficient promise to make the effort of changing worthwhile.

Lewin refers to this as 'unfreezing'. Schein (1996), summarizing the essence of these three points, argues that unless the unfreezing process offers a promise of psychological safety, any disconfirmation provided by the diagnostic phase will be denied or defended against and those involved will not be motivated to change.

The diagnostic phase leads to the articulation of 'ends', a vision of a more desirable state and the specification of change goals. The planning and implementation phases are concerned with the 'means' of achieving these goals. This involves identifying possible strategies for action, and selecting and then implementing the strategy that offers the greatest promise of success.

Prepare and plan for implementation

The links between the three aspects of Lewin's work – field theory, action research and the three-step model of change – are illustrated by Burnes (2004a), when he refers to Lewin's assertion that following unfreezing, one should seek movement (change) by taking into account all the forces at work and identifying and evaluating, on a trial-and-error basis, all the available options.

Detailed analysis of the future and present state leads to the identification of a long list of things that will need to be done in order to make the proposed change a reality. There will be different lead times associated with the various tasks, interdependencies between them and resource and other constraints. All these things need to be taken into account when developing an implementation plan. However, it is important that implementation is not viewed as only a technical activity.

Implementation has an important political dimension. It needs to address the extent to which people are ready for and accepting of change and whether the process threatens them in any way. Choices need to be made, such as which method to adopt to implement the change and whether to proceed to full implementation or start with a trial or pilot. In Chapter 15, the dangers of separating planning and implementation are discussed and the benefits of adopting a more integrated and incremental approach are explored.

Implement change

Whatever has been planned now needs to be implemented and the focus shifts from planning to action. Attention also needs to be given to monitoring and control to ensure that things happen as intended. There are two basic approaches to implementing change. Sometimes change involves moving from A to B, where, before implementation, the nature of B is known and clearly defined. This kind of change is sometimes referred to as a 'blueprint' change. Typical examples of a blueprint change include relocation, computerization of a business process, or the introduction of a new appraisal or grading system. In these circumstances, it is easier to view the management of change from the perspective of 'planned change' that involves a predetermined linear process – following step by step the successive stages in the models of change presented above.

Often, however, it is not possible to specify the end point (B) of a change in advance of implementation. While a need for change might be recognized, for example the organization is losing market share or is failing to innovate as fast as its competitors, it may be less obvious what needs to be done to improve matters. There may be a broadly defined goal and a direction for change, for example improving competitiveness, but it may not be possible to provide a detailed specification of what this end state will look like. In some situations, it may not even be helpful to think in terms of specific end states because the rate of change in the operating environment may be such that the precise definition of a desirable end state may be subject to constant revision.

In these circumstances, a blueprint approach to change is inappropriate. Change needs to be viewed as a more open-ended and iterative process that emerges or evolves over time. Buchanan and Storey (1997) argue that this is not unusual and that change often unfolds in an iterative fashion and can involve much backtracking. Burke (2002) echoes this view and argues that the change process is often more like a series of loops rather than a straight line, reflecting the reality that things rarely progress as planned, and even when plans are implemented as intended, there are often unanticipated consequences. Managers frequently report that for every step forward, they seem to fall back two steps and that they are constantly having to 'fix things' to keep the change on track.

An emergent or evolutionary approach to change involves taking tentative incremental steps in, what it is hoped is, the right direction. After each step, the step itself and the direction of the change are reviewed to establish if the step worked and if the direction still holds good. As the process unfolds, it may be possible to define the end state a bit more precisely or to take future steps with more confidence.

Even with blueprint changes, these feedback loops are important because feedback from implementation can lead to the identification of new problems and possibilities. It may have implications for the planning of further activities to bring about change and may even affect the definition of a more desirable end state, thus leading to a revision of the blueprint. Sometimes the feedback may also alert change managers to the possibility that what was originally perceived as a blueprint change might be more appropriately approached and managed as an evolutionary change. But this feedback is not always available.

Part VI examines nine different ways of intervening to implement change and move the organization towards a more desirable state.

Review

The review process is sometimes taken to imply some form of post-implementation review but in practice monitoring and reviewing progress need to be ongoing activities, as progress is measured against key milestones. All too often, however, change managers fail to deliberately seek out available feedback and only realize that the change is producing unintended consequences when some third party or unplanned happening draws it to their attention. Example 2.2 illustrates this point.

Example 2.2

Concrete Flags Ltd

Concrete Flags Ltd adopted a new business strategy, which involved a shift from manufacturing concrete paving stones for builders merchants, do-it-yourself outlets and garden centres to providing end consumers with their 'dream patio' delivered direct to their home on a pallet. This shift required a new approach to marketing and the design and installation of a more automated production technology.

Before the change, the company had manufactured a limited range of concrete paving stones in batches using a basic process that relied on a large input of low skilled labour. While reliable, it was costly because batch production required the company to hold large inventories of different paving stones. The new strategy required the company to develop the capability to manufacture a wider range of paving stones. Taking into account variations in shape, size, colour and texture, the company aimed to manufacture 150 different products on demand. Managers worked with a supplier to design the new automated production system. The plan was to install and test one machine first and then purchase additional equipment as the new marketing strategy generated additional demand.

The equipment was installed on time and appeared to be performing well, but it was not long before managers became aware that production targets were not being met. They identified the problem as wet concrete sticking in the weigh-boxes. The supplier acknowledged a minor design fault, which was quickly rectified.

It was while they were modifying the equipment that the supplier discovered, and reported to managers at Concrete Flags, that operators had attempted to keep the machine running by hitting the weigh-boxes with a large hammer. It appeared that this crude method of removing wet concrete had worked well enough with the old, less sophisticated and more robust equipment but it had caused damage to the new machine. This feedback alerted managers to an important misalignment between the new equipment and the operators' knowledge and skills. They responded by arranging a number of training sessions, which led to an immediate improvement in the way they operated and maintained the new equipment.

Within a short while, another problem emerged. Achieving the vision of delivering a tailor-made patio-on-a-pallet direct to end users included providing them with a leaflet containing laying instructions. Unfortunately, the importance of this leaflet had not been explained to the workers, who still defined their role as making concrete paving slabs. On investigation, managers found that the workers regarded inserting the leaflet before the pallet was shrink-wrapped as an unnecessary complication – it was just a bit of paper. When supplies ran out, they had continued to dispatch patios-on-pallets without laying instructions. Managers had been unaware of this problem until customers began to complain that they had not received the promised leaflet.

This feedback led managers to appreciate that while they had given a lot of attention to developing a new marketing strategy and designing and installing the new equipment, they had given relatively little attention to how the change would affect the operators. They had not consulted or reassured the workers about the change. Managers had assumed that they would welcome it, but they were wrong. The operators saw it as a 'management ploy to make money', which threatened their job security. Nobody had informed them that the plan was to purchase additional machines and increase production, thereby safeguarding jobs, in order to satisfy the anticipated growth in demand.

Many of the corrective actions required to keep the change on track had been prompted by unsolicited feedback from the suppliers of new equipment and from customers. One of the lessons learned by managers at Concrete Flags was that they could have done much more to deliberately seek out feedback that would have made it easier to monitor how the change was being implemented.

Clegg and Walsh (2004) suggest that feedback is often unavailable or not acted on because the change process is too fragmented. They cite the example of software design where the typical process involves the stages of strategy, feasibility, conceptual design, detailed design, programming, implementation, use and maintenance. Each of these stages tends to involve different people who often have different goals and priorities. This fragmentation undermines the feedback process. One group may nudge the project in a particular direction and not recognize a need to inform others about this, or may confront and address a problem without recognizing the implications of their actions for end users. Even when they are aware that others may need to know, they may not always identify who should be informed, and those who are informed may not recognize the significance of what they have been told. Clegg and Walsh observe that this lack of continuity and feedback can make it difficult for those involved in the change process to influence and learn from one another. Chapter 27 considers some of the tools that can help to facilitate this review process.

Sustaining change

Sustaining change refers to the refreezing stage of Lewin's model. It involves holding on to gains, that is, making change stick, and spreading these gains across the organization. This requires, among other things, that there are feedback mechanisms and reward systems in place that will monitor and reinforce the desired new behaviours. However, rather than attempting to simply ossify the new state, it also involves building on and updating the change as required.

Managing the people issues

As well as the steps described in the model and presented in Figure 2.2, a strategy for managing change must address a number of people issues that are ongoing throughout the process, including:

▶ power, politics and stakeholder management
▶ leadership
▶ communication
▶ motivating others to change
▶ support for others to help them manage their personal transitions
▶ the change manager's mode of intervening and the effect this has on the change relationship.

These issues will be considered in Chapters 8–13.

Change managers need to address these people issues at all stages of the change process and not just when designing a strategy for implementation. A common mistake is to treat the stages of starting the change, reviewing the present and designing the future state as purely technical activities. Too often, too little attention is given to the political and motivational issues associated with the plan for change. Diagnosing and visioning, for example, are not benign activities and must be managed carefully. Stakeholders may resist any attempt to even consider the possibility that change might be required. Nadler (1987) refers to the importance of shaping the political dynamics of change and motivating constructive behaviour.

A change strategy is essentially a plan to make things happen. It needs to address all the things that have to be done to bring about the change. When developing a strategy, change managers need to attend to each step in the change process and to the way the overall process is to be managed. However, all this needs to be regarded as something that is dynamic and evolving and not a grand plan that can be 'set in stone' from the start.

It is also important to recognize that there is no one recipe or prescription about how change 'should' be managed that can be applied to all situations. Managing change is a complex process. Change managers need to contextualize their approach and develop bespoke strategies that accommodate the cultural and political dynamics that can undermine or facilitate any attempt to manage change.

Summary

Open systems theory provides a framework for thinking about organizations as a system of interrelated components that are embedded in, and strongly influenced by, a larger system. The key to any system's prosperity and long-term survival is the quality of the state of alignment between the internal components of the organization and between the organization system and the wider system of which it is a part. Alignment is presented as a process rather than an end state. It is a dynamic search that seeks to align the organization with its environment and the various internal elements of the organization with each other.

The quest for internal and external alignment is not an easy process to manage. Drawing on the work of Lewin, a generic model of change management is presented as a process involving eight elements:

1 *Recognizing the need for change:* Recognition involves complex processes of perception, interpretation and decision making.
2 *Starting the change process:* This involves translating the need for change into a desire for change and deciding who will manage the change.
3 *Diagnosis:* This involves
   - reviewing the present state
   - identifying the desired future state.

   People are more likely to be motivated to change if the diagnostic process:
   - disconfirms their view that all is well
   - produces an appropriate level of anxiety
   - offers sufficient incentive.
4 *Preparing and planning for implementation:* Plans have to take account of different lead times, interdependencies, necessary resources and other constraints. Most importantly, plans need to address political issues.
5 *Implementing:*
   - Implementation may involve following a 'blueprint plan' to move from A to B.

- However, sometimes it is impossible to specify B. Implementation becomes an open-ended, iterative process. It involves taking tentative steps in what is hoped is the right direction and then reviewing whether the step worked and the direction still holds good.

6 *Reviewing:* Reviewing not only refers to a post-implementation review, it is also an ongoing activity, checking progress against agreed milestones.

7 *Sustaining:* This involves refreezing behaviour at the new level for as long as it is beneficial to do so. It includes consolidating and building on gains and spreading new methods and processes across the organization.

8 *Managing the people issues:* Any strategy for change must address a number of people issues that are ongoing throughout the change process, including:
    - power, leadership and stakeholder management
    - communication
    - motivating others to change
    - support for others to help them manage their personal transitions
    - training and development.

This generic model provides the framework for Chapters 3–29. The way in which Chapters 3–29 relate to the generic model is illustrated below in Figure 2.3.

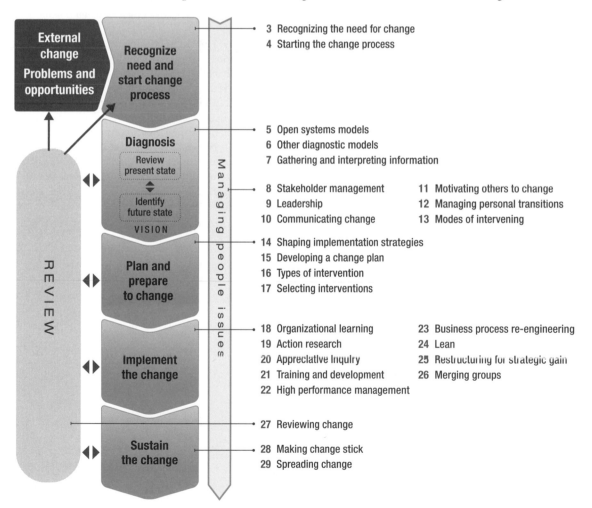

Figure 2.3   *The relationship between Chapters 3–29 and the generic process model of change*

References

Beckhard, R. and Harris, R. (1987) *Organizational Transitions: Managing Complex Change* (2nd edn), Reading, MA: Addison-Wesley.

Buchanan, D.A. and Storey, J. (1997) Role taking and role switching in organizational change: the four pluralities, in I. McLoughlin and M. Harris (eds) *Innovation, Organizational Change and Technology*, London: International Thompson.

Burke, W.W. (2002) *Organization Change: Theory and Practice*, Thousand Oaks, CA: Sage.

Burnes, B. (2004a) Kurt Lewin and the planned approach to change: a re-appraisal, *Journal of Management Studies*, 41(6): 977–1002.

Burnes, B. (2004b) Kurt Lewin and complexity theory: back to the future?, *Journal of Change Management*, 4(4): 309–25.

Clegg, C.W. and Walsh, S. (2004) Change management: time for change, *European Journal of Work and Organization Psychology*, 13(2): 217–39.

Dawson, P. (2003) *Organisational Change: A Processual Approach*, London: Chapman.

Dunphy, D. (1996) Organisational change in corporate settings, *Human Relations*, 49(5): 541–2.

Egan, G. (1996) *Change Agent Skills: Managing Innovation and Change*, Englewood Cliffs, NJ: Prentice Hall.

Ford, D.J. and Ford, L.W. (1995) The role of conversation in producing intentional change in organizations, *Academy of Management Review*, 20(3): 571–600.

Ford, W.M. and Greer, B.M. (2006) Profiling change: an empirical study of change process patterns, *Journal of Applied Behavioral Science*, 42(4): 420–46.

Hayes, J. and Hyde, P. (1998) A process model of change, unpublished workshop handout.

Hendry, C. (1996) Understanding and creating whole organisational change through learning theory, *Human Relations*, 48(5): 621–41.

Kantor, R.M., Stein, B.A. and Jick, T.D. (1992) *The Challenge of Organizational Change*, New York: Free Press.

Kotter, J.P. (1996) *Leading Change*, Boston, MA: Harvard Business School Press.

Lewin, K. (1947) Frontiers in group dynamics, *Human Relations*, 1: 5–41.

Lewin, K. (1951) *Field Theory in Social Science*, New York: Harper & Row.

Lippet, R., Watson, J. and Wesley, B. (1958) *The Dynamics of Planned Change*, New York: Harcourt Brace, Jovanovich.

Locke, E.A. and Latham, G.P. (1984) *Goal Setting: A Motivational Technique that Works*, Englewood Cliffs, NJ: Prentice Hall.

Miles, R.E. and Snow, C.C. (1984) Designing strategic human resource systems, *Organizational Dynamics*, 13: 36–52

Nadler, D.A. (1987) The effective management of organizational change, in J.W. Lorsch (ed.) *Handbook of Organizational Behaviour*, Englewood Cliffs, NJ: Prentice Hall.

Schein, E.H. (1996) Kurt Lewin's change theory in the field and in the classroom: notes towards a model of management learning, *Systems Practice*, 9(1): 27–47.

Schneider, B., Hayes, S.C., Lim, B. et al. (2003) The human side of strategy: employee experiences of strategic alignment in a service organization, *Organizational Dynamics*, 32(2): 122–41.

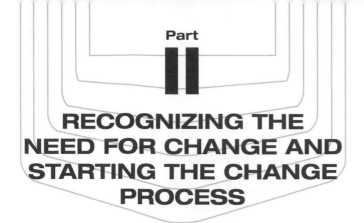

RECOGNIZING THE NEED FOR CHANGE AND STARTING THE CHANGE PROCESS

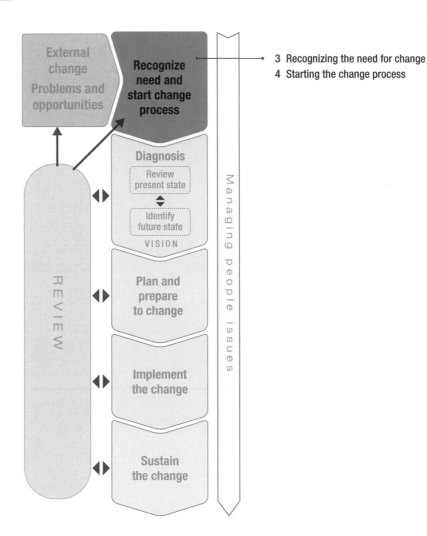

3 Recognizing the need for change
4 Starting the change process

Chapter 3   Recognizing the need for change

The focus of this chapter is recognizing of the need for change. Particular attention is given to how internal factors can affect this. These include strong organizational ideologies that inhibit learning, the composition of the top team, the way the agenda for change is formulated and the extent to which organizational members are encouraged or allowed to contribute to this process.

Chapter 4   Starting the change process

This chapter examines some of the issues associated with starting the change process. Most important is translating the need for change into a desire for change. Organizational members may be reluctant to pursue change because they lack confidence in their own and others' ability to make a difference. This chapter (and book) adopts a 'voluntaristic' perspective and argues that organizational members are not powerless pawns, unable to affect change, but are independent actors able to intervene in ways that can make an important difference. To do this, they need concepts and theories that will help them to understand the process of changing and ways of intervening, but they also need to believe in their own ability to affect outcomes.

Attention is given to who should lead the change and how they can build effective change relationships.

This chapter considers factors that can affect recognition of the need for change. Particular attention is given to internal factors, such as strong organizational ideologies, the composition of the top team, the way the agenda for change is formulated and the extent to which organizational members are encouraged or allowed to contribute to this process. The final section considers some of the indicators of organizational effectiveness that can signal a need for change.

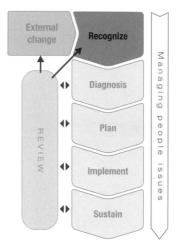

Recognizing the need for change

It was noted in Chapter 1 that some organizations (or units) are good at anticipating the need for change and this gives them time to investigate the emerging problem or opportunity and decide how best to respond. Others lack this ability. Some may fail to recognize the need for change until they have little choice but to react quickly to an unanticipated set of circumstances. Others may never recognize the problem or opportunity. In some circumstances, such failures can threaten the organization's long-term survival, but often the change may not be so critical or the organization may have sufficient 'fat' to survive. Nevertheless, the cost may be that it ends up performing at a level much below what it might have been.

Organizations may fail to recognize the need for change because members pay insufficient attention to what is happening in the wider environment. Even where organizational members are aware of what is going on outside, they may fail to recognize its implications for the organization. In Chapter 18 on organizational learning, reference is made to how ideologies and inappropriate shared mental models can undermine an organization's ability to interpret and understand what is going on in the environment. At the level of the organization, this can lead to strategic drift and at the level of the unit or subsystem, it can lead to a similar lack of alignment and consequent inefficiencies.

Nadler and Shaw (1995) illustrate this with their argument that one of the paradoxes of organizational life is that success often sets the stage for failure. This is because when organizations are successful, managers become locked into the patterns of behaviour that produced the original success. These patterns become codified or institutionalized and are rarely questioned. Nadler and Shaw elaborate their argument with the proposition that success often leads to growth and growth leads to complexity and greater differentiation. As this happens, attention shifts away from how the organization relates to the environment – it is taken for granted that this relationship will be successful – and attention is switched to managing the new and more complex relationships within the organization. Customers and suppliers receive less attention and the competitive gains of rival organizations, for example in terms of reduced costs or shorter time to market, are ignored. Where this complacency and internal focus leads to declining performance, the organization may behave as if the solution is to do more of what led to success in the past. Nadler and Shaw (1995: 11) refer to the organization becoming 'learning disabled'. Managers become incapable of looking outside, reflecting on success and failure, accepting new ideas and developing new insights. If unchecked, the ultimate outcome of this trap of success can be what they refer to as the 'death spiral' (see Figure 3.1).

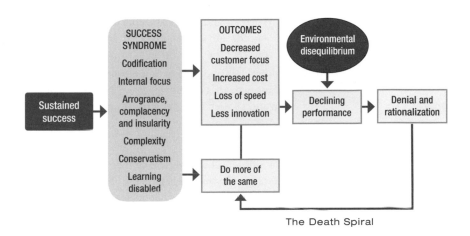

Figure 3.1   *The trap of success*
Source: Nadler and Shaw, 1995:11

Improving the organization's ability to sense the need for change

Sensing a need for change and formulating a change agenda begin when individuals notice and respond to what they perceive to be significant external or organizational events. Pitt et al. (2002) observe that sometimes the signals or events that cause them to sense that an issue is important or urgent may be relatively weak but, based on their intuition and context-particular experience, some individuals are able to anticipate the implications of these signals. It is often argued that when top teams are populated by executives with diverse backgrounds, they are more likely to be sensitive to a wider range of internal and external issues that could impact on future performance than when they are drawn from similar backgrounds, and therefore will be less likely to be learning disabled and caught in the trap of success. This proposition is based on the assumption that functional conditioning (current and past functional experience) affects cause-and-effect beliefs and directs attention to issues related to these beliefs. Various studies support the validity of this view. For example, Cohen and Ebbesen (1979) found that goals that are salient during a task amplify the salience of information related to these goals, suggesting that executives who work or have worked in various functional areas will be influenced by the information and issues related to their various and different past experiences. However, Chattopadhyay et al. (1999), in a study of 371 executives working in 58 businesses across 26 industrial sectors, found little support for this view. A key finding of their study was that the beliefs of other members of the top team had a much greater effect on collective sense making than members' functional experience. This raises the possibility that groupthink (discussed in Chapter 18) could undermine the top team's ability to recognize the need for change.

According to Pitt et al. (2002), issues emerge and are shaped to form the 'agenda for change' through various forms of individual initiative. While agenda-forming initiatives are often restricted to senior managers at the top of the organization, people located at multiple levels in the hierarchy can take action to influence the agenda for change. However, such personal actions may not be sufficient to guarantee that the organization will address the issues identified by individuals. Pitt et al. (2002) assert that if ideas and concerns are to have any impact on what the organization does, they must receive some minimal level of collective attention and be recognized as having sufficient priority to deserve further consideration. Personal concerns compete for collective attention and interpretation:

> Whether, and how fast a concern crystallizes into an issue or item *on the agenda* depends on who is involved and the opportunities they have to interact and construct the issue through conversation and debate. (Pitt et al., 2002: 157)

Political behaviour to promote self-interest and strong ideologies that marginalize minority or dissenting views and promote groupthink are some of the factors that can affect which issues emerge as part of the agenda for change.

The role of playmakers

The individuals who influence the organizational agenda are referred to by Pitt et al. (2002) as 'playmakers', a term they borrow from football, where it refers to the restless, energetic midfield role that links play, energizes the team and 'makes things happen'. They argue that these playmakers do not always have to form an exclusive elite. Top managers can encourage other organizational members to perform playmaker roles by seeking out relevant opinion from those who are close to the realities of the operating environment; however, in many organizations, this does not happen – see the discussion of organizational silence in Chapter 10.

Based on a study in a manufacturing company, Pitt et al. (2002) identified a number of roles that people from various parts of the organization can play to influence the agenda for change. These are:

▶ *Upward-facing advocates:* they promote ideas and concerns via rational arguments. Those who opt to play this kind of role are most effective when they are perceived as experts and are able to present persuasive technical evidence and well-crafted arguments. Describing his approach to influencing the top team, a systems manager who acted as an upward-facing advocate said: 'Senior people like to measure things. Arguments about change are easier to sustain if you can quantify things. If you want to justify something, get clear measurements of feasibility and benefits, proof on paper' (Pitt et al., 2002: 161).

▶ *Upward-facing emotive champions:* they use emotion and polemics rather than rational arguments to manage impressions and champion issues. Those who adopt this approach are often motivated by self-interest allied to a genuine concern for the future of the organization. Pitt et al. (2002: 161) cite a manager who adopted this approach to influencing the change agenda: 'I went to a meeting and really stirred it up. I told them what they were saying was ludicrous. I came back and said to my manager that lunatics have taken over the asylum. I created a major issue.' This approach can involve risks but the person quoted above felt so strongly about the issue that he was prepared to speak up.

> ▶ *Democratic brokers:* they facilitate lateral communication among peers. They tend to be respected organizational members with perceived expertise who function as interpreters, ideas brokers and opinion canvassers. They use their nodal position in communication networks to originate and trade concerns with peers. Because they bring together different groups and interests, brokers can make a particularly valuable contribution by promoting diverse interpretations of situations that can point to opportunities or threats that might not be identified by a narrow group of senior managers acting alone. Pitt et al. (2002: 165) refer to a planning manager who described a situation in which he acted as broker with his peers in various departments: 'We bounce problems off each other all the time. What's expected of us and how it fits in with where the company's going. How we want to restructure it, where people actually fit in. A lot is about communication ... trying to ... influence our peers. Its about networking ... talking to people, bouncing ideas off them.'

Pitt et al. (2002: 164) report that in the company they studied, notwithstanding the examples referred to above, the locus of playmaking was narrowly demarcated and tended to be confined to a select few:

> Although newcomers and junior staff were in theory free to contribute to issue debates, older and wiser hands tended to be ambivalent or dismissive when they did so, thereby limiting interpretive diversity in practice.

Widening the opportunity for organizational members to engage in playmaking can greatly improve an organization's ability to recognize the need to take action to either minimize threats or exploit new possibilities.

The Active Sports Equipment Company provides a good example of how people located at different points in the organization have the potential to make a valuable contribution to the formulation of the change agenda.

Case study 3.1

The Active Sports Equipment Company

The Active Sports Equipment Company (ASE as it will be referred to here) is a small to medium-sized manufacturer of high-quality sports equipment. It was founded 35 years ago and currently employs around 50 people to manufacture a specialist piece of sporting equipment. Current turnover is £4m and 65% of output is exported worldwide. The founder of the company is a mechanical engineer. He established ASE to produce a specialist piece of sports equipment based on his own original and highly innovative design. He is still the managing director and his obsessive concern with the details of design and engineering excellence dominate the culture of the company.

This concern for engineering excellence has served the company well, and it has built itself an enviable reputation as *the* standard by which all other sporting equipment in this specialist category is judged, despite the fact that the basic design of ASE's product has evolved little over the years. Recently, however, a number of challenges to this dominant position have emerged as other sports equipment manufacturers have sought to enter what they regard as an attractive market with newer designs. These newcomers compete effectively on price and many aspects of performance and specification, although they still fail to match ASE's product on ease and speed of assembly and the compactness of the fold for transportation. Much of the success of the ASE product is based on its well-engineered and robust construction that enables it to be folded and unfolded easily and quickly. However, it is with such challenges in mind that ASE introduced its biggest ever number of innovations in April 2005, the most significant of which was the option of a number of titanium parts that deliver important weight-saving advantages.

But what about the future? ASE might continue to focus on its core competence and seek to retain its current competitive advantage by further improving the design of its product. Product and production engineering are highly valued within the company.

There is no doubt that it is engineering that has created the ASE brand and made it what it is today. There is, however, the risk that engineering alone may not guarantee that the current record of success will be sustained.

There are a number of other possibilities that might deserve attention. For example:

- Some managers see opportunities for improving the effectiveness of the company by reviewing the way it functions. Like many small and medium-sized enterprises, ASE appears to have pursued a rather informal approach to the development of its own internal organization. This reflects the priority given to the development of product and production processes in the early years. Since then staff roles have been redefined and new ones created on an ad hoc basis to reflect the changing demands on the business. There may be, for example, advantages to be gained from improving internal communication and planning processes or reviewing the way the organization is structured. Such changes might lead to superior performance by improving internal alignment.
- Other managers are aware of opportunities in the marketplace. A marketing manager was recruited two years ago but this appointment has not had much impact on the company's overall culture, which continues to be engineering led. More attention to marketing issues might help to ensure that if and when customer needs change, this will be recognized by those who control the strategic agenda.
- Related opportunities might involve building alliances between product engineering and marketing to extend the product range and exploit the ASE brand.
- People working in the production departments are also aware of opportunities to reduce manufacturing costs, but are reluctant to voice some of these because they suspect that they may lead to job losses.

If you were a manager in ASE aware of some of these issues, would you actively try to influence the company's strategic agenda? If no, why not? If yes, how would you attempt to do this?

Source: This case study is based on contributions from Andy Shrimpton

Problems relating to the recognition of the need for change are more likely to arise in those organizations where alternative perspectives and interpretations are ignored or suppressed than in those organizations where they are actively sought out and debated. Such debates will not necessarily lead to major changes, but at least they ensure that the possibility of new threats or opportunities is properly considered. There are many examples of companies that have continued to exploit, for many years, whatever it is that has provided them with a competitive advantage. This can be a healthy state of affairs so long as care is exercised to avoid complacency and the trap of success. Organizations that are most likely to sustain their success over long periods are those that engage in the process of double loop collective learning discussed in Chapter 18. They identify and question basic assumptions and take nothing for granted. Sometimes this process points to the need for major change but sometimes it confirms the validity of the existing strategy and way of operating, and points to little more than the kind of change that fine-tunes the existing way of working.

Indicators of effectiveness

Managers are responsible for ensuring that the organization or the part of the organization they manage performs effectively. Discrepancies between actual and desired levels of performance signal a need for change. Problems arise when managers (and others) fail to pay attention to important performance indicators.

Exercise 3.1   **Indicators of effectiveness**

Before reading on, make a note, in the space provided below, of the indicators that you believe are used to assess whether or not your organization – and your department or unit within the organization – is effective.

Organization

Department/unit

When you have completed this chapter, you might like to review these indicators and consider whether any of them need to be revised.

Organization effectiveness can be defined in many ways:

▶ *Purpose:* Many commercial organizations use profit as one of the main indicators of effectiveness, but this indicator might not apply to all organizations. While financial viability may be necessary for the survival of organizations such as religious orders, universities, hospitals or charities, profit might not be viewed as a critical indicator of effectiveness. The effectiveness of hospitals in the British National Health Service (NHS), for example, might be judged on indicators such as waiting lists and mortality rates rather than 'profit'. Change managers need to attend to performance indicators that reflect the purpose of their organization.

▶ *Stakeholder perspective:* Different stakeholders often use different indicators to assess an organization's effectiveness. Profit might be more important to shareholders than to workers. Suppliers, customers, employees and people in the wider community affected by the products and services (and pollution) produced by an organization will all have their own views on what should be taken into account when assessing whether or not it is effective. When John Birt joined the BBC, he felt that programme makers were neglecting some of the corporation's key stakeholders and that this neglect was threatening the organization's survival (see Case study 1.1.1).

▸ *Level of assessment:* Effectiveness can be assessed at different levels, for example the organization, subunit or individual employee. Only paying attention to overall performance might result in major inefficiencies going undetected.

▸ *Alignment:* Assessments of effectiveness need to be aligned up, down and across the organization. Indicators of individual and group effectiveness need to be aligned with indicators of departmental effectiveness, which, in turn, need to be aligned with indicators of organizational effectiveness. The indicators used for different units also need to be aligned 'horizontally' across the organization. Figure 3. 2 depicts a simplified model of an organization and presents examples of indicators of effectiveness for each function, and objectives that each function might pursue in order to achieve an effective performance.

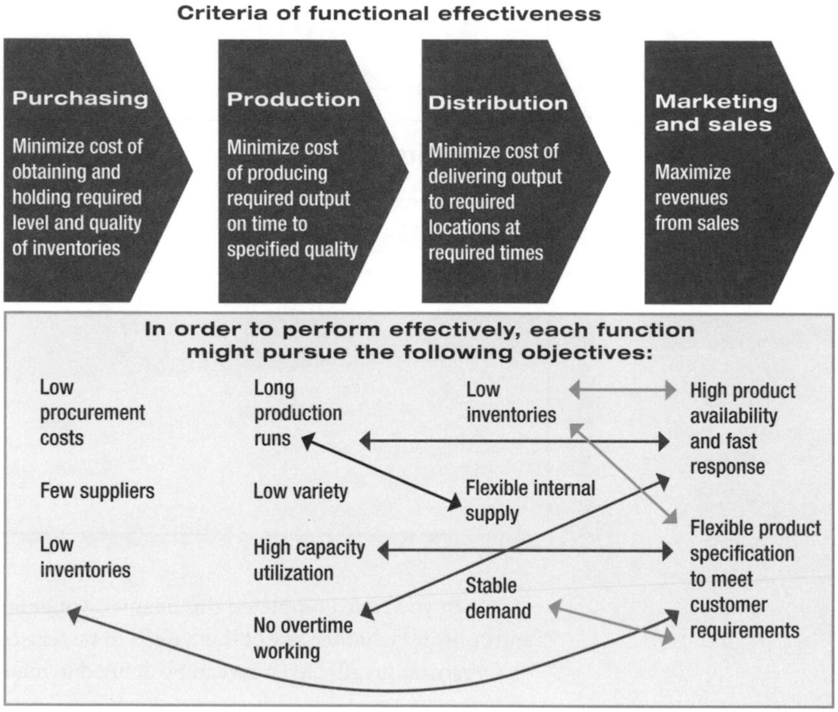

Criteria of functional effectiveness

Purchasing	Production	Distribution	Marketing and sales
Minimize cost of obtaining and holding required level and quality of inventories	Minimize cost of producing required output on time to specified quality	Minimize cost of delivering output to required locations at required times	Maximize revenues from sales

In order to perform effectively, each function might pursue the following objectives:

Figure 3.2 *Examples of functional misalignment*

Managers working in subunits of the organization represented in Figure 3.1 might lose sight of the overall goal of the organization and focus their attention on the achievement of more immediate goals related to functional performance. For example, in the face of strong price competition, sales and marketing might seek to secure increased sales (related to their goal of maximizing revenue from sales) by offering customers fast delivery and customized products. While this strategy might help sales and marketing achieve its own performance targets, it might undermine the effectiveness of the manufacturing and distribution functions – and consequently the effectiveness of the overall organization. In order to customize products and offer an immediate and flexible response to satisfy customers' just in time delivery requirements, the manufacturing function might have to introduce short product runs, make greater use of overtime working and hold higher stocks of work in progress. The distribution function might have to hold higher inventories of finished goods and, because of unpredictable demand, make more deliveries that involve part loads. The cost of meeting these new manufacturing and distribution requirements might be greater than the net benefits achieved from the increased sales revenue, and might threaten the organization's overall effectiveness.

A few examples of sources of possible misalignment are indicated by the double-headed arrows shown in Figure 3.2. As will be seen from this example, it is not uncommon for organization subunits and individual employees to be rewarded for behaving in ways that have little to do with overall organizational effectiveness. Unless organizational leaders are alert to the need to monitor internal alignment, problems may go unrecognized for some time.

Time perspective

It has already been noted that in some cases profitability can be a useful indicator of organizational effectiveness. However, just because organization A is currently more profitable than organization B does not mean that A is the most effective organization. Organization B might be incurring higher costs and lower profits today in order to invest in new plant, product development and staff training in the belief that this will help to secure survival and growth over the longer term. The implication of this is that organizational leaders need to take account of the time perspective when assessing the effectiveness of particular departments or the organization as a whole.

Benchmark

Often effectiveness is assessed in terms of some output:input ratio such as the number of units produced per man-hour. It is assumed that any increase in output with constant or decreasing inputs represents greater effectiveness and vice versa. When making this kind of assessment, reference needs to be made to a standard or benchmark. For example, all producers within a given product category or industrial sector may have experienced efficiency gains because of the introduction of a new and widely available manufacturing system. In this context, the assessment of whether one particular producer has maintained or improved its effectiveness might need to include a comparison of this producer's performance relative to the performance of others. A company may have improved its output:input ratio, and therefore improved its efficiency, but may have achieved smaller improvements than other comparable producers. In these circumstances, the company may be deemed to be more efficient than it used to be but less effective than comparable companies.

Constraints and enabling factors

Account also needs to be taken of any constraints that inhibit performance or enabling factors that boost performance relative to comparable other organizations. The new manufacturing system referred to above might produce levels of toxic emissions greater than the levels permitted by environmental regulations. These regulations may only apply to a minority of producers located in a particular region or country. In these circumstances, while a producer faced with the strict environmental regulations might not improve output:input ratios as much as some of its competitors, it might achieve considerable success in modifying its production processes in a way that enables it to adopt the new manufacturing technology and improve efficiency enough to produce sufficient profit to survive. A failure to respond in this way may have resulted in the company going out of business. In terms of its ability to minimize the effect of the constraint imposed by the environmental legislation, it might be deemed to be an effective organization.

Summarizing the discussion so far, those assessing effectiveness need to take account of:

▶ purpose and desired outcomes
▶ the stakeholder perspective from which the assessment is made
▶ level of assessment
▶ alignment with the various indicators used at different levels and across different functions
▶ specified time frame – short, medium or long term
▶ benchmark standard
▶ any special constraints or enabling factors that affect performance.

When any of these factors are ignored, those assessing performance may fail to spot problems and identify the need for change in good time.

At this point, it might be useful to distinguish between effectiveness and efficiency. Carnall (2003) defines efficiency as achieving stated goals within given resource constraints. His definition of effectiveness includes the efficient use of resources to achieve immediate goals but also embraces the need to adapt to changing circumstances in order to remain efficient over the longer term.

Effectiveness and conceptualizations of organizations

This discussion of organizational effectiveness can be elaborated further. Goodman and Pennings (1980) argue that our preferred definitions of organizational effectiveness are closely linked to the way we conceptualize organizations. They define the following four perspectives:

▶ *The goals perspective* presents organizations as rationally constructed entities that are formed, and their existence is legitimized, in the quest for certain identifiable goals. The meaning of effectiveness is derived from the accomplishment of these goals.
▶ *The systems perspective* focuses on the functional complementarity of parts of the organization and the nature of the organization's relationship with the environment. The organization is viewed as an open system that imports inputs from the environment, transforming them into outputs which are then exported (see Chapter 5). The fundamental task of the organization is to survive and this is seen to depend on the maintenance of functional complementarity within the organization and between the organization and the wider environment. According to Goodman and Pennings, the systems perspective views functional complementarity as being more important than the achievement of some particular goal.
▶ *The organization development (OD) perspective* is concerned with the processes of organizational learning that promote organizational renewal and long-term survival. This perspective emphasizes the contribution that organizational members can make to improving organizational performance and pays attention to indicators of effectiveness that embrace the quality of working life.
▶ *The political arena perspective* presents organizations as a collection of internal and external constituencies, each pursuing their own objectives. Organizational

effectiveness is defined in terms of the attributes valued by the most powerful constituencies. A constituency's power is determined, at least in part, by the importance of its contribution to the input-transformation-output process. Suppliers or customers are powerful if they are vital to the survival of the organization. Groups of employees, such as members of a particular trade union, or specific departments are powerful only as long as the organization needs to rely on them to survive. The more central the contribution of a constituency to the survival and prosperity of the organization, the greater its power. This political perspective views the organization as the product of a negotiated order that is managed by the dominant coalition of constituencies, and reflects aspects of the goals and systems conceptualizations of organizations.

There are common threads in these different conceptualizations of organizations that point to some of the factors that need to be considered when assessing effectiveness. Organizations are interdependent open systems that comprise a range of constituencies, each with their own interests and goals. The constituencies (stakeholders) that dominate the political process define the purpose of the organization and the key indicators of organizational effectiveness. Whether or not an organization performs effectively will be determined by the extent to which the various elements of the input-transformation-output system are aligned.

The balanced scorecard

In the early 1990s, Kaplan and Norton embarked on a collaborative research project to explore new ways of measuring performance that addresses many of the issues discussed above. A guiding hypothesis was that managers and employees focus their efforts on those aspects of performance that are measured and give relatively little attention, or even neglect, those aspects of organizational functioning that are not measured. This can have serious implications for the recognition of the need for change. One of Kaplan and Norton's (2004) early observations was that in the majority of organizations, the primary measurement system was financial accounting. This approach tended to treat investment, such as the development of customer relationships, employee capabilities and improved quality, as expenses in the period in which they were incurred.

These financial reporting systems fail to measure or provide a basis for managing the value created by the organization's intangible assets. Kaplan and Norton's early research led them to develop the concept of the balanced scorecard. Financial measures, which provide a useful summary of the results of actions previously taken, are supplemented by measures of three other aspects of organizational functioning that Kaplan and Norton believe are important drivers of future financial performance – customer-related measures, internal business process measures and measures of the infrastructure that facilitates long-term growth and improvement. The scorecard approach enables managers to attend to short- and long-term objectives and lagging and leading indicators through a process that reviews performance from a number of different perspectives. In Chapter 27, the ways in which the balanced scorecard can be used as a change management tool are discussed.

Recognizing the need for change is an essential step in starting the change process. You might want to reflect on your own experience and consider whether those who are best placed to recognize the need for change are able to influence those responsible for formulating the change agenda (Exercise 3.2).

Exercise 3.2

Recognizing the need for change

Think of an occasion within the last three years when your unit or organization recognized the need for change in good time and then think of another occasion when it failed to do this.

In the space below, list those factors you suspect may have contributed to these different outcomes.

Factors that contributed to the recognition of the need for change	Factors that contributed to the failure to recognize the need for change

Reflect on your unit or organization's past record of recognizing the need for change. Note, in the space below, anything that you or others could do to help ensure that, in the future, your unit or organization will be more alert to the need for change.

Summary

This chapter has considered some of the factors that can affect the recognition of a need for change. Particular attention has been given to internal factors. These include:

▶ *The inclination of organizational members to pay attention to the external environment:* Organizations may fail to recognize the need for change because members pay insufficient attention to what is happening in the wider environment. At the level of the organization, this can lead to strategic drift and at the level of the unit or subsystem, it can lead to a lack of internal alignment and consequent inefficiencies.

▶ *The extent to which organizational members are encouraged or allowed to contribute to formulating the agenda for change:* Initiatives that contribute to the formulation of the agenda for change are often restricted to senior managers at the top of the organization. However, people located at multiple levels in the hierarchy may be well placed to make a valuable input, but their effort to contribute may not be sufficient to guarantee that the organization will address the issues they identify as important.

▶ *The way the agenda for change is formulated:* Political behaviour to promote self-interest, the composition of the top team and strong ideologies that marginalize minority or dissenting views and promote groupthink are some of the factors that can affect which issues emerge as part of the agenda for change.

▶ *The indicators of effectiveness that are attended to:* Managers are responsible for ensuring that the organization, or part of the organization they manage, performs effectively. Discrepancies between actual and desired levels of performance signal a need for change. Problems arise when managers and others fail to pay attention to important performance indicators. Those assessing organizational effectiveness need to take account of:
  - organizational purpose and desired outcomes
  - the stakeholder perspective from which the assessment is made
  - level of assessment – total organization, department, work group or individual
  - the alignment of the various indicators used at different levels and across different functions
  - specified time frame – short, medium or long term
  - benchmark standard
  - special constraints or enabling factors that affect performance.

▶ *The balanced scorecard* illustrates an approach to assessing performance that attends to a wide range of factors that could signal the need for change.

References

Carnall, C.A. (2003) *Managing Change in Organisations* (3rd edn), Harlow: Prentice Hall.

Chattopadhyay, P., Glick, W.-H., Miller, C.C. and Huber, G.P. (1999) Determinants of executive beliefs: comparing functional conditioning and social influence, *Strategic Management Journal*, **20**(8): 763–89.

Cohen, C. and Ebbesen, E. (1979) Observational goal and schema activity: a theoretical framework for behavior perceptions, *Journal of Experimental and Social Psychology*, 15: 305–29.

Goodman, P.S. and Pennings, J.M. (1980) Critical issues in assessing organizational effectiveness, in E.E Lawler, D.A Nadler and C. Cammann (eds) *Organizational Assessment*, New York: Wiley.

Kaplan, R.S. and Norton, D.P. (2004) *Strategy Maps: Converting Intangible Assets into Tangible Outcomes*, Boston, MA: Harvard Business School Press.

Nadler, D.A. and Shaw, R.B. (1995) Change leadership: core competency for the twenty-first century, in D.A. Nadler, R.B. Shaw and A.E. Walton (eds) *Discontinuous Change: Leading Organizational Transformation*, San Francisco, CA: Jossey-Bass.

Pitt, M., McAulay, L. and Sims, D. (2002) Promoting strategic change: 'playmaker' roles in organizational agenda formulation, *Strategic Change*, 11: 155–72.

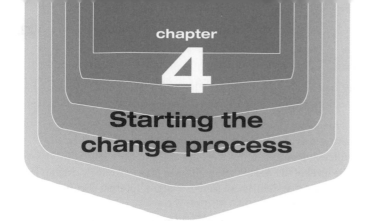

Starting the change process

This chapter considers some of the issues associ-ated with starting the change process. Most important is translating the need for change into a desire for change. Organizational members may be reluctant to pursue change because they lack confidence in their own and others' ability to make a difference. This chapter (and book) adopts a 'voluntaristic' perspective and argues that organizational members are not powerless pawns, unable to affect change, but are inde-pendent actors able to intervene in ways that can make an important difference. To do this, they need concepts and theories that will help them to understand the process of changing and ways of intervening, but they also need to believe in

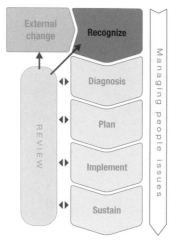

their own ability to affect outcomes. The final part of this chapter looks at who should lead the change and how they can build effective change relationships.

Beliefs about change agency

Change agency refers to the ability of a manager or other agent of change to affect the way an organization responds to change. One approach to the study of change and change management portrays the manager and other organizational members as pawns affected by change rather than as agents who can initiate and secure change. This approach is referred to by Wilson (1992) as 'determinism'.

The deterministic view

The deterministic view is that the ability of the manager to influence change is limited because the main determining forces lie outside the organization and the realms of strategic choice for managers. Wilson (1992: 42) notes that advocates of this approach view organizations as interdependent elements of a much greater open system and they regard the characteristics of the wider organization–environment linkages as the key determinant of strategic change. For example, no matter how good the CEO of an organization might be, when faced with a dramatic downturn in the trade cycle or unfavourable exchange rates, they may be able to do little to improve the immediate fortunes of the organization. Greenwood and Hinings (1996) echo this view when they discuss how, in some circumstances, an organiz-ation's institutional context can limit the possibilities for change, especially when the organization is embedded in a wider system that has tightly coupled relationships.

Mellahi and Wilkinson (2004) note that one of the points that classical industrial organization and organizational ecology scholars can agree on is the deterministic role of the environment that constrains management action.

The voluntarist view

The voluntarist view rejects the assumption that managers are powerless and argues that managers are the principal decision makers who determine the fate of the organization. The strategic choice framework provides an example of how the voluntarist approach can work. It challenges the view that there is an ideal type of organization and a one best way of managing. It recognizes functional equivalents and the possibility of equifinality, whereby organizational outcomes can be achieved in a variety of different ways. One of the key factors that determines the effectiveness of an organization is the quality of the strategic choices made by members of the dominant coalition. This approach emphasizes the role of human agency and asserts that managers can intervene to affect change in ways that will either promote or undermine organizational effectiveness.

Raynor et al. (2009) sound a note of caution about seeking insight from 'success studies'. They argue that some of the companies cited in management bestsellers such as *In Search of Excellence* and *Good to Great* may just have been lucky. They demonstrate how easily we can succumb to the temptation to 'explain' seemingly significant outcomes that are entirely random by describing an experiment one of them conducts at the beginning of her strategic management class. She starts the class by asking all the students in the room to stand up and then instructs each of them to toss a coin. If the toss comes up tails, they are to sit down, but if it comes up heads, they are to remain standing:

> Since there are around 70 students in the class, after six or seven rounds there is only one student left standing. With the appropriate theatrics, I approach the student and say, 'How did you do that? Seven heads in a row! Can I interview you in *Fortune*? Is it the T-shirt? Is it the flick of the wrist? Can I write a case study about you?' (Raynor et al., 2009: 18)

This example illustrates that chance is a factor that cannot be ignored. However, there is still evidence that managers can act in ways that contribute to the success of their organizations. For example, Pettigrew and Whipp (1991) report the outcome of a study of firms in four sectors – automobile manufacture, book publishing, merchant banking and life assurance – and conclude that there are observable differences between the ways that leaders in higher performing firms manage change compared to those in lesser performing firms.

From the perspective of change agency, the deterministic view offers an overfatalistic perspective. While, in some situations, there may be external forces that exercise a powerful effect on organizational performance, there will almost always be scope for managers to intervene in ways that will promote the organization's interests. Burnes (2004) argues that despite the constraints they face, managers have a far wider scope for shaping decisions than most organization theories acknowledge. He asserts that 'the scope for choice and the development of political influence is likely to be more pronounced where change, particularly major change, is on the managerial agenda' (2004: 198).

Problems can arise, however, when managers and others do not believe in their own ability to act as agents of change. As a consequence, they may fail to behave proactively. Their response, and therefore the response of the organization, may be to react passively in response to external forces for change.

Voluntarism and change agency

Two assumptions underpinning the approach to managing change adopted in this book are that managers can make a difference and they can learn to manage change more effectively. Effective change managers require, and can be helped to acquire:

▶ confidence in their own ability to make a difference
▶ the motivation to change
▶ conceptual models and action tools/interventions
▶ change management skills.

These factors are now explored in more detail.

Confidence in their own ability to affect outcomes

Some managers may have the conceptual knowledge and required skills to equip them to intervene and make a difference but they may fail to act because they have insufficient faith in their own ability to affect outcomes.

While optimism and overconfidence can be a problem (Thaler and Sunstein, 2009), often change managers are ineffective because they fail to act in ways that enable them to exercise the control necessary to achieve desired outcomes. Rollo May (1969) argued that in many walks of life, people are hypnotized by their own feelings of powerlessness and use this as an excuse for doing nothing. He describes the central core of modern man's neuroses as the undermining of his experience of himself as responsible, and the sapping of his will and ability to make decisions. According to May (1969):

> the lack of will is much more than merely an ethical problem: the modern individual so often has the conviction that even if he did exert his 'will' – or whatever illusion passes for it – his actions wouldn't do any good anyway.

This inner feeling of impotence is a critical problem for some managers and can undermine their ability to act as agents of change. There are two explanations for this.

Locus of control

After observing that some of their clients seemed to attribute outcomes to luck rather than to factors over which they had some control, two psychologists, Rotter and Phares, embarked on a programme of research that led to the development of the concept of the 'locus of control'. The locus of control reflects the degree to which people believe that their own behaviour determines what happens to them. Those who attribute outcomes to their own efforts are referred to as 'internals' and those who attribute outcomes to external factors, such as luck, fate, other people, the state of the economy or other factors over which they have no control, are referred to as 'externals'. In the context of change management, those who are overcommitted to a deterministic view of change may be inclined to believe that the locus of control is external to themselves and the organization and may therefore develop the view that there is little they can do to influence events. Those who think this way are less likely to attempt to adopt a proactive approach to the management of change than those who have a more internal view about the locus of control.

Learned helplessness

Locus of control is related to Seligman's (1975) theory of learned helplessness. This theory argues that a person's expectation about their ability to control outcomes is learned. It suggests that managers may begin to question their ability to manage change if, when confronted with a new problem or opportunity, old and well-tried ways of managing fail to deliver desired outcomes. Furthermore, if their early attempts to experiment with alternative ways of managing are equally unsuccessful, this questioning of their own ability may develop into an expectation that they are helpless and the associated belief that there is little they can do to secure desired outcomes. Seligman argues that this expectation will produce motivational and cognitive deficits:

▶ *Motivational deficits* involve a failure to take any voluntary actions designed to control events following a previous experience with uncontrollable events. If managers believe that they cannot exercise any control over outcomes, they will not even be motivated to try.

▶ *Cognitive deficits* involve a failure to learn that it is possible to control what happens. If managers believe that they cannot affect outcomes in a particular set of changing circumstances, this belief may stop them recognizing opportunities to exercise control, even if there is evidence that their own behaviour has actually had an important impact on outcomes.

The theory suggests that the incentive for managers and others to initiate activity directed towards managing change will depend upon the (learned) expectation that their action can produce some improvement in the problematic situation. If they do not have any confidence in their own ability to manage the change and achieve any improvements, they will not try to exercise influence.

Both individuals and organizations can develop the expectation that there is little they can do to secure desirable outcomes when confronted by change. However, individuals and organizations can also learn that they can affect their own destiny, and they can learn how to exercise this influence.

The motivation to change

Pugh (1993) argues that those who are most likely to want to change are those who are basically successful but who are experiencing tension or failure in some particular part of their work. This group will have both the confidence and the motivation to change. The next most likely to change are the successful because they will have the required confidence. However, because of their success, they may be satisfied with the status quo and lack the motivation to change. The least likely to understand and accept the need for change are the unsuccessful. While they may be the ones who need to change most, they are also the ones who are likely to lack confidence in their own ability to improve their predicament. Consequently, they may prefer the status quo (the devil they know) to the possible outcome of a failed effort to change (the devil they don't know).

Change readiness is important. Jones (2005) defines readiness as the extent to which employees hold positive views about the need for change and believe that the change will yield positive outcomes for themselves and the wider organization. Rune By (2007) studied the management of change in the UK tourism industry and found support for Armenakis et al.'s (1993) proposition that successful implementation is positively correlated with the level of change readiness.

This has implications for deciding where to initiate the change effort. When faced with the possibility of alternative starting points, the change agent might decide to start working with those who have the confidence and motivation to engage in the change process because early successes can inspire others to get involved.

Example 4.1

Failure to convince others of the need for change at AT&T

There are many instances where those who recognize the need for change want to embrace it but cannot because they are unable to convince others that the change is necessary. Werther (2003) illustrates this with the example of AT&T's telephone manufacturing division (Western Electric) following deregulation of the telecommunications sector in the USA. Prior to deregulation, consumers had no choice other than to lease their telephones from one of the Bell operating companies (another part of AT&T). These local operating companies were regulated monopolies, allowed to earn up to a set maximum return on their assets. This regulated monopoly situation encouraged AT&T to pursue a high reliability, high-cost strategy for the manufacture of its telephone instruments. This strategy was attractive for a number of reasons:

1 The cost of the phones was included as part of the asset base on which the local operating company's returns were calculated. This offered no incentive for them to persuade Western Electric to reduce its manufacturing costs.
2 Western Electric's market was protected from the threat of low-cost phones produced elsewhere because customers had to lease their phones from the local Bell company.
3 High-quality, high-cost phones were more reliable. This reduced the cost of repairs and service for the operating company and also reduced the number of complaints to the regulator about the quality of service.

All this changed after deregulation. Customers were allowed to purchase and install their own telephones and they were attracted to the many low-cost instruments that began to flood the market. This had a dramatic effect on Western Electric's share of the market and convinced senior management of the need to switch from a high reliability, high-cost manufacturing strategy to one that focused on producing low-cost phones. Werther reports that this proposed switch was fiercely resisted by engineers, managers and assemblers across the company because they believed that the company should remain committed to its traditional policy of producing high-quality if expensive phones. Their resistance was so strong that the company was forced to outsource the production of low-cost phones overseas.

This example illustrates the importance of translating the need for change into a desire for change on the part of all those who can affect the success of the change project.

Motivating others to accept the need for change can be difficult. Pitt et al. (2002) refer to how senior managers can adopt a downward-facing evangelist playmaker role to win subordinates' attention and commitment. In their study, they found evidence to suggest that spreading a message via potent, emotive symbols can be more effective than rational appeals. Pitt et al. (2002: 163) cite the case of a technical director who needed to win support for a proposed change to improve hygiene standards. His message was that the company is in a high-risk business (producing ingredients for the processed food industry) and that 'the bottom line is life and death – if you get it wrong you are going to kill people'. There are, however, circumstances where alternative ways of winning support might be more effective. These are considered in Chapter 11.

Conceptual models

Change managers can acquire a range of concepts and theories that they can use to manage change. Essentially they fall into two categories: process models that are concerned with the how of change management, and diagnostic models that focus on identifying what it is that needs to be changed. Change managers need concepts and theories that will help them to:

▶ identify the kind of change that confronts them, for example incremental or discontinuous
▶ understand the process of changing
▶ identify what needs to be attended to – through a process of diagnosis and goal setting – if they are to achieve desired outcomes.

Types of change are discussed in Chapter 1 and process models are considered in Chapter 2. Diagnosis involves the application of the many theories that exist about the behaviour of individuals and groups in organizations, about organizational processes such as power and influence, leadership, communication, decision making and conflict, and the structure and culture of organizations. These individual, group and organizational performance models can be used to help managers to identify what needs to be changed in order to protect or improve organizational effectiveness. Organizational-level diagnostic models are considered in Chapters 5 and 6.

In addition to the conceptual tools that can help change managers to understand the change process and diagnose what needs to be changed, they also need to be familiar with a range of different types of intervention that they can use to secure a desired change. These are considered in Chapters 18–26.

Change managers also need to have some basis for deciding which interventions to use in specific circumstances, taking account of contingencies such as the pace of change, the power of stakeholders to resist and so on. Models that can be used for this purpose are considered in Chapter 17.

Change management skills

While conceptual understanding is necessary, it is not sufficient to guarantee that change agents will be able to secure desired changes. When managers are acting as change agents, they need to be able to communicate, offer leadership, work with teams, confront, negotiate, motivate and manage relationships with others. Change agency requires these and many other skills that managers use in everyday life. Sometimes change agents are less effective than they might be because they fail to recognize the importance of some of these skills or they fail to apply them when required. Some of these skills are discussed in Chapters 9–12. A more detailed discussion of some of the interpersonal skills associated with helping others to change is provided in Chapter 13.

Starting the change process

After persuading others of the need for change, it is necessary to decide who will, at least in the first instance, facilitate the change. The change agent could be an insider, a member of the system or subsystem that is the target for change, or an outsider. An insider might be chosen in situations where:

▶ the person responsible for managing the unit or subsystem that is to be the (initial) target for change is committed to acting as change agent
▶ it is agreed that a particular insider has the time, knowledge and commitment to manage the change more effectively than an outsider
▶ the system does not have the resources to employ an outsider
▶ issues of confidentiality and trust prohibit the use of an outsider
▶ it proved impossible to identify a suitable outside consultant.

An outsider might be chosen where:

▶ there is nobody on the inside who has the time or competence to act as facilitator/change agent
▶ it is felt that all the competent insiders have a vested interest in the outcome and therefore might be less acceptable to other parties than a neutral outsider.

Deciding who will manage the change can have an important impact on the outcome of the change process. Often it is automatically assumed that the lead will be a technical expert rather than a manager who will be responsible for making the change work post-implementation. Clegg (2000) challenges this assumption and advocates that users should play a more central role. In Chapter 2, reference is made to the fragmented nature of many change projects. This can result in the separation of diagnosis, planning and implementation from use and maintenance. This separation can allow technical experts leading the change to focus too much attention on technical issues, such as designing a technically superior system, rather than on the needs of users. Clegg cites the example of the way a successful change project was led by a senior user at Lyons Confectionery to support his case that users need to be more centrally involved.

Example 4.2

> ## Leading change at Lyons Confectionery
>
> Lyons Confectionery makes confectionery products for sale through retail outlets across the UK. Products are distributed using a fleet of several hundred delivery vans. The sales director (who was the end user responsible for this function) was keen to improve various aspects of the performance of the van sales and delivery operation. He identified inaccuracies and delays in the feedback of information from shops as an important source of inefficiencies. This information was provided by the drivers and was an essential input for deciding manufacturing plans, inventory levels and delivery schedules.
>
> The sales director thought that it would be possible to improve the quality and speed of information flow, but rather than starting by bringing in an information technologist to develop a new information technology (IT) system, he decided to spend time with his team working out how they wanted the new way of working to operate. Their starting point was to think about how the whole van sales and delivery operation could be changed for the better before thinking about how this could be supported by new IT. They undertook a total rethink of the drivers' role. Should they, for example, continue working in their existing delivery role or could their role be expanded to include sales? They even thought about making the drivers into franchise holders.
>
> The project team included the regional sales managers, some delivery drivers and depot workers, and people from sales administration, customer services and manufacturing (all the groups linked in the process), together with the company's IT specialist (along with other experts from departments such as accounts) to advise the project team. In other words, it was the prospective users of the new system who pulled through the new working arrangements (and technology) that they needed to meet their operational needs. The team, taking advice from the IT specialist, decided that hand-held computers could deliver the required improvements, and it was the team of prospective users who organized the trials of various hand-held computers available on the market.
>
> Clegg (2000) reports that this proved to be one of the most successful change projects he ever witnessed.

Establishing a change relationship

Where the change agent is a member of the target system, entering the change relationship may simply involve agreeing with members of the target system that:

▶ there is a problem or opportunity that requires attention
▶ there is a need to engage in some form of preliminary data gathering in order to determine what further action is required.

A brand manager who is unhappy with the time it takes to introduce a change in the way a product is packaged may enlist the support of others to benchmark their performance against that of leading competitors. Similarly, a manager of a sports centre might set up a meeting with staff to consider possible reasons why an increasing proportion of existing members are failing to renew their membership.

Because the change agent is an insider and known to others, many of the issues that can be problematical and require careful attention when introducing an external consultant/change agent can often be managed informally and without too much difficulty.

Where the change agent is an outsider – coming from another part of the organiz-ation or from outside – the establishment of a change relationship can be a more complex and sometimes more formal process.

Issues that can affect the quality of the relationship

One of the key issues is building trust and confidence. Some individuals and groups are less comfortable than others when it comes to being open and discussing their affairs with outsiders. This might be because they fear that it might be difficult to communicate the nature of their problem or opportunity to others and that others may view them as incompetent or foolish. Alternatively, it may be because they fear that seeking help will threaten their autonomy and make them too dependent on others.

The early stages of the relationship-building process can be critical because clients quickly form impressions about the change agent's competence, ability to help, friendliness and inferred motives.

In terms of competence and ability, some clients want a change agent who has sufficient expertise to be able to 'see a way through' and tell them what to do. They might expect the change agent to undertake a diagnostic study and prepare a written report. In these circumstances, the competence they are seeking from the change agent is related to the 'content' of the problem or opportunity. Others might want a more collaborative relationship and expect the change agent to work with them to help them to solve their own problems. The competence that is valued in this type of relationship is related more to the process of problem solving and managing change rather than the content of a problem. (Chapter 13 reviews five ways in which change agents can work with clients.) The important point to make at this stage is that both parties need to reach some agreement about the role of the external consultant/ change agent.

In terms of friendliness and approachability, what many clients want is a helper who is, on the one hand, sympathetic to their needs and values but, on the other hand, is sufficiently neutral to offer objective comment, feedback and other assistance.

In terms of inferred motives, where clients feel that they can trust the consultant/ change agent and believe that they are 'on their side' and are 'working for them', they will be more likely to share sensitive information and be receptive to feedback or suggestions about helpful processes and so on. However, where the change agent is seen as untrustworthy, incompetent or 'not for them', the clients will be much more likely to react defensively and resist any attempt to influence their thinking. Avolio et al. (2009) draw on the work of others to provide a brief overview of 'servant leadership', which involves listening, empathy, healing, awareness, persuasion, conceptualization, foresight, stewardship, commitment and building community. These attributes can help to build effective change relationships. Van Buren and Safferstone (2009) observe that many newly appointed change managers feel under pressure to secure quick wins and this often comes across as a drive to secure an individual (personal) quick win. They argue that to be successful, leaders need to work with others to achieve 'collective' quick wins.

Developing a relationship with an external change agent can take time and sometimes clients test the helper's competence, attitudes, perceived role and trustworthiness by presenting them with what they regard as a safe or peripheral problem. If they are satisfied with the change agent's performance, the client may move on to present what they believe to be the real problem.

Identifying the client

From the perspective of the change agent, an issue that must be managed carefully is the identification of the client. The person who invites an outsider into a situation may not be the person or group that ends up as the focal client. The change agent needs to be ready to amend the definition of the client if a preliminary diagnosis suggests that the problem is not confined to one group or unit, but involves multiple units, several levels of the hierarchy or people outside the organization such as customers, suppliers, trade associations or unions.

Problems can arise when external change agents define the client as the person/group who invited them into the situation. If they are blind to the need to redefine who the client is, they may inadvertently end up working to promote or protect a sectional interest rather than the effectiveness of the organization.

One way of defining the client is in terms of the person or persons who 'own' the problem and are responsible for doing something about it. For example, the client might be either the manager who seeks help to improve the effectiveness of their department, or the organization as a whole. Cummings and Worley (2001) define the client as those organizational members who can directly impact the change issue, whether it is solving a particular problem or improving an already successful situation. This definition is more likely to identify the client as a group or the members of a subsystem rather than as an individual. Cummings and Worley specify the client in terms of all those who can directly impact on the change because they argue that if key members of the client group are excluded from the entering and contracting process, they may be reluctant to work with the change agent.

The author learned about this from direct experience. He was invited by the personnel director of an international oil company to help with a problem in a distant oil refinery. He was flown to the nearest major airport, put up in a hotel and, next morning, flown by a small plane to the refinery's own airstrip. Eventually he found himself in a meeting room in the refinery with all the senior managers. After some brief introductions, the refinery manager started the meeting by asking the consultant why he was there. It was clear that the personnel director had not involved the refinery manager in the decision to engage an external consultant. This was strongly resented and by the time the consultant had arrived at the refinery, there was little he could do to build an effective working relationship with the management team. However, some months later, the same refinery manager approached the consultant and invited him back to the refinery to work on a different problem. On this occasion, it was his problem and his decision to involve an outsider. The rejection first time round had nothing to do with the consultant's competence. The refinery manager had been unhappy that somebody else had decided he had a problem and, without any consultation, had decided he needed external help to resolve it.

Clarifying the issue

Reference has already been made to the possibility that the presented symptoms or problem may not be related to the issue about which the client is most concerned. There are other problems associated with deciding what the real issue is.

Those who seek help from consultants to resolve a problem often present the difficulty as somebody else's problem. The head of HR of a manufacturing company invited a consultant to meet the finance director over lunch. The problem the finance director, who was also the deputy chairman of the board, wanted to talk about was to do with the poor state of communications between the board and senior management. He defined the problem in terms of the quality of the senior managers. Eventually, after the consultant had met with the board, they redefined the problem as something to do with the board itself, about conflicting views regarding the role of the board and political issues that affected how the board functioned.

Another issue is that problems are often presented to others in terms of implied solutions, such as: 'We need help to

▶ improve the appraisal system
▶ build a more cohesive team
▶ improve communications.

The communications problem might be further defined in terms of improving the communicating skills of certain individuals. However, a preliminary investigation may suggest that while communications are a problem, an important factor contributing to the problem is the structure of the organization and the effect this has on communication networks. In such a situation, improving the communication skills of selected individuals or replacing existing members with others might do little to resolve the underlying structural problem.

Change agents need to keep an open mind about the nature of the problem until there has been some kind of preliminary investigation. However, it is important that the change agent pays careful attention to the felt needs of the client.

| **Exercise 4.1** | **Starting the change process** |

Think of an occasion when you acted as a change agent. It might have been at work or elsewhere (home, club and so on) and it might have involved an individual, group or larger system. Did it go smoothly from the start or did you hit problems initiating the change process?

If you did hit problems, did they relate to any of the issues considered in this chapter?

Reflect on this experience and, in the space below, make a note of any learning points that might help you to avoid similar problems in the future.

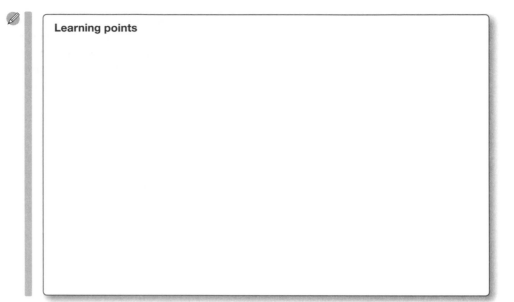

Learning points

Summary

Attention has been given to some of the issues associated with starting the change process. These include translating the need for change into a willingness to pursue change, deciding who will lead the change process and establishing an effective change relationship.

1 Translating the need for change into a willingness to pursue change: This chapter adopts a 'voluntaristic' perspective and argues that organizational members are not powerless pawns, unable to affect change, but are independent actors able to intervene in ways that can make an important difference. To do this, they need:

▶ *Confidence in their own ability to affect outcomes:* While optimism and overconfidence can be a problem, some change managers and others can be ineffective because they fail to act in ways that enable them to exercise the control necessary to achieve desired outcomes:
- The locus of control reflects the degree to which people believe in their own ability to make things happen. Those who attribute outcomes to their own efforts (internals) tend to have confidence in their own ability to make a difference.
- Seligman's theory of learned helplessness proposes that a person's expectation about their ability to control outcomes is learned. It suggests that organizational members may begin to question their ability to manage change if, when confronted with a new problem or opportunity, old and well-tried ways of managing fail to deliver desired outcomes.
▶ *The motivation to pursue change:*
- Those who are most likely to want to change are those who are basically successful but who are experiencing tension or failure in some particular part of their work. This group will have the confidence and the motivation to change.
- The next most likely to change are the successful because they will have the required confidence. However, because of their success, they may be satisfied with the status quo and lack the motivation to change.
- The least likely to understand and accept the need for change are the unsuccessful. While they may be the ones who need to change most, they are also the ones who are likely to lack confidence in their own ability to improve their predicament.

▶ *Concepts and theories that will help them understand and manage the change process:* These include concepts and theories that will help them to:

- identify the kind of change that confronts them, for example incremental or discontinuous
- understand the process of changing
- identify what needs to be attended to – through a process of diagnosis and goal setting – if they are to achieve desired outcomes.

▶ *Change management skills:* While conceptual understanding is necessary, it is not sufficient to guarantee that change agents will be able to secure desired changes. When managers are acting as change agents, they need to be able to communicate, offer leadership, work with teams, confront, negotiate, motivate and manage relationships with others.

2 Leading the change process: After persuading others of the need for change, it is necessary to decide who will, at least in the first instance, facilitate the process. The change agent could be an insider, a member of the system or subsystem that is the target for change, or an outsider. There is some evidence suggesting that change efforts are most successful when led (pulled) by users rather than (pushed) by technical experts.

3 Establishing an effective change relationship:

- The quality of the relationship between the change agent and others is highly dependent on factors such as confidence and trust.
- Associated issues for the change agent include being clear about who the client is, and keeping an open mind about the precise nature of the problem while seeking to clarify the issues that are of concern to the client.

References

Armenakis, A.A., Harris, S.G. and Mossholder, K.W. (1993) Creating readiness for organizational change, *Human Relations*, **46**(6): 681–703.

Avolio, B.J., Walumbwa, F.O. and Weber, T.J. (2009) Leadership: current theories, research, and future directions, *Annual Review of Psychology*, 60: 421–49.

Burnes, B. (2004) *Managing Change: A Strategic Approach to Organisational Dynamics*, Harlow: Pearson.

By, R.T. (2007) Ready or not … , *Journal of Change Management*, **7**(1): 3–11.

Clegg, C.W. (2000) Sociotechnical principles for system design, *Applied Ergonomics*, 31: 463–77.

Cummings, T.G. and Worley, C.G. (2001) *Organization Development and Change* (7th edn), Cincinnati, OH: West.

Greenwood, R. and Hinings, C.R. (1996) Understanding radical organizational change: bringing together the old and the new institutionalism, *Academy of Management Review*, 21: 1022–54.

Jones, R.A., Jimmieson, N.L. and Griffiths, A. (2005) The impact of organizational culture and reshaping capabilities on change implementation success: the mediating role of readiness for change, *Journal of Management Studies*, **42**(2): 361–86.

May, R. (1969) *Love and Will*, New York: W.W. Norton.

Mellahi, K. and Wilkinson, A. (2004) Organisational failure: a critique of recent research and a proposed integrative framework, *International Journal of Management Reviews*, **5–6**(1): 21–41.

Pettigrew, A. and Whipp, R. (1991) *Managing for Competitive Success*, Oxford: Blackwell.

Pitt, M., McAulay, L. and Sims, D. (2002) Promoting strategic change: 'playmaker' roles in organizational agenda formulation, *Strategic Change*, 11: 155–72.

Pugh, D. (1993) Understanding and managing organisational change, in C. Mabey and B. Mayon-White (eds) *Managing Change*, London: Paul Chapman/Open University.

Raynor, M.R., Ahmed, M. and Henderson, A.D. (2009) Are 'great' companies just lucky?, *Harvard Business Review*, **84**(4): 18–19.

Selegman, M.E.P. (1975) *Learned Helplessness*, San Francisco, CA: W.H. Freeman.

Thaler, R.H. and Sunstein, C.R. (2009) *Nudge: Improving Decisions about Health, Wealth, and Happiness*, London: Penguin.

Van Buren, M.E. and Safferstone, T. (2009) The quick win paradox, *Harvard Business Review*, **87**(1): 54–61.

Werther, W.B. (2003) Strategic change and leader-follower alignment, *Organizational Dynamics*, **32**(1): 32–45.

Wilson, D. (1992) *A Strategy for Change*, London: Routledge.

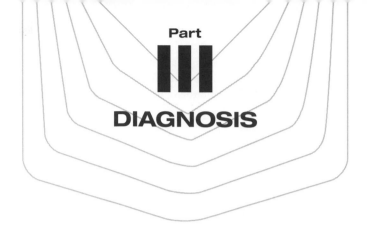

Part III

DIAGNOSIS

Organizational diagnosis is concerned with identifying what it is that needs to be changed.

Organizational behaviour, at all its different levels, is a complex phenomenon and it is impossible for managers to pay attention to every aspect of organizational functioning. Diagnostic models help change managers to cope with this complexity.

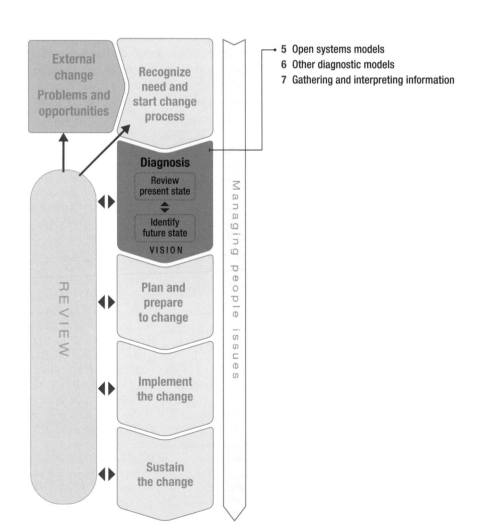

5 Open systems models
6 Other diagnostic models
7 Gathering and interpreting information

Chapter 5   Open systems models and alignment

This chapter opens with an examination the role of models in organizational diagnosis and introduces an exercise designed to help raise your awareness of the implicit models you use when thinking about organizations and assessing the need for change.

Often our implicit models provide a good basis for understanding what is going on and predicting what kinds of actions or interventions will produce desired change. Sometimes, however, they are subjective and biased; they overemphasize some aspects of organizational functioning and completely neglect others. The aim of the model-building exercise is to help you to develop a greater awareness of your own model of organizational functioning, assess whether it is consistent with or relevant to the problems or opportunities that you may need to address, and consider ways in which you can improve the efficacy of your approach to organizational diagnosis.

The second part of the chapter considers the attributes of holistic models of organizational functioning, summarizes the main features of open systems models and discusses the utility of the concept of alignment.

Chapter 6   Other diagnostic models

This chapter presents a range of other models that can be used to aid diagnosis:

▶ PEST and SWOT analyses focus attention on organization–environment fit.
▶ Stebel's model of competitive behaviour also considers organization–environment fit but does so from the perspective of an evolutionary cycle.
▶ Greiner's five phases of growth and Flamholtz's framework for organizational diagnosis are life cycle models that identify predictable stages of an organization's development and the issues that have to be managed at each stage.
▶ The Phelps et al. states framework for firm growth identifies problems (tipping points) that must be successfully addressed if growth is to continue and the knowledge that is required to address these challenges.
▶ The McKinsey 7S model and Weisbord's six-box model focus attention on internal alignment.
▶ The Burke-Litwin model is an open systems model that distinguishes between transformational and transactional change and pays special attention to the relative 'weight' of the causal relationships between variables.

It is argued that 'good' diagnostic models are those that are relevant to the issues under consideration, help to identify critical cause-and-effect relationships and focus attention on elements that change managers can affect.

Chapter 7   Gathering and interpreting information for diagnosis

This chapter examines the process of gathering and interpreting information for the purpose of diagnosis. Attention is focused on five main steps:

1 selection of an appropriate conceptual model for diagnosis
2 clarification of information requirements
3 information gathering
4 analysis
5 interpretation.

Attention is also drawn to the political issues associated with data collection that can frustrate attempts to gain an accurate impression of organizational functioning.

At the end of this chapter, you are invited to think about a recent occasion when you, or somebody working close to you attempted to introduce and manage a change, and reflect on the extent to which this change initiative was based on an accurate diagnosis of the need for change, as well as consider the extent to which the accuracy of the diagnosis was related to the appropriateness of the diagnostic model used, the nature of the information collected and the way in which it was interpreted.

The first part of this chapter examines the role of models in organizational diagnosis and introduces an exercise designed to help raise your awareness of the implicit models you use when thinking about organizations and assessing the need for change.

The second part considers the attributes of holistic models of organizational functioning, summarizes the main features of open systems models and discusses the utility of the concept of alignment.

Using models to aid diagnosis

Organizational behaviour, at all its different levels, is a complex phenomenon. It is impossible for anyone to pay attention to, or understand the interactions between, all the many elements or variables that can have an effect on how an organization functions. Consequently, we tend to simplify the real world by developing models that focus attention on:

▶ a limited number of 'key elements' that we feel offer a good representation of the real world
▶ the ways these elements interact with each other, sometimes referred to as 'causal relationships' or laws of effect
▶ the 'outputs' produced by these interactions, which provide the basis for evaluating performance and assessing effectiveness.

We all develop our own implicit theories or conceptual models about how organizations function, and we use these models to:

▶ guide the kind of information that we attend to
▶ interpret what we see
▶ decide how to act.

We develop these models on the basis of our personal experience, either as organizational members or external observers of organizational behaviour. Sometimes these models provide a good basis for understanding what is going on and predicting what kinds of actions or interventions would produce desired change. Often, however, they are subjective and biased; they overemphasize some aspects of organizational functioning and completely neglect others. Consequently, they do not always provide a useful guide for the management of change.

The aim of the first part of this chapter is to help you develop a greater level of awareness of your own model of organizational functioning. This will help you to assess whether the model you use is consistent with or relevant to the problems or opportunities you need to address. It will also help you to compare your implicit model with alternatives and point to ways of modifying it to improve its utility.

Making personal models more explicit can be of benefit to all the people involved in managing a change. It can provide an opportunity for them to share their models, debate their relative merits, and move towards the development of a shared model that can be used to provide a basis for joint diagnosis and concerted action.

Exercise 5.1

Raising awareness of your implicit model of organizational functioning

This exercise is based on a procedure for collaborative model building devised by Tichy and Hornstein (1980) and involves five steps. The first requires you to prepare a short assessment of the current state of your organization. The next four steps involve reflecting on how you arrived at this assessment to tease out the main features of your implicit model of organizational functioning.

Step 1 Assess the current state of your organization

Prepare a short note that describes your organization, either the total organization or an important unit that you are familiar with, and assesses or diagnoses its current state. Make reference to the issues you feel require attention. These issues might be problems or opportunities. If you feel there is a need for some kind of change to ensure that these issues will be managed more effectively, justify this view.

Do not explain the kinds of interventions you think may be necessary to bring about any required changes. The aim of this exercise is to diagnose the current state of the organization and assess whether it is and will continue to perform effectively, not to provide a prescription of actions required to improve matters.

Step 2 Identify the information you used to make this assessment

Think about the things you considered when making your assessment in the first step. Identify and list the 'bits of information' that you attended to. Focus on the information that you actually attended to. Try not to let the kind of information you think you 'should' have considered influence your list.

Identify, if possible, at least 25 different bits of information and record them in the space provided. Table 5.1 provides some examples of the bits of information that people might attend to when assessing the state of their organization. These are only offered as examples to stimulate your thinking; your own list may not contain any of these.

Table 5.1 *Examples of the kind of information that might be attended to*

Quality of boss–subordinate relationships	Production/operations systems	The way activities and staff are grouped together	Awareness of competitive threats
Effectiveness of coordinating mechanisms	Quality of communications	Level of commitment to the organization	Training and staff development
Knowledge management	Reward systems	Costs	Inventory levels
Margins	Staff turnover	Customer satisfaction	Cash flows
The extent to which people feel challenged in their present jobs	Match between staff competencies and task requirements	Extent to which staff understand the central purpose of the organization	Awareness of possible future sources of income/revenue
The way the business is financed	Attitudes towards quality assurance	The way conflicts are managed	Level of bureaucracy
Effectiveness of IT system	Number of levels in the hierarchy	Marketing procedures and policies	Management accounting systems

Step 3 Developing categories for organizing your diagnostic information

Some of the bits of information you used to make your assessment might be related, and it might be possible to group them together into a number of more inclusive categories:

- Group related bits of information in the category boxes provided below. Typically, people identify 4–12 categories, but there are no restrictions on the number of categories you might identify.
- When you have categorized your bits of information, describe the rationale you used for including information in each category.

These categories reflect the main elements or variables of your diagnostic model.

Category name:	Category name:
Items included in category:	Items included in category:
Briefly state rationale for including items in this category:	Briefly state rationale for including items in this category:

Category name:	Category name:
Items included in category: Briefly state rationale for including items in this category:	Items included in category: Briefly state rationale for including items in this category:

Category name:	Category name:
Items included in category: Briefly state rationale for including items in this category:	Items included in category: Briefly state rationale for including items in this category:

Category name:	Category name:
Items included in category: Briefly state rationale for including items in this category:	Items included in category: Briefly state rationale for including items in this category:

Use additional category boxes if required.

Step 4 Specifying relationships between categories/elements

The categories identified above reflect the elements of your implicit diagnostic model. Step 4 of the model-building process focuses on interdependencies and causal relationships between the elements. These can be identified by considering whether a change in any one element will have an effect on any other element:

- Using the format of Table 5.2, list the elements (categories) identified in step 3 down the left-hand column and across the top of the table.
- Take each element down the left-hand column in turn and assess the impact a change in this element might have on every other element, using a three-point scale, where 0 = no or slight impact; 1 = moderate impact; and 2 = high impact.

Table 5.2 *Interdependencies between elements*

Effect of change on Elements	1	2	3	4	5	6	7	8	9	10	11	12
1	–											
2		–										
3			–									
4				–								
5					–							
6						–						
7							–					
8								–				
9									–			
10										–		
11											–	
12												–

NB: Even though elements might be interrelated and affect each other, one element, for example A, can have a greater effect on another, for example B, than vice versa. This is illustrated in Table 5.3.

Table 5.3 *An example of a matrix of interdependencies*

Categories	A	B	C	D	E
A	–	2	1	0	2
B	1	–	1	0	0
C	0	1	–	0	1
D	0	0	1	–	2
E	2	0	1	2	–

Your implicit model can be represented diagrammatically:

- Draw a circle for each of the elements you identified in Table 5.1.
- Label each circle with the name of the element it represents.
- Draw lines between those elements that have any impact on each other. Use a solid line to show a strong relationship between elements, with the arrowhead indicating the direction of a cause-and-effect relationship, and a dotted line to show a moderate link. Do not join elements that have only a slight or no impact on each other.

The model represented by Table 5.3 is presented diagrammatically in Figure 5.1.

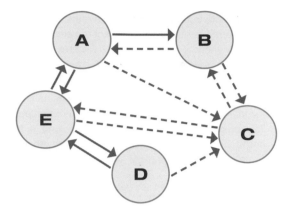

Figure 5.1 *A causal map of a diagnostic model*

Draw your model here

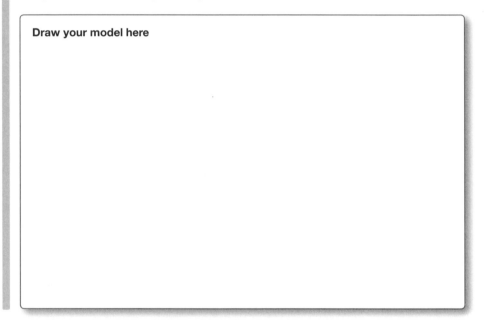

The rest of this and the following chapter present a range of models of organizational functioning that are widely used to aid diagnosis. When you have read to the end of Chapter 6, you might find it useful to compare your own model with these alternatives and consider whether they suggest ways of improving your model.

To refine your own model, you might want to reflect on the following:

▶ How do the models presented in this and the next chapter relate to your personal experience? For example, to what extent do they accommodate or ignore elements and causal relationships that your experience has led you to believe are important? It might be unwise to slavishly apply a model that ignores aspects of organizational functioning that your own experience tells you are significant.

▶ Do any of the available models include elements and/or relationships that you have never previously considered but which, on reflection, might help you make better sense of your own experience? You need to be alert to the danger of rejecting alternative models too hastily. You might find that a model that is quite different from your own personal model can provide useful new insights. Even if you decide not to adopt an alternative model in its entirety, you might decide to incorporate some aspects of it into your own model.

Giving proper consideration to these issues can help to refine and improve your personal model of organizational functioning.

Total system models

There are many theories and models – of motivation, decision making, group functioning, organization structure and so on – that change agents can use to help them understand the functioning of the various components of an organization. They can use this understanding to help identify what needs to be changed. Nadler and Tushman (1980) acknowledge the utility of such 'component models', but caution against combining, in some additive manner, the specific assessments they provide in order to produce an overview of organizational functioning and effectiveness. They argue that there is a need for frameworks and models that provide an understanding of the way in which the total system of organizational behaviour functions, and they advocate a more holistic approach.

Open systems theory

Open systems theory provides such a framework and views an organization as a system of interrelated components that transact with a larger environment. From the perspective of open systems, some of the main characteristics of organizations are that they are:

▶ *Embedded within a larger system:* Organizations are dependent on the larger system (environment) for the resources, information and feedback they require in order to survive.
▶ *Able to avoid entropy:* Through the exchange of matter, energy and information with the larger environment, organizations can forestall entropy, the predisposition to decay. They can even increase their vitality over time. People are partially closed systems, in that while they can import food, water and air to breath, there are parts of their body that cannot be renewed or replaced. Groups and organizations, on the other hand, have the potential for indefinite life. In their simplest form, as illustrated by Figure 5.2, organizations can be portrayed as open systems in a dynamic relationship with their environment, receiving various inputs that they transform in some way and export as outputs. In order to survive, organizations need to maintain favourable input–output transactions with the environment.

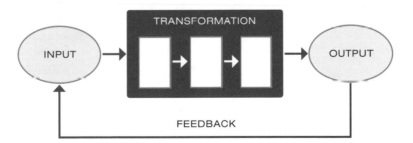

Figure 5.2   *The organization as an open system*

▶ *Regulated by feedback:* Systems rely on information about their outputs to regulate their inputs and transformation processes. Feedback loops also exist between the various internal components of the system. Consequently, changes in any one component can affect changes in other components.

▸ *Subject to equifinality:* The same outcomes can be produced by configuring the system in different ways.
▸ *Cyclical in their mode of functioning:* Events are patterned and tend to occur in repetitive cycles of input, throughput and output. For example, the revenue generated from selling outputs is used to fund inputs, purchase more raw materials, pay bank charges, wages and so on, which are used to produce more outputs.
▸ *Equilibrium seeking:* Open systems tend to gravitate to a state where all the component parts of the system are in equilibrium and where a steady state exists. Whenever changes occur that upset this balance, different components of the system move to restore the balance. (Note the links with Lewin's field theory, discussed in Chapter 2.)
▸ *Bounded:* Open systems are defined by boundaries. External boundaries differentiate the organization from the larger environment and regulate the flow of information, energy and matter between the system and its environment. Internal boundaries differentiate the various components of the system from each other and regulate the inputs and outputs of subsystems.

The notion that organizations are systems of interrelated elements embedded in, and strongly influenced by, a larger system is not new. Burns and Stalker (1961) and Lawrence and Lorsch (1967) produced interesting research findings that suggested a link between the internal characteristics of an organization and the external environment.

Contingency theories

Burns and Stalker (1961) examined the relationship between the internal structure of 20 British firms and the environments in which they operated. They found that the firms that operated in relatively stable and unchanging environments tended to have more highly structured and formal internal arrangements than firms that operated in unstable environments. They described firms that operated in stable environments as 'mechanistic', because they were characterized by many rules and procedures and were dominated by hierarchy of authority. The firms that operated in less stable environments were described as 'organic', because they tended to have a free-flowing, decentralized and adaptive internal organization. Table 5.4 summarizes the main features of mechanistic and organic organizations.

Table 5.4   *Mechanistic and organic organization forms*

Mechanistic	Organic
Specialized tasks, narrow in scope	Common tasks and interdependencies
Tasks rigidly defined	Tasks adjusted and redefined as required
Strict hierarchy of authority	Less adherence to formal authority and rules
Centralized knowledge and control	Decentralized knowledge and control
Hierarchical communication	Network communication, diffused channels

The contingency approach advanced by Burns and Stalker (1961) received further support from a later study undertaken by Lawrence and Lorsch (1967). They examined three departments (manufacturing, research and sales) in 10 US companies and found that departmental structures varied with environmental uncertainty. The results of their research indicated that production departments tended to have the highest degree of structure, followed by marketing and then research. Their results also indicated that the more complex and uncertain the external environment, the greater the internal differentiation between departments. This happened as departments developed their own attitudes, goals, work orientation and internal structures and processes to accommodate the requirements of their specialized subenvironments. Lawrence and Lorsch's findings also suggested that this internal differentiation tended to lead to problems of internal coordination between departments and, consequently, to a greater need for internal integrating mechanisms.

There are some who question the utility of contingency theory and argue that it fails to provide a convincing explanation for the way in which organizations operate (see Burnes, 2004: 79–80). Congruency theorists, however, interpret the results of these and other studies as offering support for a broader proposition that the alignment or 'fit' between an organization and the environment and also between the various internal elements of the organization is a critical determinant of organizational effectiveness.

Alignment as a determinant of organization effectiveness

Open systems theory predicts that changes to any one of the internal or external elements of an organization's system will cause changes to other elements. This implies that in order to understand the performance of an organization, one must view it as a system of interconnected choices (Siggelkow, 2001).

Kotter (1980) elaborated this proposition when he developed his integrative model of organizational dynamics. His model comprises seven major elements. Figure 5.3 shows these as a set of key organizational processes plus six structural elements.

Figure 5.3 *Kotter's integrative model of organizational dynamics*
Source: Kotter, 1980: 282

The key organizational processes are classified under two main headings, informational processes such as information gathering, communication and decision making, and processes that are concerned with the conversion or transportation of matter/energy. Specific processes can be labelled according to their purpose and might include the market research process, the product development process, the manufacturing process or the leadership process.

The six structural elements in Kotter's model are:

▶ *external environment*, including the immediate task-related environment and the wider environment, which includes public attitudes, the political system and so on
▶ *employees and other tangible assets* such as buildings, plant, inventories and cash
▶ *formal structure, job design and operating systems*
▶ *social system* including the organization's culture and social structure
▶ *technology* (or technologies) associated with the organization's core products
▶ *dominant coalition* – the objectives and strategies of those who control policy making.

Short run

In the short run, organization effectiveness can be defined in terms of the nature of the cause–effect relationships that link all the elements of the system together. For example, if demand for a major product produced by organizations operating in a particular industrial sector begins to slump, the dominant coalition in some organizations will recognize this and take corrective action much faster than the dominant coalition in other organizations. An organization's response will be influenced by the effectiveness of its information-gathering and decision-making processes and by how quickly these processes can affect other elements in the organization to adjust matter/energy conversion and transportation processes in ways that will maintain their efficiency. Adjustments might involve cutting production, finding new customers or reducing prices in order to minimize any build-up of stocks of finished goods. Any delays in reacting to changes will result in a wasteful use of resources. In the short run, therefore, effective organizations are those that have key processes that are characterized by levels of decision-making effectiveness and matter/energy efficiency that help to ensure that resources are used effectively.

Medium term

Kotter argues that over the medium term, which he defines as a few months to a few years, the effective organization is one that is capable of maintaining its short-run effectiveness. He suggests that organizations do this by maintaining the key process elements in an efficient and effective state because it is this that enables them to ensure that the other (six) structural elements are aligned to each other. Sustained misalignment (sometimes referred to as 'poor fit') leads to levels of waste that will eventually threaten the survival of the organization. He suggests that what constitutes a misaligned relationship between any two or more structural elements is often 'intuitively obvious'. He cites several examples to illustrate the point:

▶ If the goals and strategies championed by the organization's dominant coalition are based on inaccurate assumptions about the task environment, the dominant coalition and the task environment are obviously misaligned.

▶ If the size of the workforce or the organization's other tangible assets are not sufficient to take advantage of the economies of scale inherent in the organization's technologies, the two elements are obviously misaligned.

▶ If the level of specialization called for in the formal organizational arrangements are inconsistent with the skills of the workforce, then again the two elements are misaligned.

The most common sources of nonalignment are changes in the external environment and growth. Kotter argues that organizational systems correct misalignments by taking the path of least resistance; they move towards the solution that requires the minimum use of energy. This usually involves realigning around the element or elements of the organization that are most difficult and expensive to change (or emerge as the driving force over the longer term). However, if the organization can afford the waste associated with misalignment, minor examples of poor fit could go uncorrected for a considerable period of time. This argument suggests that, over the medium term, the focus of change management needs to be ensuring that the elements of the organization are appropriately aligned.

Long term

Over the longer term (6–60 years), Kotter predicts that it is the organization's driving force and the adaptability of the six structural elements that will be the underlying determinant of effectiveness. He notes that, over time, one or more of the structural elements, for example the external environment, technology, the employees or the dominant coalition, typically begin to exert more influence on the key organizational processes than the other elements. This element (or elements) emerges as the driving force that shapes the development of the company. He argues that because of the nature of the interdependence among all the elements, and the equilibrium-seeking disposition of systems, if one or two elements emerge as the driving force, the natural tendency is for the others to follow. They adapt to the 'driving force' in order to maintain internal alignment. The founder and managing director of the Active Sports Equipment Company (see Case study 3.1) illustrates this point. His obsessive concern with engineering excellence dominated the organization's culture and shaped its strategy and management practices for many years. This argument suggests that the driving force can create a 'deep structure' within an organization that can be a source of inertia and inhibit change (see the discussion of this point in Chapter 1).

The key to an organization's prosperity and long-term survival is its ability to adapt in order to maintain external alignment. According to Kotter, this adaptability is a function of the state of its structural elements. These can range on a continuum from highly constraining and hard to align with other structural elements to unconstraining and easy to align with. He provides examples of structural states that do and do not facilitate system adaptation, shown in Table 5.5. The more an organization's structural elements look like those in the left-hand column of Table 5.5, the more difficult it will be for the organization to adapt.

Adaptability is important because it is this that determines whether or not the organization will be able to maintain the required degree of alignment over the long term. Over the longer term, therefore, the focus of change management needs to be ensuring that the structural elements of the organization are as adaptable as possible.

Table 5.5 *Examples of element states that do and do not facilitate system adaptation*

Factors	States that are highly constraining and hard to align with, thus inhibiting adaptation	States that are not constraining and are easy to align with
Technology	Organization possesses a single complex technology, which is rapidly becoming outdated and requires large amounts of capital for equipment	Organization possesses the most advanced technologies for its products, services and administrative systems, along with a number of alternative technologies it might need in the future
Social system	Key norms are not supportive of organizational flexibility; little trust found in relationships; total power in the system is low; morale is low; little sense of shared purpose	Key norms are supportive of organizational flexibility; high trust found in relationships; total power in the system is high; morale is high; high degree of shared purpose
Employee and other tangible assets	Plant and equipment are run down; employees, especially middle managers, are unskilled; organization has some highly specialized human skills and equipment it doesn't need anymore	Plant and equipment in top-notch shape; employees, especially middle managers, are highly skilled; organization possesses equipment and people with skills it doesn't need now but may need in the future
Organizational arrangements	Formal systems are not sophisticated but are applied in great detail, uniformly across the organization	Different kinds of formal systems exist for structuring, measuring, rewarding, selecting and developing different types of people working on different tasks; formal systems also exist to monitor change in the organization and its environment and to change the formal systems accordingly
Dominant coalition	A small, homogeneous, reasonably untalented group with no effective leadership; all about the same age	A large, reasonably heterogeneous yet cohesive group of talented people who work well together and have plenty of effective leadership; members are of different ages
External environment	The organization is dependent on a large number of externalities, with little or no countervailing power	The organization has only a limited number of strong dependencies, with a moderate amount of countervailing power over all dependencies
	Demand for products and services is shrinking; supplies are hard to get; regulators behave with hostility and inconsistency	Demand for products and services is growing; supplies are plentiful; regulators behave consistently and fairly
	Public angry at the firm; economy in bad shape; political system isn't functioning well; overall, the environment is hostile	Public likes the organization; economy is in good shape; political system is functioning well; overall, the environment is benevolent

Source: Adapted from Kotter, 1980: 292–3

Nadler and Tushman's congruence model of organizations

An alternative open systems model, proposed by Nadler and Tushman (1982), also highlights the effect of the congruency of the component parts of the organization on organization effectiveness. In addition, it elaborates the relationship between the organization and its wider environment and focuses more explicit attention on the role of strategy.

The model identifies four classes of input:

1 *Environment:* includes any larger 'suprasystem' that the focal organization is a part of – a large corporation, markets, financial institutions, suppliers and so on – and the wider environment that includes the culture(s) within which the organization operates. It is this environment that provides the opportunities and constraints with which the organization has to contend.

2 *Resources:* such as liquid capital, physical plant, raw materials, technologies and labour.

3 *History:* this is important because past strategic decisions and the development of core values and patterns of leadership can affect current patterns of organizational behaviour.

4 *Strategy:* this involves determining how the organization's resources can be used to best advantage in relation to the opportunities, constraints and demands of the environment. Effective organizations are those that are able to align themselves with the external environment and, as required, reposition themselves to take advantage of any environmental changes such as shifts in markets, technologies and so on. Nadler and Tushman argue that the strategy, and its associated goals and plans, defines the task (purpose) of the organization and is the most important input to the organization's behavioural system. They suggest that effectiveness can be assessed in terms of how well the organization's performance meets the goals of strategy.

Nadler and Tushman define the major components of the transformation process as:

1 *Task,* which can be viewed in terms of complexity, predictability, interdependence and skill demands.
2 *Individuals* who are members of the organization and their response capabilities, intelligence, skills and abilities, experience, training, needs, attitudes, expectations and so on.
3 *Formal organizational arrangements* that include all the mechanisms used by the organization to direct, structure or control behaviour.
4 *Informal organization,* including informal group structures, the quality of intergroup relations, political processes and so on.

Like Kotter, they argue that any useful model of organizations must go beyond merely providing a simple description of the components of the organization and consider the dynamic relationships that exist between the various components. They define congruence as the degree to which the needs, demands, goals, objectives and/or structures of any one component of the organization are consistent with the needs, demands, goals, objectives and/or structures of any other component. Their general hypothesis is that, other things equal, the greater the total degree of congruence between the various components, the more effective the organization's behaviour. Figure 5.4 summarizes the congruence model and the double-headed arrows indicate the six 'fits' between the components of the transformation process (the internal organization).

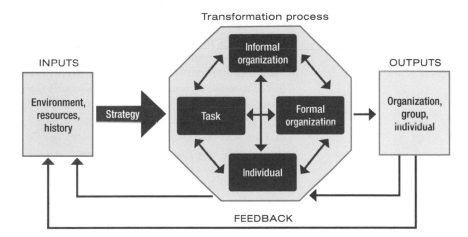

Figure 5.4 *Congruence model*
Source: Nadler and Tushman, 1980: 274

These six fits are:

1 *Individual–formal organization:* for example, to what extent are individual needs met by the formal organizational arrangements?

2 *Individual–task:* for example, to what extent do individuals have the skills necessary to meet task demands and to what extent do the tasks satisfy individual needs?

3 *Individual–informal organization:* for example, to what extent does the informal organization satisfy the needs of individuals or make best use of their talents?

4 *Task–formal organization:* for example, to what extent are the formal organizational arrangements adequate to meet the demands of the task?

5 *Task–informal organization:* for example, to what extent does the informal organization facilitate task performance?

6 *Formal–informal organization:* for example, to what extent are the goals, rewards and structures of the informal organization consistent with those of the formal organization?

Many of the components that Nadler and Tushman choose to focus on are different from those that figure in Kotter's model. All models are simplifications of the real world, and the utility of any particular model, in the context of change management, needs to be judged in terms of whether or not it provides a helpful conceptual framework for managing the change process. The four components of the transformation process in Nadler and Tushman's congruence model are derived from Leavitt (1965). The basic hypothesis underpinning congruence would still be valid if these four components were replaced with the five subsystems (production, supportive, maintenance, adaptive and managerial) identified by Katz and Kahn (1966). It is the congruence or alignment between the organization and the environment and between the internal components of the organization that is the key concept that can aid organizational diagnosis and the development of change strategies.

Internal and external alignment promotes organizational effectiveness because the various elements of the system reinforce rather than disrupt each other, thereby minimizing the loss of system energy and resources (Schneider et al., 2003). However, a state of perfect alignment is rarely achieved. Miles and Snow (1984) suggest that rather than viewing alignment as a state, it might be better to think of it as a process – a dynamic search that seeks to align the organization with its environment and the various internal elements of the organization with each other. Higgins (2005) observes that one reason why alignment is becoming a greater challenge for many organizations is that, in a fast-moving business environment, organizations are forced to revise their strategies more frequently than in the past. As noted in Chapter 1, organizations that recognize or anticipate shifts in their external environment may be better placed to initiate actions to manage this process of alignment than those that are slow to recognize the need for change. But even where a need to improve alignment is recognized, forces for inertia within the organization can make this difficult to achieve. This is especially the case in what Greenwood and Hinings (1996) and Levinthal (1997) refer to as tightly coupled systems, because the tighter the fit, the more difficult it is to modify individual elements of the system through a process of incremental change.

The utility of the concept of alignment

The concept of alignment has been criticized on the grounds that it is difficult to apply in practice. Wilson (1992) refers to difficulties relating to problems of definition. Some view the organization and the environment as 'objective' fact, readily open to description and definition, whereas others view them as 'subjective' fact. Problems can arise because managers, and others, perceive them from their own subjective point of view. This makes it difficult to establish any shared understanding of the current or desired level of alignment. Even when people can agree, there is no guarantee that this shared perception will be a reliable indicator of the conditions that will lead to organization effectiveness.

Another criticism is that alignment might be a more valid concept when the focus is the management of incremental change. When faced with discontinuous change, alignment might be a less helpful concept because the need is to break with the past and introduce radical innovation before seeking to re-establish a new state of alignment around a new task and/or new structural elements.

These criticisms may have some validity, but systems models, alignment and the concept of fit can make an important contribution to effective change management.

| Change tool 5.1 | **Checking alignment between steps in the transformation process** |

This exercise provides an opportunity to test out a useful change tool. Think of your department or unit in terms of a process that transforms inputs into outputs.

Step 1
Identify the major inputs and outputs and make a note of them in the space provided below. Depending on the time available, focus on one or more inputs and one or more outputs.

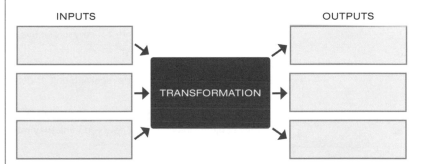

Step 2
Select one input and identify the department, unit or external supplier that provides it.

Step 3
Assess how effective you think this supplier is:

- List the indicators you use to assess the effectiveness of the supplier.
- Against each indicator, note your assessment of how effective the supplier is, using a five-point scale, where 1 = very ineffective and 5 = very effective.

Step 4
Think about how members of the supplying department or unit rate their own effectiveness:

- List the indicators you think they use to assess their own effectiveness.
- Against each indicator, note how you think they rate their own effectiveness.

Indicators I use to assess the effectiveness of the supplier	My assessment	Indicators they use to assess their effectiveness	Their assessment

Step 5

Compare the two lists. Do they suggest any actual or potential problems that could undermine organizational effectiveness? If so, specify below.

Step 6

Select one output and identify the department, unit or external customer that receives it.

Step 7

Assess how effective you think your department or unit is:

- List the indicators you use to assess the effectiveness of your department, with respect to the supply of the focal output.
- Against each indicator, note your assessment of how effective you think your unit is, using a five-point scale, where 1 = very ineffective and 5 = very effective.

Step 8

Think about how members of the receiving unit or department rate the effectiveness of your department:

- List the indicators you think they use to assess your department's effectiveness.
- Against each indicator, note how you think they rate the effectiveness of your department.

Indicators I use to assess the effectiveness of my unit	My assessment	Indicators customers use to assess the effectiveness of my unit	Their assessment

Step 9

Compare the two lists. Do they suggest any actual or potential problems that could undermine organizational effectiveness? If so, specify below.

> **Potential problems with alignment between steps in the transformation process**

Summary

The first part of this chapter examines the role of models in organizational diagnosis and introduces an exercise designed to help raise your awareness of the implicit models you use when thinking about organizations and assessing the need for change.

The second part considers the attributes of holistic (as opposed to component) models of organization functioning. It was noted that while component theories are useful for diagnosing specific problems, combining their assessments of different aspects of organization functioning might not always provide an adequate view of the factors that are affecting organization effectiveness. Open systems models are seen to provide a useful overarching conceptual framework for assessing how the total system functions.

From the perspective of open systems, some of the main characteristics of organizations are that they are:

▶ embedded within a larger system
▶ able to avoid entropy
▶ regulated by feedback
▶ subject to equifinality
▶ cyclical in their mode of functioning
▶ equilibrium seeking
▶ bounded.

The main body of the chapter:

▶ draws on contingency theory to illustrate the embeddedness of organizations within a larger system and the importance of alignment
▶ elaborates Kotter's integrative model of organizational dynamics and considers the importance of alignment and adaptability as determinants of organization effectiveness over the medium and long term
▶ reviews Nadler and Tushman's congruency model of organizations and highlights the importance of strategy in achieving and maintaining alignment.

The chapter concludes with a discussion of the utility of the concept of alignment, and a change tool for checking alignment.

References

Burnes, B. (2004) *Managing Change: A Strategic Approach to Organisational Dynamics*, Harlow: Pearson.

Burns, T. and Stalker, G.M. (1961) *The Management of Innovation*, London: Tavistock.

Greenwood, R. and Hinings, C.R. (1996) Understanding radical organizational change: bringing together the old and the new institutionalism, *Academy of Management Review*, **21**(4): 1022–54.

Higgins, J.M. (2005) The eight 'S's of successful strategy execution, *Journal of Change Management*, **5**(1): 3–13.

Katz, D. and Kahn, R.L. (1966) *The Social Psychology of Organisations*, New York: Wiley.

Kotter, J.P. (1980) An integrative model of organisational dynamics, in E.E. Lawler, D.A. Nadler and C. Cammann (eds) *Organizational Assessment*, New York: Wiley.

Lawrence, P.R. and Lorsch, J.W. (1967) *Organization and Environment*, Boston MA: Harvard Business School Press.

Leavitt, H.J. (1965) Applied organizational change in industry, in J.G. March (ed.) *Handbook of Organizations*, Chicago: Rand-Mcnally.

Levinthal, D. (1997) Adaptation on rugged landscapes, *Management Science*, 43: 934–50.

Miles, R.E. and Snow, C.C. (1984) Designing strategic human resource systems, *Organizational Dynamics*, 13: 36–52.

Nadler, D.A. and Tushman, M.L. (1980) A congruence model for organizational assessment, in E.E. Lawler, D.A. Nadler and C. Cammann (eds) *Organizational Assessment*, New York: Wiley.

Nadler, D.A. and Tushman, M.L. (1982) A model for diagnosing organizational behavior: applying a congruence perspective, in D.A. Nadler, M.L. Tushman and N.G. Hatvany (eds) *Managing Organizations*, Boston: Little, Brown.

Schneider, B., Hayes, S.C., Lim, B. et al. (2003) The human side of strategy: employee experiences of strategic alignment in a service organisation, *Organizational Dynamics*, **32**(2): 122–41.

Siggelkow, N. (2001) Change in the presence of fit: the rise, the fall, and the renaissance of Liz Claiborne, *Academy of Management Journal*, **44**(4): 838–57.

Tichy, N.M. and Hornstein, H.A. (1980) Collaborative organization model building, in E.E. Lawler, D.A. Nadler and C. Cammann (eds) *Organizational Assessment*, Chichester: Wiley.

Wilson, D. (1992) *A Strategy for Change*, London: Routledge.

Postma and Kok (1999) describe organizational diagnosis as a process of research into the functioning of an organization that leads to recommendations for improvement. In practice, diagnosis is usually a multi-stage iterative process that begins with change managers using some kind of holistic model of organizational functioning to look at the organization as a whole before moving on to investigate particular aspects of organizational functioning in more detail (see Example 6.1). Sometimes, however, this process is reversed. Change managers focus their attention on specific components of organizational functioning, such as motivation, group processes, leadership, task design, information systems, organizational struc-

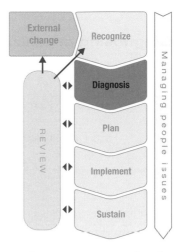

ture or culture, in order to help them understand the total picture. It was noted at the beginning of Chapter 5 that while it may be tempting to build a picture of what is going on in an organization by looking at the various components separately, the picture this approach produces may be incomplete or in some other way misleading. Nadler and Tushman (1980: 262) maintain that the systemic nature of organizations implies that:

> there are properties of the whole that cannot be understood by simply adding together the component parts. Indeed, part of the dynamic of the whole concerns the nature of the interaction among the different components of organizational behaviour.

Diagnosis starts with an assessment of how well the organization is performing. Performance indicators provide the data for identifying discrepancies between actual and desired performance and signalling the need for change (see Chapter 3). They also provide a basis for monitoring whether the change is on track and whether the change plan (based on the diagnosis) is still valid (see Chapter 27). If the change is not proceeding to plan, it may prove necessary to revisit the original diagnosis and repeat the process.

The previous chapter considered organizations as systems of interrelated parts embedded in and strongly influenced by a larger system (the environment). A review of Kotter's (1980) and Nadler and Tushman's (1980) open systems models highlighted the importance of 'fit' and pointed to internal and external alignment as key determinants of organizational effectiveness. This chapter presents a range of other holistic models that can be used to aid diagnosis:

▶ PEST and SWOT analyses focus attention on organization–environment fit.

▶ Stebel's model of competitive behaviour also considers organization–environment fit but does so from the perspective of an evolutionary cycle.

▶ Greiner's five phases of growth and Flamholtz's framework for organizational diagnosis are life cycle models that identify predictable stages of an organization's development and the issues that have to be managed at each stage.

▶ The Phelps et al. states framework for firm growth identifies problems (tipping points) that must be successfully addressed if growth is to continue.

▶ The McKinsey 7S model and Weisbord's six-box model focus attention on internal alignment.

▶ The Burke-Litwin model is an open systems model that distinguishes between transformational and transactional change and pays special attention to the relative 'weight' of the causal relationships between variables.

Diagnosing organization–environment fit

There are a number of models that focus on assessing the environment and how environmental changes might affect organizational performance, and these are discussed in detail below.

PEST analysis

PEST analysis can be used to examine the organization's environment and search for evidence of change that might signal a problem or opportunity. PEST refers to political, economic, sociocultural and technological factors:

▶ *Political* factors include new legislation in areas such as environmental management, consumer protection and employment; regulation of markets in areas such as telecommunications and broadcasting; fiscal policies and so on. Organizations that operate in international markets need to be aware of how legislative changes or changes in the level of political stability in different parts of the world might influence their operations.

▶ *Economic* factors include issues such as exchange rates, cost of borrowing, change in levels of disposable income, cost of raw materials, security of supplies, new competitors and the trade cycle.

▶ *Sociocultural* factors include demographic trends such as a fall in the birth rate or an ageing population. They also include shifting attitudes towards education, training, work and leisure, which can have knock-on effects on the availability of trained labour, consumption patterns and so on. Cultural factors can also affect business ethics and the way business is done in different parts of the world.

▶ *Technological* factors include issues such as the levels of investment that competitors are making in research and development and the outcome of this investment; the availability of new materials, products, production processes, means of distribution and so on; the rate of obsolescence and the need to reinvest in plant and people.

SWOT analysis

SWOT analysis offers a more comprehensive approach to diagnosing organization–environment fit. In addition to assessing the opportunities and threats that a PEST analysis might reveal, it also includes an assessment of the organization's strengths and weaknesses and its capability of responding to the threats and opportunities that confront it. Suggestions and templates for using a SWOT analysis are presented in Change tool 7.2.

Strebel's evolutionary cycle of competitive behaviour

Strebel's (1996) model can be used to anticipate technological and economic changes in the environment and initiate planned organizational changes that will enable a company to remain one step ahead of the competition. Strebel posits that there is an evolutionary cycle of competitive behaviour and that different phases of the cycle are marked by break points. He also suggests that, given proper attention to competitive trends, these break points can be predicted in advance. The two phases of the cycle are innovation and efficiency.

The start of the innovative phase of the cycle (bottom left of Figure 6.1) is characterized by a sharp increase in divergence and begins when an innovation by one competitor is seen to create a new business opportunity. This triggers others to innovate and gives rise to a greater variety in the offerings (products and services) available to customers. This process continues until there is little scope for further innovation that offers suppliers or customers much in the way of added value. At this point, the divergence of offerings begins to decline as the best features of past innovations are imitated by competitors.

The next phase of the cycle begins when one or more providers begin to turn their attention to efficiency rather than innovation. Cost reduction is seen as the route to maintaining market share and increasing profit. They achieve this by improving systems and processes to reduce delivered cost. While each phase of the cycle can present opportunities for some, it can also pose threats for others. In the efficiency phase of the cycle, only the fittest survive and inefficient competitors are driven out of business.

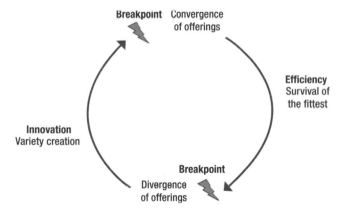

Figure 6.1 *Strebel's cycle of competitive behaviour*
Source: Strebel, 1996

When most of the opportunities for gaining competitive advantage from improving efficiency have been exploited, attention might switch once again to innovation, and the cycle will repeat itself. Strebel (1996) suggests indicators that can be used to anticipate break points. He also notes that convergence is usually easier to anticipate than divergence, because it involves a move towards greater similarity in existing products and services, whereas divergence is based on potential new offerings and their existence might not be known until a competitor offers them to customers.

Strebel's model, which focuses attention on the evolutionary cycle of competitive behaviour, has some similarities with the organizational life cycle models considered below.

Life cycle models

Life cycle models posit that organizations progress through a series of predictable stages of development and that each stage brings with it a set of alignment-related issues that have to be managed if the organization is to be effective. Two are discussed below, those of Greiner and Flamholtz.

Greiner's five phases of growth

Greiner (1972) cautions managers about the danger of only attending to the external environment and the future. He asserts that, for many organizations, the most pressing problems are rooted more in the organization's past decisions than present events and external dynamics. His view is that organizations evolve over time and progress through five phases of development. Each phase involves a prolonged period of evolutionary growth during which changes tend to be small and incremental. But these phases create their own crisis (due to internal misalignments) and end with a period of turmoil and revolution. Whereas Romanelli and Tushman (1994) believe that periods of discontinuous revolutionary change are triggered by changes in the external environment, Greiner argues that it is internal problems that trigger crises and discontinuous change (see Figure 6.2). The way these crises are managed determines whether the organization will survive and move forward to the next phase of evolutionary growth. Managers need to be aware of where their organizations, and their component parts, are in terms of the five stages of development, and recognize the kinds of problems that need to be addressed.

According to Greiner, each evolutionary period is characterized by a dominant management style, and each revolution is characterized by a dominant management problem that must be resolved if the organization is to continue to grow. The five phases are:

1 *Growth through creativity leading to a crisis of leadership:* At first, most organizations are preoccupied with identifying a market and creating a product. The founders are typically entrepreneurial and technically oriented and the organization's structure, systems and culture tend to be informal. But as the organization grows, the need for more knowledge about the efficiencies of manufacturing, more professional systems for maintaining financial control and more formal approaches for managing and developing people leads to a crisis of leadership. A new approach to managing and leading the business is required, but the founders may not be qualified to provide this. Sometimes the only effective way forward is for the founders to bring in a strong business manager from outside.

2 *Growth through direction leading to a crisis of autonomy:* During the second phase of growth, organizations often differentiate activities and develop a functional organizational structure, along with a clear hierarchy, more formal communication systems and more sophisticated accounting, inventory and manufacturing systems. Although this new level of order and direction delivers efficiencies, as the organization continues to grow, it eventually becomes less effective; for example long communication chains delay decision making and set

procedures prevent competent people taking initiatives. This leads to demands for greater autonomy.

3 *Growth through delegation leading to a crisis of control:* Delegation brings many benefits. Employees at lower levels are motivated and managers operating in a decentralized organization structure can act faster. Eventually, however, they begin to lose sight of organization-wide goals, develop parochial mindsets and begin to work too independently. This gives rise to a need for greater coordination across the organization.

4 *Growth through coordination leading to a crisis of 'red tape':* Formal systems and procedures are introduced in order to facilitate greater coordination. While these measures align separate functions, departments and work groups around corporate goals, the creeping bureaucratization of the organization eventually stifles initiative and strangles growth.

5 *Growth through collaboration:* Greater spontaneity is encouraged through developing interpersonal competencies, matrix and network structures and associated systems that enable people to work together in ways that rely more on social control and self-discipline than formal control and close monitoring from above.

According to Greiner, when organizations come to the end of one of the evolutionary phases and enter a period of crisis (revolution), the critical task for change managers is to be aware of the organization's history and its current phase of development and identify the new set of organization practices that will provide the way forward into the next period of evolutionary growth.

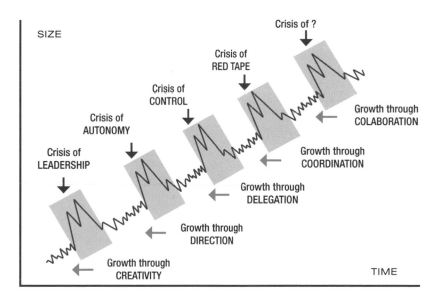

Figure 6.2   *Greiner's five phases of growth*

Flamholtz's organizational life cycle model

Flamholtz's (1995) framework for organizational diagnosis brings together a model of organizational effectiveness, which he refers to as the 'pyramid of organizational development' (see Figure 6.3), and an organizational life cycle model, and points to a number of key transformation points.

The organizational effectiveness model identifies six key tasks that determine an organization's effectiveness:

1 *Markets:* The first challenge is to identify a market for a good or service.
2 *Products and services:* The second is to develop, that is, design and produce, a product capable of satisfying that need.
3 *Resource management:* From the start, organizations have to acquire or develop the resources – financial, technological, physical and human – necessary to facilitate current and anticipated levels of production
4 *Operational systems:* In order to run the business on a day-to-day basis, organizations need systems – for accounting, billing, recruiting and so on.
5 *Management systems:* Organizations require management systems – planning, organization, management development and control – to ensure the long-term functioning of the business.
6 *Corporate culture:* Organizations also need to develop a culture that is aligned with its mission and strategy to ensure that what is important, for example in terms of product quality, customer service, treatment of employees, is consistently attended to.

All six tasks have to be performed to some degree at all stages of an organization's development, but the stage of development determines the relative importance of these tasks and how they need to be performed. The first two tasks (markets and products) reflect the business the organization is in. The next four reflect the organization's infrastructure. Resource management and operational systems provide the operational infrastructure, and management systems and corporate culture provide the management infrastructure.

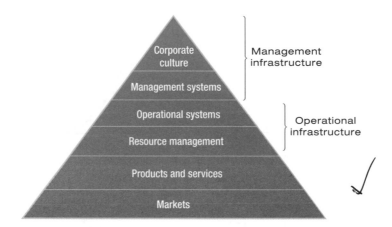

Figure 6.3 *Flamholtz's pyramid of organizational development*
Source: Flamholtz, 1995

Flamholtz asserts that organizations progress through seven stages of development from new venture to decline-revitalization. He argues that organizations are ineffective when their infrastructure is inconsistent with their stage of growth. At each stage, the criteria of organizational effectiveness change, as does the relative importance of the six tasks.

The seven stages of Flamholtz's organizational life cycle are:

1 *New venture*: The major concern is survival and critical areas for development are markets and products.

2 *Expansion:* Resources are stretched and operating systems become overwhelmed, so resource management and the development of operating systems emerge as key tasks. Flamholtz offers examples of the kinds of problems that can arise – somebody sells a product they know to be in stock only to find that someone else has taken it for their customer; some invoices are paid twice, whereas others are not paid at all; product quality drops for no apparent reason.

3 *Professionalization:* The point where more formal management systems are required.

4 *Consolidation*: Attention needs to be turned to managing the corporate culture and ensuring that the successive waves of new employees are socialized into the organization in a way that ensures that values and ways of doing things remain aligned to the organization's mission and strategic goals.

5 *Diversification:* Markets and products again emerge as key tasks.

6 *Integration:* All aspects of the organizational infrastructure require attention.

7 *Decline-revitalization:* All six tasks must be managed.

Greiner and Flamholtz both argue that change managers can use organizational life cycle models to help them recognize their organization's stage of development and identify the kinds of issues that might be adversely affecting organizational performance.

Phelps et al. states framework for firm growth

Phelps et al. (2007) propose an alternative conceptualization of firm growth. Unlike both Greiner and Flamholtz, they make no assumptions about linearity, predictability or sequence. They discard the notion of stages and suggest that, as firms grow, they encounter a series of problems (tipping points) that must be successfully addressed if growth is to continue. The issues that give rise to these tipping points are people management, strategic orientation, formalization of systems, new market entry, obtaining finance and operational improvement.

Phelps et al. (2007) argue that to continue growing, a firm must successfully resolve the challenges presented by each tipping point. In order to do this, it must have the capability to find new knowledge suited to resolving the new challenges posed by the tipping point, and the ability to implement this knowledge to navigate through the crisis.

Phelps et al. (2007) draw on the notion of absorptive capacity (Cohen and Levinthal, 1990) to propose a series of possible learning states that growing firms may occupy (Figure 6.4):

▶ The base state is ignorance: the firm does not realize that it is facing important key issues.

▶ The second state is awareness. Once the firm is aware of an issue, new knowledge can be actively sought or passively received to help resolve it.

▶ The final state involves the implementation of the action required to achieve real change.

This model can be applied to help change managers become more aware of the issues confronting their organization (potential tipping points) and the organization's capacity to identify, acquire and apply the knowledge it needs to address emerging challenges.

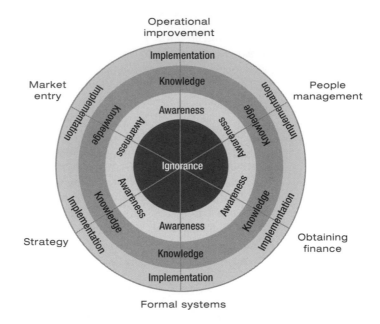

Figure 6.4 *The absorptive capacity/tipping point framework for growth firm states*
Source: Phelps et al., 2007

Diagnosing internal alignment

Two models that are widely used to diagnose internal alignment are the McKinsey 7S model and Weisbord's six-box model.

The McKinsey 7S model

The McKinsey 7S model highlights seven interrelated elements of organizations (Figure 6.5), which, when aligned, make an important contribution to organizational effectiveness (Pascale and Athos, 1981). It can be used to identify relationships that are misaligned and point to elements of the organization that need to be changed. While it considers strategy, the model does not make explicit reference to outcomes or the external environment.

The seven elements are:

1 *Strategy:* Purpose of the business and the way the organization seeks to enhance its competitive advantage.
2 *Structure:* Division of activities; integration and coordination mechanisms; nature of informal organization.
3 *Systems:* Formal procedures for measurement, reward and resource allocation; informal routines for communicating, resolving conflicts and so on.
4 *Staff:* The organization's human resources, its demographic, educational and attitudinal characteristics.
5 *Style:* Typical behaviour patterns of key groups, such as managers and other professionals, and the organization as a whole.
6 *Shared values:* Core beliefs and values and how these influence the organization's orientation to customers, employees, shareholders and society at large. Figure 6.5 shows shared values at the centre of the module.
7 *Skills:* The organization's core competencies and distinctive capabilities.

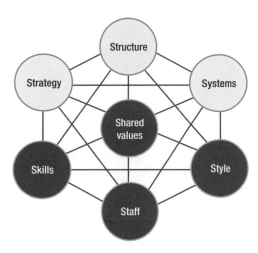

Figure 6.5   *The 7S model*

Change tool 7.1 presents the 7S matrix, a tool that change managers can use to assess the degree of alignment between the seven elements.

Higgins (2005) has elaborated the McKinsey model to provide managers with an 8S heuristic, which, he suggests, offers a more effective basis for monitoring and assessing cross-functional alignment.

Weisbord's six-box model

Weisbord (1976) presents his systemic model as a 'practice theory' that synthesizes knowledge and experience from change agents. It provides a conceptual map of six elements or boxes that can be used to apply any (component) theories to the assessment of these elements in a way that can reveal new connections and relationships between elements (Figure 6.6). It is an open systems model that recognizes the importance of organization–environment relationships but focuses most attention on what needs to be done internally to ensure that the organization becomes/remains a high performance organization able to adapt to external changes.

Weisbord (1976) argues that the effectiveness of an organization's functioning depends on what goes on in and between the six boxes. There are two aspects of each box that deserve attention: the formal and the informal. He argues that the formal aspects of an organization, for example stated goals or the structure as represented by an organization chart, might bear little relation to what happens in practice. Attention needs to be given to the frequency with which people take certain actions in relation to how important these actions are for organizational performance (see Change tool 18.2). This leads to a consideration of why people do what they do, and what needs to be changed to promote more effective behaviour. Leadership is seen to have a role to play in coordinating what goes on in the other five boxes.

Weisbord (1976) suggests that a useful starting point for any diagnostic exercise is to:

▶ focus on one major output of a unit or the total organization
▶ explore the extent to which the producers and the consumers of the output are satisfied with it
▶ trace the reasons for any dissatisfaction to what is happening in or between the six boxes that represent the unit or organization under consideration (see Change tool 5.1).

Figure 6.6 *Weisbord's six-box model*
Source: Weisbord, 1976: 9

Diagnosing internal and external alignment

Kotter's (1980) integrative model of organizational dynamics and Nadler and Tushman's (1981) congruence model of organizations, reviewed in Chapter 5, focus on internal and external alignment. A third model is presented below.

The Burke-Litwin causal model of organizational performance and change

The Burke-Litwin (1992) open systems model points to the relative weight of the elements of organizational functioning and the causal linkages that determine the level of performance and affect the process of change. The model also differentiates between two types of change: 'transformational change' that occurs as a response to important shifts in the external environment, and 'transactional change' that occurs in response to the need for more short-term incremental improvement. These features distinguish this model from the others considered in this chapter.

The model comprises 12 interrelated elements (Figure 6.7). It is an open systems model in which the inputs are represented by the external environment element at the top of the figure, and the outputs by the individual and organizational performance element at the bottom. Feedback loops go in both directions: the organization's performance affects its external environment and the external environment affects performance. The remaining 10 elements represent the process of transforming inputs into outputs, and reflect different levels of this process. Strategy and culture, for example, reflect aspects of the whole organizational or total system. Climate is an element associated with the local unit level, and motivation, individual needs and values, and job–person fit are individual-level elements.

The model is presented vertically (rather than across the page from left to right, like the Nadler and Tushman model) to reflect causal relationships and the relative impact of elements on each other. Burke and Litwin posit that those elements located higher in the model, such as strategy, leadership and culture, exert greater impact on other elements than lower elements do on higher elements. In other words, even though elements located lower down in the model can have some impact on those above them, the position in the model reflects the 'weight' or net causal impact.

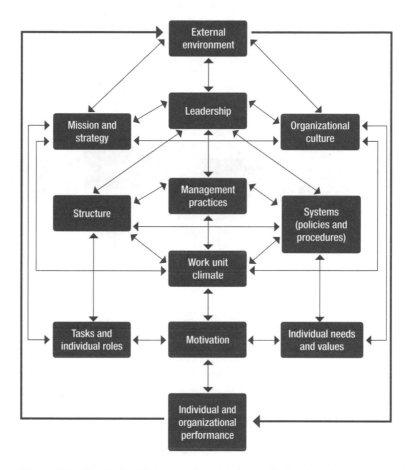

Figure 6.7 *The Burke-Litwin causal model of organizational performance and change*
Source: Burke and Litwin, 1992: 528

This said, the model does not prescribe that change should always start with elements at the top of the model. It is a predictive rather than a prescriptive model. It specifies the nature of causal relationships and predicts the likely effect of changing certain elements rather than others. The decision about where to intervene first might be influenced by whether the aim is to secure transformational or transactional change. The model elaborates these two distinct sets of organizational dynamics. One is associated with organizational transformation and the need for a fundamental shift in values and behaviour, and the other is associated with behaviour at the more everyday level.

Transformational change is required when an organization has to respond to the kind of environmental discontinuities considered in Chapter 1. This kind of change involves a paradigm shift and completely new behaviours. Instead of changes designed to help the organization do things better (incremental change), the organization needs to do things differently or do different things. As noted in Chapter 18, this calls for the principles, assumptions and values that underpin the implicit and explicit rules that guide behaviour to be revised. It involves a change in the organization's culture. It also calls for a change in the organization's mission and strategy, and for managers at all levels to provide a lead and to behave in ways that clarify the new strategy and encourage others to act in ways that will support it. Where the need is for this kind of change, attention needs to be focused on the transformational elements highlighted in Figure 6.8.

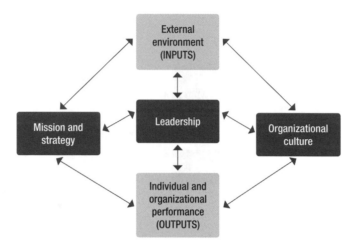

Figure 6.8   *The transformational factors*
Source: Adapted from Burke and Litwin, 1992: 523

Transactional change is associated with fine-tuning, with how the organization functions within the existing paradigm. It emphasizes single rather than double loop learning, as in the model of organizational learning discussed in Chapter 18 (see Figure 18.2). The focus of attention needs to be the structures, management practices and systems that affect the work climate, which in turn impacts on motivation and performance at both the unit and individual level.

Interventions designed to bring about organizational transformation that target 'higher level' elements in the model will eventually and inevitably have an impact on all other elements in the system because of their weight and relative impact. If, however, the target of interventions is primarily the elements in the lower part of the model, aimed at achieving what Burke and Litwin refer to as 'transactional change', the impact is more likely to remain at local unit level. Interventions targeted at this type of element might have relatively little, if any, impact on overall organizational culture and strategy. Burke and Litwin (1992) present an impressive (if selective) summary of studies that provide empirical support for the causal linkages hypothesized by their model.

Revising your personal model of organizational functioning

This and the previous chapter have presented a brief summary of some widely used models of organizational functioning and have identified some of the main differences between them. You are advised to develop a 'healthy scepticism' towards the utility of different models and constantly reassess which is most appropriate for the purpose at hand.

Characteristics of a good model

All the models that have been considered are simplifications of the real world. None are guaranteed to accommodate all circumstances, provide a reliable basis for understanding why things are the way they are, or identify actions that can be taken to produce a desired outcome. Depending on circumstances and purpose, some theories or models might have greater utility than others.

Three characteristics of 'good' diagnostic models are that they:

1 are relevant to the particular issues under consideration
2 help change agents to recognize cause-and-effect relationships
3 focus on elements that they can influence.

At the end of Chapter 5, it was recommended that, after reading this chapter, you reflect on and review your own model of organizational functioning. Points you might consider are:

▶ How the models presented above relate to your personal experience. For example, to what extent do they accommodate or ignore elements and causal relationships that your experience has led you to believe are important? It might be unwise to slavishly apply a model that ignores aspects of organizational functioning that your own experience tells you are significant.
▶ Do any of these models include elements and/or relationships that you have never previously considered but which, on reflection, might help you to make better sense of your own experience? You need to be alert to the danger of rejecting alternative models too hastily. You might find that a model that is quite different from your own personal model can provide useful new insights.

Using diagnostic models in practice

Example 6.1 below illustrates how a change manager's subjective model of organizational functioning provided a basis for developing a better understanding of the organization and identifying targets for change.

Example 6.1

The Site Security and Secure Escorts case

This case illustrates a funnel approach to diagnosis that began with a newly appointed CEO using his own model of organizational functioning to diagnose 'the big picture' and then moving on to use component models to develop a better understanding of particular issues.

Site Security and Secure Escorts (SSSE) is a company wholly owned by (what will be referred to here as) CP Security Services. The parent company provides a wide range of security services in the UK and abroad including risk assessment and management; site security and secure escort services; cash transit (armoured vehicles) and high-value courier services; detention centres and prison escorts; and technical security systems. SSSE provides manned guard and secure escort services across a range of sectors, including pharmaceuticals, financial services, telecommunications, defence and utilities, to provide protection from theft, vandalism, industrial espionage, terrorism and attacks from radical activists motivated by issues such as animal rights. A new CEO was appointed to SSSE in April 2005 and tasked to grow the business and improve profitability.

His first task was to familiarize himself with the current state of affairs and identify what could be done to improve the situation. He spent a lot of time out of his office meeting people. He had almost daily conversations with most managers at head office and, with his director of operations, visited clients and met with SSSE staff working on clients' premises. His aim, using conversations, observations and management reports, was to identify key issues and begin to formulate an agenda for change. He did not embark on this process with a 'clean sheet'. When he joined SSSE, he brought with him his own subjective model of how organizations work and the key cause-and-effect relationships that determine effectiveness (see Figure 6.9 below) and used this to direct his attention and interpret what he saw, heard and read about the organization.

He quickly realized that a number of clients were unhappy with the quality of service provided by SSSE. This not only threatened to undermine his plan to grow the business and increase margins but also raised the possibility that SSSE would lose existing business as and when contracts came up for renewal. His initial diagnosis, informed by the model presented in Figure 6.9, pointed to several factors that appeared to be contributing to this state of affairs:

- *Staff shortages:* Following 9/11 and the aggressive tactics employed by some animal rights activists, there had been a sharp increase in the demand for site security. This was accompanied by a related demand for new recruits to be more thoroughly vetted. This was a time-consuming process that reduced supply just when the demand for new staff was growing.
- *Management style:* The company's management style was top-down command and control. While this had been effective in the past when management could easily impose sanctions for poor performance, it was proving less effective in the current tight labour market. There was evidence that it was having a negative impact on motivation and some employees were paying less attention to performance standards and were ignoring operating procedures because they were confident, given the rising demand for staff, that they would not be dismissed.
- *Management structure:* The number of supervisors had not increased in line with the number of new contracts. Consequently, supervisors were overstretched. This situation was exacerbated because, in order to fulfil immediate contractual requirements for guards and escorts, supervisors had to stand in and personally cover for staff shortages.
- *Ineffective management information systems:* Decision making was highly centralized but inadequately supported by the quality of available management information. For example, managers located at headquarters did not have access to up-to-date information on operations, making it difficult for them to schedule work effectively.

This assessment was shared and debated with other senior managers and produced a number of suggestions for improvement. One of these was to explore ways of improving the performance of existing staff. The operations director and a site supervisor conducted two focus groups with guards and escorts drawn from several sites. While the guards and escorts raised different points specific to their roles, a number of common themes emerged. For example, both groups indicated that most of their job was boring and lacked any meaningful challenge, and some remarks hinted that when not directly supervised, they read newspapers or did puzzles rather than give their full attention to their duties. They also felt undervalued. They realized that there was a growing demand for personnel who had the level of security clearance required by SSSE's clients, but they felt that this 'scarcity factor' was not reflected by their rates of pay. These finding prompted a more detailed diagnosis of the roles people were required to perform, with a view to redesigning their jobs in ways that would improve their motivation and the quality of their work. Managers were introduced to Hackman and Oldham's job characteristics theory (1980) and used the job diagnostic survey to gather more information (see the theorizing mode of intervening discussed in Chapter 13).

Another suggestion for improvement was to take a detailed look at the way the organization was structured and to consider alternatives that might address some of the issues uncovered by the initial diagnosis. A consultant was brought in to facilitate a workshop on organization design. This led to the senior management team exploring the possible benefit of introducing team working on client sites, with self-managed teams being delegated responsibility for monitoring their own performance as well as executing the task. Hackman's book *Leading Teams* (2002) guided much of this work.

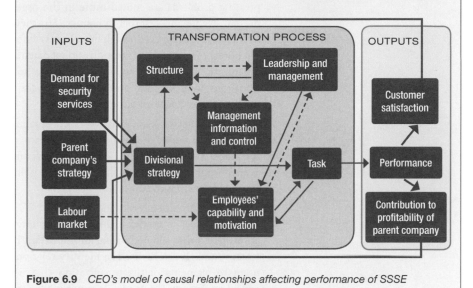

Figure 6.9 *CEO's model of causal relationships affecting performance of SSSE*

Diagnosis is not a one-off activity; it is ongoing and often begins with a review of the total system. The use of component models to investigate specific aspects of organizational functioning elaborates and helps to build a richer picture of the organization as a whole, and because this big picture exists, it is possible to align efforts to improve particular aspects of organizational performance. For example, in the SSSE case, there were obvious opportunities for synergy between the redesign of jobs and efforts to restructure the organization that involved the introduction of team working. Also, both initiatives had implications for the development of new management information systems and so on.

Summary

This chapter reviews a range of holistic models that can be used to aid diagnosis.

1. Organization–environment fit models
   - The PEST model can be used to examine the organization's environment and search for evidence of change that might signal a problem or opportunity. The acronym refers to political, economic, sociocultural and technological factors.
   - The SWOT model offers a more comprehensive approach to diagnosing organization-environment fit. In addition to assessing the opportunities and threats that a PEST analysis might reveal, it includes an assessment of the organization's strengths and weaknesses and its capability to respond to identified threats and opportunities.

- Strebel's model of competitive behaviour considers organization–environment fit but does so from the perspective of an evolutionary cycle of competitive behaviour.

2 Life cycle models

Greiner's five phases of growth and Flamholtz's framework for organizational diagnosis are life cycle models that identify predictable stages of an organization's development and the issues that have to be managed at each stage:

- Greiner cautions managers about the danger of only attending to the external environment and the future. He asserts that for many organizations the most pressing problems are rooted more in the organization's past decisions than present events and external dynamics. His view is that organizations evolve over time and progress through five phases of development.
- Flamholtz's framework for organizational diagnosis brings together a model of organizational effectiveness, which he refers to as the 'pyramid of organizational development', and an organizational life cycle model, and points to a number of key transformation points.

Phelps et al. propose an alternative conceptualization of firm growth. Unlike Greiner and Flamholtz, they make no assumptions about linearity, predictability or sequence. They discard the notion of stages and suggest that, as firms grow, they encounter a series of problems (tipping points) that must be successfully addressed if growth is to continue.

3 Models that emphasize internal alignment

- The McKinsey 7S model highlights seven interrelated elements of organizations that, when aligned, make an important contribution to organizational effectiveness. It can be used to identify relationships that are misaligned and point to elements of the organization that need to be changed. While it considers strategy, the model does not make explicit reference to outcomes or the external environment.
- Weisbord presents his systemic model as a 'practice theory' that synthesizes knowledge and experience from change agents. It provides a conceptual map of six elements or boxes. Component theories can be applied to assess each of these elements in a way that can reveal new connections and relationships between them. It is an open systems model that recognizes the importance of organization–environment relationships but focuses most attention on what needs to be done internally to ensure that the organization becomes and remains a high performance organization able to adapt to external changes.

4 Diagnosing internal and external alignment

The Burke-Litwin causal model of organizational performance and change is an open systems model that points to the relative weight of each element of organizational functioning and the causal linkages that determine performance. The model also differentiates between two types of change: transformational change that occurs as a response to important shifts in the external environment, and transactional change that occurs in response to the need for more short-term incremental improvement. These features distinguish this model from the others considered in this section.

5 Three characteristics of a 'good' model are also identified. These are:

- relevance to the issues under consideration
- ability to identify critical cause-and-effect relationships
- ability to focus attention on elements that change managers can affect.

The chapter closes with an example of how change managers can use models to aid their diagnosis.

The next chapter examines some of the issues that you need to consider when deciding how to collect information for diagnosis.

References

Burke, W.W. and Litwin, G.H. (1992) A causal model of organizational performance and change, *Journal of Management*, **18**(3): 523–45.

Cohen, W.M. and Levinthal, D.A. (1990) Absorptive capacity: a new perspective on learning and innovation, *Administrative Science Quarterly*, 35: 128–52.

Flamholtz, E. (1995) Managing organizational transition: implications for corporate and human resource management, *European Management Journal*, **13**(1): 39–51.

Greiner, L.E. (1972) Evolution and revolution as organizations grow, *Harvard Business Review*, 50: 37–46.

Hackman, J.R. (2002) *Leading Teams*, Boston, MA: Harvard Business School Press.

Hackman, J.R. and Oldham, G.R. (1980) *Work Redesign*, Reading, MA: Addison-Wesley.

Higgins, J.M. (2005) The eight 'S's of successful strategy implementation, *Journal of Change Management*, **5**(1): 3–13.

Kotter, J.P. (1980) An integrative model of organizational dynamics, in E.E. Lawler, D.A Nadler and C. Cammann (eds) *Organizational Assessment*, New York: Wiley.

Nadler, D.A. and Tushman, M.L. (1980) A congruence model for organizational assessment, in E.E. Lawler, D.A. Nadler and C. Cammann (eds) *Organizational Assessment*, New York: Wiley.

Pascale, R. and Athos, A. (1981) *The Art of Japanese Management*, New York: Warner Books.

Phelps, R., Adams, R. and Bessant, J. (2007) Life cycles of growing organizations: a review with implications for knowledge and learning, *International Journal of Management Reviews*, **9**(1): 1–30.

Postma, T. and Kok, R. (1999) Organizational diagnosis in practice: a cross-classification analysis using the DEL-technique, *European Management Journal*, **17**(6): 584–97.

Romanelli, E. and Tushman, M.L. (1994) Organizational transformation as punctuated equilibrium: an empirical test, *Academy of Management Journal*, **37**(5): 1141–66.

Strebel, P. (1996) Breakpoint: how to stay in the game, *Mastering Management*, Part 17, London: Financial Times.

Weisbord, M.R. (1976) Organizational diagnosis: six places to look for trouble with or without a theory, *Group and Organization Studies*, **1**(4): 430–47.

Gathering and interpreting information for diagnosis

Diagnosing the need for change involves a process of gathering, analysing and interpreting information about individual, group and organizational functioning. The main steps in this process are:

1 selecting a conceptual model for diagnosis
2 clarifying information requirements
3 information gathering
4 analysis
5 interpretation.

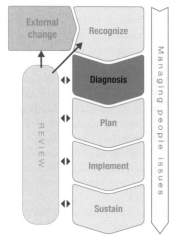

In those circumstances where the information is collected by an internal or external change agent working on behalf of a client group, the information will need to be fed back to the other organizational members who will be involved in the diagnosis. This often occurs after those who have collected the data have completed a preliminary analysis but before the information has been interpreted.

Selecting a diagnostic model

It was noted earlier that organizational behaviour, at all its different levels, is a complex phenomenon and it is impossible for managers to pay attention to every aspect of organizational functioning. We cope with this complexity, sometimes unconsciously, by developing or adopting conceptual models that simplify the real world and focus attention on a limited number of elements and relationships. Some of the explicit models of organizational functioning available to change agents relate to how the organization functions as a total system. Component models focus on selected elements of the overall system, such as leadership, structure, job design, competencies and so on. A range of holistic models was considered in the previous two chapters, and most good texts on organizational behaviour critically review a wide range of component models.

Conceptual models play a key role in the diagnostic process because they help us to decide which aspects of organizational behaviour require attention and provide a focus for information gathering. They also provide a basis for interpreting the information that has been collected.

When selecting a model for diagnosis, the obvious first point that has to be considered is the extent to which the model is relevant to the issue(s) under consideration, for example loss of market share, dysfunctional intergroup conflict, high labour turnover and so on.

An effective model is one that identifies specific elements and/or cause-and-effect relationships that contribute to the problem or opportunity, and indicates which of these have most weight (or effect) on other aspects of organizational functioning and performance. Evidence, from personal experience or published research, about the ability of a conceptual model to explain and predict cause-and-effect relationships can help the change manager to select an appropriate model for diagnosis. However, the ultimate aim of organizational diagnosis is more than improving our understanding of why something is the way it is. It also involves using this understanding to plan action to improve organization effectiveness.

Consequently, if a diagnostic model is to have any practical utility, it needs to highlight aspects of organizational functioning that, either directly or indirectly, the change manager can do something about.

Clarifying information requirements

Exercise 5.1 invited you to think about the information you would use in order to diagnose the current state of your organization. This information was then categorized and used to help you make explicit your personal model of organizational functioning.

This process can be reversed. When a diagnostic model has been selected, the change manager can identify the items of information that will be required to assess how an organization (unit or group) is performing and to distinguish what is going well and what is going not so well. Two examples illustrate what this involves.

The 7S model focuses attention on seven aspects of organizational functioning – strategy, structure, systems, staff, style, shared values and skills (see Figure 6.5). A change manager using this model will need to identify the kind of information required to describe each element. For example, under 'strategy', they may seek information about how the organization goes about matching its resources with opportunities, constraints and demands in the environment, how it plans to develop in the future and how it goes about creating and maintaining a competitive advantage. Under 'structure', a change manager may seek information about formal and informal arrangements for grouping and coordinating activities, defining responsibilities and establishing reporting relationships. An organization's structure might be described in terms of functions, divisions, a matrix or a network.

The twelve elements of the Burke-Litwin causal model of organizational performance, discussed in Chapter 6, are defined in Table 7.1, together with examples of the kind of question that might be used to elicit information about each element. The examples are taken from an instrument used in a diagnostic exercise in the BBC. The survey instrument included a minimum of four questions relating to each element of the model. Respondents were invited to respond to the questions on a five-point scale.

The way a change manager can use this kind of information to identify what might need to be changed is considered later in this chapter.

Change tool 7.2, at the end of the chapter, provides another example of how a model can help to clarify the kind of information you need to collect.

Table 7.1 *Examples of questions asked in a BBC staff survey*

	Elements	Indicative questions
External environment	Any outside condition or situation that influences the performance of the organization. Includes such things as marketplaces, world financial conditions, political/governmental circumstances and so on	Regarding the pace of change, what would you say the organization as a whole is experiencing – from static to very rapid change?
Mission/strategy	What organizational members believe is the central purpose of the organization and how the organization intends to achieve that purpose over an extended time	How widely accepted are the organization's goals among employees?
Leadership	Executive behaviour that encourages others to take needed actions	To what extent do senior managers make an effort to keep in touch with employees at your level in the organization?
Culture	'The way things are done around here.' The collection of overt and covert rules, values and principles that guide behaviour and have been strongly influenced by history, custom and practice	To what extent are the standard ways of operating in the organization difficult to change?
Structure	The arrangements of functions and people into specific areas and levels of responsibility, decision-making authority and relationships	To what extent is the organization's structure clear to everyone?
Management practices/action	What managers do in the normal course of events to use human and material resources to carry out the organization's strategy	To what extent does your manager communicate in an open and direct manner?
Systems	Standardized policies and mechanisms that facilitate work. They typically manifest themselves in the organization's reward systems and in control systems such as goal and budget development and human resource development	To what extent are the communication mechanisms in the organization effective (for example grapevine)?
Climate	The collective current impressions, expectations and feelings of the members of local work units. These affect members' relations with supervisors, with one another and with other units	Where you work in the organization, to what extent is there trust and mutual respect among employees?
Task requirements and individual skills	The behaviour required for task effectiveness, including specific skills and knowledge required for people to accomplish the work assigned and for which they feel directly responsible – the job–person match	How challenged do you feel in your present job?
Motivation	Aroused behavioural tendencies to move towards goals, take needed action and persist until satisfaction is attained	To what extent do you feel encouraged to reach higher levels and standards of performance in your work?
Individual needs and values	The specific psychological factors that provide desire and worth for individual actions and thoughts	(From disagree strongly to agree strongly) I have a job that matters.
Performance	The outcomes or results, with indicators of effort and achievement. Examples include productivity, customer or staff satisfaction, profit and service quality	To what extent is the organization currently achieving the highest level of employee performance of which they are capable?

Information gathering

This stage of the process begins with a series of planning decisions relating to which methods of data collection to employ and whether data can/should be collected from every possible source or from a representative sample of the total population of sources.

There are a number of different techniques or methods that can be used to collect information. They include individual and group interviews, questionnaires, projective methods such as drawings and collages, observation and the use of secondary data, sometimes referred to as unobtrusive measures. Cummings and Worley (2001) provide a useful discussion of most of these methods. Only their main features are summarized below.

Interviews

Individual and group interviews are a rich source of information about what is going on in an organization. People can be asked to describe aspects of the organization and how it functions, and they can also be asked to make judgements about how effectively the organization, or an aspect of it, functions and how they feel about this (their affective reaction). For example, after describing how the appraisal system operates in an organization, some employees might judge it to be ineffective but indicate that they are quite happy about this because the ineffective system works to their personal advantage.

Individual interviews have some added advantages. Respondents might be persuaded to share private views they may be reluctant to express in a more open forum. The interaction between interviewer and respondent can offer the possibility that respondents might be stimulated to articulate and make explicit vague feelings and views they had not previously formulated at a conscious level.

Interviews are adaptive. If respondents raise issues that the interviewer had not anticipated, the interview schedule can be modified to allow these emerging issues to be explored in more detail. The interview also offers the opportunity for the interviewer/change agent to build rapport and develop trust with respondents and motivate them to develop a constructive attitude towards the change programme.

Interaction between respondents in a group interview can generate information that might not be forthcoming in an individual interview. For example, if individuals from different units or levels in the organization express different views, these differences might promote a useful discussion of why the conflicting perceptions exist and what problems or opportunities they might point to.

There are, however, a number of potential problems associated with using the interview to collect information. Interviews can be time-consuming and costly, although group interviews less so than individual interviews.

Coding and interpreting responses can be a problem, especially when interviews are unstructured. Coding and interpretation can be simplified by adopting a more structured approach, asking all respondents the same set of predetermined questions and limiting the use of open-ended questions. However, the gains from adopting a more structured approach need to be balanced against the potential loss of rich data that can be gleaned from a more unstructured conversation, for example where the interviewer leads off with some general open-ended questions and then follows the respondent's chain of thought.

Bias is another problem that can arise from the way interviewers organize the order of topics to be covered and the way they formulate questions. Especial care needs to be taken to avoid the use of leading questions that signal to the respondent that there is a desired response.

Questionnaires

Questionnaires are sometimes referred to as 'self-administered interviews'. They are designed to obtain information by asking organizational members (and others) a predetermined set of questions about their perceptions, judgements and feelings. Using questionnaires to collect diagnostic information can be more cost-effective than using interviews, because they can be administered simultaneously to large numbers of people without the need to employ expensive interviewers. Also, they can be designed around fixed response-type questions that ease the burden of analysis.

However, they do have a number of disadvantages. They are non-empathic. When using questionnaires to collect information, it can be difficult for change managers to build rapport and communicate empathy with respondents. This can have an adverse effect on respondents' motivation to give full and honest answers to the questions asked.

Questionnaires are also much less adaptive than interviews. Interviewers can modify their approach in response to the interviewee's reaction to questions and can explore unanticipated issues. The format of the questionnaire, on the other hand, has to be decided in advance. Problems can arise because respondents fail to understand or misinterpret the meaning of questions. Important questions may also be omitted – a problem that is difficult to resolve once the questionnaire has been administered.

Another problem is self-report bias. Questionnaires (like interviews) collect information from people who may, either deliberately or otherwise, bias their response. Responses to questions are based on the respondents' perceptions of what is going on. These perceptions may be based on incomplete or false information. Also there is a tendency for respondents to present their own behaviour in the most positive light and protect their own interests. The design of the questionnaire can also bias responses. For example, people may fall into a pattern of answering co-located questions in a similar manner, or their attention may wander and they may take less care when answering questions towards the end of the questionnaire.

Projective methods

Projective methods such as drawings and collages can be a useful way of collecting information about issues that people may find difficult to express in other ways. Fordyce and Weil (1983) suggest that by asking subgroups to prepare a collage around themes such as 'how do you feel about this team?' or 'what is happening to the organization?' and present and explain it to the total group in a plenary session, organizational members can be helped to express and explore issues at a fairly deep and personal level. A similar procedure is to invite individuals to prepare and share drawings that show certain aspects of organizational life. For example, individuals might be asked to draw a circle for each member of their group, making the circles larger or smaller depending on the influence they have over the way the group works. They may also be asked to elaborate their drawing by locating the circles for different members of the group in terms of how closely they need to work together to get the job done. A further elaboration might be to ask them to join the circles with blue lines where the people they represent have a personally close relationship and with red lines if they are far apart in terms of communication, rapport and empathy.

These kinds of approaches to surfacing information can be good icebreakers and can provide an easy route to the discussion of sensitive issues that are rarely discussed openly. However, while they may be well received by some groups, others may reject them as childish games.

Observations

Observing behaviour as it occurs is one approach to collecting information that avoids self-report bias. One of the key issues associated with this approach is deciding how the observation can be organized to focus attention on required behaviour and avoid being distracted or swamped by irrelevant information. When collecting information about behaviour in a group setting, for example, the degree of structure for observing and recording can vary from using broad categories such as leadership or communication to the use of detailed category sets such as the interaction process analysis framework developed by Bales (1950).

An advantage of this approach to information collection is that the observer may recognize patterns of behaviour that those being observed may be unaware of and are therefore unable to report in interviews or in their responses to questionnaires.

Another advantage is that observations relate to current behaviour and are less likely than self-reports to be contaminated by historical factors. Observation is also an adaptive approach to collecting information. What is observed might cue the observer to explore connected aspects of current practice. Some of the disadvantages of this approach include problems associated with coding and interpretation, cost and possible observer bias.

Unobtrusive measures

In many organizational settings, large amounts of information are collected as a normal part of day-to-day operations, which relate to various aspects of organizational functioning, such as costs, downtime, wastage rates, absenteeism, labour turnover, delivery times, margins, complaints, number and type of meetings and so on. This kind of information is referred to as 'unobtrusive', because the fact that it is being collected for diagnosis is unlikely to prompt any specific response bias. It is also likely to be readily accepted by organizational members and, because of the nature of many of the records that contain this kind of information, it may be easy to quantify.

However, even when records are maintained, it may be difficult to access information in the required form. For example, information about individuals, such as the outcome of performance appraisals, increments awarded, absenteeism and sickness rates, may all be contained in each individual's personal record but may not be available in any aggregate form for all members of a particular department.

Sampling

Sometimes, for example when collecting information from members of a relatively small work group, it may be possible to include every member of the group in the survey. However, when a diagnostic exercise involves collecting information about a whole department, or the total organization, it may be necessary to consider ways of sampling people, activities and records in a way that will provide sufficient information to provide a representative picture of what is going on.

Important issues that need to be considered when drawing a sample relate to sample size, relative to the total population, and composition. For example, how many people should be interviewed, events observed or records inspected, and which individuals, events or records should be included in the sample? The answer to the size or 'how many' question depends on the degree of confidence in the findings that is required and, if the information is to be subjected to statistical analysis, the type of analysis that is to be used. The answer to the composition or 'which' question depends on the complexity of the total population. If the total population is relatively homogeneous, the selection of members to be included in the sample might be done on a random basis, using random number tables, or by selecting every nth member of the total population. If, however, the total population contains different subgroups, it might be important to ensure that all of them are represented in the sample. This involves segregating the total population into a number of mutually exclusive subpopulations and drawing a sample from each. The composite sample that results from this process is referred to as a 'stratified sample'.

Analysis

Once information has been collected, it needs to be analysed. For example, in response to a question such as 'How challenged do you feel in your present job?', only some of those surveyed might have offered a positive response. The change agent may want to know what proportion of the sample responded in this way compared to those who responded in the same way in other organizations, in order to be able to assess whether the lack of challenging work is a problem. It might also be useful to consider whether there is any relationship between those who do not feel challenged and the unit they work in or their level in the hierarchy. Analytical procedures organize information in ways that can provide answers to diagnostic questions. Analytical techniques are often classified as qualitative or quantitative.

Qualitative techniques

Qualitative techniques tend to be more concerned with meaning and underlying patterns than with scientific tests. Cummings and Worley (2001) refer to content analysis and force-field analysis as two qualitative analytical techniques that are frequently used in organizational diagnostic exercises.

Content analysis

Content analysis attempts to summarize respondents' comments into meaningful categories. This involves identifying comments or answers that tend to recur most frequently and grouping them in ways that provide a set of mutually exclusive and exhaustive categories or themes. For example, in response to a question such as 'What do you like best about your work?', a number of responses might refer to working with friendly colleagues, considerate supervisors and having the opportunity to communicate with co-workers while doing the job. All these comments might be regarded as referring to a common theme, the 'social aspects' of the job. A different set of comments might refer to the degree of challenge offered by the work, the opportunity to be creative and the freedom to experiment with new methods. All these comments might be regarded as referring to different aspects of the 'nature of the work' itself. These two categories might then be used as a basis for analysing the content of all the information collected from respondents. When a set of categories is exhaustive, it is possible to allocate every response to a category, and when it is mutually exclusive, each item of information will fall into one particular category. After all responses have been classified, one way of determining the importance of the different categories is to identify those that have been referred to most often.

NUDist is one example of a software tool that can be used for coding and analysing qualitative data, and provides a relatively easy method of comparing the responses from different respondents to particular questions.

Force-field analysis

Force-field analysis, discussed in Chapter 2, also involves categorizing information. The distinctive feature of force-field analysis is that it involves organizing the categories into two broad types; those relating to forces or pressures for change and those relating to forces or pressures supporting the (problematic) status quo and resisting change.

It was noted in Chapter 2 that Lewin (1951) viewed the level of behaviour in any situation as the result of a force field comprising a balance of the forces pushing for change (some different level of behaviour) and the forces resisting that change. Diagnosing situations in terms of driving and restraining forces can provide a useful basis for developing action plans to secure desired change. When the forces pushing in one direction exceed the forces pushing in the opposite direction, the dynamic equilibrium changes. The level of behaviour can be changed towards a more desirable state by increasing the strength of forces for change (the driving forces) in the desired direction or by diminishing the strength of restraining forces (Figure 7.1).

Change tool 7.3, at the end of this chapter, provides a step-by-step approach you can use to apply force-field analysis to an opportunity development or problem management issue with which you might have to deal.

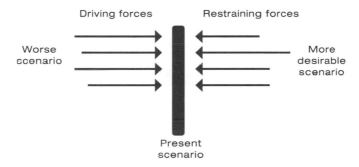

Figure 7.1   *A force field*

Quantitative techniques

Some of the basic techniques most frequently used by change agents when analysing quantitative information are means, standard deviations, correlation coefficients and difference tests. The mean is a measure that indicates the average response or behaviour. For example, over the last year, the eight employees in department X might have averaged 5 days sick leave. The standard deviation indicates the extent to which there is high or low variation around this mean, for example six members of the department may have had no sick leave, whereas the other two may have had 20 days each. Correlation coefficients measure the strength of the relationship between variables, for example sick leave might be inversely related to job satisfaction. Difference tests indicate whether the scores achieved by one group, for example an average of 5 days sick leave for members of department X, are significantly different from those achieved by members of other groups – different departments in the same organization or some benchmark score or industry norm. More details on these and other techniques can be found in any standard text on statistics.

Interpretation

Conceptual models provide a basis for interpreting diagnostic information and identifying what needs to be changed to achieve a more desirable state of affairs.

Change managers using the 7S model (described in Chapter 6) can construct a 7S matrix (see Change tool 7.1). The kind of information required about each element was considered earlier. This can be analysed to provide descriptions that can be entered on the matrix and used to assess the degree of alignment between all seven elements. For example, using a five-point scale, the change manager can assess the extent to which shared values are aligned with the organization's strategy, structure, systems, staff, skills and so on. This analysis will point to areas where it might be necessary to intervene to change an element in order to improve fit. This will not always be an easy process. Introducing a change to improve the fit between two specific elements might create misalignments elsewhere, but the model provides a framework for reviewing each change and taking further action as required.

Change tool 7.1

The 7S matrix

Strategy	Structure	Systems	Staff	Style	Shared values	Skills
Describe strategy	Strategy/ structure alignment	Strategy/ systems alignment	Strategy/staff alignment	Strategy/style alignment	Strategy/ values alignment	Strategy/skill alignment
	Describe structure	Structure/ systems alignment	Structure/ staff alignment	Structure/ style alignment	Structure/ values alignment	Structure/ skills alignment
		Describe systems	Systems/staff alignment	Systems/style alignment	Systems/ values alignment	Systems/ skills alignment
			Describe staff	Staff/style alignment	Staff/values alignment	Staff/skills alignment
				Describe style	Style/values alignment	Style/skills alignment
					Describe shared values	Values/skills alignment
						Describe skills

The results of the 1993 staff survey in the BBC, which was designed around the Burke-Litwin causal model of organizational performance, indicated some priorities for change. The elements most in need of change were structure, leadership and factors affecting motivation, but there was also evidence that there was scope for improvement in many other areas. A brief summary of the results of this survey is presented in Figure 7.2.

Change tool 7.2 at the end of this chapter provides another example of how diagnostic information can be used to identify what action needs to be taken to improve organizational performance.

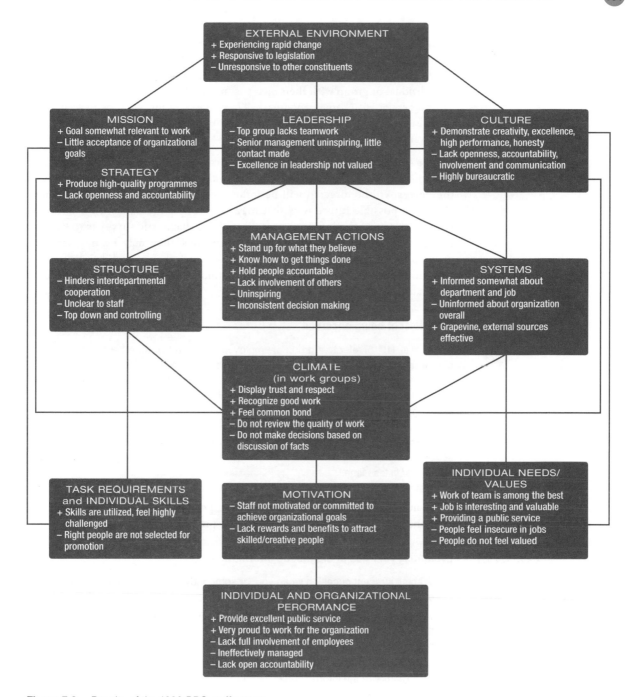

Figure 7.2 *Results of the 1993 BBC staff survey*

Political considerations

Collecting information is not an innocuous or benign activity. Nadler (1977) argues that the collection and distribution of information can change the nature of power relationships. Data collection can generate energy around the activities or behaviours that are being measured for a number of reasons. For example:

▶ It may result in information that an individual or group has previously withheld in order to secure some political advantage being widely distributed, thereby undermining their power and influence.

▶ It opens up the possibility of comparing the current performance of an individual or group with their own past performance, with the performance of others or with some benchmark. These possibilities might be perceived as threatening, especially where there is a link between performance and rewards.

The energy generated by data collection can be directed towards assisting or undermining the change agent's attempt to diagnose the need for change. How the energy will be directed will be influenced by the perceptions people have about the possible future uses that may be made of the data. If, for example, employees expect the information collected in a diagnostic survey is to be used in an open, non-threatening and helpful manner, they may be motivated to provide accurate information. If, on the other hand, they expect it to be used in a punitive manner, they may attempt to withhold or distort data. This point is illustrated in Example 7.1 below.

Example 7.1

The effect of being observed

Porter et al. (1975) refer to a group of employees who worked together to assemble complicated large steel frameworks. Their method of working varied depending on whether or not they were being observed by anyone who might influence the rate they were paid for the job. The group had discovered that by tightening certain bolts first, the frame would be slightly sprung and all the other bolts would bind and be difficult to tighten. When they used this method, they gave the impression they were working hard all the time. When they were not being observed, they followed a different sequence of tightening bolts and the work was much easier and the job could be completed in less time.

Change managers need to be alert to the possibility that they will encounter resistance even at this early stage in the change process.

Exercise 7.1

Evaluating your use of diagnostic information

Think about a recent occasion when you, or somebody working close to you, have attempted to introduce and manage a change in your part of the organization:

1 Reflect on the extent to which this change initiative was based on an accurate diagnosis of the need for change.
2 Consider to what extent this was related to:
   • the appropriateness of the (implicit or explicit) diagnostic model used
   • the nature of the information collected
   • the way in which it was interpreted.
3 Reflect on what steps you might take to help improve the quality of the way the need for change is diagnosed in your unit or department.

Notes

Using diagnostic information to develop action plans

SWOT analysis and force-field analysis provide useful frameworks for using diagnostic information to identify what needs to be changed, as shown in Change tools 7.2 and 7.3 below.

Change tool 7.2	**Using a SWOT analysis**

Anybody can do a SWOT analysis but doing it with others can provide a richer picture of how the group or organization fits with its operating environment and the issues that need to be attended to in order to secure future performance.

Strengths are the positive tangible and intangible attributes of the group, department or organization. Weaknesses are negative factors that can undermine the group, department or organization's ability to attain desired goals. The PRIMO-F framework (people, resources, innovation, marketing, operations, finance) offers a useful set of headings for reviewing strengths and weaknesses, but in some situations, it might be more appropriate to adapt this framework to include particularly relevant factors, such as scalability – the ability to rapidly expand or contract operations, or develop a bespoke framework more suited to the circumstances. It can also be useful to include a catch-all category such as 'other' to ensure that difficult to categorize factors are not ignored.

Opportunities are external factors that offer the possibility for benefit and threats are the factors that can jeopardize existing ways of working, limit possibilities and derail future plans. The PEST headings can provide a useful set of categories for exploring opportunities and threats.

A simple 2 × 2 matrix can provide a basic framework for plotting the findings and identifying issues that require attention (Table 7.2).

Table 7.2 *A simple SWOT template*

Strengths	Weaknesses
1	1
2	2
3	3
4	4
Opportunities	Threats
1	1
2	2
3	3
4	4

Table 7.3 presents a more sophisticated template, which incorporates the PRIMO-F and PEST categories and offers the possibility of assessing the relative impact of each strength, weakness, opportunity and threat.

Table 7.3 *A more detailed SWOT template*

Strengths	Major	Significant	Marginal	Weaknesses	Major	Significant	Marginal
People				People			
1				1			
2				2			
3				3			
Resources				Resources			
1				1			
2				2			
3				3			
Innovation				Innovation			
1				1			
2				2			
3				3			
Marketing				Marketing			
1				1			
2				2			
3				3			
Operations				Operations			
1				1			
2				2			
3				3			
Finance				Finance			
1				1			
2				2			
3				3			
Other				Other			
1				1			
2				2			
3				3			

Opportunities	Major	Significant	Marginal	Threats	Major	Significant	Marginal
Political				Political			
1				1			
2				2			
3				3			
Economic				Economic			
1				1			
2				2			
3				3			
Sociocultural				Sociocultural			
1				1			
2				2			
3				3			
Technology				Technology			
1				1			
2				2			
3				3			
Other				Other			
1				1			
2				2			
3				3			

Once the strengths, weaknesses, opportunities and threats that need to be addressed have been identified, they can be transposed onto the template in Table 7.4. The final steps in the process involve exploring ways of developing and making best use of strengths and using them to exploit opportunities, and finding ways of reducing weaknesses and containing threats.

Table 7.4 *Using SWOT to develop action plans*

Internal factors			
Strengths	Ways to exploit	Weaknesses	Ways to reduce
1	1	1	1
2	2	2	2
3	3	3	3
4	4	4	4
5	5	5	5
External factors			
Opportunities	Ways to exploit	Threats	Ways to reduce
1	1	1	1
2	2	2	2
3	3	3	3
4	4	4	4
5	5	5	5

Change tool 7.3

A force-field approach to opportunity development or problem management

1 Think about a problem you have to manage or an opportunity you could develop in terms of what a more desirable scenario would look like. Use this as a basis for identifying a concrete goal you wish to achieve, and write it in the box down the right-hand side of the page. An alternative might be to apply force-field analysis to Case study 8.1.

2 List the driving forces that are pushing towards the more desirable scenario down the left-hand side of the page, and down the right-hand side list the restraining forces that are blocking the achievement of your goal.

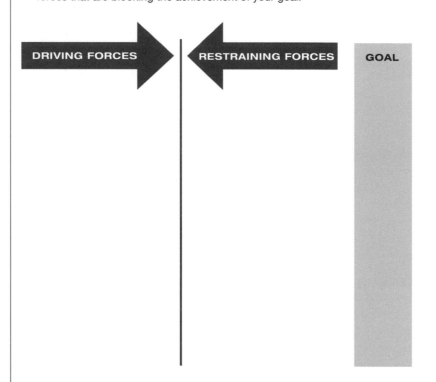

3 Review your list of driving and restraining forces and highlight those that are both powerful, in terms of either pushing for or resisting change, and manageable, that is, you anticipate that you will be able to affect the power of the force.

Driving forces: Review each of the driving forces that you have highlighted (starting with the most important) and brainstorm all the steps you could take to increase the effect of the force. Do not confine yourself to 'sensible' ideas. List everything that comes to mind.

Driving force ....
Brainstorm action steps to increase the effect of this force.

Driving force ....
Brainstorm action steps to increase the effect of this force.

Driving force ....

Brainstorm action steps to increase the effect of this force.

Driving force ....

Brainstorm action steps to increase the effect of this force.

Driving force ....

Brainstorm action steps to increase the effect of this force.

Do not evaluate any of these action steps until you have brainstormed action steps to reduce the effect of the restraining forces.

Restraining forces: Now do the same for the most important restraining forces, but this time brainstorm all the steps you could take to reduce the effect of each restraining force.

Restraining force ....

Brainstorm the steps you could take to reduce the effect of this force.

Restraining force ....

Brainstorm the steps you could take to reduce the effect of this force.

Restraining force ....

Brainstorm the steps you could take to reduce the effect of this force.

Restraining force ....

Brainstorm the steps you could take to reduce the effect of this force.

Restraining force ....

Brainstorm the steps you could take to reduce the effect of this force.

Now review all the action steps:

1 Eliminate those action steps that are totally impractical, but only after you are sure they cannot be 'twisted' or adapted to provide a useful contribution.
2 Identify the 'best of the rest'. Consider whether some action steps can contribute to the strengthening of more than one driving force or the erosion of more than one restraining force. An alternative approach to distilling out the most useful action steps is to group similar actions together and identify those from each group that seem most practical.
3 Finally, list those action steps that deserve serious consideration below.

ACTION TO INCREASE THE EFFECT OF DRIVING FORCES

ACTION TO REDUCE THE EFFECT OF RESTRAINING FORCES

GOAL

The final step involves re-evaluating the action steps from a cost–benefit perspective. The plan has to be practical and some of the proposed action steps might be too expensive in terms of time or other resources. It may be necessary to amend the plan at this stage in order to improve its viability. However, it may also be necessary to include new elements to mould individual action steps into an integrated plan. Give some thought to timescale and milestones against which progress can be assessed. Milestones are important because they provide early warning if the plan is not working and signal the need for renewed effort or the implementation of contingency plans.

Summary of action plan

Action plans that are only concerned with increasing the effect of driving forces may be less effective than plans that include reducing the effect of restraining forces. If restraining forces are weakened, the balance of the remaining forces may push the situation towards the desired scenario.

An example of how a change agent can use force-field analysis is presented in Chapter 13.

Summary

This chapter examines the process of gathering and interpreting information for the purpose of diagnosis. Attention is focused on five main steps:

1 *Selection of an appropriate conceptual model for diagnosis:* Conceptual models play a key role in the diagnostic process because they help us decide which aspects of organizational behaviour require attention and they provide a focus for information gathering. They also provide a basis for interpreting the information that has been collected. When selecting a model for diagnosis, the obvious first point that has to be considered is the extent to which the model is relevant to the issue(s) under consideration, for example loss of market share, dysfunctional intergroup conflict, high labour turnover and so on.

2 *Clarification of information requirements:* Once a diagnostic model has been selected, the change manager can identify the items of information that will be required to assess how an organization (unit or work group) is performing.

3 *Information gathering:* Factors that might determine the method of data collection – interviews, questionnaires, projective methods, observations and unobtrusive measures – are considered, together with ways of sampling people, activities and records that will provide sufficient information to provide a representative picture of what is going on.

4 *Analysis:* Qualitative and quantitative analytical techniques are reviewed.

5 *Interpretation:* Issues that need to be considered when interpreting data are reviewed. Collecting information is not an innocuous or benign activity. Attention is drawn to the political issues associated with data collection that can frustrate attempts to gain an accurate impression of organizational functioning.

References

Bales, R.F. (1950) *Interaction Process Analysis: A Method for the Study of Small Groups*, Cambridge, MA: Addison-Wesley.

Cummings, T.G. and Worley, C.G. (2001) *Organizational Development and Change* (7th edn), Cincinnati, OH: South Western.

Fordyce, J.K. and Weil, R. (1983) Methods for finding out what is going on, in W. French, C.H. Bell and R. Zawacki (eds) *Organization Development: Theory, Practice and Research*, Plano, TX: Business Publications.

Lewin, K. (1951) *Field Theory in Social Science*, New York: Harper & Row.

Nadler, D. (1977) *Feedback and Organization Development: Using Data-based Methods*, Reading, MA: Addison-Wesley.

Porter, L.W., Lawler, E.E. and Hackman, J.R. (1975) *Behavior in Organizations*, New York: McGraw-Hill.

People issues need to be attended to throughout the whole change process. Just because 'managing people issues' is presented as Part III in this book does not mean that they are unimportant prior to implementation. A common mistake is to treat the early stages of starting the change and diagnosis and goal setting as purely technical activities and too often too little attention is given to political and motivational issues. It is not unusual for 'expert' change agents to decide when and where change is required and to define change objectives without taking into account the concerns of stakeholders or recognizing the ways in which they can contribute to or sabotage

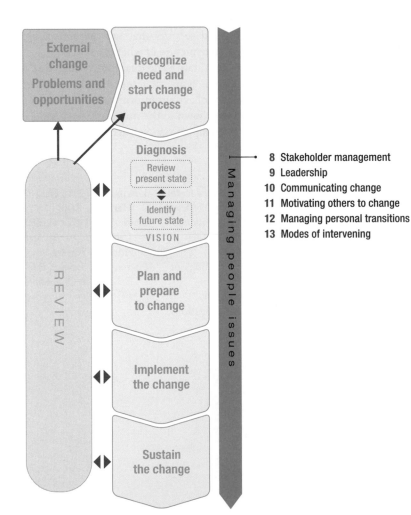

8 Stakeholder management
9 Leadership
10 Communicating change
11 Motivating others to change
12 Managing personal transitions
13 Modes of intervening

the change process. The six chapters in Part IV examine some of the people issues that change managers need to address.

Chapter 8   Power, politics and stakeholder management

This chapter explores the politics of organizational change and the need to enlist the support of key stakeholders. An instrumental theory of stakeholder management is elaborated with reference to resource dependence theory, prospect theory and life cycle models. It provides a conceptual framework for identifying which stakeholders are likely to be most important at various stages of a change project and for selecting appropriate ways of managing relationships with them. After completing an exercise designed to help you to explore some of the issues involved in stakeholder management, you will be invited to think about a recent change in your organization or elsewhere and, with the advantage of hindsight:

▶ identify the stakeholders involved in the change
▶ classify them according to their power to influence and their attitude towards the change
▶ assess the extent to which the change manager was aware of these stakeholders and took proper account of them when managing the change.

Chapter 9   The role of leadership in change management

This chapter examines the role of leadership in change management. Special attention is given the leader's role in terms of creating a vision, aligning relationships around the vision and inspiring others to achieve the vision. Leadership is also considered as a collective process and some of the issues associated with maintaining coherence in the leadership group and between the leadership group and internal and external stakeholders are reviewed. The chapter closes with a review of Kotter's eight-point checklist of what leaders can do to promote change.

Chapter 10   Communicating change

This chapter considers the role of communication in the management of change. Often the focus is exclusively on the 'what, when, who and how' of communicating from the perspective of the change manager communicating to others. In this chapter, attention is also given to issues associated with change managers perceiving, interpreting and using information communicated to them by others.

After studying this chapter, you will be invited to consider how the quality of communication has helped or hindered change in your organization, or some other situation with which you are familiar.

Chapter 11   Motivating others to change

This chapter considers how the general level of commitment in an organization can affect the level of support for change and identifies some of the most common sources of resistance to change. The utility of expectancy theory for assessing and managing resistance to change is explored.

The second half of the chapter involves an exercise designed to help you use expectancy and equity theory to motivate others to change.

Chapter 12 Managing personal transitions

This chapter addresses the way organizational members experience change. It examines the response to change, irrespective of whether the change is viewed as an opportunity or a threat, as a progression through a number of stages of psychological reaction. It also considers how an understanding of the way individuals react to change can help managers to plan and implement organizational change in ways that will maximize benefit and minimize cost for the organization and those affected by the change.

In this chapter, you will be invited to reflect on how you reacted to a change that was lasting in its effects, took place over a relatively short period of time and affected a number of key assumptions you made about how you related with the world around you. The information generated by this exercise will be used to validate a generic stage model of transition.

Chapter 13 Modes of intervening

This chapter argues that the most effective way of facilitating change is to intervene in a way that helps others to help themselves. Usually this involves adopting a collaborative approach but sometimes there may be special circumstances which call for a more prescriptive approach. Five different modes of intervening are discussed. One of these, advising, is prescriptive and the other four – supporting, theorizing, challenging and information gathering – are collaborative.

chapter

chapter

8

Power, politics and stakeholder management

This chapter explores the politics of organizational change and considers the role of stakeholder management in the change process.

When thinking about managing change, some people assume that organizations are well integrated entities within which everybody works harmoniously together. Some also believe that decisions are made logically and rationally, that people share similar views of the world around them and they act to promote the interests of the organization as a whole. This is rarely the case.

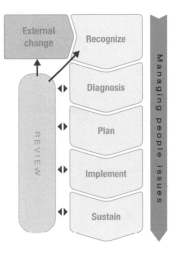

Organizations as political arenas

Organizations can be conceptualized as a collection of constituencies, each pursuing their own objectives. This view presents organizations as political arenas within which individuals and groups attempt to influence each other in the pursuit of self-interest. Those who adopt this political perspective argue that when there is a conflict of interest, it is the power and influence of the individuals and groups involved that determine the outcome of the decision process, not logic and rational argument. This perspective submits that those responsible for managing change cannot afford to ignore issues of power and influence.

Nadler (1987) argues that political behaviour tends to be more intense in times of change because individuals and groups perceive the possibility of upsetting the existing balance of power. Some may be motivated to defend the status quo, whereas others may perceive change as an opportunity to improve their position (see McNulty and Ferlie, 2003). Pettigrew (1972) also argues that some may engage in political action for ideological reasons, especially when they fear that a change may be inconsistent with their values.

Change managers need to be alert to these political dynamics and especially to the possibility that others may be motivated to act in ways that undermine their efforts to bring about change. These others may not only resist change because they feel threatened by the anticipated future state, but also because they feel threatened by the processes used to secure change. For example, some organizational members may be concerned that the collection of information for diagnosis could weaken their position because they may be asked to disclose information they had previously protected in order to secure some political advantage.

Given that different constituents or stakeholders are likely to act in ways that maximize their power and their ability to secure preferred outcomes, change managers need to be alert to the identity of important stakeholders and their predisposition to either support or resist the change.

Power

McClelland (1975) defines power as the ability to change the behaviour of others. It is the ability to cause others to perform actions they might not otherwise perform.

Power and authority

Those in authority are those who are seen to have a legitimate right to influence others, but power is not always legitimate. Sometimes individuals and groups who do not have legitimate authority are able to exercise considerable influence and may even have more power than legitimately appointed managers. Change managers need to ensure that they do not overlook or ignore powerful individuals or groups just because they do not have any formal authority to influence a proposed change.

Exercise 8.1 **Identifying the sources of power**

Consider the following questions:

1 Who are the most powerful people/units in your organization?
2 Why? What is the basis of their power?

Notes

Sources of power

Power acquisition is not just a matter of chance or personality. McCall (1979) argues that it is possible to predict where power will reside in an organization. He suggests that power accrues from position, timing, resources and past actions. The constituencies or stakeholder groups that are most powerful are those that:

▶ are in a position to deal with important problems facing the organization
▶ have control over significant resources valued by others

> ▶ are lucky or skilled enough to bring problems and resources together at the same time
> ▶ are centrally connected in the work flow of the organization
> ▶ are not easily replaced
> ▶ have successfully used power in the past.

In order to ensure the successful introduction of change, it is essential that change managers secure the assistance of powerful stakeholders and build a critical mass of support for the change.

Stakeholders

Freeman (1984) defines a stakeholder as any individual or group who can affect or is affected by the achievement of the organization's objectives. In the context of evaluating corporate performance, Clarkson (1995) widened the traditional definition to include the government and the communities that provide infrastructure and markets – whose laws must be obeyed, and to whom taxes and other obligations may be due – as well as traditional stakeholder groups such as employees, shareholders, investors, customers and suppliers. Stakeholders other than employees can exercise considerable influence over the outcome of many strategic change initiatives, but often the success of a project is highly dependent on support from other organizational members. Several examples illustrate this point.

McNulty and Ferlie (2002) attribute the lack of success of a project to change the care process for patients in the accident and emergency (A&E) department of a large UK hospital to the change agents' failure to generate sufficient support for the change from senior doctors and nurses. Clinical staff viewed the attempt to introduce change as interference from 'outside' by people who lacked adequate experience and understanding of the work of the department. They were suspicious of the change agents' objectives, and believed that the project failed to address the core problems of the department and was more concerned with achieving cost savings rather than improving the services provided to patients. McNulty and Ferlie also report that A&E doctors viewed the process-based philosophy behind the initiative as a threat to the established function of the A&E department in the broader context of the hospital and to the roles of doctors within the department.

In a large manufacturing company, a change was blocked by a senior manager who was not immediately involved in any of the departments directly affected by the change but who was pursuing a separate agenda that was inconsistent with the proposed change. The proposal was to drive down costs by centralizing procurement in order to gain economies of scale. It had many supporters but the senior manager who opposed it did so because he favoured the company adopting a more decentralized structure.

While internal stakeholders can exercise considerable influence, external stakeholders can also be important. Local residents in a UK city were offended – to the point of rioting in the streets – when a large leisure company decided to rebrand its bingo halls as 'Mecca Bingo'. The problem arose because the company failed to recognize the impact of demographic changes, which resulted in many of its bingo halls being located in neighbourhoods with predominantly Islamic populations. Another example involved the Bank of Scotland when some customers, including West Lothian Council with a £250m account, threatened to close their accounts in protest at the bank's proposed joint business venture with US evangelist Pat Robertson. Customers were unhappy with the proposal after he proclaimed that Scotland was a 'dark land' and a stronghold of homosexuality. These examples illustrate the point that it is not always easy to identify all the individuals and groups who may be affected by a change or who have the power to influence the outcome of the change.

Which stakeholders should be taken into account by change managers?

Jones and Wicks (1999) identify two divergent theoretical positions regarding stakeholder management.

Normative theories

According to normative or ethics-based theories of stakeholder management, the interests of all stakeholders have intrinsic value and should be taken into account when formulating strategy and planning and implementing change. Berman et al. (1999) note that ethics-based theories hold that many claims of stakeholders are based on fundamental moral principles unrelated to the stakeholders' instrumental value to the organization. Those who subscribe to normative theories argue that moral commitments should provide the basis for managing stakeholder relationships rather than the desire to use stakeholders to promote managerial interests.

Instrumental theories

The basic premise of instrumental theories is that managers will only attend to the interests of stakeholders to the extent that those stakeholders can affect their interests. They posit that managers are selective in who they attend to and are not motivated by a concern for the welfare of stakeholders in general. Managerial interests vary, and may range from parochial concerns such as status or the end of year bonus, to more strategic concerns such as marketplace success and organizational survival. In most formulations of the instrumental approach, however, managerial interests are equated with the firm's financial performance and the satisfaction of shareholders. Schein (1996: 15) refers to a tacit set of assumptions that CEOs and their immediate subordinates appear to share worldwide:

> This executive worldview is built around the necessity to maintain an organization's financial health and is preoccupied with boards, investors, and capital markets. Executives may have other preoccupations but they cannot get away from having to worry about the financial survival and growth of their organization.

At lower levels in the organization, however, many managers may be more concerned with managing relationships with different stakeholders who can have a more immediate impact on the performance of their department.

Implicit in the instrumental perspective is the assumption that change managers will abandon modes of dealing with stakeholders that prove to be unproductive. Berman et al. (1999) argue that while a firm might try to improve sales by adopting a total quality management approach that involves investing considerable effort in improving relationships with workers and suppliers, it might reassess its commitment to this strategy if it fails to deliver results. Similarly, an organization might adopt an employee share ownership scheme in the hope that it will motivate organizational members to work more effectively, but might abandon the scheme if it has little effect on performance.

The instrumental approach to stakeholder management is highly pragmatic. In the context of change management, regardless of the purpose of the change, it dictates that the change manager will focus attention on those relationships that will affect the success of the change.

A life cycle approach to stakeholder management

Jawahar and McLaughlin (2001) offer an approach to managing stakeholders that draws on resource dependence theory, prospect theory and organizational life cycle modules. The underlying premise is that an organization faces different pressures and threats at different stages in its life cycle. Consequently, over time, certain stakeholders will become more important than others because of their ability to satisfy critical organizational needs. Their theory identifies which stakeholders will be important at different stages in the organizational life cycle and indicates how the organization will attempt to deal with each of its primary stakeholders at every stage. Although Jawahar and McLaughlin focused their attention on stakeholder management at different stages of an organization's life cycle, their theory offers many insights into the management of stakeholders at different stages of the life cycle of specific change projects.

The contribution of resource dependence theory

Resource dependence theory conceptualizes the organization as being dependent on the resources in its environment for survival and growth. Jawahar and McLaughlin (2001) extend this theory to stakeholder management and propose that organizations will pay most attention to those stakeholder groups who control resources critical to the organization's survival. The different levels of attention that they devote to different groups of stakeholders are manifest in the form of different stakeholder management strategies. Following Carroll (1979), Clarkson (1995) and others, it is possible to identify four types of stakeholder management strategy:

▶ *Proactive* – doing a great deal to address stakeholder issues
▶ *Accommodating* – a less active approach for dealing with stakeholder issues
▶ *Defending* – doing only the legally minimum required to address stakeholder issues
▶ *Ignoring* – ignoring or refusing to address stakeholder issues.

The contribution of prospect theory

Prospect theory posits that, relative to whatever reference point is used to evaluate an outcome, which might be the current position or a level of benefit that an individual hopes to achieve, outcomes that are evaluated as losses are weighted more heavily than similar amounts of outcome that are evaluated as gains. Central to prospect theory is the notion that actual (objective) and psychological (subjective) values attributed to an outcome can and do differ. Kahneman and Tversky (1979) argue that the relationship between the actual and psychological value of an option can be depicted by an S-shaped value function that is concave in the domain of gains and convex in the domain of losses. Bazerman (2001) illustrates the effect of this relationship by suggesting that the pain associated with losing $1,000 is generally perceived to be greater than the pleasure associated with winning a similar amount. Kahneman and Tversky hypothesized that individuals will be risk seeking in the loss domain and risk averse in the gain domain, and that their choice between certain (no-risk) and risky options will depend on whether the outcome of the choice is framed in positive terms, for example jobs saved, or negative terms, for example jobs lost.

Bazerman (2001) provides an example of how this might work in practice. He describes a plant closure problem. When managers are presented with a positively framed version of the problem, the majority select plan A, the option with the 'certain' outcome (Table 8.1).

Table 8.1 *Positive frame*

Plan A 'Certain' (no-risk) outcome Selected by the majority		Plan B High-risk outcome
Save one of three plants and 2,000 of 6,000 jobs	*versus*	1 in 3 chance of saving all three plants and all 6,000 jobs, but a 2 in 3 chance of saving no plants and no jobs

However, when managers are presented with a negatively framed version of the same problem, the majority select plan D, which is the risky option (Table 8.2).

Table 8.2 *Negative frame*

Plan C 'Certain' (no-risk) outcome		Plan D High-risk outcome Selected by the majority
Lose two of the three plants and 4,000 jobs	*versus*	2 in 3 chance of losing all three plants and all 6,000 jobs, but a 1 in 3 chance of losing no plants and no jobs

Both sets of alternative plans are objectively the same. Plan A (saving one of three plants and 2,000 of 6,000 jobs) offers the same objective outcome as plan C (losing two of the three plants and 4,000 of the 6,000 jobs), and plan B offers the same objective outcome as plan D.

Jawahar and McLaughlin (2001: 404) point to the essence of prospect theory:

> in the context of gains, individuals will be risk averse and choose the option with a certain outcome over a risky option, whereas in the context of losses, individuals will be risk seeking and choose the risky option over the option with a certain outcome.

They go on to argue that addressing the concerns of all stakeholders in a proactive or accommodating manner is a certain or risk-averse option, because it is likely to persuade all stakeholders to provide the organization with the resources it requires for survival and prosperity. However, using proactive and accommodating strategies to address the concerns of only some stakeholders and using defending and ignoring strategies to address the issues of others is a more risky option.

Based on these contributions from resource dependence theory and prospect theory, Jawahar and McLaughlin (2001) take the first step towards the development of their descriptive stakeholder theory by proposing two theorems:

1 In the absence of threats to organizational survival, a 'gain frame' will be adopted, and the organization will follow a risk-averse strategy and actively address all stakeholder issues.

2 In the presence of threats to organizational survival, a 'loss frame' will be adopted, and the organization will pursue a risky strategy that involves addressing the concerns of only those stakeholders who are relevant to the immediate loss threat, while defending or denying any responsibility for the concerns of other stakeholders. For example, if a firm is in danger of being forced into administration, senior managers might do everything possible to address the concerns of creditors while giving little attention to the concerns of employees.

The contribution of organizational life cycle models

Most organizational life cycle models point to four overlapping phases in the life of an organization: start-up, emerging growth, maturity and decline/revival. The pressures, threats and opportunities, internal as well as external, that confront firms vary with the stages of the organizational life cycle. Consequently, the resources required by the firm will also vary with life cycle stages.

Jawahar and McLaughlin (2001) argue that if at any stage in the organizational (or change project) life cycle, the fulfilment of critical resource requirements is threatened, organizational decision makers will adopt a loss frame and interact with those stakeholders who control the critical resources in a proactive or accommodating manner, and with other stakeholders in a defensive or reactive manner. In those stages where the flow of resources is not threatened, decision makers are likely to adopt a gain frame, pursue a risk-averse strategy and actively address the concerns of all stakeholders.

Jawahar and McLaughlin's stakeholder theory

Drawing on organizational life cycle, resource dependence and prospect theories, Jawahar and McLaughlin (2001) argue that:

1 At any given life cycle stage, certain stakeholders become more important than others because of their potential to satisfy critical organizational needs
2 It is possible to identify which stakeholders are likely to be more or less important at each stage of the life cycle
3 The strategy that will be used to deal with each stakeholder will depend on the importance of that stakeholder relative to other stakeholders.

This stakeholder theory is based on the premise that organizations have finite resources and at times they are in short supply. Consequently, managers have to decide how best to allocate them in order to manage stakeholders in the most effective way possible. Jawahar and McLaughlin's theory suggests that different individuals and groups might need to be the focus of change managers' attention at different points in the life cycle of a particular change project. Change managers must not assume that if they engage in the kind of stakeholder analysis suggested below, they will have identified, once and for all, the key constituents who require attention. Power relationships and the ability of various individuals and groups to influence events will change over time and therefore it may be necessary to review and manage stakeholder relationships on a continuing basis.

Managing stakeholders

Building on the key player matrix developed by Piercy (1989), Grundy (1998) suggests a useful approach for managing stakeholder relationships. The first part of the process involves a stakeholder analysis to identify important stakeholders and appraise their power to influence and their attitude towards the proposed change. The second part involves developing a strategy for persuading influential stakeholders to support the change.

Case study 8.1

Stakeholder brainstorm

Familiarize yourself with this departmental merger case and list all the individuals and groups who can affect or might be affected by the outcome of the change.

You are the recently appointed human resources (HR) director of a newly merged acute hospital trust in West Yorkshire. You have been in post four weeks. The new trust has been formed from the merger of two co-located hospital trusts (A and B). The new chief executive (CE) was appointed five months ago. He was previously CE of trust B. You moved to your post from elsewhere in the NHS.

You were the last of the directors to be appointed. The board is in place but the structure of the new trust has not, as yet, been finalized. The two parts of the new trust continue to operate much as they did before the merger. However, the CE feels that the HR and finance functions need to be reorganized as quickly as possible. He also expects that the HR and finance functions will help to facilitate the merger of other parts of the new trust.

You have been tasked with merging the HR departments of the two former trusts and achieving an annual saving of £100k on the HR budget. It is obvious that the HR staff have high expectations about what you will deliver. Almost everybody wants the merger of the two departments to be completed quickly, but with minimum disruption to the status quo.

There are important differences in the culture and structure of the two original trusts and these differences are reflected in the way their HR departments operate. A potential problem is that the staff in both HR departments, and line managers in their respective former trusts, appear to be happy with the way things are operating at present and would like their way of working to be the template for the new merged department.

The members of staff who work in the two HR departments are located in hospitals 15 miles apart. Irrespective of whether the way forward will involve bringing all the staff together, the staff working in what was trust B will have to move, even if only to a new location on their present site, because their existing accommodation has been reallocated. Your impression is that people will be reluctant to move between sites.

Some of the main differences between the two original trusts are shown in Table 8.3.

Table 8.3 · *Differences between the two trusts*

Trust A	Trust B
Decentralized structure. Two big and largely autonomous directorates (surgery and medicine) each with its own operational director	Centralized structure. Many small departments led by general managers who report directly to the CE
Fragmented culture, medical staff and managers are separate groups	Collaborative culture, medical staff and managers work closely together
The HR department is only responsible for personnel information and employee relations. Training and development is located under nursing	All the HR functions, including training and development, are centralized within one department
The HR department employs a small group of staff who tend to stay within their own department and act as professional advisers to the operational managers. Operational managers are responsible for much of the HR management within their own departments	The HR department is 'staff rich'. HR staff work closely with operational managers, accompany them to meetings, take notes for them and assume responsibility for much of the day-to-day HR activity
Line managers hold personnel files in operational departments	HR holds personnel files centrally

You recognize that it may be necessary to slim down the HR establishment if you are to achieve the £100k cost savings. Additional issues that might influence your approach to managing this change are:

1 The two former heads of the HR functions, who are still leading the two departments, have different philosophies about the nature of HR.
2 Since the two trusts were merged, there has been a rapid rise in the number of grievances registered by staff across the new trust, especially from staff required to work alongside colleagues from the other former trust. Most of these grievances relate to the differences in terms and conditions that apply across the new trust. For example, there are differences in the protection agreements that safeguard an individual's pay and conditions when their work is regraded, and there are differences in holiday entitlements that lead to problems when members of the two

former trusts start working together. This has had a marked effect on the day-to-day workload of sections of your staff.

3 Managers across the new trust are seeking help from HR on issues related to the merger. This presents you with two related issues. First, it adds to the HR workload problem. At a time when HR needs to allocate resources to managing its own internal merger, it has to respond to new demands from client departments. Second, managers across the new trust, depending on where they worked previously, have different expectations regarding the support HR should provide.

You are required to develop a plan to bring together the two HR departments in order to:

- Create a new HR function that will promote excellent HR practice
- Deliver efficiency gains of £100k p.a.

Task: Brainstorm a list of stakeholders

Identifying the power and commitment of stakeholders

Grundy (1998) presents identifying the power and commitment of stakeholders as involving three steps:

1 He refers to the first step as the 'stakeholder brainstorm'. This involves identifying all those who might be affected by and/or could affect the outcome of the proposed change.

2 The second step involves assessing how much power and influence each group of stakeholders has. This can be quite difficult in practice:

- There may be people with little influence over organizational issues in general but who have considerable influence over a particular issue related to the change.
- There may be individuals who express support for the change but who cannot be relied on because their supportive efforts are undermined by other people in their departments.
- There may be people who have exercised little influence in the past but who have more power than anticipated or who have recently acquired the ability to influence others.

3 The third step involves assessing stakeholders' attitudes towards the proposed change. Again this can be difficult. For example:

- There may be individuals or groups who appear to support the proposal in public but who work against it behind the scenes.
- There may be others who misunderstand the proposed change but who would be supportive if they were better informed.

Attitudes can range from positive, through neutral to negative. Shaw and Maletz (1995) describe those who proactively work to prevent the change effort from succeeding as 'blockers', and those who proactively work to ensure that it succeeds as 'sponsors'.

The two dimensions of 'attitude' and 'power' are brought together in the stakeholder grid presented in Change tool 8.1.

Case study 8.2   Stakeholder mapping

Developing the merger case presented in Case study 8.1, imagine that your initial vision for the new HR function is one where:

- There will be a core group of HR professionals working on strategic HR issues. Most day-to-day operational matters will be devolved to line managers. The HR department will only work on operational issues where there are clear benefits from providing a centralized service. These benefits could be cost savings or service quality.
- Training and development will be moved from nursing to HR, but some delivery – especially the day-to-day aspects of work-based training – will be based in operational departments.
- The HR function will be restructured. Instead of the two existing departments (based on the former trusts), each providing a full range of services, work will be reallocated into two broad portfolios and will be managed on a new trust-wide basis. You (the new HR director) will manage one of these portfolios and the other will be managed by one of the heads of the two former HR departments.
- While you feel that it necessary for HR to have a 'presence' on each of the two major sites, you feel that on one of the sites, this should be limited to a small number of staff who will work alongside line managers as advisers.
- You want to co-locate most staff on a single site but you feel that this might be easier to achieve if everybody moved to a new location on one of the existing sites in order to avoid the feeling that one of the former departments has been 'taken over' by the other.

Before you begin to test out this vision with others or start to develop a plan to move from the current situation to your vision for the HR function, think about the others who may have a stake in the change and how they might react.

Change tool 8.1   Stakeholder grid

Task: Locate all the stakeholders who can affect or might be affected by the outcome of the change onto the stakeholder grid below.

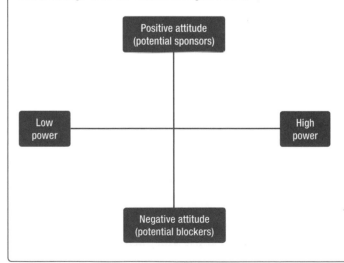

Influencing stakeholders to support the change

The second part of the process described by Grundy (1998) involves the change manager acting in ways that will ensure maximum support for the change. This might involve:

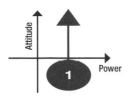

1 *Winning the support of those who oppose the change and who have the power to influence the outcome:* Changing powerful blockers into sponsors might be achieved by providing them with information that could persuade them to be more supportive, involving them in the change process in order to give them more control over the outcome, or bargaining with them to win their support.

   Listening to why they oppose the change and indicating a willingness to at least consider revising the change plan can be an effective way of winning their support. Sometimes change managers are so concerned with being right that they lose sight of their original goal. Ford and Ford (2009) argue that stubbornly pushing things through without even trying to understand the 'blockers' point of view can waste a valuable opportunity to engage the sceptics.

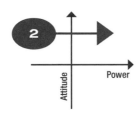

2 *Increasing the influence of those stakeholders who are already supportive:* This might be achieved, for example, by working to secure their appointment to decision-making groups that regulate matters related to the proposed change.

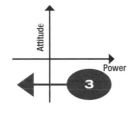

3 *Reducing the influence of powerful blockers:* This might be achieved in a number of ways. For example, managers can challenge the arguments blockers use to oppose the change. They can also take steps to marginalize them from the decision-making process by working to ensure that they are not members of the committee or group that has to sanction the change, or transferring them to another part of the organization.

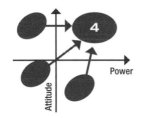

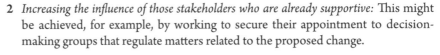

4 *Building a coalition of supportive stakeholders who will be prepared to work together to support the change:* This might involve communicating an inspiring vision that highlights mutual benefits and encourages independent groups of stakeholders to align themselves with the change manager's purpose.

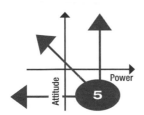

5 *Fragmenting existing coalitions who are antagonistic towards the change:* This might involve picking off key players in the coalition and providing them with information that could persuade them to be more supportive, or bargaining with them to win their support (as in 1 above) or undermining their case (as in 3 above).

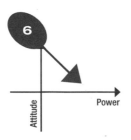

6 *Bringing new sponsors or champions into play:* This could involve persuading 'players' who have not been proactive to take a more active part in influencing events. It may also involve publicising the proposed change within the company or in the wider community, via the media, in order to seek support from powerful individuals or groups who may be unknown to the change manager. However, this kind of intervention is not without risk because it could also attract the attention of unknown others who may be opposed to the change.

Another possibility that the change manager might consider is reformulating the change in a way that will make it more acceptable to a wider range of stakeholders.

Case study 8.3

Managing stakeholder relationships

1   Review the stakeholder map you produced in Change tool 8.1 and indicate how you would attend to the concerns of stakeholders. Which stakeholders would you:

- *address proactively* – do a great deal to address their concerns? Indicate with a 'P' on your stakeholder map.
- *accommodate* – take a less active approach to dealing with their concerns? Indicate with an 'A' on your stakeholder map.
- *ignore* – do the legal minimum or refuse to address their concerns? Indicate with an 'I' on your stakeholder map.

Reflect on how the project might unfold and consider whether any of the stakeholders you decided to ignore might become more important at a later date.

2   What steps would you take to increase support or reduce opposition for your proposed way of managing the merger?

Notes

An important point to remember is that as a change project unfolds and as circumstances change, the identity of key stakeholders may also change. This can have implications for how you decide to manage stakeholder relationships over the short term because some stakeholders who may be unimportant today could become much more important in the future. If they feel that their interests have been disregarded in the past, they may be reluctant to support the change manager in the future.

How one set of stakeholders is managed can also affect the attitudes and behaviour of others. For example, the way redundancies are managed can impact the commitment and motivation of survivors. There is a widely held view that if leavers are seen to be treated badly, this will adversely affect the motivation and commitment of those who have kept their jobs. Early work on the 'survivor syndrome' (see Brockner, 1992; Doherty and Horsted, 1995) focused attention on how the good treatment of leavers can help to maintain the support of survivors. While there is evidence to support this proposition, a more recent study (Sahdev, 2004) has shown that focusing too much attention on pleasing leavers can have a negative effect on the behaviour of survivors (see Research report 8.1).

Research report 8.1 > **Perceptions of fair treatment**

Sahdev, K. (2004) Revisiting the survivor syndrome: the role of leadership in implementing downsizing, *European Journal of Work and Organizational Psychology*, **13**(2): 165–96

Sahdev's qualitative study compared the effects of two different approaches to managing redundancies. She studied two organizations, Barclaycard and SKF UK Ltd, over a four-and-a-half-year period, collecting data from company documents, one-to-one interviews and focus groups. These two organizations were selected because they were located in different sectors and had different experiences of downsizing. SKF UK had been downsizing since 1974, whereas this was the first experience of downsizing for Barclaycard. In both organizations, downsizing was accompanied by a transformation change programme.

Barclaycard, anticipating greater competition, had proactively embarked on a three-year re-engineering programme designed to reduce costs and deliver better service to customers. It involved a big investment in new technology, the redesign of roles and responsibilities and the introduction of a matrix structure. As part of the change, 1,100 employees were made redundant. Guided by state-of-the-art knowledge (including research on the survivor syndrome), the company focused strongly on accommodating leavers by pursuing a transparent redundancy process, applying fair decision rules, and providing substantial support for leavers in terms of outplacement and redundancy packages.

While the majority of those who were made redundant felt that they had been fairly treated, employees who were retained felt let down by the company. The new technology did not deliver the high service levels that had been promised. Response speeds were too slow, making it difficult to satisfy customer needs. Customer service advisers also failed to achieve their targets, creating high levels of anxiety. Employees began to question the rationale for the change and the capability of senior management to handle the re-engineering programme. Senior managers were rarely visible throughout the change process and many employees felt that the changes were implemented mechanistically with little regard for those who had to make them work. Furthermore, the way senior managers announced the impending downsizing created false expectations. Everybody assumed that they could take the severance package and many started to make plans for 'life after Barclaycard'. Unfortunately, lots of applications for voluntary redundancy were rejected and many of those who did not want to be part of the new world were forced to stay on.

The outcome, contrary to the company's expectations, was that while every effort had been made to manage the redundancy process in a positive and supportive way, this approach had failed to retain the commitment and support of those employees who were retained. Sahdev attributes this to the lack of attention that was given to the needs of survivors.

SKF UK was pushed into a major change programme because, compared with other SKF sites, the UK operation was a high-cost, low-quality producer of ball bearings. In order to avoid closure, it embarked on a lean manufacturing transformation programme. This involved shifting responsibility down the hierarchy to blue-collar workers who were directly involved in the manufacturing process, and empowering them to take whatever actions might be necessary to eliminate waste and improve quality. Managers were supportive and engaged with the production operatives to ensure that they had the resources to manage the many challenges they faced on a daily basis. Management also made a significant investment in educating the entire workforce to acquire new skills, for which they received extra pay. Overstaffing was addressed through a voluntary redundancy programme, which targeted those workers who had been with the company for a long time and who genuinely wanted to take early retirement rather than retrain and adopt the new ways of working. The severance scheme was generous and allowed people to leave with dignity.

Compared to the survivors in Barclaycard, those who stayed on in SFK were more committed to the company. Sahdev suggests that this was because, while SKF gave people the choice of leaving with a generous severance package, the company also gave high priority to the needs of those who chose to stay. Barclaycard, on the other hand, paid too much attention to the leavers and insufficient attention to winning the commitment of those who were retained.

Sahdev's study suggests that downsizing needs to be managed in a way that directly attends to the needs of both leavers and survivors. Focusing attention on leavers, while necessary, is not sufficient to ensure the commitment of those who are retained.

Reflect on the issues discussed in this chapter and addressed in Case studies 8.1–8.3 and consider how they apply to the management of stakeholders in your organization (Exercise 8.2).

Exercise 8.2 **Stakeholder analysis**

Think about a recent change in your organization and with the advantage of hindsight:

- identify the stakeholders involved in the change
- classify them according to their power to influence and their attitude towards the change
- assess the extent to which the change manager was aware of these stakeholders and took proper account of them when managing the change.

> **Notes**
>
>
>
>
>
>
>
>
>
>
>
>
>

Summary

This chapter explores the politics of organizational change and points to the importance of enlisting support from key stakeholders.

Organizations are conceptualized as a collection of constituencies, each pursuing their own objectives:

▶ Individuals and groups attempt to influence each other in the pursuit of self-interest

▶ When there is a conflict of interest, it is the power and influence of those involved that determines the outcome rather than logical and rational argument
▶ In order to ensure the successful introduction of change, it is essential that change managers secure the assistance of powerful stakeholders and build a critical mass of support for the change
▶ Stakeholders are any individuals or groups who can affect or are affected by a change.

Political behaviour tends to be more intense in times of change because individuals and groups perceive the possibility of upsetting the existing balance of power. Some may be motivated to defend the status quo, whereas others may perceive change as an opportunity to improve their position. Consequently, change managers need to be alert to these political dynamics, especially to the possibility that others may be motivated to act in ways that undermine their efforts to bring about change.

Jones and Wicks (1999) identify two divergent theoretical positions regarding stakeholder management:

▶ *Normative*: all stakeholders should be taken into account. Moral commitments should provide the basis of managing stakeholder relationships rather than the desire to use stakeholders to promote managerial interests.
▶ *Instrumental*: managers will only attend to the interests of stakeholders to the extent that they can affect their interests.

Jawahar and McLaughlin's (2001) instrumental theory of stakeholder management provides a conceptual framework for identifying and managing stakeholders. It draws on:

▶ *Resource dependence theory* – organizations are dependent on the resources in their environment for survival and growth.
▶ *Prospect theory* – outcomes that are evaluated as losses are weighted more heavily than similar amounts of outcome that are evaluated as gains. Individuals will be risk seeking in the loss domain and risk averse in the gain domain.
▶ *Organizational life cycle models* – the pressures that threaten the success of a change project will vary with the stages of the project life cycle. Consequently, the resources required will also vary with life cycle stages.

Based on contributions from resource dependence theory and prospect theory, Jawahar and McLaughlin (2001) propose two theorems:

1 In the absence of threats, a gain frame will be adopted, and the organization will follow a risk-averse strategy and actively address all stakeholder issues.
2 In the presence of threats, a loss frame will be adopted, and the organization will pursue a risky strategy that involves addressing the concerns of only those stakeholders who are relevant to the immediate loss threat, while defending or denying any responsibility for the concerns of other stakeholders.

Based on contributions from life cycle models, Jawahar and McLaughlin argue that if at any stage in the organizational (or change project) life cycle, the fulfilment of critical resource requirements is threatened, organizational decision makers will adopt a loss frame and interact with those stakeholders who control the critical resources in a proactive or accommodating manner and with other stakeholders in a defensive manner. In those stages where the flow of resources is not threatened, decision makers are likely to adopt a gain frame, pursue a risk-averse strategy and actively address the concerns of all stakeholders.

The following points emerged as important:

1　At any given stage in a change project, certain stakeholders emerge as more important than others because of their potential to satisfy critical organizational needs.
2　It is possible to identify which stakeholders are likely to be more or less important at each stage.
3　The strategy that will be used to deal with each stakeholder will depend on the importance of that stakeholder relative to other stakeholders.

The stakeholder grid is introduced as a useful tool for identifying the power of stakeholders and their predisposition to support or oppose the change.

References

Bazerman, M. (2001) *Judgement in Managerial Decision Making* (5th edn), Chichester: Wiley.

Berman, S.L., Wicks, A.C., Kotha, S. and Jones, T.M. (1999) Does stakeholder orientation matter? The relationship between stakeholder management models and firm financial performance, *Academy of Management Journal*, **42**(5): 488–506.

Brockner, J. (1992) Managing the effects of layoffs on others, *California Management Review*, **34**(4): 9–27.

Carroll, A.B. (1979) A three dimensional conceptual model of corporate social performance, *Academy of Management Review*, 4: 497–505.

Clarkson, M.B. (1995) A stakeholder framework for analyzing and evaluating corporate social performance, *Academy of Management Review*, **20**(1): 92–117.

Doherty, N. and Horsted, J. (1995) Helping survivors stay on board, *People Management*, **1**(1): 26–31.

Ford, J.D. and Ford, L.W. (2009) Decoding resistance to change, *Harvard Business Review*, **87**(4): 99–103.

Freeman, R.E. (1984) *Strategic Management: A Stakeholders Approach*, Boston: HarperCollins.

Grundy, T. (1998) Strategy implementation and project management, *International Journal of Project Management*, **16**(1): 48–50.

Jawahar, M. and McLaughlin, G.L. (2001) Toward a descriptive stakeholder theory: an organizational life cycle approach, *Academy of Management Review*, **26**(3): 397–414.

Jones, T.M. and Wicks, A.C. (1999) Convergent stakeholder theory, *Academy of Management Review*, **24**(2): 206–21.

Kahneman, D. and Tversky, A. (1979) Prospect theory: an analysis of decisions under risk, *Econimetrica*, 47: 263–91.

McCall, M.W. (1979) Power, influence and authority, in S. Kerr (ed.) *Organizational Behaviour*, Columbus, OH: Grid Publishing.

McClelland, D.C. (1975) *Power: The Inner Experience*, New York: Irvington.

McNulty, T. and Ferlie, E. (2002) *Reengineering Health Care: The Complexities of Organizational Transformation*, Oxford: Oxford University Press.

McNulty, T. and Ferlie, E. (2003) Redesigning public services, *British Journal of Management*, Supplement **1**(1): 14–35.

Nadler, D.A. (1987) The effective management of organizational change, in J.W. Lorsch (ed.) *Handbook of Organizational Behaviour*, Englewood Cliffs, NJ: Prentice Hall.

Pettigrew, A.M. (1972) Information control as a power resource, *Sociology*, **6**(2): 187–204.

Piercy, N. (1989) Diagnosing and solving implementation problems in strategic planning, *Journal of General Management*, **15**(1): 19–38.

Sahdev, K. (2004) Revisiting the survivor syndrome: the role of leadership in implementing downsizing, *European Journal of Work and Organizational Psychology*, **13**(2): 165–96.

Schein, E.H. (1996) The three cultures of management: the key to organizational learning, *Sloan Management Review*, **38**(1): 9–20.

Shaw, B.R. and Maletz, M.C. (1995) Business processes: embracing the logic and limits of reengineering, in D.A. Nadler, R.B. Shaw and A.E. Walton (eds) *Discontinuous Change: Leading Organizational Transformation*, San Francisco: Jossey-Bass.

The role of leadership in change management

Leadership is widely regarded as the key enabler of the change process but there appears to be considerable debate about what constitutes good leadership. Drawing on Northouse (2004), leadership is defined here as a process that involves influencing others to achieve desired goals.

Tichy and Devanna (1986) and Kotter (1990) draw attention to a tension between management and leadership. They argue that management is concerned with maintaining the existing organization, whereas leadership is more concerned with change. In other words, management is about 'doing things right' and leadership is about 'doing the right things' (Bennis and Nanus, 1985: 21). This chapter reviews the role of leadership,

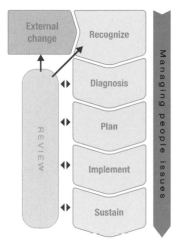

explores the proposition that in times of change, managerial work is increasingly a leadership task and considers the view that leadership needs to be viewed as a collective process.

The role of leadership

Kotter (1990) argues that there is marked difference in the orientation between management and leadership. Both involve deciding what needs to be done, developing the capacity to do it, and ensuring that it is done. However, while management is concerned with order and consistency, leadership is concerned with change.

Deciding what needs to be done

▶ *Management* involves deciding what needs to be done through a process of goal setting, establishing detailed steps for achieving these goals and identifying and allocating the resources necessary for their achievement, through planning and budgeting.
▶ *Leadership*, on the other hand, focuses on setting a direction and developing the strategies necessary to move in that direction, that is, creating and achieving a vision (see Kotter, 1990).

There is wide acceptance that a strong vision can make a valuable contribution to the success of a change initiative, but sometimes too little attention is given to the consequences of leaders developing a vision that is not fit for purpose. It is essential that those exercising leadership make a realist assessment of the opportunities and constraints facing the organization and that they are sensitive to the needs and priorities of key stakeholders. Conger (1990) suggests that sometimes this does not happen.

One reason for this is that leaders become so committed to a project or belief that they only attend to information that supports their own position and fail to recognize signals that point to, for example, changes in customer requirements or the availability of resources. A history of past successes can contribute to this condition. In Chapter 3, reference is made to the 'trap of success', where past experience promotes a sense of self-belief and arrogance. This encourages the leader to plough ahead without giving sufficient consideration to the needs or concerns raised by others. Conger (1990) provides examples of the inventor with a pet idea who succeeds in acquiring sufficient resources to initiate a venture that eventually fails to meet the market's needs, and the CEO who is motivated to accelerate the realization of a vision after early successes.

A related problem is that leaders, even when they become aware that their vision is flawed, refuse to change. Conger (1990) suggests that this can be explained by 'cognitive dissonance'. Leaders continue to pursue past commitments because a failure to do so would damage their favourable perceptions of themselves.

The leader's relationships with others can also lead to circumstances where a clearly flawed vision goes unchallenged. Subordinates may fear repercussions if they challenge the leader's view or they become too dependent on and trusting in the leader's judgement. Some writers argue that charismatic leaders who have dominant personalities can promote this kind of unquestioning dependence. This lack of challenge can also develop in those circumstances where the leadership team becomes so committed to a single ideology that they engage in what Janis (1972) described as 'groupthink'.

In terms of the ideas discussed in Chapter 18 (on organizational learning), management is more focused on developing plans to do things better, whereas leadership needs to involve more double loop thinking about what is the right thing to do. It involves attending to a wide range of cues that might signal emerging opportunities or problems and setting a direction that will maximize future benefit. Recognizing the need or opportunity for change is a key leadership task, which is discussed in Chapter 3.

Those who are in a position to formulate the agenda for change need to develop a vision that serves the interests of key stakeholders. Kotter (1995) argues that visions that ignore the legitimate needs and rights of some stakeholders, favouring certain stakeholders over others, may never be achieved. However, as discussed in Chapter 8 (on stakeholder management), sometimes leaders may have to give preference to the interests of some stakeholders over others.

Bruch et al. (2005) also argue that leadership decisions about the 'right thing to do' need to be made before the management decisions about 'how to do the change right', otherwise ongoing debates about 'does the change make sense?' will rob the project of its energy and weaken the implementation process.

Developing the capacity to do it

▶ *Management* involves developing the capacity to accomplish the organization's agenda by organizing and staffing.
▶ *Leadership* focuses on aligning people, communicating the new direction and creating coalitions committed to getting there.

Kotter (1990) asserts that a common problem is that the vision is poorly communicated. Key aspects of many change programmes are grossly undercommunicated, but insufficient communication is not the only problem. Conger (1990) points to miscommunication as a potential problem. He argues that sometimes leaders present information in ways that make their vision appear more realistic and more appealing than it really is, and they communicate in ways that foster an illusion of control when the reality is that things are out of control. In Chapter 4, the need to create a sense of confidence in order to promote a readiness to change is discussed, but this has to be done ethically. Sometimes information is manipulated in a way that encourages people, employees and investors, to make decisions that are neither in their own nor the organization's best interest.

Communicating in a way that aligns people to achieve the vision is an important role of leadership. Kotter argues that a central feature of modern organizations is interdependence, where no one has complete autonomy, and where most members of the organization are tied to many others by their work, technology, management systems and hierarchy. Kotter (1996) argues that these linkages present a special challenge when organizations attempt to change because unless individuals line up and move together, they will get in each others' way and fall over one another. Kühl et al. (2005) argue that managers throughout the organization have to engage in 'lateral leadership' to create a shared understanding, influence the political process and develop trust. Transformational leaders have the ability to identify those who might be able to support or sabotage an initiative, network with them and communicate in a credible way what needs to be done. Aligning people in this way empowers them, even people at lower levels of the organization. When there is a clear, and shared, sense of direction, committed stakeholders, including subordinates, are more likely to feel able to take action without encountering undue conflict with others or being reprimanded by superiors.

Ensuring that it is done

▶ *Management* involves ensuring that people accomplish plans by controlling and problem solving.
▶ *Leadership* is more concerned with motivating and inspiring.

Kotter (1995) believes that inspiring others and generating highly energized behaviour can help them to overcome the inevitable barriers to change they will encounter as the initiative unfolds. He identifies four ways in which leaders can do this:

▶ articulating the vision in ways that are in accord with the values of the people they are addressing
▶ involving people in deciding how to achieve the vision, thereby giving them some sense of control
▶ supporting others' efforts to realize the vision by providing coaching, feedback and role modelling
▶ recognizing and rewarding success.

Managerial work, in times of change, is increasingly a leadership task

While management and leadership are distinct activities, they are complementary and both are necessary for success in a changing business environment. Bolden (2004) argues that it can be confusing to think about managers and leaders as though they are different, and to a large extent incompatible, people. For example, some talk about leaders as dynamic, charismatic individuals with the ability to inspire others, and managers as uninspiring bureaucrats who just focus on the task in hand. Bolden (2004: 7) asserts that such a view

> does not coincide well with the lived experience of being a manager. People are generally recruited into 'management', rather than 'leadership', positions and are expected to complete a multitude of tasks ranging from day-to-day planning and implementation, to longer-term strategic thinking. None of these are done in isolation.

Kotter (1999) argues that managers are the people who, typically, are in the best position to provide the leadership required to ensure that a change will be successful. However, if they are to provide this leadership, they need to recognize that their role involves a dual responsibility, for management – keeping the system operating effectively – and for leadership – revitalizing and renewing the system to ensure that it will remain effective over the longer term.

The thrust of the argument developed in Chapter 1 is that not only is the pace of change increasing, but that there is also a shift in emphasis towards managing discontinuous or transformational change. An implication of this shift is that leadership and the provision of a sense of direction are becoming more important parts of managerial work.

What leaders do

A lot of attention has been paid to what leaders do (the behavioural view) and how circumstances affect what they do (situational leadership).

In various chapters, more detailed attention is given to particular aspects of leadership behaviour. For example:

▶ recognizing the need for change – Chapters 2, 3 and 9
▶ identifying change goals – Chapters 2, 5, 6, 7, 9, 14 and 25
▶ communicating a sense of direction – Chapters 8, 9, 25, and 26
▶ formulating a change strategy – Chapters 2, 14 and 25
▶ involving others – Chapters 2, 4, 8, 14, 16, 18, 19, 20 and 28
▶ motivating people – Chapters 4, 8, 9 and 11
▶ providing support – Chapters 12, 13, 21 and 26
▶ creating an organizational context conducive to change – Chapters 26 and 29.

How they do it: leadership style

Attention is also focused on how they do it (see, for example, Chapters 8, 10, 13, 19, 20 and 22). The assumptions leaders make about others has a powerful effect on their leadership style. McGregor (1960) suggested that some managers hold a negative view of human nature. This is reflected in his theory X:

▶ The average person has an inherent dislike of work and will avoid it if they can.
▶ Because of this dislike of work, most people must be coerced, controlled, directed and threatened with punishment to get them to put forth adequate effort towards the achievement of organizational objectives.
▶ The average person prefers to be directed, wishes to avoid responsibility, has relatively little ambition and, above all, wants security.

Managers who hold these assumptions adopt a more directive and controlling leadership style. Theory X shares many of the assumptions that underpin Beer's (2001) economic change strategy, which focuses on the drive for economic value through tough, top-down, results-driven action.

The assumptions underpinning McGregor's theory Y are completely different:

▸ The expenditure of physical and mental effort in work is as natural as play or rest.
▸ External control and the threat of punishment are not the only means for bringing about effort towards organizational objectives. People will exercise self-direction and self-control in the service of objectives to which they are committed.
▸ Commitment to objectives is a function of the rewards associated with their achievement.
▸ The average person learns, under proper conditions, not only to accept but to seek responsibility.
▸ The capacity to exercise a relatively high degree of imagination, ingenuity and creativity in the solution of organizational problems is widely, and not narrowly, distributed in the population.

Managers who see other organizational members in this way are inclined to adopt a leadership style that promotes employee commitment to the change agenda and invests effort in developing their capacity to contribute to the achievement of change goals. This commitment maximization approach assumes that commitment is generated when people are trusted and allowed to work autonomously. It is an approach that shares many of the assumptions that underpin Beer's (2001) organizational development strategy for change, insofar as it involves creating the capabilities that organizational members require in order to deliver high performance and secure competitive advantage over the long term.

Early work on leadership styles suggested that some styles were superior to others. For example, Lewin et al. (1939) studied the effect of leadership styles in classroom situations and concluded that democratic leadership was more effective than an autocratic style. Later work by academics at Ohio State University identified two dimensions of leader behaviour that appeared to influence performance (Fleishman et al., 1955). They were 'consideration', the extent to which supervisors have relationships that are characterized by mutual trust, respect for subordinates' ideas and consideration of their feelings, and 'initiating structure', which reflects the extent to which the leader is inclined to define and structure the work of subordinates. Fleishman et al.'s (1955) findings suggested that effective leaders were those who were high on both consideration and structure. This provided the conceptual basis for Blake and Mouton's (1964) managerial grid, which pointed to 'team management' as the most effective leadership style

A leader's style can have positive and negative effects. For example, an aggressive and overly controlling style may alienate followers and other key stakeholders. A considerate style that encourages some subordinates to feel 'special' may have positive outcomes for that group, but may create 'us-versus-them' feelings between members of the in-group and others. An informal style that involves being visible and relating with people at all levels might help the leader to keep in touch with what is going on but may violate the chain of command and upset and confuse managers down the line.

Situational leadership

Situational leadership challenged the notion that there is one leadership style that will be best for every manager in all circumstances. Fieldler (1967), Adair (1973) and Hersey and Blanchard (1977) are just some of those who proposed theories suggesting that the most effective style depends on situational factors such as the people, the task and the organizational context.

Charismatic leadership

The development of 'new genre' models of leadership was, at least in part, prompted by research evidence which indicated that traditional, sometimes referred to as 'transactional', leadership models – that focus on goal setting, direction, support and reinforcement – only accounted for a relatively small percentage of variance in performance outcomes (Bryman, 1992). Accumulated research on the new genre models, on the other hand, has found that charismatic and transformational leadership are positively associated with a range of important organizational outcomes, such as job satisfaction, motivation, morale and performance, across many different types of organizational setting (see Avolio et al., 2009).

Charismatic leadership draws on transformational leadership (Burns, 1978), especially the ability to motivate and empower others, together with elements of earlier trait and 'great man' theories. According to Avolio et al., it emphasizes symbolic leader behaviour, visionary inspirational messages, emotional feelings, ideological and moral values, individualized attention, and intellectual stimulation. The effect is to raise followers' aspirations, activate their higher order values and encourage identification with the leader's mission.

Bolden (2004) attributes the recent popularity of charismatic leadership to it being perceived as an antidote to the demoralizing effects of organizational restructuring, competition and redundancies. The charismatic leader is seen as someone who can rebuild morale and offer a positive vision of the future.

Conger (1991: 31) argues that the charismatic leader must have the ability to inspire others. To illustrate what this involves, he uses the story of two stonemasons who, while working on the same project, were asked what they were doing. The first replied: 'I am cutting stone;' the second: 'I am building a great cathedral.' Conger asserts that the second mason was able to describe his work in a more far-reaching and meaningful way. He argues that leaders need to embody this same ability, 'the capacity to articulate an organization's mission and communicate it in ways that inspire'. This requires two distinct skill categories. The first is 'framing', the ability to define the purpose of the organization in a meaningful way. The second is the ability to use symbolic language to give emotional power to the message, which Conger refers to as 'rhetorical crafting'. While the basic message provides the sense of direction, it is the rhetoric that heightens its motivational appeal and determines whether it will be sufficiently memorable to influence the day-to-day decision making of those involved in the change.

Mintzberg (2004) and others have some reservations about charismatic leadership theories, insofar as they focus on the individual leader and glorify the leader as a hero.

Distributed leadership

In many organizations, there has been a move from deep hierarchies, in which leader–subordinate relationships were clearly defined, towards new organizational forms where cross-functional teams, networks and communities of practice require an approach to leadership that is capable of being dissociated from organizational hierarchies.

In the first instance, the initiator of change might be an individual or a small group. These initiators might be viewed as the ones who are leading the change, but Kotter (1999) argues that this leadership has to be multiplied and shared if the change is to be successful. Throughout the system, managers have to accept that they have a leadership role to play. They have to contribute to creating a vision, aligning relationships and inspiring others. Oxtoby et al. (2002) support this view and argue that not only does a system of leadership need to cascade down the organization in the form of a distributed network of key players, each providing leadership in their part of the organization, but also that to be effective, this network needs to share a common vision of the organization's purpose that is clear, consistent and inspiring. Developing and maintaining this common approach is not always easy.

Spillane (2006) likens leadership to a two-partnered dance. While it is possible to focus attention on the actions of a single partner, to understand the performance of the dance it is necessary to pay attention to the interactions of all the dancing partners. Collinson (2005) notes that many studies of leadership have only concentrated on leaders' traits and styles and have either ignored or underestimated the importance of relations between leaders and followers. Bolden (2004) points to an increasing awareness of the importance of social relations, the need for leaders to be given authority by followers and the realization that no one individual is the ideal leader in all circumstances. This line of thinking has led to the development of less formalized models of leadership that accommodate the possibility that leadership is not the exclusive preserve of senior managers. Bolden observes that individuals at all levels in an organization (not just managers) can exercise leadership influence over colleagues and thus influence the overall direction of the organization. This perspective shifts attention away from the individual 'heroic' leader to a more collective process of sense making and direction giving.

The collective nature of leadership

In much of the literature on organizational change, the role of the CEO as leader receives considerable attention. Research evidence on the link between the CEO's leadership style and organizational performance is mixed. Avolio et al. (2009) refer to some studies that found that the charisma of the CEO was not related to subsequent organizational performance, whereas others found the opposite. This may be because, in many situations, leadership needs to be viewed as a collective process. Pascale and Sterin (2005) point out that when individuals stand out as champions of change, there is a danger that this will generate unconstructive dependence from other members of the organization. They argue that leadership needs to come from within a community. Denis et al. (2001) also caution against the glorification of individual heroes. Organizations are becoming more complex and pluralistic. Their external boundaries are becoming increasingly blurred as they engage in a variety of collaborative arrangements and as they outsource many of their operations. Within organizations, the growth of matrix and network structures and the move from functional to more process-oriented organizational forms are creating circumstances where traditional command and control cultures are being eroded and where managers are increasingly having to collaborate with others, over whom they have no direct authority, in order to get things done.

Coherence

One of the key problems associated with managing change in pluralistic settings is the development of sufficient coherence. Denis et al. (2001) argue that in situations where power is diffused and where there are divergent objectives, change initiatives need to be led by a collective leadership group rather than a single individual.

On the basis of their research in healthcare organizations (see Research report 9.1), Denis et al. (2001) argue that major change in pluralistic organizations is more likely to be achieved under unified collective leadership in which members of a 'leadership constellation' play complementary roles and work together harmoniously. In many countries, there are conventions or legally binding codes of practice that explicitly formalize the collective nature of strategic leadership by separating the posts of CEO and president or chair of the company's board of directors, but often the membership of the leadership constellation is wider than this, with members having different but complementary roles. For example, some may focus their attention on the management of external relations, whereas others may manage relationships with particular internal constituencies. Collective leadership is essential in those circumstances where a single individual is unable to formulate and implement a vision that is acceptable to a sufficient body of powerful stakeholders. Collective leadership offers the possibility of bringing together the range of skills and experience required to formulate an acceptable vision as well as the ability to influence others in a manner that is perceived to be legitimate.

Fragility

While Denis et al. (2001) argue that unified collective leadership is necessary in pluralistic settings, they found that leadership constellations are always fragile. They define fragility in terms of three types of 'coupling':

▶ *Strategic coupling* is the internal harmony between members of the leadership constellation (Figure 9.1). Constellations can become disconnected when divergent views emerge about what is important and when these differences lead to conflicts within the constellation.

Figure 9.1 *Strategic coupling*

▶ *Organizational coupling* reflects the relationship between members of the leadership constellation and their organizational constituencies, which in turn relates to the perceived conformity between the objectives of leaders, as reflected by their behaviour, and the interests of constituents (Figure 9.2). If members of the leadership constellation lose touch with their constituents, the constituents will begin to feel that their views are not being properly represented by their leaders. This can reduce the leaders' ability to influence constituents and may even threaten their membership of the leadership constellation. The reason for this is that leaders rule, at least in part, by the consent of the led. Denis et al. (2001: 825) argue that:

> In a context of fluid power relationships, the judgements of others concerning the appropriateness of one's behaviour are crucial for long-term survival in a leadership position. Actions that tend to enhance survival prospects are called credibility enhancing, and those that tend to diminish it are credibility draining. Changes in credibility directly or indirectly affect the capacity of an individual or leadership group to act in the future. Increased credibility widens the scope for action. Reduced credibility diminishes it and may lead to leader turnover.

Figure 9.2   *Organizational coupling*

This has implications for the effectiveness of different leadership styles. Denis et al. suggest that if a constellation is tightly coupled and covers all power bases, members of the constellation may find that behaving in an aggressive, secretive and authoritarian manner is an effective way of getting things done in the short term, but they suggest that in the long term, these tactics can be credibility draining. There may be a need, especially over the long term, to balance forceful leadership action with maintaining a necessary level of approval from those who are being led.

▶ *Environmental coupling* refers to the degree of coherence between the leadership constellation's vision and aspirations and the demands and constraints imposed by powerful external stakeholders (Figure 9.3). Constellations can break down if they become so detached from their environments that performance begins to decline. This happens when concerns about performance lead to pressures from the company's board or other powerful external stakeholders for members of the constellation to be replaced.

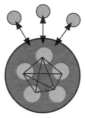

Figure 9.3   *Environmental coupling*

Denis et al. (2001) argue that it can be difficult to maintain harmony at all three levels. Sometimes too much attention is directed towards developing a close alignment between the aspirations of internal stakeholders (organizational coupling) and insufficient attention is given to the impact of external demands (environmental coupling). Accommodating different interests is easier when there is a degree of organizational slack, but when resources are limited, there is less opportunity for accommodations and compromises. In these circumstances, the stability of leadership constellations and their ability to deliver change may depend on some of the personal and interpersonal skills of members. Denis et al. (2001) refer to the importance of a tacit knowledge of how things can be done in the organization, 'social embeddedness', and creative opportunism – the ability to see opportunities to reconcile a range of aspirations with environmental pressures. Other factors might also be important. Hollenbeck and Hall (2004) highlight the effect of self-efficacy, that is, leader self-confidence, on leader performance, and while Ferris et al. (2000) agree that tacit knowledge and self-efficacy are important, they also point to the importance of a number of other social skills such as social intelligence, emotional intelligence, ego resilience and self-monitoring.

Research report 9.1 ⟩ **Collective leadership and strategic change**

Denis, J.-L., Lamothe, L. and Langley, A. (2001) The dynamics of collective leadership and strategic change in pluralistic organizations, *Academy of Management Journal*, **44**(4): 809–37

The study was designed to examine leadership from a process perspective, focusing attention on what leaders do to mobilize others in a system of interrelationships. They set out to examine the dynamic construction, deconstruction and reconstruction of leadership roles over time.

Method

The study was partly planned and partly opportunistic, and was partly deductive (inspired by theory) and partly deductive (inspired by data). A case study approach was adopted because this enabled the researchers to trace processes in their natural contexts and study the temporal sequence of events.

The research process

Five cases were studied over a 10-year period. The first involved a hospital that was negotiating with a medical school to acquire a teaching mission. The data drew the researchers' attention to the importance of collective leadership and the link between leaders' tactics and their capacity to remain in leadership positions. In this case, after an earlier change initiative had failed, a new leader emerged and mobilized the leadership team to pursue the teaching mission. But the united leadership team moved too fast for many others in the hospital and an election led to the team being dissolved and replaced, slowing down the once rapid change process.

The second case, which involved a small hospital developing a new emergency care service, was planned to replicate and test the conceptual model that was emerging from the first study. A new leader replaced the management team, built credibility with the board and achieved both internal and external support for the new mission, but a group of physicians put in place to implement the development of the emergency service pushed to develop it more extensively than the CEO and the board felt was possible. Conflict led to the departure of the physicians and a halt to the project.

Building on their emerging model of collective leadership, the third case focused on how a new CEO positioned himself within an existing leadership constellation.

Over the course of these three case studies, four observations emerged as important:

1. Periods of substantive change tend to be associated with complementary and united leadership constellations.
2. Leadership constellations are fragile because of the possibility of disconnections between members (strategic coupling), between members of the leadership constellation and their organizational bases (organizational coupling), and between the leadership constellation and environmental demands and constraints (environmental coupling).
3. Because of this difficulty of maintaining alignment at all three levels, change occurs in a cyclical fashion as opposing forces are reconciled on a sequential, rather than a simultaneous, basis. For example, after a leadership constellation has developed a commitment to change, it may need to seek support from external stakeholders. This may not be easy (problems with environmental coupling) and might require the leadership constellation to make concessions. This may lead to problems within the leadership constellation (strategic coupling). The resolution of these differences may, in turn, require further compromise, creating problems for some members with their organizational constituents (organizational coupling). These problems may have to be resolved before the change can progress.

4 Leadership affects political positions. The way others perceive and judge a leader's actions, such as conceding or failing to deliver on promises, affects their credibility and survival in a leadership role.

Denis et al. went on to observe that four factors – slack resources, internal social embeddedness, creative opportunism, and time, inattention and the protection of formal position – could help to create sufficient temporary stability to allow substantive change to become irreversible before political changes made it impossible.

Four years after the start of the project, moves to consolidate the teaching hospital network in Quebec presented a new opportunity to extend the research to more complex cases. Two cases were studied, each involving the merger of three hospitals. The researchers found that increasing the number of pluralistic dimensions made it much more difficult to establish a unified leadership constellation, to achieve anything more than partial coupling, to break free from a cycle of shifting alliances and to manage the sequential attention to different goals. Denis et al. concluded that greater complexity increases the need for counterbalancing sources of stability, such as slack resources, internal social embeddedness, creative opportunism, and time, inattention and the protection of formal position, if substantive change is to be achieved.

A checklist for leading change

Whether leadership is provided by a single individual or is more widely distributed and exercised as a collective process, some of the key leadership tasks identified by Kotter can provide those leading a change with a useful guiding framework. Kotter (1995) adopts a process perspective on change management and highlights, in terms of leadership, what needs to be done to ensure success at each stage in the process. These actions can be easily mapped on to the process model of change presented in Chapter 2.

The eight-point checklist is as follows:

1 *Establish a sense of urgency:* Change managers often underestimate how hard it can be to drive people out of their comfort zones. Unfreezing involves alerting organizational members to the need for change and motivating them to let go of the status quo. Many factors can make this difficult to attain. These include a history of past success and the lack of an immediate crisis. After British Gas was privatized, many senior managers refused to recognize that there was any real threat to the organization's monopoly position. Those attempting to lead change in the business had to work hard to convince colleagues that they should begin to prepare for major discontinuities. Chapter 4 (on starting the change process) considers a range of issues that require the leader's attention at the beginning of a change.

2 *Form a powerful coalition:* This point relates to the politics of change discussed in Chapter 8 and the collective nature of leadership discussed above. Kotter argues that unless those who recognize the need for change can put together a strong enough team to direct the process, the change initiative is unlikely to get off the ground. He suggests that while this 'guiding coalition' might not include all the senior managers, it is much more likely to succeed if, in terms of titles, information, experience, reputations and contacts, it is seen to signal a real commitment to change.

3 *Create a vision:* The guiding coalition needs to develop a shared vision that can be easily communicated to others affected by the change. In his book *Leading Change,* Kotter (1996) summarizes six criteria for an effective vision:

- *imaginable:* conveys a picture of what the future will look like
- *desirable:* appeals to the long-term interests of employees, customers, stockholders and others who have a stake in the enterprise
- *feasible:* comprises realistic, attainable goals
- *focused:* is clear enough to provide guidance in decision making
- *flexible:* is general enough to allow individual initiatives and alternative responses in the light of changing conditions
- *communicable:* is easy to communicate; can be successfully explained within five minutes.

Sometimes interventions such as visioning workshops (see Chapter 16 on types of intervention) can be helpful in developing a vision that satisfies these criteria.

4 *Communicate the vision:* People need a sense of direction. Communication is considered in more detail in Chapter 10. However, in terms of communicating the vision, people – all those affected by the change – need to hear the message repeatedly. Kotter asserts that in many change programmes, the vision is undercommunicated by a factor of ten. He also emphasizes that communicating a vision involves more that the spoken and written word. Organizational members, and other stakeholders, watch those responsible for managing the change for indications of their commitment. It is important that they 'walk the talk' and communicate the vision by example.

5 *Empower others to act on the vision:* Transformational leadership involves identifying and removing obstacles that can stop people acting to implement the vision. Some of these obstacles might include tangible aspects of the organization, such as reward systems that penalize valued behaviour, restrictive rules and regulations or inflexible organizational structures. Others may be less tangible and involve beliefs and assumptions that stifle initiative. Empowering others to act includes creating a climate in which people believe in themselves and are confident that they have the support of others to make things happen. The importance of beliefs about change agency is considered in Chapter 4.

6 *Plan for and create short-term wins:* Kotter argues that achieving major change can take time. The danger with this is that the change effort can slow down as people lose the initial sense of urgency and their attention drifts elsewhere, possibly to pressing operational matters. One way of minimizing this risk is for those leading the change to seek out short-term wins and plan for visible, interim performance improvements that can be celebrated along the way.

7 *Consolidate improvements and produce still more change:* This involves capitalizing on early wins. However, while Kotter advocates celebrating early wins, he cautions against declaring victory too soon because this can kill momentum. Leaders should capitalize on early wins to motivate others to introduce further changes to systems and structures that are consistent (aligned) with the transformation vision.

8 *Institutionalize new approaches:* Leaders need to ensure that changes are consolidated. They can help achieve this by showing others how the changes have produced new approaches, behaviours and attitudes that have improved performance. Kotter argues that leaders should take every opportunity to demonstrate benefit and reinforce these changes until they become an accepted part of the culture and the 'way things are done around here'. Embedding change is considered in Chapters 28 and 29.

Exercise 9.1 > **Validating Kotter's checklist**

Identify two change managers, or constellations of change managers, who have been key figures in attempting to introduce and manage change in your organization. One should be a person(s) who you judge to have been successful at managing change. The other should be someone who you judge to have been much less successful. Assess their approach to managing change using Kotter's checklist for leading change. Consider whether there is any evidence to suggest that successful change managers are those who attend to Kotter's eight points.

Notes

Summary

The role of leadership in change management had been summarized as:

- creating a vision
- aligning relationships around the vision
- inspiring others to achieve the vision.

While it is recognized that a strong vision can make a valuable contribution to the success of a change initiative, some of the factors that might render the vision unfit for purpose have been reviewed. These include leaders making unrealistic assessments of opportunities and constraints and formulating the vision in a way that does not address the needs and concerns of key stakeholders.

The need to communicate the vision in a way that will align people around it has been discussed along with the dangers of distorting the vision to make it more appealing to key stakeholders.

The importance of management style, the effect of situational factors and the contribution that charismatic management can make to the successful implementation of change have been considered.

The danger of focusing too much attention on individual leaders received attention. Within organizations, the growth of matrix and network structures and the move from functional to more process-oriented organizational forms are creating circumstances where traditional command and control cultures are being eroded and where managers are increasingly having to collaborate with others over whom they have no direct authority in order to get things done.

Denis et al. argue that in situations where power is diffused and where there are divergent objectives, change initiatives need to be led by a collective leadership group (constellation) rather than by a single individual. Special attention is given to:

▸ coherence and the importance of unified collective leadership
▸ fragility – leadership constellations tend to be fragile because of the possibility of disconnections between members of the leadership constellation (strategic coupling), between members of the leadership constellation and their constituents (organizational coupling), and between the leadership constellation and environmental demands and constraints (environmental coupling).

The chapter closed with an eight-point checklist of what leaders can do to promote change:

1 establish a sense of urgency
2 form a powerful coalition
3 create a vision
4 communicate the vision
5 empower others to act on the vision
6 plan for and create short-term wins
7 consolidate improvements and produce still more change
8 institutionalize new approaches.

References

Adair, J. (1973) *Action-centred Leadership*, New York: McGraw-Hill.

Avolio, B.J., Walumbwa, F.O. and Weber, T.J. (2009) Leadership: current theories, research, and future directions, *Annual Review of Psychology*, 60: 421–49.

Beer, M. (2001) How to develop an organization capable of sustained high performance: embrace the drive for results-capability development paradox, *Organizational Dynamics*, **29**(4): 233–47.

Bennis, W. and Nanus, B. (1985) *Leaders: The Strategy for Taking Charge*, New York: Harper & Row.

Blake, R.R. and Mouton, J.S. (1964) *The Managerial Grid*, Houston, TX: Gulf.

Bolden, R. (2004) *What is Leadership?*, research report, Leadership South West: University of Exeter.

Bruch, H., Gerber, P. and Maier, V. (2005) Strategic change decisions: doing the right change right, *Journal of Change Management*, **5**(1): 97–107.

Bryman, A. (1992) *Charisma and Leadership in Organizations*, Newbury Park, CA: Sage.

Burns, J.M. (1978) *Leadership*, New York: Harper Row.

Collinson, D. (2005) Leading questions: questions of distance, *Leadership*, **1**(2): 235–50.

Conger, J.A. (1990) The dark side of leadership, *Organizational Dynamics*, **19**(2): 44–5.

Conger, J.A. (1991) Inspiring others: the language of leadership, *Academy of Management Executive*, **5**(1): 31–45.

Denis, J.-L., Lamothe, L. and Langley, A. (2001) The dynamics of collective leadership and strategic change in pluralistic organizations, *Academy of Management Journal*, **44**(4): 809–37.

Ferris, G.R., Perrewe, P., Anthony, W.P. and Gilmore, D.C. (2000) Political skills at work, *Organizational Dynamics*, **28**(4): 25–37.

Fielder, F. (1967) *A Theory of Leadership Effectiveness*, New York: McGraw-Hill.

Fleishman, E.A., Harris, E.F. and Burtt, H.E. (1955) *Leadership and Supervision in Industry*, Columbus, OH: Bureau of Educational Research, Monograph 33, Ohio State University.

Hersey, P. and Blanchard, K. (1977) *Management of Organizational Behavior*, Englewood Cliffs, NJ: Prentice Hall.

Hollenbeck, G.P. and Hall, D.P. (2004) Self-confidence and leaders performance, *Organizational Dynamics*, **33**(3): 254–69.

Janis, I.L. (1972) *Victims of Groupthink: A Psychological Study of Foreign Policy Decisions and Fiascos*, Boston, MA: Houghton-Mifflin.

Kotter, J.P. (1990) What leaders really do, *Harvard Business Review*, **68**(3): 103–11, reproduced in J.P. Kotter (1999) *On What Leaders Really Do*.

Kotter, J.P. (1995) Leading change: why transformation efforts fail, *Harvard Business Review*, **73**(2): 59–67.

Kotter, J.P. (1996) *Leading Change*, Boston, MA: Harvard Business School Press.

Kotter, J.P. (1999) *On What Leaders Really Do*, Boston, MA: Harvard Business School Press.

Kühl, S., Schnelle, T. and Tillmann, F.J. (2005) Lateral leadership: an organisational change approach, *Journal of Change Management*, 5(2): 177–89.

Lewin, K., Lippitt, R. and White, R. (1939) Patterns of aggressive behavior in experimentally created social environments, *Journal of Social Psychology*, 10: 271–99.

McGregor, D. (1960) Theory X and theory Y, in D.S. Pugh (ed.) *Organization Theory: Selected Readings*, London: Penguin.

Mintzberg, H. (2004) *Managers Not MBAs*, London: FT/Prentice Hall.

Northouse, P.G. (2004) *Leadership: Theory and Practice* (3rd edn), London: Sage.

Oxtoby, B., McGuiness, T. and Morgan, R. (2002) Developing organisational change capability, *European Management Journal*, 20(3): 310–20.

Pascale, R.T. and Sterin, J. (2005) Your company's secret change agents, *Harvard Business Review*, 83(5): 72–81.

Spillane, J. (2006) *Distributed Leadership*, San Francisco, CA: Wiley.

Tichy, N.M. and Devanna, M.A. (1986) *The Transformational Leader*, Chichester: Wiley.

Communicating change

The quality of communications can have an important impact on the success or otherwise of a change programme. It can, for example, affect whether the need for change is recognized in good time and can have a major impact on the quality of collective learning (see Chapter 18). This chapter briefly considers the features of communication networks that relate to the management of change, reviews some alternative communication strategies, explores some of the factors that can deprive change managers of access to vital information, discusses the effect of interpersonal relations on the quality of communication, and considers how change communication can affect perceptions of fairness and justice.

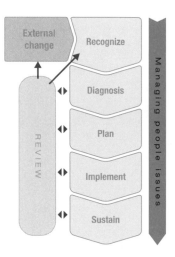

Features of communication networks

Four features of communication networks will be considered: directionality, role, content and channel.

Directionality

The management of change is often experienced as a top-down process, with those responsible for managing the change informing others lower down the organization about the need for change, what is going to happen and what is required of them. Allen et al. (2007) argue that the reason why many organizations encounter difficulties in reducing employee uncertainty during change is because of this one-way, top-down pattern of communication. Effective change communication also calls for a stream of upward communication that provides change managers with the information they require in order to clarify the need for change, and develop and implement a change programme. Beer (2001) identifies the poor quality of upward communication as one of his six 'silent killers' that block change and learning.

O'Reilly and Pondy (1979) list some of the consequences of directionality on the content of messages. Senders transmitting messages up the organization hierarchy send information that they perceive to be relevant and which reflects favourably on their, or their unit's, performance. Where possible, they screen out information that reflects unfavourably on them. Consequently, people further up the organization may not receive all the information that may be relevant to the issues they have to manage.

Senders transmitting messages downwards have a tendency to screen out any information they perceive to be not directly relevant to the subordinates' task. There is also a tendency for them to elaborate this task-related information to ensure that it is properly understood. This 'need to know' attitude can lead to problems when change managers fail to pass on information that might have helped others to understand the need for change or feel more involved in the change process (see the discussion of the 'withhold and uphold' communication strategy below).

The quality of lateral communication can also have a powerful impact on an organization's level of performance and its ability to innovate and change. Brown and Eisenhardt (1997), Orlikowski (1996) and Tjosvold (1998) all argue that intense and open communication between people within and between teams is an essential requirement for continuous improvement. This information sharing contributes to the identification of issues and the development of new possibilities. Hargie and Tourish (2000) assert that when groups work in isolation, with people sharing minimal information, 'the locomotive of change slows to a crawl'. They report finding that poor interdepartmental communication is linked to feelings of isolation and dissatisfaction and low levels of involvement in the decision-making process. In Hargie and Tourish's (2000: 7) opinion, 'poor information exchange exacerbates uncertainty, increases alienation and produces a segmented attitude to work that is inimical to the spirit of innovation'.

Morrison and Milliken (2000) discuss how, in some organizations, there is a widespread withholding of opinion and concerns that deprives change managers of vital information. This will be considered later in this chapter under the heading Organizational silence.

Role

The nature of what is communicated can be affected by the roles that organizational members occupy. The nature of an 'inter-role relationship' is important; a person might communicate certain things to a colleague that they would not communicate to an external consultant, an auditor, a member of another department, their boss, a subordinate or a customer. This issue will be discussed in more detail when the effect of trust and power on the quality of interpersonal relationships is considered.

The nature of a role can be an important determinant of whether the role occupant will be an 'isolate' or a 'participant' in the organization's affairs. Some roles are potentially more isolating than others: a finance officer may be better networked within the organization than a salesperson who is responsible for a remote territory; an employee on an assembly line may have relatively few opportunities to communicate with others and may therefore be deprived of opportunities to contribute to collective learning. This may be much less of a problem for somebody located in an open-plan office who is constantly interacting with colleagues. Some of the interventions that will be considered in Chapter 18 are designed to create opportunities for dialogue, sharing and the provision of feedback that are so important in situations characterized by uncertainty and change. When planning to communicate with people about a proposed change, it is important to take account of those who occupy isolated roles. People who feel they have been neglected or excluded are more likely to be alienated than those who feel they are in a position to participate in the change.

Some members of the organization occupy 'boundary-spanning roles' that enable them to transfer information from one constituency to another. For example, people in sales, customer support and product development occupy roles that link the organization with the wider environment. Within the organization, there are also roles that straddle the boundaries between internal constituencies; the occupants of these boundary-spanning roles may have access to important information that could be used to identify emerging problems or opportunities. MacDonald (1995) argues that critical information is often imported into organizations through informal and individual contacts and that the persons who are the boundary spanners who acquire this information may not be the people who can use it as a basis for managing change. They may have to pass their information on to others who are in a better position to respond. However, these 'others' may not recognize the importance of the information or may receive a message that is different from that which the originator of the message intended to convey.

Distortion can occur because information is passed on to others by 'gatekeepers'. Gatekeepers are those who are in a position to interpret and screen information before transmitting it to others. Almost everybody in the organization is a gatekeeper to some extent, but some roles offer their occupants considerable power to control the content and timing of the information that is passed on to decision makers. Change managers need to be aware of who controls the flows of information that are important to them. One way of reducing dependence on some gatekeepers is to build an element of redundancy into the communication network in order to provide the possibility of obtaining information from more than one source.

In Chapter 3, three different kinds of 'playmaker' roles are discussed. Pitt et al. (2002) borrowed this term from football where it refers to the restless, energetic, midfield role that links play, energizes the team and 'makes things happen'. They argue that playmakers are the individuals who seek out opinion from those who are close to the realities of the operating environment and pass it on to those who are in a position to formulate the change agenda.

Content

Allen et al. (2007) argue that one reason why many organizations encounter difficulties in reducing employee uncertainty during change is because change managers often focus on providing employees with information regarding strategic issues. They acknowledge that this might be important at first but argue that later in the change process, employee concerns are likely to shift to more job-related issues.

MacDonald (1995) distinguishes between internal and external information and draws attention to the importance of attending to information from outside the organization and integrating this with the information that is routinely available to organizational members in order to facilitate organizational learning. A common problem, however, is that this external information is often unfamiliar, and responding to it frequently leads to disruption and uncertainty. Consequently, organizational members tend to prefer the more familiar internal information that is easier to integrate into the prevailing mental models and paradigms that are used for making sense of the situation that confronts them.

Other important aspects of content are whether it is perceived as good news or bad news, and how senders expect it to be received. Change managers need to be alert to content issues and especially the need to give careful consideration to the potential relevance of information that at first sight may appear to be of little consequence (see the discussion on the trap of success at the beginning of Chapter 3).

Channel

Information and meaning can be communicated in many different ways: written communication via hard copy, electronic communication via email, videoconferencing, telephone, face-to-face communication on a one-to-one, one-to-group or group-to-group basis and so on. O'Reilly and Pondy (1979) suggest that written communication may be effective when the sender and receiver have different vocabularies or problem orientations, and that oral communication may be most effective when there is a need to exchange views, seek feedback and provide an immediate opportunity for clarification. They note, however, that while organization members may prefer certain media and certain forms of communication may have clear advantages in specific circumstances, external factors may limit the freedom to select a particular mode of communication. For example, distance may prohibit face-to-face interaction, budget constraints may demand the use of written communication rather than videoconferencing, and time constraints may rule out the use of lengthy meetings. Clampitt et al. (2000) echo this efficiency/effectiveness dilemma. They note that while it may be more efficient to send an email to all employees outlining a major change, it may not be the most effective way to create employee buy-in. They argue that face-to-face communication is a more persuasive channel because it provides a dynamic and effective way of dealing with people's concerns. However, face-to-face communication costs the organization more in terms of time and energy than a lean medium like email.

Communication strategies

These features of communication networks provide a useful backdrop for comparing the advantages and disadvantages of various communication strategies. As Clampitt et al. (2000) have observed, managers can communicate about anything but they cannot communicate about everything, so, implicitly or explicitly, they make choices about communication content. They also take decisions or unconsciously act in ways that impact on the shape of communication networks. For example, they may communicate with some organizational members but not with others and they may authorize or encourage certain others to communicate with each other. They may also influence, if only by example, preferred channels for passing on particular types of information.

Communication plays a vital role in the change process. It is an essential prerequisite for recognizing the need for change, and it enables change managers to create a shared sense of direction, establish priorities, reduce disorder and uncertainty, and facilitate learning. However, change managers often give insufficient attention to the role of communication. Clampitt et al. (2000) suggest that communication strategies emerge from existing practices with little hard thinking about communication objectives or processes and little, if any, attention to reviewing the consequences of their approach to communicating with others. On the basis of their experience in several organizations and a review of the literature, they identified five basic strategies. Sometimes the communication strategy in any particular setting closely resembles one of these, but sometimes it is a hybrid and includes a blend of elements from more than one. The five basic strategies are:

▶ *Spray and pray:* Clampitt et al. (2000) use this term to describe a communication strategy that involves showering employees with all kinds of information in the hope that they will feel informed and have access to all the information they require. It is based on the assumption that more information equals better communication, which in turn contributes to improved decision making. It is also based on an implicit assumption that all organizational members are able to differentiate between what is significant and what is insignificant. In practice, some employees may only attend to the information that is related to their own personal agendas, while others may be overwhelmed by the amount of information they are confronted with – unable to sort the wood from the trees.

▶ *Tell and sell:* This approach involves change managers communicating a more limited set of messages that they believe address the core issues related to the proposed change. First of all they tell employees about these key issues and then sell them the wisdom of their approach to managing them. Clampitt et al. (2000) observe that change managers who adopt this kind of strategy often spend a great deal of time planning sophisticated presentations but devote little time and energy to fostering meaningful dialogue and providing organizational members with the opportunity to discuss their concerns. They also assume that they possess much of the information they need and they tend to place little value on input from others.

▶ *Underscore and explore:* Like the tell and sell approach, this strategy involves focusing attention on a limited set of fundamental issues linked to the change but, unlike the tell and sell approach, change managers give others the creative freedom they need to explore the implications of these issues. Those who adopt this approach are concerned not only with developing a few core messages but also with listening attentively for potential misunderstandings and unrecognized obstacles.

▶ *Identify and reply:* This strategy is different from the first three in that the primary focus is the concerns of organizational members. It is a reactive approach that involves a lot of listening in order to identify and then respond to these concerns. It is essentially directed towards helping employees make sense out of the often confusing organizational environment, but it is also attentive to their concerns because it is assumed that organizational members are in the best position to know what the critical issues are. However, this may not always be the case. Clampitt et al. (2000) suggest that often they may not know enough to even ask the right questions.

▶ *Withhold and uphold:* This strategy involves withholding information until necessary. When confronted by rumours, change managers uphold the party line. There may well be special circumstances where commercial or other considerations require information to be shared on a need to know basis but there are also change managers whose implicit values are secrecy and control whatever the circumstances. Some of those who adopt this strategy assume that information is power and they are reluctant to share it with anyone. Others assume that most organizational members are not sophisticated enough to grasp the big picture.

Clampitt et al. (2000) use a crescent-shaped continuum to compare the effectiveness of the different strategies (Figure 10.1). On the left, the spray and pray strategy provides employees with all the information they could possibly desire, while on the right, the withhold and uphold strategy provides the absolute minimum information. Both these strategies make it difficult for employees to frame and make sense of the intended change and its consequences. The strategies towards the middle of the continuum pay more attention to prioritizing and managing content to provide guidance for those involved in the change and, to varying degrees, attend to employee concerns. Clampitt et al. (2000) argue that the strategies at the extremes are the least effective and the most effective is underscore and explore. This is because it incorporates elements of the tell and sell strategy and allows change managers to shape the change agenda, and it also incorporates aspects of the identify and reply strategy that responds to the concerns of employees.

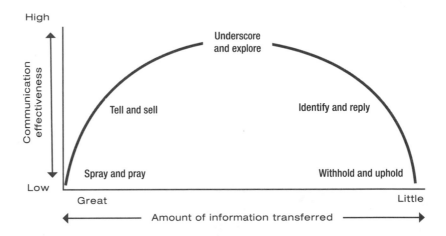

Figure 10.1 *Effectiveness of communication strategies*
Source: Clampitt et al., 2000

Hargie and Tourish (2000) recommend the regular auditing of communications. This requires change managers to have a clear idea about their communication objectives in order to assess the extent to which they are being achieved. Some of the questions they might need to ask are:

▶ Who is communicating with whom?
▶ What issues are they talking about?
▶ Which issues receive most attention and arouse most anxiety?
▶ Do people receive all the information they require?
▶ Do people understand and use the information they receive?
▶ Do people trust and have confidence in the information they receive?
▶ From what sources do people prefer to get their information?
▶ Which channels are most effective?

Organizational silence: a major barrier to change

Morrison and Milliken (2000) argue that many organizations are caught in an apparent paradox in which most employees know the truth about certain issues and problems but are afraid to voice that truth to their superiors. They refer to the widespread withholding of opinions and concerns as 'organizational silence' and assert that it can be a major barrier to organizational change and development. In Chapter 3, the importance of ensuring that multiple and divergent views contribute to the decision-making process was highlighted in the context of formulating the agenda for change, but Morrison and Milliken refer to several studies (for example Moskal, 1991; Ryan and Oestreich, 1991) indicating that in practice employees often feel compelled to remain silent and refrain from voicing their views. The dynamics that give rise to organizational silence are summarized in Figure 10.2.

According to Morrison and Milliken (2000), a climate of silence in organizations will develop when:

1 Senior managers fear negative feedback from subordinates and try to avoid it or, if this is not possible, dismiss it as inaccurate or attack the credibility of the source.

2 Senior managers hold a particular set of implicit beliefs about employees and the nature of management that make it easy for them to ignore or dismiss feedback. These beliefs are that:

- employees are self-interested, untrustworthy and effort averse
- management knows best and therefore subordinates should be unquestioning followers, especially since they are self-interested and effort averse and therefore unlikely to know or care about what is best for the organization
- dissent is unhealthy and should be avoided and unity, agreement and consensus are indicators of organizational health.

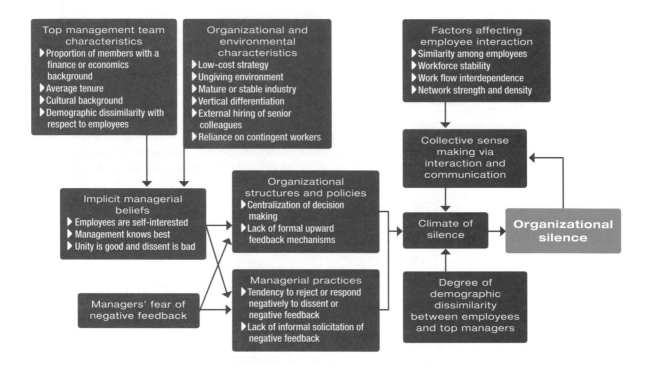

Figure 10.2 *Dynamics giving rise to organizational silence*

Source: Adapted from Morrison and Milliken, 2000

Conditions that foster these managerial beliefs

Morrison and Milliken (2000) argue that top management teams that are dominated by members with economic or financial backgrounds are more likely to subscribe to the belief that employees are self-interested because this belief is rooted in economic models of behaviour. They also argue that dissent will be less welcome by top teams that are homogeneous with respect to functional training and experience, and by teams that have experienced low turnover. This is because such teams are likely to be more cohesive and share entrenched assumptions. Distrust is also fostered when top teams are highly dissimilar to lower level employees in terms of demographic characteristics such as age, gender and race.

Organizational and environmental variables can also foster these beliefs. For example, they argue that when organizational strategies emphasize control in order to maximize economic value (see the discussion of economic change strategies in

Chapter 14), managers may view negative feedback and dissent as a threat to their authority. Furthermore, organizations operating in stable and mature environments are more likely to subscribe to beliefs that foster silence than organizations in high velocity environments because, in stable environments, a lack of upward communication is less likely to threaten their survival. They also argue that these beliefs are more likely to be fostered in organizations that have many levels in the hierarchy, hire in top managers from outside and make heavy use of temporary and agency workers. These conditions limit interaction across the hierarchy and do little to build senior managers' trust in their subordinates.

Effect of managerial beliefs and fear of feedback on structures, policies and practices

Morrison and Milliken (2000) argue that in those organizations where the dominant ideology reflects the beliefs that employees are self-interested, management knows best and disagreement is bad, it will give rise to structures, policies and managerial behaviours that create an environment that discourages upward communication. Examples include centralized decision-making procedures that exclude most employees, an absence of formal feedback mechanisms for soliciting employee feedback on decisions after they have been made, a tendency to reject employees' concerns about a proposed change because they are viewed as 'resistance' motivated by self-interest rather than a true concern that the change may be bad for the organization, and a general unwillingness on the part of managers to seek informal feedback from subordinates.

Morrison and Milliken (2000) point out that these barriers to upward communication can exist at many different levels in the organization. While it may only be top management that can impose company-wide structures and policies that foster organizational silence, managers at all levels can discourage upward communication by the way they design their bit of the organization and by reacting negatively to unsolicited inputs from subordinates and failing to seek feedback from employees on issues that affect performance. However, even when middle managers do not share the implicit beliefs held by their superiors, top management attitudes can encourage middle managers and many other supervisors to behave in ways that foster silence. For example, middle managers may choose to respond to senior managers' lack of openness to dissenting views by filtering out some of the information they receive from their subordinates before passing it up the organization. Their subordinates, in turn, notice this apparent disregard for their views and respond by not voicing their own concerns and those reported to them by their subordinates. In this way, the conditions that encourage a climate of silence trickle down the organization.

The creation of shared perceptions that lead to organizational silence

The management beliefs outlined above promote the development of structures, policies and practices that foster a climate of organizational silence. A climate of silence exists when employees believe that speaking up about problems is not worth the effort and voicing one's problems and concerns is dangerous.

Morrison and Milliken (2000) adopt an interactionist perspective to explain how these beliefs develop. They argue that it is through the sharing of perceptions and experience that employees engage in a process of collective sense making and develop a common understanding and a set of shared beliefs about whether to voice or withhold their views. They go on to argue that centralized decision making, lack of upward feedback mechanisms, managerial resistance to employee input and a lack of downward feedback-seeking behaviour are more likely to lead to a climate of silence when there is a relatively high level of interaction and communication between mid to lower level employees. This is because interaction can foster the development of a shared belief that speaking up is not worth the effort.

The amount of interaction that takes place is related to several factors. These include:

▶ similarity between direct co-workers, because there is evidence that people are more open when communicating with people they perceive to be similar to themselves

▶ relatively stable organizational membership, because this increases the likelihood that shared perceptions will persist over time

▶ work flow interdependence that necessitates regular communication, coordination and teamwork

▶ informal social networks and strong ties that promote intense and frequent contact.

This collective sense-making process can be flawed, and inaccurate perceptions may develop as employees share and collectively interpret their observations and experiences. Sources of bias include the reliance on second-hand information, because many people prefer to learn vicariously rather than risk finding out first hand, and the tendency to exaggerate the riskiness or futility of voicing dissent. However, even if they are inaccurate, these shared perceptions have a strong impact on employees' attitudes and behaviour.

The implications of organizational silence

Organizational silence can compromise decision making and elicit undesirable reactions from employees. Organizational silence deprives decision makers of the opportunity to consider alternative perspectives and conflicting viewpoints. There is considerable evidence that this can adversely affect creativity and undermine the quality of decision making. Also blocking negative feedback can inhibit organizational learning, because it affects the ability of managers to detect and correct the causes of poor performance. Morrison and Milliken (2000) also suggest that decision makers may not receive important information because employees only pass on the information they think their managers want to hear.

Organizational silence can have destructive outcomes for employees, with knock-on effects for the organization:

▶ Employees may feel undervalued and this may affect their commitment and lead to lower motivation, satisfaction, psychological withdrawal or the decision to quit.

▶ When discouraged from speaking up, employees may feel that they lack sufficient control over their working environment. This can also lead to low motivation, low satisfaction and, possibly, attempts to regain some control through acting in ways that are destructive to the organization, such as engaging in sabotage.

▶ Employees may also experience cognitive dissonance because of the discrepancy between their beliefs and behaviour, leading to anxiety and stress.

Morrison and Milliken argue that when top management adheres to the assumptions that foster silence, it makes it difficult for organizations to respond to the diversity of values, beliefs and other characteristics that are features of pluralistic organizations. The more these differences 'pull' the organization in divergent directions, the more senior managers may 'push' against these forces because they view differences as a threat that has to be suppressed. Morrison and Milliken (2000: 720) argue that 'despite "knowing" that they should encourage upward communication, organizations' dominant tendency may be just the opposite – namely, to create a climate of silence.'

Interpersonal effects on the quality of communication

Factors such as trust and influence can have an important effect on the quality of the information that is exchanged. Lines et al. (2005) argue that whether change agents gain access to the knowledge and creative thinking they need to solve problems depends largely on how much people trust them. O'Reilly and Pondy (1979) refer to studies that show that lack of trust is associated with a tendency for senders to withhold unfavourable but relevant information while passing on favourable but irrelevant information. There is also evidence that senders are guarded in what they are prepared to share with those who are able to influence what happens to them.

Change managers often have to seek out information from others (see Chapter 7 on gathering information for diagnosis), but this is not always an easy task. Interpersonal interactions are complex social encounters in which the behaviour of each party is influenced by the other. An often-used model of information gathering presents the process solely in terms of an information seeker (change manager) getting information from respondents (organizational members). This model is an oversimplification because it fails to take full account of the interactive nature of the encounter (see Figure 10.3).

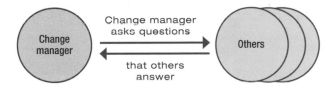

Figure 10.3 *An oversimplified model of the interview*

Organizational members are aware that change managers are observing what they say and do and that they may be making judgements about them and their future role. Consequently, they may not openly and honestly answer all the questions they are asked. They may attempt to manage the way they respond so as to maximize their personal benefit from the interaction rather than help change managers to achieve their purpose. This example could just as easily be presented in terms of organizational members 'interviewing' a change manager.

Goffman (1959), Mangham (1978) and others have used drama as a metaphor for describing and explaining a wide range of interactions, and this metaphor can usefully be applied to this kind of social encounter. Goffman talks about putting on a performance for an audience and argues that people's portrayal of action will be determined by their assessment of the audience. He also notes that actors use mirrors so that they can practise and become an object to themselves, backstage, before going 'on stage' and becoming an object to others. Similarly, organizational members may anticipate the nature of their audience, the change managers, and rehearse the way they want to present themselves.

A better representation of the interaction between change managers and organizational members is illustrated in Figure 10.4. Change managers are likely to structure the situation and behave in ways they feel will best project their definition of the purpose of the encounter and the role they want to assume in the interaction. This behaviour not only says a lot about how change managers wish to be seen, but also about who they take the other organizational members to be and the role they are expected to play. Change managers attempt to influence others' interpretation of the situation and to focus their attention on those issues which they (the change managers) regard as important, and much of what takes place at this stage involves cognitive scene setting.

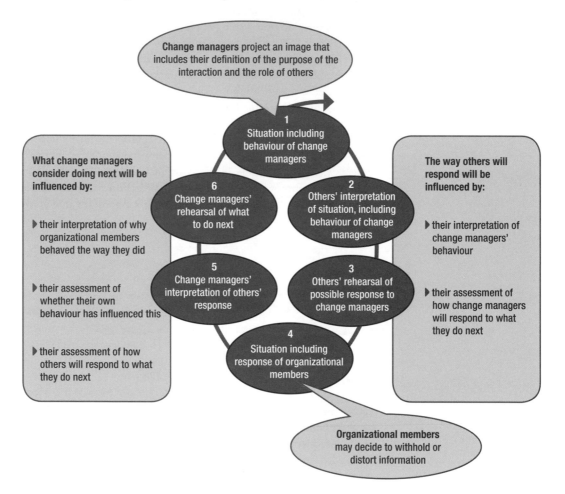

Figure 10.4 *The interaction between change agents and organizational members*

At stage 2 in Figure 10.4, organizational members seek to understand what it is that change managers are projecting and what implications this has for them. Do the change managers, for example, appear to see the encounter as an information-gathering exercise designed to provide them with the information they need to determine what has to be changed? Alternatively, do they see it as the first step towards involving organizational members in the management of the change process?

Organizational members might detect a difference between the performance change managers consciously and deliberately give, and what Mangham (1978) refers to as the information they 'give off'. Change managers may attempt to perform in a way that gives others the impression that they are committed to a shared approach to the management of change; however, they may actually 'give off' signals, verbal and nonverbal, that contradict this intended impression. Thus, as the interaction progresses through stages 3 and 4, organizational members may decide to cooperate and give change managers the information they are seeking, or they may decide to distort or withhold information until they are more confident about the change managers' intentions.

Reference has already been made to rehearsal of action. At stage 3, organizational members have to decide, on the basis of their interpretation of the situation, how to respond to change managers. Farr (1984), discussing the work of Margaret Mead, a cultural anthropologist, notes that Man not only acts but reacts to his own actions. He reacts to his own behaviour on the basis of the actual or anticipated reaction of others. He can anticipate their reactions through simulation or rehearsal. He can try out, in his own mind, a few pieces of behaviour and test them for fit. Mangham even suggests that he can simulate several stages into alternative futures for an interaction, a form of mental chess in which various moves and their consequences are tested.

Once organizational members have decided what to do and have responded to the change managers' initial behaviour, the situation changes. Both parties, at stage 4 on the circle, are faced with a situation that includes the most recent behaviour of organizational members. If change managers failed to make their purpose explicit (at stage 1), organizational members may misinterpret their behaviour and act in ways that change managers either did not anticipate or feel are inappropriate to the situation.

Change managers have to assess this situation (stage 5) and attempt to understand the meaning of organizational members' behaviour. Their interpretation of organizational members' responses offers a basis for assessing the relevance and validity of any information communicated by them. Good interviewers/information gatherers have the ability to empathize with the other party; they can assume the other's role in the interaction, putting themselves in the other's shoes and replaying in their mind the situation faced by other organizational members. And they can interpret the other's behaviour, including their answers to questions, from this perspective. Unfortunately, this is a skill that many change managers have not developed and this can lead to many misunderstandings.

On the basis of their interpretation of the situation, including organizational members' behaviour, change managers can rehearse their next move (stage 6) before deciding what to do and/or say. This then forms part of the unfolding scene to which the other organizational members will have to respond, and so the process continues.

The point of this example is that the nature of the encounter will influence how both parties will interpret what they see and hear. It will also influence the quantity and quality of the information that each is prepared to offer. Change managers need to give careful thought to how others will interpret their actions. Their interpretation will be an important determinant of what others are prepared to communicate to them and how they will behave in response to information passed to them by change managers. All this is relevant to the discussion of developing and maintaining helping relationships, which will be considered in Chapter 13.

Change communication and perceptions of fairness and justice

The way change is communicated can affect perceptions of fairness and justice that, in turn, will affect how stakeholders will respond to change. For example, organizational members value adequate notice before decisions are implemented and expect to receive adequate and accurate information. They may also want the opportunity to voice their concerns and have an input to the decision process. If they perceive that the change is being managed in a way that is unfair, this perception may have an adverse effect on their morale, organizational commitment and performance.

Colquitt et al. (2001) identify a number of ways of thinking about organizational justice:

▶ *Distributive justice* is about the equity of outcomes (see the discussion of motivation in Chapter 11).

▶ *Procedural justice* is about fair process. Thibaut and Walker (1975), after studying dispute resolution procedures, found that disputants were more prepared to give up control of the decision about outcomes if they had had sufficient control over the process used to reach the decision, especially over the presentation of their arguments and the time they had to present their case.

▶ *Informational justice* is about the explanations provided to people that convey information about why particular procedures were used or why the outcomes were distributed in a particular fashion. The discussion of realistic merger previews in Chapter 26 provides a useful insight into how the provision of information affects the way people respond to change.

▶ *Interpersonal justice* is about how people are treated by those executing procedures or determining outcomes. Greenberg (1990) studied how people reacted to a pay cut (see Research report 10.1) and found that when employees were treated with dignity by managers who were sensitive to how the changes would affect them, and when managers explained and justified the changes and demonstrated that they were being applied consistently and without bias, they reacted better than employees who were not treated in this way.

Research report 10.1   Communicating bad news

Greenberg, J. (1990) Employee theft as a reaction to underpayment inequity: the hidden cost of pay cuts, *Journal of Applied Psychology*, **75**(5): 561–8

Greenberg investigated the effect of adequate explanations on perceptions of inequity by observing employee theft rates and labour turnover when rates of pay were temporarily cut by 15%.

Participants in the study were employees working for 30 consecutive weeks in three manufacturing plants owned by the same parent company. Following the loss of two large manufacturing contracts, two of the three plants lost work and the company responded by cutting wages. The third plant was unaffected and wage rates remained unchanged.

- In plant A (the adequate explanation condition), employees were called to a meeting and informed by the company president that their pay was going to be cut by 15% for a period expected to last 10 weeks. They were told that company management seriously regretted the need to reduce their pay, but that they were taking this action to avoid layoffs, and that all plant employees, including managers, would share in the pay cuts. The reasons for the decision were carefully explained and information about cash flows was shared to reassure everybody that the need for pay cuts was only temporary. The meeting lasted 90 minutes and most of the time was given over to answering questions.

- In plant B (the inadequate explanation condition), the meeting lasted 15 minutes. Employees were informed about the pay cut, that it was expected to last for 10 weeks and that it was being imposed because of the loss of contracts. There was no expression of apology or remorse and the basis for the decision was not clearly described.

- In plant C (the control condition), the loss of the contracts had no effect and rates of pay remained unchanged.

Following the pay cuts in plant B, where the explanation had been inadequate, pilfering increased threefold compared to levels of pilfering in the control plant. In plant A, where a full and sensitive explanation had been provided, thefts also increased, but not as much as in plant B. There were, however, significant differences in turnover rates. In plant B, turnover was 23%, whereas in plants A and C, it was 5% or less.

The data support equity theory's predictions regarding likely responses to underpayment and demonstrate the mitigating effects of adequate explanations on feelings of inequity.

Often the discussion of change communication tends to focus exclusively on the 'what, when, who and how' of communication from the perspective of the change manager communicating to others. The discussion in this chapter has also empha-sized issues associated with change managers perceiving, interpreting and using information provided by others.

There are no magic formulae about the 'what, when, who and how' of communic-ation that can provide ready answers for all situations. In some circumstances, change agents may advocate a policy of complete openness about all issues to every-body as soon as possible. In other circumstances, information might be highly restricted because it is deemed to be commercially sensitive, or it might be decided that information should not be widely shared until after certain high-level decisions have been made. Counterarguments might focus on the difficulty of keeping the need for change secret and the importance of not losing control of communications to the informal grapevine. The alternative strategies, considered earlier, highlight some of the options available to change managers.

What is important is that adequate attention is given to ensuring that all relevant information is sought and is attended to by change managers, and that they pay careful attention to the information they need to communicate to others.

Exercise 10.1   ## Assessing the quality of communications

Think about a recent attempt to introduce and manage change in your organization or a particular part of the organization you are familiar with, and reflect on how the quality of communication helped or hindered the change process:

- Did the change manager(s) communicate effectively to all those involved in or affected by the change?
- If not, to what extent was this related to 'network factors', such as directionality, role, content or channel, or to interpersonal factors that interfered with the quality of communication?

Notes

What could the change manager(s) have done differently that might have improved the quality of communications?

Notes

Case study 10.1   **Galaxy**

Galaxy, as it will be referred to here, is a German company producing a wide range of heating, air-conditioning, refrigeration, cooking and laundry appliances for home and commercial use. Most of its 30,000 employees are located in the older EU states and the company has an annual turnover of €40bn. Galaxy has always been focused on making a good return on investments and growing shareholder value and has pursued this goal by giving priority to product innovation, investment in new technology and developing the capability of its staff.

Galaxy has managed to maintain the competitive position of its European manufacturing facilities in the face of growing competition from companies manufacturing in low-cost countries. However, two years ago, the board recognized that this competitive position could not be sustained and that eventually much of its manufacturing capacity would have to be moved to cheaper locations.

Galaxy already has manufacturing facilities in India and China but these were built to produce a new range of products and did not involve the relocation of work from existing plants in Europe. Over the next four years, this situation will change. The company plans to close seven plants in Germany, France, Denmark, Italy and the UK, with the loss of 12,000 jobs, and expand production elsewhere in the world.

The first closure will involve a German plant that produces refrigeration equipment. A new manufacturing facility has been acquired in China and within nine months it will be ready to commence production of a limited range of high-volume products that have few parts and are relatively easy to assemble. As the capability of the Chinese workforce is developed, the full range of products manufactured at the German plant will be relocated but it will be two years before all production, including the more complex, high-value products, can be moved. Consequently, while some staff will be laid off in nine months, others will need to be retained for up to two years.

Sixty-five per cent of the output of the plant targeted for closure is sold within Germany but the company estimates that the reduction in production costs associated with the move to China will more than outweigh the cost of transporting the refrigeration equipment back to the German market. One concern, however, is how customers will react to the company moving jobs abroad.

Employees were shocked by the news that their plant is to be closed and are planning to do everything they can to resist the closure. Employees elsewhere in the company are aware that more plants are likely to be closed.

Imagine that you have been asked to advise Galaxy about how to manage the closure of the refrigeration plant in Germany:

- What are the communication issues?
- How do you think they should be addressed?

Summary

The quality of communications can have an important impact on the success or otherwise of a change programme. It can, for example, affect whether the need for change is recognized in good time and can have a major impact on the quality of collective learning. This chapter has considered the features of communication networks that relate to the management of change, reviewed some alternative communication strategies, explored some of the factors that can deprive change managers of access to vital information, discussed the effect of interpersonal relations on the quality of communication, and considered how change communication can affect perceptions of fairness and justice.

Four features of communication networks have been considered:

Directionality:
▶ The management of change is often experienced as a top-down process, with those responsible for managing the change informing others lower down the organization about the need for change, what is going to happen and what is required of them.
▶ Effective change communication calls for a stream of upward communication that provides change managers with the information they require in order to clarify the need for change, and develop and implement a change programme.

Role:
▶ The nature of what is communicated can be affected by the roles that organizational members occupy.
▶ The nature of an inter-role relationship is important; a person might communicate certain things to a colleague that they would not communicate to an external consultant, an auditor, a member of another department, their boss, a subordinate or a customer.

Content:
▶ It is important to give careful consideration to the potential relevance of information that at first sight may appear to be of little consequence.
▶ MacDonald (1995) distinguishes between internal and external information and draws attention to the importance of attending to information from outside the organization and integrating this with the information that is routinely available to organizational members in order to facilitate organizational learning.

Channel:
▶ Information and meaning can be communicated in many different ways. It is important to select a channel that is fit for purpose.

The chapter also:

▶ Reviewed five communication strategies and some of the issues that might affect choice of strategy.

▶ Explored the concept of organizational silence and the factors that can deprive change managers of important information.

▶ Discussed the effect of interpersonal relationships on the quality of communication.

▶ Considered how change communication can affect perceptions of fairness and justice and the implications this can have for motivation and commitment.

The chapter ends with a review of some of the main issues that managers need to consider when communicating about change.

References

Allen, J., Jimmieson, N.L., Bordia, P. and Irmer, B.E. (2007) Uncertainty during organizational change: managing perceptions through communication, *Journal of Change Management*, **7**(2): 187–210.

Beer, M. (2001) How to develop an organization capable of sustained high performance: embrace the drive for results-capability development paradox, *Organizational Dynamics*, **29**(4): 233–47.

Brown, S.L. and Eisenhardt, K.M. (1997) The art of continuous change: linking complexity theory and time-paced evolution in relentlessly shifting organizations, *Administrative Science Quarterly*, 42: 1–34.

Clampitt, P.G., DeKoch, R.J. and Cashman, T. (2000) A strategy for communicating about uncertainty, *The Academy of Management Executive*, **14**(4): 41–57.

Colquitt, J.A., Conlon, D.E., Wesson, M.J. et al. (2001) Justice at the millennium: a meta-analytic review of 25 years of organizational justice research, *Journal of Applied Psychology*, **86**(3): 425–45.

Farr, R. (1984) Interviewing: the social psychology of the inter-view, in C.L. Cooper and P. Makin (eds) *Psychology for Managers*, London: British Psychological Society.

Goffman, E. (1959) *The Presentation of Self in Everyday Life*, New York: Doubleday.

Greenberg, J. (1990) Employee theft as a reaction to underpayment inequity: the hidden cost of pay cuts, *Journal of Applied Psychology*, **75**(5): 561–8.

Hargie, O. and Tourish, D. (2000) *Handbook of Communication Audits for Organizations*, London: Routledge.

Lines, R., Selart, M., Espedal, B. and Johansen, S.T. (2005) The production of trust during organizational change, *Journal of Change Management*, **5**(2): 221–45.

MacDonald, S. (1995) Learning to change: an information perspective on learning in the organization, *Organizational Science*, **6**(5): 557–68.

Mangham, I.L. (1978) *Interactions and Interventions in Organizations*, Chichester: Wiley.

Morrison, E.W. and Milliken, F.J. (2000) Organizational silence: a barrier to change and development in a pluralistic world, *Academy of Management Review*, **25**(4): 706–25.

Moskal, B.M. (1991) Is industry ready for adult relationships?, *Industry Week*, **24**(4): 18–25.

O'Reilly, C.A. and Pondy, L.R. (1979) Organizational communication, in S. Kerr (ed.) *Organizational Behavior*, Columbus, OH: Grid Publications.

Orlikowski, W.J. (1996) Improvising organisational transformation over time: a sustained change perspective, *Information Systems Research*, **7**(1): 63–92.

Pitt, M., McAulay, L. and Sims, D. (2002) Promoting strategic change: 'playmaker' roles in organizational agenda formulation, *Strategic Change*, **11**(3): 155–72.

Ryan, K.D. and Oestreich, D.K. (1991) *Driving Fear Out of the Workplace: How to Overcome the Invisible Barriers to Quality, Productivity and Innovation*, San Francisco, CA: Jossey-Bass.

Thibaut, J. and Walker, L. (1975) *Procedural Justice: A Psychological Analysis*, Hillsdale, NJ: Erlbaum.

Tjosvold, D. (1998) *Team Organization: An Enduring Competitive Advantage*, New York: John Wiley.

It was noted in Chapter 5 that organizations, like all open systems, seek to maintain a state of equilibrium; they tend to gravitate to a condition where all the component parts of the system are aligned with each other. Intentionally intervening to change the organization by modifying one component of the system can disturb this state of equilibrium and can create pressure to restore it. Restoration can be achieved by realigning other components with those that have been changed or by resisting the change and seeking to re-establish the status quo.

In all organizational systems, there is a natural tendency to resist change. This chapter will:

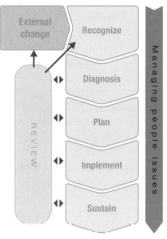

▶ consider how the general level of commitment in an organization can affect the extent to which organizational members will support new initiatives
▶ review and synthesize some of the views on resistance to change presented by Kotter and Schlesinger (1979), Zaltman and Duncan (1977), Nadler (1993) and Pugh (1993)
▶ assess the utility of expectancy theory as a basis for assessing the motivation of an individual or group to support or resist change
▶ consider how change strategies can be designed to motivate individuals and groups to change.

Organizational commitment and the level of support for change

People's past experience of change can affect their level of commitment to the organization and their willingness to support further change. Around 50 years ago, Argyris (1960) first defined the psychological contract as the perceptions of both parties to the employment relationship of their obligations implied in the relationship. More recently, Guest et al. (1996) referred to it in terms of perceptions of fairness, trust and the extent to which the 'deal' is perceived to have been delivered. It is an unwritten set of expectations between every member of an organization and those who represent the organization to them, and it incorporates concepts such as fairness, reciprocity and a sense of mutual obligation. For example, organizations may expect employees to:

▶ be loyal
▶ keep trade secrets
▶ work hard and do their best for the organization.

In return, employees may expect that they will:

> ▶ receive an equitable level of remuneration
> ▶ be treated fairly and with dignity
> ▶ have some level of security of employment
> ▶ have some level of autonomy
> ▶ have an opportunity to learn and develop.

If employees feel that their employer/managers have kept their side of the psychological contract, they are likely to respond by displaying a high level of commitment to the organization. If, on the other hand, they feel that the organization has failed to keep its side of the bargain, they may respond by redefining their side of the psychological contract. They may invest less effort in their work, be less inclined to innovate and less inclined to respond to the innovations or changes proposed by others.

Exercise 11.1

Violations of the psychological contract

Think of an incident at work when the organization/management fell short of what might have been reasonably expected of them in their treatment of an individual or group of employees.

In the space below, list any effects this incident had on the level of commitment of the individual or group and on their willingness to support change.

Notes

You might also consider the effect on others. People observe how colleagues are treated and this affects their views about how they may be treated in the future if they are involved in some kind of change. Note, in the space below, any 'ripple effect' this incident had on the commitment of others and their willingness to support change.

Notes

Managers often expect that those who have been retained after a programme of redundancies will be relieved and grateful and will respond with higher levels of commitment and performance. Research on survivor syndrome (see Doherty and Horsted, 1995) suggests that this may not be the case. Survivors may respond in a number of ways, ranging from shock, anger, animosity towards management, guilt, concern for those gone, and anxiety, to relief that they still have a job or fear of losing their job in the future. The evidence suggests that survivors often display less confidence in and a lack of commitment, trust and loyalty to the organization (see Research report 8.1). As Sir Robert Worcester, founder of MORI, once said: 'Don't worry about those staff who turn off and go: worry about those who turn off – and stay!'

Reasons for resisting specific changes

Kotter and Schlesinger (1979) identify four main reasons why people resist change, which are discussed below.

Parochial self-interest

People resist change when they think that it will cause them to lose something of value. It is not uncommon for stakeholders to focus on their own best interests rather than those of the organization.

Pugh (1993) suggests that all too often managers fail to anticipate resistance because they only consider change from a rational resource allocation perspective and fail to appreciate that many organizational members are much more concerned about the impact it will have on them personally. They will assess its impact in terms of how it might affect ways of working, job opportunities, career prospects, job satisfaction and so on, and in terms of how it might undermine or enhance their power and status, and the prestige of the groups to which they belong.

Zaltman and Duncan (1977) view threats to power and influence as one of the most important sources of resistance to change. They observe that the prospect of a merger often gives rise to fears on the part of individuals, groups and even entire organizations that they will lose control over decision making. They also note that managers, even senior managers, may resist the use of certain approaches to the management of change if they feel that these may undermine their power and authority. They illustrate this with an example of head teachers who were resistant to the use of a survey feedback approach to organization development because it enabled teachers and district-level personnel to have access to data and to use it, along with the heads, to propose solutions to problems. Some head teachers were concerned that this approach would increase the power of teachers and undermine their own power to influence how the schools were managed.

Misunderstanding and lack of trust

Misunderstandings can be a frequent source of resistance. Stakeholders often resist change because they do not understand the implications it may have for them. Such misunderstandings may lead them to perceive that the change will cost them more than they will gain.

Misunderstandings are most likely to arise when trust is lacking between the person(s) initiating the change and the stakeholders who feel that they will be affected by it. Lines et al. (2005) note that several studies have linked trust to levels of openness in communication and information sharing, levels of conflict and the acceptance of decisions or goals. When organizational members do not trust change managers, they are likely to resist any change they propose.

Managers and change agents often fail to anticipate this kind of resistance, especially when they are introducing a change they perceive will be of benefit to those involved. A consultant was asked by the CEO of a chemical company to investigate why the workforce had rejected a productivity agreement that senior management believed offered considerable advantage to both the organization and process workers. It turned out that the message that had been communicated to the workforce was, in some important respects, different to the proposal the senior management team had agreed to make (see Chapter 10 on communication problems). These differences had arisen as the proposal had been passed down the management chain. However, this communication problem had been compounded by the fact that the process workers felt that the offer was too good to be true and that management was intent on manipulating them in some way.

Different assessments

Kotter and Schlesinger (1979) suggest that another common reason why some stakeholders resist change is that they assess the situation differently from those initiating the change and see more costs than benefits resulting from it, not only for themselves but also for the organization or other constituencies that are important to them. They argue that managers who initiate change sometimes assume that they have all the relevant information required to conduct an adequate organization analysis and that those who will be affected by the change have the same facts. Often neither assumption is correct. Also, those initiating change often fail to take account of how the change might affect stakeholders who are not organizational members. External stakeholders can be an important source of resistance. This problem was discussed in Chapter 8.

Zaltman and Duncan (1977) point to how selective attention and retention can prevent individuals or groups appreciating that the current state of affairs is unsatisfactory. The mental models that influence how they perceive, interpret and make sense of their environment (referred to in Chapter 18 on collective learning in organizations) can have a strong effect on how organizational members assess their circumstances and whether or not they perceive any problems. Their mental models can also affect the kind of solution that will be favoured if a problem is perceived to exist. It is not unusual for resistance to occur, even when organizational members and their managers have a shared view of the nature of a problem, because both parties have conflicting views about what should be done to resolve it.

Ford and Ford (2009) argue that, all too often, when people voice their different assessments about a situation, change managers interpret this as resistance when it might be viewed more usefully as valuable feedback. Dismissing this kind of feedback too quickly can not only deprive change managers of potentially valuable information, but can also cost them goodwill and jeopardize important relationships.

Low tolerance for change

Stakeholders also resist change when they are concerned they will not be able to develop the new skills and behaviours that will be required of them. All people are limited in their ability to change, but some are more limited than others. In Chapter 1, reference was made to Toffler's view that people respond to the increasing rate of change in different ways and that some are more able than others to internalize the principle of acceleration, modify their durational expectancies and make an unconscious compensation for the compression of time. Toffler also considers the phenomenon of adaptive breakdown, what he calls future shock.

Even when stakeholders intellectually understand the need for change, sometimes they are emotionally unable to make the transition (see Chapter 12). The change may involve a grieving process similar to that which occurs when a person loses a loved one. Perceived loss can affect people in different ways but often this involves some element of denial and a reluctance to 'let go'.

Expectancy theory and the motivation to support or resist change

Expectancy theory considers how expectations influence motivation. It offers a useful conceptual framework for assessing whether a stakeholder is likely to support or resist an impending change. Expectancy theorists (for example Vroom, 1964; Porter and Lawler, 1968) argue that behaviour is a function of two factors; expectancies about the future and the attractiveness of outcomes:

▸ *Outcomes* can be evaluated in terms of their value or attractiveness. Vroom (1964) refers to this as 'valence'. If stakeholders expect the change to reduce the availability of valued outcomes, they are likely to offer resistance. If, on the other hand, they expect it to increase the availability of valued outcomes, they are more likely to offer support.
▸ *Expectancies:* Stakeholder motivation will also be influenced by expectancies about the likelihood that they will actually receive valued outcomes in practice. The theory focuses attention on two expectancies about the future:
   • *effort to performance expectancy:* This refers to the person's expectation, that is, subjective probability about the likelihood, that they can perform at a given level, in other words, that effort will lead to successful performance.
   • *performance to outcome expectancy:* This refers to a person's expectation that some level of performance will lead to desired outcomes, or the avoidance of negative outcomes.

From a motivational perspective, it is the expectation or belief about the relationship between effort, performance and valued outcome that will determine whether a stakeholder will be motivated to support or resist a change. The basic elements of this theory are illustrated in Figure 11.1.

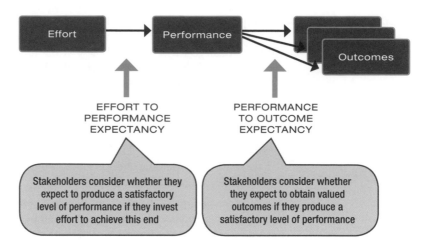

Figure 11.1 *The expectancy model of motivation*

Equity of treatment

The model can be extended to include stakeholder expectations about the equity of outcomes in the changed situation. If stakeholders believe that comparable others will receive more favourable treatment (in terms of valued outcomes) as a result of the change, this will affect their assessment of the attractiveness of the outcomes they expect to receive. Some stakeholders who expect, in absolute terms, to receive a net increase in valued outcomes may resist the change because they feel that they are being treated unfairly relative to comparable others.

Understanding and competence

The model can also be extended to include key factors that may affect effort to performance expectancies. These include the stakeholder's understanding of the nature of the required performance, and the rules that govern how a performance should be produced, and the competencies required to deliver a satisfactory level of performance (Figure 11.2). These will be discussed below.

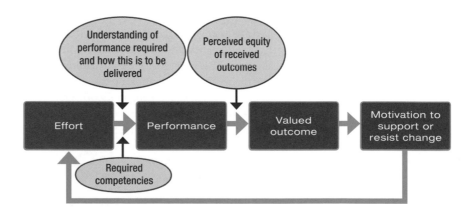

Figure 11.2 *An expectancy model of the motivation to support or resist change*

Assessing the availability of valued outcomes

The first step in assessing how stakeholders will respond to change is to identify how the change will affect the availability of valued outcomes in the changed situation. In order to do this, the change manager needs to:

▶ be aware of the kinds of outcomes that are valued by the stakeholders who will be affected by the change

▶ have some understanding of the extent to which the current situation provides these outcomes

▶ have some understanding of the extent to which valued outcomes will be (at least potentially) available in the changed situation.

This assessment will provide a useful first indication of the extent to which stakeholders will support or resist the change. It will also indicate the extent to which they are likely to be motivated to perform in ways that will contribute to organizational effectiveness in the changed situation.

When people are confronted by an impending change, they often fear that they will lose some of the outcomes they value in the existing situation. However, they may also anticipate some gains. These gains might be more of the outcomes they already enjoy or some completely new benefits. In order to anticipate how stakeholders will feel about a change, it is necessary to empathize with them in order to construct a balance sheet of what (we think) they will perceive as gains or losses.

Different people value different outcomes. Even the same person may value different outcomes at different points in time. The more we know about stakeholders, the better placed we will be to construct a balance sheet of their gains and losses. Listed below are some broad headings that might suggest the kinds of outcomes that could be important to stakeholders:

▶ Pay
▶ Working conditions
▶ Interesting/meaningful work
▶ Autonomy
▶ Opportunity for competition or collaboration
▶ Opportunities to be creative
▶ Power and influence
▶ Belonging/involvement
▶ Location
▶ Security
▶ Working with considerate supervisors
▶ Satisfaction
▶ Challenge
▶ Achievement
▶ Recognition
▶ Status
▶ Openness/sharing
▶ Opportunity to use knowledge and skills.

Each of these headings can be elaborated to include a more detailed list of associated outcomes. For example, under the heading of pay, employees might feel that the impending change is likely to reduce the availability of a valued outcome because they will be required to work longer hours or at a faster rate for the same pay. On the other hand, the change might be viewed as enhancing valued outcomes if it leads to a regrading that will boost pay. This might also be the case if it offers a shift to annualized hours that will eliminate unpredictable variations in weekly pay and provide a guaranteed annual income that can be used, for example, to secure a bank loan or a mortgage.

The broad headings listed above are intended as prompts. They do not provide an exhaustive list. Different kinds of stakeholders may value different kinds of outcomes.

Change tool 11.1

Assessing the availability of valued outcomes

1 Think about a recent or impending change at work or elsewhere, home, church and so on, and identify a key stakeholder affected by the change.
2 List all the valued outcomes you believe the stakeholder receives in the current situation. Review the list and indicate whether you feel that the change will produce a gain (✓), no change (?) or a loss (✗) for each outcome.

Valued outcome in existing situation	✓	?	✗	Rank

3 Next, extend the list by adding any new outcomes you anticipate will be available to the stakeholder in the changed situation and indicate your assessment of whether the stakeholder will view them as a gain (✓), neutrally (?) or as a loss (✗).

New outcome in changed situation	✓	?	✗	Rank

4 Then review the content of both tables and rank how you think the stakeholder will value the outcomes. In the column headed Rank, enter 1 next to the most valued outcome, 2 next to the second most valued and so on.
5 In order to make an overall assessment of the potential net gain or loss for the stakeholder, it is necessary to take account of both the number of gains and losses identified in the above tables, and also the relative importance of the different valued outcomes to the stakeholder. The ranking is intended to provide a basis for weighting the significance of each gain and loss. Is the stakeholder likely to view the net effect of the change as a gain or a loss?

6 Consider whether those responsible for managing the change were/are aware of how the change was/is likely to affect the availability of outcomes that are valued by the selected stakeholders.

7 Consider whether this information might have improved the way the change was/is being managed.

Notes

Expectancies about effort–performance and performance–outcome relationships and equity of net benefits

Although the change manager may see potential net gains for the people affected by the change, the individuals concerned may not share this assessment. Whether stakeholders will be motivated to support or resist the change will depend on their expectations about:

▶ their ability to deliver a satisfactory level of performance in the changed situation
▶ whether a satisfactory (or even exceptional) level of performance will lead to the achievement of valued outcomes in the changed situation
▶ whether the net benefits accruing to them will be equitable when compared to the net benefits accruing to comparable others in the changed situation.

In order to understand better the extent to which stakeholders will resist or support change, the change manager needs to consider these three issues.

Anticipate stakeholder expectations regarding whether they will be able to produce a satisfactory level of performance in the changed situation

There will be less resistance (more support) in those situations where stakeholders expect to be able to deliver a satisfactory level of performance in the changed situation. Individuals or groups are more likely to resist a change when they expect that, irrespective how hard they work, the change will undermine their ability to produce a satisfactory level of performance.

Diagnosis

In order to anticipate how the change might affect stakeholder expectations about their ability to produce a satisfactory level of performance in the changed situation, the change manager needs to:

▶ Consider whether any misunderstandings might arise about the processes and procedures that will apply in the changed situation. Stakeholders may assume that any new rules that define the nature of a satisfactory level of performance, or new rules that regulate working practices may undermine their ability to produce a satisfactory level of performance.

Example: Individuals may assume that in the changed situation they will have less autonomy and that they will be required to work in a group setting. They may also fear that in this group setting their performance will be dependent on inputs from others who are poor or unreliable performers. Their fears may be well founded, but they may also be based on misunderstandings about the nature of the change or the other people they may have to work with.

Possible action

The change manager may be able to reduce resistance from this source by:

- helping people to develop a clear understanding of how the change will affect the way they will be required to work – *education*
- helping them to understand the consequences these new processes and procedures may have for their ability to deliver a performance – *education and persuasion*
- providing them with an opportunity to be involved in the planning of the change. This might reassure them that the change will be managed in a way that will minimize those factors that could undermine their ability to deliver a satisfactory level of performance – *participation and involvement*.

Diagnosis

The change manager also needs to:

▶ Consider the relevance of existing core competencies in the changed situation.

Example: In those situations where a stakeholder's core competencies become more highly valued, the individual is more likely to support the change. However, where core competencies are perceived to be less relevant, or even redundant, the change is more likely to be resisted because stakeholders may fear that they will not be able to produce a satisfactory level of performance.

Possible action

The change agent may be able to reduce the resistance from this source by:

- considering possibilities for redeploying people to roles that will better utilize existing competencies – *planning*
- involving people in identifying possibilities for redeployment – *participation*
- providing training to develop more relevant competencies – *training and development*.

Anticipate stakeholder expectations about the relationship between performance and the achievement of valued outcomes in the changed situation

There will be less resistance (and more support) for a change in those situations where stakeholders expect that the delivery of a satisfactory level of performance will be linked to the achievement of valued outcomes. In those situations where they expect the change to undermine the achievement of valued outcomes, they are more likely to resist the change and to be less motivated to perform in the changed situation.

Diagnosis

In order to anticipate how the change might affect stakeholder expectations about the relationship between performance and the achievement of valued outcomes, the change agent needs to:

▶ Empathize with the stakeholders affected by the change in order to develop a better understanding of how they might expect the change to affect the link between performance and the achievement of valued outcomes.

Example: If an individual values promotion and expects that in the changed situation there will be a closer link between advancement and level of performance, they may support the change and be motivated to perform well in the changed situation. If, however, the individual expects the change to weaken this link, this will increase the possibility that the change will be resisted.

Possible action

The change agent may be able to reduce resistance from this source by:

- considering ways of modifying the change to strengthen the links between performance and the achievement of valued outcomes – *planning*
- persuading individuals that the change will actually strengthen these links – *persuasion*
- involving stakeholders in the diagnosis, planning and implementation of the change. This might reassure them that the change will be managed in a way that will strengthen links between performance and valued outcomes – *participation*.

Anticipate stakeholder perceptions of their net benefits (or losses) compared to those enjoyed by comparable others

There will be less resistance (and more support) in those situations where stakeholders feel that they are being treated equitably relative to others. Where they feel that they are being treated unfairly, they may be more likely to resist the change.

Diagnosis

In order to anticipate the effects of perceived equity on the level of resistance or support for change, the change agent needs to:

▶ Identify those who may regard themselves as being treated inequitably.

Possible action

The change agent may be able to reduce resistance from this source by:

- helping people who feel this way recognize all the potential gains available to them and ensuring that they fully understand the possible losses if the change is not implemented – *education and persuasion*

- exploring possibilities for improving the availability of valued outcomes for those who feel that they have received inequitable treatment – *planning*
- exploring the possibility of redistributing costs and benefits between those affected by the change in order to produce greater equity – *planning*
- involving stakeholders in the diagnosis, planning and implementation of the change. This might reassure them that the change will be managed in a way that will maximize equity of treatment – *participation*.

Resistance and the need to motivate people to change

Attempts to introduce change often founder because the new initiative is resisted. Earlier sections of this chapter have considered why resistance might be encountered and presented an expectancy-based model for diagnosing resistance and identifying possible ways of managing it. This section provides a more detailed discussion of how change strategies can be designed to motivate individuals and groups to change. Kotter and Schlesinger (1979) identify six methods for dealing with resistance to change, which are discussed below.

Education and persuasion

One of the most frequently used ways of minimizing resistance is to educate people about the need for change. Zaltman and Duncan (1977) refer to educative strategies as those that provide a relatively unbiased presentation of the facts in order to provide a rational justification for action. This approach is based on the assumption that organizational members and other stakeholders are rational beings capable of discerning fact and adjusting their behaviour accordingly when the facts are presented to them.

A related approach is the persuasive strategy that aims to motivate people to change by biasing the message to increase its appeal. Most advertising is persuasive in nature. When the level of commitment to change is low, persuasive approaches are likely to be more effective than rational educative strategies. Persuasive approaches can increase commitment by stressing (realistically or falsely) either the benefits of changing or the costs of not changing. The way a persuasive argument is framed is important. Thaler and Sunstein (2009) argue that people are more likely to be persuaded to change if attention is focused on what they will lose by not changing rather than on what they will gain if they do change. This is because people are loss averse: 'Roughly speaking, losing something makes you twice as miserable as gaining the same thing makes you happy' (Thaler and Sunstein, 2009: 36). However, if a persuasive message is so false/biased as to deceive the change target, the approach is better classified as manipulative (see below).

Nadler (1993) builds on Lewin's notion of 'unfreezing' and argues that one of the most effective ways of motivating people to change is to expose or create a feeling of dissatisfaction with the current state. This can be accomplished via education or persuasion, but there is evidence to suggest that focusing attention on the weaknesses of the change target's current practice is less effective than informing them of the potential benefit associated with the adoption of alternative practices, or the potential losses if these alternative practices are not adopted. Confronting people about problems associated with current practice can be interpreted as criticism and blame, and can provoke a defensive reaction. Instead of motivating people to change, the effect can be to motivate them to save face by justifying current practice and denying the need to change.

Participation and involvement

Nadler (1993) argues that another effective way of surfacing and creating dissatisfaction with the current state and motivating people to change is to involve them in the collection, analysis and presentation of information. Information that people collect for themselves is more believable than information presented to them by external experts or other advocates of change.

A potential benefit of participation and involvement is that it can excite, motivate and help to create a shared perception of the need for change within a target group. When change is imposed, the change target is likely to experience a lack of control and feel the 'victim' of change. The more people are involved, the more likely they are to feel that the change is something they are helping to create. In addition to increasing motivation, participation and involvement can also produce better decisions because of the wider input and can help to sustain the change once implemented because of a greater sense of ownership.

The classic study by Coch and French (1948) demonstrated that workers are much more accepting of a change in work practices when they are involved in the planning of the change. Their findings suggested that participation led to the acceptance of new practices because it encouraged the group to 'own' them as a group goal (see Research report 11.1). This ownership offered the bonus of new group norms that helped to implement and sustain the changes. Acceptance, and the effect of acceptance on productivity, was most marked when the basis of participation was the whole group. When participation was by representation, there was an initial decline in productivity. This suggests that when people are not personally involved, it can take them longer to understand and accept new practices. Lines (2004) reports a study of change management in a national telecommunications firm that demonstrates a link between participation and the acceptance of change. Findings indicate a strong positive relationship between participation, goal achievement and organizational commitment and a strong negative relationship with resistance.

Involvement can be encouraged at any stage of the change process and can include all of a target group or only a representative sample. Organizational members might be invited to participate in the initial diagnosis of the problem, in the development of solutions and the planning of implementation strategies, in the actual implementation of the change plan and/or in the evaluation of the effectiveness of the change. Some of these possibilities will be discussed in more detail in Chapter 16 when different types of intervention are considered.

Some managers have an ideological commitment to participation and involvement, whereas others feel that it threatens their power and authority and is almost always a mistake. Kotter and Schlesinger (1979) maintain that both attitudes can lead to problems because neither is realistic. They argue that where change initiators do not have all the information they need to design and implement a change, or when they need the wholehearted commitment of the change target, involving others can make good sense. However, involvement does have some costs. It can be time-consuming and, if those who are involved have less technical expertise than the change initiators, it can result in a change plan that is not as good as it might be. Factors that can affect the decision to involve others are discussed in Chapter 14.

Facilitation and support

Kotter and Schlesinger (1979) suggest that when fear and anxiety lie at the heart of resistance, an effective approach to motivating change is to offer facilitation and support. They suggest that this might involve the provision of training in new skills, giving time off after a demanding period or simply listening and providing emotional support.

Nadler (1993) refers to the need to provide time and opportunity for people to disengage from the current state. This can be especially helpful when they feel a sense of loss associated with the letting go of something they value or feel is an important part of their individual or group identity. He also refers to the value of group sessions that provide organizational members with the opportunity to share their concerns about the change. However, he acknowledges the possibility that such sessions might also have the effect of increasing rather than reducing resistance.

Ceremonies and rituals that mark transitions can also help people to let go of the past and begin to think constructively about the future.

The provision of emotional support can be particularly effective in circumstances where feelings and emotions get in the way and undermine people's ability to think clearly and objectively about a problem. Some examples of facilitation and support will be considered in Chapter 12.

Negotiation and agreement

People can be motivated to change by rewarding those behaviours that will facilitate the change. The explicit provision of rewards is a useful approach when the change target is unlikely to perceive any obvious gains associated with the original change proposal.

Kotter and Schlesinger (1979) suggest that negotiated agreements can be a relatively easy way to avoid resistance when it is clear that someone, who has sufficient power to resist a change, is going to lose out if the change is implemented. The problem associated with this approach is that others who may have been content to go along with the change may now see the possibility of improving their lot through negotiation. The long-term effect can be to increase the cost of implementing changes and increase the time required to negotiate the change with all the interested parties.

Manipulation and cooption

Manipulation is the covert attempt to influence others to change and it can involve the deliberate biasing of messages, as considered above. It can also involve cooption. Kotter and Schlesinger (1979) note that coopting usually involves giving an individual or group leader a desirable role in the design or implementation of the change. The aim is not to seek access to any expertise they may have, rather it is to secure their endorsement.

While this approach may be quicker and cheaper than negotiation, it runs the risk of those who are coopted feeling that they have been 'tricked' into supporting the change. Also those who are coopted may exercise more influence than anticipated and steer the change in a direction not favoured by the change initiators.

Direction and a reliance on explicit and implicit coercion

The ability to exercise power exists when one person or group is dependent on another for something they value. Coercive strategies involve change managers using their power to grant or withhold valued outcomes in order to motivate people to change. While the result may be a willingness to comply and go along with the change, the change target's commitment to the change may be low. Consequently, compliance may only be sustained so long as the change manager continues to monitor the situation and maintains the threat of withholding valued outcomes.

In spite of the risks of long-term resentment and the possibility of retaliation that are often associated with coercive change strategies, there may be occasions where their use is appropriate. These may include situations where the target group has a low perceived need for change, where the proposed change is not attractive to the target group and where speed is essential.

Research report 11.1) Effect of group participation on resistance to change

Coch, L. and French, J.R. (1947) Overcoming resistance to change, *Human Relations*, 1: 512–32.

Coch and French designed one of the first experiments to explore the effect of group participation on resistance to change. They observed, in the Harwood Manufacturing Corporation, that changing people's jobs and rates of pay often led to drops in performance and higher levels of grievances, aggression and labour turnover.

They examined the effect of two different ways of including workers in the design of the change. The first involved participation through representation and the second involved the participation of the whole group. The effects of these two methods were compared with the outcome of the normal procedure for introducing change.

The normal way of introducing change was for management to define the new job and then set the new rate of pay before calling a meeting to inform the workers why the change was necessary (a response to competitive pressures) and what it would involve. Questions were answered before the meeting was closed.

The first experimental treatment (participation through representation) involved a group meeting with all operators before any changes had been designed. Managers explained the need for change and encouraged discussion before proposing a six-stage process that involved studying the job as it was being done, eliminating all unnecessary work, training representative operators in the new methods, setting the new piece rates using time studies of these operators, explaining the new job and pay rates to all operators and, finally, involving the representatives in training all the other operators. Coch and French report that this approach was successful and that the representatives referred to 'our job' and 'our rate'. The second experimental treatment was applied to two groups. It was similar to the first but involved all operators rather than just representatives.

Results

There was little improvement in the performance of the control group (where change had been introduced in the normal way) and resistance to the change developed almost immediately. However, there was significant improvement in the performance of both experimental groups (participation through representation and participation of the whole group) and the changes were introduced without any significant resistance. The rate of performance improvement was higher when all operators participated in designing the change.

Coch and French conducted a second experiment 10 weeks after the control group involved in the first experiment had been dispersed to other jobs in the company. The original group was brought together again and they were transferred to a new job using the total participation procedure (no reference was made to their previous behaviour on being transferred). The results were in sharp contrast to the results when they had been moved to new work using the company's normal procedure. Performance improved and there was no resistance.

The first set of experiments indicated that:

1 performance improvement was directly proportional to the amount of participation
2 the rate of turnover and aggression was inversely proportional to the amount of participation.

Q

The second experiment with members of the original control group suggested that the results depended on the experimental treatment (amount of participation) rather than personality factors or differences in skill level.

Summary

This chapter has considered:

1 How the general level of commitment in an organization can affect the extent to which organizational members will support new initiatives:
   - people's past experience of change can affect their level of commitment to the organization and their willingness to support further change
   - the psychological contract is an unwritten set of expectations between every member of an organization and those who represent the organization to them and incorporates concepts such as fairness, reciprocity and a sense of mutual obligation
   - if employees feel that the organization has failed to keep its side of the 'bargain', they may respond by redefining their side of the psychological contract and invest less effort in work, be less inclined to innovate and be less inclined to respond positively to changes.

2 Why people resist change:
   - parochial self-interest
   - misunderstandings and lack of trust
   - different assessments of costs and benefits
   - low tolerance for change.

3 Expectancy theory and the motivation to support or resist change
Expectancy theory considers how expectations influence motivation and provides a basis for assessing whether a stakeholder is likely to support or resist an impending change. Whether stakeholders will be motivated to support or resist the change will depend on their expectations about:
   - their ability to deliver a satisfactory level of performance in the changed situation
   - whether a satisfactory, or even exceptional, level of performance will lead to the achievement of valued outcomes in the changed situation
   - whether the net benefits accruing to them will be equitable when compared to the net benefits accruing to comparable others in the changed situation.

4 Methods for dealing with resistance to change:
   - education and persuasion
   - participation and involvement
   - facilitation and support
   - manipulation and cooption
   - direction and a reliance on explicit and implicit coercion.

References

Argyris, C.P. (1960) Organizational socialisation tactics: a longitudinal analysis of links to newcomers' commitment and role orientation, *Academy of Management Journal*, 33: 847–58.

Coch, L. and French, J.R. (1947) Overcoming resistance to change, *Human Relations*, 1: 512–32.

Doherty, N. and Horsted, J. (1995) Helping survivors stay on board, *People Management*, 1: 26–31.

Ford, J.D. and Ford, L.W. (2009) Decoding resistance to change, *Harvard Business Review*, **87**(4): 99–103.

Guest, D., Conway, N., Briner, R. and Dickman, M. (1996) *The State of the Psychological Contract in Employment*, London: Institute of Personnel and Development.

Kotter, J.P. and Schlesinger, L.A. (1979) Choosing strategies for change, *Harvard Business Review*, **57**(2): 106–14.

Lines, R. (2004) Influence of participation in strategic change: resistance, organisational commitment and change goal achievement, *Journal of Change Management*, **4**(3): 193–215.

Lines, R., Selart, M., Espedal, B. and Johansen, S.T. (2005) The production of trust during organizational change, *Journal of Change Management*, **5**(2): 221–45.

Nadler, D. (1993) Concepts for the management of organisational change, in C. Mabey and B. Mayon-White (eds) *Managing Change* (2nd edn), London: Paul Chapman.

Porter, I. and Lawler, E.E. (1968) *Managerial Attitudes and Performance*, New York: Irwin.

Pugh, D. (1993) Understanding and managing organisational change, in C. Mabey and B. Mayon-White (eds) *Managing Change* (2nd edn), London: Paul Chapman.

Thaler, R.H. and Sunstein, C.R. (2009) *Nudge: Improving Decisions about Health, Wealth, and Happiness*, London: Penguin.

Vroom, V.H. (1964) *Work and Motivation*, London: Wiley.

Zaltman, G. and Duncan, R. (1977) *Strategies for Planned Change*, London: John Wiley.

Further reading

Arnold, J. (1996) The psychological contract: a concept in need of closer scrutiny, *European Journal of Work and Organisational Psychology*, **5**(4): 511–20.

Herriot, P., Manning, W. and Kidd, J. (1997) The content of the psychological contract, *British Journal of Management*, **8**(2): 151–62.

Chapter 11 considered some of the factors that determine whether stakeholders will view a change as an opportunity that promises personal benefit or a threat that could reduce access to valued outcomes. It also considered some of the steps that change managers can take to motivate stakeholders to support a change.

This chapter addresses the way organizational members experience change, irrespective of whether they view it as an opportunity or threat. It examines the individual's response to change as a progression through a number of stages of psychological reaction. It also considers how an understanding of the way individuals react to change can help managers to plan and implement

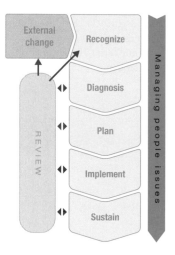

organizational change in ways that will maximize benefit and minimize cost for both the organization and individual stakeholders.

Organizational change involves a change in contextual or situational factors, such as technology, structures, systems and required competencies, and a series of personal transitions for all those affected. Bridges (1980) suggests that while many managers are wise about the mechanics of change, they are often unaware of the dynamics of transition.

Personal transitions are important because, even though some situational factors can be changed relatively quickly, the new organizational arrangements may not work as planned until the people involved let go of the way things used to be and adjust to the new situation. Commenting on the factors that can undermine the successful implementation of change, Bridges (1991: 3) claims: 'It isn't the changes that do you in, it's the transitions.'

The nature of personal transitions

Individuals, like organizations, can be confronted with both incremental and discontinuous changes. Some changes happen slowly, for example ageing. This process of gradual incremental change rarely presents any abrupt challenges to the assumptions people make about how they relate to the world around them. But this is not the case for all types of change.

A sudden merger, and the announcement that key personnel will have to reapply for their jobs in the new organization, will raise many questions in the minds of those affected about what the future will hold for them. This is an example of a change that poses a serious challenge to an individual's assumptive world.

Parkes (1971) argues that this assumptive world is the only w are aware. It includes everything we know or think we know. It affec tion of the past and our expectations of the future, our plans and ou or all of these may need to change as a result of an organizational c not these changes are perceived as gains or losses.

When changes are lasting in their effects, take place over a relatively short period of time and affect large areas of the assumptive world, they are experienced as personal transitions. The change manager might perceive the promotion of a team member to team leader as a simple and quickly accomplished organizational change. However, from the perspective of the individual who is promoted, the personal transition associated with this organizational change might be a more protracted process. It might be difficult for the newly promoted team leader to let go of their former role as team member, and the close friendships this involved with some colleagues and the distant, businesslike relationships it involved with others. The newly promoted team leader might feel isolated in the new role and might be unsure about how to behave towards others, especially subordinates who used to be both colleagues and close friends. It might take some time and quite a lot of experimenting to discover a style of managing that works. In some cases, the individual may be so unhappy with the new role that they might give up the struggle and resign, leaving the change manager with the job of finding a new team leader.

Loss of employment, whether through redundancy or early retirement, is another example of a personal transition. Parkes (1971) suggests that loss of job deprives a person of a place of work, the company of workmates and a source of income. It also removes a familiar source of identity, self-esteem and sense of purpose. Adjustment to this change will require, for example, new assumptions about the way each day will be spent and about sources of income. It might also affect the individual's faith in their capacity to work effectively and to earn a living. This kind of disruption to the assumptive world will cause an individual to set up a cycle of internal and external changes aimed at finding a new fit between self and the changed environment.

Even the loss of a job that was wanted but not secured can be difficult to cope with because a person's assumptive world contains models of the world as it is and also as it might be. People who might be promoted to works manager rehearse in their mind the world they hope to create. They engage in a kind of anticipatory socialization aided by the rich imagery of their comfortable new office, efficient secretary, challenging assignments and respectful subordinates. It may be almost as hard to give up such expectations and fantasies as it is to give up objects that actually exist. Thus the people who are not promoted may actually lose something important and they may have to make new assumptions about how things will be in the future.

Marks (2007: 724) observes that in many work organizations, discontinuous transitions have become a way of life: 'an acquisition, followed by a downsizing, a restructuring, a change in strategy, a subsequent restructuring, another wave of downsizing and so on'. He argues that the effects of stressful events are cumulative and the costs of ongoing change mount. He refers to O'Toole (1995) who notes that continual discontinuous change is not a natural condition of life, and that resistance is a to-be-expected response. He echoes Burke (2002) when he goes on to argue that the phenomenon of resistance to change is not necessarily that of resisting the change per se but is more accurately a resistance to losing something of value to the person – loss of the known and tried in the face of being asked, if not forced, to move into the unknown and untried.

personal cost of coping with transitions

Personal transitions require those affected to engage in some form of coping behaviour. Holmes and Rahe (1967) developed a social readjustment rating scale that attributed mean values to the degree of adjustment required after individuals experience a series of life events. The scale was originally constructed by telling 394 subjects that marriage had been given an arbitrary value of 50 and asking them to attribute a score to 42 other life events, indicating whether each life event would require more or less adjustment than marriage. The mean values attributed to the 43 events included in the social readjustment rating scale ranged from 100 for death of spouse to 11 for a minor infringement of the law (Table 12.1). Social readjustment was defined in terms of the amount and duration of change in one's accustomed pattern of life following a life event, irrespective of the desirability of the event. Various retrospective and prospective studies using the social readjustment rating scale, reported by Holmes and Masuda (1973), found that the magnitude of life change is highly significantly related to the time of illness onset. An example of a prospective study of this relationship is one that involved recording the life changes experienced by 2,500 officers and enlisted men aboard three US navy cruisers. It was found that there was a clear correlation between life changes experienced in a given period before the cruisers put to sea and the onset of illness during the period at sea. The studies reported by Holmes and Masuda indicate that the higher the score over the last 12 months, the greater the likelihood of illness onset over the next 12 months.

Table 12.1 *The social readjustment rating scale*

Rank	Life event	Mean value
1	Death of spouse	100
2	Divorce	73
3	Marital separation	65
4	Jail term	63
5	Death of close family member	63
6	Personal injury or illness	53
7	Marriage	50
8	Sacked from work	47
9	Marital reconciliation	45
10	Retirement	45
11	Change in health of family member	44
12	Pregnancy	40
13	Sexual difficulties	39
14	Gain of a new family member (child or 'oldster' moving in)	39
15	Business readjustment	39
16	Change in financial state	39
17	Death of close friend	37
18	Change to a different line of work	36
19	Change in number of arguments with spouse	35
20	Taking on a large mortgage (for example for house purchase)	31
21	Foreclosure of mortgage or loan	30
22	Change in responsibilities at work	29
23	Son or daughter leaves home	29
24	Trouble with in-laws	29
25	Outstanding personal achievement	28
26	Spouse beginning or ceasing work	26
27	Begin or end school (formal education)	26

Rank	Life event	Mean value
28	Change in living conditions	25
29	Revision of personal habits (dress, manners, associations and so on)	24
30	Trouble with boss	23
31	Change in work hours or conditions	20
32	Change in residence	20
33	Change in schools/college	20
34	Change in recreation	19
35	Change in church (mosque) activities	19
36	Change in social activities	18
37	Taking on medium level loan (for TV, computer and so on)	17
38	Change in sleeping habits (amount, time of day and so on)	16
39	Change in number of family get-togethers	15
40	Change in eating habits	15
41	Holidays	13
42	Christmas	12
43	Minor violations of the law	11

Source: Adapted from Holmes and Rahe, 1967: 215

This relationship may be moderated by individual differences in the ability to cope with personal transitions. People may perceive the same event and/or assess their ability to cope with it in different ways. This can be influenced by many factors, including past experience of the event and personality variables such as hardiness, self-esteem, self-reliance and so on.

You might find it interesting to use the social readjustment rating scale (Table 12.1) to assess the amount of life change that you have experienced in the last 12 months. Total the values of the life change events you have experienced over this period. A life crisis is defined as 150 or more life change units in any one year:

▶ a mild life crisis is defined as 150–199 life change units
▶ a moderate crisis is 200–299 life change units
▶ a major life crisis is defined as more than 300 life change units.

The relationship between life change and illness susceptibility highlights the personal cost associated with adjusting to change, irrespective of whether the change is viewed as desirable or undesirable. It also points to the possibility that different people may react to the same organizational change in different ways, because for some it is an isolated event, whereas for others it is one of a number of changes, at work and elsewhere, that push them towards a major life crisis.

Adjusting to organizational change

When individuals adjust to organizational changes that:

▶ are lasting in their effects
▶ take place over a relatively short period of time
▶ affect large areas of the assumptive world

they experience a process of personal transition. Exercise 12.1 invites you to reflect on how you have reacted to a change that involved a personal transition. The information generated by this exercise will enable you to compare your reactions with the typical pattern of reaction described by the stage model of transition presented later in this chapter.

Your experience of a transition

Think of a change that was lasting in its effects, took place over a relatively short period of time and affected the assumptions you made about how you related to the world around you.

Examples of this kind of change could be redundancy, job change, promotion, relocation, bereavement, illness or accident that affected your mobility or some other aspect of your functioning, marriage, or birth of first child. For the purpose of this exercise, the change need not be an organizational change. Answer the following questions.

Entry
When did you realize that the transition was to take place?

How did you know?

What did you feel at the time?

What did you do/how did you behave?

During the transition
Did your feelings and/or behaviour change during the transition? Are you able to identify any stages that highlighted differences in the way you reacted to the change? If so, what were these stages?

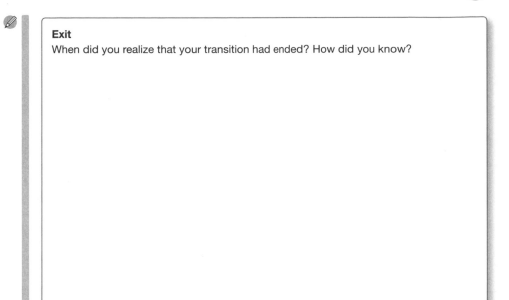

Exit
When did you realize that your transition had ended? How did you know?

Think about your answers to the questions posed in Exercise 12.1 when the stages of psychological reaction to a change are considered below.

Organizational change and personal transition

Organizational change involves the ending of something and the beginning of something else. For example, it might involve the introduction of a new organizational structure, a more automated production process, revised procedures, the merger of two units, the closure of a plant, a redundancy programme, job transfers, a new project or a promotion. While these changes might be carefully planned and happen on a predetermined date, it might be some time before those involved have adapted to their new circumstances. Managers need to develop an understanding of how people respond to change. They need to know the course of events associated with the process of transition and the kinds of actions they can engage in to facilitate adaptation.

A model of change as a transition

The model presented below is based on the work of William Bridges (1980, 1991). It conceptualizes transition as beginning with an ending and then going on to a new beginning via a neutral zone (Figure 12.1). These three phases are not separate stages divided by clear boundaries. Phases can overlap and an individual can be in more than one phase at any one time. Bridges sees the movement through a transition as being marked by a change in the dominance of one phase as it gives way to the next.

Endings involve letting go of the old situation and the identity that went with it. It is impossible to fully engage in a new role or have a new purpose until those involved have let go of the old role or old purpose. For example, as noted above, a promotion, especially when it is in the same work group, involves letting go of the role of group member and internalizing the new role of group leader. Fink et al. (1971), drawing on the work of Lewin, argue that every human system has within it forces for the maintenance of the status quo and forces for growth. While these forces tend to operate counter to each other, the balance between maintenance and growth is constantly shifting. Endings are often associated with a predominance of maintenance forces that manifest themselves in a resistance to change and a reluctance to let go.

The neutral zone is the in-between state. It involves a recognition of the need to change and uncertainty about the nature of more desirable end states. It is a period of disorientation, self-doubt and anxiety, but it can also be a period of growth and creativity in which new opportunities are identified. However, there is a danger that people may be so uncomfortable with the ambiguity and disorientation associated with this stage of transition that they push prematurely for certainty and closure. Consequently, they may lock on to the first opportunity that offers any promise of a more satisfactory state of affairs and, in so doing, lock out the possibility of a creative search for better alternatives.

TRANSITION

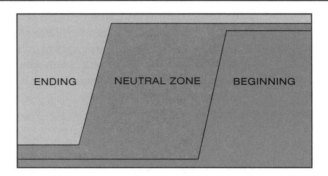

Figure 12.1 *Bridges' model of transition*
Source: Bridges, 1991: 70

Beginnings involve reorientation to a new situation and the development of a new identity. Initially the forces for growth predominate but eventually, as the new situation is more clearly defined and a new identity is internalized, the forces for maintenance and growth achieve a new balance.

The stages of psychological reaction

People going through change experience a variety of emotional and cognitive states. Transitions typically progress through a cycle of reasonably predictable phases described below. This applies to all kinds of transitions: voluntary and imposed, desirable and undesirable. There is a widely held view that, in each case, the person experiencing the transition will have to work through all the stages if the transition is to be successfully completed. Understanding this process can help both individuals and managers.

The model presented below has been developed by Hayes and Hyde from an earlier version that originally appeared in *Transitions: Understanding and Managing Personal Change* by Adams et al. (1976). The cycle reflects variations in the degree to which people feel able to exercise control over the situation. The seven transition stages are shown in Figure 12.2 and discussed below.

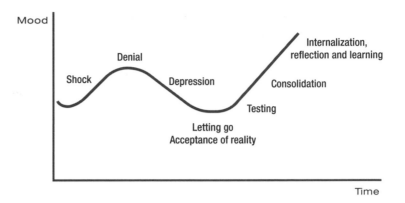

Figure 12.2 *Transition phases*

Awareness/shock

Often people have little warning of changes and they experience the initial phase of a transition as a shock. They feel overwhelmed, frozen, paralysed. Feelings of anxiety and panic can undermine their ability to take in new information, think constructively and plan. This leads to a state of immobilization. People behave as though they are on 'autopilot' and show little response to new developments. While their mood may be more positive if the transition is perceived as a desirable gain, for example winning first prize on the lottery, they may still experience a state of immobilization and have difficulty planning and taking constructive action. In those circumstances where people develop a gradual awareness of a pending change, they often focus on what they might lose and engage in 'worry work' that diverts their attention from other matters that might require their attention. The intensity of this phase will be influenced by the degree of preparedness and the desirability of the transition – immobilization will be greater when the transition is unexpected and unwanted.

Denial

This phase is characterized by a retreat from the reality of change. Negative changes may be denied or trivialized and attention may be displaced onto other more immediate but less important matters. Energy and activity are devoted to the known and the familiar and any perceived threat to the status quo is managed by behaving in habitual ways. Clinging to the past and refusing to consider the need to change can lead to a reduction in anxiety. Anything or anyone who challenges this false sense of security is likely to provoke an angry response. Resistance to change is at its highest at this point. Positive changes may induce euphoria together with an unwillingness to consider any possible negative consequences. In some cases, denial may be functional if it provides the opportunity to recharge 'emotional batteries' and helps a person face up to the need to change.

Depression

Eventually the reality of the change becomes apparent and the individual acknowledges that things cannot continue as they are. In terms of Bridges' model, this corresponds to the start of the neutral zone. This provokes a feeling of depression often associated with a feeling that the situation is beyond one's control. This phase may be characterized by anger, sadness, withdrawal and confusion. This depressed mood occurs even in changes that were initially embraced enthusiastically whenever practical difficulties are encountered. It is in the depression phase therefore that the change really starts to be experienced as stressful. If the change was a voluntary one, this may be the point at which the person gives up. In involuntary changes, the person may seek to leave the situation.

Letting go

This phase involves accepting reality for what it is. It implies a clear letting go of the past. This may be experienced as a 'little death' and often entails a process of mourning. It can help at this point to remember that the lowest ebb is the turn of the tide.

Testing

A more active, creative, experimental involvement in the new situation starts to take place. New ways of behaving and being are tried out. More energy is available but anger and irritability may be easily aroused if the new behaviour is not successful. This phase may involve trial-and-error behaviour or a more active plan-do-study-act cycle (see Chapter 23). As some patterns are found that seem to work, this phase gradually gives way to the next.

Consolidation

Out of the testing process come some new ways of being and behaving that are gradually adopted as new norms. This corresponds to the beginning stage in Bridges' model. This stage progresses in parallel with testing but to begin with there is often more testing and rejecting than testing and consolidating. It involves reflecting on new experiences and assessing whether they offer a basis for a constructive way forward. Sometimes there is little consolidation. Early experiments with new roles and relationships are rejected and the person experiencing the transition learns little from the experience. When consolidation occurs, it involves reflecting on the new experience (the outcome of a test) and using any learning to build on this experience and inform the choice of further 'testing' experiences.

Internalization, reflection and learning

The transition is complete when the changed behaviour is normal and unthinking and is the new natural order of things. Ideally, the past has been left behind and little or no 'unfinished business' remains. Reflection is a cognitive process involving reflecting on what all the activity and emotion have really meant. It is at this point that learning and personal growth, which may benefit future transitions, may be recognized.

At this point, you might find it interesting to reflect on the answers you gave to the questions in Exercise 12.1. Does the stage model of psychological reaction presented above provide a useful conceptual framework for understanding the process of adjustment you went through?

Some observations on the stage model of transitions

Each individual's experience of a transition will be influenced by a number of factors. These include the importance of the transition, whether it is perceived as a gain or loss, the intensity of its impact, the existence of other simultaneous transitions (and the magnitude of any associated life crisis), personal resilience and so on. It follows therefore that there can be no absolutely standard pattern of reaction. Some possible variations are noted below:

▶ The wave (shown in Figure 12.2) can be shallower or deeper and the overall shape of the curve may be skewed one way or the other. For example, if the change is perceived as a desirable opportunity, the individual might find it easier to let go of the past, whereas if it is perceived as a threat or loss, the individual might be reluctant to let go and resist the change for as long as possible.

▶ The time taken to pass through all the phases can vary greatly. Just as some people take longer than others to come to terms with the loss of a loved one, so organizational members can vary in terms of the time it takes for them to adjust to a work-related transition.

▶ Although presented as a purely linear process, people may regress and slip back to an earlier stage in the process.

▶ People can get stuck at any phase and not complete the cycle. They may, for example, continue to deny the need to change or fail to recognize the new opportunities associated with the change.

Where multiple transitions are involved, people handle the situation in different ways. Some people keep the transitions firmly compartmentalized and deal with one at a time; others throw their energy into one as a displacement activity to get away from another, which is therefore held in denial; in other cases, one major transition predominates and swamps the others.

Implications for individuals and change managers

Hayes and Hyde (1996) summarize some of the implications for individuals and change managers going through a transition.

For individuals:

▶ it takes time for people to make the adjustments required in transitions

▶ it can help them to know that their own experience is normal, it will involve ups and downs and it will eventually come to an end

▶ the process can be managed: there are things they can do to facilitate their own transitions.

For change managers:

▶ it is important to recognize that there will often be a time lag between the announcement of a change and an emotional reaction to it: it is easy to mistake the apparent calm of the immobilization and denial phases for acceptance of the change

▶ because any given change will have different implications for different individuals or groups, different parts of the organization will progress through the cycle at different rates and in different ways

▶ change managers need to beware of getting out of phase with their staff. They tend to know about the change before others and so it is not unusual for them to have reached an acceptance of change long before other organization members. This can create great potential for ineffective communication

▶ the cycle cannot be avoided, but there is much that change managers can do to facilitate people's passage through it.

Facilitating progress through a transition

This final section outlines some of the interventions that change managers can make to help facilitate other people's progress through a transition. This kind of facilitation is particularly important where people have become stuck at a particular stage in the process.

The interventions are presented in relation to each stage of the process of transition. What follows is not meant to be a prescriptive list of what the change manager should do. It is a set of suggestions, based on observations and anecdotal evidence of what seems to have worked in practice, supplemented by managers' reports about what they have done that appeared to help others to manage their personal transitions. These suggestions might alert you to some of the issues that have to be managed and possible ways of intervening that might be appropriate in a particular set of circumstances.

Shock

The shock reaction associated with the announcement/discovery of a change affecting an individual's assumptive world can sometimes be minimized by:

▶ preparing the ground and creating a climate of receptivity to change
▶ consulting and involving people in the decision making.

If this is not possible, the change manager might consider possible ways of announcing the change. Anecdotal evidence suggests that the following points might be worth considering:

1 *Who should make the announcement:*
   • This might be a senior manager in order to signal the importance of the change and the organization's concern for the people involved.
   • Alternatively, it might be decided that a relatively junior manager should make the announcement because they have a better relationship with those affected.
2 *Timing:*
   • Should the announcement be made simultaneously to all staff or should some be told before others?
   • Should people be told as soon as possible or should the announcement be delayed?
3 *Method:*
   • Should it be done face to face, via a video link, by email or by letter?
   • In face-to-face encounters, it is important to keep calm and avoid becoming defensive or aggressive in the face of questions.
4 *Content:*
   • Should a consistent message be given to all?
   • How much information should be communicated?
   • Should the message be kept as simple as possible?
   • Should explanations be given about why the change is necessary?
5 *Dialogue:*
   • It often helps to show empathy and understanding for how people will feel, for example 'I know this will be upsetting for you and I feel very sad about it myself, but ... .'
   • Should questions be encouraged?

It is important to allow time for people to digest the information and share their feelings with others.

When people are in shock, the change manager needs to recognize that:

▶ performance might be temporarily impaired and in some circumstances this might lead to dangerous or costly consequences, which could influence the timing of the announcement
▶ some people might need more support than others.

Denial

The change manager needs to diagnose what it is that is being denied, for example the change isn't necessary, is not real, does not affect me and so on, and then consider whether it would be helpful to:

▶ confront what is being denied gently and supportively
▶ repeat the message
▶ draw people's attention to relevant examples, evidence and experience
▶ arrange demonstrations of what the change will involve, if possible
▶ establish and keep to a timetable to provide milestones and evidence of change
▶ find ways to ensure that they have to engage with the reality of the change
▶ take early action if at all possible. The longer the gap between the announcement of a change and the change taking effect, the easier it is for an individual to ignore that the change is for real
▶ get people to do practical things related to the change.

Depression

The change manager can intervene in order to help others understand and accept the situation by:

▶ providing support
▶ listening
▶ adopting an accepting and non-critical reaction to their expression of feelings.

The change manager can also help others to work on their feelings about the situation by:

▶ helping them to get it off their chest
▶ providing space to grieve
▶ providing appropriate opportunities to vent emotion.

They can also help them to identify opportunities to move on by:

▶ not letting them wallow in feeling bad: gently confronting and challenging
▶ helping them to identify other things they are good at
▶ providing further information about the change to help people to envisage what the future will be like
▶ helping them to identify options and possible benefits
▶ helping them to focus their attention on the things they can do or can influence
▶ where possible, providing opportunities for the exercise of influence, for example consultation and involvement.

Letting go

The change manager can help people let go of the past by:

▶ explaining the need for change in terms of benefits rather than problems associated with past practice. Rubbishing the past can provoke a defensive reaction

▶ providing challenging targets associated with the movement towards a more desirable state
   ▶ drawing attention to deadlines
   ▶ eliminating the symbols of the past
   ▶ reminiscing in a way that leads to a process of taking the best forward from the past
   ▶ marking the ending by rituals and ceremonies, wakes and leaving parties
   ▶ letting people take souvenirs and mementoes.

Testing

Some of the ways in which the change manager can encourage testing include:

   ▶ creating the space, time and resources required to test
   ▶ promoting creative thinking
   ▶ helping people to identify options
   ▶ encouraging risk taking and experimentation
   ▶ discouraging premature closure
   ▶ avoiding punishing those who make mistakes
   ▶ injecting new processes, tools and competencies that will help people to help themselves
   ▶ eliminating the drivers of old behaviours
   ▶ acting as a mentor
   ▶ praising and supporting successes
   ▶ encourage networking and cross-fertilization
   ▶ providing feedback.

Consolidation

Consolidation can be facilitated by:

   ▶ reviewing performance and learning
   ▶ helping others to identify the desirable characteristics of the new state
   ▶ recognizing and rewarding achievement
   ▶ getting them to help others and share their experience
   ▶ helping them to build on successes
   ▶ broadcasting their successes.

Reflecting, learning and internalization

Reflecting, learning and internalization can be facilitated by:

   ▶ helping them to review the experience of change – asking questions, running review workshops and so on
   ▶ conducting formal post-implementation reviews
   ▶ getting them to help others and share their experience.

Summary

This chapter has addressed the way organizational members experience change:

   ▶ Organizational change not only involves a change in situational factors, such as technology, structures and systems, but also a series of personal transitions for all those affected.
   ▶ New structures and systems may not work as planned until organizational members let go of the way things used to be and adjust to the new situation.

Incremental and discontinuous changes:

▶ Individuals, just like organizations, can be confronted with incremental or discontinuous changes.
▶ Incremental changes do not present any serious challenge to the assumptions we make about how we relate to the world around us, but discontinuous changes do.
▶ Discontinuous changes are those that are perceived to be relatively lasting in their effects, take place over a relatively short period of time and affect large areas of an individual's assumptive world.

The personal cost of coping with transitions:

▶ Studies have found a link between the magnitude of life changes – irrespective of the desirability of the changes – and illness susceptibility.
▶ This relationship can be moderated by individual differences, for example hardiness and self-esteem, and past experience.

The process of personal transition involves a number of stages of psychological reaction:

▶ *Awareness/shock* – when awareness is sudden, the individual can be overwhelmed – anxiety can undermine the ability to think constructively and plan, leading to a state of immobilization.
▶ *Denial* – individuals cling to the past in order to reduce anxiety – attention is focused on the known and the familiar.
▶ *Depression* – following acknowledgement that things cannot continue as they are, individuals experience a feeling of loss of control. This can lead to depression, anger, sadness, withdrawal and confusion.
▶ *Letting go* – the need to change is accepted.
▶ *Testing* – experimental involvement in new situations begins to occur. Frustration is experienced when experiments fail. As some experiments appear to work, the individual begins to consolidate successes.
▶ *Consolidation* – this stage progresses in parallel with testing and leads to new ways of behaving and being.
▶ *Reflection, learning and internalization* – the transition is completed when the changed behaviour is accepted as normal.

An individual's experience of a transition will be influenced by a number of factors:

▶ the importance of the transition
▶ whether it is perceived as a gain or loss
▶ the existence of other simultaneous transitions
▶ personal resilience.

Implications for managers:

▶ Recognize that there will often be a time lag between the announcement of a change and an emotional reaction to it. It is easy to mistake the apparent calm of the initial awareness and denial phases for acceptance of the change.
▶ Different individuals or groups will progress through the cycle at different rates and in different ways, because the change might affect them differently.
▶ Change managers need to beware of getting out of phase with their staff. They tend to know about the change before others and so it is not unusual for them to have reached an acceptance of change long before other organization members.

References

Adams, J., Hayes, J. and Hopson, B. (1976) *Transitions: Understanding and Managing Personal Change*, London: Martin Robertson.

Bridges, W. (1980) *Transitions*, Reading, MA: Addison Wesley.

Bridges, W. (1991) *Managing Transitions: Making the Most of Change*, Reading, MA: Addison Wesley.

Burke, R.J. (2002) Organizational transitions, in C.L. Cooper and R.J. Burke (eds) *The New World of Work*, Malden, MA: Blackwell.

Fink, S.L., Beak, J. and Taddeo, K. (1971) Organisational crisis and change, *Journal of Applied Behavioral Science*, **7**(1): 15–37.

Hayes, J. and Hyde, P. (1996) Transitions workshop, unpublished manual, Hyde Management Consulting, Woodvale House, Basingstoke Road, Reading RG7 1AE.

Holmes, T.H. and Masuda, M. (1973) Life change and illness susceptibility, in J.P. Scott and E.C. Senay (eds) *Separation and Depression*, Washington DC: American Association for the Advancement of Science.

Holmes, T.H. and Rahe, R.H. (1967) The social readjustment rating scale, *Journal of Psychosomatic Research*, 11: 213–18.

Marks, M. (2007) A framework for facilitating adaptation to organizational transition, *Journal of Organizational Change Management*, **20**(5): 721

O'Toole, J. (1995) *Leading Change*, San Francisco, CA: Jossey-Bass.

Parkes, C.M. (1971) Psycho-social transitions: a field of study, *Social Science and Medicine*, 5: 101–15.

Further reading

Stuart, R. (1995) Experiencing organizational change: triggers, processes and outcomes of change journeys, *Personnel Review*, **24**(2): 1–87.

13

Modes of intervening

There are many ways in which change agents can intervene to facilitate change. Blake and Mouton (1983) argue that even where change agents have correctly diagnosed the issue or problem that is of concern to the client, their efforts may not be successful if they adopt an inappropriate mode of intervening. The focus of this chapter is modes of intervening to facilitate change.

When people think about change agents, they often only think about external consultants, but within organizations, there are many people who occupy roles that are almost exclusively concerned with facilitating change. Examples include systems analysts, business development advisers, operations researchers, management development

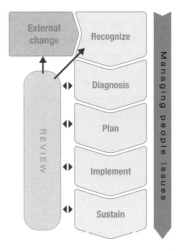

specialists, trainers, project managers and the transition managers referred to in Chapter 15. There are also many managers who, as part of their normal day-to-day responsibilities, intervene to facilitate change. They intervene to facilitate the introduction of new working practices, find ways of reducing costs, help staff to develop better relationships with customers, help others to identify and exploit opportunities offered by changing circumstances, or to help colleagues who are experiencing problems that are affecting their performance or general wellbeing. Throughout this chapter, all those who facilitate change will be referred to as change agents or helpers and those who are being helped – be they colleagues, subordinates or clients in the more conventional sense – will be referred to as clients.

Paraphrasing Mangham (1986: 4), successful change agents are those who can conduct themselves in the complexity of the organization as subtle, insightful, incisive performers. They require a highly developed ability to read the actual and potential behaviour of others around them and to construct their own conduct in accordance with this reading. We all have this is ability to a greater or lesser extent but, according to Mangham, 'the most successful among us appear to do social life with a higher degree of skill than the rest of us manage'.

Much has been written about the skills required by change agents. Greiner and Metzger (1983) refer to a wide range of skills but argue that consulting and facilitating change are essentially human enterprises and, irrespective of whether the problem being addressed concerns a new accounting system or the need for better strategic planning, the success of the project will be largely determined by the quality of the change agents' interaction with the client or client group. Margerison (2000) echoes this view and highlights the importance of personal and interpersonal skills.

Intervention styles

Change agents can intervene to help in many different ways. The intervention style indictor has been designed to help you to identify your preferred approach to facilitating change. You might find it useful to complete it now and refer back to your intervention style profile as you read on. It will provide you with a point of reference when thinking about how you might improve the effectiveness of your helping interventions.

Exercise 13.1

The intervention style indicator

Five cases (problem situations) are presented and, for each case, there are five examples of how a change agent/helper could respond. For each of the five responses to each case, circle the number on the scale that most closely reflects the probability that you would use that response. For example:

NEVER USE →	1	②	3	4	5	← DEFINITELY USE

There are no right or wrong answers.

CASE A

A newly appointed supervisor has complained to you that her subordinates are hostile, moody, only hear what they choose to hear and often fail to obey instructions. She likened their behaviour to rebellious school children who are determined to 'break' the new teacher. Her account placed all the blame for the rapidly deteriorating situation onto her subordinates. You had not expected this kind of conversation because she had joined the company with glowing references and a 10-year record of successful people management. In addition, her work group has never created problems before. All of them have been with the company for at least 10 months, most are well qualified and two have recently been through the company's assessment centre and been identified as having potential for promotion.

How likely is it that you would use each of the following responses? Circle one number on each of the five scales

1 Introduce the supervisor to a theory that might help her better understand the situation. For example, you might explain the basics of transactional analysis and ask her to apply it to her problem and consider whether her subordinates see her as a controlling parent dealing with a group of inexperienced children rather than an adult interacting with other competent adults, and then speculate how she might apply the theory to improve the situation.

A1 NEVER USE →	1	2	3	4	5	← DEFINITELY USE

2 Tell her that she has failed to recognize the quality of her subordinates, she is undervaluing the contribution they can make, and she needs to delegate more and give them greater responsibility.

A2 NEVER USE →	1	2	3	4	5	← DEFINITELY USE

3 Listen carefully and attempt to see the problem through her eyes, in the hope that by being supportive you can encourage her to open up and tell her story, which in turn may help her to develop a better understanding of the problem and what needs to be done about it.

A3 NEVER USE →	1	2	3	4	5	← DEFINITELY USE

4 Suggest to her that it may not only be her subordinates who hear what they choose to hear, and ask her if she has really paid attention to all the messages she has been sent by the members of her work group.

A4 NEVER USE →	1	2	3	4	5	← DEFINITELY USE

5 Help her to get to the bottom of the problem by assisting her to gather more information, which she can use to develop a better understanding of what is going on and what can be done to improve matters.

A5 NEVER USE →	1	2	3	4	5	← DEFINITELY USE

CASE B

You have been approached by the head of a strategic business unit in your organization with a request for help. She has been in post for six months and has come to the view that the way her top team is working together is adversely affecting performance.

How likely is it that you would use each of the following responses? Circle one number on each of the five scales

1 Offer to collect information from people who are affected by how well the team is performing and feed this back to her and her senior colleagues to help them review their performance and agree what they need to do to improve matters.

B1 NEVER USE →	1	2	3	4	5	← DEFINITELY USE

2 Offer to bring in a trainer to run a workshop for her top team, which would introduce colleagues to the concept of team roles and help them to use Belbin's (1993) model of team roles to diagnose how well they are working together and what they might do to improve their performance.

B2 NEVER USE →	1	2	3	4	5	← DEFINITELY USE

3 Adopt a supportive approach and encourage her to talk about her concerns in order to help her clarify her own thoughts and feelings and develop for herself a better understanding of the situation.

B3 NEVER USE →	1	2	3	4	5	← DEFINITELY USE

4 Interview all members of her top team and the people who are affected by how well the team is performing in order to prepare a report that lists a set of recommendations that she should implement to improve the situation.

B4 NEVER USE →	1	2	3	4	5	← DEFINITELY USE

5 Focus attention on her behaviour and consider whether this might be contributing to the problem. This approach might involve challenging some of the assumptions she is making and/or drawing attention to discrepancies between what she says she does and what you observe her doing.

B5 NEVER USE →	1	2	3	4	5	← DEFINITELY USE

CASE C

You are the human resources manager of a large utility company. An employee, a 40-year-old widower, was recently promoted and moved from a busy office in the city, where he had spent most of his working life, to manage a small but strategically important office in a relatively isolated small town. He has come to see you because he is unhappy with the new job. He misses his friends, does not enjoy being the boss in a situation where he has no colleagues he can relate to, and he reports that the people who live locally are cliquish, aloof and unfriendly.

How likely is it that you would use each of the following responses? Circle one number on each of the five scales

1 Tell him that there is a vacancy at his old grade in the department he used to work in and indicate that you think the best solution would be for him to move back.

C1 NEVER USE →	1	2	3	4	5	← DEFINITELY USE

2 Explore how he feels about the situation without passing judgement or jumping to conclusions. Make sure that you really understand why he is unhappy and do everything you can to help him clarify his own feelings about what the problem might be. You might listen hard to what he has to say and then reflect back to him the essence of what you think you heard. For example, 'What you seem to be saying is … Have I got it right?'

C2 NEVER USE →	1	2	3	4	5	← DEFINITELY USE

3 Help him adopt a balanced problem-solving approach and encourage him to thoroughly explore every aspect of the problem and, where necessary, gather information that might help him to identify and evaluate possible solutions, for example by helping him to identify opportunities to meet new people.

C3 NEVER USE →	1	2	3	4	5	← DEFINITELY USE

4 Give him the kind of feedback that might push him into taking a new initiative, for example by telling him that you have listened to what he has said and not once heard him mention anything he has done to try to make new friends – all he seems to do is moan about others and complain that they do nothing to make him welcome. You might try to encourage him into action by asking him if he has thought about what he might do that would make others want to get to know him better.

C4 NEVER USE →	1	2	3	4	5	← DEFINITELY USE

5 Lend him a copy of Dale Carnegie's (1936) book *How to Win Friends and Influence People* and suggest that if he could master some of the techniques and skills it contains, making friends might be something he could do more easily.

C5 NEVER USE →	1	2	3	4	5	← DEFINITELY USE

CASE D

The CEO of a fast-growing software company has approached you for help following the second time in 12 months that a project team has failed to deliver a major project within budget and on time. She told you that on both occasions similar problems appeared to have been associated with the failures. She also told you that relationships between members of the project team have deteriorated and they all appear to be blaming each other for the failures.

How likely is it that you would use each of the following responses? Circle one number on each of the five scales

1 Interview the CEO and the manager in charge of the project team to ensure that you have a good understanding of what happened before advising the CEO what she should do to ensure that future projects will be managed more efficiently and effectively.

D1 NEVER USE →	1	2	3	4	5	← DEFINITELY USE

2 Run a workshop on new approaches to managing projects and use the models presented to help team members to review the way they managed the last two projects and identify lessons they might use to inform the way they will manage the next project.

D2 NEVER USE →	1	2	3	4	5	← DEFINITELY USE

3 Talk to each member of the team individually in order to help them to express any frustrations, anxieties or other feelings that might be inhibiting their ability to make an objective assessment of the situation.

D3 NEVER USE →	1	2	3	4	5	← DEFINITELY USE

4 Interview all members of the project team and other stakeholders in order to identify key issues related to the failures, then convene a workshop where you can feed this information back and use it to stimulate a discussion of the problem and help them to explore ways of improving their performance.

D4 NEVER USE →	1	2	3	4	5	← DEFINITELY USE

5 Work with the CEO to help her clarify the issues she wants to raise with the project team, and then facilitate a meeting where she can confront members with her concerns.

D5 NEVER USE →	1	2	3	4	5	← DEFINITELY USE

CASE E

A colleague has come to you for help. He does not want to be an autocratic boss and believes that people work best when they are given the freedom to get on with their job. However, his department is beginning to get itself a reputation for not getting it right. He has explained that while he always tries to pursue an open-door policy, there are some people who never cross his threshold. Consequently, he is badly informed and avoidable mistakes have been made. He is obviously upset and you suspect that his boss has just had him in and torn a strip off him.

How likely is it that you would use each of the following responses? Circle one number on each of the five scales

1 Share with him a similar problem you once had and tell him what you did about it. Also, suggest that there can come a time when democracy has to go out of the window and you have to read the riot act, which is what he should do now.

E1 NEVER USE →	1	2	3	4	5	← DEFINITELY USE

2 Tell him about a theory you are familiar with that argues that the best style of leadership might vary from one situation to another, and suggest that one way forward might be for him to consider whether his current style appears to be a 'best fit' or whether the theory would suggest an alternative leadership style.

E2 NEVER USE →	1	2	3	4	5	← DEFINITELY USE

3 On the basis of what you have observed, challenge his view that he always operates an open-door policy. You might, for example, tell him that you have heard that he is never around when he is needed, and that while he might believe he is approachable, others see him as aloof and distant. You might follow this up by asking him to consider how true this is.

E3 NEVER USE →	1	2	3	4	5	← DEFINITELY USE

4 You can see that he is upset, so decide that the best thing you can do is to sit him down with a cup of coffee and let him get it off his chest.

E4 NEVER USE →	1	2	3	4	5	← DEFINITELY USE

5 Help him to identify some specific circumstances where things have gone wrong and then question him about a number of these problems to sort out precisely what happened and whether there are any patterns that he could do something about.

E5 NEVER USE →	1	2	3	4	5	← DEFINITELY USE

SCORING

In the grid below, all the available responses to each case have been arranged into columns that reflect five different styles of helping.

- Taking each case in turn, enter the number you circled for each response alongside the appropriate response code in the grid. For example, for case A, you may have circled 2 for response A1, so enter 2 in the square for A1; and you may have circled 5 for response A2, so enter 5 in the square for A2, and so on.

NB: For cases B to E, the response codes are presented in different sequences and are not arranged in order from 1 to 5.

- Calculate the total score for each column and enter this in the box provided.

The total score for each column indicates your relative preference for the different helping styles.

Response grid									
	Theorizing		Advising		Supporting		Challenging		Information gathering
Case A	A1		A2		A3		A4		A5
Please note that from B to E the response codes are not arranged in order from 1 to 5									
Case B	B2		B4		B3		B5		B1
Case C	C5		C1		C2		C4		C3
Case D	D2		D1		D3		D5		D4
Case E	E2		E1		E4		E3		E5
TOTAL									

You should now have a score for all five modes of intervening. Note whether your scores are equally spread across all five intervention styles or whether your response pattern indicates that you prefer to use one or two approaches more than the other modes of intervening.

The goal of intervening

Egan (1988) argues that the management of change is not about planning or action but about achieving results – system-enhancing outcomes such as innovations realized, problems managed more effectively and opportunities developed, or new organization-enhancing behaviours put in place.

Change agents intervene to facilitate change. Blake and Mouton (1986) describe their interventions as cycle-breaking endeavours. They argue that behaviour tends to be cyclical in character, that is, sequences of behaviour are repeated within specific time periods or particular contexts or settings. Some of these patterns of behaviour are advantageous to the client or client group but some do little to promote their interests and may even be harmful. They go on to argue that individuals, groups or larger client systems such as entire organizations may engage in behaviour cycles by force of habit. They may not be conscious of the possibility of harmful or self-defeating consequences. They may be aware that things are not going well, but they may not understand why or what they could do to improve matters. The change agent's function is to help clients identify and break out of these damaging kinds of cycles.

This cycle-breaking endeavour can take many forms. It can be prescriptive or collaborative. Egan (2004) argues that problem management and opportunity development are not things that helpers do to clients. He advocates a collaborative approach that involves clients achieving their goals through the facilitation of the helper. However, much of the help offered by external consultants and internal change agents is not collaborative in nature.

The five modes of intervening featured in the intervention style indicator – advising, supporting, theorizing, challenging and information gathering – are now discussed.

Prescriptive mode of intervening: advising

The mode of intervening referred to as 'advising' on the intervention style indicator is prescriptive. Many change agents intervene by giving advice and telling others what to do in order to rectify problems or develop opportunities. Change agents who adopt this mode of intervening assume that they have a greater level of relevant expertise than their clients and can discern their real needs. They also appear to assume that clients lack the necessary competence to either make a sound diagnosis or plan corrective actions for themselves.

In many circumstances, consultants or change managers can see a solution because they are more experienced than their clients/subordinates, but if they intervene by offering advice and telling people what to do, they deprive them of the opportunity to learn how to solve the problem for themselves. Clients can become dependent on the change agent and the next time they experience a difficulty, they again have to seek help.

Often clients actively seek advice, especially when they are under great pressure to find a solution and/or when they are at their wits' end. Steele (1969) argues that the needs of both the client and the change agent may propel the change agent towards exclusive occupancy of the role of expert in their relationship, and in those circumstances where the client accepts the change agent as expert, there may be some benefits. However, he also identifies some costs. One is the increased dependency, which has already been mentioned, and the other has to do with the change agent's neglect of the clients' knowledge about their own problem. Even where clients do not attempt to withhold this knowledge, the helper may choose to ignore it:

> The client often has great wisdom (intuitive if not systematic) about many aspects of his own situation, and an overweighing of the consultant's knowledge value may indeed cause poorer choices to be made than if there were a more balanced view of that which each can contribute to the situation. (Steele, 1969: 193)

Although clients often seek advice, there are circumstances when they may reject any advice they are offered. For example, they are likely to reject advice when they lack confidence in the expertise of the change agent, or when it is offered by a change agent who appears to be insensitive to their needs.

Collaborative approach

The other four modes of intervening – supporting, theorizing, challenging and information gathering – are non-prescriptive. Change agents adopting these approaches work with clients to help them develop opportunities or manage their own problems rather than intervene by telling them what they should do.

A number of factors can contribute to clients being ineffective opportunity developers or problem managers. Emotional states such as anger or insecurity may undermine their ability to function normally. They may lack the information they need to understand the problem or develop a plan for change. They may be locked into an ideology or set of beliefs that inhibit their ability to respond effectively. They may not have access to concepts and models that can help them identify the cause-and-effect relationships that maintain the status quo or offer opportunities for change. There is also the possibility that they have already tried to introduce changes and their efforts have failed to deliver desired outcomes. All these conditions can contribute to clients lacking confidence in their own ability to develop opportunities or manage problems.

Seligman's (1975) theory of learned helplessness, mentioned in Chapter 4, states that when individuals are subjected to events that are uncontrollable, that is, when the probability of an outcome is the same irrespective of how they respond, they will develop expectations of non-contingency between response and outcome. The theory suggests that the incentive for clients to initiate activity directed towards resolving a problem depends upon their expectation that responding will produce some improvement to the problematic situation. If clients have no confidence in their own ability to achieve any improvement, they will not try. Hiroto (1974) illustrated this effect with an experiment that exposed one group of college students to loud controllable noises they could terminate by pressing a button four times and a second group to uncontrollable noises that were terminated independently of what they did. A third group included in the experiment was not exposed to any noise. All subjects were then tested in a situation in which it was possible for them to exercise control over noise termination. Hiroto found that the groups that had either been subjected to controllable noise or no noise learned to terminate the noise in the later test situation, whereas subjects who had previously been subjected to uncontrollable noise failed to terminate noises during later tests.

Abramson et al. (1978) distinguish between universal helplessness – where the client believes that the problem is unsolvable by anyone – and personal helplessness – where the client believes that the problem is solvable, for example by the helper but not by self. The danger with the prescriptive/advising approach to helping is that it can promote a sense of personal helplessness in the client and the client may become dependent on the help of others.

Egan (2004) discusses the notion of 'empowerment' in the helping relationship. He notes that some clients learn, sometimes from an early age, that there is nothing they can do about certain life situations. They engage in disabling self-talk (see Ellis, 1977) and tell themselves that they cannot manage certain situations and they cannot cope. Egan's position is that whether clients are victims of their own doing or the doings of others, they can and must take an active part in managing their own problems, including the search for solutions and efforts towards achieving those solutions. He also argues that helpers can do a great deal to help people develop a sense of agency or self-efficacy. Change agents can help clients to challenge self-defeating beliefs and attitudes about themselves and the situation. They can help clients to develop the knowledge, skills and resources they need to succeed and they can encourage them to take reasonable risks and support them when they do. The function of the change agent, according to Egan, is to encourage clients to apply a problem-solving approach to their current problem situation and to learn from this experience, so that, over the longer term, they will apply a problem-solving approach to future problem situations. In other words, his approach is one that is directed towards eliminating feelings of personal helplessness and empowering clients to act.

Supportive approach

The supportive mode of intervening involves the change agent working with others to help them clarify their views and express feelings and emotions that impede objective thinking about a problem or opportunity.

Margerison (2000) refers to change agents helping clients to give themselves permission. In the first instance, this involves giving themselves permission to talk about difficult issues, which leads on to giving themselves permission to act rather than to worry. He reports that in his consulting experience, an effective intervention has sometimes been to just listen and help managers to open up difficult areas and talk about matters they have so far avoided. He observes that clients appear to experience this kind of intervention as a great relief. It is as though a load has been taken off their mind.

Change agents adopting a supportive mode of intervening listen empathetically, withhold any judgement and help clients develop for themselves a more objective view of the situation. It is assumed that this new level of awareness will often be sufficient to help them go on and solve the problem for themselves.

Supportive interventions have many similarities with the way client-centred counsellors work with their clients (Rogers, 1958). They listen, reflect and sometimes interpret what clients have to say about themselves and their relationship with others and the situation, but they do not intervene or develop any active strategies for dealing with clients' problems. It is a person-centred, as opposed to a problem-centred, approach to helping.

Example 13.1 will help to clarify how this approach can be effective. Blake and Mouton (1986) describe a case in which a consultant, who was working in the Hawthorn Plant of Western Electric, used a supporting approach to help a shop-floor worker.

Example 13.1

Using a supportive approach

The consultant overheard the worker complaining, in an emotional tone, about his supervisor and decided to intervene. He asked what had been going on and was told, in the same emotional tone: 'The bosses are not worth a damn because when you have a rise coming to you, they will not give it.' The worker went on to tell the consultant that he thought the place stank and he wanted to get out. The consultant's response was to avoid siding with either the worker or the supervisor, but to invite the worker into his office to 'talk it over'. As the interaction progressed, the worker unloaded his feelings about his supervisor. As he went on, he began to ramble from one complaint to another. He had been refused a rise, and because he was at the top of his grade, he could not advance any higher. He then complained about the machine setters who did everything they could to protect their own position and stop others learning anything that would help them to improve the work they do. All the way through this interaction, the consultant maintained his neutral stance and refrained from making any evaluation of the worker's complaints. He assumed the role of active listener and did little more than reflect his sympathetic understanding by repeating what he had been told. For example, in response to the complaint about the machine setters, he said: 'I see, they seem to be pretty selfish about their knowledge of screw machines.'

In this case, the consultant's strategy was to allow the worker to vent his anger because he believed that until he had done this, he would be too wound up to think straight. It appeared to work. Slowly, as the tension eased, the conversation moved away from gripes towards problem solving. The consultant confined his interventions to supportive listening and clarifying but eventually the worker (client) began to work through his problems for himself.

Supportive modes of intervening can be effective but there are situations where this approach to helping clients develop a better understanding of their situation may not be sufficient to produce change. In these circumstances, other modes of intervening might be required, but supporting can still have an important role to play in the early stages of helping.

Theorizing approach

The theorizing approach involves change agents identifying theories and conceptual models that are pertinent to the clients' problem situation, presenting these to clients and helping them to learn to use them to facilitate a better understanding of their situation in an analytical cause-and-effect fashion. The change agents then build on this understanding and use it to help clients to identify what they can do to move towards a more desirable state of affairs.

This mode of intervening might be adopted when change agents feel that some kind of theoretical framework could help clients to organize their thoughts and provide the basis for a fresh appraisal of their predicament. For example, the stakeholder grid discussed in Chapter 10 might be used to help a management team identify important stakeholders and develop strategies for winning their support, or the Burke-Litwin causal model of organizational performance (Chapter 6) might be used to focus attention on important cause-and-effect relationships that affect performance. Change agents can also use theories to facilitate the discussion of potentially delicate or sensitive issues. For example, a discussion of Belbin's (1993) team roles might provide a relatively safe and non-threatening way of exploring how members of a management team work together. This theory-based approach can also provide a way of exploring and testing implicit assumptions and values in a way that avoids direct confrontation, and it can provide a basis for increasing the client's capacity for independent action. Force-field analysis also offers an approach that clients can use to help understand their predicament and identify a viable course of action, as shown in Example 13.2.

Example 13.2

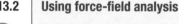

> **Using force-field analysis**
>
> Bill had been recruited by a large multinational auto components manufacturer to transform the organization's manufacturing capability so that the company could regain its previous world-class status and ensure its survival in an increasingly competitive environment. Sometime after his appointment he began to worry about his lack of progress. The senior managers of the operating divisions located in several countries around the world were resisting his efforts to introduce change. A consultant met Bill when he was working on another project in the company. They talked about the problem for 20 minutes and Bill suggested a further conversation, which happened the following week.
>
> The story Bill told revealed a complex set of related problems but eventually he focused on an immediate goal, which was to engage more effectively with senior managers and persuade them to provide him with detailed information about the current situation in the manufacturing units for which they were responsible. Initially Bill

focused on why managers should provide him with this information. He needed it to be able to assess how well the group was doing in relation to leading competitors and to assess the company's strengths and weaknesses in terms of its current manufacturing technology. He also wanted to be in a position to identify opportunities for rationalization and areas where efforts to introduce new technologies might be productive. He expressed a genuine desire to help divisions raise their performance and felt that the information he was seeking would help him make this contribution. He also felt that the information would be valuable to managers for their own use within their own divisions. Given all these powerful reasons why the provision of this information was in the company's best interests, he failed to understand why divisional managers insisted on keeping him at arm's length and were resistant to his requests for information.

In terms of Lewin's force field, Bill had focused his attention on the driving forces. His initial plan for achieving his goal was to further increase these driving forces by enlisting the support of the CEO and asking him to instruct the divisional managers to comply with his requests for detailed information. At this point, the consultant introduced Bill to force-field analysis, suggesting that before he pursued this course of action, Bill might consider some of the restraining forces. Why were the divisional managers resisting his requests and was there anything Bill could do to lower this resistance? (In Chapter 2 it was noted that Lewin favoured action directed towards reducing restraining forces.) The consultant suggested that Bill might find it helpful to view the situation through the eyes of the divisional managers. As he did this, Bill began to speculate about whether they truly understood his role and what he was trying to achieve. He also recognized the possibility that they feared that the detailed reporting he was requesting could threaten their autonomy, unfavourable comparisons might be made between the divisions, and the information – in its raw form – might be misinterpreted by others at corporate headquarters, who might access it when making decisions about resources, promotions and bonuses. He also recognized that he had not involved the divisional managers in specifying the information requirements, nor had he given them the opportunity to discuss the information that would be of help to them in their own businesses. There was also a possible problem relating to the cost of collecting this information. Who was to pay for it? This analysis helped Bill develop a better understanding of the situation and provided a good basis for planning action to achieve his goal.

Bill decided that his first initiative would not be to appeal to the CEO to increase pressure on the divisional managers to comply with his requests. He didn't rule this out, but decided that actions directed towards reducing the restraining forces might be more productive, especially bearing in mind that achieving this particular goal was only one part of his overall plan for change. The consultant continued to work with Bill to help him prioritize the forces he wanted to work on and to identify specific actions he could take to achieve his aim. In this case, it transpired that all Bill's priorities for action involved reducing the power of selected restraining forces. It is not essential that plans should only be based on reducing the power of restraining forces, but plans that only involve actions to increase the power of driving forces might deserve another look.

Blake and Mouton (1986) argue that theories can help clients free themselves from blind reliance on intuition, hunch, common sense and conventional wisdom and enable them to see situations more objectively. Theories can be applied to all classes of problems in a wide range of situations, so long as the theory is valid and the clients are willing and able to internalize the theory and make it a personally useful source of guidance. Theory-based interventions might be less effective than other approaches if the change agent introduces clients to a theory they perceive to be invalid, irrelevant or too complicated, or if the client is unreceptive to the possibility of using theory as a basis for managing problems. Even valid, user-friendly theories may be rejected, for example when clients are emotionally charged. In such circumstances, a supportive mode of intervening might be used before adopting a theory-based approach to helping.

Challenging approach

The challenging mode of intervening has great potential for facilitating change. It involves the change agent confronting the foundations of the client's thinking in an attempt to identify beliefs, values and assumptions that may be distorting the way situations are viewed. Blake and Mouton (1986: 210) observe that:

> Values underlie how people think and feel and what they regard as important and what is trivial. Sometimes guidance from a particular set of values is sound – things go smoothly, results are good. Sometimes values cause problems – they are inappropriate, invalid, or unjustified under the circumstances. Often people who must work in concert hold different values; failure to achieve agreement in such situations results in antagonisms, disorder or outright chaos.

An assumption underlying this challenging mode of intervening is that effective action can be undermined by the clients' inability or unwillingness to face up to reality. They may not be aware of some aspects of their behaviour or its consequences, or they rationalize or justify their behaviour and in so doing create or perpetuate an unsatisfactory situation. Challenging interventions are designed to call attention to contradictions in action and attitude or challenge precedents or practices that seem inappropriate. The aim of this approach is to challenge values and assumptions and identify alternatives that might facilitate the exploitation of opportunities or lead to the development of more effective solutions to problems (Example 13.3).

Example 13.3

> **Using a challenging approach**
>
> The head teacher of a successful primary school had worked hard to improve the school's external reputation and had invested a great deal of effort in building a good team spirit among his staff. When one of them applied for a job elsewhere, the head teacher interpreted this as a sign of disloyalty. He communicated his reaction to the individual concerned and made his disapproval public by excluding him from management team meetings. The deputy head intervened. He reminded the head about his own early career progress and pointed out how this was little different from the progress the teacher who had applied for the job elsewhere was seeking. The deputy pointed out that the head had rarely stayed in one job for more than three years, whereas this individual had already been in post and had performed satisfactorily for almost four years. He asked the head how he thought others would interpret his action and what effect it was likely to have on the team spirit he prized so highly. Eventually, the head accepted that the teacher's application was a timely and appropriate step to take, and that he had not only overlooked the career development needs of this individual but had given insufficient attention to the career development of all his staff. He also accepted that his response had been inconsistent with the management culture he was trying to create.

Great care needs to be exercised when change agents adopt a challenging style. Egan (2004) argues that confrontation can be strong medicine and, in the hands of the inept, can be destructive. Effective challenges are those which are received by clients as helpful invitations to explore aspects of a problem from a new perspective. Change agents adopting this approach ask questions or provide feedback that draws the client's attention to inappropriate attitudes, values, discrepancies and distortions, but they avoid telling the client how they should think or act. Challenges that clients perceive as personal attacks or a public unmasking of possible inadequacies are likely to be met with some form of strong defensive reaction and will rarely be effective. Even in circumstances where a challenging style of intervention promises to be effective, this promise may not be realized if change agents are inept at challenging and confronting.

Information-gathering approach

The information-gathering approach to helping involves change agents assisting clients to collect data they can use to evaluate and reinterpret a problem situation. Hayes (2002) illustrates this with the example of a sales trainer (Example 13.4).

Example 13.4

> ### Using an information-gathering approach
>
> A trainer in the sales department of a machine tool company was faced with a demotivated young representative who had recently lost three important accounts. The trainer suggested that he got in touch with the buyers he used to deal with and ask them why they had changed suppliers. The trainer suspected that it was because the representative had not been attentive to their needs but he felt that it would be more effective if the representative discovered this for himself and then decided what he needed to do about it.

The assumption underlying this approach is that information deficiencies are an important cause of malfunctioning. The helpers' objectives are to help clients arrive at a better level of awareness of the underlying causes of a problem and help them to identify what action is required to resolve it. Many change agents adopting this approach assume that any information they might present will be less acceptable and less likely to be understood than information that individuals or groups generate for themselves. Another assumption often made by change agents adopting this approach is that clients will be less resistant to proposals and action plans they generate for themselves. Pascale and Sterin (2005) point to 'positive deviance' as an example of an intervention that relies on helping others to gather and use information for themselves. It involves helping clients to identify and investigate examples of innovation and superior performance in order to share their findings and use them as a basis for exploring ways of spreading this best practice. Pascale and Sterin argue that because the process of information gathering is undertaken by members of the client system, ownership is high, and because the innovators who are responsible for superior performance are members of the same system ('just like us'), disbelief and resistance are easier to overcome.

Sometimes change agents might be more directly involved in the collection of data but when this happens, they are often working on behalf of their clients and they feed the information back to them for them to use to develop a better understanding of their problem and explore ways of improving the situation.

Developing collaborative relationships

Collaborative modes of intervening are most effective when change managers have a genuine respect for the people they are working with. This requires that they:

▶ *Signal that the other's viewpoint is worth listening to:* This reflects their willingness to commit to working with others. It also suggests a minimum level of openness to their point of view. Too often, even when change managers go through the motions of asking others for their views, they are not really committed to listening. If collaborative working is to be effective, change managers need to respect others' views and clearly signal this respect.

▶ *Suspend critical judgement:* If change managers are really committed to working collaboratively with others, they need to keep an open mind and avoid reaching premature conclusions. Egan (2004) and Reddy (1987) assert that this does not mean that they should signal approval of everything they hear or observe, rather it involves communicating that their point of view has been heard and understood. The act of suspending judgement, and trying to understand the other's viewpoint, can encourage them to explore their position. It avoids pushing them into defensive positions and gives them the freedom to change their view.

Exercise 13.2 | **Monitoring your respect for others**

Next time you are involved in a helping relationship, observe yourself. Open up a second channel and monitor what you are thinking when you are relating with a client. What does this tell you about your respect for others and their points of view?

• Are you able to suspend critical judgement?
• Do you believe that the client's point of view is worth listening to?

According to Reddy (1987), suspending judgement and keeping an open mind do not come naturally. He argues that we have been conditioned to persuade others to our point of view. At school, there is nearly always a debating society but rarely a listening club. It may be that we often fail to keep an open mind because if we listen, we may end up agreeing, and if we agree, we may appear to have lost. However, the aim of a collaborative helping relationship is not to win. Signalling to others that their views are worth listening to and suspending judgement can encourage them to believe that the change agent is prepared to help them to achieve the best outcome, whatever that might be.

Prescriptive versus collaborative modes of intervening

It has been argued that the most effective way of helping others is to help them to help themselves, and that this will normally involve adopting a collaborative mode of intervening. There may, however, be occasions when a more prescriptive style might be appropriate. Clients may be faced with a critical problem that, if not resolved quickly, could have disastrous consequences. If the change agent has the expertise to help them avoid this disastrous outcome, it might be appropriate to adopt a prescriptive mode to provide the required help quickly. While this kind of intervention is only likely to provide a 'short-term fix', it might be effective if it can buy time to help clients to develop the competencies they require to manage any similar situations they might encounter in the future.

Helping skills

The focus of attention in this chapter has been on intervention styles and how they can be applied to facilitate change over the course of the helping relationship. Passing reference has also been made to some of the specific helping skills that change agents need to use to intervene effectively. These 'helping skills' are not a special set of skills reserved exclusively for the helping relationship (Hopson, 1984). Helping involves the appropriate use of a wide range of 'everyday and commonly used' interpersonal skills. Some of these are:

▶ self-awareness
▶ establishing rapport and building relationships
▶ empathy
▶ listening to facts and feelings
▶ probing for information
▶ identifying themes and seeing the bigger picture
▶ giving feedback
▶ challenging assumptions.

These and many other relevant interpersonal behaviours are considered in detail in *Interpersonal Skills at Work* (Hayes, 2002).

Exercise 13.3 is designed to help you reflect on the discussion so far and on your experience of being a client.

Exercise 13.3 **Identifying effective helping behaviours**

Think of a number of occasions when others have tried to help you.

1 Identify people whose behaviour towards you was very helpful:
   • What did they do that you found helpful?
   • How did you respond to this behaviour?
   • Why was it helpful?

Record you observations below.

List the helpful behaviours	Explain why the behaviours were helpful

2 Identify people who, while trying to help, behaved towards you in ways that you found unhelpful:
   • What did they do that you found unhelpful?
   • How did you respond to this behaviour?
   • Why was it unhelpful?

List the unhelpful behaviours	Explain why the behaviours were unhelpful

Reflect on your findings and consider how they relate to the modes of intervention referred to in this chapter. Does your experience highlight any skills not discussed but which appear to have an important bearing on the outcome of the helping relationship?

Summary

The goal of intervening is not about planning or action but about achieving results – system-enhancing outcomes such as innovations realized, problems managed more effectively and opportunities developed, or new organization-enhancing behaviours put in place.

Paraphrasing Mangham, those change agents who are effective at intervening are those who can conduct themselves in the complexity of the organization as subtle, insightful, incisive performers:

▶ They require a highly developed ability to read the actual and potential behaviour of others around them and to construct their own conduct in accordance with this reading.

▶ This is an ability we all have to a greater or lesser extent but, according to Mangham (1986: 4), 'the most successful among us appear to do social life with a higher degree of skill than the rest of us manage'.

Blake and Mouton describe intervening as a 'cycle-breaking endeavour'. This chapter has considered five modes of intervening to facilitate change:

▶ *Advising:* this involves change agents drawing on their own knowledge and experience and telling clients what they should do to resolve their problem.

▶ *Supporting:* this involves listening empathetically; withholding judgement and helping clients to express the feelings and emotions that impede clear and objective thinking about their problem. The prime focus is the client rather than the problem.

▶ *Theorizing:* the change agent presents the clients with a theory relevant to their problem and helps them to use the theory to understand the problem and plan remedial action.

▶ *Challenging:* this involves confronting the foundations of the clients' thinking in order to identify beliefs and values that may be distorting the way they view the situation.

▶ *Information gathering:* this involves helping clients to collect data they can use to evaluate and reinterpret the situation.

In many circumstances, consultants or change managers can see a solution because they are more experienced than their clients/subordinates and this encourages them to intervene by giving advice and telling others what to do:

▶ Telling people what to do may deprive them of the opportunity to learn how to solve the problem for themselves.
▶ Clients can become dependent on the change agent and the next time they experience a difficulty, they again have to seek help.

While acknowledging that advising may be an appropriate mode of intervention in some circumstances, this chapter has highlighted the benefits of those approaches that helps clients to help themselves.

Helpers are most effective when they demonstrate a genuine respect for the people they are working with. They can do this by:

▶ signalling that the other person's viewpoint is worth listening to
▶ suspending critical judgement.

Helping involves the appropriate use of a wide range of 'everyday and commonly used' interpersonal skills. Some of these are:

▶ self-awareness
▶ establishing rapport and building relationships
▶ empathy
▶ listening to facts and feelings
▶ probing for information
▶ identifying themes and seeing the bigger picture
▶ giving feedback
▶ challenging assumptions.

References

Abramson, L.Y., Seligman, M.E.P. and Teesdale, J.D. (1978) Learned helplessness in humans: critique and performulations, *Journal of Abnormal Psychology*, **87**(1): 49–74.

Belbin, R.M. (1993) *Team Roles at Work*, Oxford: Butterworth Heinemann.

Blake, R.R. and Mouton, J.S. (1986) *Consultation: A Handbook for Individual and Organization Development*, Reading, MA: Addison-Wesley.

Carnegie, D. (1936) *How to Win Friends and Influence People*, New York: Simon & Schuster.

Egan, G. (1988) *Change Agent Skills: Managing Innovation and Change*, San Diego, CA: University Associates.

Egan, G. (2004) *The Skilled Helper: A Problem Management and Opportunity Development Approach to Helping*, Pacific Grove, CA: Brooks/Cole.

Ellis, A. (1977) The basic clinical theory of rational-emotive therapy, in A. Ellis and G. Grieger (eds) *Handbook of Rational-emotive Therapy*, Monterey, CA: Brooke/Cole.

Greiner, L.E. and Metzger, R.O. (1983) *Consulting to Management*, Englewood Cliffs, NJ: Prentice Hall.

Hayes, J. (2002) *Interpersonal Skills at Work*, Hove: Routledge.

Hiroto, D.S. (1974) Locus of control and learned helplessness, *Journal of Experimental Psychology*, 102: 187–93.

Hopson, B. (1984) Counselling and helping, in C. Cooper and P. Makin (eds) *Psychology for Managers*, Leicester: British Psychological Society.

Lewin, K. (1951) *Field Theory in Social Science*, New York: Harper & Row.

Mangham, I.L. (1986) *Power and Performance in Organisations: An Exploration of Executive Process*, Oxford: Blackwell.

Margerison, C.J. (2000) *Managerial Consulting Skills*, Aldershot: Gower.

Pascale, R.T. and Sterin, J. (2005) Your company's secret change agents, *Harvard Business Review*, **83**(5): 72–81.

Reddy, M. (1987) *The Manager's Guide to Counselling at Work*, London: British Psychological Society/Methuen.

Rogers, C.R. (1958) The characteristics of a helping relationship, *Personnel and Guidance Journal*, 37: 6–16.

Seligman, M.E.P. (1975) *Helplessness*, San Francisco, CA: W.H. Freeman.

Steele, F.I. (1969) Consultants and detectives, *Journal of Applied Behavioural Science*, **5**(2): 193–4.

Part V

PLANNING AND PREPARING FOR CHANGE

The four chapters in Part V examine some of the issues that change managers need to attend to, after they have diagnosed what needs to be changed, in order to decide how to achieve the required change.

Chapter 14   Shaping the implementation strategy

This chapter looks at the broad picture and considers the strengths and weaknesses of three approaches to managing change, explores some of the situational variables

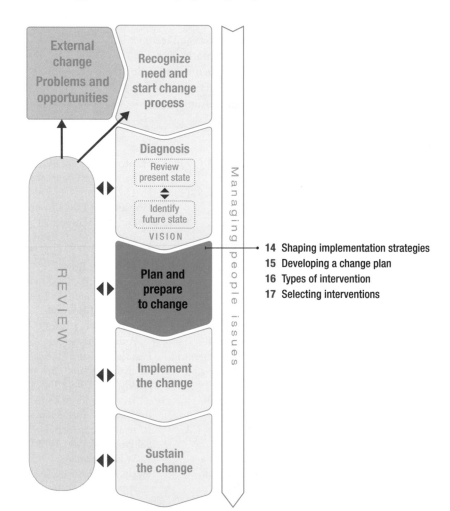

14 Shaping implementation strategies
15 Developing a change plan
16 Types of intervention
17 Selecting interventions

that need to be considered when shaping an implementation strategy and considers how and why a change strategy may need to change over time. The chapter concludes with a brief review of some alternative starting points for change.

After reading this chapter, you will be invited to critically assess the strategy used to manage a recent change within your organization or some other situation with which you are familiar.

Chapter 15   Developing a change plan

It is not unusual for change to disrupt normal work and undermine existing management systems. This chapter considers some of the steps that need to be considered when developing a change plan. These are:

▸ appoint a transition manager
▸ identify what needs to be done
▸ produce an implementation plan, with clear targets and goals, which can indicate progress and signal any need for remedial action
▸ use multiple and consistent leverage points for change
▸ schedule activities
▸ ensure that adequate resources are allocated to the change and that an appropriate balance is maintained between keeping the organization running and implementing the changes necessary to move towards the desired future state
▸ implement reward systems that encourage experimentation and change
▸ develop feedback mechanisms that provide the information required to ensure that the change programme moves forward in a coordinated manner, especially where the plan calls for change in a number of related areas.

After reading this chapter, you will be invited to reflect on an occasion when you were involved in the management of a change, at work or elsewhere, and consider what you or others might have done differently to develop an effective implementation plan.

Chapter 16   Types of intervention

Interventions are intentional acts designed to disrupt the status quo and move the organization towards a more effective state. Change efforts can be less successful than they might be because those responsible for managing the change are unaware of the full range of interventions available to them. This chapter reviews interventions using two contrasting typologies.

The first focuses attention on who does the intervening and what it is they do to bring about change. Four classes of intervention are discussed:

▸ experts applying scientific principles to solve specific problems
▸ groups working collaboratively to solve their own problems
▸ experts working to solve system-wide problems
▸ everybody working to improve the capability of the whole system for future performance.

The second classifies interventions in terms of the issues they address. Again, four main types of intervention are identified, which focus on:

▸ human process issues
▸ technology/structural issues
▸ human resource issues
▸ strategic issues.

Chapter 17   Selecting interventions

This chapter reviews some of the factors that need to be considered when selecting which kind of intervention to use. They include the nature of the diagnosed problem, the level of change target – individual, group, organization and so on – and the required depth of intervention. These factors are combined to provide a three-dimensional model to aid choice.

Attention is also given to the factors that can affect the sequencing of interventions. These include the intent or purpose of the change, organizational politics and how they can affect the support for different interventions, the need for an early success to maintain motivation, the stakes involved, and causal links that affect the dynamics of change.

Shaping implementation strategies

This chapter considers the strengths and weaknesses of three approaches to managing change and explores some of the situational variables that need to be considered when shaping an implementation strategy.

Read the Asda case study before reviewing the content of this chapter and consider how you would have managed the situation if you had been the newly appointed CEO.

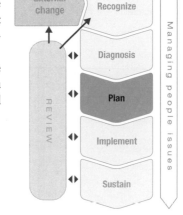

Case study 14.1

Asda: a winning formula

Asda was the first company in the UK to invest in large, out of town superstores, with ample free car parking, selling food and related products.

Asda was created in 1965 as a subsidiary of Associated Dairies. It started business by opening a string of large discount stores in converted mill and warehouse premises. In the early days, shoppers were offered a limited range of competitively priced products.

When Asda went public in 1978, it was the third largest food retailer in the UK, selling an ever widening range of food and non-food products. Its success continued to be based on high volumes, low margins and good value for money (Asda price).

A change of strategy: the pursuit of higher margins

In 1981, Asda began to shift towards a new strategy focused on raising margins. A range of new initiatives involved seeking efficiencies to reduce costs and introducing more high-margin products such as prepared foods and a wider range of non-food items.

There was also a drive to expand in the south of England where customers had greater spending power:

- This expansion policy was slow to get off the ground, partly because planning permissions for large retail developments were more difficult to secure in the south, the price of land was significantly higher and many of the best sites were already being developed by competitors.
- Sales were less than anticipated because Asda's value for money image and its relatively austere store layouts tended to be unattractive to relatively wealthy southern customers who were used to shopping in more upmarket stores. Asda attempted to brighten up some of its stores and further distance itself from its 'pile-them-high and sell-them-cheap' image but this did not generate the anticipated contribution to operating profits.
- Another related problem was that long-standing customers in the north appeared to be confused by what Asda was beginning to offer them and many switched their allegiance to new cut-price retailers who were more focused on offering value for money.

Diversification

Towards the end of the 1970s, senior management began to consider the possibility that saturation may limit future growth in food retailing and the decision was taken to diversify into non-foods.

Some of the most notable acquisitions included:

1977 Wades Department Stores, with over 70 prime high-street sites.

1978 Allied Retailers (Allied Carpets, Ukay Furniture and Williams Furnishings), but unfortunately this acquisition did not make the anticipated contribution to profitability because the recession in the early 1980s led to heavy discounting. Ukay furniture faired worst and was sold in 1982. While the recession hit Allied Carpets, it continued to make modest profits and by 1985 had improved to the point where it was decided to expand this side of the business.

1985 Asda merged with the MFI furniture group, but this merger, the biggest in British retailing up to that point, was another disappointment. Asda-MFI attributed the poor performance to one-off problems, such as a new range of kitchens that failed to sell. It was anticipated that the problems would be short-lived but performance failed to pick up as expected.

1986 Asda launched Asdadrive, a car retailing business at sites adjacent to six of its superstores, with the intention of rolling it out to about 75% of all sites.

Refocusing on the core business

Following the merger with MFI, Asda-MFI's shares significantly underperformed. In 1987, the company surprised the market with a major change of strategy. Instead of continuing with the policy of diversification, it decided to refocus on the Asda superstores.

The Asda-MFI merger ended with a management buyout of MFI, although Asda then bought a 25% stake in this new company. Asdadrive and most of the associated fresh foods business were also disposed of and it was intended to dispose of the Allied Carpets business. However, following the collapse of the equity market, it proved impossible to obtain the anticipated profit from the sale of Allied Carpets, so the business was retained and later expanded with the acquisition of Marples in 1989.

In order to develop the core business, it was decided to invest up to £1bn over a period of three years. Most was earmarked for accelerating the opening of new stores, especially in the south, but there were also other demands. Asda had lagged behind its competitors in a number of areas:

- *Own-label products:* They had all invested heavily in own-label products, which offered higher margins and better value to customers, whereas Asda had only started to introduce them in the mid-1980s, and on a much smaller scale.
- *Computerized point-of sale equipment:* Competitors had invested heavily in technology that improved stock control and provided better customer service at checkouts.
- *Centralized distribution networks:* The competition had also developed centralized distribution networks for fresh foods that pushed down costs, enabled stores to receive fewer 'just in time' deliveries from vehicles carrying full loads, and reduced the requirement for store-related warehousing space.
- *Store refurbishment:* Asda had neglected many of its stores, which were beginning to look tired and in urgent need of refurbishing.

Asda recognized the need for investment in all these areas.

A leap forward that contributed to a major debt problem

In 1989, a consortium that was planning to buy Gateway agreed that, if its bid was successful, it would sell 62 superstores to Asda for £705m. This was seen as an attractive proposition. It offered Asda the possibility of making up for lost ground and regaining its old position as the third largest British food retailer. It also promised to double the number of Asda stores in the south of England and contribute an extra £1bn to sales. Asda bought the stores in October 1989.

Asda's performance following the purchase of the Gateway stores was poor. Profits were down and Asda's stake in MFI contributed a loss. Allied-Marples was also in trouble. Asda had net debts of over £900m. From the end of 1989, Asda's share price began to slide compared with major competitors and in September 1991, it dropped a further 29%. The announcement of a rights issue at the end of the month led to another massive fall in the share price.

The appointment of Archie Norman

Archie Norman was offered the role of CEO in October 1991 and took up his appointment in December. By the time he arrived, the company was fast running out of cash. He found a company that was bureaucratic, hierarchical and highly centralized. There was a large headquarters staff located in the new custom-built Asda House. Directors had little contact with their subordinates. The culture was risk averse. People at all levels appeared to be intimidated by their bosses and told them what they thought they wanted to hear. They also seemed reluctant to take any initiatives that would call attention to themselves. Morale was low.

The trading department was dominant. Buyers, located at Asda House, determined what the stores would sell but they had little contact with store managers. The new CEO had concerns about the quality of management and the apparent unwillingness, throughout the organization, to make best use of the talent that existed.

Store managers felt ignored and found it impossible to have any meaningful input to thinking at Asda House. There were also problems within stores. Vertical communication was poor and customers were not valued.

If you had been Archie Norman in December 1991, what would have been your strategy for change?

Notes

The trap of success

It was noted in Chapter 3 that one of the paradoxes of organizational life is that success often sets the stage for failure. This is because when organizations like Marks & Spencer continue to be successful year after year, managers become locked into the patterns of behaviour that produced the original success. These patterns become codified or institutionalized (part of the deep structures discussed in Chapter 1) and are rarely questioned. Successful firms can become complacent, internally focused, and caught in what Nadler and Shaw (1995) refer to as the 'trap of success'. They take their eyes off the competition and fail to pay enough attention to what is going on in their external environment. Even those organizations that invest heavily in continuous improvement can become victims of strategic drift. They may change, but fail to change fast enough to keep pace with the rate of change in their external environment. Part of the problem is that continuous improvement tends to focus attention on 'doing things better' and insufficient attention is given to the potential benefit of 'doing things differently' or even 'doing different things'. This argument supports the punctuated equilibrium paradigm and predicts that, at some point, almost all organizations will be faced with the need to transform themselves in order to survive.

How can companies transform themselves? Beer (2001), a leading US consultant and professor at Harvard Business School, has identified two well-tried strategies (economic and organization development), but argues that the most effective strategy is a third way that combines the best of both. As you read this chapter, reflect on your own experience to test the validity of this proposition and consider which strategy you would have adopted if you had been Archie Norman at Asda.

Economic strategies

Economic strategies focus on the drive for economic value through tough, top-down, results-driven action. These actions involve the imposition of technical solutions to those problems that are seen to undermine organizational effectiveness. There are a wide range of such solutions including restructuring, re-engineering, drives for efficiencies and layoffs. Often large groups of consultants are employed to help top management drive them into the organization. Sometimes a new CEO or other senior executive might be appointed to act as a 'turnaround' manager.

There are many examples where economic strategies have led to improved shareholder returns. Many believe that they made a major contribution to the success of Lord Hanson and colleagues at Hanson Trust. However, economic strategies have been criticized on the grounds that they often destroy human commitment. Consequently, while they might deliver short-term results, they may not guarantee longer term success.

Organization development strategies

Organization development (OD) strategies focus on creating the capabilities required to sustain competitive advantage and high performance. Beer and others identify some of these capabilities as:

▶ coordination and teamwork
▶ commitment and trust
▶ competence – technical and leadership
▶ open communications
▶ creativity
▶ the capacity for constructive conflict
▶ learning.

OD strategies emphasize the importance of shared purpose, a strong culture, bottom-up change and involvement rather than financial incentives as the motivator for change. This approach can improve shareholder value but it has been criticized on the grounds that it is too indirect and takes too long, especially when the need for change is urgent.

The BBC offers good examples of the implementation of both economic and OD strategies. During the 1990s, the dominant strategy was economic, but when Greg Dyke was appointed director general in 2000, he began to pursue more of an OD strategy.

Example 14.1

| **The implementation of an economic strategy at the BBC** |

After a long period of sustained success during which the BBC established itself as the world's leading public broadcaster, it began to become complacent. It knew that it was the best in the field and, because of the way it was funded via a compulsory licence fee, felt that it was financially secure. But then the world began to change and the BBC was faced with a range of pressing problems. These included:

- *A new political climate:* In 1979, Margaret Thatcher and a Conservative government came to power with an agenda for change that included plans to transform the public sector. Although the BBC was not the new government's first target, Thatcher viewed it as a bloated bureaucracy that was overmanned, inefficient and ripe for reform. The government (like many before and since) was also unhappy with the BBC's editorial policy and was particularly irritated by what it perceived as unpatriotic reporting of issues such as Northern Ireland and the Falkland's War.
- *Wide-ranging technological change:* Possibly the biggest challenge came from the development of digital technologies that opened up the possibility of many more channels, better technical quality, video-on-demand and interactivity.
- *Increased competition* from new players and the launch of BskyB.

In order to fend off the possibility of privatization, protect the licence fee, which the government had reduced in real terms, and prepare the BBC for the digital world, John Birt, director general of the BBC between 1992 and 2000, introduced a range of tough reforms. His mission was to make the BBC the best managed organization in the public sector. At the time he was appointed, it was almost impossible to determine how much it cost to make a programme or use an in-house facility such as a studio. The core values were about quality rather than cost.

Birt was determined to make the organization more efficient. He introduced 'Producer Choice' and created an internal market that shifted the balance of power away from programme makers to managers and accountants. Departments became cost centres that had to break even, and producers were required to reduce the cost of programme making by using external suppliers whenever they could provide a more cost-effective service than in-house providers. This top-down drive to introduce new structures and systems slashed the cost of making programmes, but the reorganization led to nearly 10,000 people being made redundant or opting to leave the organization.

By the time Birt retired in 2000, his strategy for change had delivered results that secured the future of the BBC. He had gained the confidence of the government and other opinion formers – the public sector equivalent of shareholders – and had successfully introduced a range of 'technical' solutions that helped to secure the licence fee for a further six years, plus extra funding to develop new digital services. However, his change strategy had neglected the social system. He had done little to win the hearts and minds of the majority of staff. His reforms fragmented what had been a collaborative organization. People became much more focused on achieving their own targets, and were inclined to 'play safe' rather than take risks and innovate.

Example 14.2

| **The implementation of an OD strategy at the BBC** |

When Greg Dyke took over as director general at the BBC, he inherited an efficient organization but he detected a climate of fear and was worried about whether this increased efficiency had been won at the expense of other factors that would begin to have a negative impact on the BBC's performance. Efficiency was still on his agenda but he pursued it via a more inclusive approach. He also began to pursue a bottom-up strategy to identify what inspired people and to develop the capabilities required to ensure that the BBC retained its position as the world's leading public broadcaster.

He introduced a new vision. In place of striving to make the BBC the best managed organization in the public sector, his vision was to turn the BBC into the most creative organization in the world, where people enjoy their work and feel supported and powered to excel.

In February 2002, he launched the 'One BBC – Making it Happen' initiative. While he had some ideas about how to make it happen, he wanted the detailed plans to emerge from within the organization. The aims of Making it Happen were to:

- put audiences at the heart of the BBC
- inspire creativity
- develop current leaders and nurture those of the future
- provide an environment where people feel valued and encouraged to give of their best
- cut through the bureaucracy and build greater collaboration between divisions.

Dyke decided that he and the executive team would take every opportunity to demonstrate their commitment to the process. For example, they brought together the top 400 managers for two days to create a collective sense of responsibility for leading change. Dyke also led many discussions with staff and introduced the notion of the 'big conversation'.

He was determined to consult with a critical mass of employees. In order to promote buy-in and ownership, this process was managed by in-house staff rather than external consultants. The first phase involved a search for 'quick wins'. These included modest changes such as refurbishments and reward schemes that recognized people when they made a special contribution. In the news division, for example, one of the first winners was a travel desk clerk.

The second phase involved 10,000 staff, a third to the entire workforce, participating in 180 half-day workshops. Local managers and their staff were invited to 'Just Imagine' what the organization could be like and to identify what needed to be changed in order to make it happen.

In each of the BBC's 17 divisions, Make it Happen teams were established to coordinate the Just Imagine sessions and introduce change at the local level. For example, in the news division, various measures were introduced to improve the working climate and encourage staff to take risks and give of their best. The change plan also included a number of simple, inexpensive measures designed to address other issues that emerged from the Just Imagine sessions. These included 'back to the floor' days for managers and short secondments to enable staff to better understand what was happening in other departments.

In addition to what was happening within divisions, there were organization-wide initiatives that emerged from the Making it Happen process. These included giving more attention to providing a thorough induction to all new staff, a shift away from the extensive use of short-term contracts in an attempt to build more commitment, and a big investment in leadership and management training.

The third way: a combined economic/OD strategy

Beer (2001) asserts that while both economic and OD strategies can produce improvements, neither of these strategies is as effective as one that combines top-down, results-driven change with the slower bottom-up development of organizational capability. With the benefit of hindsight, it could be argued that change at the BBC was successful because it did embrace Beer's combined strategy – but implemented sequentially rather than simultaneously. However, change at the BBC was not planned as a combined strategy. This emerged because Dyke recognized a need to address issues that had not been addressed by his predecessor. The real challenge for change managers is to implement a combined strategy simultaneously.

Beer (2001) argues that change strategies that are capable of delivering sustained high performance require:

1 *The development of a compelling and balanced business and organization development direction:* This requires the CEO to lead change at the top and create an effective executive team that can speak with one voice and articulate a coherent story about why and what type of change is needed. This story is more likely to win the support of key stakeholders if it not only provides an explanation of why the change is necessary but also offers an inspiring vision of a preferred future, which includes a business direction that will lead to the achievement of key results and an overview of the organizational capabilities required to achieve and sustain this vision.

2 *The management of key stakeholders in order to buy time to develop organization capability:* Often, but not always, this will involve managing shareholder expectations. Making overambitious commitments about the achievement of economic results can push change managers into short-term cost-cutting strategies rather than longer term strategies designed to create the capability required to generate revenue, or achieve the other outcomes that are required to sustain organizational success.

3 *The adoption of a sociotechnical approach that involves the development of down the line managers:* When tightly prescribed change programmes are rolled out across the organization, they typically focus on improving the technical system, and the interaction between the technical and social system tends to be ignored. Problems can arise when this type of programmatic change strategy fails to:
   - respond to local conditions
   - adequately involve local managers in a way that enables them to take real responsibility for moving the organization forward
   - provide local managers with the opportunity to reflect on and learn from their experience of managing change.

Beer (2001: 242) argues that

top down initiatives undermine one of the key capabilities needed for sustained performance – down-the-line leaders who can lead a process of organizational learning.

He advocates the management of corporate change on a unit-by-unit basis with a high involvement of local staff because this:

▶ enables organizational members to engage with senior managers and contribute to shaping the change process
▶ facilitates the development of down the line leaders.

Top management's reluctance to adopt a combined drive and develop approach

Beer's (2001) research suggests that CEOs and their top teams have a mindset that promotes a top-down drive for results. The three key aspects of this mindset are:

1 *The importance given to shareholder interests:* Shareholders have gained considerable power relative to employees, and even customers. Low share prices lead analysts, the financial community at large and board members to press CEOs for change. Those who do not respond risk being fired. Consequently, the top team is focused

on the need to maximize economic value. Guerrera (2009) reports that former GE chief Jack Welsh, widely recognized as the father of the shareholder value movement, now challenges this approach. He claims that it is a 'dumb idea' for analysts and executives to focus so heavily on quarterly profits and share price gains. He believes that more attention should be given to increasing the long-term value of the company. Shareholder value should be regarded as a result, not a strategy. He goes on to argue that more attention needs be given to employees, customers and products. Nonetheless, many executives still appear to give high priority to achieving short-term improvement in shareholder value. Their attention to shareholder interests echoes Schein's (1996) view that chief executives and their immediate subordinates tend to see themselves as embattled lonely warriors championing the organization in a hostile economic environment. They develop elaborate management information systems to stay in touch with what is going on in the organization and impose control systems to manage costs. They view people as 'resources' and regard them as costs rather than human assets. People and relationships are merely a 'means to the end of efficiency and productivity, not an ends in themselves. If we must have human operators, so be it, but let's minimize their possible impact on the operations and their cost to the enterprise' (Schein, 1996: 16).

2 *The assumption that it is the organization's technical rather than social system that is the prime determinant of performance:* Change strategies are designed to improve the organization as a technical system and interventions such as business process re-engineering, total quality management and performance management tend to be viewed as technical solutions. Beer (2001) extends this argument to include the introduction of new human resource management systems such as performance appraisal, succession planning and training programmes. They are implemented without too much thought being given to how they might affect roles, responsibilities, relationships and the power, status, self-esteem and security of individuals and groups across the organization. This neglect can erode trust, commitment and communication.

3 *The assumption that there is little to be gained from dialogue with employees:* When top teams are planning and implementing transformational change, they often overrely on top-down communication. Beer (2001: 238) notes how the thoughts and feelings of the CEO and the top team can be shaped by pursuing a 'drive' strategy:

> To avoid the dissonance aroused by the opposites of tough, top-down action to lay off employees and sell businesses on the one hand, and the need to gain commitment to change on the other, they distance themselves from employees. They begin to assume that employees are part of the problem.

Ford and Ford (2009: 100) argue that rather than regarding questions and complaints as resistance, change managers might benefit from viewing this 'feedback' as a resource: 'Even difficult people can provide valuable input when you treat their communications with respect and are willing to reconsider some aspects of the change you're initiating.'

Morrison and Milliken (2000) suggest that senior managers are more likely to discourage upward communication when they believe that employees are self-interested and effort averse and are therefore unlikely to know or care about what is best for the organization. This kind of thinking can lead to a situation where top managers are deprived of vital information that can signal a need for further change or provide feedback about the effectiveness of change initiatives that have already been implemented (see Chapter 10). It can also lead to a situation where the top team begins to rely on outside consultants and new managerial hires. Beer notes that when this happens, it can further alienate people down the line, leading to an erosion of trust and the capabilities required for high performance such as coordination, commitment, communication and learning.

Beer (2000) and Beer and Nohria (2000) summarize the main differences between economic (E) and OD strategies and highlight the main features of combined strategies:

1 *Leadership:* E strategies involve top-down leadership, OD strategies involve participative leadership, and combined E and OD strategies involve senior managers setting the direction and then engaging people throughout the organization.

2 *Focus:* E strategies focus on changing structures and processes (the technical systems), OD strategies focus on changing the organization's culture (the social systems), and combined E and OD strategies focus simultaneously on changing technical and social systems.

3 *Process:* E strategies are programmatic and involve the development and implementation of plans, OD strategies are more emergent and encourage experimentation, and combined E and OD strategies involve plans that accommodate spontaneity.

4 *Reward systems:* A feature of E strategies is a reliance on extrinsic motivation and the use of financial incentives, OD strategies rely on intrinsic motivation and the development of commitment, and combined E and OD strategies use financial incentives and other extrinsic motivators but only to reinforce change rather than to drive it.

5 *Use of consultants:* E strategies involve using consultants to analyse problems and prescribe solutions, OD strategies involve using consultants as facilitators to help managers diagnose problems and shape their own solutions, and combined E and OD strategies involve using consultants who are experts but who are able to use their expertise to empower organizational members.

Reflect on the strategy you would have adopted if you had been Archie Norman at Asda. Would your strategy have been primarily an economic strategy that involved a drive to maximize economic value, a development strategy that focused on developing organizational capabilities, or a combined drive and development strategy?

Situational variables that can shape an implementation strategy

The strategy Archie Norman implemented at Asda was a combined drive and development strategy. When he arrived, the company was facing bankruptcy and there was an urgent need to generate cash to ensure short-term survival, but there was also a need to transform the business in ways that would ensure its long-term success. His approach to managing change was 'tough', at times he was very directive and many people ended up leaving, but he also encouraged people at all levels to participate in the process of transforming the business. He went to great lengths to involve others and to ensure that managers down the line engaged with their subordinates. He also integrated careful planning with a willingness to let the details of the change strategy emerge over time.

There is no simple formula for designing implementation strategies based on Beer's 'third way'. After studying the merger of the Swedish pharmaceutical company

Astra AB with the British company Zeneca, Eriksson and Sundgren (2005) concluded that while there are benefits from combining E and OD theories, the ideal balance between the two may vary from case to case.

Kotter and Schlesinger (1979) argue that successful change strategies are those that are internally consistent and compatible with key situational variables. In practice, many managers vary their approach to managing change at different stages of the change process. For example, some may decide not to involve others in the preliminary diagnostic phase, but might draw more people into the latter stages of problem definition and the specification of a more desirable future state. They may then move on to involve many more in the details of implementing the change plan. Factors that might lead to a variation in approach over time will receive more attention below.

Some of the main situational variables that can influence the shape of an implementation strategy are illustrated in Figure 14.1 and discussed below.

DIRECTIVE	COLLABORATIVE
Urgent requirement for change	Non-urgent requirement for change
Desired end state clearly specified from the start	Problem/opportunity recognized but what needs to be done to resolve problem or exploit opportunity not clear from the start
Little resistance anticipated	Great resistance anticipated
Change managers have access to all the information they need to diagnose the need for change, develop a change plan and monitor its implementation	Change managers need information from other stakeholders
Others have high trust in change managers	Others have low trust in change managers
Change managers do not have to rely on the commitment and effort of others to implement the change plan	Successful implementation of the change plan is highly dependant on the commitment and effort of others

Figure 14.1   *A continuum of intervention strategies*

The main situational variables are:

1 *Urgency and stakes involved:* The greater the short-run risks to the organization if the current situation is not changed quickly, the more change managers may have to adopt a directive strategy towards the left-hand side of the continuum. Involvement and participation take time, and this time might not be available if the need for change is urgent.

2 *Clarity of desired future state:* Reference has already been made to two different types of change; blueprint change and evolutionary change (see Chapter 2). Blueprint changes are those where the desired end state can be clearly specified from the start, whereas evolutionary changes are those where the need for change is recognized but it is difficult to anticipate what a more desirable future state will look like.

Depending on other factors, such as the power of change managers relative to other stakeholders, it may be easier to adopt a more directive approach to implementation when confronted with a blueprint-type change than when the change involves an incremental process of action learning. Implementing an evolutionary change involves hypothesizing about what might be a useful next step, planning how to achieve it, taking action to implement the plan, reflecting on what happened, and then hypothesizing about what needs to be done next. This process is more likely to be successful when change managers seek inputs and feedback from others and adopt a more collaborative approach.

3 *The amount and type of resistance that is anticipated:* All other factors being equal, the greater the anticipated resistance, the more the change manager will have to work at persuading others to accept the need for change. This might require the adoption of a more collaborative approach towards implementation.

4 *The extent to which change managers have the required data for designing and implementing the change:* The more change managers anticipate that they will need information from others to help design and implement the change, the more they will have to adopt a collaborative approach and move towards the right-hand side of the continuum.

5 *Degree to which other stakeholders trust change managers:* The more other stakeholders trust change managers, the more likely they are to be prepared to follow their direction. The lower the level of trust, the more change managers may have to involve others in order to win their trust and build their commitment to the change plan.

6 *Degree to which change managers have to rely on the commitment and energy of others to implement the plan:* The more change managers have to rely on the energy and commitment of others to engage in discretionary behaviours to make the change plan work, the more they may have to adopt a collaborative approach and involve them in the change process.

Kotter and Schlesinger (1979) argue that one of the most common mistakes made by change agents is that they often rely on a single approach to implementing change, regardless of the situation. They refer to:

▶ the autocratic manager whose only approach is to coerce people
▶ the people-oriented manager who typically tries to involve and support people
▶ the cynical manager who always tries to manipulate others
▶ the intellectual manager who relies too much on education as an influence strategy
▶ the lawyer-type boss who typically tries to negotiate and bargain.

The model presented here emphasizes the need for change managers to adopt a contingent approach to the choice of implementation strategy that accommodates and balances a number of interdependent factors.

Variations over time

Balogun and Hailey (2008) suggest that the focus of the change strategy may need to change over time. For example, in the short term, the critical requirement might be to secure the organization's survival. In order to do this, it might be necessary to adopt a tough top-down, results-driven strategy that involves radical cuts and closures, or it may be necessary to redefine the purpose of the organization. Over the longer term, the focus may switch to a more incremental strategy of fine-tuning and the major concern may become continuous improvement. Associated with this change in focus may be a move towards a more collaborative approach to implementation.

Zaltman and Duncan (1977) cite complexity, communicability, compatibility, relative advantage and divisibility as factors that might influence the way change managers attempt to influence others. These factors might also affect the styles of influence that will be most effective at different stages of the transition phase:

▶ *Complexity and communicability:* If the required change is complex and difficult to communicate, the initial style of influence might involve a high level of explanation and education. However, once people understand the problem and what is required, other means of influence might be more effective.

▶ *Compatibility and relative advantage:* Similarly, a change that is compatible with the change targets' preferences and offers relative advantages over current practice might lend itself to a persuasive strategy. In other cases, negotiation or high levels of involvement might be the most effective way forward.

▶ *Divisibility:* Where the change is divisible and quick action is required, it might be decided to direct a part of the organization to adopt a small-scale trial before making a decision about how to proceed. If it is decided to go ahead, speed may be less of an issue and commitment might be more important. Consequently, at this stage, a less directive approach may be adopted.

Alternative starting points

Balogun and Hailey (2008) consider the advantages and disadvantages of different starting points for change. These are:

▶ *Pilot sites:* A small-scale change might be introduced into a pilot site that might be a single unit or a completely new site. At Asda, for example, three stores were selected for the early experimental phase of the change. An alternative approach is to introduce changes in new sites, with new staff. They can provide effective test beds for initiatives that might be resisted elsewhere because of ingrained traditional attitudes and practices. Once a change initiative has been proven on the pilot site, other parts of the organization might find it more difficult to resist the change. However, as the Asda case illustrates, care needs to be exercised when rolling change out to other parts of the organization (see the discussion of 'spread' in Chapter 29).

▶ *Pockets of good practice:* Another type of small-scale change is the kind of development that is led by an individual or group who takes an initiative and promotes a pocket of good practice that, eventually, might be copied by others.

▶ *Top down versus bottom up:* An advantage of a bottom-up approach is that organizational members who are in a position to recognize problems long before they are obvious to top management can take initiatives and introduce changes at an early stage. Bottom-up strategies also encourage commitment. However, they may not produce widespread action fast enough. In times of crisis, when a rapid organization-wide response is essential, a top-down approach might be most effective. Also coordination may become a problem if a number of separate and incompatible change initiatives begin to emerge at different points across the organization. In some cases, coordination from the top may be an essential ingredient of an effective change strategy, even if many of the initiatives originate at lower levels in the organization.

Exercise 14.1 > **Change strategies**

1 In your experience, which is the most frequently used change strategy? What are the reasons for this?

> **Notes**

2 In your opinion, can a change strategy that combines a top-down drive for results and the development of organizational capability offer the best chance of achieving sustained high performance rather than one that focuses on either results or capability? Why?

> **Notes**

Exercise 14.2 > **Critically review a change strategy you have observed**

Identify a recent change in your organization and critically assess the effectiveness of the strategy used to implement it.

> **Notes**

Case study 14.2

Direct Banking

Direct Banking is a successful Dutch telephone and internet bank that serves customers across much of Europe. It is a wholly owned subsidiary of a large international bank, but since its launch over 10 years ago, the parent company has allowed Direct Banking considerable autonomy.

Over that time, Direct Banking has developed an organizational culture that values the customer and focuses everybody's attention on delivering exceptional customer service. Service centre staff, for example, are not restricted to narrow 'scripts' when talking to customers and are encouraged to develop relationships with them in order to help them identify and satisfy customers' needs. Over 85% of Direct Banking's customers have recommended the bank to their friends and family and the quality of its communication with customers has been a major factor contributing to its success.

Over the last 12 months, costs have risen faster than in any other period in the bank's history. The parent company has responded by appointing a new CEO and tasking him to grow profits. Soon after taking up his appointment, the new CEO informed his management team that he wanted to introduce voice activation and routing as a way of radically reducing staff costs in all its service centres.

He argued that voice automation could be used to drive down costs by using speech recognition-based technology to analyse inbound calls to identify callers, why they were calling and what kind of transaction they required. In those cases where full automation of the transaction would not be possible, he suggested that partial automation could provide an intermediate solution by collecting routine data, such as account numbers and the service required, and routing the call to a specialized agent who could complete the transaction.

The new CEO was a champion of technical innovation in the parent bank before he was appointed CEO of Direct Banking, but he has had no experience of running the kind of service-oriented brand that is the central plank of Direct Banking's strategy.

The new CEO feels under pressure to deliver higher profits in the shortest possible time and he has approached you for advice about how he can best achieve this aim.

- With reference to Beer's (2001) typology of change strategies, what kind of change strategy is the new CEO seeking to implement?
- In order to achieve the goal of delivering higher profits, what are the issues that will require special attention?
- What advice would you give to the new CEO?

Summary

This chapter has considered the strengths and weaknesses of three approaches to managing change:

1 *Economic strategies* focus on the drive for economic value through tough, top-down, results-driven action. These actions involve the imposition of technical solutions to those problems that are seen to undermine organizational effectiveness. While economic strategies might deliver short-term results, they may not guarantee longer term success.

2 *Organization development (OD) strategies* focus on creating the capabilities required to sustain competitive advantage and high performance. Beer and others identify some of these capabilities as:
   - coordination and teamwork
   - commitment and trust
   - competence (technical and leadership)
   - open communications
   - creativity
   - the capacity for constructive conflict
   - learning.

OD strategies emphasize the importance of shared purpose, a strong culture, bottom-up change and involvement rather than financial incentives as the motivator for change. This approach can improve shareholder value but it has been criticized on the grounds that it is too indirect and takes too long, especially when the need for change is urgent.

3 *The third way: a combined economic/OD strategy*: Beer asserts that while both economic and OD strategies can produce improvements, neither of these is as effective as one that combines top-down, results-driven change with the slower, bottom-up development of organizational capability. Such combined strategies require:

- the development of a compelling and balanced business and organization development direction
- the management of key stakeholders in order to buy time to develop organization capability
- the adoption of a sociotechnical approach that involves the development of down the line managers.

CEOs and their top teams often have a mindset that promotes a top-down drive for results. The three key aspects of this mindset are:

▶ the importance given to shareholder interests
▶ the assumption that it is the organization's technical rather than its social system that is the prime determinant of performance
▶ the assumption that there is little to be gained from dialogue with employees.

Some situational variables that need to be considered when shaping a change strategy were explored. These included:

▶ urgency and stakes involved
▶ clarity of desired future state
▶ the amount and type of resistance that is anticipated
▶ the extent to which change managers have the required data for designing and implementing the change
▶ degree to which other stakeholders trust change managers
▶ degree to which change managers have to rely on the commitment and energy of others to implement the plan.

The chapter concludes with a brief review of some alternative starting points for change.

References

Balogun, J. and Hailey, V.H. (2008) *Exploring Strategic Change*, London: Prentice Hall.

Beer, M. (2000) Cracking the code of change, *Harvard Business Review*, **78**(3): 133–41.

Beer, M. (2001) How to develop an organization capable of sustained high performance: embrace the drive for results-capability development paradox, *Organizational Dynamics*, **29**(4): 233–47.

Beer, M. and Nohria, N. (2000) *Breaking the Code of Change*, Boston, MA: Harvard Business School Press.

Eriksson, M. and Sundgren, M. (2005) Managing change: strategy or serendipity – reflections from the merger of Astra and Zeneca, *Journal of Change Management*, **5**(1): 15–28.

Ford, J.D. and Ford, L.W. (2009) Decoding resistance to change, *Harvard Business Review*, **87**(4): 99–103.

Guerrera, F. (2009) Welch slams the obsession with shareholder value as a 'dumb idea', *Financial Times*, 13 March.

Kotter, J. and Schlesinger, L. (1979) Choosing strategies for change, *Harvard Business Review*, **57**(2): 106–14.

Morrison, E.W. and Milliken, F.J. (2000) Organizational silence: a barrier to change and development in a pluralistic world, *Academy of Management Review*, **25**(4): 706–25.

Nadler, D. and Shaw, R. (1995) Change leadership, in D. Nadler, R. Shaw and A.E. Walton (eds) *Discontinous Change*, San Francisco, CA: Jossey-Bass.

Schein, E.H. (1996) The three cultures of management: the key to organizational learning, *Sloan Management Review*, **38**(1): 9–20.

Zaltman, G. and Duncan, R. (1977) *Strategies for Planned Change*, London: Wiley.

Beckhard and Harris (1987) define the period of time between the identification of the need for change and the achievement of a desired future state as the 'transition state'. Often key phases of this state are unique and different from either the state that exists before the change or the state that will exist after the change. For example, if an organization recognizes that it needs to improve the way it manages information and, after exploring a number of possibilities, decides to move to an enterprise resource planning integrated information system, it will experience a period of transition. There will come a point when the organization continues to rely on the old system while the new one is being developed, installed and debugged. During this period, people affected by the change will have to keep the old system going while learning how to work with the new system and develop the work roles and relationships that will have to be in place when the new system is up and running.

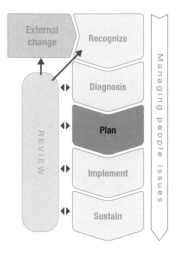

It is not unusual for many types of change to disrupt normal work practices and undermine existing systems of management. Nadler (1993) argues that during this period, one of the major challenges facing management is one of control. To abandon previous management systems before new ones have been developed can frustrate any attempt to manage the change unless some form of temporary management system is put in place. Nadler refers to the need for 'transition devices'. These include the appointment of a transition manager, the development of a plan for the period of transition between the old state and the proposed future state, the allocation of specific transition resources such as budgets, time and staff, and the development of feedback mechanisms to facilitate monitoring and control.

Planning for implementation is a key step in the change process. This chapter focuses attention on the following eight tasks:

1 appoint a transition manager
2 identify what needs to be done
3 produce an implementation plan, with clear targets and goals, which can indicate progress and signal any need for remedial action
4 use multiple and consistent leverage points for change
5 schedule activities
6 ensure that adequate resources are allocated to the change and that an appropriate balance is maintained between keeping the organization running and implementing the changes necessary to move to the desired future state

7 implement reward systems that encourage experimentation and change
8 develop feedback mechanisms that provide the information required to ensure that the change programme moves forward in a coordinated manner, especially where the plan calls for consistent change in a number of related areas.

Appoint a transition manager

It is not always obvious who should be in charge during the transition phase. Should the person in charge of the pre-change state continue to be in charge during the transition, should management responsibility pass to a temporary project manager or to the person who will be in charge post-transition? Beckhard and Harris (1987) suggest that there is no cut and dried answer to this question. Typically, the transition state is characterized by high levels of ambiguity and conflict and the individual (or group) tasked with managing the transition needs the:

▶ 'clout' to mobilize the resources necessary to keep the change moving. In situations where resources are scarce, those responsible for keeping the old system going may resist giving up the staff time and other resources required to develop the new system. The transition manager needs the power and authority to ensure that resources are allocated as required
▶ respect of both the existing operational leadership and those who are working on the development of the new system
▶ ability to get things done in ways that will win support and commitment rather than resistance and compliance.

Depending on the nature of the change, there may be several possible candidates for the transition management role. A very senior person in the organization may step in and take control. A project manager may be appointed on a temporary basis (see the discussion of this possibility in Chapter 4). The person in charge of the pre-change state may be given responsibility for the transition in addition to their current operating role. A task force or temporary team may be established. Where a team approach is adopted, consideration needs to be given to team composition. It might include representatives from the constituencies affected by the change, a diagonal slice of staff representing different levels of the organization, 'natural leaders' (people who have the confidence and trust of large numbers of their colleagues), or a group who are drawn together because of their technical skills.

Avoid unnecessary fragmentation

The problem with some of these options, such as the appointment of a temporary project manager, is that they can fragment the change process. Clegg and Walsh (2004) observe that many change processes appear to be designed with little reference to the powerful logic underlying business process thinking. They refer to software development projects that are often managed through various sequential stages including, for example, strategy, feasibility, conceptual design, detailed design, programming, implementation, use and maintenance. Even when change projects involve fewer steps, they may still be fragmented, with recognition, initial diagnosis and visioning being undertaken by one (often senior) group who then hand over to others for more detailed work and implementation, who in turn hand over to users who have to make the changes work. Clegg and Walsh (2004) suggest that this can give rise to a number of problems:

1 the different people involved at each stage can make different assessments and prioritize different objectives, resulting in confusion, conflict and waste

2 feedback loops are limited

3 consequently, opportunities to influence and learn from each other are restricted.

So while it is important to appoint a capable person to lead the transition, it is also important to ensure that this transition manager keeps in close contact with others involved at an earlier stage in the process and the post-transition manager who will have to live with the consequences of the change.

Identify what needs to be done

Once a change objective has been identified (see below), attention needs to be given to what has to be done to achieve the change.

Change tool 15.1

The Awakishi diagram

A useful tool to stimulate thinking about what needs to be done is the Awakishi diagram (Newman, 1995).

Let us assume that the change involves the closure of a plant to achieve cost savings. An individual (or group) could brainstorm ideas about what needs to be done to achieve this goal. The brainstorm might generate a large number of issues that require attention. These can be grouped into categories. The most important categories provide the main 'bones', which connect to the spine of the skeleton (see Figure 15.1). These could be plant to be closed, surplus equipment, inventories and people.

Using these bones as prompts, the other things that will need to be done can be identified and prioritized. For example, what needs to happen in order to identify which plant to close, which equipment to dispose of and which people to let go? Attention can then be given to what needs to be done to actually close the target plant, dispose of surplus equipment and manage the relocation/severance of surplus staff. Attention can also be given to issues such as stakeholder management, communications and the like.

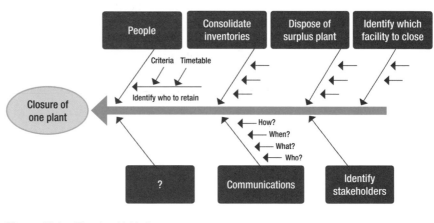

Figure 15.1 *The Awakishi diagram*

Develop an implementation plan

There are two factors that will influence the change plan. These are:

▶ the change participants' perceptions of the proposed change in terms of its appeal and the likelihood that it will happen

▶ the clarity of the desired end state – is the change a 'blueprint change' where the desired end state is known, or an emergent change where the desired end state is, as yet, unknown?

Change participants' perceptions

Dibella (2007) points to four scenarios regarding change participants' perceptions (see Figure 15.2). The first is where participants view the change as desirable and consider it inevitable. In these circumstances, the transition manager's task is clear. There will be little resistance so the main requirement is to develop an implementation plan that lays out critical tasks and time frames. This will help to avoid the possibility that, because the change is viewed as inevitable, those involved may relax and overlook the need to complete some necessary tasks.

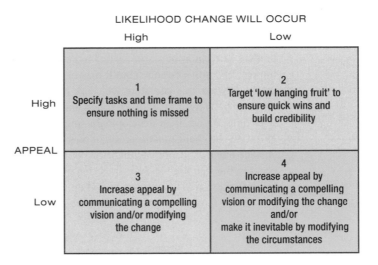

LIKELIHOOD CHANGE WILL OCCUR

	High	Low
APPEAL High	**1** Specify tasks and time frame to ensure nothing is missed	**2** Target 'low hanging fruit' to ensure quick wins and build credibility
Low	**3** Increase appeal by communicating a compelling vision and/or modifying the change	**4** Increase appeal by communicating a compelling vision or modifying the change and/or make it inevitable by modifying the circumstances

Figure 15.2 *Change participants' perceptions of the appeal and likelihood of the change*

The second scenario is where participants view the change as desirable but are not convinced it will happen. In these circumstances, the transition manager needs to act in ways that will shift perceptions and increase participants' conviction that the change will be accomplished. Dibella (2007) suggests this can be achieved by developing a change plan that focuses, in the first instance, on achieving small victories by addressing 'low hanging fruit'. This will help to secure early successes that will build credibility.

The third scenario is where participants do not view the change as desirable but anticipate that it is inevitable. This fits the stereotypical condition where resistance to change is expected. Dibella (2007) suggests that, overtly or covertly, participants will strive to alter the conditions and make it less inevitable by reducing their engagement. Delaying tactics, for example, might hold back the change until it is eclipsed by a crisis or some other initiative that diverts attention elsewhere. In these circumstances, transition managers need to focus attention on making the change more desirable. There may be features of the change that can be modified to make it more appealing. As a minimum, the transition manager will need to communicate a compelling vision.

The final scenario is where participants perceive the change to be undesirable and unlikely to happen. Under these conditions, there is no clear incentive for participants to engage in the change. They may be openly defiant and act in ways that will test the transition manager's credibility. Dibella (2007) suggests that, in these circumstances, the transition manager's options include modifying the change to make it more appealing or altering the environment to make it seem more inevitable. One possibility for altering the environment might be to recruit into the process a set of champions or advocates who view the change in more positive terms or remove some of the most resistant participants from the scene (see the discussion of stakeholder management in Chapter 8).

Clarity of the end state

Planning is easier when the desired end state is known. With a blueprint change, it is normally relatively easy to define the change goal, but sometimes it is not possible to articulate a clear vision of what the end state will look like. There are circumstances, described in Chapter 2, where a need for change might be recognized – because, for example, the organization is losing market share or is failing to innovate as fast as its competitors – but it may be far from obvious what needs to be done to improve matters. There may be a broadly defined goal and a direction for change, for example improving competitiveness, but it may not be possible to provide a detailed specification of what this end state will look like. In this kind of circumstance, change needs to be viewed as an open-ended and iterative process that emerges or evolves over time. Rather than developing a single grand plan to achieve a clearly defined end state, the change manager might need to think in terms of developing a series of smaller but reasonably well-defined plans. After each step in the implementation process, the step itself and the direction of the change can be reviewed, and the plan for the next step in the process firmed up.

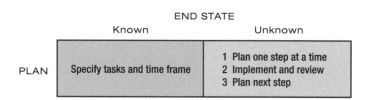

Figure 15.3 *Clarity of end state and content and structure of the plan*

Quinn (1993) suggests that this kind of incremental approach to planning and implementing change can have advantages even when change managers do have a view of where they want the organization to be. He argues that taking small steps, reflecting on progress and building on the experience gained can be effective because it:

▶ improves the quality of the information used in key decisions
▶ helps overcome the personal and political pressures resisting change
▶ copes with the variety of lead times and sequencing problems associated with change
▶ builds the overall awareness, understanding and commitment required to ensure implementation.

Based on his observations of senior managers in Xerox, GM and IBM, Quinn (1993: 83) concludes that often, in practice, by the time change plans begin to crystallize, elements of them have already been implemented. He reports that by consciously adopting this kind of incremental process, change managers can build sufficient momentum and gain sufficient commitment to change plans 'to make them flow towards flexible and successful implementation'.

While recognizing the importance of planning, Nadler and Tushman (1989) caution against developing an uncompromising commitment to an implementation plan. Early actions will have unintended consequences, some welcome, some not, and it is inevitable that some unforeseen opportunities as well as problems will be encountered. They assert that to ignore unanticipated opportunities just because they are not in the plan could be 'foolish'. Planned change involves learning and constant adjustment. Planning needs to be balanced with what they refer to as 'bounded opportunism'. Change managers should not feel compelled to respond to every problem, event or opportunity, because doing so could involve adopting courses of action that are inconsistent with the intent of the change, but within certain boundaries, being opportunistic and modifying plans can deliver benefits.

Beckhard and Harris (1987) identify seven characteristics of effective transition plans. Effective plans are:

▶ *purposeful:* the planned activities are clearly linked to the change goals and priorities
▶ *task specific:* the types of activities involved are clearly identified rather than broadly generalized
▶ *integrated:* the discrete activities are linked
▶ *temporal:* events and activities are timetabled
▶ *adaptable:* there are contingency plans and ways of adapting to unanticipated opportunities and problems
▶ *agreed:* by top management, and other key stakeholders, as required
▶ *cost-effective:* to avoid unnecessary waste.

This list might be extended to include some of the issues considered below, for example the provision of adequate resources and rewards for desired behaviours.

Use multiple and consistent leverage points for change

It was noted earlier that organizations are equilibrium-seeking systems. If only one component of the system is changed, this can trigger forces that will work to realign all the components of the system and re-establish the status quo. One way of avoiding this is to use multiple and consistent leverage points for achieving change. For example, if it is decided to change the structure of an organization, it may be necessary to modify other elements of the system at the same time, such as culture and career management systems, in order to secure the intended benefits (see Example 15.1).

Example 15.1

Matrix structures

Managers in an auto components manufacturing company decided that, in order to improve performance, they needed to introduce a new structure that would be more responsive to the complex technical issues associated with production and the unique project requirements of their customers (see Figure 15.4). This kind of dual focus has long been recognized as a requirement in the aerospace industry where products are technically complex and customers very demanding.

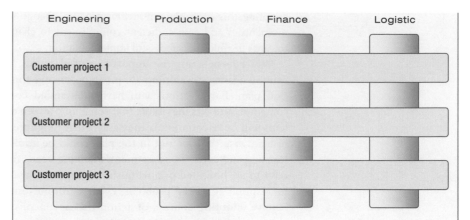

Figure 15.4 *A matrix organization structure*

In this case, the promise of improved performance was not realized because the transition plan did not incorporate multiple and consistent leverage points for change. It failed to recognize the need, when introducing the new structure, to adjust a range of other elements of the wider organization, such as the organization's systems and culture.

Matrix structures will only be effective if they are supported by organizational systems concerned with planning, controlling, appraising and rewarding that serve the needs of the functional and customer project dimensions of the new structure. If appraising and rewarding are left in the hands of functional managers, such as the heads of engineering and production, the managers responsible for the customer-related projects might find that they have little influence over the members of their project teams who also report to a functional manager. In the example of the auto components manufacturing company, team members gave priority to the demands of their functional managers because they continued to exercise most influence over their career and reward package. The new systems failed to accommodate the new dual focus.

There was also no attempt to modify the pre-change organization culture to ensure it would be compatible with the new matrix approach to management. In this case, there was a rigid bureaucratic tradition, a belief in the sanctity of the unity of command and a commitment to immediate departmental objectives. This culture undermined attempts to achieve the dual strength of technical competence and customer focus. A matrix organization will only be effective when members are aware of and willing to work towards these broad goals and when they have the skills and competence to expand their contribution to embrace responsibility for managing the relationship between their subtask and the broader organizational purpose.

Schedule activities

It was noted in Chapter 2 that any plan for change will involve managing a long list of things that will need to be done in order to make the proposed change a reality. There will be different lead times associated with the various tasks, interdependencies between them and resource and other constraints. All these things need to be taken into account when developing an implementation plan. Careful scheduling can help to ensure that all the necessary actions occur when required.

Change tool 15.2

Critical path analysis

A useful tool for scheduling and identifying resource requirements is critical path analysis. It focuses attention on:

- the tasks that need to be completed
- the order in which they have to be undertaken
- dependencies between activities. It may not be possible to start some activities until others have been completed, whereas others might not be dependent on the completion of other tasks and can be started at almost any time – so long as they are completed when required by later stages in the change process (see task 8 below)
- the resources needed to complete the project and when they will be required
- milestones to monitor progress
- the shortest time to complete the project to specification and within budget
- possible ways of shortening this project time if circumstances require – crashing the critical path.

Drawing the critical path

The first step is to list all the tasks that need to be undertaken, the time required to complete each task and the dependencies between tasks. A simple table can help.

Task	Duration	Start date	Completed by
Task 1	5 days	To be completed first	Day 5
Task 2	3 days	On completion of task 1	Day 10 (2-day float)
Task 3	5 days	On completion of task 1	Day 10
Task 4	5 days	Anytime	Day 15 (10-day float)
Task 5	5 days	On completion of task 3	Day 15
Task 6	3 days	On completion of tasks 4 and 5	Day 21 (3-day float)
Task 7	2 days	On completion of tasks 4 and 5	Day 17
Task 8	1 day	Anytime	Day 22 (21-day float)
Task 9	5 days	On completion of task 7	Day 22

The data can be used to create a diagram (see Figure 15.5), in which the arrows show the activities and time required to complete each task. Circles show the beginning and end of tasks. The numbers in each circle shows the required end date, and the milestones for the critical path (in bold).

The coloured arrows in Figure 15.5 show the critical (longest) sequence of dependent tasks and the shortest time to complete the project. Unless tasks on the critical path are started and completed on time, it will take longer than necessary to complete the overall project. The table and diagram also show those tasks that have spare or 'float' time. For example, task 8 can be started anytime so long as it is completed by day 22.

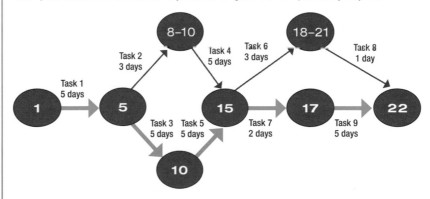

Figure 15.5 *A critical path analysis*

> **Crashing the critical path**
> If part of the project is delayed or for some other reason it is necessary to complete the project quickly, the critical path analysis will indicate how this might be achieved. Just throwing extra resources at every task to speed things along may be less effective than targeting extra resources at those tasks that are part of the critical path.

Provide resources for the transition

There is always a cost associated with change. For example, there may be a need for training, new equipment, the development of software, the design of new structures, and staff time for all of this. When the need to change is anticipated, it is more likely that the resource requirements will have been foreseen. However, when change is imposed as an urgent response to a pressing problem, the organization may find itself stretched. In some circumstances, it may be so stretched that it cannot resource the change and has no option but to go out of business. In less pressing circumstances, it is not unusual for management to assume that much of the staff burden of change will be borne by employees working longer and harder. While people often rise to the challenge in the short term, goodwill cannot be relied on forever. In situations where change is a constant feature of organizational life, this needs to be recognized and the required resources made available.

Nadler and Tushman (1989) suggest that one of the most scarce resources is senior staff time and observe that when senior managers are so overloaded that they are unable to invest sufficient time – to attend planning meetings, make presentations, attend special events, get involved in training and so on – change initiatives are more likely to fail.

Reward transition behaviours

In situations where people are required to continue working in accordance with the pre-change system, in order to 'keep the show on the road' and maintain operations while simultaneously developing the new system, they might give insufficient attention to the change. This can happen because existing control systems reward current practice and offer little incentive for development work. Consequently, people are discouraged from investing their time in this work and from experimenting with new behaviours that might be required in the future. Steps need to be taken to ensure that transition behaviour is not penalized and every opportunity to reward this kind of behaviour needs to be explored.

Develop feedback mechanisms

A key requirement for maintaining control in the transition phase is the development and installation of new feedback devises and control systems that will facilitate the monitoring of progress towards the desired future state. Nadler (1993) is a particularly strong advocate of customized feedback mechanisms during the transition phase, because the feedback processes that managers normally use to collect information about how the organization is functioning might be less appropriate during this period. Additional sources of feedback might include organization-wide surveys, focus group discussions and feedback from individual organizational members. Bruch et al. (2005) argue that a comprehensive system for monitoring and reporting is essential to maintain people's attention on the change. This point receives more attention in Chapter 27.

Exercise 15.1 — **Maintaining control during the transition stage**

Reflect on some of the changes that you have been responsible for managing at work or elsewhere:

- Did you have an implementation plan that actually worked?
- Why was this?
- Could you have done anything to improve the implementation plan?

Notes

Summary

It is not unusual for many types of change to disrupt normal work practices and undermine existing systems of management. Nadler (1993) argues that during this period, one of the major challenges facing management is one of control. To abandon previous management systems before new ones have been developed can frustrate any attempt to manage the change, unless the change is carefully planned and some form of temporary management system is put in place.

This chapter has considered eight steps that can be taken to develop a change plan and maintain control of the change process. These are:

1 *Appoint a transition manager:* Typically the transition state is characterized by high levels of ambiguity and conflict and the individual (or group) tasked with managing the transition needs the:
   - 'clout' to mobilize the resources necessary to keep the change moving
   - respect of the existing operational leadership and those who are working on the development of the new system
   - ability to get things done in ways that will win support and commitment rather than resistance and compliance.

   It is also important to avoid unnecessary fragmentation in the way the change is managed.
2 *Identify what needs to be done:* An Awakishi diagram can help achieve this.
3 *Produce an implementation plan:* This must appeal to stakeholders and have clear targets and goals that can indicate progress and signal any need for remedial action.
4 *Use multiple and consistent leverage points for change:* If only one component of the system is changed, this can trigger forces that will work to realign all the components of the system and re-establish the status quo. One way of avoiding this is to use multiple and consistent leverage points for achieving change.

5 *Schedule activities:* Careful scheduling can help ensure that all the necessary actions occur when required.

6 *Ensure that adequate resources are allocated to the change:* Also ensure that an appropriate balance is maintained between keeping the organization running and implementing the changes necessary to move to the desired future state.

7 *Implement reward systems that encourage experimentation and change:* In situations where people are required to continue working in accordance with the pre-change system in order to 'keep the show on the road', they might give insufficient attention to the change.

8 *Develop feedback mechanisms:* These need to provide the information required to ensure that the change programme moves forward in a coordinated manner, especially where the plan calls for consistent change in a number of related areas.

References

Beckhard, R. and Harris, R.T. (1987) *Organizational Transitions: Managing Complex Change*, Reading, MA: Addison-Wesley.

Bruch, H., Gerber, P. and Maier, V. (2005) Strategic change decisions: doing the right change right, *Journal of Change Management*, **5**(1): 97–107.

Clegg, C. and Walsh, S. (2004) Change management: time for change?, *European Journal of Work and Organizational Psychology*, **13**(2): 217–39.

Dibella, A.J. (2007) Critical perceptions of organisational change, *Journal of Change Management*, **7**(3/4): 231–42.

Nadler, D.A. (1993) Concepts for the management of organizational change, in C. Mabey and B. Mayon-White (eds) *Managing Change*, London: Paul Chapman/Open University.

Nadler, D.A. and Tushman, M.L. (1989) Organizational frame bending: principles for managing reorientation, *Academy of Management Review*, **10**(3): 194–204.

Newman, V. (1995) *Made-to-measure Problem Solving*, Farnham: Gower.

Quinn, J.B. (1993) Managing strategic change, in C. Mabey and B. Mayon-White (eds) *Managing Change*, London: Paul Chapman/Open University.

Change efforts can be less successful than they might be because those responsible for managing the change are unaware of the full range of interventions that are available. Cummings and Worley (2001: 142) define interventions as 'a set of sequenced planned actions or events intended to help an organization increase its effectiveness'. They are deliberate acts that disturb the status quo. This chapter reviews some of the main types of intervention.

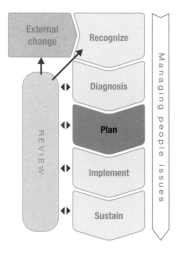

The first section of this chapter considers how the development of interventions over the past century has been influenced by theoretical perspectives. Burnes (2004) identifies the three main perspectives as the individual perspective, the group dynamics school and open systems thinking. These different perspectives focus attention on different aspects of organizational life and have implications for the focus of change efforts and how change is managed. Weisbord (1989) adopts a similar view and traces the development of interventions in terms of who should do what. He identifies four main types of intervention:

▶ experts applying scientific principles to solve specific problems
▶ groups working collaboratively to solve their own problems
▶ experts working to solve system-wide problems
▶ everybody working to improve the capability of the whole system for future performance.

The second section introduces an alternative typology that classifies the types of intervention in terms of the issues they address. Again, four main types of intervention are identified. They focus on:

▶ human process issues
▶ technology/structural issues
▶ human resource issues
▶ strategic issues.

A number of specific interventions are briefly considered under each of these headings and a selection of interventions is considered in more detail in Part VI.

A classification of interventions based on who does what

Weisbord (1989) observes that there has been a continuous development of new types of intervention over the past century and suggests that this has been a response to environmental changes, particularly the trend towards greater turbulence and uncertainty.

He classifies the range of interventions available to change agents into four categories according to who does the intervening and what it is they do to bring about improvement. In terms of who does the intervening, he notes that 100 years ago, the typical intervention relied on an expert to solve a problem, whereas today interventions often involve the whole system, including experts. In terms of what it is that the interventions focus on, he notes that there has been a shift from problem solving past mistakes in particular parts of the system to improving the capability of the whole system for future performance. This evolution in interventions is illustrated in Figure 16.1.

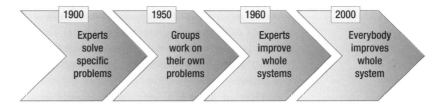

Figure 16.1   *Developments in types of intervention over the past century*
Source: Adapted from Weisbord, 1989

The use of technical experts to solve problems

Fredrick W. Taylor published his *Principles of Scientific Management* in 1911 in which he advocated a systematic experimental approach to problem solving. His principles involved a careful analysis of tasks and experimentation to determine, from the perspective of efficiency, how the task should be divided into segments and how the work in each segment should be done. One of the most frequently quoted examples of Taylor's work involves an assignment at the Bethlehem steel plant designed to find the most efficient way of moving 100lb pigs (slabs) of iron from a loading dock into a railroad truck. He enlisted the help of a pig iron handler called Schmidt and studied him while, on instruction, he moved the pigs in different ways. The outcome was an ideal approach to doing the job that also specified rest periods and included an incentive system that rewarded the job holder for working efficiently. The new approach increased productivity by 280%.

Taylor's approach led to the widespread use of experts to solve problems, such as methods engineers to identify the most efficient way of accomplishing a task and time and motion analysts to set standard times for the completion of each segment of the work.

Today many organizations still employ experts to solve specific problems, for example to develop a new payments system or design a new information management system. Experts are often used when a unit (or the organization) only has occasional need for a specific kind of expertise, when the need is for cutting-edge expertise that might only be obtained from specialist departments or external consultants, or when a solution has to be found urgently and the quickest approach is to buy in external help. A potential problem associated with the use of experts is that members of the system may not share the expert's diagnosis of the problem and therefore may not be committed to implementing the prescribed solution. Also, members of the system may not learn how to solve the problem for themselves, so should it reoccur, they will continue to be dependent on the expert for the solution.

Interventions that involve groups working on their own problems

Half a century later, the work of Kurt Lewin and his associates at the Research Center for Group Dynamics at MIT began to produce evidence that supported the proposition that the behaviour, attitudes, beliefs and values of individuals are all based in the groups to which they belong. This led to the view that groups exert a strong influence over whether individuals will accept or resist a change. A consequence was the development of new kinds of interventions that involved all members of a work group working together to solve problems. Interventions focused on changing the groups' norms, roles and values.

Cartwright (1951) summarized eight principles, which emerged from the early research on group dynamics, that influenced the design of interventions. The first five are concerned with the group as a medium of change and with how the group is able to exert influence over its members. The final three focus on the potential benefits of making the group the target of change, even when the prime aim is to change individual behaviour. Evidence suggests that by changing the standards, style of leadership and structure of a group, it is possible to change the behaviour of individual group members. The eight principles are:

1 **If the group is to be used as a medium of change, those people who are to be changed and those who are to exert influence for change must have a strong sense of belonging to the same group.**

This implies that in situations where the change agents are regarded as part of the group, and when a strong 'we' as opposed to an 'us and them' feeling exists, those trying to bring about change will have more influence over others. Cartwright cites research findings that show that there is greater change in members' opinions when discussion groups operate with participatory rather than supervisory leadership.

2 **The more attractive a group is to its members, the greater the influence it will exert over its members.**

When individuals find a group attractive and want to be members of the group, they are more ready to be influenced by other members of the group. Attractiveness promotes cohesiveness and a willingness, on the part of members, to conform with others when conformity is a relevant matter for the group.

A group is more attractive to members the more it satisfies their needs. Some of the ways that group attractiveness can be increased include:

▶ increasing the liking of members for each other
▶ increasing the perceived importance of the group goal
▶ increasing the prestige of the group in the eyes of others.

3 **A group has most influence over those matters that attract members to it.**

Research evidence suggests that in attempts to change attitudes, values or behaviour, the more relevant they are to the basis of attraction to the group, the greater the influence the group is able to exert upon them. This helps to explain, for example, why a member of a local branch of a trade union might be willing to follow a union recommendation to engage in industrial action to influence the outcome of a pay negotiation but refuse to join a wider political protest targeted at government policies. While some members might be attracted by the union's political agenda, others might not share the union's political affiliation. However, all may be attracted by the role the union can play in protecting their interests in the workplace.

> **4** The greater the prestige of a member in the eyes of other group members, the greater the influence that member can exert.

The relevance of this principle, in the context of change management, is that the person who has greatest prestige and who exerts most influence may not be the manager or formal leader designated by the organization. Also, in peer groups, the most influential person may not be the person who behaves in ways that are valued by superiors. For example, in a classroom situation, the teacher's pet may have low prestige in the eyes of other members of the class and therefore will have low influence over them.

> **5** Efforts to change individual members or subparts of a group, which, if successful, would have the effect of making them deviate from the norms of the group, will encounter strong resistance.

In many groups, the price of deviation is rejection. Consequently, especially where group membership is valued, there is pressure to conform to the norms of the group. This principle helps to explain why training interventions that involve taking individuals from different groups and training (changing) them often have a poor record in terms of transfer of learning when compared with training interventions that are directed at all members of a natural work group. Where the focus is on changing an individual, that individual may be reluctant to continue to behave differently after training for fear of rejection. Where the intervention is targeted at the whole group, this problem is less likely to arise.

> **6** It is possible to create strong pressures for change in a group by establishing a shared perception of the need for change, thus making the source of pressure for change lie within the group.

When groups are presented with 'facts' by an outsider, for example a manager, an internal or external consultant, even where, to the outsider, the facts 'prove' the case for change, the facts may not be accepted by the group. The group may reject the facts because it does not own them.

When groups collect and test their own facts, they are more likely to accept the evidence. Cartwright (1951) notes that there appears to be all the difference in the world between those cases where external consultants are hired to do a study and present a report and those in which a technical expert collaborates with the group in doing its own study. Often external reports are not acted on, but are left to gather dust rather than stimulate lasting change.

> **7** Information relating to the need for change and the consequences of change, or no change, must be shared by all relevant people in the group.

This principle is about getting people talking about the need for change. Changes can be blocked unless action is taken to improve communication. Evidence suggests that where the prospect of change creates feelings of threat, mistrust or hostility, people avoid communicating openly and freely about the issues that concern them. Just at the point when the need for communication is at its highest, people act defensively and communicate less.

8 Changes in one part of the group or system produce strain in other parts of the group or system that can be reduced only by eliminating the initial change or bringing about readjustments in the related parts.

This principle is about alignment. For example, a training programme that has produced changes in one subgroup, say nurses working on a hospital ward, will have implications for other subgroups working above, below and around them as part of the total group of people dealing with patients on that ward.

The use of experts to solve systemic problems

Following the impact of von Bertalanffy's (1950) seminal paper on the theory of open systems in physics and biology, social scientists began to pay more attention to organizations as systems of interrelated units that transact with a larger environment. (Some of the main implications of systems thinking for organizations are summarized in Chapter 5.) This interest led to the development of a new class of intervention. Attention shifted from solving isolated problems to looking at more systemic issues. Organizations began to employ experts, such as operations researchers and systems analysts, to guide this approach to problem solving.

In the UK, social scientists at the Tavistock Institute of Human Relations began to develop interventions based on sociotechnical theory. Much of their work was based on the principle that, in any situation, there is rarely only one single social system (work relationship structure) that can be used to accomplish a given task. Usually, there are a number of such systems that can be used to operate the same technology and therefore there exists an element of choice in designing the work organization (see Trist, 1969). This gives rise to the question of which social system will provide the optimum conditions and contribute most to the outcomes valued by various stakeholders. The ground-breaking work on sociotechnical systems was undertaken by Trist and Bamforth (1951) in the UK coal mining industry. Their study (see Research report 16.1) demonstrates how the introduction of a new technology, in this case a new technology for coal getting, had a profound negative impact on miners and their social system. Their study led to further work that explored ways of modifying the long-wall system to minimize this negative impact. The outcome was the 'composite' long-wall system, which not only produced impressive improvements in the work life of miners, including a marked increase in group cohesiveness, personal satisfaction and attendance, but also a significant improvement in performance.

Research report 16.1 ⟩ **Sociotechnical systems**

Trist, E.L. and Bamforth, K.W. (1951) Some social and psychological consequences of the long-wall method of coal-getting, *Human Relations*, 1: 3–38

The introduction of the long-wall method of coal getting into UK mines failed to achieve the level of performance improvements that had been anticipated. Trist and Bamforth investigated the impact of the new technology on the social quality of work at the coalface. Their research method involved following and maintaining relatively continuous contact with 20 coalface workers over a period of two years. Group discussions with all grades of manager provided additional data.

Their findings indicated that the 'room-and-pillar' method, which preceded the long-wall system, provided workers with greater social balance than the more mechanized system. The outstanding feature of the room-and-pillar system was its emphasis on autonomous small groups. It was common practice for two colliers – a hewer and his mate – to make their own contract with colliery management and work their own small face, with the assistance of a 'trammer' who loaded the hewn coal into tram-tubs and removed it from the coalface. This group had responsibility for the complete coal-getting task, was self-regulating and could set its own targets, adjusting work rate to take account of age, stamina and changing working conditions. The choice of workmates was also made by the men themselves.

The introduction of coal cutters and mechanical conveyers required radically different work relationships. Colliers worked in units of 40 or more men along a single long coalface, and their work was broken down into a series of component operations that followed each other in rigid succession over three shifts. In the first shift, two men worked across the top of the coalface boring holes for explosives. Another two men used a cutter to undercut the coal to a depth of 2 m, 15 cm from the floor. Four more men removed the coal from this 15 cm undercut, making a gap so that the coalface could drop when the explosive shots were fired. Finally, temporary 'noggins' were inserted in this gap so that the coalface would not sag while it was left standing during the next shift. While all this was happening, two more men dismantled the conveyor belt and got it ready for moving.

During the second shift, two men moved and rebuilt the conveyor belt close to the new face. A separate team of eight reinforced air and haulage ways and ripped down the remaining roof of the old face to make the new working area safe. When all this had been done, the explosive shots were fired to collapse the coalface.

The third shift of 20 'fillers' worked independently of each other to extract all the coal from their designated section of the coalface. This had to be completed before the cycle could begin again, but many factors could make this difficult.

There were many close interdependencies between all the above tasks. Failure to achieve 100% performance of any task seriously disrupted the cycle, but despite this interdependence, workers were only qualified to perform their own task, had little or no contact with others and had no sense of belonging to a whole work group. Trist and Bamforth document many of the problems that workers had to contend with in this situation of 'dependent isolation' – where they were split off from any sense of belonging to either a shift or a total production group – and observed that one of the ways the miners adapted was to adopt a norm of low productivity.

Trist (1969) reports that the early 'conventional' long-wall system eventually gave way to a 'composite' system in which miners were multiskilled and worked in self-selected autonomous teams responsible for allocating themselves to the various jobs management required the team to undertake. This increased flexibility allowed an oncoming shift to take up the production cycle at whatever point the previous shift had left it and carry on with whatever jobs had to be done next.

This kind of development gave rise to a proliferation of other interventions in different settings that were directed towards systemic issues such as managing the organization's relationship with its environment and helping to promote a better alignment of the elements within the organization. While most early systemic interventions were led by experts, many of those that were developed later integrated representatives of the target system into the process of managing change. This development has been taken a stage further in whole systems interventions.

Whole system interventions to improve capability for future performance

The most recent development has been whole systems interventions in which everybody is involved in whole system improvement. Many examples of this type of intervention, such as Weisbord's strategic search conference, adopt a 'whole system in the room' or conference model format. Some of the principles that underpin the whole system approach are summarized below:

▶ *Parallel organization versus 'whole system in the room' approaches:* The effectiveness of attempts to introduce change, especially at the strategic level, is dependent on the actions and behaviours of everybody affected by the change. Therefore, wherever practicable, everybody should be involved in the change process.

A typical intervention used to develop a shared vision and an agreed strategic plan is to set up a temporary parallel organization involving representatives from different groups (and levels) across the regular organization to work together in various committees and task forces to produce the desired output. It is assumed that this kind of approach creates a wide feeling of involvement and gains the commitment of all organizational members. Often, however, only the representatives and those close to them feel involved. While this minority may become excited and passionate about the changes, others may feel left out and unable to influence developments. This can undermine their commitment to the vision and strategic plan produced by this process.

An alternative approach, embedded in the whole system in the room or conference model, involves a significant part of the whole system rather than a parallel organization of representatives. This permits everybody to contribute. It is not uncommon to accommodate 500 or more members of the organization in a single conference. In large organizations, several conferences may be required, with some mechanism for integrating the findings from the different meetings at key stages.

▶ *Problem-solving versus preferred future approaches:* Lippitt (1983) argues that trying to 'fix the past' by problem solving depletes energy, whereas focusing attention on planning for a new future releases energy. Dannemiller and Jacobs (1992) report that when Lippitt compared a problem-solving group and a group using a 'preferred futures' approach, the latter group envisioned the future they preferred and developed plans to achieve it, whereas the former group restricted itself to problem identification and action planning. He also found that the preferred futures approach was associated with higher levels of energy, greater ownership of the situation and more innovative and future-oriented goals and plans. The focus of whole systems approaches tends to be on what the organization might become, rather than the current problems that need to be solved.

▶ *Organizational biographies – understanding the past and present as a basis for exploring a preferred future:* All too often organizational members are unaware of the assumptions and consistent patterns that guide how they interpret and respond to situations, yet these assumptions and consistent patterns may blind them to threats and opportunities and may lead them to develop unrealistic strategic plans.

What an organization is today has been influenced by the way organizational members have interpreted and responded to opportunities and threats in the past. But organizations are not victims of the past. It is possible to learn from past experience and to use this learning to challenge and modify assumptions, identify new possibilities and identify what needs to happen if these possibilities are to become reality. An element of many interventions, therefore, is the development of a better understanding of where the organization has come from, where it is today and how it moved from where it was to where it is.

▶ *Overcoming resistance to change:* Change occurs when organizational members experience a tension that results from a discrepancy between their awareness of current reality and their desired future state (Fritz, 1984). They are motivated to reduce the tension by acting in ways that will help the organization move towards the more desired future state. The conference method is designed to create this necessary tension across the whole organization. Dannemiller and Jacobs (1992) advance this view and adapt Gleicher's change formula to argue that change will occur when the product of dissatisfaction with the present situation (D), a vision of what is possible (V), and practical first steps towards reaching the vision (F) are greater than the cost of change/resistance (R):

$$C = (D \, V \, F) > R$$

The conference method involves a process that openly explores organizational members' satisfaction with the status quo, develops a clear vision of future possibilities and identifies practical first steps in order to motivate people to change.

▷ *Open systems planning*: Jayaram (1977) and others strongly advocate open systems planning. In the conference method, external stakeholders, such as suppliers and customers, are invited to contribute their views about the organization's current performance and the opportunities and threats it will have to respond to in the future. This kind of input enriches the database available to organizational members.

Essentially, large group methods involve getting people together to deal with issues of importance. These issues might relate to problems affecting performance in a particular organizational unit, managing relationships with customers or suppliers, or the future of the whole system. Alban and Bunker (2009) suggest that they tend to be most effective where the issue affects the whole system, it is important to the organization's future, it would benefit the organization to have broader ownership of the issues and where new and creative ideas are required. Large group methods can help promote bottom-up change but they can also form part of a management-led initiative and do not need to take away management's responsibility for charting the way forward.

The past 100 years have seen many developments in the types of intervention available to change agents, but all four types considered so far can be used to good effect in appropriate circumstances. The next section of this chapter will review interventions from a different perspective.

A classification of interventions based on focal issues

Cummings and Worley (2001) offer an alternative typology for classifying interventions based on the kinds of issues they are designed to resolve. Figure 16.2 shows the four main types of intervention. Systemic interdependencies are indicated by the double-headed arrows. Specific interventions within each of the four types can differ in terms of their intended target: individual, group or whole organization. For example, under the heading of 'human resource management interventions', there might be some interventions, such as those concerned with reward systems, that could be targeted at all three levels, whereas other interventions, such as those concerned with performance appraisal, might only be targeted at the individual and group levels.

Human process interventions

Human process interventions focus on people and the processes through which they accomplish organizational goals, such as communication, problem solving, decision making and leadership.

Interpersonal and group process approaches include the following interventions:

▶ *T-groups*, sometimes referred to as sensitivity training, involve trainees exploring group dynamics and providing each other with feedback about the impact of their behaviour on others.

▶ *Process consultation* typically involves a consultant helping group members diagnose what is going on in their group as they work on real issues, and helping them devise solutions to problems that undermine group effectiveness.

▶ *Third-party interventions* involve an outsider helping organizational members resolve conflicts.

▶ *Team-building interventions* are designed to improve team working, often by re-examining the group's task, members' roles and the strategies they use for completing the task.

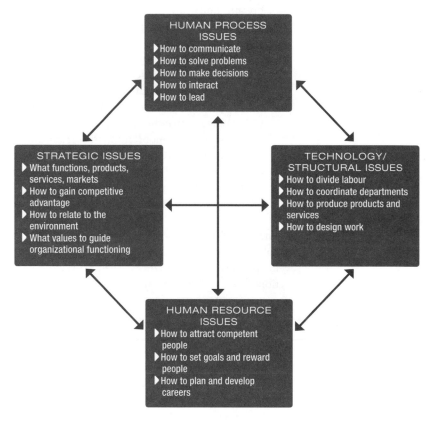

Figure 16.2 *Cummings and Worley's typology of interventions based on focal issues*
Source: Adapted from Cummings and Worley, 2001: 146

Human process interventions can be applied at the organizational level to deal with more systemic issues. These include the following interventions:

▶ *Confrontation meetings* are interventions designed to mobilize organization-wide resources to identify problems, set priorities and targets and devise plans for action. They are often employed to bridge the gap between senior management and the rest of the organization.

▶ *Intergroup relations interventions* can take a number of forms such as microcosm groups with members representing different interests coming together to work on issues relating to diversity, and interventions designed to help two or more groups work to resolve dysfunctional conflicts.

▶ *Large group interventions* go under a number of labels, such as whole system in the room conferences, search conferences, open space meetings and future searches, and are designed to involve many people, including external stakeholders, in the management of issues that affect the whole organization.

▶ *Grid interventions*, and Likert's System 4, are normative in the sense that they specify a one best way to manage organizations and involve processes that help organizations move to this ideal.

Action research and appreciative inquiry (see Chapters 19 and 20) are examples of human process interventions that adopt different approaches to accomplishing organizational goals. Action research involves the application of scientific principles to problem solving, whereas appreciative inquiry involves the identification and amplification of best practice.

Technostructural interventions

Technostructural interventions focus on the three areas of structure, task methods and job design.

Interventions relating to the design of organizations include the grouping of activities, downsizing and re-engineering:

▶ *Structural design* encompasses interventions that aim to identify and move towards more effective ways of structuring activities. It often involves moving towards more process-based and network-based structures in order to provide the flexibility to cope with increasing turbulence and uncertainty.

▶ *Downsizing interventions* are aimed at reducing the size of the organization.

▶ *Business process re-engineering* involves a fundamental rethink and radical redesign of business processes to achieve a step change in performance. It often involves the use of IT systems to help organizational members control and coordinate work processes more effectively. This kind of intervention is considered in more detail in Chapter 23.

Interventions designed to increase employee involvement in order to enhance their commitment and performance often involve moving decision making downwards in the organization, closer to where the work is done. To achieve this, employees, at all levels, have to be provided with the power, information, knowledge and skills required to act effectively. Interventions of this type include:

▶ *General interventions* designed to improve the quality of work life such as job enrichment, self-managed teams and labour/management committees.

▶ *Interventions of various types* that involve the creation of a parallel structure that operates in tandem with the formal organization to provide alternative settings, such as awaydays, project groups or quality circles, in which organizational members can address problems and search for solutions.

▶ *Other broad-based interventions* designed to increase employee involvement are high-involvement organizations, which entail a joint manager-worker redesign of the organization to promote high levels of involvement and performance, rather that the addition of parallel structures, and total quality management, which is a long-term effort designed to focus all the organization's activities around the concept of quality.

Work/job design interventions for groups and individuals include the following approaches:

▶ *Engineering approaches* to work design focus on efficiency and job simplification.
▶ *Motivational approaches* focus on enriching the work experience and are designed to motivate employees to work more effectively.
▶ *Sociotechnical approaches* to work design focus on integrating the technical and social aspects of work. They often involve the introduction of self-managed work groups.

Human resource management interventions

Human resource management interventions focus on personnel practices such as selection, training and development, goal setting, performance appraisal, incentives, internal promotion systems, career development and so on, and how they can be used to integrate people into the organization.

Interventions designed to develop and assist organizational members can be grouped under three headings:

▶ *Career planning and development interventions* are often introduced to help employees manage their own careers and prepare themselves to respond to the uncertainties and lack of job security that are increasingly becoming a feature of organizational life.
▶ *Workforce diversity interventions* are designed to respond to the different needs, preferences and expectations of the various groups of employees who bring different resources and perspectives to the organization. A key aim of these interventions is to help the organization retain a diverse workforce and use it to gain competitive advantage.
▶ *Employee wellness interventions* are designed to promote the wellbeing of organizational members and to contribute to the development of a productive workforce. They include employee assistance and stress management programmes.

Performance management interventions focus on how goal setting, performance appraisal and reward systems can contribute to organizational effectiveness by aligning members' work behaviour with business strategy and workplace technology.

High performance management is a human resource management intervention that involves developing and implementing a 'bundle' of HR practices that are internally consistent and aligned with the organization's strategy to achieve improvements in organizational effectiveness. This type of intervention is considered in Chapter 22.

Strategic interventions

Strategic interventions link the internal functioning of the organization with the wider environment. They aim to align business strategy with organizational culture and the external environment.

Cummings and Worely (2001) highlight three interventions designed to improve the organization–environment fit:

▶ *Open systems planning* is an intervention designed to help an organization systematically assess its environment and develop strategic responses to it.
▶ *Integrated strategic change interventions* are directed towards integrating strategic planning and operational and tactical actions.

▶ *Trans-organizational development* is an intervention that focuses on the creation of beneficial partnerships with other organizations to perform tasks or solve problems that are beyond the capability of a single organization.

Another subcategory of strategic interventions are those that focus more directly on changing the organization's culture and mental models. They involve diagnosing the existing culture and assessing the cultural risks associated with planned changes.

Exercise 16.1

Types of intervention

Review some of the change programmes that have been pursued within your organization and consider the types of intervention used. Do they all tend to fall within one or two of the categories reviewed in this chapter or have a wide range of different types of intervention been employed?

Notes

Summary

Interventions are 'a set of sequenced planned actions or events intended to help an organization increase its effectiveness' (Cummings and Worley, 2001). They purposely disrupt the status quo in order to move the organization towards a more effective state.

This chapter has presented two contrasting typologies to provide a brief overview of the wide range of interventions available to change agents.

The first focuses attention on who does the intervening and what it is they do to bring about change. Four classes of intervention are discussed:

1 *Experts applying scientific principles to solve specific problems:* Experts tend to be brought in when there is only an occasional need for a particular expertise within a business unit and/or when there is a need for cutting-edge expertise. Problems can arise if:
   - the expert disregards local knowledge
   - insiders are reluctant to share their knowledge and experience with the expert
   - the expert's diagnosis and prescription for change is resisted by insiders
   - insiders may become too dependent on the expert.

2 *Groups working collaboratively to solve their own problems:* Coch and French demonstrated that people are much more accepting of change when they are involved in the process of planning and implementing the change. Action research offers an example of how a facilitator can work with a group to help it solve its own problems.

3 *Experts working to solve system-wide problems:* Experts such as operations researchers, systems analysts and manufacturing systems engineers typically focus on changing the technical system. Trist and Bamforth were the first to recognize the importance of changing the social and technical systems together – the sociotechnical systems approach.

4 *Everybody working to improve the capability of the whole system for future performance:* The most recent development has been whole systems interventions in which everybody is involved in whole system improvement.

The second typology classifies interventions in terms of the issues they address. Again, four main types of intervention are identified. They focus on:

1 *Human process issues:* Human process interventions focus on the development of better working relationships and the processes people use for communicating, problem solving, decision making and so on.

2 *Technology/structural issues:* Technostructural interventions are typically associated with shifts from rigid and bureaucratic to more adaptive and cost-efficient organizational forms, and address such issues as the division of labour, coordination between departments, processes used to produce goods and services and the design of work.

3 *Strategic issues:* Strategic interventions address issues such as the formulation and implementation of strategy, ensuring that strategy is aligned with organizational structure and culture and that all three are aligned with the external environment, and seeking and maintaining competitive advantage.

4 *Human resource issues*: Human resource interventions focus on personnel practices and how they can be used to integrate people into the organization. They address issues such as how to attract and retain competent people, set goals and reward people, develop employee competences and plan and develop careers.

These different perspectives draw attention to different aspects of organizational life and have implications for the focus of change efforts and how change is managed.

References

Alban, B. and Bunker, B.B. (2009) Let your people take you higher, *People Management*, February: 22–5.

Burnes, B. (2004) *Managing Change*, Harlow: Pearson Education.

Cartwright, D. (1951) Achieving change in people: some applications of group dynamics theory, *Human Relations*, **4**(2): 381–92.

Cummings, T.G. and Worley, C.G. (2001) *Organizational Development and Change*, Cincinnati, OH: South Western.

Dannemiller, K.D. and Jacobs, R.W. (1992) Changing the way organizations change: a revolution of common sense, *Journal of Applied Behavioural Science*, **28**(3): 480–98.

Fritz, R. (1984) *The Path of Least Resistance*, Salem, MA: Stillpoint.

Jayaram (1977) Open systems planning, in T. Cummings and S. Srivastra (eds) *Management at Work: A Socio-technical Systems Approach*, San Diego, CA: University Associates.

Lippitt, R. (1983) Future before you plan, in R.A. Ritvo and A.G. Sargent (eds) *The NTL Managers' Handbook*, Arlington, VA: NTL Institute.

Trist, E.L. (1969) On socio-technical systems, in W.G. Bennis, K.D. Benne and R. Chin (eds) *The Planning of Change*, New York: Holt, Rinehart and Winston.

Trist, E.L. and Bamforth, K.W. (1951) Some social and psychological consequences of the long-wall method of coal-getting, *Human Relations*, 1: 3–38.

Von Bertalanffy, L. (1950) General systems theory, in *General Systems: Yearbook of the Society for the Advancement of General Systems Theory*, 1:1–10.

Weisbord, M. (1989) *Building Productive Workplaces: Change Strategies for the 21st Century*, Blue Sky Videos.

Selecting interventions

This chapter examines the factors that need to be considered when selecting which type of intervention to use. Consideration is also given to the factors that can affect decisions regarding the sequencing of interventions in those circumstances where it might be necessary to use more than one type of intervention. This is important because sometimes an inappropriate sequence can undermine the effectiveness of a change programme.

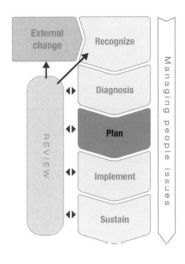

Beware fashions and fads

There is a real danger that change agents underuse many traditional well-tried interventions in favour of those that are new and 'fashionable'. Ettorre's (1997) life cycle theory of management fads suggests that the adoption of an intervention follows five stages:

1 *discovery:* intervention just begins to come to people's attention
2 *wild acceptance:* uncritical adoption
3 *digestion:* critics begin to suggest that it is not a panacea
4 *disillusionment:* recognition of problems associated with the intervention
5 *hard core:* only a minority continue with the intervention.

But the most fashionable interventions may not always be the most effective. After surveying the 100 largest *Fortune* 500 firms, Staw and Epstein (2000) found that while the use of popular interventions, such as total quality management, empowerment and team working, was positively associated with corporate reputation – organizations were admired, seen as more innovative and rated as having higher quality management – and positively related to CEO pay, it was not associated with improvement in economic performance – assessed over a one to five year period. It is important to select and apply those interventions that will be effective in a particular context. At times this might involve using interventions that have been around for some considerable time.

Factors indicating which interventions to use

Consideration is given first to those factors that need to be taken into account when deciding which interventions are likely to contribute most to achieving the goals of a change programme. Attention is given to three main factors: the nature of the problem or opportunity that the intervention has to address (diagnosed issue), the level of change target (individual, group and so on) that is to be the focus for change, and the depth of intervention required. Two additional factors are also considered. These are the time available for the change and the efficacy of different types of interventions.

Diagnosed issue

A key determinant of the appropriate intervention is the nature of the diagnosed problem or opportunity. This underpins the aim of the change programme and indicates the issues that have to be attended to in order to move an organization or unit from the current position to a more desirable future state.

At a macro-level, the issue might be defined in terms of either transformational or incremental change. Where the issue is defined in terms of a need for 'transformational change', Burke and Litwin (1992) suggest that the most effective interventions will be those that are targeted at changing system-wide elements such as mission and strategy, leadership and culture. Interventions that successfully change these elements will have knock-on effects that will affect just about every other element in the system.

On the other hand, where the issue is defined in terms of 'incremental change', or fine-tuning, the most effective interventions may be those that address elements that, if changed, might have a more localized impact in terms of units or levels affected. These include interventions targeted at elements such as structure, systems, climate, tasks and roles. For example, the focal issue might be to improve task performance in a particular department. The intervention selected to address this issue might be work redesign. Redesigning the work to improve task performance may affect other factors such as the competencies required of those who do the work or departmental structure if redesigning the work involves reducing the number of levels in the hierarchy. However, this kind of intervention may have relatively little impact on how the entire organization functions, even if it does have some implications for how the target unit interacts with related units.

At a micro-level, issues might simply be defined in terms of the organizational elements that are most closely associated with the diagnosed problem or opportunity. The 12 elements of the Burke-Litwin model could provide a basis for classifying issues in this way (see Chapter 6). An alternative, used in the three-dimensional model presented below, is the typology used by Cummings and Worley (2001) to classify interventions (see Chapter 16). It points to four broad types of diagnosed issue:

▶ *human process issues*, which include communicating, problem solving, decision making, interpersonal and intergroup interactions, and leadership
▶ *technology and structural issues*, which include horizontal and vertical differentiation, coordination, technology and production processes, and work design
▶ *human resource issues*, which include attracting, selecting, developing, motivating and retaining competent people
▶ *strategic issues*, which include managing the interface between the organization and its environment, and deciding which markets to engage in, what products and services to produce, how to gain competitive advantage and what values should guide the organization's development.

Level of change target

Schmuck and Miles (1971), Blake and Mouton (1986), Pugh (1986) and others all include the individual, group, intergroup and organization in their classifications of units that can be the target for change. Blake and Mouton also include the larger social system as the potential client or target for change and Schmuck and Miles include dyads/triads as a separate unit.

In the three-dimensional model for selecting interventions presented below (Figure 17.1), five levels are identified. These are individual, group, intergroup, organization and trans-organization. For example:

▶ A diagnostic analysis might indicate that the critical issue has to do with a mismatch between task demands and individual competencies, suggesting that the target for change is at the *individual* level.

▶ Alternatively, the diagnosis might point to poor working relationships within a group, indicating that the *group* should be the target for change.

▶ Another possibility is that the diagnosis focuses on poor relationships between groups, suggesting that *intergroup* relations should be the target.

▶ The diagnosis may suggest that organizational strategy is not matched to market conditions or is not properly appreciated by organizational members at all levels, indicating that the target for change is the whole *organization*.

▶ At the *trans-organizational* level, the diagnosis may suggest that there is a need to create a lean enterprise including all the organizations contributing to a value stream, or that the way forward might involve seeking a partner for a joint venture or merger.

Depth of intervention required

Harrison (1970) argues that the depth of individual emotional involvement can be a key factor in determining whether an intervention will be effective. This factor is concerned with the extent to which core areas of personality or self are the focus of change events. He posits a dimension running from surface to deep. Interventions that focus on external aspects of an individual and deal with the more public and observable aspects of behaviour are located at the surface end of the continuum. Interventions that touch on personal and private perceptions, attitudes or feelings and attempt to affect them are located at the deep end.

Operations research is an example of an intervention that can be classified at the surface end of the continuum because it is a process of rational analysis that deals with roles and functions without paying much attention to the individual characteristics of the persons occupying these roles. An example of a deeper intervention is management by objectives. This involves a boss and subordinate establishing mutually agreed goals for performance and monitoring performance against these goals. Typically, the exchange of information is limited to that which is observable. Further along the continuum are interventions such as management counselling that, for example, might involve a consultant working with managers to increase their awareness of how their personality, role relationships and previous experience affect their management style. Deeper interventions might involve members of a group discussing with peers the interpersonal processes that affect their contribution to group performance. This kind of intervention can involve group members sharing personal information about themselves, how they perceive their own behaviour and the behaviour of others and exploring with them how they and others might modify their attitudes, roles and behaviour to improve group performance.

Harrison (1970) argues that as the level of intervention becomes deeper, the information needed to intervene becomes less available. For example, the information needed by the operations researcher is easily obtained because it is often a matter of record. The information required by those engaged in management by objectives can often be observed. However, people may not be prepared to discuss freely their attitudes and feeling towards others or to be open to feedback from others about their own interpersonal style. These considerations led Harrison to suggest the following criterion:

> **Change agents should intervene at a level no deeper than that required to produce an enduring solution to the problem at hand.**

However, this criterion, while necessary, is not sufficient for determining the depth of intervention. While the change agent may have a view about the nature of the information required and the depth of intervention necessary to produce this information, the change target (individual, group or system) may not be comfortable working at this level. Harrison (1970) argues that any intervention, if it is to be successful, must be legitimized in the norms of the group or organization and must be seen to relate to the felt needs of organizational members. This led him to suggest a second criterion:

> **Intervene at a level no deeper than that at which the energy and resources of the client can be committed to problem solving and change.**

Harrison (1970) suggests that in those circumstances where change agents suspect that the required information is located at a depth greater than that at which the client is comfortable working, they should resolve the dilemma by selecting an intervention on the basis of the second criterion. Once the client has gained confidence, they may be prepared to engage in an intervention that will involve the sharing of information such as attitudes and feelings that they would normally regard as private and confidential.

A three-dimensional model to aid choice

The factors considered so far can be combined to produce a three-dimensional model that can be used as a rough guide for selecting the type of intervention that might be most effective in a given situation. This is presented in Figure 17.1.

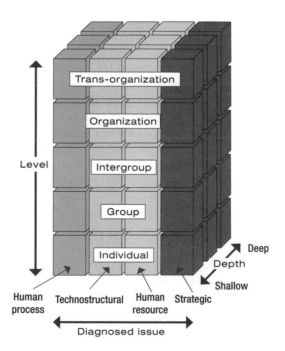

Figure 17.1 *A three-dimensional model to aid choice of interventions*

Figures 17.2–17.5 provide examples of interventions for each of the four diagnosed issues.

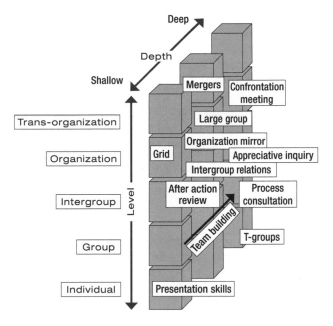

Figure 17.2 *Examples of human process interventions*

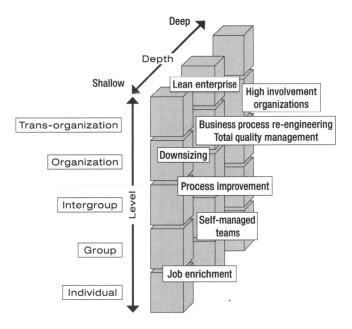

Figure 17.3 *Examples of technostructural interventions*

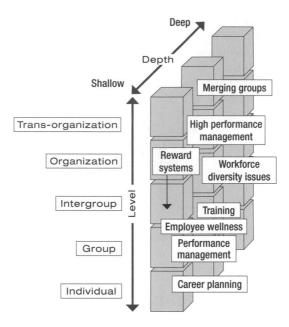

Figure 17.4 *Examples of human resource interventions*

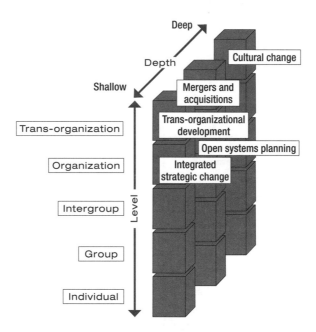

Figure 17.5 *Examples of strategic interventions*

Some cells in Figures 17.2–17.5 are blank because they represent situations that are unlikely to call for an intervention that complies with all three criteria. For example, there may not be many (any?) situations that call for a deep level techno-structural intervention targeted at the individual.

Some interventions could appear in more than one cell. Team building, for example, is an instance of a human process intervention that is targeted at the group. In terms of depth, however, some team-building interventions are shallow and others rather deep. At the shallow end, interventions might only be concerned with agreeing the purpose of the group, indicators of effective performance and performance strategies that could contribute to achieving this level of performance. On the other hand, at the deep end, interventions could involve an exploration of interpersonal relationships and how these promote or undermine performance.

Figures 17.2–17.5 contain only a sample of the interventions available to change agents. The literature on the management of change is a rich source of other possibilities. Two additional factors might also influence choice of intervention.

Time available to implement change

Where the need for change is urgent and the stakes are high, there may be insufficient time to employ some of the more time-consuming interventions that offer organizational members the opportunity to be involved in deciding what needs to be changed or how the change will be achieved. It might be necessary to restrict choice to those interventions that can be implemented quickly and this might, for example, involve the use of experts who can rapidly prescribe solutions. Prescriptive/directive interventions can be effective, especially over the short term and where organizational members recognize the need for this kind of action. However, there is always the possibility that organizational members may resent the way the change was managed, experience little sense of ownership of the process or the outcome and therefore may only go along with the change so long as their behaviour is being closely supervised and there is a perceived threat of sanctions for non-compliance.

Where the need for change is less pressing, the change agent may be able to consider a much wider range of interventions.

Efficacy of interventions

A basic question that needs to be addressed when considering whether or not to choose a particular intervention is: 'Will it produce the intended result?' Some popular interventions are not always as effective as many would like to believe. There are frequent reports in academic journals and the business press indicating disappointment with the outcome of major change programmes that have involved interventions such as business process re-engineering, total quality management, job design or interpersonal skills training.

Sometimes the problem is that the change agents select an ineffective intervention. This kind of problem can be avoided by seeking evidence about the efficacy of interventions from reports, colleagues and elsewhere. Often, however, the problem is not that the intervention is ineffective, but that its success is dependent on a number of contingent factors. In these circumstances, it is important to take account of these factors when selecting interventions. There are many examples of interventions that are affected by contingent variables, three of which are now briefly discussed.

T-group training

T-group training is a form of social skills training that provides participants with an opportunity to increase their awareness about themselves and their impact on others in order to learn how to function more effectively in groups. Some of the early evidence on the effectiveness of T-groups indicated that they can be effective. Cooper and Mangham (1971), for example, report that they can improve skills in diagnosing individual and group behaviour, lead to clearer communication, greater tolerance and consideration and greater action skill and flexibility. However, other reports suggest that, while there is evidence of learning and behaviour change, this may not always be transferred to the work situation. Transfer is dependent on a number of factors, one of which is the match between the structures and norms that characterize the work and training situations; the closer the match, the greater the transfer and vice versa.

Job design

Job design is often presented as the universal answer to low commitment and poor performance in situations where people are required to perform repetitive, sort cycle, simple tasks. Motivation theory suggests that people will be more committed and will perform best when they are engaged in varied and challenging work that

- provides feedback about how well they are doing
- allows them to feel personally responsible for outcomes
- offers them the possibility of producing outcomes that are perceived to be worthwhile and meaningful.

In practice, job design has been found to be effective in some circumstances and not in others. One of the most important contingent variables related to the success of this intervention is the level of need that employees are seeking to satisfy at work. Job design appears to be most effective where employees are seeking to satisfy higher order needs for personal growth and development through their work.

Total quality management

Total quality management (TQM) is an organization-wide, long-term change effort designed to orient all an organization's activities around the concept of quality. Cummings and Worley (2001) report that in the USA, a survey of *Fortune* 1000 companies showed that about 75% of them had implemented some form of TQM. They also report that the overwhelming majority (83%) rate their experience with TQM as either positive or very positive. However, other reports of the success of TQM initiatives are less optimistic. Crosby (1979), for example, asserts that over 90% of TQM interventions by US companies fail and Burnes (2004) lists a number of studies that suggest that European companies have experienced a similar rate of failure. It is not immediately obvious why TQM interventions are successful in some settings and less so in others, but one possibility relates to the attitude of top management. In those settings where TQM is viewed in instrumental terms, for example as a way of gaining a kite mark such as ISO 9000 that will provide competitive advantage, it may be less successful than where there is a genuine commitment to routinely meeting or exceeding customer expectations. Where the aim is merely to gain a kite mark, organizational members may experience the intervention as a requirement to comply with a new set of rules. This may have little long-term effect on their values and attitudes towards customers. Also, once the kite mark has been secured, top management may shift attention elsewhere, and any movement towards a more customer-focused culture may be short-lived.

Where there is a need to use more than one type of intervention

Often because of the nature of the problem or opportunity, systemic interdependencies and the need to maintain alignment, it may not be possible to think in terms of selecting a single intervention to respond to an isolated issue. For example, the recognition of a new opportunity and the decision, by senior management, to intervene in order to develop a strategy to exploit it might require a range of further interventions. The organization may have to introduce a new technology, adapt its structures and systems, introduce new management practices, redesign tasks, reallocate employees to new roles and provide training to equip people to perform as required. The change agent has to decide whether to pursue them all simultaneously or to sequence them in some way.

Sequencing interventions

The organization's capacity to cope with change is often limited. Consequently, decisions have to be made about priorities and the sequencing of interventions. Several factors can influence these decisions. These include the overall purpose or intention of the change, organizational politics, the need for an early success, the stakes involved, and causal links in the change process.

Intent

Where the intention is to transform the organization, interventions that address the transformational variables, such as mission and strategy, leadership and culture, need to be given priority (see above and Chapter 6 on diagnostic models). Where, on the other hand, the intention is to seek an incremental change, the focus of attention might be on the transactional variables identified by Burke and Litwin, such as structure, management practices, systems, work climate and so on.

Politics

The change agent needs to be aware of how political factors can affect who is prepared to support different kinds of interventions. Some of the issues that relate to this have been considered elsewhere (for example Chapters 8 and 11 and earlier in this chapter). Other issues include:

▶ *Professional orientation:* Many managers have been socialized, over the course of their training and work experience, to focus attention on certain variables rather than others. For example, many managers are more comfortable with interventions that focus on changing structures, technology, and manufacturing and information systems rather than with interventions that focus on 'softer' people issues.
▶ *Fashions and fads:* These can influence the choice of intervention. In the 1990s, many managers were keen to adopt certain interventions, such as performance-related pay, in order to be seen as progressive and attuned to the latest developments. Change agents who propose favoured interventions might receive more encouragement than those who propose an intervention that has 'gone out of fashion', even if is the most appropriate intervention to deal with the issue at hand.
▶ *Past experience with certain interventions:* Change agents who have a track record of success with certain interventions may be more inclined to recommend their use than interventions with which they are less familiar. While it may be wise to

take account of a change agent's skills and experience, other factors also need to be considered. Just because a change agent is skilled at hammering does not mean that nails are the only means of 'fixing things'. There may well be occasions when 'screws or glue' may be much more effective.

Need for an early success

It has already been noted in Chapter 8 that long-term change efforts can slow down if people lose their initial sense of urgency. One way of countering this is to select problems and interventions that offer the promise of some early successes.

Stakes involved

Priority needs to be given to those interventions that can resolve issues that threaten the survival of the organization. Where survival is not an issue, priority might still be given to issues where the potential gains and losses are relatively high.

Dynamics of change

In some circumstances, the dynamics of change may suggest that the best way to proceed is to adopt an indirect approach rather than addressing the prime issue or change target first. The following three issues could be considered:

▶ *Causal links:* Consideration needs to be given to causal links and the relative strength of the interrelationships between the elements of the organizational system. The Burke-Litwin model points to the relative strength of high-level elements such as strategy, leadership and culture over lower level elements such as structure, systems and management practices. While culture and systems can affect one another, culture is seen to have a stronger influence over systems than vice versa. This kind of consideration can influence which elements are selected as the initial targets for change, thereby influencing the sequencing of interventions.

▶ *The effect of groups on individuals:* A related dynamic relationship that can affect the sequencing of interventions is the effect that the group can exert over individual behaviour. This was discussed in Chapter 16. Research evidence suggests that there may be occasions where the most effective way of changing individual behaviour is to intervene at the level of the group. Group-level interventions, such as team-building activities designed to produce a more cohesive group that has high prestige in the eyes of other organizational members, might motivate individuals to change their behaviour to support group goals. A follow-up intervention might involve training selected individuals to provide them with the competencies they might need to make a more effective contribution to group performance. If individual training had been the first intervention, it might only have had limited success because of low member motivation. After a group-level intervention, individual members might be much more highly motivated to acquire the competencies that will enable them to play a full and active part in the work of the group.

▶ *The effect of attitudes on behaviour and vice versa:* There have been many debates about whether the most effective route to lasting change is to target attitudes and values first or behaviour first. While there is support for the view that strongly held values and attitudes influence behaviour, the evidence that interventions targeted at values and attitudes can change behaviour is more equivocal. An alternative view is that the most effective route to lasting change is to intervene to create conditions that require people to behave differently, because over the longer term, attitudes and values will be realigned with the new behaviour.

Porter et al. (1975) offer a third way, suggesting that an effective route to change is to intervene in ways that simultaneously modify structures, in order to create the conditions that will elicit new and desired behaviours, and modify interpersonal processes – to address issues of managerial style, attitudes and the social climate of the organization. This approach employs structural interventions to support intra-personal and interpersonal learning.

They suggest that structural interventions might include:

▸ modifying work structures in order to change how individual employees actually spend most of their time
▸ modifying control structures in order to determine what individuals attend to
▸ modifying reward structures in order to influence what individuals will do when they have choice.

While there are no hard and fast rules about whether interventions should address interpersonal processes or structures first, there is a growing body of opinion that intervening to change one without the other is less effective than intervening to change both.

Conclusion

There is no easy formula that can be used to identify the most effective intervention for all types of situation. However, there are some useful principles that can be applied to aid the selection of appropriate interventions and assist with decisions about how they should be sequenced.

Exercise 17.1

Choice of interventions

Review some of the change programmes that have been pursued within your organization and, with reference to the content of this chapter, critically assess the choice of interventions. Are you able to identify occasions when inappropriate interventions have been used? Give reasons and suggest interventions than might have been more effective.

Notes

Summary

This chapter has examined the factors that need to be considered when selecting which type of intervention to use. Consideration has also been given to the factors that can affect decisions regarding the sequencing of interventions in those circumstances where it is necessary to use more than one type of intervention.

Some of the factors that need to be considered when selecting interventions are:

1 *Diagnosed problem*:
   - Where the issue is defined in terms of a need for transformational change, Burke and Litwin suggest that the most effective interventions will be those that are targeted at changing system-wide elements such as mission and strategy, leadership and culture.
   - Where the issue is defined in terms of a need for incremental change (or fine-tuning), the most effective interventions may be those that address elements that, if changed, might have a more localized impact in terms of units or levels affected. These include interventions targeted at elements such as structure, systems, climate, tasks and roles.
   - The typology of issues used in the three-dimensional model (Figure 17.1 above) focuses on four broad type of diagnosed issue: human process issues, technology and structural issues, human resource issues and strategic issues.
2 *Level of change target:* This might be defined in terms of the individual, group, intergroup, organization or trans-organization.
3 *Depth of intervention required:* Harrison argues that the depth of individual emotional involvement can be a key factor in determining whether an intervention will be effective. This factor is concerned with the extent to which core areas of personality or self are the focus of change events.

These three factors have been combined to provide a three-dimensional model to aid choice. Two additional factors are also referred to; the time available to implement the change and the efficacy of interventions.

Attention has also been given to the factors that can affect the sequencing of interventions. These include:

▶ intent or purpose of the change
▶ organizational politics and how they affect the support for different interventions
▶ the need for an early success to maintain motivation
▶ the stakes involved
▶ causal links that affect the dynamics of change.

Case studies: selecting and designing interventions

Before reading the nine chapters of Part VI, you are invited to complete at least two of the following four case studies. Imagine that you are a consultant and have been invited to design an intervention to address the issues raised in each case. Case study 17.1 is set in southwest India and involves improving the effectiveness of primary healthcare centres. Case study 17.2 involves designing an intervention to increase the motivation and flexibility of the workforce of a Danish dairy company operating in the UK. Case study 17.3 involves designing an intervention to improve the treatment offered by the trauma orthopaedic care department of a large UK hospital. Case study 17.4 involves reducing absenteeism in the elderly care sector of the Silkeborg Council in Denmark.

After reading Chapters 18–26, you might find it useful to review your approach to designing an intervention for each of the following cases. You might also consider the nature of your change strategy in the light of the strategies considered in Chapter 14.

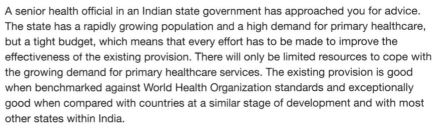

Case study 17.1

Designing an intervention to improve the effectiveness of primary healthcare centres in southwest India

A senior health official in an Indian state government has approached you for advice. The state has a rapidly growing population and a high demand for primary healthcare, but a tight budget, which means that every effort has to be made to improve the effectiveness of the existing provision. There will only be limited resources to cope with the growing demand for primary healthcare services. The existing provision is good when benchmarked against World Health Organization standards and exceptionally good when compared with countries at a similar stage of development and with most other states within India.

There are about 500 primary healthcare centres spread across the state, many in isolated rural areas. Their role is to offer medical care, mother and child welfare, family planning, improvements in environmental sanitation, control of communicable disease, health education and school health. In addition, they are required to collect statistics and provide a referral service. Each centre is managed by a chief medical officer and has approximately 60 staff. There is typically a main facility that has accommodation for clinics, operating theatres for minor surgery, three wards for short-stay patients and a pharmacy. Various outreach services may also be located at satellite sites in the community served by a centre.

Up until now attempts to improve the effectiveness of primary healthcare provision have been limited to sending chief medical officers and other doctors who have been identified as candidates for promotion on a lengthy training programme at the state's Institute for Management in Government. The senior health official who has approached you for advice believes that there has been relatively little transfer of learning back into the primary healthcare centres and that the heavy investment in training has had little effect on performance.

Your task

- Design an intervention that will improve the capability of the staff working in the health centres to improve the effectiveness of the services they provide.
- Identify issues that might affect the success of your proposed intervention and explain how you would address these issues.

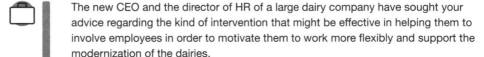

Case study 17.2

Designing an intervention to increase the motivation and flexibility of the workforce in a large dairy company

The new CEO and the director of HR of a large dairy company have sought your advice regarding the kind of intervention that might be effective in helping them to involve employees in order to motivate them to work more flexibly and support the modernization of the dairies.

The company is Danish owned. It began production in the UK six years ago following the acquisition of a number of British dairies. It now employs 2,400 people at six dairies and one other plant that produces fruit drinks. The past few years have been a difficult time for the dairy industry in the UK and many companies have gone out of business. Supermarkets are selling milk at very competitive prices, presenting a fierce challenge to the doorstep delivery business, and the abolition of the Milk Marketing Board has led to a sharp increase in the price of raw milk.

After the new CEO was appointed, he initiated a restructuring of the UK business, creating strategic business units serving particular segments of the market and major customers such as the large supermarket chains. The company has also invested heavily in state-of-the-art processing and packaging equipment. But further action is still needed to ensure the company's success.

Labour requirements fluctuate considerably as the demand for dairy products varies over the week and over the year. Operations managers cope with peak periods by making extensive use of overtime working. Many of the workers at the company's processing sites are low paid and make a living wage by working overtime. It is not unusual for workers to work between 50 and 70 hours over a six-day week. There is always plenty of overtime at peak times such as Christmas, but in order to ensure that overtime is available at other times, employees operate machines inefficiently.

Managers experience great difficulty persuading employees to work flexibly or accept new practices. Over the years they have used supplementary payments as a way of getting things done. There are over 90 different rates of pay and no formal grading system to justify differences. The state of industrial relations varies across sites, ranging from good to difficult. Absenteeism is high, running at about 10%. The company needs a skilled and well-motivated workforce able and ready to react flexibly to customers' demands and willing to support the modernization of the dairies.

Your task

- Design an intervention that will involve the employees in order to motivate them to work more flexibly and support the modernization of the dairies.
- Identify issues that might affect the success of your proposed intervention and explain how you would address these issues.

Case study 17.3 **Designing an intervention to improve the treatment offered by the trauma orthopaedic care department in a large NHS hospital**

The general manager responsible for orthopaedic services in a large acute NHS hospital has sought your advice regarding the kind of intervention that might be effective in helping to improve the treatment offered to patients who are admitted for trauma orthopaedic care. (This case is based on a situation that existed in 2001.)

Trauma orthopaedic care, which typically involves an emergency admission via the A&E department and immediate treatment for a condition such as a broken leg, and elective orthopaedic care, which involves non-emergency treatment such as a hip replacement operation, are provided by separate departments located in neighbouring hospitals within the same city. Because of a government initiative to reduce waiting times for elective treatments, extra resources have tended to be allocated to elective care rather than to trauma services. The situation confronting trauma orthopaedic care has worsened over the past three years because the department has had to cope with an 11% increase in emergency admissions. This has undermined the department's ability to provide the quality of care that it, and other stakeholders, believe patients should receive. While the hospital recognizes that trauma services are underresourced and has agreed to appoint more orthopaedic surgeons and increase their access to operating theatres, everybody recognizes that these changes will not be in place for some time. As a result, staff morale is low.

Several orthopaedic surgeons and departmental managers are highly motivated to change what they refer to as a 'desperate situation' in trauma orthopaedic care. They are particularly concerned to improve patient care for one of the largest groups of patients, those admitted with a broken neck of femur. There are approximately 800 such admissions each year and the average patient stay is 24 days.

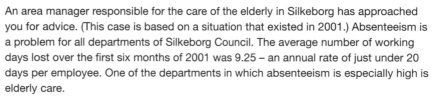

The department has a traditional structure with four wards, each headed by a ward sister – a senior nurse who acts as ward manager. Occupational therapists and physiotherapists work with patients to facilitate their rehabilitation. Doctors, nurses, occupational therapists and physiotherapists maintain their own care notes and treatment plans. Many patients with this condition are elderly and require support in the community post discharge. Social workers, who work for the local authority's social services department, assess this need and arrange social care packages.

Your task

- Design an intervention that will improve the situation in trauma orthopaedic care. This could include delivering outcomes such as improved patient care and reduced length of stay in hospital.
- Identify issues that might affect the success of your proposed intervention and explain how you would address these issues.

Case study 17.4 ⟩ **Designing an intervention to reduce absenteeism in the elderly care sector of Silkeborg Council, Denmark**

An area manager responsible for the care of the elderly in Silkeborg has approached you for advice. (This case is based on a situation that existed in 2001.) Absenteeism is a problem for all departments of Silkeborg Council. The average number of working days lost over the first six months of 2001 was 9.25 – an annual rate of just under 20 days per employee. One of the departments in which absenteeism is especially high is elderly care.

Over a period of several years, the council had taken several initiatives to reduce absenteeism. In the area of elderly care, these have included:

- analysing the reasons for lost time
- introducing a 'stop-lift' policy to improve practices in moving and handling in order to reduce lost time caused by back injuries
- helping group leaders develop their supervisory skills
- educating the management team in the area of supervision and leadership
- helping the management team and care staff to work together to develop an absenteeism policy.

An important element of the new absenteeism policy is that illness should be regarded as a common concern for both employer and employee rather than a private issue for the employee alone. If people are off sick frequently, or for a prolonged period of time, their managers should engage in a dialogue with them about work, health and satisfaction in order to explore ways of improving the situation for the individual and the department.

These various initiatives have produced short-term improvements but little long-term change.

Your task

- Design an intervention that will help the elderly care department provide a better service for patients and the wider community by ensuring that the 250 frontline staff are present more of the time and making a full contribution to the work of the department.
- Identify issues that might affect the success of your proposed intervention and explain how you would address these issues.

References

Blake, R.R. and Mouton, J.S. (1986) *Consultation: A Handbook for Individual and Organization Development* (2nd edn), Reading, MA: Addison-Wesley.

Burke, W.W. and Litwin, G.H. (1992) A causal model of organizational performance and change, *Journal of Management*, **18**(3): 523–45.

Burnes, B. (2004) *Managing Change: A Strategic Approach to Organisational Dynamics* (4th edn), Harlow: Pearson.

Cooper, C. and Mangham, I.L. (1971) *T-groups: A Survey of Research*, London: Wiley.

Crosby, P.B. (1979) *Quality is Free*, New York: McGraw-Hill.

Cummings, T.G. and Worley, C.G. (2001) *Organizational Development and Change* (7th edn), Cincinnati, OH: South Western.

Ettorre, B. (1997) What's the next management buzzword?, *Management Review*, **86**(8): 33–5.

Harrison, R. (1970) Choosing the depth of organizational interventions, *Journal of Applied Behavioral Science*, **6**(2): 182–202.

Porter, L.W., Lawler, E.E. and Hackman, J.R. (1975) *Behavior in Organizations*, London: McGraw-Hill.

Pugh, D. (1986) *Planning and Managing Change*, Milton Keynes: Open University Business School.

Schmuck, R.A. and Miles, M.B. (1971) *Organization Development in Schools*, Palo Alto, CA: National Press Books.

Staw, B. and Epstein, L.D. (2000) What bandwagons bring: effects of popular management techniques on corporate performance and reputation, *Administrative Science Quarterly*, **45**(3): 523–60.

Part

VI

IMPLEMENTING CHANGE

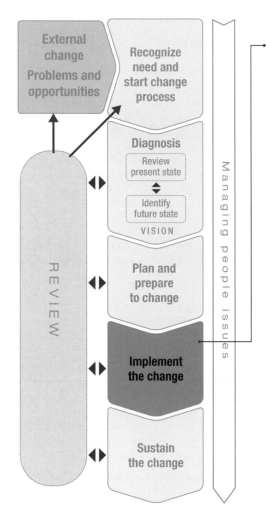

18 Organizational learning
19 Action research
20 Appreciative inquiry
21 Training and development
22 High performance management
23 Business process re-engineering
24 Lean
25 Restructuring for strategic gain
26 Merging groups

Implementation is the step in the change process that involves taking action to bring about change. Part VI reviews the theory that underpins types of intervention and considers how each can be used to secure change. The first three chapters address interventions that focus on human process problems, the next two focus on interventions that address human resource issues, the following two chapters review technostructural interventions and the final two focus on interventions that address strategic issues.

Chapter 18　Collective learning in organizations

This chapter reviews how collective learning can contribute to organizational effectiveness and presents examples of interventions that promote learning in different situations. It is presented first because learning is an essential element of almost all interventions.

Different kinds of collective learning are discussed. Single loop learning is concerned with continuous improvement through doing things better. Double loop learning involves challenging current thinking and exploring the possibility of doing things differently or doing different things. Attention is also been given to the role of knowledge transfer within and between organizations.

Chapter 19　Action research

Action research is the basic model underpinning most organizational change interventions. It involves the application of scientific methods (fact finding and experimentation) to organizational problems and underpins the generic process model of change presented in Chapter 2.

Action research is based on the premise that people learn best and are more willing to apply what they have learned when they manage the problem-solving process for themselves. The learning process involves:

▸ observing what is going on
▸ developing hypotheses that specify cause-and-effect relationships and point to actions that could help organizational members to manage their problem more effectively
▸ taking action
▸ collecting data to evaluate the effect of the action and test the hypothesis.

Chapter 20　Appreciative inquiry

Appreciative inquiry is a process that involves exploring the best of what is and amplifying this best practice. It seeks to accentuate the positive rather than eliminate the negative; it focuses attention on what is good and working rather than on what is wrong and not working.

Whereas action research promotes learning through attending to dysfunctional aspects of organizational functioning (problems), appreciative inquiry is concerned with embracing possibilities. This involves:

▸ Discovering the best of whatever is the focus of the inquiry, for example team working, leadership and so on
▸ Understanding what creates the best of …
▸ Amplifying the people or processes that create the best of … .

This chapter examines appreciate inquiry from three perspectives; a philosophy of knowledge, an intervention theory, and a methodology for intervening in organizations to improve performance and the quality of life.

Chapter 21　Training and development

This chapter considers how training can contribute to the change process. Attention is directed towards the main elements of an effective approach to training. These are:

1　A training needs analysis, which involves three steps:

- a system-level review to determine which parts of the organization will be affected by the change
- a more focused task analysis to determine how the pattern of task demands and required competencies will change
- a person analysis to identify the extent to which existing organizational members possess the required competencies.

2 The design and delivery of training.
3 The evaluation of the training.

The final section reviews the development of training practice in Australia over a 10-year period and highlights a number of trends in training provision.

Chapter 22 High performance management

This chapter considers how people management practices can affect performance by:

1 improving employees' knowledge and skills
2 motivating them to engage in discretionary behaviours that draw on their knowledge and skill
3 modifying organizational structures in ways that enable employees to improve the way they perform their jobs.

Rather than focusing on separate people management practices, high perform-ance management involves developing and implementing a 'bundle' or system of practices that are internally consistent, aligned with other business processes and with the organization's business strategy. Alignment is the defining feature of high performance management interventions.

Chapter 23 Business process re-engineering

This chapter examines the nature of business process re-engineering (BPR). While it is often regarded as a fundamental rethinking and radical redesign of business proc-esses to achieve dramatic change, the benefits of less ambitious approaches that adopt BPR principles to improve existing processes are also considered.

The seven stages of BPR are discussed. These are:

1 process mapping
2 identifying processes for re-engineering
3 understanding the selected process
4 defining key performance objectives
5 designing new processes
6 testing
7 implementation.

Chapter 24 Lean

This chapter traces the development of lean thinking and presents Womark and Jones's five lean principles:

- specifying value for each product or product family
- identifying value streams for each product to expose waste
- making value flow without interruption
- letting customers pull value from the producer
- pursuing perfection by searching out and eliminating further waste.

A number of lean tools and techniques are reviewed along with issues to be considered when implementing lean. The chapter ends with an exploration of how lean has been applied in manufacturing and non-manufacturing settings.

Chapter 25   Restructuring for strategic gain: mergers and acquisitions

Acquisition success depends on both strategic and organization fit. This chapter adopts a process perspective and considers some of the conditions and critical junctures that can affect the quality of strategic fit and the integration process. Some of the issues that those leading the acquisition need to recognize and address are identified.

Many of the problems that undermine the acquisition process can be avoided, or at least minimized, if careful attention is given to:

▶ specifying acquisition objectives
▶ developing an acquisition overview that provides the bridge between the acquisition objectives and what needs to happen if they are to be achieved
▶ elaborating this overview to develop an implementation plan
▶ taking care to avoid managing the actual implementation in a heavy-handed way.

Chapter 26   Merging groups: combining people for effective performance

This chapter draws on social identity and acculturation theories to provide a conceptual framework for thinking about how managers can intervene to promote people synergy and achieve merger success. Attention is focused on three types of intervention:

▶ culture profiling – to pre-screen potential merger partners and, later in the merger process, guide the integration process
▶ change communication – to provide organizational members with clear and unambiguous information about what is going to change as a result of the merger
▶ socioemotional support – to care for those affected by the change, minimize alienation and promote post-merger organizational identity.

Collective learning in organizations

According to Miles (1982), organizations have leeway and choice in how they adjust to a changing environment and it is this choice that offers the opportunity for learning. Lank and Lank (1995) argue that the quality of individual and organizational learning is an important determinant of organization effectiveness, and de Geus (1988) suggests that the ability to learn faster than competitors may be the only sustainable competitive advantage. Learning is a core element of almost all interventions, for example action research, appreciative inquiry, training, high performance management, business process re-engineering, lean and so on. This chapter reviews how collective learning can contribute to organizational effectiveness and presents examples of interventions that promote learning in different situations.

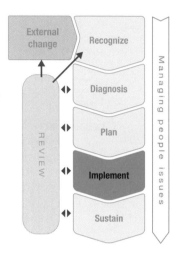

Organizational learning

Organizational learning involves enhancing the collective ability to act more effectively. The collective nature of learning is especially important in complex and turbulent environments because senior managers may not be the best placed individuals to identify opportunities and threats. Organizational members, at all levels, who are involved in boundary-spanning activities such as procurement, technical development or sales, may have data that could provide a valuable input to strategy formulation. Furthermore, the quality of response to any threats or opportunities that are identified may require individuals and groups located in different functions to collaborate and learn from each other in order to design and produce high-quality products or services in ever shorter time frames.

Shared mental models, rules and behaviour in organizations

Swieringa and Wierdsma (1992) conceptualize organizations as a set of explicit and implicit rules that prescribe the way members behave (see Figure 18.1). These rules are based on insights that represent what is known and understood. They relate to everything that happens in the organization. For example, there are rules about the structure of the organization that prescribe how activities will be grouped and responsibilities allocated, and rules about how resources are procured and used and how people are managed and rewarded. These rules reflect the mental models, that is, subjective theories and shared meanings and beliefs, through which organizational members examine and make sense of their experience. The shared mental model represents the basic assumptions that underpin the organization's culture. Schein (1990: 111) defines culture as (a) the pattern of basic assumptions, (b) invented, discovered or developed by a group, (c) as it learns to cope with its problems of external adaptation and internal integration, (d) that have worked well enough in the past to be considered valid and, therefore, (e) are taught to new members as (f) the correct way to perceive, think and feel in relation to these problems.

Learning to behave in accordance with the rules

So long as the rules lead to behaviours that produce desired results, there will be no need to change the rules. The only requirement will be for individual learning. Organizational members will have to learn to behave in accordance with the rules. For example, if an individual is promoted into a position that involves being responsible for a budget, they will not only have to develop an understanding of the rules relating to the management of budgets, but will also have to acquire the knowledge and skills necessary to behave in accordance with these rules.

Figure 18.1 *Individual learning*

This kind of learning, however, may not always be sufficient to guarantee organizational success. In today's turbulent and complex environment, old ways of behaving may fail to produce the required results and the organization may be faced with the need to change, to modify the rules and encourage new behaviours in order to ensure its continued competitiveness and survival.

Collective learning and the modification of rules

Collective (organizational) learning occurs when a group recognizes something that offers a more effective way of functioning. It has already been noted (see Chapter 5) that organizations are more effective when their major components, such as structure, technology, systems and people, are aligned with each other and when there is a good fit between the organization and the environment. Collective learning can facilitate this fit. It involves organizational members diagnosing the organization's predicament, integrating this understanding into their shared mental models and using it as a basis for modifying, as required, the rules that guide decision making and action. This process is similar to that referred to by Daft and Weick (1984) when they describe organizations as open social systems that seek and interpret information about their environment in order to provide a basis for action.

Modifying the rules via single and double loop learning

Argyris and Schön (1978) distinguish between two kinds of collective learning:

▶ *Single loop learning* entails the detection and correction of errors leading to a modification of the rules within the boundaries of current thinking (Figure 18.2). It involves organizational members collectively refining their mental models about how the organization operates and identifying ways of doing things better. This might involve, for example, revising reporting relationships, redesigning jobs, modifying decision-making procedures and so on. Single loop learning does not fundamentally challenge the organizational paradigm. It leads to the modification of the rules but not the mental model on which they are based.

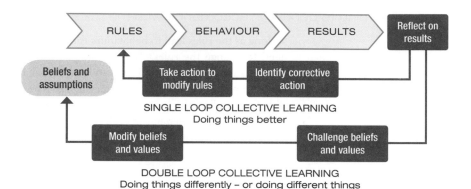

Figure 18.2 *Individual and collective learning in organizations*
Source: Adapted from Swieringa and Wierdsma, 1992

▶ *Double loop learning* is a more cognitive process; it occurs when the assumptions and principles that constitute the governing variables that underpin the shared mental model are examined and challenged (Figure 18.2). This kind of learning challenges accepted ways of thinking and can produce a new understanding of situations and events, which in turn can lead to the development of new rules that require organizational members to change their behaviour and do things differently or even do different things.

Example 18.1

> **first direct**
>
> Midland Bank – once one of the big four banking groups, but acquired by HSBC in 1992 – provides a good example of double loop learning. Managers challenged the assumption that the only way to do business with retail customers was face to face via a costly high-street branch network. This thinking led to the creation of first direct, the first telephone bank with no branch outlets, in 1989 and within six months it had over 100,000 customers. By April 1994, the customer base was over 500,000. This double loop thinking led first direct to be the first bank to launch internet banking in 1997 and to launch text message (SMS) banking in 1999.

While double loop learning is often seen as a desirable goal, it can be difficult to achieve in practice, a point that will receive further consideration below.

Triggers for double loop learning

When there is a good fit between the organization and its environment and when this leads to the achievement of desired levels of performance, there is a high chance that the prevailing shared mental model will be reinforced. Most collective learning will be single loop learning associated with the detection and correction of errors. This kind of learning is often associated with continuous improvement.

Double loop collective learning is most likely to occur when desired performance levels are not achieved and when feedback signals a need to re-examine the relevance of the shared mental model. Leroy and Ramanantsoa (1997) refer to incongruous events that violate conceptual frameworks as triggers for this kind of learning, and Fiol and Lyles (1983) assert that some type of crisis is necessary to trigger higher level or double loop learning. Triggers are often associated with discontinuities such as the appointment of a new leader or dramatically altered market conditions.

Crises, however, are not always required to trigger double loop learning. In the most effective organizations, such as first direct, double loop learning can occur as a matter of course. There are also occasions when someone in a position to make a difference can stimulate others to think creatively. Johnson et al. (2008b) report that when Ratan Tata, chairman of Tata Group, looked out over the streets of Mumbai and saw motorcycles in traffic carrying entire families – father, mother and children – he began to think about the possibility of providing a safe enclosed car for these scooter families at a price they could afford. This thinking led to the development of the Tata Nano, the cheapest car in the world, costing £1,300. Johnson et al. (2008b) also point to other examples where assumptions that underpin a business model were successfully challenged. The iPod revolutionized portable entertainment and transformed Apple because the company developed a ground-breaking new business model that combined hardware, software and service. Apple essentially gave away the low-margin iTunes music to lock customers into buying the high-margin iPod.

Can organizations learn or is it only individuals that learn?

The approach to organizational learning presented here focuses on the development of supra-individual or shared mental models that provide a basis for effective action. These shared mental models furnish organizations with a conceptual framework for perceiving and interpreting new information and determining how stored information can be related to any given situation. They persist over time, despite changes in organizational membership. This implies that organizations have collective memories that are not wholly dependent on the knowledge stored in the minds of current members. It is assumed that knowledge can also be stored in files, procedural manuals, routines, traditions and conventions and that this collective memory enables past experience to be applied to current problems.

Douglas (1986) challenges the view that organizations can learn. She concedes that institutional thinking can exist in the minds of individuals and she accepts that much of the learning that goes on in an individual's head is influenced by what other organizational members know and by the kind of information present in the organizational environment. She refers to this process as the 'squeezing' of each others' ideas into a common shape. However, she does not go along with the view that organizations, as collective entities, can learn.

Daft and Weick (1984) are more comfortable with the concept of collective or organizational learning. They base their view of organizations as 'interpretation systems' on the assumption that they have cognitive systems and memories. While they recognize that it is individuals who send and receive information and in other ways carry out the interpretation process, they argue that the organization interpretation process is something more than that which is undertaken by individuals. Individuals come and go, but there is an order and regularity in the way that organizational members continue to respond. The implication is that organizations, as well as individuals, develop mental models.

March (1991) appears to support this view. He presents learning in organizations as a mutual process that leads to a convergence between organizational and individual beliefs. While there may be an external reality that is independent of beliefs about it, individuals and organizations develop their own mental models and beliefs about reality. The organization stores the knowledge that it accumulates, over time, from the learning of its members in the form of an organizational code of received truth. This code or mental model, which influences the explicit and implicit rules and procedures that regulate behaviour in the organization, is modified by the beliefs of individuals, and at the same time, individual organizational members are socialized into the beliefs about reality that are associated with the shared mental model or organizational code. Thus, over time, the organization's mental model affects the beliefs of individuals while it is being affected by those beliefs.

Although March (1991) argues that this convergence is generally useful for the individual and the organization, he recognizes a potential threat to the effectiveness of organizational learning if individuals adjust to the shared mental model or organizational code before the code can learn from them. This threat is most likely to manifest itself and undermine organizational learning when a group develops a strong ideological commitment to the code or shared mental models and dismisses or suppresses deviant thinking as either irrelevant or potentially dangerous. De Holan and Phillips (2004) argue that the failure to unlearn old dominant logics can inhibit collective learning and organizational change.

The revision of shared mental models: the key to collective learning

Shared mental models need to be fluid and open to modification if they are to provide an effective basis for assessing the environment and planning action. Codified patterns of behaviour can contribute to the 'trap of success' referred to in Chapter 3. Unfortunately, once established, shared mental models may be resistant to change. Johnson et al. (2008a) refer to the strategic drift that can occur when the need to modify the organizational paradigm is not recognized and when managers, blinkered by an outdated set of taken-for-granted beliefs and assumptions, fail to detect changes in the organization's competitive position. It may not be until this strategic drift manifests itself in an unacceptable poor level of performance that the need to modify the paradigm is eventually recognized.

Shared mental models are one of the main sources of inertia identified by Gersick (1991), and Hodgkinson and Healey (2008) point to ingrained schemata as important barriers to organizational change. Unless they are open to revision, they can seriously limit an organization's ability to adapt, and can promote an episodic rather than a continuous response to threats and opportunities (see the discussion of punctuated equilibrium in Chapter 1).

The role of knowledge transfer in organizational learning

Organizational learning involves the acquisition of knowledge, the recognition of its potential and its application to improve organizational performance.

Knowledge may exist within an organization but it may not be available to those who can make best use of it. Huber (1991) draws attention to the importance of distributing information. As organizational members gain access to new information, they may be better able to create new knowledge by piecing together patterns that had not previously been apparent or identify and apply superior practices that are being used elsewhere in the organization. But information does not always flow freely and consequently valuable learning opportunities are missed. In many organizations, innovative work practices that are a great success in one location often remain 'islands of innovation'. Nicolini et al. (2008) review knowledge management policies and practices in the healthcare sector and Walton (1975) notes that the failure to diffuse innovation often forces organizations to invest in a costly duplication of effort in order to reinvent similar practices in other locations. Zell (2001) reports that best practices often linger in isolated locations within companies for years, unrecognized and unshared. Szulanski (1996) also observes that in many organizations there are surprising performance differences between different units, suggesting that knowledge is not being utilized as effectively as it could be. For example, IBM had only limited success transferring re-engineering logistics and hardware design processes between business units, and General Motors experienced problems trying to transfer manufacturing processes between divisions. These observations prompted Szulanski to study 122 best practice transfers in eight companies in order to better understand the 'internal stickiness' that impedes the transfer of knowledge. He found that, contrary to conventional wisdom, which attributes internal stickiness to poor motivation, the major barriers to internal knowledge transfer are:

▶ a lack of capacity to value, assimilate and apply new knowledge
▶ ambiguity regarding the precise reasons for the success or failure in replicating a practice in a new setting
▶ the quality of relationships.

Some of these issues are considered in more detail in Chapter 28.

Intra- and interorganizational learning

Most of the literature on organizational learning focuses on collective learning, including knowledge transfer, within a single organization. There is, however, a growing awareness of the importance of interorganizational learning.

Knowledge transfer between unrelated organizations

Leseure et al. (2004) examine the use of superior knowledge and the adoption of best or 'promising' practices from unrelated or competing organizations. They prefer to use the term 'promising' rather than 'best' practice because while a collection of ideas, values, procedures, techniques and tools may work well in some organizations, they may not be 'best practice' in all. Imported practices may not be aligned with the organization's culture, structure and other practices and, if they are to work at all, they may need to be customized before they can offer any benefit. They refer to TQM, just in time practices, business process re-engineering and high performance management as examples of some of the promising practices organizations may wish to adopt.

Leseure et al. (2004) developed a model that posits that both 'need pull', associated with performance gaps, and 'institutional push', normative pressures applied by customers, suppliers and regulators, can trigger efforts to adopt promising practices. Based on earlier work by Szulanski (1996) and Bessant et al. (2003), they suggest that the adoption process involves several steps:

▶ *Initiation*: The process may start with the discovery of a need for performance improvement that prompts a search for superior knowledge and best practices that address this need. Szulanski (1996) also suggests the possibility that the discovery of superior knowledge may cause organizational members to reframe as unsatisfactory a situation that, hitherto, was regarded as satisfactory.

▶ *Set-up and adaptation:* Following the decision to proceed, attention is focused on pre-empting implementation problems by exploring the feasibility of adapting the promising practice to suit the identified need (adaptation versus exact copying is discussed in Chapter 29). There are indications that this step in the process often receives insufficient attention.

▶ *Implementation:* Launch the change programme, giving attention to short-term actions such as training, modifying structures, writing new procedures and so on.

▶ *Ramp-up:* This begins when the organization starts to use the new practices.

▶ *Integration:* This involves the embedding of superior knowledge and the routinization of the new practices.

Change managers can design interventions to facilitate the transfer of knowledge between unrelated organizations. They can, for example, arrange for managers from the 'home' organization to visit a 'host' organization to learn about how it functions and explore promising practices that might offer benefits to the 'home' organization. The essential features of this kind of intervention are summarized in Change tool 18.1.

Change tool 18.1

Organizational visits

The purpose is for a leadership group from one organization to visit another organization to see how it operates and develop insights into how their own and the other organization works. The process involves four steps:

1 *Preparation:*
- the group meets to agree the focus of their inquiry and nature of the sample they would like to interview
- a facilitator visits the host organization to make arrangements for the inquiry
- the visiting group design their inquiry. For example, they may divide into two subgroups, each undertaking a separate stream of interviews, for example senior managers and others.

2 *Interviews:*
- members of each subgroup work in pairs, each pair interviews up to four individuals or groups.

3 *Analysis and preparation for presentation:*
- the visitors meet in subgroups to make sense of their visit
- they then share their analysis with the total group and prepare to present their observations to representatives of the host organization.

4 *Presentation:*
The visiting group shares with their hosts:
- what it has learned about the host organization and how it works
- insights that the visit has given them into how their own organization works.

Steps 3 and 4 in this process require the visiting managers to share their findings and build a common view they can articulate to their hosts. This joint construction of meaning is the essence of organizational learning (see below). When managers recognize this, they are more likely to appreciate the value of attending to the views of others who might have different insights about how their own organization functions.

Knowledge transfer within networks of related organizations

Bessant et al. (2003) discuss the importance of learning and development across networks of related organizations. These networks can take many forms, for example strategic alliances, shared product development projects and regional small firm clusters. Bessant et al. (2003: 167) focus their attention on supply chains and assert that: 'The competitive performance of the value stream depends upon the learning and development of the whole system, not just the leading players.' A common pattern in such networks is that learning is championed by a leading firm or some external institution such as a government department or trade association. Interfirm learning is often facilitated by a sense of shared crisis or a shared perception of a common opportunity. Based on a study of six UK supply chains, Bessant et al. report that learning does not typically cascade throughout the supply chain and that it tends to be confined to lead firms and first-tier suppliers.

Advocates of 'lean' thinking emphasize the importance of applying lean principles to the whole lean enterprise rather than restricting attention to a single organization. Wal-Mart, for example, has helped companies in its supply chain to eliminate waste by providing them with access to point-of-sale information, which allows them to track their own products on a real-time basis (see Chapter 24).

Impediments to organizational learning

The essence of collective learning is the joint construction of meaning. This occurs through sharing and dialogue. However, this process is rarely problem free. Several sources of difficulty will be considered.

Poor appreciation of the systemic qualities of organizations

Many individuals and groups have a parochial and limited view of their role and this restricts their ability to contribute to organizational learning. Often they focus all their attention on the immediate task and fail to appreciate how this relates to the overall purpose of the organization. Egan (1988) discusses the need to promote 'business thinking' that relates to the organization's overall mission and the importance of markets, competitors, customers and the products and services that satisfy customers' needs and wants. 'Organization thinking' is more blinkered and is essentially inward looking, concerned with the way the firm organizes its structures and processes to engage in its business. Organization thinking is important, but sometimes people become too preoccupied with the details of their particular bit of the organization and ignore how what they do affects others and how this impacts on the overall effectiveness of the business.

Lean thinking, discussed in Chapter 24, seeks to shift attention away from 'departmental' or functional thinking to thinking about value-creating processes across the enterprise. Another intervention that promotes systems thinking is business process re-engineering (see Chapter 23). McNulty and Ferlie (2002), commenting on attempts to re-engineer processes within a large hospital, suggest that process mapping enabled doctors, nurses and other stakeholders to analyse and understand the end-to-end care process and develop a vision of how the process could be improved.

There are a number of techniques that can facilitate a better appreciation of an organization's systemic qualities. Two are outlined below: a process for reviewing priorities and the organization mirror (Change tools 18.2 and 18.3).

Change tool 18.2

Priority review

Malby and Fischer (2006) argue that organizations get more of whatever they pay attention to and suggest that helping senior managers to examine what they actually do can provide a sense of what really counts in the organization. Mapping this onto the declared purpose and values of the organization can identify issues that might be adversely affecting organizational performance. The process presented here is based on an organizational feedback process described by Malby and Fischer. The process has seven steps:

1 Invite members of the top team, individually, to write down what they think the organization exists to do and what they think they pay attention to.
2 Help them to gather evidence about what individuals and top groups actually focus their attention on. This might involve reviewing the minutes of board and other senior management meetings over the past six months, reviewing diaries to see how people spent their time and reviewing the content of corporate communications.
3 Analyse the evidence and work out what issues receive most and least attention.
4 Display the results in a way that highlights what gets most and least attention.
5 Help members to identify patterns and any surprises. How do the issues that receive most attention relate to the purpose of the organization? Is there any evidence of 'drift'? Are people getting caught up in issues of the moment and neglecting what is important?
6 In the light of findings about what people actually do, consider whether the declared purpose of the organization is still valid. If not, consider revision.
7 Consider whether the most important issues are receiving sufficient attention and whether the ways of working on these issues are as effective as they might be.

Change tool 18.3

Organization mirror

This is an intervention that helps a unit or department to see itself as others see it and to use this new awareness to improve its working relationships with other groups. Essentially, data are gathered from other units or departments and fed back to the focal unit for consideration. Typically, members of the other groups are present when the data are fed back and participate in the analysis and discussion.

Before the mirror meeting
The person facilitating the process works with the focal group to help members understand how they fit into the business and identify the other units who are affected by what they do. Representatives of these 'outsider' groups are invited to meet with and provide feedback to the focal group. The facilitator may interview these representatives before the meeting to gain a sense of the key issues and brief them on the process.

The mirror meeting
The leader of the focal group welcomes the representatives of 'outsider' groups and invites them to give their feedback. The outsiders sit in an inner circle with members of the focal group forming a second outer circle – a configuration often referred to as a 'fishbowl'. Those on the outside listen as those in the fishbowl share their views about the focal group. Members of the focal group observe and listen but do not intervene.

The two groups then change places and members of the focal group, now in the fishbowl, talk about and seek to understand what they have heard, asking for clarification if required. The aim, so far, is to uncover problems, not to work on them.

The next step, working on the issues, begins by prioritizing the issues that have been uncovered and identifying what needs to be done to improve the effectiveness of the focal group. This is done by subgroups, each comprising members of both the focal and outsider groups.

The total group then convenes to share views, formulate action plans and agree who needs to do what by specific dates; some actions may require joint work by insiders and outsiders.

Lack of accessible channels for dialogue and the sharing of meaning

When learning is shared, the data on which it is based are open to challenge. Others can reassess the reasoning and logic that led to conclusions. In other words, meanings are not just exchanged. Dixon (1997) argues that shared meaning is 'constructed' in the dialogue between organizational members. She believes that in the process of articulating one's own meanings and comprehending the meanings others have constructed, people alter the meanings they hold. This joint construction of meaning is the essence of organizational learning. Unfortunately, the conditions that facilitate this process are often lacking. This has prompted many organizations to experiment with interventions designed to overcome some of the barriers to understanding between individuals and groups. Some of these interventions include the organization mirror process presented above, team approaches such as action research and Revans' (1980) action learning, and 'whole system in the room' processes such as General Electric's work-out, Weisbord's strategic search conferences and the conference model for developing a 'preferred future', which is presented in Change tool 18.4.

The active participation of organizational members is a critical element in collective learning. Bessant et al. (2003) highlight the importance of feedback and the challenge and support that others can provide.

Change tool 18.4

A conference method for developing a 'preferred future'

The conference method is a process that involves one or more meetings of organizational members, and other stakeholders as appropriate, to:

- examine key issues affecting the organization's future from a variety of perspectives
- learn from each other
- develop a shared understanding.

This shared understanding can be used either to facilitate real-time decision making by the organizational members participating in the conferences, or as an input to guide the decision making of a smaller strategic planning group.

Elements of the conference method
The details of the process will differ depending on circumstances, and will normally be decided by an in-company design team, facilitated by a consultant. However, the elements of the process typically include the following steps (Figure 18.3):

1 *Past:* the development of a shared understanding of the organization's strengths and weaknesses and opportunities and threats at an agreed point in time, say, three years ago.
2 *Present:* the exploration of the organization's current strengths, weaknesses, opportunities and threats, as perceived by organizational members and external stakeholders.

3 *Lessons about change:* an assessment of how the change (from past to present) was managed. Key questions might be: What did we get right? What might we have done better?

4 *Futures:* the development, by a number of subgroups, of a range of alternative visions of the future, based on the views of organizational members and external stakeholders.

5 *Criteria:* an examination and critique of these alternative visions to identify the criteria that should be used for selecting a 'preferred future'. Justifying choice when voting for preferred futures can help to surface criteria.

6 *Shared vision:* the generation of a shared vision of what a preferred, achievable future would be like.

7 *Implementation plan:* the development of a shared understanding about the best way of managing the change required to move to the desired future state, taking account of lessons learned from reviewing the management of past changes (step 3).

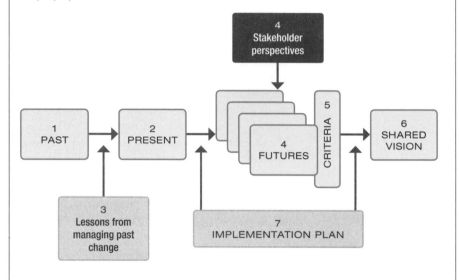

Figure 18.3 *A conference method for developing a 'preferred future'*

In Chapter 3, it was noted that senior managers can act in ways that encourage subordinates to share information and contribute to the formulation of the change agenda, but it was also noted in Chapter 10 that managers' fear of negative feedback and their negative beliefs about the commitment of employees lower down the organization can create a climate and give rise to the development of structures and processes, such as centralized decision making and the absence of formal mechanisms for soliciting feedback, that make it difficult for some organizational members to get their views heard. Whole system in the room-type interventions, awaydays and temporary groups, such as quality circles, can provide channels for dialogue and learning. Example 18.2 illustrates how soliciting feedback and encouraging dialogue can produce benefits.

Example 18.2

Bone density scans

Bone density scans at an NHS hospital were scheduled for 30-minute slots to accommodate variations in scan times, which varied from 10 to 50 minutes, and manage patient waiting times.

> At a departmental awayday, a junior member of staff pointed out that the main factor determining the length of a scan was the patient's body weight. This information was not requested on the patient referral form.
>
> Amending the form and adjusting scan times to match patient needs led to a marked increase in the number of scans completed in each session and to a reduction in patient waiting times. The member of staff who had triggered this improvement admitted that he had been aware that it was possible to reduce the average scan time for a long time but had not said anything because nobody had asked.

The context in which sharing and dialogue must occur

Brown and Eisenhardt (1997) illustrate the importance of context when describing the characteristics of firms that are able to manage change as a continuous process (see Chapter 1). They refer, for example, to organizational structures (semi-structures) that facilitate improvisation and the modification of work practices through mutual adjustments. Szulanski (1996) also reports that formal structures and systems, sources of coordination and expertise, and behaviour-framing attributes of the organizational context affect the quality of knowledge transfer.

The acquisition of knowledge, the recognition of its potential and its application to improve organizational performance often require numerous individual exchanges. Reference has already been made to the availability of channels for communication but the quality of relationships between organizational members can also affect the quality of organizational learning. Szulanski (1996) suggests that this is particularly important in those situations where knowledge has tacit components (see Nonaka, 1994) and where the reasons for the success or failure of knowledge transfers are ambiguous.

Attitudes towards mistakes and failures can have an important impact on the quality of learning. Husted and Michaiova (2002) argue that mistakes are often the result of exploring unknown territory and can be a vital source of new insights, but they are often buried and kept secret. This happens when organizational members are uncertain about how others will react and especially when they fear that they will be blamed for wasting resources. Blame cultures limit information sharing and increase the possibility of the same mistake being made repeatedly. They also inhibit creativity and learning because people are motivated to play safe and avoid experimentation.

Postmortems and post-implementation reviews are frequently used to dissect past events, identify mistakes and produce reports that include recommendations for improvement. They can be a useful source of single and double loop learning but the experience of the US army was that bringing in a highly qualified officer to conduct a post-combat review, identify mistakes and leave the platoon with a checklist to follow next time produced little real learning. The army responded by developing the 'after action review' (AAR). It facilitates learning by comparing the commander's intent, stated at the start of a mission, with what subsequently happens. Parry and Darling (2001) report that the vivid intersection between army doctrine and the standard practices (the 'rules') that govern situations, such as 'movement to contact with an enemy unit', and direct battle experience allows espoused theory and actual practice to shape each other on a daily basis – it facilitated the testing and, where necessary, modification of the rules.

Change tool 18.5

> ## The after action review
>
> It is an intervention that involves a leader (platoon commander) gathering the team on a regular basis to address the following questions:
>
> - *What was supposed to happen?*
>   This question helps the group to clarify and develop a shared understanding of what was expected of them.
> - *What actually did happen?*
>   This question helps the group to construct a shared picture of what actually happened. It has to be a collective process because typically no one person will be aware of the total picture. This shared understanding is then used to identify discrepancies between what was supposed to happen and what actually happened, but at this stage, no attempt is made to identify why things happened as they did.
> - *Why did it happen this way?*
>   This step involves exploring deeply what Malby and Fischer (2006) refer to as the relationship rules that guide the way people work together, the information rules that govern the availability of information and anything else that is perceived to have influenced performance.
> - *What are we going to change?*
>   This step involves considering what individuals and the group as a whole can do to deliver intended outcomes and to minimize unintended consequences. In the battle context, the aim is to generate insights into what needs to be changed to improve effectiveness and provide the basis for planning the next day's action.

Parry and Darling (2001) note how this approach has been applied in business settings. Harley-Davidson applied it to improve the process of introducing new models. After each 'pre-build', it conducted a series of AARs to compare actual with anticipated performance and use the learning to improve the way it conducted the next pre-build. A wine retailer conducted quarterly AARs with his team, focusing on a single event that happened in that quarter; in one quarter, for example, it was how they had managed a pre-holiday spike in demand. This example gave the team some insights into how they and the system worked under pressure. Power Construction used AAR principles to develop their 'lessons learned workshops' that brought multi-firm project teams together at the beginning, middle and end of large projects.

Example 18.3

> ## Google: a good example of a learning organization
>
> Throughout the whole organization, there is a good appreciation of the systemic qualities of Google and a clear understanding that success not only depends on being aligned with the external environment but on taking initiatives that will shape the external environment. For example:
>
> - Products are often launched early, in pre-mature stages, to receive input from users and developers. In this way, Google learns about what the market demands.
> - Many products are released 'open source', with all the source codes being shared freely with developers all over the world, so that they can build on Google's initial offering to develop a better core product and, importantly, use this as the basis for developing component products.
>
> In house, creativity is fostered by allowing employees to spend 20% of their time to experiment with whatever they want to explore. This has been the source of many well-known Google products.

The value of dialogue and open communication is widely recognized. Google has developed a transparent approach to knowledge management to ensure that no opportunities are missed for learning from colleagues or joining forces with others to develop new ideas. This is helped by structures that have few layers and a culture that promotes team working.

The culture also encourages risk taking and learning from mistakes. It is absolutely understood that exploration and learning involve taking risks. Failure is not a problem, it is regarded as a sign of having explored, and it teaches the organization what works and what does not. People are not motivated to hide failures because it is only when they are shared that the learning effect is achieved.

The big question is whether Google will be able to retain this learning culture over the next 10 years. Google was founded in 1998 by Larry Page and Sergey Brin while they were students at Stanford University. In 2004, they floated Google to raise new capital. The initial public offering raised US$1.67bn, implying a value for the entire corporation of US$23bn. One implication of this development is that the company will now have to pay more attention to shareholder value.

Greiner's (1972) life cycle model posits that as companies grow and mature, they move through a predicable series of stages of development. He describes the first as 'growth through creativity' (see Chapter 6). He argues that many company founders are entrepreneurial and technically oriented and the organization's structure, systems and culture tend to be informal. But as the organization grows, the need for more knowledge about efficiencies, more professional systems for maintaining financial control and more formal approaches for managing and developing people can lead to a crisis of leadership. Greiner suggests that a new approach to managing and leading the business may be required, and often the way forward is for the founders to bring in a strong business manager from outside. This happened at Google when Eric Schmidt joined the company as chairman and CEO in 2001. Prior to joining Google, Eric had been the chairman and CEO of Novell and before that the chief technology officer at Sun Microsystems. Google employs over 20,000 people and is still growing, so the challenge will be how to sustain this growth without compromising the organization's capability for double loop learning.

Characteristics of the sources and recipients of knowledge

An important factor that can influence an organization's ability to learn is the willingness of individual organizational members to share with others the meaning they have constructed for themselves as they encountered new experiences and ideas. Issues of confidentiality may prevent some sharing but there are occasions where knowledge is withheld for what Dixon (1997) describes as political and logistical reasons. These include gaining a personal competitive advantage, or a perceived lack of interest, on the part of others, in what the individual might want to share. Trust is also an issue. Lines et al. (2005) argue that whether change agents and others gain access to the knowledge and creative thinking they need to solve problems depends largely on how much people trust them.

Husted and Michaiova (2002) cite organizational members' reluctance to spend time on knowledge sharing as an impediment to organizational learning. This reluctance may arise because people are overwhelmed with other tasks or believe that their time can be invested more profitably elsewhere. They may also be reluctant to share information because they fear that this will encourage 'knowledge parasites', those who fail to invest much effort in acquiring their own knowledge, benefiting at their expense.

A related problem, referred to by Dixon (1997), is that some organizational members may be reluctant to consider the relevance of knowledge that others are willing to share with them. Individuals and groups may prefer to develop their own ideas and knowledge and reject knowledge that is 'not invented here'. They may also reject knowledge because they have reservations about the source's reliability or trustworthiness.

The motivation to consider and utilize knowledge from other sources is not the only problem. Cohen and Levinthal (1990) suggest that a lack of absorptive capacity, which manifests itself in the ability to value, assimilate and apply new knowledge, might render recipients incapable of exploiting the knowledge available to them. Szulanski (1996) also refers to a lack of retentive capability, the ability to institutionalize the utilization of new knowledge, as a block to organizational learning because it undermines persistence.

Ideologies

Reference has already been made to how ideology can distort the free flow of meaning. Walsh (1995) notes how shared mental models can be detrimental to organizational learning. He cites a number of case studies that link 'organizational blunders' to dysfunctional information processing among the organizations' top leadership groups, for example the Facit Corporation's inability to recognize the electronic calculator as a threat to its mechanical calculator business, and the Allied commanders' unwillingness to accept the futility of the saturation bombing of Europe in the Second World War. In both these examples, the group could be seen as holding a supra-individual schema that distorted its understanding of the information world in a way that made it blind to certain important aspects of its environment. In terms of Swieringa and Wierdsma's (1992) model, the consequence was that the 'rules' used to guide behaviour were based on an inadequate understanding of the environment, that is, flawed assumptions and beliefs, and they failed to promote behaviours that would contribute to the organization's success.

Weick (1979: 52) points to the phenomenon of groupthink as an example of the dysfunctional consequences when people are dominated by a single, self-reinforcing schema (mental model):

> Having become true believers of a specific schema, group members direct their attention towards an environment and sample it in such a way that the true belief becomes self-validating and the group becomes even more fervent in its attachment to the schema. What is underestimated is the degree to which the direction and sampling are becoming increasingly narrow under the influence of growing consensus and enthusiasm for the restricted set of beliefs.

Janis (1972) describes groupthink as a deterioration of mental efficiency, reality testing and moral judgement that is the result of in-group pressure. He defines eight symptoms of groupthink:

1 The group feels invulnerable. There is excessive optimism and risk taking.
2 Warnings that things might be going awry are discounted by the group members in the name of rationality.
3 There is an unquestioned belief in the group's morality. The group will ignore questionable stances on moral or ethical issues.
4 Those who dare to oppose the group are called 'evil', 'weak' or 'stupid'.
5 There is direct pressure on anyone who opposes the prevailing mood of the group.
6 Individuals in the group self-censor if they feel that they are deviating from group norms.
7 There is an illusion of unanimity. Silence is interpreted as consent.

8 There are often self-appointed people in the group who protect it from adverse information. These people are referred to as 'mind guards' by Janis.

All too often individuals and organizations fail to exploit the full potential for learning because they are unaware of the extent to which their mental models filter out important information. Covey (1989: 29) contends that while people think they are objective and see things as they are, they actually see what they have been conditioned to see. He argues that:

> The more aware we are of our basic paradigms, maps or assumptions, and the extent to which we have been influenced by our experience, the more we can take responsibility for those paradigms, examine them, test them against reality, listen to others and be open to their perceptions, thereby getting a larger picture and a far more objective view.

This points to the importance of double loop learning (Figure 18.4). It is important to raise awareness of, and challenge, the paradigms, maps and assumptions that regulate organizational functioning.

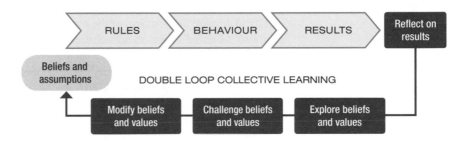

Figure 18.4 *Double loop learning*

Dysfunctional interactions between competing ideologies

Schein (1996) argues that in almost every organization, there are three important subcultures that have a major impact on the organization's capability to innovate and learn – the operator culture, the engineering culture and the executive culture. The operator culture is essentially an internal culture but the engineering and executive cultures have their roots outside the organization in wider occupational communities. CEOs, for example, share common problems that are unique to their role and engineers have common educational backgrounds and are influenced by the external professional bodies that license them to practise.

Operations managers value people as human assets. They tend to be sensitive to the interdependencies between the separate elements of the production process and recognize that, regardless of how carefully engineered a process is, its effective functioning will be determined by the quality of human interaction. Openness, mutual trust, commitment and the ability of people to learn and adapt to unanticipated circumstances are highly valued.

According to Schein (1996: 14), engineers, systems designers and technocrats (broadly defined) are attracted to their profession because it is abstract and impersonal. They are pragmatic perfectionists who prefer people-free solutions. They 'recognize the human factor and design for it, but their preference is to make things as automatic as possible'.

CEOs and their immediate subordinates tend to be preoccupied with the financial survival and growth of the organization, and focus much of their attention on boards, investors and capital markets. Schein (1996) argues that their self-image tends to be the embattled lonely warrior championing the organization in a hostile economic environment. They develop elaborate management information systems to stay in touch with what is going on in the organization and impose control systems to manage costs. People tend to be viewed as 'resources' and are regarded as costs rather than human assets.

Dysfunctional interactions arise when the three cultures are misaligned. Schein (1996) provides examples from a range of different organizational contexts. One relates to how the managers of operational units in a nuclear power generating company had their various plans for performance improvement overruled by the corporate engineering community who wanted to find standard solutions to common problems and the executive culture that was anxious to control costs. Another focused on teachers (operators) who valued human interaction with their students, and the advocates of computer-based learning (engineers) on the one hand and school managers on the other who wanted to control costs by increasing class size, and consequently reducing the human interaction valued by the teachers.

Schein (1996) argues that a root problem is that we have come to accept conflict between the three cultures as 'normal' and this has encouraged members of each culture to devalue the concerns of the other cultures rather than look for integrative solutions. As noted above, an organization's ability to learn is largely determined by the receptiveness of organizational members to the concerns and knowledge presented by others and their willingness to be open and share their knowledge and concerns with others. All three cultures are valid and can be a source of valuable learning. CEOs do need to worry about the financial health of the organization and engineers can make a valuable contribution by developing systems or solutions that eliminate human error. The way forward, therefore, is not to allow one of the three cultures to define reality for the others, but to seek greater alignment by developing sufficient mutual understanding to allow members to develop and implement integrative solutions.

However, because members of the executive and engineering cultures belong to wider occupational communities, even when organizations make great efforts to align these three cultures, the effect might be short-lived. Schein (1996) suggests that executive succession, for example, might lead to the appointment of a new CEO who may take the organization back to where it used to be.

Schein (1996) concludes that until executives, engineers and operators realize that they use different languages and make different assumptions about what is important, and until they come to accept that the assumptions of the other cultures are valid and worthy of attention, organizational learning efforts will continue to fail.

There are a number of interventions that change managers can use to facilitate learning between groups and members of different subcultures. Beckhard (1969), for example, describes a method for managing differences between groups.

Change tool 18.6 	**Beckhard's process for improving intergroup relations** • The first step involves the leaders, or the total membership, of two groups meeting to agree to commit some time and effort to working together to develop a joint understanding about the issues that are causing friction. • The two groups meet in separate rooms. Their first task is to develop a list that summarizes their attitudes and feeling about the other group, which might include their perceptions about what the other group is like and the way members behave. They do not have to reach a consensus about the items on their list.

- Their second task is to develop another list that summarizes what they think the other group might be saying about them.
- The groups then come together to share their lists. They start by sharing their first list – what they think about the other group. They have to listen to each other without comment at this stage. They then share their second lists – what they thought the other group would write about them.
- The groups return to their separate rooms to discuss their reactions to what they have heard and to prepare a new list of issues they think both groups should work on. Beckhard reports that in this meeting, group members discover that at least some of the issues on their first list reflected misunderstandings that were cleared up by simply sharing information. Their lists of key issues for attention are usually much shorter than their original lists.
- The two groups then meet, compare their lists of issues and make one joint list that reflects their agreed views about importance and immediacy. They then begin working together to agree what needs to be done.

Exercise 18.1

Assessing the quality of organizational learning in your organization

Consider the quality of organizational or collective learning in your organization, or in a part of the organization you are familiar with. When making your assessment, reflect on the following:

- What is the balance between single and double loop collective learning and how does this relate to the kinds of changes (continuous or discontinuous) confronting the organization or unit?
- Do people fully appreciate the systemic nature of the organization and are they aware of how what they do affects overall organizational effectiveness?
- Are people motivated to share experiences and ideas, and seek a more effective way of operating?
- Is there an ideological commitment to an established way of doing things that discourages innovation and the exploration of new possibilities?

Notes

Summary

Organizational learning involves enhancing the collective ability to act more effectively. The collective nature of learning is especially important in complex and turbulent environments, because senior managers may not be the best placed individuals to identify opportunities and threats. Responding to threats or opportunities may require individuals and groups located in different functions to collaborate and learn from each other.

This chapter opened with an examination of the nature of organizational learning and how it contributes to organizational effectiveness. Different kinds of collective learning have been discussed:

▶ *Single loop learning* entails the detection and correction of errors. It is concerned with continuous improvement through doing things better.
▶ *Double loop learning* occurs when the assumptions and principles that underpin the shared mental model are examined and challenged. It involves challenging current thinking and exploring the possibility of doing things differently or doing different things.

Attention has also been given to the role of knowledge transfer within and between organizations. Organizational learning involves the acquisition of knowledge, the recognition of its potential and its application to improve organizational performance. Knowledge may exist but it may not be available to those who can make best use of it. Information may not flow freely and consequently valuable learning opportunities may be missed.

The final section focuses on impediments to intra- and interorganizational learning. These include:

▶ *A failure to appreciate the systemic nature of organizations:* Many individuals and groups have a parochial and limited view of their role and this restricts their ability to contribute to organizational learning.
▶ *The lack of accessible channels for dialogue and the sharing of meaning:* When learning is shared, the data on which it is based are open to challenge. Others can reassess the reasoning and logic that led to conclusions. In other words, meanings are not just exchanged, they are constructed. Unfortunately, the conditions that can facilitate this process are often lacking.
▶ *Context:* While formal structures and organizational systems affect the possibility for dialogue, other factors affect the extent to which these possibilities are realized:
    • pressure of work and time for dialogue
    • level of trust between parties
    • the extent to which mistakes are viewed as opportunities for learning
    • attitudes towards sharing information and voicing concerns
    • the extent to which people actively seek feedback
    • attitudes towards dissent and receptivity to other people's ideas.
▶ *Sources and recipients of knowledge:* A lack of motivation to consider and utilize knowledge from other sources and a lack of absorptive capacity, which manifests itself in the ability to value, assimilate and apply new knowledge, might render recipients incapable of exploiting the knowledge available to them.
▶ *Pressures for conformity that constrain creative thinking:* Strong ideologies can promote groupthink and distort the free flow of information.
▶ *Dysfunctional interactions between competing ideologies:* Schein argues that in almost every organization, there are three important subcultures that have a

major impact on the organization's capability to innovate and learn. Members of each subculture often devalue the concerns of the other cultures rather than look for integrative solutions.

A number of change tools are described to provide a sense of some of the things change managers can do to improve the quality of collective learning in organizations.

References

Argyris, C. and Schön, D. (1978) *Organizational Learning*, London: Addison-Wesley.

Beckhard, R. (1969) *Organization Development: Strategies and Models*, Reading, MA: Addison-Wesley.

Bessant, J., Kaplinsky, R. and Lamming, R. (2003) Putting supply chain learning into practice, *International Journal of Operations and Production Management*, **23**(3): 167–85.

Brown, S.L. and Eisenhardt, K.M. (1997) The art of continuous change: linking complexity theory and time-paced evolution in relentlessly shifting organizations, *Administrative Science Quarterly*, 42: 1–34.

Cohen, W.M. and Levinthal, D. (1990) Absorptive capacity: a new perspective on learning and innovation, *Administrative Science Quarterly*, **35**(1): 128–52.

Covey, S.R. (1989) *The Seven Habits of Highly Effective People*, London: Simon & Schuster.

De Geus, A. (1988) Planning as learning, *Harvard Business Review*, **88**(2): 70–4.

De Holan, P.M. and Phillips, N. (2004) Remembrance of things past? The dynamics of organizational forgetting, *Management Science*, **50**(11): 1603–13.

Daft, R.L. and Weick, K.E. (1984) Toward a model of organisations as interpreting systems, *Academy of Management Review*, **9**(2): 284–95.

Dixon, N. (1997) The hallways of learning, *Organizational Dynamics*, **25**(4): 23–34.

Douglas, M. (1986) *How Institutions Think*, Syracuse, NY: Syracuse University Press.

Egan, G. (1988) *Change-agent Skills: Assessing and Designing Excellence*, San Diego: University Associates.

Fiol, C.M. and Lyles, M.A. (1983) Organizational learning, *Academy of Management Review*, **10**(4): 803–13.

Greiner, L.E. (1972) Evolution and revolution as organizations grow, *Harvard Business Review*, 50: 37–46.

Gersick, C.J.G. (1991) Revolutionary change theories: a multilevel exploration of the punctuated equilibrium paradigm, *Academy of Management Review*, 16: 10–36.

Hodgkinson, G.P. and Healey, M.P. (2008) Cognition in organizations, *Annual Review of Psychology*, 59: 347–417.

Huber, G. (1991) Organizational learning: the contributing processes and the literature, *Organizational Science*, **2**(1): 88–115.

Husted, K. and Michaiova, S. (2002) Diagnosing and fighting knowledge-sharing hostility, *Organizational Dynamics*, **31**(1): 60–73.

Janis, I.L. (1972) *Victims of Groupthink: A Psychological Study of Foreign Policy Decisions and Fiascos*, Boston: Houghton-Mifflin.

Johnson, G., Scholes, K. and Whittington, R. (2008a) *Exploring Corporate Strategy*, London: Prentice Hall.

Johnson, M.W., Christensen, C.M. and Kagermann, H. (2008b) Reinventing your business model, *Harvard Business Review*, **86**(12): 50–9.

Lank, A.G. and Lank, E.A. (1995) Legitimising the gut feel: the role of intuition in business, *Journal of Managerial Psychology*, **10**(5): 18–23.

Leroy, F. and Ramanantsoa, B. (1997) The cognitive and behavioural dimensions of organizational learning in a merger situation: an empirical study, *Journal of Management Studies*, **34**(6): 871–94.

Leseure, M.L., Bauer, J., Birdi, K. et al. (2004) Adoption of promising practices: a systematic review of the evidence, *International Journal of Management Reviews*, **5/6**(3/4): 169–90.

Lines, R., Selart, M., Espedal, B. and Johansen, S.T. (2005) The production of trust during organizational change, *Journal of Change Management*, **5**(2): 221–45.

Malby, B. and Fischer, M. (2006) *Tools for Change: An Invitation to Dance*, Chichester: Kingsham.

March, J.E. (1991) Exploration and exploitation in organisational learning, *Organizational Science*, **2**(1): 71–87.

McNulty, T. and Ferlie, E. (2002) *Reengineering Health Care: The Complexities of Organisational Transformation*, Oxford: Oxford University Press.

Miles, R.H. (1982) *Coffin Nails and Corporate Strategies*, Englewood Cliffs, NJ: Prentice Hall.

Nicolini, D., Powell, J., Coleville, P. and Martinez-Solano, L. (2008) Managing knowledge in the healthcare sector: a review, *International Journal of Management Reviews*, **10**(3): 245–63.

Nonaka, I. (1994) A dynamic theory of organizational knowledge creation, *Organizational Science*, **5**(1): 14–37.

Parry, C.S. and Darling, M.J. (2001) Emergent learning in action: the after action review, *The Systems Thinker*, **12**(8): 1–5.

Revans, R. (1980) *Action Learning*, London: Blond and Briggs.

Schein, E.H. (1990) Organisational culture, *American Psychologist*, **45**(2): 109–19.

Schein, E.H. (1996) Three cultures of management: the key to organizational learning, *Sloan Management Review*, **38**(1): 9–20.

Swieringa, J. and Wierdsma, A. (1992) *Becoming a Learning Organization*, Reading, MA: Addison-Wesley.

Szulanski, G. (1996) Exploring internal stickiness: impediments to the transfer of best practice within the firm, *Strategic Management Journal*, **17**(S): 27–43.

Walsh, J.P. (1995) Managerial and organisational cognition: notes from a trip down memory lane, *Organisational Science*, **6**(3): 280–321.

Walton, R. (1975) The diffusion of new work structures: explaining why success didn't take, *Organizational Dynamics*, **3**(3): 3–21.

Weick, K.E. (1979) Cognitive processes in organizations, in B.W. Staw (ed.) *Research in Organizational Behaviour*, Greenwich, CT: JA Press.

Zell, D. (2001) Overcoming barriers to work innovations: lessons learned at Hewlett-Packard, *Organizational Dynamics*, **30**(1): 77–86.

Action research is the basic model underpinning most organizational change interventions. It involves the application of scientific methods (fact finding and experimentation) to organizational problems and underpins the generic process model of change presented in Chapter 2.

Lewin developed the action research model in the 1940s when he identified the need for social scientists to base their theory building on research into practical problems. Early projects involved Coch and French (1948) working with employees at the Harewood Manufacturing Company to overcome resistance to change and Lewin working in the community to reduce violence between Catholic and Jewish teenage gangs (see Marrow, 1969). These early projects involved social scientists collaborating with members of social systems to understand and take action to resolve problems. The action research methodology helped members to apply scientific methods to guide their actions and helped social scientists to develop knowledge about social processes that they could generalize to other situations.

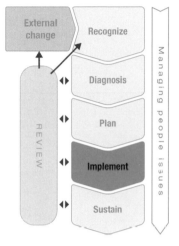

Dickens and Watkins (1999) observe that Lewin originally conceived of action research as a process that involved cycling back and forth between an ever deepening surveillance of the problem situation and a series of research-informed action experiments. These experiments formed an important part of the process. Action research is based on the traditional scientific paradigm that involves experimental manipulation and observation of the effects of the manipulation. However, as Dickens and Watkins note, there are important differences between action research and traditional science. Action research, unlike traditional science, does not attempt to set tight limits and controls on the experimental situation. Also action research uses information to guide behaviour in order to solve immediate problems, whereas traditional science involves studying information for the purpose of learning and typically ends at the point of discovery. Over time, this dual focus on problem solving and theory building has changed, as those concerned with facilitating change have focused more of their attention on improving organizational functioning within a particular context rather than helping social scientists contribute to the development of theoretical understanding. However, over the past few years, there has been a growing body of social scientists using action research as the basis for developing theory. Brydon-Miller et al. (2001) refer to Lewin's (1951: 169) assertion that 'there is nothing so practical as a good theory' as a major influence on their work. Brydon-Miller et al. (2001: 15) argue that:

> action research goes beyond the notion that theory can inform practice, to a recognition that theory can and should be generated through practice, and ... that theory is really only useful insofar as it is put in the service of a practice focused on achieving positive social change.

Action research and organizational learning

Hendry (1996) reviews the role of learning in the management of change and refers to Lewin's three-stage process of change as a learning process. The motive force for learning and change is cognitive dissonance and the experience of disconfirmation. The initial questioning and unlearning associated with this 'unfreezing' experience provides the motivation for individuals and groups to engage in the information gathering, diagnosis and experimentation that leads to new learning.

Individuals, groups and whole systems are constantly faced with the need to learn and change in order to adapt to changing circumstances. Those who are best able to adapt are those who are able to learn from their experiences. Kolb (1984) elaborated Lewin's model and articulated a theory of experiential learning that conceptualizes learning as a four-stage cycle, which translates experience into concepts that are used to guide the choice of new experiences (Figure 19.1).

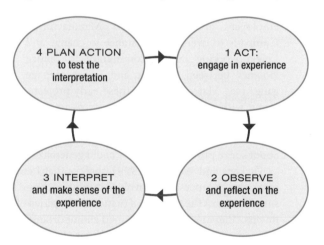

Figure 19.1 *The experiential learning model*

The first stage involves engaging in immediate concrete experience in order to provide the basis, at stage two, for observation and reflection. At stage three, these observations are interpreted and assimilated into a 'theory' from which new implications for action can be deduced. These implications or hypotheses then serve as guides when planning, at stage four, how to act to create new experiences. If individuals and groups are to be effective learners and action researchers, they must be able to:

▶ involve themselves fully, openly and without bias in their experiences
▶ reflect on and observe these experiences from many perspectives
▶ create concepts that integrate their observations into logically sound theories
▶ use these theories to make decisions and solve problems.

Role of the facilitator

This process can be facilitated by a change agent. Fifty years ago, Shepard (1960) was advocating a collaborative relationship between consultant and client. His view was that the role of the consultant is to 'help' the client or client group to design their fact-finding procedures and plan their actions in such a way that they can learn from them in order to serve the end of discovering better ways of organizing.

The role of the change agent as facilitator rather then prescriber of solutions has received considerable attention. Action learning (Revans, 1980), for example, advocates an approach to learning that involves solving real problems. Mumford (1985) made the point 25 years ago that those who wish to assist learners should do so by helping them to learn from exposure to problems and each other. The role of the facilitator/trainer is to help learners to formulate their own plans for action and test them through implementation.

Over the past 60 years, action research has spawned many related action strategies that have been applied to individual learners, groups, organizations and even wider networks of institutions (see the special edition of *Management Learning*, edited by Raelin, 1999, and the special issue of *Human Relations*, edited by Eldon and Chisholm, 1993). In addition to the classical model of action research, Raelin (1999) refers to five other models: participatory research, action learning, action science, developmental action inquiry and cooperative inquiry. Appreciative inquiry is also regarded by many as a contemporary development of the classical action research model. This will receive separate and detailed attention in Chapter 20.

The participative nature of action research

All these action strategies are inherently participative. According to Raelin (1999: 117), facilitators and members of the target system

> mutually open themselves up to an inquiry process that seeks to 'unfreeze' the assumptions underlying their actions. Their methodologies are experimental and predominantly conducted in group settings.

Reason and Bradbury (2001: 1) define action research as

> a participatory, democratic process concerned with developing practical knowing in the pursuit of worthwhile human purposes … It seeks to bring together action and reflection, theory and practice, in participation with others, in the pursuit of practical solutions to issues of pressing concern to people, and more generally the flourishing of individual persons and their communities.

Most of those who advocate a collaborative approach to problem solving in organizations do so because they believe that much of the information relevant to resolving problems is widely disseminated throughout the organization. Participation increases the likelihood that those who hold important information will share it with others. Collaborative approaches to problem solving also build commitment and facilitate the implementation of actions designed to resolve the problem.

Action research at the Harewood Manufacturing Company

Blake and Mouton (1983) report one of the early examples of action research to illustrate the importance of participation. It was undertaken at the Harewood Manufacturing Company, a pyjama factory in rural Virginia, at a time when the company was planning to recruit older workers to ease the labour shortage created by the Second World War. The proposal was fiercely resisted by supervisors who feared that older workers would be inefficient and difficult to manage. The director of personnel responded by providing the supervisors with scientific 'proof' that older workers did possess the skills and aptitude necessary to perform effectively. But the supervisors rejected the evidence and were not persuaded. However, rather than moving ahead and imposing the new hiring policy, the director of personnel decided to try to change attitudes by involving the supervisors in a research project designed to investigate the efficiency of older workers. The study focused on older workers already employed in the plant. Some had been with the company for many years and others had been employed more recently for social reasons, for example because they had been widowed. Members of staff were given full responsibility for designing the project and deciding how to collect the data. The findings of the study were a surprise to the supervisors. They found that it was not age but a range of other factors that were the main determinants of performance. Blake and Mouton report that while the supervisors had rejected 'expert' evidence, they were convinced by their own findings. Their involvement in the project helped them to unlearn some of the beliefs they had held to be true and changed their attitudes towards the employment of older workers.

The process of action research

The classical model of action research involves collecting and analysing data about the nature of a problem, taking action to bring about a change and observing the effects of the action in order to inform further actions to improve the situation. Sometimes the process starts following the identification of a problem by a senior member of the organization who has the power and influence to make things happen. However, this top-down approach is not the only way of introducing action research methodologies into organizations. Sometimes group members are aware that a problem exists but, for a variety of reasons, find it difficult to manage the problem more effectively. This may motivate them to take the initiative and seek help from an external facilitator. Whatever the starting point, Lewin (1946) argued that an essential prerequisite for action research is a 'felt need', an inner realization that change is necessary. Unless the group is willing to work on their problem, this kind of collaborative intervention is unlikely to succeed.

Following the identification of an issue that requires attention, action research involves successive cycles of action and evaluation. Each cycle comprises five steps. Succeeding cycles begin with the collection and analysis of data to evaluate the consequences of the action taken at the end of the preceding cycle. (Figure 19.2) The five steps are:

1 *Data gathering for diagnosis:* This involves collecting data about the problem. This can be done in a number of ways. Several methods of collecting data have been discussed in Chapter 7, such as interviews, questionnaires, observations and reference to performance data and other records that are collected as a normal part of day-to-day operations. The choice of method needs to be influenced by the nature of the problem and the people involved. For example, the 'organization mirror' (see Change tool 18.3) is a techniques that might be appropriate when the problem involves the quality of relationships between a group and other organizational units or external parties such as suppliers and customers. These other units reflect back to the focal group their perceptions and information about its performance. They act as a mirror and provide the group with their view of the situation. Data can be collected by the whole focal group in a meeting with

representatives of other units, or by a designated person interviewing others on behalf of the group.

2 *Data feedback to client group:* Often members of the focal (problem-solving) group are delegated to investigate particular aspects of the problem or an external facilitator collects data on behalf of the group. Consequently, in order for the process to be truly collaborative, data need to be fed back to all group members.

3 *Discussion of the data and diagnosis of the problem:* One of the defining features of action research is that system members collaborate with each other and with an external facilitator to review the data, clarify issues and formulate hypotheses about cause and effect.

4 *Action planning:* This involves identifying possible interventions to improve the situation and selecting a preferred way forward.

5 *Implementation of action plan:* This involves taking action to improve the situation.

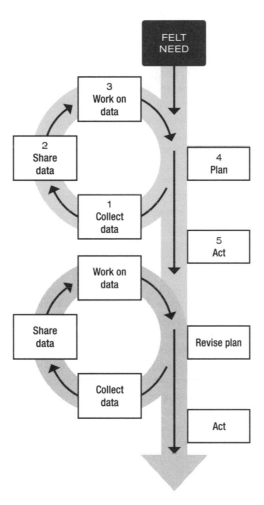

Figure 19.2 *The action research process*

Following the first cycle of the process, the original hypothesis about cause and effect and the action taken to improve the situation are evaluated through a further cycle of data gathering, feedback and analysis. This evaluation might suggest ways of refining the original hypothesis, or the implementation of alternative actions, or it might prompt the formulation of a completely different hypothesis regarding the nature of the problem. And so the process continues. Example 19.1 provides an example of how the process can unfold in practice.

Example 19.1

> ## Action research at Freedman House
>
> Freedman House is a 10-bed voluntary hostel for ex-offenders who have recently been released from prison. Shortly after the hostel was opened, the management committee decided to review how things were going.
>
> The initial energy for the Freedman House project had come from probation officers who worked in the community to rehabilitate offenders. They were aware that of the 250 people from their city who were committed to prison each year, over 20% had no fixed abode. Many had been to prison before and homelessness was identified as a factor contributing to their recidivism.
>
> One of the probation officers noticed that there were two houses located near the city centre that had been boarded up and left uninhabited for some considerable time. He thought they might provide the possible basis for a hostel and brought the idea to a volunteer group attached to the local probation office. The group agreed to establish a working party, which eventually obtained planning permission to convert the houses into a hostel. Their next step was to call a public meeting, elect a management committee and launch a fundraising campaign. The committee worked with enthusiasm, but because cash was short, it was impossible to employ contractors to undertake all the necessary work. Consequently, members and volunteers did much of the work to convert the houses. Eventually a warden was appointed, the first residents selected and the hostel opened. Unfortunately, this was a short honeymoon, soon to end with the premature departure of the first warden. The hostel had to close until a replacement could be found. Two candidates were interviewed and one was appointed. Soon after accepting the post, the successful candidate announced that he would not be able to take up the appointment. Time was short. The hostel was empty and it was decided, rather than embark on a new round of advertising and interviewing, that the unsuccessful candidate would be offered the job, which he accepted.
>
> A few months after the hostel was reopened, the office holders of the management committee decided it was time to take stock and identify priorities to carry the project forward. A national charity concerned with the welfare of offenders agreed to sponsor a consultant to facilitate this work. The office holders had an initial meeting with the consultant, where they provided him with a brief history of the project and outlined, in broad terms, the kinds of issues they felt needed to be addressed. While a number of the group were familiar with action research, some were not and had expected the consultant to introduce them to 'best practice' and offer advice. This minority was a little uncomfortable with the consultant's proposal that he acted as a catalyst to help them move forward, but as the meeting progressed, they warmed to the idea and it was agreed that the group would take the proposal to the next meeting of the full management committee. The full committee agreed to embark on the project and mandated the lead group of office holders to work with the consultant to begin data gathering.
>
> The lead group and consultant discussed the kind of information they would need to help themselves and the full committee understand how the 'system' currently operates, identify problems and explore what could be done to improve matters. They also thought about what they needed to do to gather this information and who should be involved. Because all the group had 'day jobs' elsewhere, they invited the consultant to take the lead collecting data and agreed that he would interview all

office holders, the warden, two members of the committee who were not office holders, an external stakeholder (a member of the voluntary group attached to the probation service) and two groups of residents (those under 20 and older residents). Interviews with the warden and management committee focused on the goals of the hostel, the hostel organization, strengths and weaknesses, decision making, communications and 'important issues'. Interviews with residents focused on the goals of the hostel, their expectations before arrival, what it was like now and what they would change.

The way the process unfolded is shown in Figure 19.4. A number of issues emerged from the initial feedback meeting. These were:

- *Finance:* It was felt that raising funds to keep the hostel going would be more difficult than it had been to establish the 'exciting new project' in the first place.
- *The relationship between the management committee and the warden:* A majority of the management committee felt that its role was to closely supervise the warden and the general running of the hostel. They also felt that the warden frequently stepped out of role and assumed too much responsibility, thus preventing the management committee from managing. The warden, on the other hand, felt that the management committee was bureaucratic, unwieldy and too reluctant to delegate. It was decided that this issue needed to be one of the first they would work on.
- *The management committee's contact with residents:* Some committee members felt that it was their right to 'drop in' to see how things were going at the hostel. The warden felt that this was inappropriate and insensitive. Other members of the committee supported the warden on this point, and data from residents indicated that they perceived committee members to be authority figures – most were magistrates, probation officers and so on – and felt uncomfortable when they were around.
- *The liaison officer's role:* One member of the committee had been designated as liaison officer responsible for communications between the committee and the warden and residents. It transpired that there were almost as many views about the role of the liaison officer as there were members of the committee. A clear brief had never been agreed and a complicating factor was that many probation officers on the committee had clients who were residents in the hostel.
- *Original vision versus current reality:* Some members of the committee were becoming disappointed with the project because they had had to compromise on some of their aims. Others were more pragmatic and reasonably satisfied that, at last, the hostel was 'up and running' and appeared to be 'ticking over' with few problems.
- *The future role of the management committee:* Early on everybody had been involved in lots of talking, planning and fundraising. As the project progressed, attention shifted to making things happen. Following the launch (and relaunch), attention shifted again to ensuring things worked as required, but the committee was much bigger than required to manage this task.

There was insufficient time to work on all these issues at the first meeting, so attention was focused on the management committee's relationship with the warden, their contact with residents and the role of the liaison officer. As a first step, it was agreed that only the liaison officer would visit the hostel on a regular basis. However, it was agreed that he could visit unannounced, at least on some occasions, in order to reassure the committee that all was well. With regard to the warden's role, it was anticipated that reducing visits from committee members would allow the warden more freedom to get on with managing day-to-day matters. The committee also asked the liaison officer to work with the warden to review their relationship and how this might be changed to improve the way the hostel was managed.

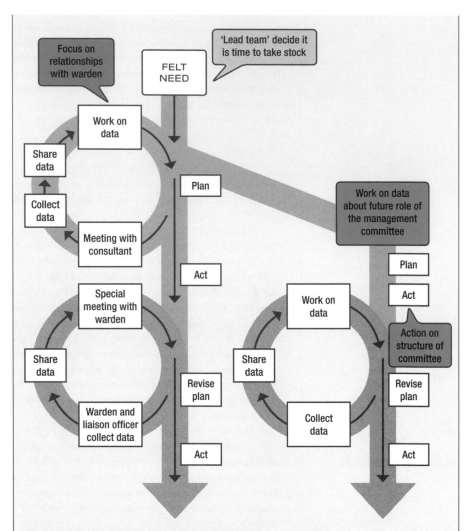

Figure 19.3 *The action research process at Freedman House*

Taking action to improve relations between the warden, liaison officer and management committee was not an easy or comfortable process, but some progress was made. The warden wrote and circulated a frank report for the committee, in which he aired a number of delicate issues that, up until then, had been avoided by all parties. The committee responded by arranging a special meeting with the warden and sharing some of their concerns about the way he ran the hostel and the way he related to members of the committee.

Working on these issue raised a number of concerns, chief of which was that the warden might 'take umbrage' and leave, but almost everybody felt that the free discussion at the special meeting and the respectful way in which it was managed produced some positive outcomes. It helped to improve relationships, reassure the committee that the warden was both competent and committed to the committee's strategy, and reassured the warden that he had support from the committee for what he was trying to do.

While this was happening, the management committee also met to work on some of the other issues identified at the first meeting of the full committee. Attention was focused on the future role of the management committee. It was agreed that the project had entered a new phase and that the existing, large management committee was no longer appropriate. It was recognized that there was a need for a smaller core group supported by a wider network of 'friends' and a separate subcommittee focused on fundraising to finance day-to-day operating expenses.

It was at this point that the consultant began to withdraw, leaving the original lead team to take matters forward.

The action research process sometimes focuses on natural work groups and sometimes brings together people who do not have close working relationships. A useful framework for managing meetings in a way that encourages maximum involvement is provided by the Axelrod meeting canoe (Change tool 19.1).

Change tool 19.1

The Axelrod canoe: a blueprint for getting people involved in meetings

The meeting canoe is a blueprint for making meetings dynamic and energy creating rather than spirit sapping and energy draining. The canoe represents the opening up phase, the body of the meeting and the closing down phase.

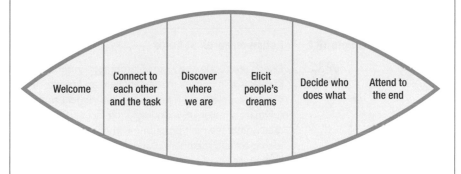

Figure 19.4   *The meeting canoe*
Source: Axelrod et al., 2004

The steps are as follows:

1   *Start by making people feel welcome:* Pay attention to how you greet people, make them feel welcome. Also pay attention to seating arrangements. A circle or semicircle may work better that seating people in rows with senior people at a top table.

2   *Find ways to create connections among people.* Conversations help us to connect. Find a way to get everybody to engage with others. If they are strangers or semi-strangers, you might start by asking them to share something about themselves that others may not know, or you might initiate a quick once round the group with people saying why they are there or what they hope to get out of the meeting.

3   *Discover the way things are: build a shared picture of the current situation:* How you do this will depend on the purpose of the meeting. If the purpose is to explore alternative futures, you might begin by asking people to explain where they fit in and what their job is in order to help them understand better how the system currently operates. If the purpose is to solve a particular problem, you might start by encouraging people to talk about how the problem impacts on them and their bit of the organization.

4   *Elicit people's dreams: build a shared picture of where you want to go:* One way of doing this is to get people to pretend it is five years on and ask them what they would like to be telling outsiders about what the organization has become. For

example, what is it like working here or what it is like being one of our customers? Pay attention to the themes that emerge. Is there a shared picture?

5 *Decide on who does what to create the future you've agreed upon:* Clarify how decisions will be made; consensus, majority vote or by the leader. Identify what needs to be done. Sometimes brainstorming can help. Finally, decide who will do it.

6 *Attend to the end:* Put as much thought and attention into saying goodbye as you did to saying hello. You might end by reviewing decisions and agreements so that everyone is sure what has been decided and what the next steps are.

Results from action research

Action research is widely acknowledged as an effective means of bringing about change. Reference has already been made to the Harewood Manufacturing Company project, illustrating how it can be used to overcome resistance to changes proposed by senior management. Greenwood et al. (1993) report a successful action research project in the Xerox Corporation that involved employees (union members and managers at plant level) persuading senior management to radically change their proposal to outsource the manufacturing of selected components.

Example 19.2

Action research at Xerox

During the 1980s, the Xerox Corporation introduced a series of major changes in response to a decline in market share and profits. One outcome of this process was the development of an employee involvement programme at the Webster plants, the company's major US manufacturing facility. Some time later, this was integrated with a quality improvement programme and was jointly administered at plant level by local managers and members of the union. They received training in group problem solving so that they could be involved in the programme as internal consultants and facilitators. This high level of collaboration provided the context of a successful action research project.

As part of a competitive benchmarking programme, Xerox decided to outsource the production of parts that could be manufactured externally at lower cost. The first outsourcing decision targeted the production of wire harnesses. Benchmarking and cost comparison studies indicated that the company could save $3.2m a year by outsourcing production and shutting down the wire harness department. It was anticipated that an immediate outcome of this outsourcing decision would be the loss of 180 jobs, but the union feared that this might be just the beginning of a major programme of redundancies as the competitive benchmarking exercise was rolled out to include a wider range of components, and local managers also recognized that their jobs were at risk.

Greenwood et al. (1993) report that after several weeks of discussions with high level union and management officials, it was decided to institute a cost study team, composed of six workers and two members of management. The team was established to determine whether Xerox could cut its manufacturing costs sufficiently to meet the outside bid and thus save the jobs. Inputs were sought from many sources including industrial engineers, cost accountants and a social psychologist. Greenwood et al. describe the outcome of this action research intervention as spectacular. The team was able to demonstrate cost savings sufficient to persuade senior management to retain wire harness production within the company. The exercise was successfully extended to include four other cases and led to 900 jobs being saved.

Greenwood et al. (1993) also reported other benefits following the action research project at Xerox. Management developed greater trust in workers' abilities and this led to them promoting a variety of other initiatives involving workers in new plant design and the restructuring of the research and development programme for discovering new products and new manufacturing methods. Union leaders and workers experienced a raised level of confidence in their own ability to make an intellectual contribution to the solving of manufacturing problems. In terms of contributing to theory, the cost study teams learned how conventional forms of allocating indirect costs to industrial products could lead management to make decisions against the economic interests of the company and workers. Greenwood et al. also assert that their analysis led to a theoretical reformulation of the relations between worker participation and productivity.

Summary

Lewin created action research as a vehicle for using communities and work organizations as laboratories for field experiments that were designed to help scientists to develop theories about social processes and to help members of the focal community to understand and manage their circumstances more effectively. During the 1960s, organization development practitioners began to use action research as a basis for intervening to promote change in organizations.

Action research is based on the premise that people learn best and are more willing to apply what they have learned when they manage the problem-solving process for themselves. The learning process involves:

▶ observing what is going on
▶ developing hypotheses that specify cause-and-effect relationships and point to actions that could help manage the problem more effectively
▶ taking action
▶ collecting data to evaluate the effect of the action and test the hypothesis.

The client group is often helped by a facilitator who works with members to help them design their own fact-finding procedure, work on the data they have collected, plan what to do, take action and then evaluate their actions in such a way that they can test their cause-and-effect hypotheses and learn from what they did.

It is a collaborative process because:

▶ many people may have information that is relevant to the problem
▶ their 'rich knowledge' about issues might be different to an outside consultant's understanding of reality
▶ involvement promotes psychological ownership of the problem
▶ involvement facilitates the implementation of the action that has been planned.

Action research, according to the typology presented in Figure 16.2, is a human process intervention that addresses processes such as learning, problem solving, communication and decision making.

A wide range of change management interventions are rooted in action research methodologies, insofar as they involve some form of fact finding and action taking designed to improve the way problems are managed. Many also reflect the principles of interactive or participatory action research, insofar as they involve organizational members in the problem-solving process in order to promote the kind of learning that will support the ongoing development of their group or organization.

References

Axelrod, R.H., Axelrod, J.B. and Jacobs, R.W. (2004) *You Don't Have to Do it Alone: How to Involve Others to Get Things Done*, San Francisco, CA: Berrett-Koehler.

Blake, R.R. and Mouton, J.S. (1983) *Consultation: A Handbook for Individual and Organization Development* (2nd edn), Reading, MA: Addison-Wesley.

Brydon-Miller, M., Greenwood, D. and Maguire, P. (2001) Why action research?, *Action Research*, **1**(1): 9–14.

Coch, L. and French, J.R. (1948) Overcoming resistance to change, *Human Relations*, 1: 512–32.

Dickens, L. and Watkins, K. (1999) Action research: rethinking Lewin, *Management Learning*, **30**(2): 127–40.

Eldon, M. and Chisholm, R.F. (1993) Emergent varieties of action research: introduction to the special issue, *Human Relations*, 46: 121–42.

Greenwood, D.J., Whyte, W.F. and Harkavy, I. (1993) Participatory action research as a process and as a goal, *Human Relations*, **46**(2): 175–93.

Hendry, C. (1996) Understanding and creating whole organizational change through learning theory, *Human Relations*, **49**(5): 621–41.

Kolb, D.A. (1984) *Experiential Learning*, Englewood Cliffs, NJ: Prentice Hall.

Lewin, K. (1946) Action research and minority problems, *Journal of Social Issues*, **2**(4): 34–46.

Lewin, K. (1951) *Field Theory in Social Science*, New York: Harper.

Marrow, A.J. (1969) *The Practical Theorist: The Life and Work of Kurt Lewin*, New York: Teachers College Press.

Marrow, A.J., Bowers, D.G. and Seashore, S.E. (1967) *Management by Participation*, New York: Harper & Row.

Mumford, A. (1985) A review of action learning, *Management Development*, **11**(2): 3–18.

Raelin, J. (1999) Preface to special issue on action strategies, *Management Learning*, **30**(2): 115–25.

Reason, P. and Bradbury, H. (eds) (2001) *Handbook of Action Research: Participative Inquiry and Practice*, London: Sage.

Revans, R.W. (1980) *Action Learning*, London: Blond & Briggs.

Shepard, H.A. (1960) An action research model, in *An Action Research Program for Organization Improvement*, Ann Arbor, MI: The Foundation for Research on Human Behaviour.

chapter 20

Appreciative inquiry

Appreciative inquiry is a process that involves exploring the best of what is, or has been, and amplifying this best practice. It seeks to accentuate the positive rather than eliminate the negative; it focuses attention on what is good and working rather than what is wrong and not working

This chapter examines appreciate inquiry from three perspectives; a philosophy of knowledge, an intervention theory, and a methodology for intervening in organizations to improve performance and the quality of life.

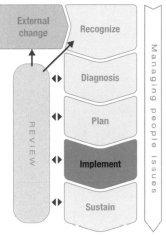

The social construction of reality

Social constructionist thinking challenges the view that there is an objective universe 'out there' that is in some sense enduring and physically observable. It posits that reality is a social construction. Elliot (1999) describes a simple exercise that illustrates how readily we make and defend our own versions of reality, even when the data we use are ambiguous. The exercise involves presenting a group with a set of squiggles on a flip chart and inviting each person to take a couple of minutes to decide what they represent. He reports that after a short while, each person begins to see, or think they can see, some emergent shape. If they are then allocated to small groups of three or four and asked to come to a consensus about what the squiggles really mean, members usually start with different interpretations, imagine that their interpretations are correct and try to convince the others that this is the case.

Everything we encounter and experience is open to multiple interpretations. Social constructionists assert that our perceptions of reality are the product of dialogue and negotiation. Dixon (1997), for example, argues that organizational members construct a shared mental model of the organization through a process of dialogue and interaction. She believes that, in the process of articulating one's own meanings and comprehending the meanings others have constructed, people alter the meanings they hold. There is no single objective reality.

The way we behave and the consequences of our behaviour are critically dependent on the way we construct reality – the way we see the world. And the way we see the world is determined by what we believe. Srivastva and Cooperrider (1990) argue that our beliefs govern what we look for, what we see and how we interpret what we see. Our beliefs, therefore, can lead to self-fulfilling expectations. Cooperrider and Srivastva (1987) argue that to the extent that action is predicated on beliefs, ideas and meanings, people are free to seek a transformation in conventional conduct by modifying their beliefs and idea systems.

A widely held belief is that organizational life is problematic. This belief promotes a deficiency perspective that focuses attention on the dysfunctional aspects of organizations and has led to many interventions being designed on the assumption that organizations are 'problems to be solved'. Such interventions typically involve:

▶ identifying key problems
▶ analysing causes
▶ analysing solutions
▶ developing action plans to manage these problems more effectively.

Cooperrider and Srivastva (1987) argue that this kind of organization development intervention is conservative, insofar as the formulation of a problem implies that somebody has knowledge of what 'should be' and therefore any remedial action is bounded by what is already known. Advocates of appreciative inquiry argue that this deficiency approach often only leads to single loop learning – continuous improvement within the existing paradigm – and is relatively ineffective when it comes to facilitating organizational transformation.

An alternative belief about organizations, and one that underpins appreciative inquiry, is that rather than 'problems to be solved', they are 'possibilities to be embraced'. Advocates of appreciative inquiry argue that not only are organizations social constructions open to revision, but that this process of revision can be facilitated by a collective inquiry. They also argue that this collective inquiry should attend to the life-giving forces of the organization rather than to a set of problems that have to be resolved. It involves appreciating the best of 'what is' and using this to ignite a vision of the possible. The process is generative; it takes nothing for granted and challenges the beliefs and assumptions that guide behaviour. The organization is viewed as an unfathomable mystery, offering many as yet unknown possibilities. The advocates of appreciative inquiry argue that this social constructionist perspective is more likely to produce double loop learning, which will lead to the organization doing things differently or even doing different things, than a perspective that is more narrowly focused on organizational dysfunction.

A theory of intervention

Cooperrider (1990) refers to the 'heliotropic hypothesis' as the core of a powerful theory of change. The essence of this theory is that social systems have images of themselves that underpin self-organizing processes and they have a natural tendency to evolve towards the most positive images held by their members. They are like plants, they evolve towards the 'light' that gives them life and energy. This leads to the proposition that interventions that promote a conscious evolution of positive imagery offer a viable option for changing social systems for the better.

It has already been noted that a widely held belief about organizations is that they are problematic. There is a tendency to focus on what is wrong rather than to celebrate what is working and going well. Elliot (1999) reports that when he asked a group of 45 managers to write down 20 adjectives that accurately caught the flavour of their organization:

▶ 72% of the words they used were critical, negative or hostile, for example chaotic, inefficient, inward-looking, lazy, poorly structured, overbureaucratic, slow, careless, unaware
▶ 13% were neutral, for example mainstream, average, contented, unambitious

▷ But only 15% were positive and approving, for example creative, exciting, thrilling, cutting edge, determined, satisfying, customer oriented, high-tech, achievement oriented.

While the members of many organizations focus attention on things that are not working well, some organizations (a minority?) have a very positive construction of themselves. Example 20.1 highlights one of these exceptions.

Example 20.1

Médecins Sans Frontières

Médecins Sans Frontières (MSF) has a culture that celebrates what is working and going well. Over a period of 40 years, MSF has grown from a small, radical organization into a highly respected and professional organization employing 26,000 people who work in over 70 countries. A recent survey found that staff described their organization and the work they do in very positive terms:

- we are a hands-on organization
- we are non-political, outspoken and neutral
- we are financed independently
- we are independent
- we can be trusted
- we have uncompromising commitment and focus
- we are reluctant to admit defeat
- we have passion for our work
- we are optimistic
- we are international
- we provide emergency-based, hands-on healthcare
- we help people neglected by everyone else
- we save lives, and are not involved in longer term development
- we help those in need irrespective of their situation or beliefs
- we are neutral, impartial and independent
- we do short-term emergency healthcare, and then hand over to the authorities or development agencies
- we provide specialist emergency medical care.

Appreciative inquiry is based on the assumption that we are free to choose which aspects of our experience we pay attention to. Elliot (1999: 12) suggests that one of the most important things that appreciative inquiry seeks to achieve is

> the transformation of a culture from one that sees itself in largely negative terms – and therefore *is inclined to become locked into its own negative construction of itself* – to one that sees itself as having within it the capacity to enrich and enhance the quality of life for all the stakeholders – *and therefore move toward this appreciative construction of itself.*

Elliot highlights the role of memory and imagination. Memory is important because every organization has a history, but this history is not an indisputable fact, it is an artefact of those who do the remembering. Organizational memory is based on how those who do the remembering interpret what happened, and one of the factors that influences their interpretations is where they are now and how they construct the present. Elliot (1999: 37) argues that it is this plasticity of memory and our freedom to remake the history of our organizations that are essential for the appreciative approach:

> For what is at stake is the capacity to construct a narrative of the organization that highlights the worthwhile and life-enriching themes without denying the darker

or more sombre tones that are likely to be present. It is only when we can read the history from this perspective that we are likely to transcend the problematic present or the fearsome future.

The way organizational members construct and reconstruct the present and the past is a prelude to the way they imagine the future. Appreciative inquiry does not promote the imagination of unachievable fantasies. It promotes the imagination of a future that is based on an extrapolation of the best of what is or has been.

Cooperrider (1990) maintains that one of the greatest obstacles to the wellbeing of an ailing group is the affirmative projection that currently guides that group. He argues that to affirm means to 'hold firm' and it is the strength of affirmation, 'the degree of belief or faith invested, that allows the imagery to carry out its heliotropic task'. He goes on to argue that when a group finds that its attempts to fix problems create more problems, or that the same problems never go away, the group's current affirmative projection is inadequate. Like Elliot, Cooperrider (1990) contends that 'every new affirmative projection of the future is a consequence of an appreciative understanding of the past or present'. We do not have to appreciate the present in terms that accentuate the negative. We can appreciate the present and build affirmative images of the future in terms that accentuate the positive. The heliotropic hypothesis posits that the future we imagine is the future we create. Strong affirmative images create a powerful 'pull effect' that can help the organization to evolve towards this more positive future.

Advocates of appreciative inquiry point to studies of the Pygmalion and placebo effects as sources of evidence that support the validity of the heliotropic hypothesis. The Pygmalion effect refers to the power of self-fulfilling prophesies. Many studies have shown that the performance of individuals and groups such as soldiers (Eden and Shani, 1982), trainee welders (King, 1970) and students (Rosenthal and Jacobson, 1968) is shaped by the expectations of others. Rosenthal and Jacobsen, for example, argue that teachers convey messages of expected success and failure to their students and their students live up to these expectations. However, we not only behave in response to the mental attitudes of those around us, especially those in authority over us, but we also behave in response to our own mental attitudes and expectations of ourselves. In the field of medicine, studies of the placebo effect have shown that those who expect an improvement in their condition are more likely to improve than those who expect no improvement. Similarly, those who remain hopeful and determined in extreme life-threatening circumstances are the ones who are most likely to survive. In other words, nothing succeeds like the expectation of success and nothing fails like the expectation of failure.

While this provides the basis for an attractive theory of intervention, Golembiewski (1999) sounds two notes of caution. The first concerns the outcome of appreciative inquiries. As predicted by the heliotropic hypothesis, social forms gravitate towards an imagined future that amplifies 'peak experiences' because people are motivated to move in that direction. People are less likely to resist this kind of change because, as Golembiewski says: 'You can catch more flies with honey than with vinegar.' However, the search for social forms faces a far larger issue than whether or not people are motivated to change. Golembiewski raises the question 'motivation for what purpose?' and notes that there are many examples where people have been motivated to level down human systems to the bestial (see, for example, Chang, 1997) as well as level them up to pursue some noble purpose. He advises that consultants should cultivate a sense of the difference: 'A powerful learning design may attract, but well-targeted ones make more progress, more safely, more of the time.' He acknowledges that appreciative inquiry can induce powerful forces but he is concerned that those who adopt a social constructionist view may pay insufficient attention to the normative character of the social form that is the imagined future: '[appreciative inquiry] in its dominant form assumes the social constructionist view that there is nothing special about any social form or norm'. This said, the evidence seems to indicate that appreciative inquiry not only engages the attention of organizational members but facilitates a process of organizational learning that moves the organization in a direction that yields benefits for all stakeholders.

His second note of caution relates to appreciative inquiry's apparent aversion to 'negative' stories. He suspects that this could encourage an incautious optimism about facts or beliefs. Elliot (1999), however, is less concerned. He argues that non-blaming, non-judgemental appreciative conversations enable people to acknowledge that the best is not the norm. For example, someone might describe an example of the best of what is and then go on to elaborate: 'But it isn't usually like this. Usually we spend too much time arguing or hating the other department, distrusting them, seeing what is bad about them.' While this kind of comment acknowledges deficiencies, it can facilitate positive thinking. Elliot (1999: 76) suggests that a skilled interviewer might achieve this be asking questions along the lines:

▶ 'What is special about the good times?
▶ What do you think you and your colleagues need to do or to be in order to be able to maximize the chances that the good times will become the norm?'

A methodology for intervening in organizations

The essence of appreciative inquiry is the generation of a shared image of a better future through a collective process of inquiry into the best of what is. It is this imagined future that provides the powerful pull effect that guides the development of the group or organization.

The critical part of the intervention is the inquiry. The mere act of asking questions begins the process of change. Based on the assumption that the things we choose to focus on and the questions we ask determine what we find, it follows that the more positive the questions, the more positive the data. And the more positive the data, the more positive the beliefs that people are likely to develop about what contributes to peak experiences. And the more positive these beliefs, the more positive the vision of the organization at its best. And the more positive this image is, the more energy it generates for change.

Bushe (1999) describes the process of appreciative inquiry as consisting of three parts:

▶ *Discovering the best of ...* involves discovering the best examples of organizing and organization within the experience of organizational members
▶ *Understanding what creates the best of ...* involves seeking insights into the forces that lead to superior performance and what it is about the people, the organization and the context that creates peak experiences at work
▶ *Amplifying the people or processes that exemplify the best of ...* involves reinforcing and amplifying those elements of the situation that contribute to superior performance.

A widely accepted methodology for discovering, understanding and amplifying the best of what is involves five steps, shown in Figure 20.1, and discussed in detail below.

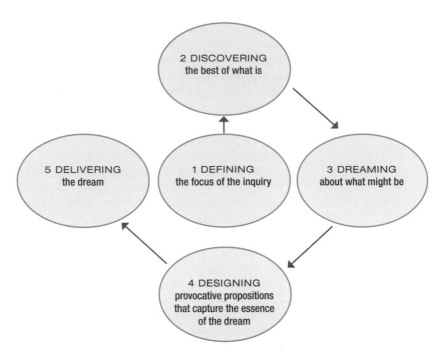

Figure 20.1 *The five steps of an appreciative inquiry*

Defining the focus of the inquiry

In the early 1990s, appreciative inquiry was often viewed as a macro-organizational intervention that studied the organization as a whole. More recently, however, the scope of appreciative inquiries has been extended to include more focused inquiries into issues such as retention, team building, leadership, customer service, conflict management, cross-gender relationships and culture change.

Defining the precise field of inquiry is often undertaken by some kind of steering group, possibly one that represents the different categories of organizational members who might be involved in the inquiry. The inquiry needs to be defined in a way that focuses attention on the positive rather than negative aspects of people's experience. For example, if an organization has an issue with high labour turnover, rather than focusing attention on why people leave, the inquiry might focus attention on why people choose to stay. Similarly, if there is an issue related to sexual harassment, rather than focusing on the problems associated with cross-gender interactions, the inquiry might focus on the conditions and factors that promote good cross-gender working relationships.

Discovering examples of excellence and achievement

Appreciative inquiry involves getting people to tell stories about the best of what is. It can involve pairs of people interviewing each other or a group of interviewers, each having appreciative conversations with 10 or 20 other people and then reporting their findings back to a core group. Whatever the format of the inquiry, interviewers need to be good listeners, able to attend to what others are saying and understand their thoughts and feelings from their perspective. They also need to be good at getting others to tell their stories of excellence and achievement. Key to this is the questions they ask. Whitney et al. (2002) have produced an *Encyclopedia of Positive Questions* that some practitioners might find helpful.

The questions the interviewer asks frame the way people look at an issue. Consider, for example, alternative ways of framing questions designed to discover the factors that contribute to good cross-gender working relationships. Even apparently neutral questions such as 'Tell me about male–female relationships here' may elicit stories about problems rather than about the best of what is. An alternative approach is to frame questions along the following lines.

▶ 'You have been identified as someone who has a good cross-gender relationship. Can you tell me about it, starting with how it began?'

This kind of opening question might be followed with questions such as:

▶ 'Reflect on your experience of this relationship. What have been the high points when you felt that the relationship was working well and you were making a real contribution to what the organization is trying to achieve?'
▶ 'Select an example of one of these high points and describe the circumstances: what were you doing, who was involved, what were they doing, what was the result, why did it feel good?'
▶ 'Tell me about another example.'

There is considerable evidence that people enjoy being interviewed appreciatively. It creates a feel-good experience but, as Bushe (1999) observes, care must be exercised to ensure that talking about peak experiences does not degenerate into social banter. The successful appreciative interview is one that provides at least one insight into the root causes of success. The interview needs to go beyond identifying what it is that works well and explore why it works well and how this success can be reinforced, amplified and extended to other parts of the organization.

A final step in this discovery phase involves sharing the stories that have been collected and identifying themes about the strengths of the organization. This can be done in a number of ways. Interviewers can verbally report their stories in an open meeting to all who have been involved in the inquiry process or they can share their stories with a core group that has been tasked to interpret the data and identify important themes. All those present can then be involved in a discussion of the stories to identify and reach a consensus about what the key themes are.

Bushe (1999) suggests that when there are lots of stories to review, organizing the data according to an 'inquiry matrix' can help to focus attention on themes relating to the purpose of the inquiry. He suggests that prior to data collection, the steering group might highlight the elements of the organization they want to attend to and amplify the best of, for example cross-gender working relationships, teamwork or customer service, and identify an organizational model they feel captures the major categories of organizing, for example structure, technology, culture, leadership, job design, rewards and so on. This information can be used to construct a matrix that can be used to categorize emerging themes from the stories. The matrix might be relatively simple and include, for example, cells for teamwork and structure, teamwork and technology, and teamwork and rewards, or it might be more complex and include a similar set of cells for other elements that may have been part of the inquiry, such as customer service.

An alternative but less structured approach, similar to one reported by Elliot (1999), involves each member of the core group of interviewers reviewing a sample of written reports of the appreciative conversations in their own time and then coming together to agree key themes. In the case reported by Elliot, a core group of 10 had conducted 100 interviews. In order to manage the workload, 3 members of the group read all 100 reports and everybody else read and analysed 10 reports plus the 10 reports of the interviews they had conducted. To aid their analysis, the facilitator, who had been closely involved with every stage of the inquiry, distributed a list of issues he thought might emerge as key themes. This kind of list provides a category set that group members can use to help them to identify key themes, but it is important they do not feel that they must restrict themselves to simply testing the validity of this suggested list. If the inquiry is to be an inclusive and collaborative process, everybody must feel free to identify other clusters of statements that might suggest alternative themes. Members bring their impressions of the content of the reports to a meeting and share and discuss their findings until they are able to agree a list of key themes that reflect the positive present and past.

Dreaming about what might be

Drawing on these themes to inspire a vision of a more positive future is the essence of the dreaming phase. Organizational members are encouraged to envision what the future might be like if the best of what is or has been became the new norm. Elliot (1999: 137) provides the following guidance to those who are involved with analysing the stories of excellence and achievement:

> You are looking for repeated themes which, together, point to a possibility that currently lies just outside the grasp of the company. You are *not* looking for a majority view nor a way-out odd-ball, but for a gathering set of ideas that, pulled together, given coherence and shape, will command an 'Ah, yes …' from a large majority of stakeholders who will recognise it as building on the best of the past but unlocking a new future.

Elliot suggests that despite all the emphasis in the literature on visioning, relatively few organizational members believe that their imagination is a significant resource that they can bring to the workplace. Consequently, many employees do not do much of it as part of their everyday work activity. He goes on to argue that imagination is like many of our faculties, from memory to muscles – if they are not used, they wither. It is possible, therefore, that some organizational members may need to be helped and encouraged in order to use their imagination to envision a more positive future. Elliot suggests some 'warm-up' exercises that might help people gain the confidence to envision new possibilities. These include asking people if they have ever visited another organization and seen things they would like to introduce here, or asking them, if one of their grandchildren were eventually to work here, what they would hope it might be like for them.

When organizational members have arrived at a consensus about their preferred future, the process moves on to the design phase.

Designing provocative propositions that will achieve the dream

In order to facilitate the achievement of the vision, it has to be translated into a set of statements of intent. These are 'provocative propositions' that will stretch organizational members and show them the way to an achievable preferred future.

Designing the provocative propositions typically generates considerable energy and involvement and it is through the dialogue associated with testing, redrafting and refining them that the possibilities for amplifying the best of the present and past are realized.

If the provocative propositions have been developed by a subgroup, it is essential that they are presented to and validated by other organizational members, thus widening the net of those involved in the dialogue. Bushe (1999) suggests that when many people need to be involved, it is possible to test the propositions using an organizational survey. Alongside each proposition there might be questions such as: 'To what extent do you believe this proposition is an important component of the topic under study?' and 'To what extent do you believe the organization exemplifies the proposition?' He argues that simply filling out the questionnaire can generate energy and do a lot towards spreading the ideas across the organization. People are encouraged to reflect on future possibilities and debate them with others. Communicating the results of the survey and informing everybody about the strength of feeling regarding each proposition can also stimulate action, licensing organizational members to begin implementing the propositions in their everyday work.

These provocative propositions are design principles that can be used to identify the structures, processes and practices that will move the organization towards the 'dream'. Finegold et al. (2002) describe them as filters that can be used to evaluate any proposed changes.

Delivering the dream

Guided by the design principles embedded in the provocative propositions, the system (group or organization) is propelled to fulfil its destiny. Sometimes those leading the inquiry help organizational members to write implementation strategies and action plans and develop scorecards or other procedures for monitoring progress. However, amplifying the best of what is and moving the organization towards a more positive future do not necessarily require those leading the appreciative inquiry to get involved with the details of implementation. While there are some who see this as important, most practitioners restrict their involvement to the point where organizational members develop and validate their vision. If the vision and its associated provocative propositions are sufficiently compelling, they not only generate the energy for change but also provide the guiding focus for individual and group initiatives and action taking across the organization.

Joep de Jong, a Dutch consultant interviewed by Elliot (1999), offers a slightly different perspective. He observes that once organizational members move back into their normal day-to-day roles, they may not find it easy to use the provocative propositions to steer their every action, but they may frequently use them as an encouragement to get back into the appreciative way of thinking. While it can be difficult to constantly pursue the realization of the provocative propositions, the process of developing them changes their way of conceiving of themselves, their colleagues and their organization. This, according to de Jong, changes their day-to-day work in a manner that makes it more probable that the essence of the provocative proposition will become reality.

Dick (2004) draws attention to a number of publications that practitioners might find useful when designing appreciative inquiries. Cooperrider et al. (2003) have published the *Appreciative Inquiry Handbook* that provides a practical guide and rich collection of resources, and Whitney and Trosten Bloom (2003) have produced what Dick describes as a practical and informative introduction to appreciative inquiry 'suitable for novices'.

Applications

Appreciative inquiry has been used in a wide range of different situations. Sorensen et al. (2003), after reviewing 350 papers on appreciative inquiry, report that there is considerable evidence pointing to its successful application in many settings. Projects vary in terms of scale, organizational context and focus. Elliot (1999) presents a detailed account of an appreciative inquiry with a private healthcare provider in the UK and several accounts of the use of appreciative inquiry to develop communities in developing countries. The interventions he describes extend over relatively long periods and involve a considerable investment of time on the part of members of the core work group. This contrasts with Jeop de Jong's much shorter (two-day) interventions with three secondary schools that had to merge and with two fast-growing computer dealers who were also involved in a merger (see Elliot, 1999).

Zemke (1999) refers to a number of large-scale projects. An appreciative inquiry at Nutrimental Foods in Brazil involved 700 stakeholders interviewing each other over the course of half a day, after which, over a period of four days, 150 of them used the data generated from these interviews to develop a new corporate vision. He reports that this led to three new business initiatives and a massive increase in sales. In Chicago, a project involved 4,000 school children conducting one million 'peak experience' interviews with older city residents to vision what the city could be like if the norm became Chicago at its best. Avon had a problem with male–female relationships and used appreciative inquiry to address the issue. Following a request on the company's email system for male–female pairs who believed they exemplified high-quality communication in the workplace, 15 pairs were selected to interview 300 other exemplary pairs. Their stories were used to generate 30 principles for positive cross-gender working relationships.

Finegold et al. (2002) describe an appreciative inquiry in a midwestern university. It started with 400 members of the administrative and finance division being asked, in pairs, to reflect on their whole span of employment at the university and tell each other a story about a peak experience, a time when they felt most energized, alive and valued. They were then invited to tell each other what they valued about themselves, their work and the university and to think about the way they wanted the university to be. For many, it was the first time they had been invited to give voice to their hopes and visions. They were able to present propositions for staff training and development and for better communication between departments and senior management. The intervention was so successful that it became the methodology for annual strategic planning in the division and eventually developed into a university-wide process where the focus was 'Discovering the power of partnership: Building a University-wide community to advance to the next tier of nationally recognized excellence.'

Example 20.2

Using collective inquiry for organization development at Médecins Sans Frontières

Médecins Sans Frontières' secretary general has launched an organization-wide programme to 'unlock potential'. Eight cross-functional working groups have been set up to look at how the organization functions and identify what MSF is best at doing in order to consolidate successes as a basis for levering further development.

The discovery phase involved the eight working groups collecting information, through interviews and surveys, and cascading this approach down the organization in order to ensure that everybody had the chance to contribute to defining best practice and developing ideas ('dreaming') about how to evolve new practices and procedures that will enable MSF to respond to new challenges.

MSF adopted this approach because it wanted to maintain its passion, maverick character and ability to go against the grain and help where others won't or can't. Appreciative inquiry was seen as a way of protecting these assets, and not stifling or suffocating them by pursuing a top-down, problem-centred approach. Senior managers recognize the need to further professionalize, but not at the expense of its culture and principles.

Bushe (1998) describes the use of appreciative inquiry in the context of team development. His basic approach involves asking team members to recall their best team experience. Each member, in turn, describes their best team experience and other members are encouraged to question the focal person about what it was about the person, situation and task that contributed to the peak experience. When everybody has told their stories, the group reviews the stories and tries to reach a consensus on the attributes of highly effective teams. His final step involves members mapping these attributes onto their experience with their current team, acknowledging anything they have seen in others that has helped the group to be like any of the listed attributes and identifying possibilities for amplifying these attributes. This approach can be applied to new teams as well as existing teams, because even though members of a new team may not have much, if any, shared experience, everybody will be able to talk about some examples of best team experiences in other contexts. Bushe (1998) actually recommends that members of ongoing teams do not use examples of best team experiences drawn from their experience with the current group because it is likely that members may recall the same experience and, after it has been talked about a few times, the process may lose steam.

Change tool 20.1	Using appreciative inquiry to clarify values at Hammersmith Hospital NHS Trust

Using appreciative inquiry to clarify values at Hammersmith Hospital NHS Trust

The chief executive of the trust wanted to create a vision for the future and develop a clear strategy based on the values of the organization. The problem was that nobody knew what the values were. It is not unusual in this kind of situation for the top team to get together and come up with a list of values they think should be part of the organization's culture, but adopting this approach provides no guarantee that the values will be owned by employees across the organization. The new head of organization development persuaded the chief executive to conduct a study to find out what members of the organization actually valued. They did this using appreciative inquiry.

A steering group was established to design the inquiry. It was agreed that exploring what happens when the organization works at its best would provide useful insights into what members valued, and it was decided to do this by inviting people from across the organization to participate in a series of workshops. Thirty 'project champions' were asked to use their personal networks to encourage people to take part. There were some reservations that people might view the inquiry as a bit 'happy-clappy' and that it would not be well received by staff who value a scientific approach to their work, but this was not a problem – 560 people attended 40 workshops.

Members of the trust were trained as internal facilitators to lead the 40 one-hour 'discovery' workshops. Between 12 and 14 people attended each workshop along with two facilitators. Each workshop started with tea and biscuits to create a relaxed atmosphere while the facilitators explained the purpose of the inquiry and what would happen over the next hour. Everybody was invited to introduce themselves (name and department) but not status. Hospitals can be hierarchical organizations and those leading the inquiry did not want this to get in the way.

Participants were invited to turn to interview the person sitting next to them for 10–15 minutes. A interviewed B and then switched roles. The interview questions were:

1 'Reflecting back over your time with the trust, please tell us a story about when you felt most alive, excited or committed about being part of a team or the trust as a whole.'

Interviewers were advised to listen carefully to:
- what made the story an exciting experience
- what factors contributed to making it a significant experience
- what was the interviewee's contribution?

2 'Without being too humble or modest (feel free to boast), what do you value most about yourself as a person and your work at the trust?'

Interviewers were advised to help the interviewee to stay positive and encourage them to focus on strengths and values, not their weaknesses. Ruth Dunlop, who led the inquiry, found that people often said 'I am good at this but I need to improve that', probably because this is the kind of response that most appraisal processes encourage.

3 'Based on your answers to the last question, could you give examples of how these values are demonstrated in the way you and others behave in the trust?'

Interviewers were advised to focus on concrete behaviours. For example, 'I value honesty in myself. This means that in practice I am open with my team and patients when breaking bad news.'

These first three questions were clearly focused on 'discovery'. The final question invited participants to engage in some 'dreaming'.

4 'If you had just one wish that would improve how we deliver care for patients, what would it be?'

Participants were asked to make a note of keywords and a brief account of each story, and in the last part of the workshop, they were invited to go round the table and share what they had talked about.

After the workshops, the keywords and stories were typed up and the facilitators were invited to a meeting to review the stories and tease out the main themes. These were recorded on flip charts. Later, Ruth Dunlop and Eleanor Murray reviewed the flip charts and distilled out four values and associated behaviours. The four values were the centrality of patients, the importance of team working in delivering high-quality healthcare, an energized atmosphere, and an emphasis on innovation. These were communicated back to members of the organization at normal team meetings to check that these four values did indeed reflect what staff felt was important. Finally, the values were reported to the top team for endorsement and were then communicated across the whole organization via leaflets, posters and a DVD about the four values for team discussion.

It will be evident from the examples of applications presented above that appreciative inquiry can be adapted to provide a methodology for intervening in many different settings and for addressing a range of different issues.

Summary

This chapter has examined appreciate inquiry from three perspectives.

1 A philosophy of knowledge linked to social constructionist theory:
   - reality is a social construction
   - everything we experience and encounter is open to multiple interpretations
   - perceptions of reality are the product of dialogue and interaction
   - the way we behave is influenced by how we see the world (construct reality).

Many people perceive organizational life as problematic and focus their attention on 'problems to be solved'. This belief promotes a deficiency perspective. An alternative belief is that organizations are 'possibilities to be embraced'. Beliefs (social constructions) about organizations are open to revision and this revision can be facilitated by a process of collective inquiry.

2 An intervention theory:
   - the 'heliotropic hypothesis' – organizations, like plants, evolve towards the light that gives them energy (this can be the most positive images held by members)

- interventions that promote a conscious evolution of positive imagery offer a basis for changing organizations for the better
- appreciative inquiry is based on the assumption that we are free to choose which aspects of reality we pay attention to
- appreciative inquiry seeks to achieve: 'The transformation of a culture from one that sees itself in largely negative terms – and therefore *is inclined to be locked into its own negative construction of itself* – to one that sees itself as having within it the capacity to enrich and enhance the quality of life for all stakeholders – *and therefore move towards an appreciative construction of itself*' (Elliot, 1999: 12).

3 A methodology for intervening in organizations

Appreciative inquiry is a process that involves exploring the best of what is and amplifying this best practice. The essence of appreciative inquiry is the generation of a shared image of a better future – 'What would the future be like if the best of what is became the norm?' Whereas action research promotes learning through attending to dysfunctional aspects of organizational functioning, appreciative inquiry seeks to accentuate the positive rather than eliminate the negative. Attention is given to:

- discovering the best of ...
- understanding what creates the best of ...
- amplifying the people or processes that create the best of ... .

The chapter ends with a number of examples of how appreciative inquiry has been used in a variety of settings.

References

Bushe, G.R. (1998) Appreciative inquiry with teams, *Organization Development Journal*, **16**(3): 41–9.

Bushe, G.R. (1999) Advances in appreciative inquiry as an organization development intervention, *Organization Development Journal*, **17**(2): 61–8.

Chang, I. (1997) *The Rape of Nanking*, New York: Basic Books.

Cooperrider, D. (1990) Positive image, positive action: the affirmative basis of organizing, in S. Srivastva and D.L. Cooperrider (eds) *Appreciative Management and Leadership*, San Francisco, CA: Jossey-Bass.

Cooperrider, D. and Srivastva, S. (1987) Appreciative inquiry in organizational life, *Research in Organizational Change and Development*, 1: 129–69.

Cooperrider, D., Whitney, D. and Stavros, J. (2003) *Appreciative Inquiry Handbook*, San Francisco, CA: Berrett-Koehler.

Dick, B. (2004) Action research literature: trends and themes, *Action Research*, **2**(4): 425–44.

Dixon, N. (1997) The hallways of learning, *Organizational Dynamics*, **25**(4): 23–34.

Eden, D. and Shani, A.B. (1982) Pygmalion goes to boot camp: expectancy, leadership, and trainee performance, *Journal of Applied Psychology*, 67: 194–9.

Elliot, C. (1999) *Locating the Energy for Change: An Introduction to Appreciative Inquiry*, Winnipeg: International Institute for Sustainable Development.

Finegold, M.A., Holland, B.M. and Lingham, T. (2002) Appreciative inquiry and public dialogue: an approach to community change, *Public Organization Review*, 2: 235–52.

Golembiewski, R.T. (1999) Fine-tuning appreciative inquiry: two ways of circumscribing the concept's value-added, *Organization Development Journal*, **17**(3): 21–6.

King, A.S. (1970) Managerial relations with disadvantaged work groups: supervisory expectations of the underprivileged worker, PhD dissertation, Texas Tech University.

Rosenthal, R. and Jacobson, L. (1968) *Pygmalion Effect in the Classroom: Teachers' Expectations and Pupil Intellectual Development*, New York: Holt, Rinehart and Winston.

Sorensen, P.E., Yaeger, T.F. and Bengtsson, U. (2003) The promise of appreciative inquiry: a 20-year review, *OD Practitioner*, **35**(4): 15–21.

Srivastva, S. and Cooperrider, D. (1990) *Appreciative Management and Leadership: The Power of Positive Thought and Action in Organizations*, San Francisco, CA: Jossey-Bass.

Whitney, D., Cooperrider, D., Trosten-Bloom, A. and Kaplan, B.S. (2002) *Encyclopedia of Positive Questions*, vol. 1: *Using Appreciative Inquiry to Bring Out the Best in your Organisation*, Euclid, OH: Lakeshore Communications.

Whitney, D. and Trosten-Bloom, A. (2003) *The Power of Appreciative Inquiry: A Practical Guide to Positive Change*, San Francisco, CA: Berrett-Koehler.

Zemke, R. (1999) Don't fix the company, *Training*, **36**(6): 26–34.

chapter
21
Training and development

Organizational change is typically associated with some degree of individual change. Often this individual change is the outcome of an informal and natural process of learning and development. However, there may be occasions when those responsible for managing an organizational change decide that some form of deliberate training intervention is required in order to help individuals to develop new knowledge, skills, attitudes and behaviours. Such interventions can be highly structured and very focused on the achievement of closely specified outcomes, or they can be designed to help organizational members learn how to learn and encourage them to actively involve themselves in a self-directed process of professional development.

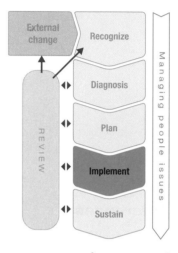

Training interventions tend to be targeted at two main types of organizational member. On the one hand, there are those who are required to perform new roles associated with managing the change. They may require training, for example, in order to lead a task force charged with diagnosing organizational problems and identifying what needs to be changed. On the other hand, there are those who, as a result of the change, will be required to behave differently and may require training in order to be able to achieve new standards of performance.

This chapter will consider, briefly, how training can help to re-establish alignment between the competencies of organizational members and other elements of the system such as task and structure. Attention will also be given to the main aspects of a systematic approach to the development of effective training interventions. The final section will review some Australian studies that have investigated recent trends in the provision of training.

Achieving a match between organizational members and changing task demands

When change calls for new behaviours on the part of organizational members, a number of factors will determine whether or not these new behaviours will be forthcoming. These include the quality of the match between competencies and task demands, the effect of reward systems on the motivation to deliver revised performance outcomes, and the availability of feedback to enable individuals and their managers to assess whether the new performance standards are being achieved. This chapter is concerned with the first of these.

Sometimes organizational members will already possess all the competencies they require in order to achieve the new performance standards. All that such people will need, in terms of their ability to perform in new ways, is information about the revised performance outcomes that they will have to achieve.

At other times the people affected by the change may not posses the competencies they will need. In these circumstances, a number of options may be available to those managing the change. They may explore ways of redesigning the task to match the existing competencies of organizational members, replace existing staff with others who already have the required competencies or help existing staff to acquire the required new competencies.

A systematic approach to training

Goldstein (1993) and others argue that effective training involves three main steps: the analysis of training needs, the design and delivery of training and the evaluation of training effectiveness, which are now discussed.

Training needs analysis

A training needs analysis also involves three steps: systems-level review, task analysis and person analysis.

Systems-level review

A systems-level review determines how the proposed change will affect organizational goals, objectives and task demands. This overview provides the information necessary to identify where more specific task and person analyses are required. For example, the move from an optical to a digital scanning technology in the reprographics equipment sector changed the nature of the tasks performed by many organizational units. In this case, a system-level review might have pointed to a need for a more detailed analysis in departments such as product design, assembly, technical support, sales and so on. However, in other departments, such as finance, the system-level review might have identified few implications for the nature of the task performed and the competencies required.

Task analysis

A task analysis focuses on specific jobs or roles and examines how modifications to the task of a unit will affect the nature of the performance that will be demanded from members of that unit. It also points to the competencies – knowledge, skills, attitudes or behaviour – that people performing these new or modified roles will require in order to perform to the new standard. Elaborating the example of the reprographics equipment manufacturer, a task analysis of, for example, the selling function might have revealed how the introduction of digital scanning technology changed the nature of the performance required by salespeople to sell digital as opposed to optical reprographics equipment.

Person analysis

A person analysis seeks to identify discrepancies between the required competencies, as determined by the task analysis, and the existing competencies of the organizational members available to perform these revised tasks. This analysis provides the information necessary to identify which individuals or groups will require training and specify training objectives in terms of what trainees need to know and how they will be required to behave.

The most useful way of expressing training objectives is in terms of behavioural objectives that specify what trainees will be able to do after training. For example, some of the training objectives for the reprographics equipment sales representatives might include being able to:

▶ accurately describe how the new technology affects the performance of the new range of copiers produced by the company
▶ demonstrate to customers how to maintain the equipment to keep it operating at peak efficiency.

The design and delivery of training

Smith (1991) suggests that the choice of training method should, at least in part, be determined by the kinds of competencies that the training is designed to impart. For example, where the aim is to impart knowledge and information, some of the most effective training methods might include lectures and reading books and manuals. Where the focus is attitudes, the most effective methods might include role play or informal discussion groups. Where the aim is to develop cognitive strategies, case studies, simulations, projects or mentoring might be used. Where the focus is perceptual and motor skills, a variety of methods might be considered. These could include the discrimination method, which is designed to help trainees detect differences between items that are very similar, and the progressive parts method, which is a schedule for organizing the practice of complex motor skills.

Reid and Barrington (1999) classify training methods under five main headings: on-the-job training; planned organization experience; in-house courses; planned experience outside the organization; and external courses. They recommend four criteria to determine which of these strategies will be most appropriate:

1 compatibility with training objectives
2 estimated likelihood of transfer of learning to the work situation
3 availability of resources, such as time, money and skilled staff
4 trainee-related factors.

These criteria can be used, for example, to help identify an effective way of training members of a new change project team. Each is now discussed in turn.

Compatibility with training objectives

The training objectives for the members of the new project team might include:

▶ *imparting knowledge,* so that trainees will understand, be able to describe to others and recognize actions that will help achieve the aims of the change programme
▶ *developing positive attitudes,* so that trainees will be committed to the aims of the programme and to working constructively with other members of the team to achieve these aims
▶ *developing group process skills,* so that trainees will be able to diagnose what is going on in the group and act in ways that will contribute to group effectiveness.

The change manager might quickly reject some methods because they are incompatible with the training objectives and may recognize that others may only be used after adaptation.

On-the-job training might be rejected because there may be no project teams currently operating in the company that could provide relevant on-the-job work experience.

External courses, such as outward bound-type team training, might offer a good way of developing positive attitudes towards colleagues and developing group process skills. However, in order to satisfy some to the other training needs, the change agent or somebody else from the company would have to be involved and the course would have to be adapted to provide some sessions that deal with the aims of the change programme. This would also require the external course to be restricted to managers from the one company and to those managers who will have to work together in the new project team.

A specially designed in-company course might be an attractive option. It could include a mix of formal inputs on the aims of the change programme, informal discussion sessions to explore trainees' reactions to these aims, and group activities that could be used as a vehicle for developing group process skills.

Transfer of learning

In terms of the transfer of learning, both the external course, if it were restricted to prospective members of the project team, and the in-house course could facilitate the transfer of group process skills and positive attitudes towards other trainees to the work situation. The in-house course could also score high on the transfer of learning if the group activities involved working on real issues that the team would have to deal with once it 'went live'.

Availability of resources

In terms of the availability of resources, time might be a factor that would preclude the use of internal or external planned work experience. Also cost, in terms of money in the budget rather than the opportunity cost of the change agent's time, might be a factor that would work against an expensive external course. The in-house course might cost less but the change agent would have to find the time to develop the training materials and the work-related group activities. The change agent may be confident that they have the necessary skills to design and deliver the in-house programme. They might also be aware of an external consultant who could be employed to help at a fee that would be considerably less than the cost of the external course.

Trainee-related factors

In terms of trainee-related factors, from a business perspective, it may be impossible to release all the managers at the same time to participate in a week-long external course. Also, for domestic reasons, some members of the proposed project team may find it difficult to be away from home for a whole week.

Taking into account all these factors, the change agent may opt for the in-house course, which could, if necessary, be scheduled as a series of short modules to fit in with the availability of trainees.

The evaluation of training effectiveness

The role of evaluation in the context of change management will be discussed in some detail in Chapter 29, together with some of the issues that can affect the validity of evaluation exercises. The focus of attention here is the kinds of criteria that can be used when evaluating the effectiveness of training interventions. Aguinis and Kraiger (2009) note that Kirkpatrick's (1983) four-level approach to training evaluation continues to be the most widely used training evaluation model among practitioners:

1 At level one, the criterion is how trainees *reacted* to the training. Did they feel it was relevant, interesting, demanding and so on?

2 At level two, the criterion is *what they learned*. It is not unknown for trainees to react favourably to the training but to learn relatively little, or only achieve acceptable standards of learning in respect of some, but not all, of the learning goals. This kind of feedback has obvious implications for those responsible for selecting and designing the details of the learning activity.

3 At level three, the criterion is *behaviour*. Trainees may have reacted positively to the training and learned what it was intended they should learn. However, back on the job, their behaviour may have changed little, if at all. In other words, what was learned on the course may not have been transferred to the work situation. It is relatively easy to apply the relevant principles of learning to design a training activity that will encourage learning. It is much more difficult to design a training activity that will ensure that the learning is transferred and used in the work situation. A common problem that inhibits transfer is the social pressure that trainees are subjected to after they return from training. While they may have learned best practice when on the course, back on the job, colleagues often pressure them to revert back to the traditional ways of working.

4 At level four, the criterion is *results*. It is possible for the training to produce the intended changes in behaviour, but this behaviour change may not produce the intended results. Sales representatives may have started to call more regularly on customers but this may not produce the increase in sales that had been anticipated. This kind of feedback indicates a need for a fundamental rethink of the training strategy.

Training for change: the Australian experience

Studies in several countries have found that organizational change is closely associated with the level of training activity in organizations (Cappelli and Rogovsky, 1994; Osterman, 1995). Smith (2005) reviewed two major studies of enterprise-level training in Australia that confirm this relationship (Research reports 21.1 and 21.2).

Research report 21.1 | ### Enterprise-level training in Australia

Smith, A. and Hayton, G. (1999) What drives enterprise training? Evidence from Australia, *International Journal of Human Resource Management*, **10**(2): 251–72

Smith and Hayton investigated the drivers of enterprise-level training. Their research involved 42 case studies in five industry sectors – construction, electronic manufacturing, food processing, retail and financial services – and a national survey of 1,760 organizations across all sectors.

In terms of the systematic approach to training outlined in this chapter, they found evidence that organizations did adopt some form of training needs analysis and in many cases this was based on a system of performance appraisal. However, the evaluation of training was relatively underdeveloped. None of the case study organizations went much beyond the use of traditional end-of-course evaluation forms.

Senior managers in some organizations adopted a proactive strategic approach to training and viewed it as a vehicle for building skill sets that could provide the basis for sustainable competitive advantage, but attitudes towards training were often fragmented, and middle and junior managers tended to be more reactive and viewed training as a short, sharp, focused response to immediate operational problems. These included workplace change, quality improvement and new technology.

Workplace change was the most important driver for change. New technology was less important than anticipated. The introduction of new products frequently required only minimum changes to existing production processes and could be introduced with little additional training. New production processes, on the other hand, often involved fundamental changes to the way work was carried out and therefore triggered a more extensive need for training. However, the required training was often short and simple and was frequently outsourced to the vendors of the new process technology.

New forms of work organization and structural change accounted for most of the increase in training activity and emphasized behavioural rather than traditional technical skills. Smith and Hayton suggest that this shift towards behavioural skills training reflects a growing concern in Australian enterprises to develop adaptability to changes in work organization.

Research report 21.2

Relationship between enterprise-level training and organizational change

Smith, A., Oczkowski, E., Noble, C. and Macklin, R. (2003) New management practices and enterprise training in Australia, *International Journal of Manpower*, **24**(1): 31–47

The study involved a survey of 3,415 HR managers and follow-up interviews with 78 of them.

While training activity was clearly associated with the introduction of new management practices, such as total quality management (TQM), team working and business process re-engineering, few of the managers surveyed felt that training had played a major role in the implementation of change. Typically, training played a 'catch-up role', dealing with the consequences of change rather than playing a major role in its planning or implementation.

Findings relating to the kind of training associated with the introduction of new management practices confirm the move away from technical skills to a new training paradigm that emphasizes the development of broad sets of generic behavioural skills. For example, the introduction of TQM involves the implementation of team working, the development of interpersonal and problem-solving skills and, especially in service industries, customer service skills. There is also a requirement to train large numbers of staff in specific TQM skills such as data collection and analysis.

Team working had been introduced by about two-thirds of the organizations included in the survey and was clearly linked to an increase in training activity. Training was focused on team-working skills for team members and management training for more senior staff.

Banker et al. (1996) found that training is a key determinant of the success and longevity of teams. Team working often changes the role of the supervisor or involves people being appointed to a new role of team leader. This calls for training to help leaders facilitate their teams. Team members may also receive training in group process skills and training to cover jobs other than their own and/or to take on greater responsibility for their work.

One new management practice that was not always associated with an increase in training activity was the introduction of lean production. Smith et al. (2003) found that lean production was consistently associated with cost cutting and this included measures to cut the cost of training. Typically, the level of formal training and the level of training infrastructure (training facilities and dedicated training staff) were reduced. Most of the training that was undertaken tended to be on the job and skewed in favour of managers.

The studies undertaken by Smith and Hayton (1999) and Smith et al. (2003) provide an overview of enterprise-level training in Australia from 1994 to 2003. This was a period of rapid change, because from the early 1980s, companies operating in Australia have been exposed to increasing levels of international and domestic competition. A number of trends in the development of enterprise-level training emerged from these studies.

The first relates to the link between training and business strategy. Notwithstanding the finding reported by Smith et al. (2003) that training did not play a major role in the planning and implementation of change, Smith (2005) reports that there has been an increase in the number of organizations that are conscious of the need to link training to business strategy if they are to capitalize more effectively on their investment in training. He notes that where enterprises have made this link, the result has been a substantial increase in all forms of training and a greater embedding of training into the management of the enterprise.

The second trend relates to the individualization of training. There has been a shift away from delivery methods that impose uniform training programmes on large groups of employees towards a more focused training provision linked to individual performance management. This trend has been associated with the demise of large centralized training departments and the devolution of responsibility for training to line managers.

Finally, much of the growth in training activity has involved the development of broad sets of generic behavioural skills rather than technical skills and has been linked to the introduction of new management practices.

Another trend identified by studies in Australia and elsewhere is that the scale of the training input often requires the use of non-training specialists, which in turn requires the provision of trainer training programmes.

Exercise 21.1 — Assessing the way training is used in the change process

Reflect on either an organization-wide change or a change targeted at a particular department or unit in your organization.

Consider the following points and then make a brief assessment of the way training was used to help achieve change:

- Was there any evidence indicating that the organization and/or particular change managers were prepared to invest in training to support change?
- Was the attention given to training inadequate, about right or 'over the top'?
- Was the training targeted at the individuals and groups most in need of training?
- Was the training that was provided compatible with training requirements and delivered in a way that maximized the transfer of learning to the work situation?

Assessment of the way training was used to help achieve change

Summary

Organizational change is typically associated with some degree of individual change. Often this individual change is the outcome of an informal and natural process of learning and development. However, there may be occasions when those responsible for managing the change decide that some form of deliberate training intervention is required in order to help individuals to develop new knowledge, skills, attitudes and behaviours.

This chapter has considered how training can help to re-establish alignment between the competencies of organizational members and other elements of the system such as task and structure. Attention has been directed towards the main elements of an effective approach to training. These are a training needs analysis, design and delivery of the training intervention and the evaluation of the training.

1 The training needs analysis involves three steps:
- *Systems-level review:* This investigates how the proposed change will affect organizational goals, objectives and task demands. This overview provides the information necessary to identify where more specific task and person analyses are required.
- *Task analysis:* This focuses on specific jobs or roles and examines how modifications to the task of a unit will affect the nature of the performance that will be demanded from members of that unit. It also points to the competencies (knowledge, skills, attitudes or behaviour) that people performing these new or modified roles will require in order to perform to the new standard.
- *Person analysis:* This step seeks to identify discrepancies between the required competencies, as determined by the task analysis, and the existing competencies of the organizational members available to perform these revised tasks.

The most useful way of expressing training objectives is in terms of behavioural objectives that specify what trainees will be able to do after training.

2 The design and delivery of training
The choice of training strategies, for example on-the-job training, private study, internal and external placements, in-house and external courses, will depend on:
- compatibility with training objectives – knowledge, skills, attitudes
- likelihood that learning will be transferred to job – individual or work group focus and relevance of training content
- available resources
- trainee-related factors – availability, domestic considerations.

3 The evaluation of the training
The effectiveness of training can be evaluated at four levels:
- how trainees reacted to the training
- what they learned
- whether the training changed their behaviour as intended
- the impact of new behaviours on performance.

The final section of this chapter has reviewed the development of training practice in Australia over a 10-year period and highlighted a number of trends in training provision.

References

Aguinis, H. and Kraiger, K. (2009) Benefits of training and development for individuals and teams, organizations, and society, *Annual Review of Psychology*, 60: 451–74.

Banker, R.D., Field, J.M., Schroeder, R.D. and Sinha, K.K. (1996) Impact of work teams on manufacturing performance: a longitudinal field study, *Academy of Management Journal*, **39**(4): 867–90.

Cappelli, P. and Rogovsky, N. (1994) New work systems and skill requirements, *International Labour Review*, **133**(2): 205–20.

Goldstein, I.L. (1993) *Training in Organisations* (3rd edn), Monterey, CA: Brooks/Cole.

Kirkpatrick, D.L. (1983) Four steps in measuring training effectiveness, *Personnel Administrator*, **28**(11): 19–25.

Osterman, P. (1995) Skill, training and work organisation in American establishments, *Industrial Relations*, **34**(2): 125–46.

Reid, M. and Barrington, H. (1999) *Training Interventions*, London: Institute of Personnel and Development.

Smith, A. (2005) The development of employer training in Australia, discussion paper, Charles Sturt University, Australia.

Smith, A. and Hayton, G. (1999) What drives enterprise training? Evidence from Australia, *International Journal of Human Resource Management*, **10**(2): 251–72.

Smith, A., Oczkowski, E., Noble, C. and Macklin, R. (2003) New management practices and enterprise training in Australia, *International Journal of Manpower*, **24**(1): 31–47.

Smith, M. (1991) Training in organisations, in M. Smith (ed.) *Analysing Organizational Behaviour*, Basingstoke: Macmillan – now Palgrave Macmillan.

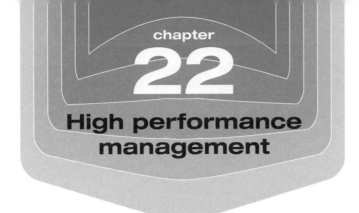

High performance management

'High commitment', 'high involvement' and 'high performance' are terms that are often used interchangeably to refer to an approach to managing an organization's human resources (HR) that involves employing HR practices to achieve sustainable improvements in productivity and financial performance.

Rather than focusing on separate HR practices, high performance management involves developing and implementing a 'bundle' or system of HR practices that are internally consistent, aligned with other business processes, and aligned with the organization's business strategy. It is an approach to improving organizational performance that is consistent with open

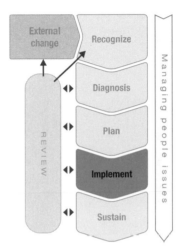

systems thinking and the concept of 'fit' discussed in Chapter 5.

Bailey (1993) contends that human resources are frequently underutilized because employees perform below their maximum potential. High performance management seeks to improve performance through HR practices that elicit discretionary efforts from employees.

MacDuffie (1995) argues that high performance management systems can contribute to improved economic performance when:

▶ employees possess knowledge and skill that managers lack
▶ employees are motivated to apply this skill and knowledge through discretionary effort
▶ the organization's business strategy can only be achieved when employees contribute such discretionary effort.

He goes on to argue that skilled and knowledgeable workers who are not motivated are unlikely to contribute any discretionary effort, and motivated workers who lack knowledge and skill may contribute discretionary effort, but with little effect on performance.

Soft and hard models of human resource management

Walton (1985) identified two profoundly different approaches to human resource management (HRM): one based on imposing control and the other on eliciting commitment. This distinction is similar to that made by Truss et al. (1997) when they referred to 'hard' (control) and 'soft' (commitment) strategies when investigating

HRM practice in eight organizations in the UK. Arthur (1992) found empirical support for Walton's control and commitment categorization when he studied HR policies and practices in 30 US steel minimills. He identified six clusters of practices that could be grouped under two broad headings, cost reduction and commitment maximization. These approaches are based on fundamentally different views about human nature and the most effective way of exercising control.

The cost reduction or control approach

The cost reduction or control approach focuses on the use of controls to reduce direct labour costs and improve efficiency. This is achieved by enforcing compliance through the application of specific rules and procedures. It is an approach that shares many of the assumptions that underpin Beer's economic change strategy, which focuses on the drive for economic value through tough top-down, results-driven action. Truss et al. (1997) observe that this 'hard' approach is based on the economic model of man and McGregor's (1960) theory X proposition that people dislike work and must be controlled and directed to get them to put forth adequate effort towards the achievement of organizational goals. Walton (1985) refers to the kind of situation in which control strategies flourish. He describes a plant in which employees are responsible for fixed jobs and are required to perform up to a minimum standard, and where peer pressure keeps them from exceeding this standard and from taking initiatives to improve performance. In such circumstances, because motivation is low, management seeks to secure adequate work effort through close monitoring and supervision and, what MacDuffie (1995) refers to as, 'efficiency wages'.

The commitment maximization approach

The commitment maximization approach is based on the assumption that people work best and contribute most to organizational performance when they are fully committed to the organization. It is an approach that shares many of the assumptions that underpin Beer's OD strategy for change, insofar as it involves creating the capabilities required to sustain competitive advantage and high performance over the long term. Truss et al. (1997) argue that 'soft' HRM has its roots in the human relations movement, the utilization of individual talents and McGregor's theory Y, which proposes that 'man will exercise self-direction and self-control in the service of objectives to which he is committed'. It focuses on developing committed employees who can be trusted to use their discretion to work in ways that are consistent with organizational goals. This approach assumes that commitment is generated when employees are trusted and allowed to work autonomously. It assumes that individuals can work hard and smart without being controlled through sanctions and other external pressures. It is the commitment maximization approach that underpins high performance management practices.

Theoretical foundations: how commitment strategies work

Huselid (1995), building of the work of Bailey (1993), argues that HRM practices can affect an individual's performance by:

▶ improving employees' knowledge and skills
▶ motivating them to engage in discretionary behaviours that draw on their knowledge and skill

▶ modifying organizational structures in ways that enable employees to improve the way they perform their jobs.

Some of the practices that contribute to these outcomes are listed below.

Improving employee knowledge and skills

There are a number of practices that can enhance employee knowledge and skill. These include:

▶ *Recruitment practices that provide a large pool of qualified applicants:* It may be possible to improve recruitment practices by focusing attention on what the organization does to attract appropriately qualified individuals and how this affects the kind of people who present themselves for selection.

▶ *Selection practices that identify those individuals who possess the required competencies:* It may be possible to improve selection practices by focusing attention on how the organization goes about selecting new employees and what steps it takes to identify and validate its selection criteria. Pfeffer (1998), for example, argues that emphasis should be placed on screening for cultural fit and attitudes rather than skills. He makes a case for 'selecting' on those attributes that are important and difficult, or impossible, to change, and 'training' people in those behaviours or skills that are more readily learned.

▶ *Induction practices that affect the way people are socialized into the organization:* It may be possible to improve induction practices by focusing attention on what happens to new employees after they join the organization and how this affects the development of competencies. Induction might also be considered as a practice that affects employees' motivation to engage in discretionary behaviours and influence their motivation to work harder and smarter.

▶ *Training practices that develop knowledge and skills required by organizational members:* It may be possible to improve training practices by focusing attention on the kinds of issues considered in Chapter 21 and questioning whether sufficient attention is given to the development of those competencies that are critical to the achievement of the organization's purpose. Pfeffer (1998) argues that training is an essential component of high performance work systems because these systems rely on frontline employees exercising their skill and initiative to identify and resolve problems, introduce changes in work methods, and take responsibility for quality. However, some organizations fail to invest sufficiently in training and many more are too quick to cut training budgets when times are hard:

> because training budgets often fluctuate with company economic fortunes, a perverse, procyclical training schedule typically develops: training funds are most plentiful when the firm is doing well. But when the firm is doing well, its people are busiest and have the most to do, and consequently, can least afford to be away for training. By contrast, when the firm is less busy, individuals have more time to develop their skills and undertake training activities. But that is exactly the time when training is least likely to be made available. (Pfeffer 1998: 89)

▶ *Other development activities that develop the knowledge, skills and job behaviours required for effective performance*: Consideration might be given to whether these practices, such as coaching, mentoring, on-the-job learning, secondments and job rotation, are as effective as they might be and whether there is an appropriate balance between these practices and more formal training activities. Performance appraisal is listed below as a practice that affects employees' motivation to engage in discretionary behaviours, but it can also provide a vehicle for developing competencies.

▶ *Retention practices that encourage valued employees to stay with the organization:* Do these motivate those most likely to be poached away by competitors to remain with the organization?

▶ *Attendance practices:* Do these encourage employees to attend regularly and work their contracted hours?

▶ *Information-sharing practices that provide employees with knowledge about immediate job-related issues and wider business matters they require in order to perform effectively:* Consideration might be given to how and when information is provided and whether it is the right kind of information.

Motivating employees to engage in discretionary behaviours

Huselid (1995) argues that the effectiveness of even the most highly skilled employees will be limited if they are not motivated to perform. A number of HR practices can encourage organizational members to work harder and smarter. These include:

▶ *Employment security:* Consideration might be given to whether employees are regarded as a variable cost or a valued asset and how this affects their commitment to the organization.

▶ *Redeployment and severance:* When workers are no longer required in their current roles, how does the organization manage this situation and how does this affect the motivation of those who are to be redeployed and their colleagues?

▶ *Performance appraisal:* It may be possible to improve the benefits from appraising performance by considering questions such as: What are the objectives of the performance appraisal system? What does it measure? Are individuals or groups appraised? Who does the appraising? Is the process perceived to be fair?

▶ *Incentives:* A wide range of factors can affect the link between incentives and performance (see Chapter 11) but some of the questions under this heading include: How are individuals compensated? Are rewards linked to the acquisition of skills or the achievement of performance targets? If they are linked to performance, is compensation based on individual, group or organizational performance?

▶ *Internal promotion systems:* How are people identified and prepared for promotion?

▶ *Status distinctions:* These can affect motivation, so it might be useful to review the kinds of status distinctions that exist and the effects they have on performance.

Enabling motivated employees to engage in discretionary behaviours

Bailey (1993) notes that the contribution of highly skilled and motivated employees will be limited unless their jobs are structured in ways that allow them to apply their knowledge and skills in order to improve the way they perform their jobs. There are a number of interventions that enable employees to engage in such discretionary behaviours. These include:

▶ *Organization structures:* How is the organization structured and how does this affect the ability of individuals to improve the way they do their jobs? For example, does the organization have a functional structure with people working in silos, or is it process based?

▶ *Parallel and temporary structures:* Does the organization use structures such as quality circles and awaydays to facilitate the sharing of ideas about performance improvement?

▶ *Job design:* Are people employed to perform narrowly defined tasks that require little skill or does job design emphasize a whole task and combine doing and thinking? Do people work on their own or in teams?

▶ *Locus of decision making:* Is decision making concentrated high up in the organization or is it decentralized and delegated?

▶ *Employee voice:* Is employee input encouraged? Is it allowed on a narrow agenda or a wide range of issues? What methods are used to facilitate upward, lateral and downward communication?

Pfeffer (1998) advocates the adoption of self-managed teams and decentralized delegated decision making as the guiding principles for organizational design. He argues that teams offer several advantages. They can substitute peer-based control for hierarchical control. Peer-based control can be powerful, for example when a team member is absent, all the difficulties of that absence fall on other team members, producing enormous peer pressure against absenteeism (Parker and Slaughter, 1988). Pfeffer also points to other advantages. Team working encourages people to pool ideas and come up with better ways of addressing problems and provides a framework within which workers can more readily help each other and share their production knowledge (Shaiken et al., 1997).

Other benefits from high performance management practices

Pfeffer (1998) argues that high commitment work practices can produce savings by reducing administrative overheads. Delegating more responsibility to people further down the organization eliminates the need for many supervisory roles. High commitment work practices can also reduce many of the costs associated with having an alienated workforce that is engaged in an adversarial relationship with management.

The alignment of HR management practices

Many attempts to improve performance through the introduction of new HRM practices fail because changes are introduced piecemeal and are focused on particular practices, such as selection, performance appraisal, compensation or training. Investing more resources in just one practice, such as training, may have little effect if other practices remain unchanged. For example, the potential benefits of training may be wasted if jobs are not redesigned in ways that give workers the freedom to apply their new knowledge and skills. HRM practices need to be aligned with each other if employees and the organization are to benefit from what MacDuffie (1995: 197) refers to as 'multiple, mutually reinforcing conditions'.

Some view alignment as the defining feature of high performance management systems and they do not believe that it is necessary to prescribe the kinds of practices that are applied so long as the practices are internally consistent. However, there is a strong body of opinion that the most effective way of securing high performance is through high commitment. Those who subscribe to this school of thought advocate a configuration of practices that support the commitment rather than the control approach to management (see Pfeffer, 1998: 56). The theoretical foundation of the three-pronged approach to improving performance outlined above is based on the assumption that HR practices should be targeted at increasing commitment in order to elicit discretionary behaviour. Pfeffer's (1998) seven practices that characterize systems that produce profits through people – employment security, selective hiring, self-managed teams and decentralized decision making, high compensation contingent on performance, extensive training, reduced status distinctions, and extensive sharing of information – are all high commitment management practices.

Implementation is not always easy. Moving from a control- to a commitment-oriented set of management practices can be difficult because many managers are wedded to a control philosophy. Pfeffer (1998: 29) refers to 'the one eighth rule', which states that only about half of all senior managers believe that there is a possible connection between how organizations manage their people and the profits they earn. Of these, only about a half will do more than attempt to change a single people management practice, not realizing that the effective management of people requires a more comprehensive and systematic approach. In those organizations where managers do make comprehensive changes, only about a half will persist with these changes long enough to derive any economic benefit.

The introduction of a commitment-based high performance management system often requires a paradigm shift in the way some managers think. Pfeffer argues that if managers see their staff as costs to be reduced, as recalcitrant employees prone to opportunism, shirking and free riding, as people who can't be trusted and who need to be closely controlled through monitoring, rewards and sanctions, then any attempt to introduce high performance management practices is likely to fail. Successful implementation requires a mindset that regards people as fundamentally trustworthy, intelligent and motivated.

Results from high performance management systems

Pfeffer (1998) presents an impressive review of studies that provide evidence of substantial gains from implementing high performance management systems. His review includes a study of five-year survival rates of initial public offerings (Welborne and Andrews, 1996); studies of profitability and stock price in a large sample of companies from multiple industries (Huselid, 1995); and detailed research in the automobile industry (MacDuffie, 1995), apparel (Dunlop and Weil, 1996), semiconductors (Sohoni, 1994), steel (Arthur, 1995), oil refining (Ricketts, 1994) and service industries (Schneider, 1991; Johnson et al., 1994). These findings suggest that high performance management can produce economic benefits in a wide range of settings, including low- and high-tech industries and in manufacturing and service settings.

| Change tool 22.1 | **Diagnosing the alignment of HR practices** |

One of the first things that needs to be done when developing and implementing a high performance management system is to diagnose the extent to which existing management practices are aligned with each other and with the organization's business strategy. Pfeffer (1998) describes the essential steps of an 'alignment diagnosis' that provides the basis for the diagnostic exercise presented below. You might find it useful to complete this exercise for your organization or some other organization that you are familiar with.

The alignment diagnosis is in two parts. The first is concerned with external alignment and involves diagnosing the extent to which management practices are congruent with the organization's business strategy. The second part is concerned with internal alignment and involves diagnosing the extent to which HRM practices are aligned with each other.

Diagnosing external alignment

Diagnosing external alignment involves four steps:

1 reviewing the organization's strategy
2 identifying the critical behaviours and related competencies that are required to achieve the strategy
3 identifying practices that the organization uses to manage people
4 assessing the alignment of each people management/HR practice with the competencies and behaviours required to achieve the organization's strategy. Does each practice support the availability and application of critical competencies and behaviours?

Each step will be considered in turn.

1 *Specifying the organization's strategy*
   Strategy is a statement of purpose that indicates how the organization will match its resources with the opportunities, constraints and demands in the environment. Implicit in this statement are the value propositions the organization offers to stakeholders.

   Summarize your organization's strategy in the space below.

2 *Identifying the critical behaviours and related competencies required to achieve the strategy*
   If the organization's strategy is premised on the provision of excellent customer service and if the majority of staff are customer facing, then the organization needs people who have the competencies necessary to support this value proposition. If, on the other hand, the strategy is premised on being first to market with innovative products, then a different set of competencies will be required. Pfeffer recommends that attention is restricted to the six or so behaviours and related competencies that are the most important. These can be entered at the head of the columns of the external alignment matrix presented below.
3 *Identifying practices that the organization uses to manage people*
   The external alignment matrix is divided into three parts in line with Bailey's (1993) model of how HR practices can affect performance. The first part relates to the policies and practices that affect the 'availability and development' of the competencies necessary to deliver required behaviours. These practices include recruitment, selection, induction, training, other development activities, attendance, and information sharing.

The second part relates to practices that affect employees' 'motivation' to engage in discretionary behaviours that involve applying critical competencies in order to improve performance. These practices include employment security, redeployment and severance, performance appraisal, incentives, internal promotion systems, and status distinctions.

The third part relates to practices that 'enable' motivated employees to engage in discretionary behaviours that lead to performance improvements. These practices include organization design, parallel and temporary structures, job design, locus of decision making, and employee voice.

Review your organization's HR practices and amend the list included in the external alignment matrix below to reflect your organization's current approach to HRM. You might also amend this list to include additional practices that, if applied appropriately, could contribute to high performance.

4 *Assessing the alignment of each HRM practice with the competencies and behaviours required to achieve the organization's business strategy*
This step involves assessing the extent to which each of the HR practices listed in your external alignment matrix is likely to promote the competencies and behaviours you identified as critical for the implementation of the strategy. Pfeffer suggests using a three-point scale, where +1 indicates that the practice is aligned with the organization's business strategy and will support the development of required competencies and behaviours, 0 where the practice has a neutral effect and −1 where it is misaligned. This procedure is a useful way of identifying where there is substantial misalignment and a clear need for action to develop and implement a revised HR practice.

Pfeffer (1998: 111) identifies some of the most common alignment-related problems. Two of these involve the link between training activities and competencies, and the link between compensation and the achievement of key performance targets:

- With regard to training and required competencies, in many organizations training activities are focused on generally useful topics, such as negotiating skills and time management, but neglect the crucial competencies that are tightly linked to the achievement of strategic objectives.
- With regard to compensation and key performance targets, Pfeffer highlights the problem with an example of a firm rewarding managers for 'making budget numbers' when the really important targets had to do with being innovative, fast and customer focused.

External alignment matrix								
Practices that affect:	Critical behaviours/competencies required to implement the organization's strategy							
1 The development and availability of competencies								
Recruitment								
Selection								
Induction								
Training								
Other developments								
Information sharing								
Other								

2 Motivation								
Employment security								
Performance appraisal								
Incentives								
Internal promotion systems								
Status distinctions								
Other								
3 Ability to use competencies to improve performance								
Organization structures								
Job design								
Locus of decision making								
Employee voice								
Other								

Diagnosing internal alignment

Diagnosing internal alignment involves assessing the internal consistency of the HRM practices. One way of doing this is to list the management practices identified as part of the external alignment exercise across the top as well as down the left-hand side of a matrix and taking each practice in turn and reviewing it for alignment against each of the other practices. For example, in terms of job design, if work is allocated to self-managed teams, are employees given training that supports this practice? Also, is performance appraisal focused on individuals or teams and is compensation based on individual or team performance? Again the three-point scale can be used to signal the degree of alignment and highlight potential problems.

Internal alignment matrix															
Practices that affect:	Management practices														
1 The development of competencies	a	b	c	d	e	f	g	h	i	j	k	l	m	n	o
Recruitment	-														
Selection	-	-													
Induction	-	-	-												
Training	-	-	-	-											
Other developments	-	-	-	-	-										
Information sharing	-	-	-	-	-	-									
2 Motivation															
Employment security	-	-	-	-	-	-	-								
Performance appraisal	-	-	-	-	-	-	-	-							
Incentives	-	-	-	-	-	-	-	-	-						
Internal promotions	-	-	-	-	-	-	-	-	-	-					
Status distinctions	-	-	-	-	-	-	-	-	-	-	-				
3 Use of competencies															
Organization structures	-	-	-	-	-	-	-	-	-	-	-	-			
Job design	-	-	-	-	-	-	-	-	-	-	-	-	-		
Locus of decision making	-	-	-	-	-	-	-	-	-	-	-	-	-	-	
Employee voice	-	-	-	-	-	-	-	-	-	-	-	-	-	-	-

This kind of alignment diagnosis can help change agents to identify the system of HR practices that will assist the organization to achieve its strategic objectives.

You might find it useful to reflect on your findings regarding the extent of external and internal alignment in your organization and the areas where alignment problems might arise.

Summary

This chapter has considered how HR practices can affect performance by:

1 improving employees' knowledge and skills
2 motivating them to engage in discretionary behaviours that draw on their knowledge and skill
3 modifying organizational structures in ways that enable employees to improve the way they perform their jobs.

Some of the people management practices that can help to improve employee knowledge and skill include recruitment, selection, induction, training, other development activities, such as coaching, mentoring, on-the-job learning, secondments, job rotation, retention of skilled staff, attendance, and information sharing.

Some of the people management practices that can help motivate employees to engage in discretionary behaviours include employment security, redeployment and severance policies, performance appraisal, incentives, internal promotion systems and minimal status distinctions.

Some of the practices that enable motivated employees to engage in discretionary behaviours include designing appropriate organization structures, implementing parallel and temporary structures, job design, pushing decision making down the organization and facilitating upward communications so that employees can voice their concerns and contribute to organizational learning.

Rather than focusing on separate HR practices, high performance management involves developing and implementing a bundle or system of practices that are internally consistent, aligned with other business processes, and aligned with the organization's business strategy.

Diagnosing external alignment involves four steps:

1 reviewing the organization's strategy
2 identifying the critical behaviours and related competencies that are required to achieve the strategy
3 identifying practices that the organization uses to manage people
4 assessing the alignment of each HR practice with the competencies and behaviours required to achieve the organization's strategy. Does each practice support the availability and application of critical competencies and behaviours?

Diagnosing internal alignment involves ensuring that all people practices are aligned with each other. For example, the potential benefits of training may be wasted if jobs are not redesigned to give workers the freedom to apply their new knowledge and skills.

Alignment is the defining feature of high performance management interventions. However, while some argue that any HR practices can be effective so long as they are aligned, others such as Pfeffer advocate a configuration of practices that support a commitment rather than a control approach to people management.

In terms of the typology presented in Figure 16.2, high performance management is an HRM intervention.

References

Arthur, J.B. (1992) The link between business strategy and industrial relations systems in American steel minimills, *Industrial and Labor Relations Review*, 45: 488–506.

Arthur, J.B. (1995) Effects of human resource systems on manufacturing performance and turnover, *Academy of Management Journal*, **37**(3): 670–87.

Bailey, T. (1993) Discretionary effort and the organization of work: employee participation and work reform since Hawthorne, working paper, Columbia University, New York.

Dunlop, J.T. and Weil, D. (1996) Diffusion and performance of modular production in the US apparel industry, *Industrial Relations*, 35: 337–8.

Huselid, M.A. (1995) The impact of human resource management practices on turnover, productivity, and corporate financial performance, *Academy of Management Journal*, **38**(3): 635–72.

Johnson, R.H., Ryan, A.M. and Schmit, M.J. (1994) Employee attitudes and branch performance at Ford Motor Credit, paper presented to the ninth annual conference of the Society of Industrial and Organizational Psychology, Nashville, TN, April.

MacDuffie, J.P. (1995) Human resource bundles and manufacturing performance: organizational logic and flexible production systems in the world auto industry, *Industrial and Labor Relations Review*, **48**(2): 197–221.

McGregor, D. (1960) Theory X and theory Y, in D.S. Pugh (ed.) *Organization Theory: Selected Readings*, London: Penguin.

Parker, M. and Slaughter, J. (1988) Management by stress, *Technology Review*, **91**(43).

Pfeffer, J. (1998) *The Human Equation: Building Profits by Putting People First*, Boston, MA: Harvard Business School Press.

Ricketts, R. (1994) Survey points to practices that reduce refinery maintenance spending, *Oil and Gas Journal*, 4 July: 38.

Schneider, B. (1991) Service quality and profits: Can you have your cake and eat it, too?, *Human Resource Planning*, **14**(2): 151.

Shaiken, H., Lopez, S. and Mankita, I. (1997) Two routes to team production: Saturn and Chrysler compared, *Industrial Relations*, 36: 31.

Sohoni, V. (1994) Workforce involvement and wafer fabrication efficiency, in C. Brown (ed.) *The Competitive Semiconductor Manufacturing Human Resources Project: First Interim Report*, Berkeley, CA: Institute of Industrial Relations.

Truss, C., Gratton, L., Hope-Hailey, V. et al. (1997) Soft and hard models of human resource management: a reappraisal, *Journal of Management Studies*, **34**(1): 53–73.

Walton, R.E. (1985) From control to commitment in the workplace, *Harvard Business Review*, 63: 77–84.

Welbourne, T. and Andrews, A. (1996) Predicting performance of initial public offering firms: Should HRM be in the equation?, *Academy of Management Journal*, 39: 910–11.

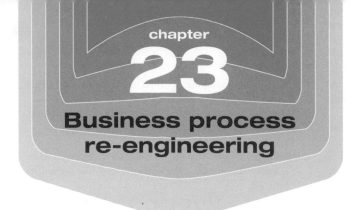
Business process re-engineering (BPR) is often presented as a top-down, organization-wide approach to transforming organizations.

The structure of most organizations has been influenced by the principle of the division of labour, first articulated by Adam Smith (1776) in *The Wealth of Nations*. Smith observed that it was much more efficient to break the process of pin making down into several steps that could be undertaken by specialist workers rather than to delegate the whole process to one generalist worker. This principle manifests itself today in organizations that structure activities according to specialist functions rather than value-creating processes. Hammer and Champy (1993) argue

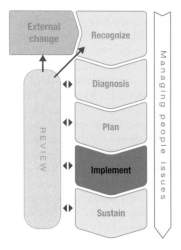

that 'companies today consist of functional silos, or stovepipes, vertical structures built on narrow pieces of a process'. They illustrate how this affects organizational functioning with reference to the order fulfilment process that starts when a customer places an order and ends when the goods are delivered:

> The person checking a customer's credit is part of the credit department, which is probably a part of the finance organisation. Inventory picking is performed by workers in the warehouse, who may report to the vice president of manufacturing. Shipping, on the other hand, is part of logistics. People involved in a process look *inward* towards their department and *upwards* towards their boss, but no one looks *outwards* toward the customer. (Hammer and Champy, 1993: 28)

BPR involves switching attention away from fragmented, functional-based thinking towards cross-functional processes that create value for the organization. Kaplan and Murdock (1991) argue that focusing attention on and redesigning core processes can make them faster and more flexible, and make organizations more responsive to changes in competitive conditions, consumer demands, product life cycles and technologies.

The nature of BPR

Hammer and Champy (1993) define BPR as the fundamental rethinking and radical redesign of business processes to achieve dramatic improvements in performance. Some of the competing views around BPR are examined below.

Fundamental rethink or incremental improvement?

Hammer and Champy (1993) argue that BPR is 'fundamental' because it involves asking the most basic questions about how an organization operates, questions that challenge many widely held assumptions. Rather than simply asking whether it is possible to improve the way something is done, BPR involves questioning why the organization does what it does. For example, those responsible for re-engineering the order fulfilment process, referred to above, might question the need to perform credit checks rather than assuming that they are an essential part of the process. It is possible that checking a customer's credit fails to add any value because the cost of performing a check is greater than any losses that might be incurred from bad debts. Hammer and Champy state that new thinking should not be influenced by embedded assumptions or any existing processes, activities and systems. They advocate a 'clean sheet' approach to process redesign.

Davenport and Stoddard (1994) challenge this view. Based on conversations with managers from more than 200 companies and rigorous research on 35 re-engineering initiatives (Javenpaa and Stoddard, 1993), they assert that in practice a clean sheet approach is rarely found. Those companies that do adopt this approach tend to make a clear distinction between clean sheet design and clean sheet implementation. They may adopt a clean sheet approach to design because it can provide a vision of a 'best-of-all-processes' world towards which the organization can focus its change efforts. They quote one manager who said: 'You can design assuming a clean slate, but you must implement assuming the existing state.' Davenport and Stoddard (1994: 123) also report that designers often start with a 'dirty slate', taking into account the opportunities for enabling a new process and the constraints that disable it:

> With both design elements in mind, the design team [can] construct the best possible process given the enablers and the constraints. Whereas this is a less exciting and more difficult design method, 'designing with a dirty slate' will normally yield a more implementable process.

Organization-wide change or piecemeal improvement?

Hammer and Champy argue that BPR is 'radical and dramatic' because, to be successful, it must entail rapid and wholesale transformation rather than incremental and piecemeal change. Davenport and Stoddard (1994), however, do not see re-engineering as incompatible with continuous improvement. While they agree with the proposition that re-engineering is a process that can contribute to organizational transformation, they do not agree that it is synonymous with it. They report observing numerous firms trying to change too many processes at once and failing in their ambition to achieve radical transformation. However, they also report observing several firms that were successfully creating hybrid configurations, adding a process dimension to their functional structures. McNulty and Ferlie (2002), in their in-depth study of BPR within the Leicester Royal Infirmary, report findings that support Davenport and Stoddard's position (see Case study 1.1.3). They found that while the intended strategy was radical and revolutionary, the emergent strategy of re-engineering proved to be evolutionary and convergent in overall approach and impact:

> as the reengineering programme unfolded the initial radical ambition for organisational process redesign was tempered and reshaped in line with functional organisational principles that underpinned the existing pattern of specialties and clinical directorates. Reengineers learned quickly that they were dependent on the support of managers and clinicians ... to effect change at specialty and clinical directorate levels. (McNulty and Ferlie, 2002: 116)

A top-down or participative process?

Those who argue that re-engineering offers a system-wide and radical approach to change also tend to view it as an essentially top-down process. Hammer and Champy (1993: 208), for example, believe that people near the front line lack the broad perspective that re-engineering demands:

> They may see – probably better than anyone else – the narrow problems from which their departments suffer, but it is difficult for them to see a process as a whole and to recognise its poor overall design as the source of their problems.

They also argue that middle managers lack the required authority to change processes that cross organizational boundaries. There are, however, those who believe that re-engineering can be a more participative process. While Davenport and Stoddard (1993) accept that innovative designs for broad processes are unlikely to come from those whose heads are 'buried deep in the bowls of existing process', they see no reason why all members of design teams must be high in the organizational hierarchy. They argue that those who are at the front line may make a valuable contribution to the design of detailed process activities. They also cite examples of organizational members who have failed to implement newly designed processes because they had had no hand in their creation.

Re-engineering at the Leicester Royal Infirmary started as a top-down programme to identify, redesign and roll out core processes across the hospital. A central re-engineering capability was created using an infrastructure of re-engineering committees, re-engineering laboratories – physical spaces in which teams or re-engineers could work on the redesign of processes – and internal and external change agents. This initial strategy began to flounder and was eventually replaced by a decentralized approach, which involved responsibility for re-engineering shifting from a dedicated team of re-engineers to managers located within clinical directorates. McNulty and Ferlie (2002) note that it was at this point that the energy and momentum for change increased because individuals felt more able to 'adopt, adapt and customise' re-engineering ideas to suit local circumstances and purposes.

The application of BPR

BPR typically involves seven steps, which are now discussed in detail.

Process mapping

A process is a series of actions that lead to an outcome. Process maps show how work flows through an organization. People tend to be more familiar with organizational units, such as manufacturing, research and development or marketing, than with the processes to which these units contribute. Examples of processes in a business organization are order fulfilment (order to payment – including intermediate steps such as manufacturing), product development (concept to prototype) and sales (prospect to order). Examples of processes in a healthcare organization include patient test (referral to diagnosis) and patient stay (admission to discharge). In most organizations, there are relatively few core processes, but each of these might involve a number of subprocesses. The starting point for any BPR project is to map the processes that contribute to the organization fulfilling its purpose.

Identifying processes for re-engineering

Even when the ambition is to use BPR to radically transform the organization in the shortest possible time, it will normally prove impossible to re-engineer all the organization's processes simultaneously. Hammer and Champy (1993) suggest three criteria for choosing which processes to re-engineer and the order in which this might be done. They are:

- ▶ *dysfunction:* which processes are in deepest trouble
- ▶ *importance:* which processes have the greatest impact on the organization's customers
- ▶ *feasibility:* which processes are most susceptible to successful redesign.

Understanding the selected process

The re-engineering team needs to understand the process, what it does, how well it does it and any critical issues that govern its performance, but it does not, according to the classical school of BPR, need to undertake any detailed analysis. Hammer and Champy (1993) caution against too much analysis because it directs attention inside the process and directs attention away from challenging embedded assumptions. They argue that attention should be focused on seeking a high-level understanding, starting with what the process delivers and how well these outcomes match what customers really want. This high-level overview provides the basis for a clean sheet design activity.

There are those, however, who see value in starting with a 'dirty slate' and looking for opportunities for incremental process improvement. While improving the patient journey in a healthcare setting might involve starting from a clean sheet and radically transforming a process, it might also involve working with an existing process and seeking out opportunities for incremental improvement. For example, the aim of a re-engineering project might be to improve the service provided to patients who go to their local doctor (GP) with symptoms that require a diagnostic test involving an X-ray. The process might be defined as starting when the patient first goes to their GP with symptoms, and ending when the doctor communicates the X-ray results to the patient (Figure 23.1).

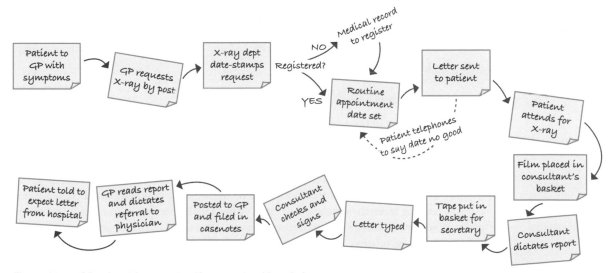

Figure 23.1 *GP referral for a routine X-ray at a local hospital*

There are several ways of mapping this process. One method is to gather all the stakeholders together for a mapping workshop. Another is for members of the re-engineering team to physically walk through the process and record what happens at each stage. This mapping for understanding might involve identifying:

▶ the number of steps in the process for the patient
▶ the number of hand-offs – occasions when the patient or information related to the patient's diagnostic test is passed from one person to another
▶ task time – the time taken for each step
▶ wait time – the time between each step
▶ dead time when nothing happens – a letter sits on a dictated tape for three days before being typed
▶ steps that fail to add any value – can they be eliminated?
▶ blockages – steps that slow the rest of the process down.

Mapping a targeted process is often done in two steps. The first involves producing a high-level process map that provides an overview of how inputs are transformed into outputs, focuses attention on the relative value of the outputs produced by the process (Are they worth the effort required to produce them? Do they really satisfy customers' needs?) and the value added by particular steps in the process (Can a step be eliminated, integrated with another step or replaced with an entirely different subprocess?). Experience suggests that analysing this kind of high-level map helps to expose embedded assumptions and identify those parts of the overall process that offer the greatest potential for improvement. The second step involves mapping these parts in more detail.

Defining key performance objectives

Key performance objectives are based on what the re-engineering team and other stakeholders believe the customer requires from the process. They provide a basis for specifying measures that will indicate whether the changes have been successful. Sometimes benchmarking is used to help define performance objectives but re-engineers need to be alert to the possibility that benchmarking may limit ambition to what is currently being achieved by 'the best of the rest' and inhibit out-of-the-box thinking about what the process could deliver. Baselining, collecting and recording data about existing (pre-re-engineered) performance can also help with the definition of realistic performance targets and provide a basis for assessing the successes of the re-engineering project.

Designing new processes

According to Hammer and Champy (1993: 134):

Redesign is the most nakedly creative part of the entire reengineering process. More than any other, it demands imagination, inductive thinking, and a touch of craziness.

They illustrate this with the example of an insurance company that believed it was costing more than it should to settle claims relating to motor accidents. There is no set format for redesigning a process, but it often involves people sharing ideas about how the process might be changed and others 'piggybacking' on these ideas to suggest other possibilities. In Hammer and Champy's example of the claims settlement process, somebody noted that it cost the same per hour to work on a big claim as it did to work on a small claim. This led to two related suggestions: introduce a step early in the process that would separate out those claims that will cost a lot to settle (usually those involving a claim for personal injury) and those that will not, and redesigning the process for small claims that will cut the time required to settle them. One suggestion was to immediately settle any claim for less that a certain amount. Some team members felt that this could encourage fraud and escalate the cost of claims but others felt that this danger could be managed by only offering immediate settlement to policy holders who had a good no-claims record. A related idea was to let the agent handle claims below a specified amount. This led to somebody else suggesting that the garage should be allowed to deal with the claim, thereby eliminating the need for many steps in the existing process. This proposal was initially dismissed because it was feared that garages might inflate the cost of repairs. However, somebody brought the team back to this idea and suggested that there would be many garages willing to work for modest margins if this enabled them to win more business from the insurance company. It was also recognized that not only could this reduce costs for the insurance company, but it would also lead to greater customer satisfaction. What customers wanted most was their car back on the road as quickly as possible.

This first meeting came up with some challenging new ideas, some of which merited further attention and testing. It also involved the application of a number of re-engineering principles, such as organizing work around outcomes, for example reduced cost and increased customer satisfaction, and involving as few people as possible in the process to reduce hand-offs and waiting time. In addition, it involved destroying some embedded assumptions such as garages cannot be trusted.

Testing

An important part of BPR is the testing of ideas to see if they will work in practice. Langley et al. (1996) advocate a plan, do, study, act (PDSA) cycle for process improvement that involves:

▶ *planning* a change that can be tested on a small scale or over a limited period – an hour, day or week
▶ *doing* or carrying out the test
▶ *studying* baseline data and the effect of the test and looking for improvements
▶ *acting* to implement the tested change.

This process has many similarities with action research and can involve several iterations before final implementation.

Change tool 23.1

The plan, do, study, act (PDSA) cycle

The PDSA cycle is a tool for testing ideas by putting changes into effect on a small scale and learning from their impact before full implementation.

The four stages are:

- *Plan:* plan the change to be tested
- *Do:* carry out the test (change)
- *Study:* study data before and after the change and reflect on what was learned
- *Act:* plan implementation or, if the test was not successful, plan the next PDSA cycle.

ACT | PLAN

STUDY | DO

Implementation

If the tests are successful, the redesigned process can be implemented and rolled out, as appropriate, to other parts of the organization. However, great care needs to be exercised if the redesigned process is to be rolled out to powerful individuals or groups who were not part of, and committed to, the re-engineering process. BPR can be highly politicized and often involves jurisdictional disputes when managers are required to let go of activities and decisions they value.

Results from BPR

Research findings regarding the results of BPR are mixed. Cummings and Worley (2001) cite a study of 497 companies in the US and 1,245 companies in Europe. While 60% of US firms and 75% of European firms had engaged in at least one re-engineering project, only 15% of them reported positive outcomes. This is quite different to the findings reported by Caron et al. (1994). They found that while only half of 20 BPR projects undertaken by CIGNA, a leading provider of insurance and related financial services, were successful first time round, the impact of re-engineering was very positive and the company saved more than $100m overall. They also reported that some of the most successful projects were those undertaken in self-contained areas.

McNulty and Ferlie (2002) report that attempts to radically transform a large hospital through process re-engineering were highly contested and the outcome of the change was uneven across the organization. Contextual factors had an important effect on outcomes, especially those relating to the extent to which doctors retained control over work practices. They also found that it was easier to secure change in those processes or parts of processes that did not cross boundaries between clinical directorates or between directorates and external agencies. This echoes one of the findings reported by Caron et al. (1994) that some of the most successful projects were those that were undertaken in self-contained areas. Despite the many difficulties encountered when trying to re-engineer the hospital, McNulty and Ferlie observed that the re-engineering methodology did make an important contribution to securing change. For example, in trauma orthopaedic care, there were a number of positive outcomes. The baselining activity produced 'facts' about patient activity on which the case for change could be built. Process mapping enabled the re-engineers and other stakeholders, such as doctors, to analyse and understand the care process and develop a vision of change. Finally, piloting allowed some changes to be introduced, often without people realizing that an important change had taken place.

Summary

This chapter has examined the nature of BPR. BPR involves switching attention away from fragmented functional thinking towards cross-functional processes.

Fundamental rethink or incremental improvement?

▶ Hammer and Champy argue that BPR involves a 'fundamental rethinking' of business processes. They argue that new thinking should not be influenced by embedded assumptions or any existing processes or activities. They advocate a 'clean sheet' approach.

▶ A consequence is that BPR initiatives should not be led by people who are involved in the processes. Interventions need to be led by top management or external experts.

▶ Davenport and Stoddard challenge this view. While they recognize the value of 'clean sheet' thinking at the design stage, they argue that, more often than not, implementation needs to be piecemeal and incremental.

Organization-wide change or piecemeal improvement?

▶ Hammer and Champy argue that BPR involves a 'radical redesign' of business processes. They argue that to be successful, BPR must entail a rapid and wholesale transformation rather than an incremental piecemeal change.

▶ Again there are competing views. Davenport and Stoddard see re-engineering as compatible with continuous improvement. While they agree with the proposition that re-engineering is a process that can contribute to organizational transformation, they do not agree that it is synonymous with it.

▶ Davenport and Stoddard report observing numerous firms trying to change too many processes at once and failing in their ambition to achieve radical transformation. However, they also report observing several firms that were successfully creating hybrid configurations, adding a process dimension to their functional structures.

BPR involves seven stages:

1 *Process mapping:* Process maps show how work flows through an organization.

2 *Identifying which process to reengineer:* Criteria might include dysfunction (which processes are in deepest trouble?), importance (which have greatest impact on customers?) and feasibility (which are most susceptible to successful redesign?).

3 *Understanding the selected process:* Mapping for understanding can involve identifying the number of steps in the process, number of hand-offs, task time, wait time, dead time when nothing happens, steps that fail to yield any value and blockages.

4 *Defining key performance objectives:* These need to be based on what the customer requires from the process.

5 *Designing new processes:* 'Redesign is the most nakedly creative part of the entire reengineering process. More than any other, it demands imagination, inductive thinking, and a touch of craziness' (Hammer and Champy, 1993: 134).

6 *Testing:* This involves implementing a proposed process improvement on a small scale, or for a limited time to see if it works in practice.

7 *Implementation:* If the test is successful, the redesigned process can be rolled out across the organization.

Great care may need to be exercised, especially with implementation, because BPR can be highly politicized and often involves jurisdictional disputes when managers are required to let go of activities or decisions they value.

In terms of the typology presented in Figure 16.2, BPR is a technostructural intervention.

References

Caron, J.R., Jarvenpaa, D.L. and Stoddard, D. (1994) Business reengineering at CIGNA Corporation: experience and lessons learned from the last five years, *MIS Quarterly*, September: 233–50.

Cummings, T.G. and Worley, C.G. (2001) *Organization Development and Change* (7th edn), Cincinnati, OH: South-Western College Publishing/Thomson Learning.

Davenport, T.H. and Stoddard, D.B. (1994) Reengineering change in mythic proportions, *MIS Quarterly*, June: 121–7.

Hammer, M. and Champy, J. (1993) *Reengineering the Corporation: A Manifesto for Business Revolution*, London: Nicholas Brealey.

Javenpaa, D.L. and Stoddard, D.B. (1993) Managing IT-enabled radical change, research proposal, University of Texas/Harvard Business School.

Kaplan, R. and Murdock, L. (1991) Core process design, *McKinsey Quarterly*, 2: 27–43.

Langley, G., Nolan, K., Norman, C. and Provast, L. (1996) *The Improvement Guide: A Practical Approach to Enhancing Organisational Performance*, San Francisco, CA: Jossey-Bass.

McNulty, T. and Ferlie, E. (2002) *Reengineering Health Care: The Complexities of Organisational Transformation*, Oxford: Oxford University Press.

Smith, A. (1776) *The Wealth of Nations*, 1950 edn, London: Methuen.

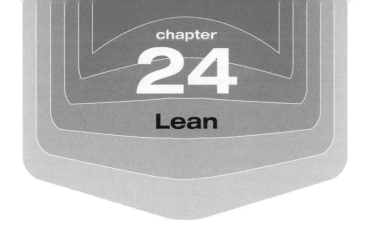

chapter

24

Lean

Womack et al. (1990) coined the phrase 'lean' to describe a production system that does more with less and less. It is a customer-focused process that aims to provide customers with precisely what they want, free of defects, exactly when they want it. Womack and Jones (1999) summarize their approach to lean in five principles: precisely specify value for each product or product family; identify value streams for each product to expose waste; make value flow without interruption; let customers pull value from the producer; and pursue perfection by searching out and eliminating further waste.

Scherrer-Rathje et al. (2009) differentiate between lean as a set of tools and techniques and lean as a philosophy. Many practitioners focus their attention on tools (such as control charts, 5S, seven wastes, total productive maintenance, just in time inventories and so on) and direct their efforts towards applying some of them to achieve specific outcomes. Sometimes change efforts are restricted to particular parts of the organization or directed towards the achievement of limited goals, such as cost reduction. Others view lean as a philosophy and focus more attention on acting in accordance with guiding principles and overarching aims to create a lean enterprise. They adopt a more holistic approach and consider how the interrelationships between and synergistic effects of related practices can affect performance across the whole enterprise.

Although originally developed in the context of manufacturing, lean thinking has spread beyond the shop floor and is now widely applied in sectors such as finance, health and education.

This chapter traces the development of lean thinking, introduces some lean tools and techniques, reviews issues to be considered when implementing lean and explores how lean has been applied in manufacturing and non-manufacturing settings.

Antecedents of lean thinking

In 1913, Henry Ford introduced the first 'flow' production line to assemble Model T Fords. It was a remarkable innovation. It involved the manufacture of vehicle components using special purpose machines that produced identical and interchangeable parts. These components were delivered to the required point on a moving assembly line and because they were identical and could be inserted without any last-minute modification, workers used standardized processes to fit them and quickly assemble their part of the car as it moved down the line.

Ford's assembly line was revolutionary, incorporating flow and inventory control to deliver cheap cars to an expanding market. But it had some important limitations. For example, as customers became more sophisticated and sought greater variety, the production system could not respond. It was inflexible. Almost all the machines involved in fabricating components produced a single part. Cycle times could be measured in years. Product development was a slow process. For example, the chassis that were being produced when production ended in 1926 were essentially the same as those when production began in 1913. This inflexibility severely limited the variety available to customers, summed up by the often-quoted expression: 'You can have any colour you want so long as it's black.' Eventually, customers were offered some variety in body styles but this was achieved by 'dropping' different bodies onto identical vehicles at the end of the assembly line.

Attempts to increase flexibility eroded some of the benefits of flow production. Companies developed production systems that involved manufacturing batches of components on bigger and faster machines. When a sufficient quantity of a particular component had been manufactured, machines were reset to produce a new batch of different components. This batch system delivered greater flexibility and reduced the unit cost of components, but these benefits had associated costs. Steps in the production process were often separated. Throughput times increased. Batch production required larger inventories, as components had to be stored until required, and levels of waste often increased – a whole batch of substandard components could be manufactured and the fault might go undetected until an item from that batch was used.

Some time before Ford developed his first production line, Sakichi Toyoda, the founder of the Toyota Group, invented a loom that automatically stopped if a thread snapped. This led to the development of other self-monitoring machines that could detect defects (deviations from a standard) as soon as they occurred. Process stopping, to detect and eliminate the cause of defects (jidoka), eventually became an important part of the Toyota Production System and was extended beyond self-monitoring machines. Workers were encouraged to intervene to stop production whenever they identified a problem. Doing this enabled problems to be contained. Resources were immediately directed to eliminating the root cause, thus contributing to continuous improvement.

Many others were involved in work that is reflected in lean thinking. F.W. Taylor contributed to the development and deployment of standardized work practices. Taiichi Ohno, an engineer at Toyota, developed just in time scheduling systems driven by customer demand rather than sales or production targets.

W.E. Deming's early work in the interwar years on the statistical control of processes laid the foundation for his later work on 'common' and 'special' causes of variation and the concept of quality. Almost immediately after the end of the Second World War, he began working with Japanese manufactures to apply his ideas to improve quality while reducing costs, by eliminating waste, and increasing market share, by providing customers with what they valued. His approach involved systems thinking to optimize end to end processes, using statistics to understand and manage variation, motivating employees by helping them see how their actions affected performance, aligning their objectives on real customer needs, and adopting a systematic approach to learning using a plan, do, study, act (PDSA) approach.

In the 1930s and again after end of the Second World War, members of the Toyoda family studied Ford's assembly lines and other developments in Japan and elsewhere to explore the possibility of creating a production system that could provide high variety, low cost, high quality and rapid throughput times. Taiichi Ohno is credited with drawing these themes together and developing the Toyota Production System.

Womack and Jones's five principles of lean thinking

Lean thinking involves specifying value, lining up value-creating activities in the most effective sequence, conducting these activities without interruption whenever 'pulled' to do so by customer demand, and continuously seeking new ways to improve this process. Each of Womack and Jones's (1996) five principles will be considered in turn.

Specify value

Specifying value is the essential first step in lean thinking and needs to be done from the perspective of the end customer. All too often, other stakeholders, such as shareholders, provide the starting point for defining value.

Womack and Jones (1996) argue that it can be hard to define value because many producers focus too much attention on the products or services they are already making and many customers only think in terms of some variant of what they are already getting. If they do attempt to rethink value, they may simply fall back on well-tried formulae such as lower cost, increased variety or instant delivery rather than challenging what is known and exploring what is really needed. They illustrate this point with numerous cases. For examples, Doyle Wilson House-builders introduced a radical TQM initiative that was welcomed by customers and helped the company increase market share. But Doyle Wilson recognized that only 22% of those purchasing a home bought a new house and began to wonder why the other 78% of homebuyers preferred old (second-hand) houses. Rather than restricting his attention to what his existing customers, the buyers of new homes, valued, he began to explore why the 78% of non-customers preferred older properties. This produced some valuable insights. They shied away from buying new homes because of the perceived hassle involved in negotiating the build specification, the long lead times before moving in, the inevitable 'snag' or 'to-be-done' lists of work still to be completed after moving in, and the 'phoney choices' available from builders who promised customized homes but then loaded them with standard equipment. Womack and Jones describe how this new perspective stimulated a complete rethink about what customers valued and what a builder of new houses needed to provide.

The specification of value in terms of the whole product or service

Typically, many departments within an organization or many firms within a supply chain contribute to producing value. Problems arise when any one of these elements in the value stream fails to appreciate how their actions affect value from the perspective of the end customer. For example, a company dedicated to producing well-designed, high-quality furniture and marketing its products direct to customers might decide to reduce costs by outsourcing delivery to an independent haulage contractor. The haulage contractor, in turn, might decide to cut costs by paying drivers on a commission basis. The effect of this might be to encourage drivers to complete as many 'drops' as possible in order to maximize their earnings, and to discourage them from spending time with customers to help them remove and dispose of packaging, check the quality of their purchase before signing for delivery, or carry the furniture from the front door to the required location. These may all be services that customers value. The furniture company's effort to deliver value to the customer can be easily undermined by this final link in the value stream. By focusing attention on their own immediate goals, the haulage contractor and the drivers they employ can destroy customer loyalty and adversely affect demand for the product.

Rethinking value not only requires producers to engage in a searching dialogue with customers, but also for all contributors to the value stream to talk to each other about how they each contribute to the value of the whole product or service from the perspective of the end user.

Target cost

Once value has been defined, it is possible to specify target cost. This, according to Womack and Jones (1996), is the amount of resource and effort required to produce the product or service to the required specification once all currently visible waste is removed from the process. It is this target cost that provides the lens for examining every step in the value stream.

Identify the value stream and eliminate wasteful steps

Identifying and mapping value streams is an effective way of exposing waste. Womack and Jones (1996) define a value stream as all the actions required to bring a specific product or product family through the three critical management tasks of:

1 problem solving – from concept through detailed design to product launch
2 information management – from order taking through detailed scheduling to delivery
3 physical transformation – from raw materials to finished product or service in the hands of the customer.

Chapter 23, on BPR, reviews many of the steps that need to be considered when identifying and mapping value streams.

While many actions in the value stream create value, others create waste (sources of waste are discussed in Change tool 24.1). Mapping a value stream involves identifying every action that, from the perspective of the customer, adds value and categorizing those activities that add no value into 'type one' and 'type two' waste. Type one waste includes all those activities that create no value but are unavoidable, given current technologies and production assets. Type two waste refers to those activities that fail to add value but are immediately avoidable.

Once type two waste has been eliminated, the way is clear to go to work on eliminating the remaining (type one) non-value-adding steps through the application of flow, pull and the other lean techniques considered later in this chapter.

Value stream mapping should not be restricted to the boundaries of a single organization in the supply chain. The concept of the lean enterprise embraces the whole value stream, which will often include contributions from more than one organization.

Flow

Once value has been specified, the value stream mapped and obviously wasteful steps eliminated, attention can be focused on making the remaining value-creating steps flow. Re-engineering to create flow can involve radical change. For example, a batch and queue production system might require considerable modification. This could involve the development of smaller machines, faster methods of switching tools to facilitate the manufacture of smaller batches, and the co-location of related steps in the production process to eliminate waste associated with transporting part-finished components between locations. A continuous flow layout often involves arranging related production steps in a sequence within a single 'cell' and quickly moving the product from one step to the next without any (wasteful) buffers of work in progress in between.

Womack and Jones (1996) advocate a three-prong approach to making value flow. The first, once value has been defined and the end-to-end value stream identified, involves following the product as it moves along the value stream. The second, reminiscent of the 'clean sheet' approach to BPR discussed in Chapter 23, involves ignoring traditional boundaries and other impediments to continuous flow, and the third involves rethinking specific work practices and tools to eliminate backflows, scrap and all sources of unnecessary stoppages so that the process can proceed continuously.

While some lean principles are similar to some aspects of BPR, Womack and Jones (1996) are critical of the re-engineering movement. In their view, although re-engineers seek to shift attention away from suboptimal departmental/functional thinking to value-creating processes, they believe that they pay too much attention to aggregated processes, such as order taking for a whole range of products, rather than the value-creating activities for a specific product or product family. They also argue that re-engineers typically limit their attention to delivering change within a single organization, and that they adopt an expert-driven, top-down approach that often fails to engage employees. They contrast this with their lean philosophy, which encourages employee engagement, focuses attention on specific products, and adopts a lean enterprise perspective that includes all the steps in a value stream even if they span many organizations.

Pull

While flow is necessary, it is not sufficient. Flow needs to be pulled through the production system. The pull principle involves no one producing anything until someone downstream requests it. Womack and Jones (1996) make an important distinction between pull and push. When products are 'pushed' through a production system to meet a sales forecast, any unanticipated fall in demand can lead to a rapid build-up of unwanted finished goods (waste) that, if not scrapped, may have to be sold off at a heavy discount.

Lean production involves making exactly what customers want when they want it. Figure 24.1 illustrates flow being pulled through the system in response to downstream requests. Customers pull the product from the producer and within the production system, every downstream production stage pulls inputs from adjacent upstream stages in the production process.

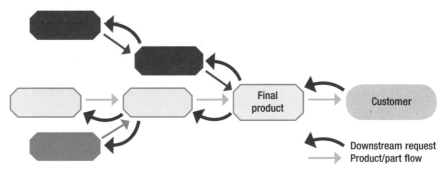

Figure 24.1 *Parts being pulled in response to customer requests*

Perfection: a continuous search for improvement

Early steps in the lean change process often involve discontinuous change such as a radical realignment of the value stream, for example moving from batch and queue to a continuous flow system pulled by customer demand. But the search for improvement should not stop there. An important principle of lean is the ongoing search for continuous improvement (kaizan).

Perfection is the complete elimination of waste. Womack and Jones see the quest for perfection as never ending and liken perfection to infinity: 'Trying to envision it (and get there) is actually impossible but *the effort to do so provides inspiration and direction essential to making progress along the path*' (1996: 94). They assert that the first four lean principles interact with each other to create a virtuous circle. Efforts to get value to flow faster expose hidden sources of waste. Efforts to pull products through the system highlight impediments to flow, and efforts to work with customers to refine the meaning of value inevitably point to new ways of adding value, facilitating flow and improving pull.

The pursuit of perfection involves assessing the gap between the current reality and perfection and, rather than trying to do everything at the same time, prioritizing the main sources of waste and focusing energy on these to close the gap. Womack and Jones (1996) advocate that when seeking perfection, attention should be focused on one thing at a time and working on it continuously until the desired improvement has been achieved.

The Toyota Production System

The Toyota Production System is widely regarded as the most successful example of lean. Its systemic qualities have has been represented as a house, all parts (foundations, pillars and roof) needing to work together to create the whole (Figure 24.2).

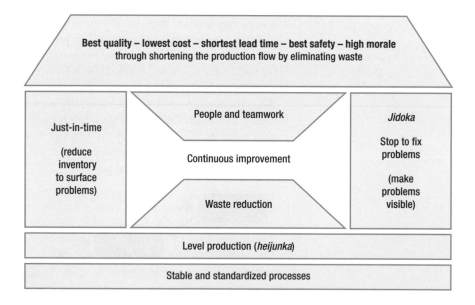

Figure 24.2 *The Toyota Production System house*
Source: Liker and Morgan, 2006: 7

Liker and Morgan (2006) point to some of the key elements of the Toyota Production System:

▶ *Just in time* was developed to facilitate smooth flow by ensuring that the right part is delivered to the right place at the right time. In ideal circumstances, material moves from operation to operation one piece at a time without interruption, but sometimes this continuous flow is not possible because components have to be produced in batches. Batch production requires the holding of inventories. Just in time refers to the way these inventories are replenished. Where fast set-up times enable machines to be quickly switched from manufacturing one component to another, it is possible to produce tiny batches. This, in turn, facilitates the holding of tiny inventories that are only replenished as required. Replenishment occurs when, and only when, the inventory is drawn down as parts are used in the next process downstream.

▶ *Jidoka* has already been described. It involves workers stopping production and immediately fixing problems as they occur. It ensures that problems are constantly surfaced and processes are improved on a continuous basis. To work effectively, people need to be skilled and motivated to solve problems quickly.

▶ *Heijunka* means levelling. It involves sequencing orders in a way that smoothes out short-term variations in demand. Level schedules make it possible to standardize processes. Without some element of levelling and stability, it would be impossible to maintain minimum level inventories that can be replenished on a just in time basis. For an example of how heijunka works, see Womack and Jones (1996: 306).

Some other lean tools and techniques

There is a wide range of other tools and techniques that lean practitioners use. A selection is provided in Change tools 24.1–24.3.

Change tool 24.1

The seven wastes

Value stream mapping, the basic tool for implementing lean, provides the basis for identifying waste. Taiichi Ohno's seven wastes offer employees a useful framework for searching out and eliminating all those activities that fail to add value. The seven wastes are:

* *overproduction:* making more than required, or making it earlier than required
* *waiting:* products waiting on the next production step, or people waiting for work to do
* *unnecessary transportation:* moving products farther than required
* *overprocessing products or parts:* this can occur because of poor design or inefficient tools
* *inventory:* holding more inventory than is minimally required
* *unnecessary motion:* people moving or walking more than minimally required, for example looking for tools, or bending to pick up a part or a tool from the floor rather that picking it off a waist-high, non-stoop scaffold
* *defective parts:* requiring effort to inspect and fix.

Womack and Jones (1996) added an eighth source of waste, producing goods and services that fail to meet the needs of the customer.

A useful starting point is to ask a group of employees to use the types of waste checklist and identify as many sources of waste as they can in their workplace.

Change tool 24.2	**The 5S methodology**
	Another technique for improving the way work is performed is 5S. Kocakülâh et al. (2008) describe how it can be applied in a kaizen event when a cross-section of managers and production workers are taken from their daily routines to focus on the 5Ss in a specific area. A typical sequence is: 1 *Separate:* evaluating and removing anything that is not required from the production area. 2 *Sort:* specifying and labelling locations for all remaining items required to perform the task. Locations are chosen to minimize motion. 3 *Sweep:* the area is cleaned and kept clean to facilitate efficient working. 4 *Standardize:* making everything consistent. Machines are set up identically and tasks are performed in a standardized way to support the flexibility of employees between work stations. 5 *Sustain:* maintaining the discipline of the preceding steps.

Change tool 24.3	**The five whys**
	This is a diagnostic tool that can be used to identify and eliminate the root cause of problems. The NHS Improvement Network (www.tin.nhs.uk/index.asp?pgid=1134) offers examples of how the five whys can be used to solve problems in healthcare settings: 1 The patient was late in the operating theatre – *Why?* 2 There was a long wait for a trolley – *Why?* 3 A replacement trolley had to be found – *Why?* 4 The original trolley's safety rail was worn and had eventually broken – *Why?* 5 It had not been regularly checked for wear – *Why?* Answer: We do not have an equipment maintenance schedule. The root cause is the absence of an equipment maintenance schedule, not the broken safety rail. Repairing the safety rail, or even a one-off safety rail check of all trolleys, will not guarantee that patients will never be late for theatre because of faulty equipment.

Other tools and techniques include total productive maintenance, single minute exchange of dyes, six sigma, control charts, cause-and-effect diagrams, the PDSA cycle and many more. Wikipedia is a rich source of further information.

Implementing lean in manufacturing contexts

Scherrer-Rathje et al. (2009) describe two attempts to implement lean in a Swiss food processing machines and equipment manufacturing company. The first attempt, in 1997, failed but a second, nine years later, was successful. The first attempt was initiated by a production supervisor who was struggling to maintain quality and delivery. While senior management agreed to fund the project, they adopted a hands-off approach, leaving the production supervisor and four colleagues to manage it. None of the project team were released from any of their day-to-day functional duties and, along with all those affected by the project, they had to cope with a number of other competing and uncoordinated change projects. This made it difficult to maintain focus and engage others. Eventually the project was terminated.

In 2006, a second project to introduce lean was launched. The trigger was increasing costs and an inability to satisfy customer requirements. In some cases, customers were having to wait up to 12 months for delivery and were threatening to move their business elsewhere. The CEO felt that a 'pull system' would help to eliminate waste, reduce costs and improve throughput times.

A key difference between the two attempts to introduce lean was that, second time round, there was sustained management commitment to the project. Managers also recognized the importance of getting employees involved and attempted to do this by concentrating resources on a pilot project, selected because it appeared most likely to deliver an early success, and using this early win to demonstrate the value of lean to the entire company. A review of the 1997 project pointed to decision-making bottlenecks, caused in part by management's hands-off approach and in part by their unwillingness to delegate sufficient autonomy to the project team. They addressed this issue by creating 'just-do-it' rooms in each business unit. In each room, the entire customer order process was displayed and, every morning, each order was tracked by an interdisciplinary team who had the authority and autonomy to make and implement decisions. The wide representation in the just-do-it room offered a macro-view of the whole process and detailed information (a micro-view) about any issues that might arise.

After reflecting on these two projects, Scherrer-Rathje et al. (2009) point to a number of lessons that might help to secure the success of future lean projects:

▶ *Visible management commitment*: Lack of management support can restrict access to required resources, lengthen decision-making processes, contribute to communication breakdowns up and down the value chain, and undermine employee commitment. Management support is a necessary condition for success.

▶ *Formal mechanisms to encourage and enable autonomy*: The 'just-do-it' rooms and procedures that enabled workers to stop production to immediately fix problems (jidoka) are examples of mechanisms that bring people working on the process together and empower them to make and implement decisions to quickly solve problems.

▶ *Communication of lean wins from the outset*: The second attempt to implement lean involved a pilot project that was used to quickly demonstrate the benefits of lean. In Chapter 29, it is argued that new initiatives are more likely to spread when they are seen to offer clear benefits and when others are able to observe these benefits in demonstration sites.

▶ *Continual evaluation of the lean project:* Early on in the second project, managers decided that while they would fully involve employees in current implementation tasks, they would not disclose the long-term strategic goal of building a lean enterprise. They took this decision to avoid overwhelming people with the scale of the project. However, as the project progressed, it transpired that some employees started to fear that they might be heading off in the wrong direction and sought reassurance that all the bits fitted together. Six months into the project, management changed their communication strategy and introduced monthly lean briefings for everybody involved. The importance of continually reviewing any change project is discussed in Chapters 2 and 27.

▶ *Implementing mechanisms to ensure the long-term sustainability of lean:* Scherrer-Rathje et al. (2009) draw attention to a number of things managers can do to help sustain and spread lean initiatives. More detailed consideration of measures that can promote sustainability can be found in Chapter 28.

Implementing lean in non-manufacturing contexts

Lean was originally developed in manufacturing companies and applied on the shop floor, but has since been applied in many non-manufacturing contexts. Liker and Morgan (2006) present an account of how Toyota applied lean principles to the product development process (PDP). They note that technical and service operations are challenging because work is often less repetitive than work on the shop floor and the product is less tangible. Nevertheless, Toyota was able to standardize the PDP, refine it, eliminate waste and, on a continuous basis, reduce both lead time and cost. Their account identifies 13 principles for applying lean in service contexts that relate to process, people, tools and technology. Four process principles are summarized here:

1 *Establish customer-defined values:* In the Toyota PDP case, this helped to reduce wasteful conflict between those who styled the car and product engineers who were more concerned with functionality and manufacturability than looks.
2 *Front load the product development process:* This helped to get everything right first time and avoid costly downstream design changes.
3 *Create a level PDP flow:* Years of experience enabled the company to predict the engineering hours required at various points in the PDP and assign engineers to programmes in a level way. People, over and above the core complement, were drawn from a central pool of technicians and engineers from outside suppliers as and when required.
4 *Standardization:* The key challenge for Toyota was to reduce variation while preserving creativity. Liker and Morgan (2006) point to a number of ways in which this was accomplished. For example, design standardization was achieved by developing a common architecture, modularity and shared components, and standardized skill sets were developed to provide flexibility in staffing.

Three other non-manufacturing contexts where lean principles have been applied are now explored.

Finance

Swank (2003) reports how lean principles were applied by Jefferson Pilot Finance (JPF) in the insurance industry. JPF was a full-service life insurance and annuities company in competition with specialized niche companies that were able to offer lower premiums and faster handling of policies. JPF's customers were independent life insurance advisers who sold and serviced policies to end users. The company's aim was to beat off the competition and establish itself as the 'partner of choice' for these advisers.

JPF identified many areas for improvement. Processing times varied between locations and, across the company, high levels of errors required many policy applications to be reworked. Swank (2003) reports that JPF believed it could benefit from lean production because its operations involved the processing of an almost tangible 'service product', with each insurance policy going through a series of processes, from initial application to underwriting, much like an automobile on an assembly line.

The company decided to pilot lean in one cell before rolling it out across the company. A number of changes were trialed. For example, linked processes, which were originally located by function in various parts of the organization, were brought together. Co-locating employees who received applications with those who sorted and processed them eliminated long delays. Files were transferred between groups in a matter of minutes rather than days. In addition to speeding throughput, this innovation also helped employees to develop a new awareness of the whole process and how what they did contributed to satisfying advisers and policy holders.

Standardized work processes, such as requiring everybody to store files in the same way, alphabetically rather than by policy number or date received, and in the same drawer at each work station, made it easier to move people between work stations in order to balance loads. It also made it easier for employees to cover for absent colleagues.

Work flows were smoothed by calculating the time for each operation so that the rate of production could be set to satisfy customer demand and people could be deployed as required to complete all steps in the process.

Product families were identified by clustering applications into separate groups according to complexity and allocating each their own performance goals. Performance measures that focused on eliminating waste and adding value from the perspective of the customer were developed. For example, processing time was measured in terms of the total time between a customer mailing an application to the company and the adviser receiving a completed policy, rather than the time taken to complete an intermediate step in the process.

Swank (2003) reports that the initiative delivered impressive results. The company halved the average time from receipt of an application to issuance of a policy, reduced labour costs by 26%, and trimmed the rate of reissues due to errors by 40%, all of which contributed to a 60% increase in new annualized life premiums in just two years.

Retailing

Up until the late 1970s, mass retailers achieved a cost advantage over smaller competitors by using their purchasing power to achieve economies of scale. This model required the retailer to hold large inventories and push products onto customers. Abernathy et al. (1999) note that Wal-Mart was one of the first to break away from this model and use emerging information technologies to pull the supply chain. Customer sales were tracked at checkouts, inventories within and across stores were monitored, and the data used to pull goods from suppliers as required. Supplies were delivered to stores from centralized distribution hubs on a just in time basis, enabling the company to drastically reduce inventories and in-store warehousing capacity.

Attention was then focused on developing a lean enterprise by extending this system to suppliers. In 1987, Wal-Mart established a 'Wal-Mart Retail Link' with Proctor & Gamble, providing the supplier with access to Wal-Mart point-of-sale information, allowing it to track its own products on a real-time basis. This development enabled Proctor & Gamble to manage its own inventories more effectively.

Healthcare

Young et al. (2004) argue that an obvious application of lean thinking in healthcare lies in eliminating delay, repeated encounters, errors and inappropriate procedures. Ben-Tovim et al. (2007) describe a successful lean implementation programme at Flinders Medical Centre in Australia. The initial project involved the emergency department. It was so congested that patients overflowed into the recovery area of the operating suite, disrupting the work of the emergency department and the division of surgery. Some elective surgery had to be cancelled at short notice, surgical training was disrupted, the safety of care in the emergency department was becoming compromised, and staff turnover was high.

The project started with a multidisciplinary group of emergency department staff mapping patient journeys. This demonstrated that the use of a five-point measure of patient acuity to prioritize care contributed to many problems, including the distress of patients who were 'bumped' down the queue when later patients were seen first because they had been allocated to a different triage category. Staff attempted to rescue this situation by instituting ad hoc and hard-to-manage strategies to push through 'bumped' patients when the build-up became excessive.

Streaming was introduced to help resolve this and related problems. Patient care families (groups whose care process was sufficiently similar for them to be managed together) were established on the basis of 'likely to go home' or 'likely to be admitted to hospital'. The process for each group was simplified by creating 'production cells' in which steps in the value stream were lined up to facilitate a steady flow. Patients were treated in these cells as they arrived rather than treating them in batches. The result was a halving of patients leaving the emergency department without completing their care, a reduction in congestion by decreasing the time patients spent in the department by 45 minutes, and the freeing of capacity to cope with a 10% increase in demand over the following 12 months.

Following this early success, lean thinking was disseminated across the hospital. Process mapping created detailed pictures of how work was done and generated a commitment to change. This led to the identification of improvement opportunities and the engagement of staff in PDSA cycles to eliminate waste and deliver value. Ben-Tovim et al. (2007) illustrate how this worked with an example that eradicated waste by speeding patient discharge. It became clear that the discharge of some inpatients was delayed because they had to wait for a date for a crucial follow-up test. A search for the root cause revealed that the clinical laboratory was under such pressure to perform tests that, when the laboratory receptionist left, it was decided to appoint a new technician rather than a replacement receptionist. The result was that appointments could only be made when a laboratory staff member was free to pick up and respond to messages left on the telephone answering system. This delay had the knock-on effect of increasing congestion in the emergency department while new patients who needed to be admitted waited for a bed.

Case study 24.1

Grampian Police

Members of the public were frustrated because they were finding it difficult to contact Grampian Police. There were over 70 different telephone lines the public could use. Some went to a central switchboard, others directly to various departments or local police stations, many of which were so small that they were not manned on a continuous basis. Consequently, many calls were not answered or were answered by somebody who was not in a position to resolve the caller's problem. Grampian Police responded by creating a new state-of-the-art call centre. Operators could use a geographical information system to identify where a caller was calling from, and could access a crime information system so that they were instantly aware of criminal activity in that area and the contact details of local officers and those leading current inquiries. The new service was well received, not least because call centre staff were able to deal with many calls in their entirety to the complete satisfaction of the caller. As word got round, more people started to ring in. The call centre became a victim of its own success. Workloads increased and the call centre manager appealed for more staff. But setting up the call centre had already stretched resources, so another way of managing the workload had to be found.

How might lean thinking help to resolve this workload problem?

Attention was focused instead on why people were calling the police. After analysing the reasons, it was found that a significant percentage of all calls related to firearms licensing matters. Grampian is a large rural area with many farmers and others who own firearms and shotguns that have to be licensed. A more detailed analysis of this category of calls revealed that almost all of them were prompted by problems and delays associated with the process of obtaining or renewing licences. It was predicted that eliminating these problems could free up to 14% of the call centre's capacity.

The first step was to study the existing process and identify sources of problems and waste arising from the design of the system. The licence renewal process, for example, started with a notice to renew being posted out to certificate holders. They then had to return a completed form to police headquarters together with other documents. After the forms had been returned and checked, a police officer was dispatched to visit the gun owner's premises. This was to inspect the guns and ensure that they were stored in a secure gun cabinet, as well as checking the suitability of the applicant. It was also necessary to inspect the land where the guns were to be used to ensure that it was compatible with the intended use. Unfortunately, many application forms were not completed correctly or some supporting documents were not supplied. The documentation had to be logged and filed and the applicant had to be written to with a request for further information or missing documents. Resubmissions then had to be reconciled with the original documentation before they could be processed. Gun owners were often frustrated because, for a variety of reasons, they often experienced delays in renewing their licences.

After the existing process had been studied, attention was focused on redesigning it to eliminate unnecessary steps and provide gun owners with a speedy and hassle-free service. The new licensing process was made to flow without interruption. Once the renewal application had been posted to the applicant, a specialist enquiry officer contacted the gun owner and arranged a home visit to complete the application process. During that visit, the enquiry officer helped the gun owner to correct any errors on the application form, checked that all the supporting documents were in order, inspected the gun, ensured that it was fit for purpose and checked the security arrangements. If the enquiry officer was satisfied that the gun owner was a fit applicant, he could accept payment on the spot and forward his recommendation to the firearms licensing manager who could then issue a licence. A process that used to take a considerable time and prompt many telephone calls to the police could now be completed expeditiously without any need for the applicant to phone into the call centre.

Summary

Womack et al. (1990) coined the phrase 'lean' to describe a production system that does more with less and less. It is a customer-focused process that aims to provide customers with precisely what they want, free of defects, exactly when they want it. Scherrer-Rathje et al. (2009) differentiate between lean as a set of tools and techniques and lean as a philosophy:

▶ Many practitioners focus their attention on tools, such as control charts, 5S, seven wastes, total productive maintenance, just in time inventories and so on, and direct their efforts towards applying some of them to achieve specific outcomes. Sometimes change efforts are restricted to particular parts of the organization or directed towards the achievement of limited goals, such as cost reduction.

▶ Others view lean as a philosophy and focus more attention on acting in accordance with guiding principles and overarching aims to create a 'lean enterprise'. They adopt a more holistic approach and consider how the interrelationships between and synergistic effects of related practices can affect performance across the whole enterprise.

This chapter traces the development of lean thinking and presents Womark and Jones's five lean principles:

1 *Precisely specify value for each product or product family:* Specifying value is the essential first step in lean thinking and needs to be done from the perspective of the end customer. Value also needs to be specified in terms of the whole product or service. Typically, many departments within an organization or many firms within a supply chain contribute to producing value. Problems can arise when any one of these elements in the value stream fails to appreciate how their actions affect value from the perspective of the end customer.

2 *Identify value streams for each product to expose waste:* Mapping a value stream involves identifying every action that, from the perspective of the customer, adds value and categorizing those activities that add no value into type one and type two waste. Type one waste includes all those activities that create no value but are unavoidable, given current technologies and production assets. Type two waste refers to those activities that fail to add value but are immediately avoidable.

3 *Make value flow without interruption:* A continuous flow layout could, for example, involve arranging related production steps in a sequence within a single 'cell' and quickly moving the product from one step to the next without any (wasteful) buffers of work in progress in between.

4 *Let customers pull value from the producer:* The pull principle involves no one producing anything until someone downstream requests it.

5 *Pursue perfection by searching out and eliminating further waste:* Perfection is the complete elimination of waste. Womack and Jones see the quest for perfection as never-ending, and liken perfection to infinity: 'Trying to envision it (and get there) is actually impossible but *the effort to do so provides inspiration and direction essential to making progress along the path*' (1996: 94).

A number of lean tools and techniques are reviewed along with issues to be considered when implementing lean. The chapter ends with an exploration of how lean has been applied in manufacturing and non-manufacturing settings.

Ben-Tovim et al.'s account of applying lean thinking at Flinders Medical Centre illustrates a key tenet of lean: learning and change only come from working on problems in the workplace. Lean is not a top-down process where senior managers diagnose the problem, design and then implement a solution. It is a process that involves people in the workplace developing a detailed understanding of how the work is done, searching out the root causes of waste and identifying more effective ways of delivering value to end users. Lean initiatives not only require visible and continuing management support but also a commitment from those directly involved in the workplace to engage in a bottom-up process to bring about change.

References

Abernathy, F.A., Dunlop, J.T., Hammond, J.H. and Weil, D. (1999) *A Stitch in Time: Lean Retailing and the Transformation of Manufacturing – Lessons from the Textile and Apparel Industries*, Oxford: Oxford University Press.

Ben-Tovim, D.I., Bassham, J.E., Bolch, D. et al. (2007) Lean thinking across a hospital: redesigning care at the Flinders Medical Centre, *Australian Health Review*, **31**(1): 10–16.

Kocakülâh, M.C., Brown, J.F. and Thomson, J.W. (2008) Lean manufacturing principles and their application, *Cost Management*, **22**(3): 16–28.

Liker, J.K. and Morgan, J.M. (2006) The Toyota way in service: the case of lean product development, *Academy of Management Perspectives*, **20**(2): 5–20.

Scherrer-Rathje, M., Boyle, T.A. and Deflorin, P. (2009) Lean, take two! Reflections from a second attempt at lean implementation, *Business Horizons*, **52**(1): 79–88.

Swank, C.K. (2003) The lean service machine, *Harvard Business Review*, **81**(10): 123–9.

Womack, J.P. and Jones, D.T. (1996) *Lean Thinking*, London: Simon & Schuster.

Womack, J.P., Jones, D.T. and Roos, D. (1990) *The Machine that Changed the World*, New York: Rawson Associates.

Young, T., Brailsford, S., Connell, C. et al. (2004) Using industrial processes to improve patient care, *British Medical Journal*, **328**(7432): 162–4.

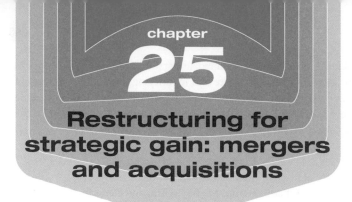

Restructuring for strategic gain: mergers and acquisitions

Judged from the perspective of value creation and value capture, relatively few mergers and acquisitions are successful (Tuch and O'Sullivan, 2007). This is the first of two chapters that explores what change managers can do to facilitate the combination process.

Although the failure of attempts to add value through acquiring or combining with other organizations is often explained in terms of poor strategic fit, problems associated with organization fit also need to be addressed. This chapter adopts a process perspective (Poole et al., 2000) and points to a set of frequently experienced early conditions and critical junctures that, if not managed carefully, can adversely affect the outcome of the acquisition process.

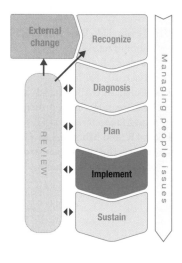

Restructuring for strategic gain

Mergers and acquisitions involve the combination of separate units. When most people think about mergers, they think about bringing together separate organizations to form a new organizational entity, but mergers can also involve internal combinations within a single organization. For example, similar units might be merged in order to eliminate duplication or different units might be brought together as part of a restructuring designed to reduce the number of separate functions.

There are many different ways in which units or whole organizations can be combined. From the perspective of 'relatedness', it is possible to identify four broad types of combination:

▸ *horizontal mergers* involve the combination of units or organizations that are engaged in similar activities
▸ *vertical mergers* involve the bringing together of units or organizations that are engaged in successive stages of a production process
▸ *concentric mergers* involve unrelated organizations in the same sector combining to secure some mutual advantage, for example a building society acquiring a firm of estate agents
▸ *conglomerate mergers* involve the combination of completely unrelated organizations.

Both mergers and acquisitions are high-risk undertakings that do not always deliver the anticipated strategic gains. Joint ventures and strategic alliances are alternative and less risky ways in which organizations can join forces for mutual advantage.

Joint ventures

Joint ventures involve the creation of a new organizational entity that enables the partner organizations to work together while protecting their core businesses.

Example 25.1

> ### GNER and MTR
>
> GNER, a train operating company, decided to form a joint venture with the Chinese MTR Corporation to bid for the integrated Kent franchise in the UK. The franchise included the commuter rail services between southeast England and London and the high-speed line from London to the Channel Tunnel. GNER operated long-distance intercity routes but had no experience of operating commuter trains. MTR ran the highly successful mass transit railway in Hong Kong and was one of the most efficient operators of commuter networks in the world. The company wanted to expand into Europe but had no experience of the British railway industry. The joint venture enabled both companies to continue running their own core businesses, while providing the opportunity to combine their technical expertise to bid for the new franchise.

Strategic alliances

Strategic alliances can vary in form from the informal cross-referral of business to more formal arrangements that involve the cross-ownership of shares. They are often adopted as the most effective way of joint working in circumstances where government regulations complicate or even prohibit the possibility of one company acquiring control of another. In other circumstances, organizations may decide to commit to a strategic alliance in order to test out the possibility of a more formal merger at a later date.

Acquisitions

The majority of combinations referred to as 'mergers' actually involve one organization acquiring control of another, but they are often referred to as 'mergers' in order to make the takeover more palatable to the stakeholders of the acquired organization.

Brenntag, the global chemical distribution company, is one of many organizations that has grown by acquiring other businesses (Example 25.2).

Example 25.2

> ### Brenntag's history of restructuring for strategic gain
>
> The German company Brenntag has a 135-year history of restructuring for strategic gain. A long line of acquisitions, divestments, joint ventures and strategic alliances has transformed the original Berlin-based egg wholesaling business into the leading distributor of chemicals, with more that 11,000 staff employed at 300 locations worldwide. As the company grew, it diversified. It began to trade in other foodstuffs and drugs, and then expanded into chemicals, crude oil and motor fuels. Eventually, however, it began to concentrate on the distribution of chemical products to industrial users.
>
> Divestments helped to provide this strategic focus. For example, Brenntag sold its network of 120 service stations for retailing petrol and related products to Total. It also

disposed of its heating and heating oil distribution operations to Raab Karcher in exchange for its chemical distribution business.

Acquisitions helped to:

- secure key links in the value-added chain, for example several shipping operations were purchased
- extend the range of chemical products it distributed – serving the needs of industrial users in sectors ranging from paints, plastics, pharmaceuticals and food processing to energy and personal care products
- gain footholds in new markets, for example Eastern Europe, Russia, Asia and the Americas
- consolidate its position in existing markets.

As well as acquiring control of many companies, Brenntag also forged strategic alliances with leading chemical manufactures to distribute their products and launched joint ventures, for example in Japan and Russia, to gain access to new sources of supply and new markets.

Brenntag's successful history of restructuring for strategic gain is the product of successive management teams' ability to articulate clear strategic objectives and develop robust criteria for assessing joint venture partners and acquisition targets in terms of their potential to add value.

The company also has a strong track record in terms of achieving organization fit. Sometimes acquired companies have been closely integrated with Brenntag's existing businesses in order to realize synergies, but there are also examples where acquired companies have been allowed to maintain considerable autonomy when this was judged to be the most effective way of securing added value.

The acquisition process

The acquisition process has received attention from many writers. Marks and Mirvis (1998, 2001) refer to three phases; pre-combination, combination and post-combination. Hubbard (1999) describes a four-phase process that involves pre-acquisition planning, communication, implementation and stabilization. She draws particular attention to the importance of three critical steps in the pre-acquisition planning phase: the identification of acquisition objectives, the development of an acquisition overview and the formulation of an implementation plan (see Figure 25.1). Hubbard argues that the way this pre-acquisition process is managed can have a powerful effect on the way the subsequent phases of the acquisition process unfold. Jemison and Sitkin (1986) also adopt a process perspective and liken the acquisition process to a courtship. They propose that factors such as context, composition of the buy team, expectancy ambiguities, pace, and the nature of early decisions affect the flow of subsequent events and the eventual success of the marriage.

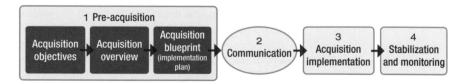

Figure 25.1 *The acquisition process*

Source: Based on Hubbard, 1999

This chapter examines some of the early conditions and critical junctures that need to be recognized and addressed in the pre-combination and combination phases if the acquisition is to deliver added value.

Acquisition objectives and strategic fit

The motive for most acquisitions is some form of value creation for one or more of the main stakeholder groups. This can take the form of increased shareholder wealth, improved benefits for customers or improved benefits for organizational members, such as enhanced prestige, greater challenges and opportunities for salary growth.

Some of the most frequently cited strategic objectives are:

▶ financial synergies
▶ market penetration
▶ market entry
▶ market protection
▶ product extension
▶ technical expertise
▶ vertical expansion
▶ access to resources
▶ operational synergies
▶ managerial expertise
▶ economies of scale
▶ enhanced prestige.

Exercise 25.1 **Securing strategic gains**

Think about an acquisition that you have experienced or know something about:

- What did the acquiring organization or merger partners seek to gain? List the acquisition objectives in the table below.
- Were the intended gains actually achieved?

	Acquisition objective(s)	Assess the extent to which each objective was achieved (1 = not at all, 5 = completely) and explain why
1		Rating: Why:
2		Rating: Why:
3		Rating: Why:

You might find it helpful to reflect back on your answers when you have read Chapters 25 and 26.

Value creation and value capture

Judged from the perspective of value creation and value capture, relatively few mergers and acquisitions are as successful as those leading the process initially anticipate. Jemison and Sitkin (1986) define strategic fit as the degree to which the target (acquired) organization augments or complements the parent (acquiring) organization's strategy and makes an identifiable contribution to the parent organization's financial or non-financial goals.

Acquisitions sometimes fail to yield much in the way of added value because, even though strategic fit tends to receive a lot of attention in the early part of the pre-acquisition process, those leading the process misjudge the potential benefit that the acquisition will generate. Even in those cases where some added value is created, this benefit may not be captured by the acquiring organization. Several firms may believe, for example, that they have the capability to restructure an ailing target and improve its performance. In this kind of 'restructuring scenario' (see Chatterjee, 1992), the value resides with the target rather than the acquiring organization and the process of bidding to acquire the target may drive up the price to a point where any added value is competed away from the successful bidder.

Capron and Pistre (2002) developed this line of thinking. They define synergy as the increase in the merging firms' competitive strengths and resulting benefits beyond those they would have achieved if they had continued to operate independently. They identify three broad cases of how potential synergies can impact the added value that is actually captured by the acquiring organization:

1 *The synergistic benefits stem from the target organization's resources:* In this situation, the acquiring firm is unlikely to capture much of the added value. In the restructuring example referred to above, the value resides with the underutilized target firm's resources. The target firm is likely to have a number of potential bidding firms, who all have the necessary managerial capability to improve its performance, to choose from and, therefore, to enjoy a superior bargaining position. The competition to acquire the target organization drives up the price of the acquisition and it is the shareholders of the acquired organization rather than the acquiring organization who end up capturing most of the added value.

2 *The synergistic benefits stem from the acquirer's resources:* It is in this situation that the acquiring firm in likely to capture most of the added value. Examples typically involve the acquiring firm controlling some unique resource, for example a patent on a new product, which it can lever into the target organization's context to create synergies that competing bidders cannot duplicate. In such cases, the value of the acquiring firm's resources does not depend on the participation of a specific target organization. Consequently, the acquiring firm has the greatest bargaining strength because it has a broad selection of target firms to choose from and minimal or no competition from rival bidders.

3 *The synergistic benefits stem from both the acquirer's and the target organization's resources:* When opportunities to exploit synergies are associated with both organizations' resources, the synergetic benefits (value created) are likely to be divided between parent and target. How the benefits will be divided will depend on the relative bargaining position and negotiating skill of the acquiring organization and the target. Capron and Pistre (2002) identify the extreme case where one unique acquirer's resources fit one unique target organization's resources, leading to the equal distribution of synergetic gains. Moving away from this position, where one organization controls resources that contribute more to the synergetic gains or has alternative opportunities to select organizations to deploy its resource with, it is likely to have superior bargaining power and, therefore, gain the greater share of the added value.

This argument indicates that even though strategic fit tends to receive a lot of attention from the buy team, especially in the pre-combination phase of the acquisition process, those driving the acquisition may be overoptimistic about how much value the acquisition will actually deliver. Cartwright and Schoenberg (2006) refer to several studies indicating that 44–50% of all acquisitions fail to meet the objectives set for them, and that, over a 30-year period, there have been few signs of improvement in merger and acquisition performance.

Assessing organization fit in the pre-acquisition phase

While issues relating to the management of strategic fit are important, there is a growing body of opinion that the quality of organization fit and the management or mismanagement of the integration process also contributes to the poor record of acquisition success. Clarifying acquisition objectives is not only an essential first step in the process of identifying a suitable acquisition target, but is also a necessary prerequisite for planning the integration process.

A number of factors interact to shape the focus and quality of early attempts to explore and test the viability of a proposed acquisition, and these are discussed in more detail below.

The range and complexity of issues

Due diligence needs to consider more than just a search for and appraisal of financial information about the target company. Depending on the acquisition objectives, it may need to include an industry and competitor analysis, a product and market analysis, an assessment of the target's management talent, an analysis of management fit in terms of philosophy and attitudes and a wider assessment of culture fit, an assessment of potential synergies and any technical issues that could affect whether these synergies will be realized, a review of terms and conditions of employment, an assessment of the compatibility of pension funds and so on. Jemison and Sitkin (1986) suggest that this complexity results in these analyses being allocated to separate members of the buy team or delegated to external specialists. This segmentation and delegation often has the effect of increasing the influence of external specialists, who tend to be more focused on assessing strategic fit rather than the practicalities involved in integrating the two businesses after the deal has been agreed. A further complication is that in some cases, little attention is given to synthesizing these disparate analyses.

Pressure to complete the due diligence review quickly

Jemison and Sitkin (1986) observe that there is often an escalating momentum in the acquisition process that results in premature solutions and insufficient attention being given to the quality of organization fit and the integration process. They point to many factors that stimulate this escalating momentum, including:

▶ the 'thrill of the chase' that can blind members of the buy team to the 'consequences of the catch'
▶ the problems associated with maintaining secrecy – to avoid unsettling customers, key staff who must be retained, suppliers and financial markets
▶ the buy team's limited tolerance for ambiguity, which motivates them to seek early closure.

The relative ease of assessing strategic rather than organization fit

It can be difficult to gather all the information required in order to assess the quality of organization fit and identify the likelihood that the desired level of integration can be achieved at a reasonable cost. This is especially so if secrecy has to be maintained or the target's management team are hostile to the bid. For example, in such circumstances, it will be difficult to obtain information about the target firm's management talent (particularly middle management talent), determine the compatibility of IT systems or gather information about the target's organization culture. The information required to assess the target company's financial health, on the other hand, is usually more accessible. This might not be a problem if the reason for acquiring a particular target centres on financial synergies, but could be a problem if gaining market share or achieving economies of scale are key acquisition objectives.

Mindset of the buy team

Marks and Mirvis (2001) report that the mindset of the buy team is an important determinant of acquisition success. They found that in the less successful cases they studied, the buyers tended to exhibit financial tunnel vision. They concentrated their attention on the numbers and focused on what the target was worth. Their decision to do a deal was typically framed in terms of the combined balance sheet of the companies, projected cash flows, and hoped-for return on investment. In the more successful cases, the buyers adopted a more strategic mindset and positioned the financial analysis in the context of an overarching set of strategic objectives.

They also found that the buyers' mindset was related to the composition of the buy team. When members had predominantly financial backgrounds, they appeared more inclined to assess potential acquisition targets from a financial perspective and make judgements about possible synergies on the basis of financial models and ratios. Hard criteria dominated and if the numbers looked good, issues relating to organizational and cultural differences tended to be ignored. However, when the buy team included influential members with operational and technical backgrounds, there was a greater chance that hoped-for synergies would be made more explicit and their value more realistically assessed and given a more central role in the early decision-making process.

Acquisition overview and the assessment of organization fit

One of the issues that needs to be considered in the pre-acquisition phase is the degree of integration sought between the parent and target companies. This issue might be addressed early when the acquisition objectives are being identified. If not, it must be addressed before any workable implementation plan can be formulated.

Hubbard (1999) presents a continuum of integration possibilities ranging from total autonomy to full integration. Four points on this continuum are specified in Figure 25.2. These are:

▶ *total autonomy:* where the acquired firm is controlled by financial measures but is not required to engage in any physical integration
▶ *restructuring followed by financial control:* where the acquired company is modified in some respect, for example new technologies, more efficient working practices or a new management team are introduced, and is then left to operate in a stand-alone capacity, subject only to financial controls
▶ *functional integration:* where one or more departments or functions are integrated to achieve cost savings or economies of scale
▶ *full integration:* where both companies merge their operations.

Hubbard (1999) argues that the strategic objectives that are driving the acquisition will determine the possible range of integration possibilities. For example, if a company is acquired in order to achieve financial synergies, total integration might not be the best way forward; however, if the aim is market penetration, almost any degree of integration might be compatible with achieving this strategic objective (see Figure 25.2).

Degree of integration chosen

Reason for acquisition	Financial controls	Change with controls	Funtional integration	Total integration
Financial synergies	LIKELY	POSSIBLE	UNLIKELY	UNLIKELY
Market entry	LIKELY	POSSIBLE	UNLIKELY	UNLIKELY
Vertical integration	POSSIBLE	LIKELY	POSSIBLE	UNLIKELY
Asset potential	POSSIBLE	LIKELY	POSSIBLE	UNLIKELY
Market penetration	POSSIBLE	POSSIBLE	LIKELY	POSSIBLE
Economies of scale	UNLIKELY	UNLIKELY	POSSIBLE	LIKELY

Figure 25.2 *Acquisition objectives and the required degree of integration*
Source: Adapted from Hubbard, 1999: 53

Hubbard (1999) describes the acquisition overview as the step in the acquisition process that provides the bridge between acquisition objectives and the acquisition blueprint (implementation plan). It specifies, in general terms, how these strategic objectives can be achieved. She offers the example of one building society acquiring another in order to achieve market penetration and economies of scale. The simple act of acquiring the other building society will help to achieve market penetration by reducing competition and consolidating the position of the acquirer in the market-place, but more may need to be done. For example, the sales teams of both companies may need to engage in cross-selling and the joint development of new products and services. Careful attention will need to be given to how this will be done.

Similarly, with regard to the objective of achieving economies of scale, thought will have to be given to how these economies will be delivered. If it will involve rationalizing branch networks, on what basis will decisions be made about which branches will be closed? Where will the new headquarters be located and what will happen to any redundant facilities? Which departments and/or processes in the two building societies could be combined and what criteria will guide decisions?

The acquisition blueprint (implementation plan)

The acquisition blueprint, according to Hubbard (1999), takes the acquisition overview and divides it into task-specific actions that can be managed on a project-by-project basis. It specifies what actions are to be taken, when they will occur, who will be affected, who will be responsible for implementing them and how they will take place. Hubbard also argues that the logic behind these changes needs to be thought through so that it can be articulated to those affected (see the section on communications below and in Chapter 26). The focus at this stage in the process is achieving the required level of integration.

Organization integration

Integration is an important issue within as well as between organizations. Within a single organization, the natural tendency to identify and communicate with those who share common problems and experiences often has the effect of diverting attention away from common objectives, as employees focus attention on the goals of their immediate subgroup. Organizations attempt to overcome this kind of problem by introducing integrating mechanisms such as rules and procedures that promote standardized ways of working, planning mechanisms that focus attention on common goals, coordinator roles that promote direct and continuous contact between groups, and organizational structures (such as matrix structures) that facilitate the management of conflicting priorities.

Shrivastava (1986) observes that these problems of within-firm integration are vastly compounded when two independent firms are merged. He identifies three levels of integration associated with mergers and acquisitions:

1 The first and easiest to achieve is procedural integration. This involves combining the accounting systems of the two organizations and creating a single legal entity.
2 The second involves the integration of physical assets, production lines, production systems and technologies.
3 The third and most critical level of integration is managerial and sociocultural.

At each of these levels, three key issues need to be addressed – coordination, control and the management of differences, that is, conflict resolution. Table 25.1 provides some examples of typical post-merger integration tasks.

Table 25.1 *Post-merger integration tasks*

	Coordination	*Control*	*Conflict resolution*
Procedural	Design accounting systems and procedures	Design management control systems	Eliminate contradictory rules and procedures Rationalize systems
Physical	Facilitate sharing of resources	Measure and manage the productivity of resources	Allocate resources Redeploy assets
Managerial and sociocultural	Establish integrator roles Introduce new organization structures Develop a consistent corporate culture and frame of reference to guide decision making	Design compensation and reward systems Allocate authority and responsibility	Stabilize power sharing Eliminate incompatible frames of reference and conflicting priorities

Source: Adapted from Shrivastava, 1986: 67

Procedural integration

Reference has already been made to the creation of a single legal entity and the merging of accounting systems, but attention might also be given to integrating other control systems and procedures in order to standardize aspects of strategic planning, management control and operations. This may involve developing new systems and procedures or the transfer of existing ways of working from one organization to the other.

Physical integration

Following a merger, there is often a need to redeploy assets in the process of resource sharing. Both organizations may have assets that could be combined to produce operational synergies. This might require the relocation of some plant and equipment, the consolidation of inventories and so on. There may also be duplication of assets, which could give rise to the need for disposals. For example, where there is duplication of IT systems or product lines, the most efficient may be retained and the least efficient discarded. Disposals may also be based on fit with the acquiring firm's strategy.

Managerial and sociocultural integration

Shrivastava (1986) defines this as a complex combination of issues, including the selection or transfer of managers, changes in organizational structure, the development of a consistent corporate culture and frame of reference to guide decision making, the gaining of commitment and motivation from all organizational members, and the establishment of new leadership.

Conflicting frames of reference illustrate the importance of achieving integration at this level, because if different frames persist, they can lead to inconsistent decision making, confusion and conflict. For example, managers from the acquiring organization may have a shared belief that the way to improve financial performance is to drive down costs, including labour costs, in order to increase market share. This will have important implications for how they will seek to manage the business postmerger. Managers from the acquired firm, on the other hand, may believe that overall performance and long-term profitability are affected by a completely different set of causal relationships. Their decision making may be guided by the belief that employee motivation and commitment are key performance drivers, because it can positively affect customer satisfaction and customer loyalty, which, in turn, will promote revenue growth and profitability. Such different frames of reference can have important implications for the way managers across the new organization work together.

Communication

Communication between the buy and sell teams during the due diligence phase is important. Marks and Mirvis (1986) observe that partners in successful acquisitions often share a common view about aims and objectives and the terms of their relationship. They note, however, that, as with marriage contracts between individuals, many aspects of the proposed relationship between the two organizations tend to be implicit rather than explicit, and, as a consequence, can be open to misinterpretation and misunderstanding at a later date.

Jemison and Sitkin (1986) draw attention to the deliberate use of ambiguity in the early phases of the acquisition process. Ambiguity can provide both parties with room for manoeuvre during negotiations and can help them to find a common dominator for agreement when faced with seemingly intractable issues. It can also help them save face when public announcements are made. However, later in the acquisition process, this once helpful ambiguity can become a problem. Jemison and Sitkin (1986) argue that when seeking agreement on parts of the new arrangement, especially those relating to how both organizations will be integrated, highlights significant

differences of interpretation, the relationships that were established during the negotiation process, including fragile bonds of trust, may begin to unravel. In worst-case
situations, the outcome can be 'a cycle of escalating conflict leading to further distrust
and polarization of preconceived attitudes about the other party'.

There is an oft-cited apocryphal story about how a failure to communicate led to
an acquisition disaster. The strategic objective for acquiring a company was its
wealth of technical talent in the field of product innovation and development. Many
parts of the acquired firm were of limited value to the new parent company. Some
production facilities were closed or relocated; the sales force was reduced and
remaining staff absorbed into parts of the new parent. The head office was closed.
The product development team watched these developments with mounting
concern. Nobody bothered to communicate with them about their future prospects.
They feared the worst. The result was that the whole team up and left and, as a
complete unit, joined a competitor organization.

Developing a communication strategy, including a detailed plan for communication to all stakeholder groups when the acquisition is announced, can have an
important impact on the outcome of the process. Hubbard (1999) provides a
comprehensive overview of the many issues that need to be considered and argues
that communication planning is important for four reasons:

1 to maximize the likelihood of successful communication on the day of announcement
2 to coordinate the communication of 'secret' information during the early pre-
 acquisition phase, while continuing to communicate openly about day-to-day
 operational matters
3 to coordinate internal and external messages
4 to provide a contingency plan if early negotiations are leaked.

Issues relating to stakeholder mapping discussed in Chapter 8 and communication
channels discussed in Chapter 10 are relevant when planning what messages are to
be communicated to which audiences, when and via which channels. Some techniques for facilitating communication are discussed in Chapter 26.

Acquisition implementation

Acquisitions are based on some kind of strategic vision, although sometimes poorly
conceived, which provides managers in the acquiring organization with a view about
how their and the acquired organization can be integrated to generate added value.
When this phase of the acquisition process is well managed, integrating both
organizations can be relatively straightforward. However, because of the heavy costs
that may have been incurred, managers in the acquiring organization often feel
under pressure to deliver quick wins. Jemison and Sitkin (1986) argue that this pressure, coupled with an overconfidence in their own management capabilities, can
lead managers in the acquiring organization to adopt a heavy-handed approach,
which typically involves imposing their way of doing things on the acquired
business. They observe that the target firm's fundamental competencies and capabilities, which may have been a part of what attracted the parent organization to acquire
the target in the first place, are often dismissed or ignored. According to Jemison and
Sitkin (1986), members of the acquired firm may experience this 'parent firm arrogance' in three ways:

1 They may perceive some measure of interpersonal arrogance in the way members
 of the acquired organization relate with them: 'Because we acquired you, we are
 smarter than you.'

2　They may also perceive a degree of cultural arrogance and the presumption that the acquiring firm's style, values, beliefs and practices are superior.

3　Finally, they may perceive a level of managerial arrogance manifest in a presumption that the parent firm's systems and processes are superior. Members of the acquired firm are unlikely to react well if everything they experience during the implementation phase signals that they are incompetent rather than just different.

Summary

Acquisition success depends on strategic and organization fit. This chapter adopts a process perspective and considers some of the conditions and critical junctures that can affect the quality of strategic fit and the integration process. Some of the issues that those leading the acquisition need to recognize and address are identified.

Acquisitions sometime fail to yield as much value as anticipated because the buy team is unclear about the acquisition objectives, misjudges the potential benefit that the acquisition will generate and overestimates the extent to which any added value will be captured by the acquiring organization.

A number of factors, such as the range and complexity of the issues that have to be investigated, the pressure to complete the due diligence review quickly, the difficulty of obtaining data to assess organization fit, and the mindset of the buy team, can deflect attention away from organization fit and the management of the integration process.

Many of these potential problems can be avoided, or at least minimized, if careful attention is given to:

1　Specifying acquisition objectives. The motive for most acquisitions is some form of value creation for one or more of the main stakeholder groups. Some of the most frequently cited strategic objectives are financial synergies, market penetration, market entry, market protection, product extension, technical expertise, vertical expansion, access to resources, operational synergies, managerial expertise, economies of scale, and enhanced prestige.

2　Developing an acquisition overview to provide a bridge between the acquisition objectives and what needs to happen if they are to be achieved. One of the issues that needs to be considered at this stage is the degree of integration sought between the parent and target companies.

3　Elaborating this overview to develop an implementation plan. This involves taking the acquisition overview and dividing it into task-specific actions that can be managed on a project-by-project basis. It specifies what actions are to be taken, when they will occur, who will be affected, who will be responsible for implementing them, and how they will take place. Integration can occur at three levels:

   •　*Procedural integration:* At a minimum, this involves creating a single legal entity and the merging of accounting systems, but it can also involve integrating other control systems and procedures.

   •　*Physical integration:* Following an acquisition, there is often a need to redeploy assets in the process of resource sharing.

   •　*Managerial and sociocultural integration:* This is a complex combination of issues including the selection or transfer of managers, changes in organizational structure, the development of a consistent corporate culture and frame of reference to guide decision making, the gaining of commitment and motivation from all organizational members, and the establishment of new leadership.

4　Avoiding a heavy-handed way of managing the actual implementation. Because of the high costs that may have been incurred, managers in the acquiring organization often feel under pressure to deliver quick wins. This pressure, coupled with an overconfidence in their own management capabilities, can lead managers in the acquiring organization to adopt a heavy-handed approach, which typically involves imposing their way of doing things on the acquired business.

References

Capron, L. and Pistre, L. (2002) When do acquirers earn abnormal returns?, *Strategic Management Journal*, 23: 781–94.

Cartwright, S. and Schoenberg, R. (2006) Thirty years of mergers and acquisitions research: recent advances and future opportunities, *British Journal of Management*, **17**(S): 1–5.

Chatterjee, S. (1992) Sources of value in takeovers: synergy or restructuring – implications for target and bidder firms, *Strategic Management Journal*, **13**: 267–86.

Hubbard, N. (1999) *Acquisition: Strategy and Implementation*, Basingstoke: Macmillan – now Palgrave Macmillan.

Jemison, D.B. and Sitkin, S.B. (1986) Corporate acquisitions: a process perspective, *Academy of Management Review*, **11**(1): 145–63.

Marks, M.L. and Mirvis, P.H. (1998) *Joining Forces*, San Francisco, CA: Jossey-Bass.

Marks, M.L. and Mirvis, P.H. (2001) Making mergers and acquisitions work: strategic and psychological preparation, *Academy of Management Executive*, **15**(2): 80–92.

Poole, M.S., van de Ven, A.H., Dooley, K. and Holmes, M.E. (2000) *Organizational Change and Innovation Processes: Theory and Methods for Research*, Oxford: Oxford University Press.

Shrivastava, P. (1986) Postmerger integration, *Journal of Business Strategy*, **7**(1): 65–76.

Tuch, C. and O'Sullivan, N. (2007) The impact of acquisitions on firm performance: a review of the evidence, *International Journal of Management Reviews*, **9**(2): 141–70.

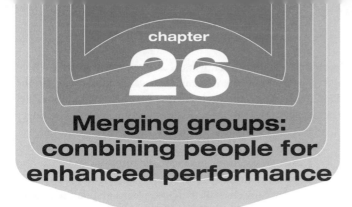
Theories of social identity and acculturation provide the conceptual framework for considering what change managers can do to promote people synergies when organizations are being combined. Social identity theory is introduced to explain how acquisitions and mergers threaten employees' organizational identity, exacerbate 'us and them' dynamics and adversely affect merger success. Acculturation theory is used to explore how employees' preferences for combining their organizational cultures, practices and systems affect acquisition and merger outcomes.

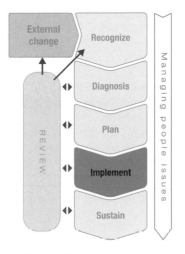

Attention is given to three ways in which managers can intervene to promote people synergy: culture profiling to pre-screen potential merger partners and, later in the merger process, guide the integration process; change communication to provide organizational members with clear and unambiguous information about what is going to change as a result of the merger; and socioemotional support to care for those affected by the change, minimize alienation and promote post-merger organizational identity.

People's response to acquisitions and mergers

Many of the benefits that are anticipated when an acquisition or merger is being planned depend on employees' commitment to the new organization and their willingness to work together to deliver high performance. Often this required level of people synergy is not achieved.

Cartwright and Cooper (1990) observe that poor post-merger performance is often explained in terms of poor strategic fit, the payment of an overinflated purchase price for the acquisition, financial mismanagement or sudden and unanticipated changes in market conditions. They note, however, that these explanations fail to take account of what they believe is the most fundamental factor contributing to merger success – 'the positive combination of people, their expertise, and their organizational cultures'.

Employees respond to acquisitions and mergers in many different ways. Some identify and welcome opportunities for career development, greater challenges and improved scope and variety of work, or they see the merger as a way of achieving greater job security or enhanced status through association with the new organization. Others have a less positive view. Members of acquired firms may feel that they have been 'sold out' and, especially if the acquisition was contested, that they have been overwhelmed and defeated. Members of acquiring and acquired organizations may be concerned about job security and, even if redundancy is not an immediate threat, may feel less in control of their immediate working arrangements and longer term career prospects. All this can have a powerful effect on job satisfaction, motivation and organizational commitment and can lead to outcomes such as anxiety, stress, poor performance, greater absenteeism and increased turnover.

There are many reports of these negative outcomes. Cartwright (2005) cites several studies which indicate that lower morale and perceptions of unfair treatment lead to lower post-merger performance. Ashford (1988) and Cooper and Payne (1988) report that stress and mental health problems undermine performance. Cabrera (1982) points to examples of non-productive behaviours such as spending time gossiping about merger-related issues, political manoeuvring and jockeying for position to gain advantage or guard against loss. Walsh (1988) reports that 25% of top executives of acquired companies leave within the first year, a rate of turnover significantly higher than 'normal' top team turnover.

Organizational identity and negative effects: social identity theory

Several writers (Ashforth and Mael, 1989; Bartels et al., 2006; van Dick et al., 2006) suggest that social identity theory offers a conceptual framework for understanding why many employees react negatively. Acquisitions and mergers threaten an important aspect of their social identity – their sense of belonging to an organization. People not only identify themselves in terms of 'I' – their idiosyncratic characteristics such as physical features, interests, abilities and personality traits – but also in terms of 'we' – affiliations with social categories such as nationality, occupation and religion. For many, work group and organizational affiliation are important parts of their social identity.

Social identity theory was developed following a series of seminal studies by Tajfel and colleagues on intergroup discrimination (see Tajfel and Turner, 1979). Their laboratory experiments investigated the minimal conditions that lead members of one group (the in-group) to discriminate in favour of their group and against another group. Participants were allocated to groups on the flimsiest of criteria, for example their preferences for an abstract painter or the toss of a coin. Findings indicated that when individuals categorize themselves as members of a group, even when the basis of this categorization was trivial, this could give rise to a sense of belonging that affected their behaviour. However, Tajfel and Turner recognized that in-group favouritism was not an inevitable consequence of group membership. They identified three conditions that give rise to intergroup discrimination and in-group bias. These are:

▶ the extent to which individuals identify with an in-group and internalize membership of that group as a part of their self-concept
▶ the extent to which the prevailing context provides grounds for comparison and competition between groups
▶ the perceived relevance of the comparison group, which, in turn, depends on the relative and absolute status of the in-group.

Acquisitions and mergers present all three of these conditions. For many employees, organizational affiliation is an important aspect of their self-concept. Acquisitions and mergers clearly provide opportunities for comparison and competition between groups and in many merger and almost all acquisition scenarios, there are status differences between the merging organizations.

Van Dick et al. (2006) argue that acquisitions and mergers affect employees' social identity because they redraw or dissolve the boundaries that once categorized the two distinct organizations. When employees perceive the merger or acquisition as a threat to the distinctiveness of their pre-merger group identity, this identity becomes more salient and both in-group differences and out-group similarities are minimized. Employees focus on the positive aspects of their own pre-merger organization and develop negative perceptions of the other organization (the out-group). This motivates them to maintain all that they value about their pre-merger organizational identity and resist any changes that threaten it. However, this is not always the case, as shown in Example 26.1.

Example 26.1

BT Cellnet's acquisition of Martin Davies
When the mobile communications network operator BT Cellnet embarked on a strategy of vertical integration and acquired Martin Davies, the UK's leading service provider, in 1998, the majority of the 1,600 Martin Davies employees were not seriously alienated by their loss of organizational identity. This was, in large measure, because BT Cellnet was widely perceived to have invested in the future in a way that opened up the possibility of new career opportunities that may not have been accessible if they had not been acquired. The acquisition was also seen to offer other benefits. BT Cellnet's terms and conditions of employment and pension scheme were more generous than those offered by Martin Davies, the acquisition involved a move to a new and attractive purpose-built site, and BT Cellnet wanted to retain all the acquired employees and worked hard to win their support.

In acquisitions, and those mergers where there is a dominant partner, it is the members of the weaker organization who are most likely to experience the greatest threat to their organizational identity. Members of the dominant organization are the ones who are more likely to experience continuity and to perceive fewer differences in their organization's culture and their daily work life. This enables them not only to preserve their identification with their former organization but also to transfer this identification to the new post-merger entity.

Continuity, and the lack of continuity, can have a profound impact on organizational identity. Van Dick et al. (2006) cite a study of two merging banks (Venbeselaere et al., 2002) that demonstrates the positive effect of continuity. The more people were satisfied with the way their pre-merger bank lived on in the merged bank, the stronger their identification with the merged bank and the more positive their attitudes towards people from the merger partner. In many cases, however, the acquiring organization will not seek to preserve continuity for members of the acquired organization. It will want to introduce changes that will disrupt continuity and these discontinuities will threaten members' organizational identity.

Evidence that high levels of identification with the post-acquisition/merger organization result in increased work motivation, performance and organization citizenship behaviours led Cartwright (2005) to suggest that a proxy measure of successful merger and acquisition integration is the speed with which employees put aside their separate pre-existing 'us and them' identities and assume a new shared organizational identity.

In all acquisitions and mergers, both organizations have their own cultures, which comprise a socially acquired set of shared values and beliefs that give rise to a collective frame of reference for determining how things are done and how people relate to others. Elsass and Veiga (1994) argue that the processes of social identification provide a useful theoretical foundation for examining the cultural differentiation that occurs when organizations merge. Acquisitions and mergers involve the bringing together of at least two different cultures: 'The tenets of social identity theory would indicate that the mere existence of these two subcultures is enough to lead to feelings of in-group out-group bias, discrimination and conflict' (Elsass and Veiga, 1994: 438).

Hubbard (1999) suggests that one of the factors that make cultural differences problematic is that while employees tacitly understand their own culture, they often cannot explain it to new colleagues. Consequently, the learning of the unwritten ways of doing business in the new merged organization is usually discovered via a painstaking process of trial and error.

Before reading on, you might find it helpful to complete Exercise 26.1.

Exercise 26.1 〉 Level of integration

Think of an acquisition that you have experienced or know something about.

Refer back to the discussion of strategic objectives in Chapter 25 and Hubbard's continuum of integration possibilities (Figure 25.1) and consider whether the acquiring organization sought to achieve a level of integration consistent with the acquisition objectives.

What was the targeted level of integration?		Was it appropriate, given the objectives of the acquisition?	Was this level of integration achieved?
Complete assimilation			
Functional integration – involving some changes for both parties			
Separation – financial controls only			
Other			

To what extent were people issues either a help or a hindrance in achieving the targeted level of integration? What kinds of people issues were important?

> **Notes**
>
>

Acculturation

Berry (2005) defines acculturation as the dual process of cultural and psychological change that takes place as a result of contact between two or more cultural groups and their individual members. Early work on acculturation focused on the domination of indigenous people by colonial powers and on how immigrants changed as they settled into a receiving society. More recently, Nahavandi and Malekzadeh (1988) and Elsass and Veiga (1994) have applied theories of acculturation to the study of how organizational members adapt to acquisitions and mergers.

Nahavandi and Malekzadeh draw on the work of Berry (1983, 1984) to identify the different ways in which members of acquired and acquiring organizations can combine their organizational cultures, practices and systems:

▶ *Integration* involves some degree of change for both organizations but allows both to maintain many of the basic assumptions, beliefs, organizational practices and systems that are important to them and make them feel distinctive.
▶ *Assimilation* is a unilateral process in which one group willingly adopts the identity and culture of the other.
▶ *Separation* involves members of the acquired organization seeking to preserve its own culture and practices by remaining separate and independent of the dominant organization. If allowed to do so, it will function as a separate unit under the financial umbrella of the parent company.
▶ *Deculturation* (Berry's marginalization) involves organizational members rejecting cultural contact with both their and the other organization. It occurs when members of an acquired company do not value their own culture, maybe because the organization has failed, and do not want to be assimilated into the acquiring organization.

NB: Hubbard's types of integration referred to in Chapter 25 and Exercise 26.1 do not correspond exactly to Berry's categories. Berry's 'assimilation' might be viewed as similar to Hubbard's 'total integration', Berry's 'integration' to Hubbard's 'functional integration' and Berry's 'separation' as spanning Hubbard's 'restructuring followed by financial control' and 'total autonomy subject to financial control'.

The process of acculturation that actually occurs depends on the degree of congruence between the acquired and acquiring organizations preferred modes of combining, and the ability of each partner organization to impose its preference.

The acquired organization's preferred mode of acculturation

The acquired organization's preferred mode of acculturation depends on the extent to which members of the acquired organization value and want to preserve their own culture, and their perception of the attractiveness of the acquiring organization's culture (see Figure 26.1).

So, for the *acquired organization*:

▶ *Integration* will be its preferred mode of acculturation when its members value their own culture and many of their organizational practices and want to preserve them, but also perceive some attractive aspects of the acquiring organization's culture and practices they would like to adopt.
▶ *Assimilation* will be its preferred mode when members do not value their own culture and practices and, therefore, do not want to preserve them, and when they are attracted to the acquiring organization's culture and practices.
▶ *Separation* will be its preferred mode of acculturation when members value their own culture and organizational practices and want to preserve them, and when they are not attracted to the acquiring organization's culture and practices.
▶ *Deculturation* will be its preferred mode when its members feel alienated because they do not value the culture and practices of either their own or the acquiring organization.

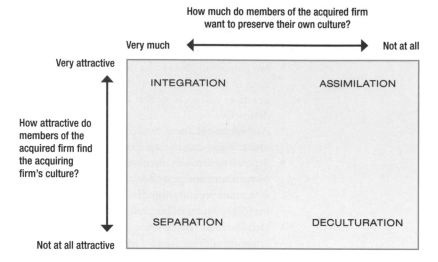

Figure 26.1 *Acquired firm's preferred mode of acculturation*
Source: Adapted from Nahavandi and Malekzadeh, 1988

The acquiring organization's preferred mode of acculturation

The acquiring organization's preferred mode of acculturation also depends on two factors; the extent to which the acquiring organization is multicultural and its acquisition strategy (see Figure 26.2). If the acquiring organization is unicultural and values conformity, it will be more likely to impose its culture and systems on the acquired firm. If, on the other hand, it is multicultural, that is, contains and values many subcultures, it will be more likely to allow the acquired firm to retain its own culture.

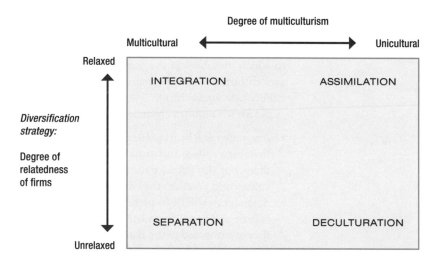

Figure 26.2 *Acquiring firm's preferred mode of acculturation*
Source: Adapted from Nahavandi and Malekzadeh, 1988

The degree of integration sought by the acquiring firm is discussed in Chapter 25. It is often related to the degree of relatedness between the merging organizations. For example, the motive for acquiring an unrelated business may be to increase the size of the acquiring organization or to decrease its dependence on some part of the environment. When this is the case, the acquirer may be happy to pursue a hands-off approach, seeking little beyond essential procedural integration. However, the motivation for acquiring a related business is more likely to be synergies gained from integrating physical assets, operating procedures and so on. This will call for a higher level of physical and cultural integration.

So, for the *acquiring firm*:

▸ *Integration* will be its preferred mode of acculturation when it is a multicultural organization and the merger is with a related company.
▸ *Assimilation* will be its preferred mode when the firm is unicultural and the merger is with a related company.
▸ *Separation* will be the preferred mode when the acquirer is multicultural and the merger is with an unrelated company.
▸ *Deculturation* is unlikely to be a mode of acculturation that will be preferred, unless it is committed to developing a completely new culture for the new organization.

Low levels of congruence between the acquiring and acquired organizations' preferred mode of acculturation are likely to produce high levels of merger stress for organizational members. This can give rise to negative emotions, such as denial, depression and anger, undermine morale, increase confusion and intergroup conflict, and lead to unproductive behaviours that disrupt the integration process. High levels of congruence, on the other hand, can have the opposite effect and promote people synergies and organization fit (see Figure 26.3).

Whether people synergies will be realized depends on how the acquisition is managed. The next section focuses attention on what managers can do to mitigate the dysfunctional consequences of cultural differentiation and the lack of continuity that is often experienced by those involved in mergers and acquisitions.

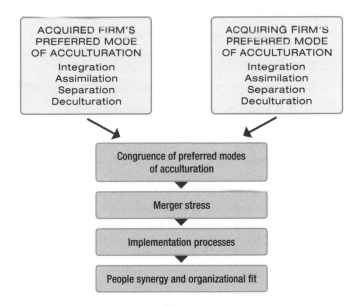

Figure 26.3 *Acculturative model for implementing organizational fit*
Source: Adapted from Nahavandi and Malekzadeh, 1988

Managing the implementation process

There are many ways in which managers can intervene to promote people synergy. At an early stage in the acquisition process, the acquiring organization can pre-screen potential target organizations for cultural compatibility. In some cases, major differences in organization culture and preferred mode of acculturation might persuade the acquiring organization to seek an alternative, more compatible partner. At a later point, a culture audit might provide data that can be used for exploring similarities and differences between the partner organizations, in order to identify which aspects of organizational functioning will be most difficult to integrate and which aspects of the merger process are most likely to produce merger stress. Such a culture audit might:

▶ inform the choice of integration strategy. It might be that valuable synergies can be achieved without seeking complete assimilation. A looser form of integration might reduce the scale of the discontinuities experienced by employees and yield added value by avoiding some of the disruption that is often triggered by high merger stress.

▶ guide how the various aspects of the integration process can be managed by, for example
  • involving, at an early stage of the acquisition process, those managers who will be responsible for managing the acquired business, and focusing their attention on possible people problems
  • ensuring adequate change communication, involving staff from both the acquiring and acquired businesses in joint task forces to plan how particular aspects of the organizations will be combined
  • cross-posting employees to learn, first hand, about the other organization
  • providing socioemotional support
  • exploring transition arrangements that will ease the introduction of common terms of employment and so on.

Attention will be given here to three ways in which managers can intervene to promote people synergy: identifying and managing cultural differences; providing effective change communication; and delivering socioemotional support.

Culture profiling and the management of cultural differences

Schein (1990) defines organizational culture as the pattern of basic assumptions that are invented, discovered or developed by a group as it learns to cope with its problems of external adaptation and internal integration. These give rise to work practices and ways of relating with others that are often referred to as 'the way things are done around here'.

There has been a robust debate about how best to measure organizational culture. Some advocate qualitative measures based on observations or employees' accounts of their organizational experience and others favour quantitative measures. Goffee and Jones (1996) developed a quantitative measure that classifies cultures according to two types of human relations: sociability and solidarity. Harrison (1972, 1986) developed a typology of organizational cultures and a measure (see Handy, 1976) that provides a basis for differentiating cultures and identifying the level of perceived empowerment, trust and cooperation associated with each.

Cartwright and Cooper (1992, 1993a, 1993b) used Harrison's measure to examine the impact of cultural dynamics on the acculturation and integration process across three acquisitions and two mergers. They found, in line with the discussion above, that the pre-existing cultures of the merging organizations could either facilitate or undermine the integration strategy adopted by the integration teams. Their research indicates that pre-existing cultures facilitate the merger in those cases where the direction of change offers employees increased autonomy, but obstruct change and undermine organizational performance when employees perceive that the merger will erode their autonomy. Their findings have been applied, through culture profiling, to help managers to anticipate how cultural differences might affect the integration process.

Assimilation strategies will only be successful when members of the acquired organization are prepared to let go of their old ways of doing things and fully embrace the culture and work practices of the acquiring organization. According to Cartwright and Cooper (1993b), this is most likely to happen when members of the acquired organization perceive the acquiring organization's culture to be less constraining than their existing pre-merger culture.

Similar factors will affect the success of acquisition strategies that stop short of complete assimilation. Successful integration depends on both partnering organizations valuing aspects of the other organization's culture and on the development, across both organizations, of a collaborative 'win–win' rather than competitive 'win–lose' approach to their engagement in the integration process. Integration will be easier when the differences between the cultures are relatively small, but even then the journey will not always be problem free.

Harrison (1972, 1986) identified four types of culture: power, role, task/achievement and person/support. Cartwright and Cooper (1993b) conceptualized the relationship between these cultures along a continuum ranging in terms of the degree of constraint they place on employees. The four cultures are briefly outlined below.

Power cultures

Power cultures impose the greatest degree of constraint and require employees to do what they are told. The main characteristics of power cultures are:

▶ centralized power
▶ unequal access to resources and a strong leader who can satisfy or frustrate others by giving or withholding rewards and sanctions
▶ behaviour influenced by precedent and the anticipation of the wishes of the central power source
▶ few rules, little bureaucracy, decisions made by individuals not committees.

Role cultures

Role cultures provide more freedom and employees are allowed to act within the parameters of their work role and job description. The main characteristics of role cultures are:

▶ limited communication between employees working in functional silos; coordination concentrated at the top
▶ hierarchical
▶ roles/job descriptions are more important that the individuals who fill them
▶ methods rather than results predominate.

Task/achievement cultures

Task/achievement cultures are even less constraining and allow employees to act in ways most suitable for completing the task. The main characteristics of task/achievement cultures are:

▶ job or project orientation
▶ resources and people are brought together as required to get the job done
▶ influence based more on expert power than on position or personal power
▶ unity of effort towards mutually valued goals
▶ adaptable – groups and project teams are formed and disbanded as required
▶ individuals and groups have a high degree of control over their work
▶ top management retains control via allocation of projects, people and resources, but find it difficult to exercise day-to-day control over methods of working.

Person/support cultures

Person/support cultures impose the least constraint and allow employees to use their own initiative and to do their own thing. The main characteristics of person/support cultures are:

▶ mutual trust between individuals and the organization
▶ members believe they are valued as human beings, not just cogs in a machine
▶ members help each other beyond the formal demands of the job
▶ members know the organization will go beyond the requirements of the employment contract to look after them if they need support
▶ structure is the minimum required to help individuals do their job.

Table 26.1 shows the suitability of culture matches between organizations of similar and dissimilar culture types. For example, an acquisition target with a role culture will experience fewer problems integrating with an acquiring organization that has a task culture than one that has a power culture (see shaded area in Table 26.1 and Figure 26.4).

Table 26.1 *Suitability of culture matches*

Culture of the acquirer/ dominant merger partner	Culture of the acquired or other merger partner	Likely outcome	Comments
Power	Power	Problematic	Success dependent on the choice and charisma of the leader. Can lead to political infighting
Power	Role Task Person/ support	All potentially disastrous	Assimilation will be resisted. Culture collisions will be inevitable. Labour turnover likely to be high
Role	Power	Potentially good	Assimilation likely to be accepted. Most will welcome the 'fairness' of a role culture
Role	Role	Potentially good	Smooth assimilation likely as effectively rewriting or presenting a new rule book is all that is required
Role	Task	Potentially problematic	Many in the acquired organization may have chosen to work in a task culture to escape the bureaucracy and red tape of role cultures

Role	Person/ support	Potentially disastrous	Anarchy likely. In above case, members of a task culture may eventually accept that the increased size of the merged organization will require greater infrastructure, but members of a person/ support culture will not
Task	Power Role Task	Potentially good	Smooth assimilation likely for those in existing power and role cultures. There will be pleasant but potentially disturbing culture shock. Those who will lose positional power may feel that their status will be eroded. Many will find the new culture demanding and potentially stressful
Task	Person/ support	Potentially problematic	While person cultures nurture self-development, they are not conducive to team working and consensual decision making

Source: Adapted from Cartwright and Cooper, 1993b: 67

The greater the dissimilarity between cultures, the greater the changes members of each organization will have to make and the more difficult it will be to integrate the organizations. Cartwright and Cooper (1993b) suggest that if the partner organizations do not have similar cultures, they should at least be adjacent types, for example task/role. If they have different cultures, for example at the opposite ends of Harrison's continuum (Figure 26.4), it could be difficult to achieve much, if anything, in the way of people synergy.

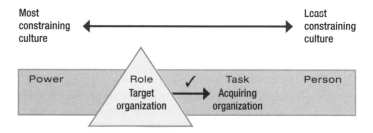

Figure 26.4 *Suitable culture*

Culture profiling as part of the due diligence process can help with the selection of appropriate merger partners. Strategic fit might be necessary but it is not a sufficient condition for merger success.

Culture profiling at a later stage in the merger process, as mentioned above, can provide data that can be used for exploring similarities and differences between the partner organizations and highlighting issues that may require special attention. For example, people who have been used to working in a more constraining power or role culture may need help to modify their management or other work style to fit in with a new 'task/achievement' culture. While they may welcome greater autonomy, they may be uncertain about how best to fit in with new working arrangements and may feel deprived of feedback that could help them to improve their performance. Similarly, employees who have been used to working in a less constraining task or person culture may find it difficult to adjust to a more constraining work environment. Exploring ways of helping people to adjust to the new culture might be more effective than just leaving them to muddle through as best they can. Also, managers who are responsible for assessing the competence of acquired employees need to be aware of the danger of making judgements about their potential contribution before they have had time to adjust to working in the new post-acquisition culture.

Managing communications to minimize the sense of discontinuity

There is ample evidence that ambiguous acquisition environments create intergroup differentiation, promote win–lose attitudes, confusion, anxiety and a general climate of mistrust. Effective communication can do much to reduce the uncertainties that unsettle organizational members; however, it is often sadly lacking. In Chapter 10, various communication strategies are reviewed. 'Withhold and uphold' strategies (see Clampitt et al., 2000), which involve withholding information until necessary and, when confronted by rumours, upholding the party line, often typify the approach adopted by managers in merger and acquisition scenarios. There are many reasons for this. They may be reluctant to communicate information because they fear that unanticipated events may render this information incorrect. They may worry about making commitments that threaten their ability to respond flexibly to changes later in the merger process, or they may fear that early communication could alert competitors or cause employees to leave. Whatever the reason, employees react to a paucity of information by fearing the worst and sharing their views with colleagues in ways that feed the acquisition grapevine and lead to even greater confusion and anxiety. If managers step in later in the acquisition process to counter these growing uncertainties, their efforts may have only limited success because, by then, employees are suspicions about their intentions and are reluctant to trust the belated information they receive.

One way of reducing these problems is to provide all employees with clear and unambiguous information about what is going to change as a result of the acquisition. Hubbard (1999) observed that those organizations with a record of successful acquisition tend to have sophisticated communication strategies for dealing with the acquired organization's internal and external stakeholders. Good communication is essential throughout the acquisition process, but it is especially important on day one because the impression the acquirer makes at the start of the process will influence how those affected will interpret all subsequent actions. However, such communication requires considerable pre-acquisition planning. Hubbard outlines a process that enables the senior managers in charge of the acquisition to develop an 'acquisition blueprint' during the pre-acquisition phase, which specifies what actions are to be taken, when they will occur, who will be affected and who will be responsible for implementing the changes (see Chapter 25). She makes the obvious point that if the acquiring organization has not done sufficient integration planning before the acquisition is announced, there will not be enough substance of information to communicate to employees. Similarly, even if the acquirer has the most well-developed acquisition plan, much of its value will be lost if it is not adequately communicated.

Schweiger and DeNisi (1991) report a study that found that the provision of unambiguous information about what would change reduced employees' perceptions of possible dysfunctional outcomes and produced higher levels of organizational commitment (see Research report 26.1).

When designing their study, they compared the amount of information desired by an employee going through an acquisition with the information a newcomer to an organization might want. New recruits, like employees involved in an acquisition or merger, face high levels of uncertainty that can result in dysfunctional outcomes. 'Realistic job previews' have been used to provide complete and realistic information about a job, including its positive and negative aspects, and have been found to be effective for reducing newcomers' uncertainty, bringing their expectations in line with reality, and helping them to cope with the transition to their new jobs. Studies show that new employees who receive previews tend to be more satisfied with their jobs and more committed to their organizations, to experience less stress, and to be less likely to leave than employees socialized through more traditional methods (see Premack and Wanous, 1985). Realistic job previews appear to work by serving two functions: they reduce uncertainty and they communicate to employees that their new employer cares about them and can be trusted.

Research report 26.1 · The realistic merger preview

Schweiger, D.M. and DeNisi, A.S. (1991) Communication with employees following a merger: a longitudinal field experiment, *Academy of Management Journal*, 34: 100–35

Schweiger and DeNisi argued that the functions served by realist job previews – reducing uncertainty and communicating that change managers care and can be trusted – are important to employees facing mergers and acquisitions. They adapted the realistic job preview concept and created a communication programme, which they called the 'realistic merger preview'. They tested the effectiveness of this approach by conducting a longitudinal experiment involving the merger of two *Fortune* 500 companies. Data were collected in two plants, an experimental plant in which the preview was introduced and a control plant in which the merger was managed more traditionally.

Employees in both plants received a letter from the CEO announcing the merger. This was the only information workers in the control plant received. Their plant manager, who was not aware of the realistic merger programme in the experimental plant, was simply told that further information would be coming as soon as it was available. In the experimental plant, employees were provided with much more information. Schweiger and DeNisi report that the aim of the realistic merger programme was to:

1 provide employees with frequent, honest, and relevant information about the merger
2 provide them with fair treatment
3 answer their questions and concerns to the fullest extent possible.

They received information about layoffs, transfers, promotions, demotions, changes in pay, jobs, and benefits. This information was communicated as soon as it was available.

A merger newsletter was sent to each employee in the experimental plant twice a month containing details of changes that the merger had created, together with answers to questions solicited from employees. There was a telephone hotline answered during working hours by a personnel manager who continually received updated information from the vice president of HR. The hotline manager answered questions about general organizational changes but did not provide answers to specific questions concerning individual employees. After working hours, employees calling the hotline reached an answering machine. Answers to questions left on the answering machine were posted on bulletin boards around the plant, and most also appeared in the next issue of the newsletter. Finally, the experimental plant's manager met weekly with the supervisors and employees of each of the eight departments in the plant. Separate meetings were arranged for each department to ensure that changes affecting that department could be specifically addressed and weekly briefings were prepared jointly by the plant manager and the vice president of HR to supplement these meetings and maintain communication consistency and accuracy across the plant.

Following the merger announcement, employees in the experimental and control plants reacted negatively. However, once the realistic merger preview programme was introduced in the experimental plant, the situation in that plant began to stabilize. Schweiger and DeNisi report that while uncertainty and its associated outcomes did not decline, they stopped increasing, and, over time, employees' perceptions of the company's trustworthiness, honesty and caring and their self-reported performance actually began to improve and move back towards the pre-announcement levels. The results of this experiment provide empirical evidence that open communications can reduce uncertainty and increase employees' perceptions that their company cares and is prepared to offer socioemotional support.

Hubbard (1999) argues that people expect change, such as redundancies, relocations and modifications to working practices, after an acquisition and will be generally accepting of it so long as they are kept informed prior to events occurring and are treated fairly when they happen. She asserts that employees will react badly to being kept in the dark, being treated unfairly or being misled. Evidence suggests that employees prefer to know the truth rather than be fobbed off with false platitudes.

In terms of Clampitt et al.'s (2000) typology of communication strategies, the realistic merger preview described above primarily involves an 'underscore and explore' approach (see Chapter 10). The change managers decided which issues they would communicate about (underscore), but they also ensured that employees had the opportunity to discuss these issues with managers in order to explore how they would be affected by them. However, change managers were also willing to respond to questions over the telephone hotline and in newsletters, indicating that they were willing to allow employees some freedom to influence the communication agenda in line with an 'identify and reply' strategy.

Delivering socioemotional support

Acquisitions and mergers, as noted above, are often associated with discontinuities and feelings of loss. Marks (2007) argues that while the personal transitions associated with these discontinuities disrupt the current equilibrium and jar people from their status quo, many respond by 'holding on' rather than 'letting go'. Adaptation can be a difficult process. Employees typically react by passing through a number of stages of psychological reaction, for example shock, denial, anger, feelings of helplessness and depression, before they can let go of their pre-merger organizational identity and begin to develop a new sense of identity with the post-merger organization (see Figure 26.5). In Chapter 12, attention is given to some of the ways that managers can intervene to facilite this process of adjustment.

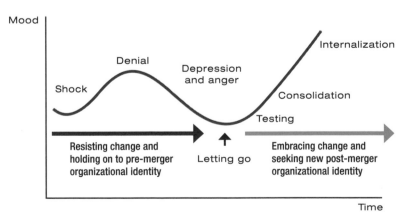

Figure 26.5 *Transition phases*

Rhoades and Eisenberger (2002) argue that employees develop global beliefs about the extent to which the organization values them and cares about their well-being, and that these beliefs affect the degree to which they incorporate organizational membership into their social identity. Employees who feel that managers are doing their best to support them through the merger are less likely to feel alienated and more likely to identify with the merged organization than those who experience little socioemotional support.

Perceptions of fairness and procedural justice are related to the way change communications are managed (see the discussion of this point in Chapter 10). Organizational members value adequate notice before decisions are implemented and expect to receive adequate and accurate information. They may also want the opportunity to voice their concerns and have an input into the decision process. If employees perceive unfairness in the way decisions are made, about pay, allocation of roles and resources, relocation, severance and so on, this can have an adverse effect on their morale, organizational commitment and performance. Equity theory (Adams, 1963) holds that motivation is a function of fairness in social exchange and posits that if people feel that they have been treated unfairly, they will take corrective action, which could involve behaving in ways that resist the merger. Greenberg's (1990) study of employee thefts as a reaction to underpayment inequity (see Research report 10.1) indicates that people reacted better to bad news when they believe that senior managers are sensitive to their viewpoints, decisions are adequately explained and justified, and they are applied consistently and without bias.

Guest (1998) notes that people who feel that they have received fair and respectful treatment engage in more positive 'organizational citizenship behaviours' and contribute more to the organization than they are contractually obliged to. Such high levels of organizational citizenship behaviour are desirable post-merger because they can contribute to greater employee flexibility and help to accommodate the inevitable increase in workload.

Trust is also important. Allen et al. (2007) discuss the role of trust in organizational change and, drawing on previous research, argue that trust is facilitated by management practices such as participative decision making, support and the meeting of expectations. Management practices that promote feelings of social justice are especially important, because when organizational members feel that they have been treated with respect and dealt with fairly, even if they are unhappy with the consequences of a decision, they will be less likely to engage in dysfunctional behaviours than those who feel that they have received little support and have been unjustly treated.

There are occasions when the discontinuity associated with an acquisition is great and largely unavoidable, but even in such circumstances, effective communication, coupled with a genuine concern for the welfare of those affected, can help those involved to cope with the change (Example 26.2).

Example 26.2

United Distillers & Vintners

When United Distillers merged with International Distillers & Vintners to create United Distillers & Vintners, part of the massive merger between Guinness and Grand Met in 1997, it was decided to locate the new HQ at Harlow and close the former HQ of United Distillers at Perth. This decision presented a major discontinuity for those working at the Perth site. The merger team worked hard to ensure that employees were fully aware of the consequences of the closure and did everything they could to help them through the transition. They provided opportunities for them and their families to visit the Harlow site so that they could consider the possibility of relocating and, for those who did not want to move away from Perth, they opened a 'career options office', provided support preparing CVs, offered training in interview skills and provided independent financial advice. They sold the Perth site to the Bank of Scotland, even though a better sale price could have achieved, because the bank planned to create 150 new jobs on the site. They also established a Bell's Heritage Centre as a way of retaining some aspects of the United Distillers organizational identity in the region.

Summary

This chapter draws on social identity and acculturation theories to provide a conceptual framework for thinking about how managers can intervene to promote people synergy and achieve merger success.

Social identity theory is introduced to explain how acquisitions and mergers threaten employees' organizational identity, exacerbate 'us and them' dynamics and adversely affect merger success:

▶ people not only identify themselves in terms of 'I', but also in terms of 'we'
▶ work group and organization can be an important source of social identity
▶ mergers and acquisitions affect social identity because they redraw or dissolve the boundaries that once categorized distinct groups
▶ people respond by focusing on the positive aspects of their pre-merger group and developing negative perceptions of the post-merger organization.

Acculturation theory is used to explore how employees' preferences for combining their organizational cultures, practices and systems affect acquisition and merger outcomes. Ways of combing cultures include:

▶ *Integration:* This involves some change but allows both parties to maintain many aspects of their culture that are important to them.
▶ *Assimilation:* A unilateral process in which one group willingly adopts the identity and culture of the other.
▶ *Separation:* Members of the acquired organization seek to preserve their own culture and practices.
▶ *Deculturation:* Organizational members reject cultural contact with both their and the other organization.

In all acquisitions and mergers, both organizations have their own cultures, which comprise a socially acquired set of shared values and beliefs that give rise to a collective frame of reference for determining how things are done and how people relate with others.

The processes of social identification provides a useful theoretical foundation for examining the cultural differentiation that occurs when organizations merge. Acquisitions and mergers involve the bringing together of at least two different cultures: 'The tenets of social identity theory would indicate that the mere existence of these two subcultures is enough to lead to feelings of in-group out-group bias, discrimination and conflict' (Elsass and Veiga, 1994: 438).

Low levels of congruence between the acquiring and acquired organizations' preferred mode of combining their cultures can lead to high levels of merger stress. This can undermine morale, increase confusion and intergroup conflict, and lead to unproductive behaviours that disrupt the integration process.

High levels of congruence, on the other hand, can have the opposite effect and promote people synergies and organization fit. Whether people synergies will be realized depends on how the acquisition is managed.

Change managers can intervene to mitigate the dysfunctional consequences of cultural differentiation and the lack of continuity. Attention has been focused on three types of intervention:

▶ *Culture profiling:* to pre-screen potential merger partners and, later in the merger process, guide the integration process
▶ *Change communication:* to provide organizational members with clear and unambiguous information about what is going to change as a result of the merger
▶ *Socioemotional support:* to care for those affected by the change, minimize alienation and promote post-merger organizational identity.

Exercise 26.2 | **Review of case studies at the end of Part V**

Reflect on the content of Chapters 18–26 and review your approach to designing an intervention for each of the four case studies presented at the end of Chapter 17. You might also consider the nature of your change strategy in the light of the strategies considered in Chapter 14.

In the light of what you have read, would you now revise the design of any of your proposed interventions? Why would you do this?

Learning points

References

Adams, J. (1963) Towards an understanding of inequity, *Journal of Abnormal and Social Psychology*, November: 422–36.

Allen, J., Jimmieson, N.L., Bordia, P. and Irmer, B.E. (2007) Uncertainty during organizational change: managing perceptions through communication, *Journal of Change Management*, 7(2): 187–210.

Ashford, S.J. (1988) Individual strategies for coping with stress during organisational transition, *Journal of Applied Behavioural Science*, 24(1): 19–36.

Ashforth, B.E. and Mael, F. (1989) Social identify theory and the organization, *Academy of Management Review*, 14(1): 20–39.

Bartels, J., Douwes, R., de Jong, M. and Pruyn, A. (2006) Organizational identification during a merger: determinants of employees' expected identification with the new organization, *British Journal of Management*, 17(3): 49–67.

Berry, J.W. (1983) Acculturation: a comparative analysis of alternative forms, in R.J. Samunda and S.L. Woods (eds) *Perspectives in Immigrant and Minority Education*, Lanham, MD: University Press of America.

Berry, J.W. (1984) Cultural relations in pluralistic societies: alternatives to segregation and their psychological implications, in N. Miller and M.B. Brewer (eds) *Groups in Contact*, Orlando, FL: Academic Press.

Berry, J.W. (2005) Acculturation: living successfully in two cultures, *International Journal of Intercultural Relations*, 29: 697–712.

Cabrera, J.C. (1982) Playing fair with executives displaced after the deal, *Mergers and Acquisitions*, September/ October: 42–6.

Cartwright, S. (2005) Mergers and acquisitions: an update and appraisal, in G.P. Hodgkinson and J.K. Ford (eds) *International Review of Industrial and Organisational Psychology*, vol. 20, Chichester: John Wiley & Sons.

Cartwright, S. and Cooper, C.L. (1990) The impact of mergers and acquisitions on people at work: existing research and issues, *British Journal of Management*, 1: 65–76.

Cartwright, S. and Cooper, C.L. (1992) *Mergers and Acquisitions: The Human Factor*, Oxford: Butterworth-Heinemann.

Cartwright, S. and Cooper, C.L. (1993a) The psychological impact of merger and acquisition on the individual: a study of building society managers, *Human Relations*, 46: 327–47.

Cartwright, S. and Cooper, C.L. (1993b) The role of culture compatibility in successful organizational marriage, *Academy of Management Executive*, 7(2): 57–70.

Clampitt, P.G., DeKoch, R.J. and Cashman, T. (2000) A strategy for communicating about uncertainty, *Academy of Management Executive*, 14(4): 41–57.

Cooper, C.L. and Payne, R. (1988) *Causes, Coping and Consequences of Stress at Work*, Chichester: John Wiley & Sons.

Elsass, P.M. and Veiga, J.F. (1994) Acculturation in acquired organisations: a force field analysis, *Human Relations*, 47(4): 431–53.

Goffee, R. and Jones, G. (1996) What holds the modern company together?, *Harvard Business Review*, 74(6): 133–48.

Greenberg, J. (1990) Employee theft as a reaction to underpayment inequity: the hidden cost of pay cuts, *Journal of Applied Psychology*, 75(5): 561–8.

Guest, D. (1998) Is the psychological contract worth taking seriously?, *Journal of Organizational Behavior*, 19(S): 649–64.

Handy, C.B. (1976) *Understanding Organisations*, Harmondsworth: Penguin.

Harrison, R. (1972) Understanding your organization's character, *Harvard Business Review*, 50(3): 119–28.

Harrison, R. (1986) *Understanding your Organization's Culture*, Berkeley, CA: Harrison.

Hubbard, N. (1999) *Acquisition: Strategy and Implementation*, Basingstoke: Macmillan – now Palgrave Macmillan.

Marks, M. (2007) A framework for facilitating adaptation to organizational transition, *Journal of Organizational Change Management*, 20(5): 721.

Nahavandi, A. and Malekzadeh, A.R. (1988) Acculturation in mergers and acquisitions, *Academy of Management Review*, 13(1): 79–90.

Premack, S.L. and Wanous, J.P. (1985) A meta-analysis of realist job preview experiments, *Journal of Applied Psychology*, 87: 706–19.

Rhoades, L. and Eisenberger, R. (2002) Perceived organizational support: a review of the literature, *Journal of Applied Psychology*, 87(4): 698–714.

Schein, E.H. (1990) Organizational culture, *American Psychologist*, 45(2): 109–19.

Schweiger, D.M. and DeNisi, A.S. (1991) Communication with employees following a merger: a longitudinal field experiment, *Academy of Management Journal*, 34(1): 100–35.

Tajifel, H. and Turner, J.C. (1979) An integrative theory of intergroup conflict, in W.G. Austin and S. Worchel (eds) *Psychology of Inter Group Relations*, Monterey, CA: Brooks/Cole.

Van Dick, R., Ullrich, J. and Tissington, P.A. (2006) Working under a black cloud: how to sustain organizational identification after a merger, *British Journal of Management*, 17(S): 69–79.

Venbeselaere, N., Boen, F. and de Witte, H. (2002) Intergroup relations after a merger: the relative impact of ingroup prototypicality and satisfaction with ingroup representation, paper presented at the 5th Jena workshop on intergroup processes, Castle Kochberg, 19–23 June.

Walsh, P. (1988) Top management turnover following mergers and acquisitions, *Strategic Management Journal*, 9: 173–83.

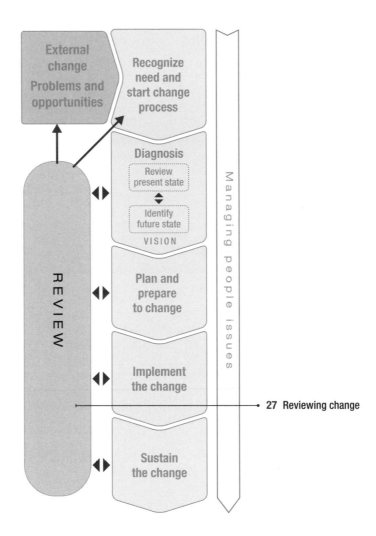

Chapter 27   Reviewing change

This chapter focuses special attention on how the process of reviewing progress can provide change managers with feedback they can use to assess whether interventions are being implemented as intended, whether the chosen interventions are having the desired effect and whether the change plan continues to be valid.

chapter
27
Reviewing change

This chapter focuses special attention on how the process of reviewing progress can provide change managers with feedback that they can use to assess whether interventions are being implemented as intended, whether the chosen interventions are having the desired effect and whether the change plan continues to be valid.

The utility of the balanced scorecard as a template for designing a system for managing change is also discussed.

Managing the implementation stage of the change process

It was noted in Chapter 2 that there are two main approaches to implementation:

1 *Implementing blueprint change:* Here, the desired end state is known in advance and change managers are in a position to formulate a clear plan of action to achieve this vision. Implementation involves rolling out this plan, monitoring the effect of interventions and taking corrective action as and when required in order to ensure that the desired end state is achieved. Often the validity of the blueprint is taken for granted and the learning associated with this kind of change tends to be restricted to single loop learning. Assumptions about what needs to be changed and how the change will be achieved tend to go unchallenged unless the feedback from implementation is so unexpected that it shocks change managers into a radical reassessment.

2 *Implementing evolutionary change:* Here, it may be difficult or impossible to specify an end point in advance. Change managers have to develop an implementation plan on the basis of broadly defined goals and a general direction for change. Sometimes, because of a high rate of change in the operating environment, ideas about the desired future state have to be constantly revised, even in those cases where the original vision has only been defined in the broadest of terms. In such circumstances, change managers have to adopt an open-ended approach to planning and implementation. Managing evolutionary change involves taking tentative incremental steps and, after each step, reviewing the intervention(s) that constituted that step (did it/they work as planned?) and the general direction of change (does it still hold good or does it need to be revised?). This questioning of the validity of the desired future state and the plan for achieving it calls for double loop learning.

Monitoring the implementation of the change plan

A plan for change reflects a set of hypotheses about cause and effect. Kaplan and Norton (1996) view the measurement and review process as a means of making these hypothesized relationships explicit. They argue that once they are clearly articulated and widely understood, the change process can be more easily managed. The process of managing change involves validating or, where necessary, revising the assumptions and hypotheses that underpin the change plan. The desired future state (vision) is reflected in the outcome measures embedded in the change plan. Performance drivers are the variables that determine whether the desired outcome will be achieved. Speci-fying these in the change plan signals to organizational members what they need to do in order to contribute to the achievement of the desired future state.

Some of the questions that need to be addressed when managing change and vali-dating the hypothesized cause-and-effect relationships that underpin the change plan are considered below.

Are interventions being implemented as intended?

Sometimes it is more difficult than anticipated to roll out a plan for change. The change manager may respond by reviewing the situation and identifying those factors that have hindered implementation first time round. These might include a lack of commitment and motivation on the part of those immediately affected by a proposed intervention, a lack of political support from those in a position to cham-pion or sabotage the change, or insufficient resources to ensure that the change initi-ative receives the attention it requires. The content of previous chapters points to ways of addressing these kinds of problems.

Are interventions producing the desired effect?

Change managers need to be alert to the possibility that while the intervention might have been implemented as intended, it might not be producing the effect that was anticipated.

An example will illustrate this possibility and indicate ways in which the change manager might address the situation:

▶ A company might be losing market share because it is lagging behind competitors in the time it takes to bring new products to market.
▶ A factor contributing to this predicament might be diagnosed as the high level of conflict between members of the product engineering department, responsible for developing new products, and members of the production engineering department, responsible for developing the manufacturing system required to produce a new product.
▶ Informed by this diagnosis, the change manager might send members of both departments on a variety of external courses to learn about intergroup dynamics and the management of conflict.
▶ After monitoring the effect of this intervention, the change manager might discover that while members of both departments are much more aware of constructive ways of behaving in conflict situations, this awareness has had little effect on the level of manifest conflict between the two departments.

An initial response might be to explore ways of modifying the original intervention in order to make it more effective, for example by seeking out opportunities to improve the transfer of learning from the training activity to the work situation.

▶ Rather than sending individuals on external courses, the change manager might decide to facilitate an in-house workshop that involves members of both departments working together to identify ways of managing their differences in a more constructive way.

If modifying the original intervention in this way still fails to produce the desired effect on the targeted performance driver, that is, the quality of interdepartmental relationships, the change manager might begin to question the assumed cause-and-effect relationship between poor conflict management skills and high levels of interdepartmental conflict. This questioning might point to other possible causes of the immediate problem (high levels of interdepartmental conflict) and lead the change manager to consider ways of modifying the change plan to include interventions that target them:

▶ It might be found that the original diagnosis was valid, insofar as it identified the level of interdepartmental conflict as a major cause of delay in getting new products to market, leading to a loss of market share. However, it may have been flawed when it focused on poor conflict management skills as the root cause of this damaging behaviour.
▶ A re-examination of the situation might suggest that the main source of conflict is rooted in the way the company is structured. This broad heading could include a number of possible causal factors. One might be the siting of work groups in locations that make it difficult for members of one department to communicate on a face-to-face basis with members of the other. Another might be misaligned performance criteria that result in competing sets of priorities in the two departments.

This questioning of the taken-for-granted, cause-and-effect assumptions involves a process of double loop learning.

Is the change plan still valid?

There may be occasions where the interventions have been implemented as intended and have produced the desired effect. However, this chain of events may have had little or no impact on overall organizational performance. This kind of outcome poses another challenge to the validity of the change plan and the hypothesized cause-and-effect relationships on which it is based.

Faced with this kind of outcome, the change manager may decide to embark on a further re-examination of the original diagnosis and the causal models that were used to inform the design of the change plan:

▶ This further re-examination might reveal that, despite what many managers in the company accept as given wisdom, improvements in the time it takes to get new products to market may have had little effect on the gradual decline in market share. Further investigations might suggest that customers are more concerned about other value propositions, such as product reliability, price and so on, and might feel that competitors are better able to satisfy their needs in these areas.
▶ On the other hand, it may be that the further investigations reveal that the original diagnosis was correct at the time, but has been overtaken by new developments, for example changes in customer requirements, that challenge its validity, with obvious implications for the change plan.

There may also be (hopefully many) occasions when the interventions have been implemented as intended, have produced the desired effect and this has had a positive impact on organizational performance. This kind of positive outcome signals a need to consolidate this achievement and use it, as appropriate, as a basis for achieving further improvements in performance.

The role of performance measures in the management of change

Some of the issues that encourage or inhibit learning are considered in Chapter 18 and towards the end of Chapter 2. This chapter focuses attention on how the cycle of monitoring, reviewing, planning, acting and further reviewing can minimize some of the problems relating to the fragmented nature of the change process and can facilitate double loop learning. Central to this review process is the collecting and feeding back of information about how interventions affect performance.

Attention has already been given to some of the different ways in which performance can be measured (see Chapter 3). It is essential that performance measures should be related to the outcomes that are important to key stakeholders and to the hypotheses about cause-and-effect relationships that are embedded in the change plan. Without the feedback that such measures can provide, change managers will be unable to monitor what is going on and determine what further action may be required to successfully implement the change plan.

Approaches to measuring performance

It was noted in Chapter 15 that many control systems are designed to reward current practice and offer little incentive for people to invest effort in changing the organization to promote long-term effectiveness. Even in those organizations where change is given a high priority, the monitoring and feedback process may only focus attention on a limited set of performance measures. Many organizations direct most of their attention on financial measures. Often too little attention is given to other performance indicators that relate to important outcomes and key cause-and-effect relationships that are central to the change plan.

One of the early attempts to widen the base of performance monitoring on an organization-wide and systematic basis was the development of a 'corporate scorecard' by Analog Devises. Alongside a number of traditional financial measures, this included measures of customer delivery time, quality and cycle times of manufacturing processes, and effectiveness of new product development.

Kaplan and Norton (2004) report that they became interested in new ways of monitoring performance when they recognized the importance of knowledge-based assets, such as employees and information technology, as determinants of competitive success. They believe that managers and others pay attention to what is measured and they are not good at managing that which is not measured. Therefore, if they are to manage, develop and mobilize the organization's intangible assets, managers need a performance management system that measures how these assets are used. This led them to develop what is now referred to as the 'balanced scorecard'.

The balanced scorecard

The balance scorecard (Kaplan and Norton, 1996) integrates financial measures of past performance with measures of the 'drivers' of future performance. It provides a template that can be adapted to provide the information that change managers need to monitor and review the effects of their interventions and to plan what they might do next to move the organization towards a more desirable future state. The scorecard includes four categories of measure: financial, customer, internal business process and innovation and learning:

▷ *Financial measures*, such as return on investment, economic value added, sales growth and generation of cash flow, summarize the economic consequences of past actions. This financial perspective considers how the organization needs to appear to its shareholders if it is to achieve its vision.

▷ *Customer-related measures* include indicators of business performance that relate to the customer and market segments that are important to the organization. Examples include measures of satisfaction, retention, new customer acquisition, customer profitability, account share and market share. They might also include measures of those performance drivers that affect the value propositions that influence customer loyalty, such as on-time delivery and product innovation. This customer perspective considers how the organization needs to appear to its customers if it is to achieve its vision.

▷ *Internal business process measures,* such as quality, response time and cost, relate to the internal business processes that make a critical contribution to the organization's current and future performance. They might measure the performance of the processes that enable the organization to deliver value propositions that attract and retain important customers, satisfy shareholders by contributing to the delivery of excellent financial returns, or deliver other outcomes that are important to key stakeholders.

▷ *Innovation and learning,* which come from three principle sources: people, systems and organizational procedures. Kaplan and Norton suggest that the financial, customer and internal business process objectives typically reveal large gaps between the existing capabilities of people, systems and procedures and the capability that is required to achieve a performance breakthrough. In order to transform an organization, or even achieve a more modest level of change, these gaps have to be addressed. This can involve intervening in the normal process of organizational functioning to enhance this infrastructure and improve the organization's capacity for innovation and learning

The balanced scorecard can be adapted to focus on those performance drivers and measures that are identified as important in specific situations. Figure 27.1 illustrates how the balanced scorecard can be used as a framework to translate a change strategy into operational terms.

Developing tools to help monitor implementation

The balanced scorecard approach can be adapted to focus on those performance drivers and measures that are identified as important in specific situations and used as a change management tool to clarify and gain consensus about the change strategy. Translating the vision and change strategy into an agreed set of operational goals (see Figure 27.1) is likely to stimulate a debate that will ensure that the change management team develop a shared understanding of what they are seeking to achieve. Specifying operational goals can also help the change management team to think about their plan for change in systemic terms and develop a shared view of how and why the various change goals are related in terms of cause and effect.

The feedback that this kind of tool can provide on how the organization or unit of an organization is performing will enable change managers to test the validity of the cause-and-effect relationships embedded in the change plan.

Figure 27.1 *Translating the change strategy into a set of operational goals*

Kaplin and Norton (1996) cite the example of Echo Engineering where change managers were able to test and validate their assumption that employee morale was a key performance driver. They found that employee morale correlated with a number of important performance indicators; for example the most satisfied customers were those who were served by employees with the highest morale, and the most satisfied customers were the ones who settled their accounts in the shortest period.

Several studies report findings that suggest that favourable employee perceptions are related to superior business performance. Koys (2001) found that the level of employee satisfaction and commitment in a chain of restaurants was positively related to profitability. Gelade and Young (2005) cite a meta-analysis by Harter et al. (2002) of 7,939 work units in 36 companies that found small but significant correlations between business unit productivity and profitability, and a composite of items they labelled 'employee engagement'. They also cite a study by Patterson et al. (2004) that reports significant associations between company climate and productivity in a sample of 42 manufacturing companies.

Heskett et al. (1994) argue that customer satisfaction is a critical intervening variable in the employee attitude–profit relationship. Their work has stimulated a lot of interest in the service profit chain (Figure 27.2). The basic premise is that employee satisfaction is positively related to employee commitment and that increased commitment promotes customer satisfaction and motivates customers to stay with the company longer and recommend the company's products and services to others. This, in turn, stimulates revenue growth and profitability. Culbertson (2009) confirms that this is indeed a winning proposition.

Figure 27.2 *The service profit chain*

Management tools, such as the balanced scorecard, not only facilitate the development of a shared view of how and why the various change goals are related in terms of cause and effect, but can also help change managers to communicate their change plan throughout the organization and provide a framework for consultation and debate about what a more desirable future state will look like and what needs to happen if it is to be achieved. This kind of management tool can also help to ensure that the range of change initiatives that might be started in different units and at different levels in the organization will be aligned to contribute to the strategic goals of the change programme.

The balanced scorecard approach is presented here as one example of a tool that can help change managers to manage the change process. In any change programme, plans have to be operationalized and communicated widely. Furthermore, targets for change have to be specified as clearly as possible if progress is to be monitored and if the change plan is to be kept under review and adjusted as circumstances require.

Reviewing how people are responding to the change

Over the long term, change managers can use measures such as customer satisfaction, customer retention and the bottom line to assess the validity of the change plan. Over a shorter timescale, they may focus attention on whether interventions are being implemented as intended and are producing the immediate outcomes that were anticipated. Another source of feedback is employees' collective perceptions of the way the changes are being managed and the effect this has on their experience of and attitudes towards the changes. Just as normal day-to-day management practices can have a powerful impact on the work climate and the willingness of organizational members to contribute to organizational performance, so the way changes are managed can have a powerful impact on how organizational members experience change, their attitudes towards the change and their readiness to support it.

It could be argued that resistance to change is inevitable and therefore employees are not good judges of how well a change is being managed. However, since one of the main imperatives of change is to win over hearts and minds and get people to buy in to change, their feedback is important. One way to gain this feedback is given in Change tool 27.1.

| Change tool 27.1 | **The change management indicator** |

Hayes and Hyde have developed the change management indicator (CMI) as a structured means of providing this feedback. It is available as an online survey (www. peterhyde.co.uk) and can be used in a number of ways:

- as a one-off diagnostic instrument to identify major areas of concern for remedial action
- as a barometer of opinion at a series of points in time, indicating whether the trend is in the desired direction
- to compare the situation in different departments, functions, locations and organizational levels and thereby identify localized problems
- as an intervention in its own right, to get people thinking about the issues and to promote dialogue
- to benchmark against other organizations undergoing similar changes.

The model underpinning the CMI proposes that people's experience of organizational change and their attitudes towards the change are influenced by four key elements.

Two of these can be difficult to affect, especially over the short term:

1 The inherent nature of the change itself. It will be hard, for example, to get positive feedback about a change if it is inherently painful, such as the closure of a facility.

2   The personality and temperamental characteristics of the people involved. Some people will be more receptive to change and others more resistant.

There are, however, two important elements of the model that change managers can do something about:

3   The change management practices they adopt, such as developing the vision for the change, leadership, planning and organization, communication, consultation, and support.

4   The way their overall strategy for change is represented 'down the line' by local management. Middle managers often struggle to find the right way to position themselves, but it seems clear that if they are not actively supportive of the corporate strategy for change, it is highly unlikely that their subordinates will buy into it.

Failure to pay attention to the way a change is being managed can adversely affect the achievement of change objectives and/or the timescale for implementing the change. It can also undermine staff morale and commitment to the organization, cause reputational damage and tie up scarce resources firefighting and managing the unintended consequences of the change process.

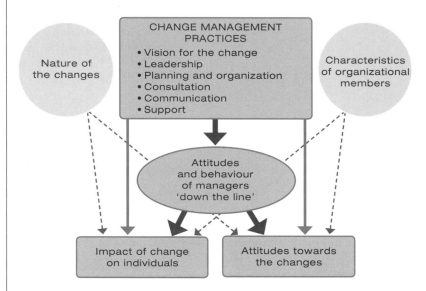

Figure 27.3   *Factors affecting how people respond to the change*

Source: Hayes and Hyde 2008, www.peterhyde.co.uk

Summary

This chapter has considered how monitoring and reviewing the implementation of a change can help managers to adjust and adapt the plan for change to help ensure that the organization moves towards a more desirable future state.

Attention has been given to the kind of information change managers need in order to, at one level, determine whether interventions are being implemented as intended and assess whether they are having the anticipated effect, including their impact on key stakeholder groups, and, at a higher level, to assess whether the change plan continues to be valid. Assessing the continued validity of the change plan, and updating it as required, is especially important when managing evolutionary-type change. Key questions that change managers need to address are:

▶ *Are interventions being implemented as intended?* Sometimes it is more difficult than anticipated to roll out a plan for change. The change manager may respond by reviewing the situation and identifying those factors that have hindered implementation first time round. These might include a lack of commitment and motivation on the part of those immediately affected by a proposed intervention, a lack of political support from those in a position to champion or sabotage the change, or insufficient resources to ensure that the change initiative gets the attention it requires.

▶ *Are interventions producing the desired effect?* Change managers need to be alert to the possibility that while the intervention might have been implemented as intended, it might not be producing the effect that was anticipated.

▶ *Is the change plan still valid?* There may be occasions where the interventions have been implemented as intended and have produced the desired effect. However, this chain of events may have had little or no impact on overall organizational performance.

When the interventions have had a positive impact on organizational performance, this achievement needs to be consolidated and used as a basis for achieving further improvements in performance.

It has been argued that change managers need to identify measures of organization effectiveness that relate to those outcomes that are important to the organization's long-term survival and growth. This might involve attending to more than just the short-term interests of shareholders.

It has also been argued that, when monitoring the effectiveness of interventions, attention needs to be paid to the cause-and-effect hypotheses that have influenced the design of the change plan. Where feedback raises questions about the validity of these hypothesized relationships, the change manager needs to review the change plan and consider whether alternative ways of intervening to move the organization towards a more desirable future state might be more effective.

The balanced scorecard has been considered as an example of a management tool that can help the manager attend to these points when managing change.

References

Culbertson, S.S. (2009) Do satisfied employees mean satisfied customers?, *Academy of Management Perspectives*, **23**(1): 76–81.

Gelade, G. and Young, S. (2005) Test of a service profit chain model in the retail banking sector, *Journal of Occupational and Organizational Psychology*, **78**(1): 1–22.

Harter, J.K., Schmidt, F.L. and Hayes, T.L. (2002) Business unit-level relationship between employee satisfaction, employee engagement, and business outcomes: a meta-analysis, *Journal of Applied Psychology*, **87**(2): 268–79.

Heskett, J.L., Jones, T.O., Loveman, G.W. et al. (1994) Putting the service-profit chain to work, *Harvard Business Review*, **72**(2): 164–74.

Kaplan, R.S. and Norton, D.P. (1996) *The Balanced Scorecard: Translating Strategy into Action*, Boston, MA: Harvard Business School Press.

Kaplan, R.S. and Norton, D.P. (2004) *Strategy Maps: Converting Intangible Assets into Tangible Outcomes*, Boston, MA: Harvard Business School Press.

Koys, D.J. (2001) The effects of employee satisfaction, organizational citizenship behaviour and turnover on organizational effectiveness: a unit-level, longitudinal study, *Personnel Psychology*, **54**(1): 101–14.

Patterson, M., Warr, R. and West, M.A. (2004) Organizational climate and company productivity: the role of employee affect and employee level, *Journal of Occupational and Organizational Psychology*, **77**(2): 193–216.

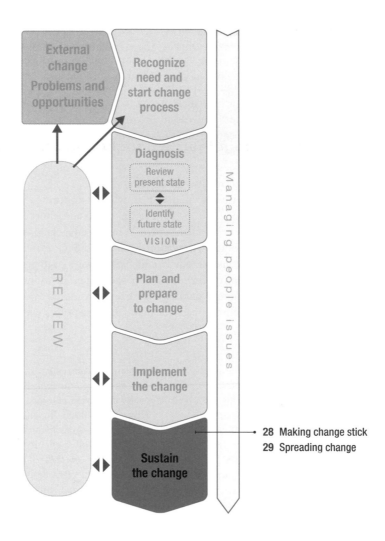

Lewin (1951) argued that all too often change is short-lived. After a 'shot in the arm', life returns to the way it was before. In his view, it is not enough to think of change in terms of simply reaching a new state. The first two chapters in part VIII look at what managers can do to sustain change. The final chapter presents a case study that provides an opportunity to reflect on and pull together all the concepts and ideas discussed in the book.

Chapter 28   Making change stick

This chapter looks at at 'stickability' and what managers can do to consolidate a change and hold on to gains. Attention is focused on two key issues:

▶ The way the change process is managed from the beginning. It is argued that tough top-down (push) strategies are more likely to foster compliance than commitment and ownership. Compliance often evaporates when the pressure to maintain the change is eased.

▶ How change managers can act to sustain change after the initial change goals have been achieved.

Chapter 29   Spreading change

This chapter looks at 'spreadability', the extent to which new methods and processes that have delivered gains in one location are applied, or adapted and then applied elsewhere across the organization. Attention is given to what managers can do to promote the spread of change.

Chapter 30   Pulling it all together: a concluding case study

This book covers a lot of ground. Chapter 30 introduces a concluding case study designed to provide you with an opportunity to review what you have read and think about how the many theories, models, techniques and tools can be applied to the management of a single case. You can do this on your own or with others.

chapter
28
Making change stick

Lewin (1951) argued that all too often change is short-lived. After a 'shot in the arm', life returns to the way it was before. In his view, it is not enough to think of change in terms of simply reaching a new state. Attention also needs to be given to maintaining this new state for as long as it is relevant. He conceptualized change as a three-stage process. The first involves unfreezing the individual, group or system from the status quo and creating a readiness for change. The second involves moving to a new state, and the final stage involves refreezing behaviour at this new level, for as long as it is beneficial to do so.

This caveat, for as long as it is beneficial, is important because there are circumstances where

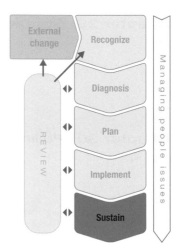

it may not be beneficial to continue to maintain a change. The change may not have been successful or it may have produced unanticipated consequences that are inconsistent with the change plan. Buchanan and Fitzgerald (2007: 25) also argue that sustaining change can be counterproductive when:

▶ changes in the wider environment render recently implemented working practices, outcomes and lines of development obsolete
▶ maintaining recently implemented practices impedes further and more significant developments.

This chapter reviews evidence from different sectors, which indicates that it is often difficult to achieve Lewin's stage of refreezing and sustaining change. After discussing two aspects of sustainability, this chapter takes a closer look at 'stickability' and what managers can do to consolidate a change and hold on to gains. The next chapter takes a closer look at the second aspect of sustainability, how successful changes can be rolled out across the organization.

Sustainability

Sustainability has been defined in many different ways. Some definitions focus on the embedding of new processes, whereas others focus attention on performance improvements 'independent of the methods employed' (Buchanan et al., 2005). Some definitions are relatively static, focusing on the maintenance of improvements within a particular setting, whereas others are more dynamic and are concerned with translating initial gains into a process of continuous improvement. Dale (1996), for example, defines sustainability in terms of increasing the pace of improvement while holding the gains made. The NHS Modernisation Agency (2002: 12) defines it as the state where 'new ways of working and improved outcomes become the norm' and where 'the thinking and attitudes behind them are fundamentally altered and the systems surrounding them are transformed in support'. In other words, according to the Modernisation Agency, change is sustained when it becomes an integrated or mainstream way of working rather than something 'added on'. Buchannan and Fitzgerald (2007: 22) conclude that while sustainability can be defined in different ways in relation to work methods, goals or continuous improvements, covering differing timescales, 'the definintion and timing that matter are those applicable to a particular organizational setting'.

Bateman and David (2002) developed a model to investigate the level of sustainability achieved in 21 companies following intensive shop-floor process improvement interventions. The model operationalizes some of these different ways of conceptualizing sustainability. It consists of two elements. The first identifies five different levels of sustainability at cell level, ranging from realizing but then failing to hold on to gains to not only maintaining the new way of working but also applying the tools and techniques learned to new problems as they arise (see Figure 28.1). The second element of the model focuses on factory-level improvements and identifies the degree to which tools and techniques have been spread between cells (see Figure 28.2). The two elements are:

1 *Cell-level sustainability:* Bateman and David's (2002) research indicated that while all cell-based interventions led to significant improvements, beyond that point, there were considerable variations in the extent to which these improvements were sustained (see Figure 28.1 and Research report 28.1 for more details).

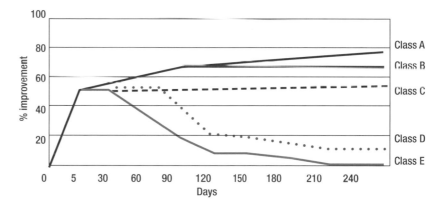

Figure 28.1 *Classes of sustainability at cell level*
Source: Bateman and David, 2002: 520

2 *Sustainability at factory level:* While cell-level improvements (factory level 1 in Figure 28.2) are often the initial focus of many lean manufacturing interventions, the longer term aim is usually a more broadly based change at factory level. However, cell-level changes may not always spread across the factory. Bateman and David (2002) report that there are often immediate possibilities for replicating improvements made in the initial activity to other manufacturing cells where the machines or processes are the same or similar (factory level 2). It may be more difficult to apply the same tools and techniques used to achieve

improvements to cells where different machines or processes are used (factory level 3). Achieving factory level 4 is even more difficult. This is where further process improvements involve changes in new areas that require the learning and application of new tools and techniques. Sustainability at factory level 5 is achieved when improvements are coordinated in a value stream across the site.

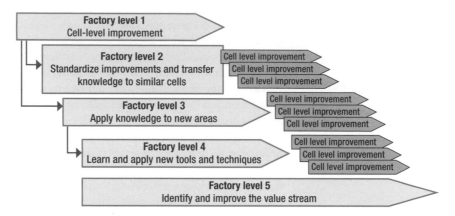

Figure 28.2 *Factory-level improvement model*
Source: Adapted from Bateman and David, 2002: 520

This chapter draws on Bateman and David's (2002) model and explores just one aspect of sustainability – the extent to which gains are held. The extent to which changes are spread across the organization is considered in Chapter 29.

Before reading further, complete Exercise 28.1.

Exercise 28.1

Factors undermining 'stickability'

Reflect on your experience of change and identify some of the occasions when new ways of working and performance gains were not maintained. List below some of the factors that you think undermine stickability and contributed to change decay.

	Factors contributing to change decay	Reason
1		
2		
3		

Stickability: holding on to gains

Research on sustainability indicates that while many change initiatives are successful, there is considerable variation in the level of sustainability achieved. Kotter (1995) reports many examples of the failure to sustain change. Gains achieved in 10 out of 12 re-engineering change programmes evaporated because 'victory' was declared too soon, for example as soon as the first major project was completed. According to Kotter, within two years, the initial gains had slowly disappeared and in 2 of the 10 cases, it was soon hard to find any trace of the re-engineering. He reports seeing the same thing happen to a vast number of other organization development projects.

Buchanan et al. (2007a) studied the problem of sustainability and spread in the UK's NHS, the largest organization in Europe and the third largest organization in the world. In 2000, the NHS embarked on a 10-year modernization initiative. Priorities were established, resources were committed, changes were implemented and many improvement targets were achieved. But, in line with evidence from the manufacturing sector, Buchanan and Fitzgerald (2007) report that there was considerable variation in the levels of sustainability that were achieved. In some areas, gains were maintained but in others improvements evaporated. For example, some clinical services developed ways of dramatically reducing patient waiting times, but found it extremely difficult to maintain these new performance levels and, over time, the improvements were eroded and performance fell back to the original level.

Sustainability can be affected by what change managers do early on and towards the end of the change process.

Acting early to promote sustainability

The way a change is managed, from the start, can affect stickability. When Lewin's theories were discussed in Chapter 2, it was noted that the behaviour of an individual, group or wider system is maintained in a condition of quasi-stationary equilibrium by a force field comprising a balance of forces pushing for and resisting change. This level of behaviour can be changed by either adding forces for change in the desired direction or reducing the opposing or resisting forces.

Both approaches can result in change but, according to Lewin, the secondary effects associated with each approach will be different. Where change is brought about by increasing the forces pushing for change, this increases the tension experienced by those affected by the change. If this rises beyond a certain level, it may be accompanied by high emotionality and low levels of constructive behaviour. Increasing the driving forces for change can be likened to pushing on a coiled spring (Figure 28.3). If change managers exert enough pressure, people will be forced to comply, but if this pressure is released, the lack of commitment on the part of those forced to comply could cause the change to evaporate and the situation to 'spring back' to its former state.

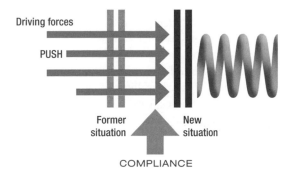

Figure 28.3 *A push approach to securing change*

On the other hand, where change is brought about by diminishing the forces that oppose or resist the change, the secondary effect is likely to be a state of relatively low tension. This argument led Lewin to advocate an approach to managing change that focused attention on reducing the restraining forces in preference to a high pressured approach that only focused on increasing the forces pushing for change. He argued that approaches that reduced the restraining forces were more likely to generate commitment and create the pull effect that will result in a more permanent change.

These principles underpin action research. This approach to improving performance is more bottom up than top down. It recognizes that many people may have information that is relevant to the problems that undermine performance and seeks to involve them in the change process. Evidence (see Chapter 19) suggests that this involvement promotes psychological ownership of the problem and gains commitment to the problem-solving process. There is also evidence that it facilitates the implementation of new methods and processes, and there is every reason to believe that this same involvement will help build the commitment that will sustain change.

Promoting sustainability later in the change process

Successful change efforts can be undermined because too little attention is given to holding on to gains once the change objectives appear to have been achieved.

Reference has already been made to change managers declaring victory too soon. This can encourage them to switch their attention and resources to other projects. Kotter (1995) advocates that instead of declaring victory early on, change managers should use the credibility afforded by early wins to go on and modify some of the systems and structures that may not be consistent with the transformation vision.

Attention also needs to be given to the attitudes and priorities of those affected by the change. Fine et al. (2008) assert that too many companies emphasize the technical aspects of change and neglect many of the related softer issues. The rush to implement toolkit-led solutions without first ensuring that employees – including managers – are prepared to adapt and work with them can contribute to the evaporation of any early performance gains. Involving people at an early stage can help to win over their hearts and minds. Kotter (1995), like those who lead the NHS Modernisation Agency, believes that change sticks when it is rooted in the organization's social norms and shared values. Until this has been achieved, change will be subject to degradation as soon as the pressures to maintain it are removed.

In his seminal *Harvard Business Review* paper, Leading change: why transformation efforts fail, Kotter (1995) identifies ways in which managers can help to embed change in the organization's culture. The first involves providing feedback and drawing people's attention to how new ways of doing things are making a difference. When people are left to make their own connections, they may attribute any successes to the wrong factors and overlook their own contribution. Relevant, understandable and focused feedback can help to keep people's efforts directed to those things that are really making a difference. Several writers (Beckhard and Harris, 1987; Nadler, 1993) argue that tailored feedback mechanisms not only facilitate monitoring and control during the transition phase of a change, but can also be effective in helping to sustain change. Change managers need to work with those operational managers who will have ongoing responsibility for day-to-day management once the change has been implemented to design feedback mechanisms that they can use for themselves to monitor and manage the situation over the longer term.

Kotter's (1995) second factor relates to the constant churn in many organizations that results in managers moving on partway through a change project. Kotter argues that care needs to be exercised to ensure that the next generation of senior managers continues to support the new approach.

Many researchers have pointed to specific ways in which sustainability can be promoted. For example, Bateman (2005) found that with shop-floor interventions in the manufacturing sector, two categories of enablers appeared to stand out as most important:

1 processes for promoting 'contribution and buy-in' during the early stages of implementation
2 processes promoting 'maintenance of standards and continuous improvement' once the initial changes had been successfully implemented (see Research report 28.1).

Brown (2009) surveyed the opinion of 15 fellow change consultants at KPMG about sustainability and found that 65% of their comments focused on three barriers to sustainability:

▶ the organization's approach to change
▶ the quality of leadership
▶ employees' level of understanding about what was expected of them following the change.

There was less agreement about enablers but engagement and communication were referred to most frequently.

Buchanan et al. (2005) report a more complex picture. On the basis of a thorough review of the literature, they identify 10 categories of factors that interact in different ways to affect sustainability, including the scale and type of change, individual commitment and competencies, managerial style, the quality of leadership, organizational culture and political processes. The relative importance of these factors is determined by context. For example, a management style that elicits enthusiastic commitment in one setting may trigger cynicism, resentment and a lack of support for change in another. Consequently, Buchanan et al. (2005) felt that more work would have to be done before they could offer change managers any simple prescription for sustaining change. However, they did point to three issues that seem to affect the extent of initiative decay:

1 *How the change is perceived.* Is it peripheral or central to organizational performance and is it perceived as acceptable or threatening by key stakeholders? Often change managers can influence the way a change is perceived and this will have consequences for sustainability.
2 *How the change is implemented.* As noted above, there is no one implementation process that will be effective in all settings, but doing everything possible to identify and adopt an appropriate process can affect whether or not the change will be sustained.
3 *The timing, sequencing and pacing of the change process.* For example, while a relaxed timetable might help people to digest the need for change, delays can undermine commitment and divert attention to other pressing issues. On the other hand, when a change is rushed, people may not feel involved and a succession of change initiatives may lead to initiative fatigue.

Research report 28.1 **Two enablers that help to promote stickability**

Bateman, N. (2005) Sustainability: the elusive element of process improvement, *International Journal of Operations and Production Management*, **25**(3/4): 261–76

Bateman studied the application of a standard process improvement intervention (the SMMT Industry Forum MasterClass) at 40 sites across 21 companies in order to identify enablers for sustaining change.

The intervention was in three parts:

1 *A diagnostic phase* to establish a baseline in terms of quality, cost and delivery, and to identify what needed to be done to achieve improvement
2 *A five-day workshop* in which an improvement team learned about and applied process improvement tools (such as 7 wastes) using a PDSA cycle. This led to the identification of new working methods and a list of technical changes that needed to be made
3 *A follow-up phase* during which the improvement team worked to maintain new methods and close out the technical issues identified in the workshop.

The 40 interventions were reviewed after 90 days and again some time later in order to assign them to one of five classes in terms of the extent to which process improvements had been sustained:

- Class A interventions succeeded in maintaining the new working practices, completing outstanding issues identified in the workshop and applying the new process improvement tools to new problems.
- Class B interventions succeeded in maintaining the new working practices and completing outstanding issues.
- Class C interventions succeeded in maintaining the new working practices but failed to complete the outstanding issues identified in the workshop.
- Class D interventions succeeded in completing the technical issues identified in the workshop but failed to maintain the new operating procedures. This led to some improvements in operating performance through technical solutions but possibilities for improvements through changes in working practices were not realized.
- Class E interventions failed to maintain new operation procedures or to close out technical issues.

Classification	Improvement in workshop?	Maintained new procedure?	Closed out technical issues?	Continuous improvement?
Class A	✓	✓	✓	✓
Class B	✓	✓	✓	✗
Class C	✓	✓	✗	✗
Class D	✓	✗	✓	✗
Class E	✓	✗	✗	✗

A list of potential enablers was generated after consulting Japanese and British 'master engineers' and reviewing the literature. This long list was then refined by screening out those potential enablers that could not be measured or were not amenable to modification by the change agents or others involved in the intervention. Data were collected to identify which enablers were associated with each class of sustainability.

Bateman found that the enablers that differentiated class A and B from class C, D and E interventions could be grouped into two categories:

1 *Processes for promoting 'contribution and buy-in' by cell members:*
   - methods for recording issues and ideas

- methods for reviewing and prioritizing issues and ideas
- processes that enable operators to act on ideas and make team decisions about the way they work
- processes for enabling team members to review actions and identify further action required.

2 *Process promoting maintenance of standards and continuing focus on process improvement activity:*
- allocating time, on a daily basis, for maintaining standards
- measuring improvement
- managers staying focused on performance improvement.

Following extensive research in the NHS, while still recognizing the complex interplay of factors that affect sustainability, Buchanan et al. (2007b: 259) identified 10 recurrent problems and offered practical advice about how each might be addressed:

1 *Those who initiated the change move on:*
- design career development and reward policies to motivate and retain key change agents
- choose successors with similar competencies and aspirations.

2 *Accountability for development becomes diffused:*
- establish clear project and line management responsibilities
- ensure appropriate and visible rewards for those responsible for driving change.

3 *Knowledge and experience of new practices is lost through turnover:*
- develop retention strategies to minimize such losses
- develop a 'buy-back' policy to involve leavers in induction and training for new staff.

4 *Old habits are imported with recruits from less dynamic organizations:*
- strengthen the induction and training regime for recruits.

5 *The issues and pressures that triggered the change initiative are no longer visible:*
- communicate in a way that keeps these issues in the forefront of staff thinking
- identify new reinforcing issues and pressures.

6 *New managers want to drive their own agenda:*
- support where appropriate but also ensure that they are given an explicit remit to work with and not dismantle particular changes introduced by their predecessors.

7 *Powerful stakeholders are using counter-implementation tactics to block progress:*
- when reason fails, develop a 'counter-counter-implementation' strategy to reduce their influence.

8 *Pump-priming funds run out:*
- start to revise budget allocations well in advance, so that the extra costs of new working practices can be absorbed gradually in a phased manner.

9 *Other priorities come on stream, diverting attention and resources:*
- develop a time-phased change implantation strategy to provide periods of planned stability between change projects
- avoid diverting resources before initiatives are embedded.

10   *Staff at all levels suffer initiative fatigue and enthusiasm for change falters:*

- beware the 'bicycle effect', where lack of forward momentum leads to a crash. Relaunch with new focus, themes and gaols
- sell the benefits and clarify what's in it for them.

Reflect back on the content of this chapter and think about what you and/or others could do to promote stickability.

Exercise 28.2   **Action steps to promote stickability**

Think of a current or pending change in your organization and identify at least three things that could be done to help ensure that the change will be embedded and sustained for as long as required.

	Actions that will help sustain the change	Reason
1		
2		
3		

Summary

Lewin conceptualized change as a three-stage process. The first involves unfreezing and creating a readiness for change. The second involves moving to a new state, and the final stage involves refreezing behaviour at this new level, for as long as it is beneficial to do so. This caveat is important because there are circumstances where it may not be beneficial to continue to maintain a change.

Sustainability has been defined in many different ways. Some definitions are relatively static, focusing on the maintenance of improvements within a particular setting, whereas others are more dynamic and are concerned with translating initial gains into a process of continuous improvement.

The maintenance of improvements (stickability) is affected by:

▶ The way the whole change process is managed from the beginning. Tough top-down (push) strategies are more likely to foster compliance, which can evaporate when the pressure to maintain the change is eased.

▶ How change managers act to sustain change after initial change goals have been achieved.

A number of studies point to issues that can affect sustainability and what change managers can do to help ensure that gains are held. While Buchanan et al. felt that more work would have to be done before they could offer change managers any simple prescription for sustaining change, they did point to three issues that seem to affect the extent of initiative decay:

▶ *How the change is perceived:* Is it peripheral or central to organizational performance and is it perceived as acceptable or threatening by key stakeholders? Often change managers can influence the way a change is perceived and this will have consequences for sustainability.

▶ *How it is implemented:* There is no one implementation process that will be effective in all settings, but doing everything possible to identify and adopt an appropriate process can affect whether or not the change will be sustained.

▶ *The timing, sequencing and pacing of the change:* While a relaxed timetable might help people to digest the need for change, delays can undermine commitment and divert attention to other pressing issues. On the other hand, when a change is rushed, people may not feel involved and a succession of change initiatives may lead to initiative fatigue.

Buchanan et al. identified 10 recurrent problems and offered practical advice about how each might be addressed. The problems are:

1 those who initiated the change move on
2 accountability for development becomes diffused
3 knowledge and experience of new practices is lost through turnover
4 old habits are imported with recruits from less dynamic organizations
5 the issues and pressures that triggered the change initiative are no longer visible
6 new managers want to drive their own agenda
7 powerful stakeholders are using counter-implementation tactics to block progress
8 pump-priming funds run out
9 other priorities come on stream, diverting attention and resources
10 staff at all levels suffer initiative fatigue and enthusiasm for change falters.

References

Bateman, N. (2005) Sustainability: the elusive element of process improvement, *International Journal of Operations and Production Management*, **25**(3): 261–76.

Bateman, N. and David, A. (2002) Process improvement programmes: a model for assessing sustainability, *International Journal of Operations and Production Management*, **22**(5/6): 515–26.

Beckhard, R. and Harris, R.T. (1987) *Organizational Transitions: Managing Complex Change*, Reading, MA: Addison-Wesley.

Brown, A. (2009) *Making Change Stick: The Holy Grail?*, White Paper, KPMG.

Buchanan, D.A. and Fitzgerald, L. (2007) Improvement evaporation: why do successful changes decay?, in D.A. Buchanan, L. Fitzgerald and D. Ketley (eds) *The Sustainability and Spread of Organizational Change*, London: Routledge.

Buchanan, D.A., Fitzgerald, L. and Ketley, D. (eds) (2007a) *The Sustainability and Spread of Organizational Change*, London: Routledge

Buchanan, D.A., Fitzgerald, L. and Ketley, D. (2007b) Sustaining change and avoiding containment: practice and policy, in D.A. Buchanan, L. Fitzgerald and D.

Ketley (eds) *The Sustainability and Spread of Organizational Change*, London: Routledge.

Buchanan, D.A, Ketley, D., Gollop, R. et al. (2005) No going back: a review of the literature on sustaining organizational change, *International Journal of Management Reviews*, **7**(3): 189–205.

Dale, B. (1996) Sustaining a process of continuous improvement: definition and key factors, *TQM Magazine*, **8**(2): 49–51.

Fine, D., Hansen, M.A. and Roggenhofer, S. (2008) From lean to lasting: making operational improvements stick, *The McKinsey Quarterly*, November, www. mckinseyquarterly.com.

Kotter, J.P. (1995) Leading change: why transformation efforts fail, *Harvard Business Review*, **73**(2): 59–67.

Lewin, K. (1951) *Field Theory in Social Sciences*, New York: Harper & Row.

Nadler, D.A. (1993) *Feedback and Organizational Development: Using Data Based Methods*, Reading, MA: Addison-Wesley.

NHS Modernisation Agency (2002) *Improvement Leaders' Guide to Sustainability and Spread*, Ipswich: Ancient House Printing Group.

chapter
29
Spreading change

This chapter looks at 'spreadability', the extent to which new methods and processes that have delivered gains in one location are applied, or adapted and then applied elsewhere across the organization. Attention is given to what managers can do to promote the spread of change. Before reading further, complete Exercise 29.1.

Exercise 29.1

Factors undermining the spread of change across an organization

Reflect on your experience of successful change efforts and identify examples where the new methods and processes were not spread to other locations. List below some of the factors you think have limited spread and fostered containment.

	Factors limiting spread	Reason
1		
2		
3		

Spreading change

Containment is a problem that affects many organizations; innovative methods and processes that have been developed and are working well in one part of an organization remain as isolated examples of good practice. This phenomenon is often referred to as the 'best practice puzzle' (Szulanski, 2003). Examples abound. Walton (1975) describes eight projects that involved work restructuring and the enlargement of the workers' scope for self-management. Only one of these eight projects, at Volvo's assembly plant in Lundby, was followed by similar changes elsewhere in the organization. Buchanan et al. (2007) report many examples of containment in the NHS along with a few outstanding successes, such as the spread of 'see and treat' (Lamont, 2005), an innovation that reduced waiting times in hospital A&E departments.

Klein and Sorra (1996) refer to two types of stage model that have been used to describe the spread of innovations – innovation here refers to anything newly introduced that involves a change to what went before. The model informing the discussion of spread in this chapter is a user-based model. It traces the innovation process from the users' perspective, from when they first become aware of the innovation to the incorporation of the innovation into their behavioural repertoire and normal way of working. Clearly, unless potential users are aware of the innovation, they cannot consider its adoption. However, attention here is focused on the implementation stage, which Klien and Sorra (1996) describe as the 'critical gateway' between the decision to adopt a new way of working and the routine use of the new methods, structure and processes. Implementation is affected by at least three factors: attributes of the innovation, attributes of the organization, and the values of the potential or targeted users of the innovation.

Attributes of the innovation

Greenhalgh et al. (2005), Tornatzky and Klein (1982) and Walton (1975) point to a long list of attributes that could help to explain why some innovations in methods and working practices spread, while others remain contained in one part of the organization. Rogers (1995) suggests that six attributes are important. New ways of working are more likely to be spread when potential users perceive them to be:

▶ *Advantageous when compared with existing practices:* Perceptions of relative advantage are based on social as well as financial costs and benefits.
▶ *Compatible with existing practices:* The more an innovation is perceived to be compatible with existing norms, values, technologies and social structures, the more likely it is to be adopted. Schein (1992), for example, notes that the introduction of quality circles, self-managed teams and autonomous working groups in many highly individualistic and competitive North American organizations can be so countercultural that it can be difficult to make them work.
▶ *Easy to understand:* Complex innovations are more likely to be resisted than those that are relatively straightforward and easy to understand. A related attribute is 'pervasiveness' (Walton, 1975). This refers to the number of aspects of the system that are affected by the innovation. Innovations that are less pervasive will spread more easily.
▶ *Observable in demonstration sites:* Potential users will be more able to assess relative advantage, compatibility with existing practices and ease of use when they can observe the new way of working first hand.
▶ *Testable:* Spread is more likely to happen when potential users can experience and test out new methods or ways of working for themselves before committing to the change.
▶ *Adaptable to fit local needs:* Rogers and others argue that where users can adapt the innovation to be more compatible with existing practices and/or deliver greater relative advantage, the more likely it is to be adopted. This view has been contested and will be considered in greater detail below.

Tornatzky and Klien (1982) conducted a meta-analysis of 75 studies of innovation attributes. They found that three of Rogers' six attributes had most influence on whether an innovation would be implemented in new sites. Relative advantage and compatibility were positively related and complexity was negatively related to the adoption of innovations in organizational settings.

Attributes are not fixed qualities

These attributes, as perceived by potential users, are not fixed qualities; they are perceptions that are potentially amenable to change. Providing potential users with more information may help to change their views. For example, they may not be aware of all the advantages that an innovation could deliver for them or for the organization. Improved communication may address this problem. Perceptions relating to compatibility might be modified if potential users are allowed to experience the new way of working first hand. Perceived complexity might be addressed by breaking the innovation down into separate, more manageable parts that could be introduced on an incremental basis.

Exact copying

There are opposing views about the value of adapting innovations to fit local needs. Szulanski and Winter (2002) advocate that when the aim is to capture and lever existing, rather than generate new, knowledge, innovative practices should be copied exactly to avoid what they refer to as 'spread errors'. Spread errors arise when those responsible for disseminating a new practice assume that they understand what it is about the new practice that delivers value. Often this may not be the case. Szulanski and Winter (2002) suggest that many details of a new working practice may be invisible because critical elements of the innovation that may be known to individual workers are not shared with supervisors. Other critical elements may be tacit – learned on the job and well known to those involved in the initial change project – but difficult or impossible to document or describe to 'outsiders'. There may also be some elements of the innovation that are deliberately kept secret because they make individual workers' jobs easier or they run counter to an organization's formal work rules. Because those responsible for disseminating the new practice assume that they understand what it is about the innovation that delivers value, this overconfidence leads them to immediately start trying to improve on the original example of good practice, cherry-picking parts of a process that appear to offer greatest advantage, or customizing it to make it more compatible with what already exists. In order to avoid these 'spread errors', Szulanski and Winter (2002) advocate that the original template of the innovation should be copied as closely as possible. They cite Rank Xerox's dissemination of nine best sales practices, Intel's 'Copy Exactly!' method of transferring semiconductor manufacturing know-how, and the successful spread of franchised operations, such as McDonald's, to support their exact copy philosophy.

Example 29.1

Asda's roll-out of 'Store Renewal'

Shortly after Archie Norman was appointed CEO of Asda in 1991, with a remit to turn the business around, he authorized radical experimentation in three of the company's stores. Cross-functional task forces were established to work with store managers to reinvent the concept of the Asda store – its design, retail proposition, and approach to organizing and managing people. The first store renewal took six months to complete but the results were very encouraging – sales rose 40%. After the other two renewal stores were successfully launched, it was decided to roll out 'Renewal' across the company. In three months, 20 stores were renewed, but the results were disappointing.

Eventually, it was recognized that the poor results were related to the way the renewal programme had been rolled out. After the early experimental phase, the pressure to turn the business around led to Renewal being rolled out as a top-down technical solution. Local store managers had been less involved than their colleagues in the experimental stores, and less attention had been given to creating the right store culture. Compromises had also been made to the way the stores were organized and managed, for example it proved difficult to implement self-managed teams in the required timescale. Compromises had also been made to the physical aspects of Renewal, because it took too long to implement the radical new layouts that were part of the first three renewal stores.

This learning led to a separation of physical renewal and cultural change. Renewal was redesignated as a physical store refurbishment programme. There was recognition of the importance of down the line leadership and store culture. Funding for Renewal was only made available after a store had demonstrated that it had fully embraced an innovation template, a codified set of principles that were referred to as the Asda 'Way of Working'. Each store had to pass a 'Driving Test' that clearly indicated that it had developed a culture that was customer friendly and responsive, and had adopted a flatter hierarchy and team working.

Reinvention

Buchanan and Fitzgerald (2007a) argue that there is no best way of spreading innovations and that best practice is contingent. They go on to argue (Buchanan and Fitzgerald, 2007b) that in the health service, many innovations involve introducing changes into multifaceted complex operating environments and that in such contexts, it is unlikely that a set of new working practices can be simply codified and copied from one location to another without some adaptation. They cite Locock (2001: 42), who, commenting on several cases of effective service improvement in the health service, asserts that these successes were arrived at by going through a redesign process:

> lifting the outcome off the shelf to re-use somewhere else without going through the redesign process may or may not work, but would miss the point that redesign is about analysing what is done in each local context now, and how local staff believe it could be done better in the interests of their patients.

Locock goes on to argue that 're-inventing the wheel' can be a vital part of creating a climate for change and gaining ownership, and ensuring that changes are embedded, a point echoed by Beer (1988).

Attributes of the organization

Klein and Sorra (1996) cite a range of studies that highlight a number of separate organizational and managerial policies, practices and characteristics that influence the spread of new practices and bring them together under an umbrella concept, which they refer to as the organization's 'climate for implementation'. They assert that a strong implementation climate fosters innovation use by:

1 ensuring employees have the skills to use the innovation
2 incentivizing them for innovation use and imposing sanctions for innovation avoidance
3 removing obstacles that hamper the adoption of new working practices.

They suggest that the attributes of a strong implementation climate could include:

▶ providing training to support innovation use to targeted employees – *ensuring skill*
▶ providing additional assistance in innovation use following training – *ensuring skill*
▶ providing employees with ample time to learn about the innovation and use it on an ongoing basis – *ensuring skill, removing obstacles*

▶ responding to employees' concerns and complaints – *removing obstacles*
▶ ensuring that the innovation can be easily accessed by targeted users, for example scheduling TQM meetings at times convenient for users – *removing obstacles*
▶ ensuring that the employees' use of the innovation is monitored and praised by managers – *providing incentives for use and disincentives for avoidance.*

Greenhalgh et al. (2005) highlight the political aspects of organizational context and argue that it is important to pay attention to how different stakeholders view the attributes of an innovation. For example, individual adopters, those who represent different aspects of the organization's interests or customers who might be affected by an innovation, may have different perceptions of the relative advantage an innovation will offer. The same innovation might be perceived as offering advantages and being worthy of support by some stakeholders, while just the opposite by others.

Walton (1975) points to another aspect of context, the 'star envy syndrome'. This relates to how people's perceptions of the incentives for adopting an innovation can affect take-up. He describes an innovation in Norsk Hydro, a Norwegian fertilizer company, in which the change project and those who led it received top management approval and considerable outside recognition. Walton reports that this attention engendered resentment and envy from other managers who were expected to adopt the innovation. This resentment led to resistance. A second related dynamic involved perceived changes to the reward structure. Those who were expected to adopt the innovation felt that they would get less praise for success than those who had led the original project but more blame for failure, so they avoided failure by not taking up the innovation in the first place.

Klein and Sorra (1996) argue that a strong supportive implementation climate encourages the diffusion of innovations, provided that employees are committed to innovation use. This caveat is important. They assert that effective implementation requires the dual influence of an organization's climate for implementation and target users' perception of a good fit between the innovation and their values.

The values of potential users

Klein and Sorra (1996) argue that an important attribute of potential users that influences the motivation to adopt an innovation is their values and their perception of whether the innovation will foster or inhibit the fulfilment of their values. They refer to this as 'innovation/values fit'. They draw on Schein (1992) and define group and organizational values in terms of shared beliefs about how the group or organization should relate to customers, competitors and other external constituencies, and how members should relate to and work with each other. This concept of innovation/values fit relates to Rogers' (1995) 'relative advantage' and 'compatibility' attributes of an innovation. Innovations that are perceived to offer a relative advantage in terms of their capacity to fulfil values and are compatible with existing norms, values and social structures are likely to have high innovation/values fit.

Depending on the extent to which the innovation is perceived by potential users to either foster or inhibit the fulfilment of their values, they will:

▶ resist and not implement the innovation
▶ comply with the requirement to adopt the new ways of working in order to gain rewards and avoid punishments
▶ internalize and enthusiastically adopt the innovation as the new way of doing things.

The combined effects of implementation climate and innovation/values fit

Klein and Sorra (1996) illustrate the combined effects of implementation climate and innovation/values fit with the example of a university that has historically valued and rewarded teaching far more than research. The university develops a new strategy that emphasizes research and pursues this strategy by attempting to spread the good research practice that exists in a few isolated departments. It supports this endeavour by introducing new policies and practices that create a strong climate for research. However, members of the university's faculty, while recognizing this supportive climate for implementation, may be reluctant to commit to the change because they perceive it to be incongruent with their values, which centre on teaching rather than research. Table 29.1 illustrates the combined effects of implementation climate and innovation/values fit.

Table 29.1 *Implementation climate and innovation/values fit: effects on employees' affective responses and innovation use*

Climate	Innovation/values fit		
	Poor	*Neutral*	*Good*
Strong implementation climate	**1** Employee opposition and resistance	**2** Employee indifference	**3** Employee enthusiasm
	Compliant innovation use, at best	Adequate innovation use	Committed, consistent and creative innovation use
Weak implementation climate	**4** Employee relief	**5** Employee disregard	**6** Employee frustration and disappointment
	Essentially no innovation use	Essentially no innovation use	Sporadic and inadequate innovation use

Source: Klein and Sorra, 1996: 1066

The six cells predict the influence of varying levels of implementation climate and innovation/values fit on employees' motivation to adopt new ways of working:

▸ In cell 3, innovation/values fit is good and the organization's implementation climate is strong. These are the ideal conditions for innovation implementation.
▸ In cell 6, innovation/values fit is good but the organization's implementation climate is weak. This is not a sufficient condition to produce skilful and consistent innovation use.
▸ In cell 1, although the organization's implementation climate is strong, innovation/values fit is poor. This is a condition that is likely to lead to compliant behaviour at best.
▸ In cell 4, innovation/values fit is poor and the organization's implementation climate is weak. Targeted innovation adopters are likely to regard this weak implementation climate with some measure of relief, because they will encounter little pressure to implement an innovation they do not value. In these circumstances, there is unlikely to be any move to adopt the innovation.
▸ In cell 2, innovation/values fit is neutral and the organization's implementation climate is strong. In these circumstances, innovation use is likely to be more than compliant but less than fully committed.
▸ In cell 5, innovation/values fit is neutral and the organization's implementation climate is weak. In these circumstances, there is unlikely to be any move to adopt the innovation.

The foregoing discussion recognizes that implementation is a multidimensional phenomenon. While there are no easy prescriptions that guarantee spread, there are things that change managers can do to facilitate the dissemination of new ways of working. For example, potential users' perceptions of the attributes of an innovation are not fixed qualities but are amenable to revision. Change managers can do many things to affect these perceptions, ranging from education and persuasion to involving users in a process of adapting the innovation to fit with local requirements and their own values. In addition, they can work to create a strong implementation climate that fosters innovation use. They can also be alert to different stakeholder interests and how these impact the innovation/values fit of different groups. This kind of awareness can help change managers to disseminate new ways of working in ways that maintain equity of treatment and minimize opportunities for conflict.

Exercise 29.2

Action steps to promote the spread of change

Think of a current or pending change in your organization and identify at least three things that could be done to help ensure that the change will not be contained and will be adopted by other users elsewhere in the organization.

	Actions that will help spread the change	Reason
1		
2		
3		

Summary

This chapter has considered 'spreadability' – the extent to which innovative methods and processes that were successfully introduced in one part of the organization are adopted by others elsewhere.

Spread is affected by three factors:

▶ attributes of the innovation
▶ context – reflected by the organization's climate for implementation
▶ the values of potential users, and their perception of the extent to which the innovation will foster or inhibit the fulfilment of their values.

The three attributes of innovations that have the greatest impact on spread are relative advantage, compatibility and complexity. It was noted that Rogers' view that adaptability is important has been contested and some of the arguments supporting adaptation and exact copying are reviewed.

A strong implementation climate fosters innovation use by:

1 ensuring employees have the skills to use the innovation
2 incentivizing them for innovation use and imposing sanctions for innovation avoidance
3 removing obstacles that hamper the adoption of new working practices.

The interaction between users' values and the implementation climate was highlighted as being particularly important.

It was also noted that many of the factors that promote stickability also support spread. Buchanan and Fitzgerald observe that the manner in which a change is spread can influence the degree to which it will be sustained. When changes are rolled out hastily, without much consultation, with few incentives and with inadequate training, they may quickly decay. Similarly, changes that do not have support and are not sustained are unlikely to spread elsewhere.

References

Beer, M. (1988) The critical path for change: keys to success and failure in six companies, in R.H. Kilmann and J.T. Covin (eds) *Corporate Transformations*, San Francisco, CA: Jossey-Bass.

Buchanan, D.A. and Fitzgerald, L. (2007a) The best practice puzzle: why are new methods contained and not spread?, in D.A. Buchanan, L. Fitzgerald and D. Ketley (eds) *The Sustainability and Spread of Organizational Change*, London: Routledge.

Buchanan, D.A. and Fitzgerald, L. (2007b) The sustainability and spread story, in D.A. Buchanan, L. Fitzgerald and D. Ketley (eds) *The Sustainability and Spread of Organizational Change*, London: Routledge.

Buchanan, D.A., Fitzgerald, L. and Ketley, D. (2007) Sustaining change and avoiding containment: practice and policy, in D.A. Buchanan, L. Fitzgerald and D. Ketley (eds) *The Sustainability and Spread of Organizational Change*, London: Routledge.

Greenhalgh, T., Robert, G., Bate, P. et al. (2005) *Diffusion of Innovation in Organizations: A Systematic Literature Review*, Oxford: Blackwell/BJM Books.

Klein, K.L. and Sorra, J.S. (1996) The challenge of innovation implementation, *Academy of Management Review*, **21**(4): 1055–80.

Lamont, S.S. (2005) See and treat: spreading like wildfire? A qualitative study into factors affecting its introduction and spread, *Emergency Medical Journal*, 22: 548–52.

Locock, L. (2001) *Maps and Journeys: Redesign in the NHS*, Health Services Management Centre, University of Birmingham.

Rogers, E. (1995) *The Diffusion of Innovation* (4th edn), New York: Free Press.

Schein, E.H. (1992) *Organizational Culture and Leadership*, San Francisco, CA: Wiley.

Szulanski, G. (2003) *Sticky Knowledge: Barriers to Knowing in the Firm*, London: Sage.

Szulanski, G. and Winter, S. (2002) Getting it right the second time, *Harvard Business Review*, **80**(1): 62–9.

Tornatzky, L.G. and Klein, K.J. (1982) Innovation characteristics and innovation adoption-implementation: a meta-analysis of findings, *IEEE Transactions on Engineering Management*, **29**(1): 28–45.

Walton, R.E. (1975) The diffusion of new work structures: explaining why success didn't take, *Organizational Dynamics*, **3**(3): 3–22.

This book has covered a lot of ground. This final chapter is designed to provide you with an opportunity to review what you have read and to think about how the many theories, models, techniques and tools can be applied to the management of a single case. You can do this on your own or with others.

After reading the KeyChemicals case study below, reflect on the content of the whole book, or those parts of the book you are familiar with, and identify the concepts, theories and tools you feel would be most helpful if you were invited to advise the CEO of KeyChemicals how best to manage the situation.

If you undertake this assignment with others, follow these three steps:

1 Working in small groups, identify the three concepts or theories you feel are most relevant to this case.
2 Share your views with members of the other groups and justify your selection.
3 Working in small groups, taking account of the views expressed by other groups in the plenary discussion, formulate the advice you would give to the CEO of KeyChemicals.

Case study 30.1 | **KeyChemicals**

KeyChemicals is a Swiss company that distributes specialist chemicals throughout Europe. Between 1970 and 2002, a long line of successful acquisitions, divestments, joint ventures and strategic alliances transformed the original Vevey-based distributer of chemicals to the food processing industry into a distributor of a wide range of specialist chemicals.

Despite a long history of growth through acquisition, some of the company's recent acquisitions, which have been led by a relatively new top team, have not delivered the anticipated level of benefit. The CEO has turned to you for advice about the management of a current acquisition.

As part of a strategy to grow its share of the specialist chemicals market in Denmark, the company has recently finalized a deal to acquire a local distributor, Eco-Pure, a family-owned company that dominates the water treatment chemicals market in Denmark. A strategic analysis has indicated that the only cost-effective way for KeyChemicals to enter the water treatment market in Denmark is to acquire Eco-Pure.

The key asset that makes Eco-Pure an attractive acquisition target is the company's sales and technical support teams. The 15 people who work in these areas are technically extremely competent, have excellent relationships with customers and a deep knowledge of their businesses. KeyChemicals aims to integrate these teams into its own sales and technical support teams. Post-acquisition priorities will include:

1 consolidating existing sales in Eco-Pure's water treatment market

2 generating additional business by requiring former Eco-Pure sales staff to cross-sell KeyChemicals' products to their formerly Eco-Pure customers

3 jointly developing new products and services to secure future business.

Eco-Pure has two distribution depots in Denmark, located in Aarhus and Copenhagen, which duplicate existing KeyChemicals depots. One depot at each location will have to be closed in order to achieve operating synergies. This will require the relocation of some equipment, the consolidation of inventories and a large reduction in the number of depot staff.

The KeyChemicals and Eco-Pure tanker fleets will be relatively unaffected. About four drivers will be surplus to requirements but it is anticipated that early retirements and normal labour turnover will deliver this reduction within 6–12 months – without the need for compulsory redundancies. Some of the remaining drivers will have to work out of new depots.

There will be some overcapacity of middle and senior managers. It is anticipated that most of Eco-Pure's middle managers will be redundant as will the finance, HR and operations directors. KeyChemicals wants to retain the marketing director.

As yet, only the CEO, executive directors and the owners of Eco-Pure are aware of the planned acquisition. Eco-Pure executive directors have negotiated generous financial terms (golden parachutes) to compensate them when their employment is terminated.

Imagine that you have been asked to advise KeyChemicals about how to manage the integration of Eco-Pure as part of KeyChemicals Denmark:

• What advice would you give to the CEO?

• Which theories and concepts would inform the advice you would offer?

Author index

Note: The page numbers in brackets indicate the page where the full reference can be found. There are some entries that are only bracketed, which indicates that the entry refers to additional reading cited at the end of the chapter. The names of some authors will not be found on the page indicated as they are included in the et al. reference on that page, for example Hayes, T.L. is part of the Harter et al. ref on p. 432, and is found in the full ref on p. 435.

Subject index

16.30